MANAGEMENT
BASICS
FOR INFORMATION
PROFESSIONALS

D0112040

Instructors adopting this textbook for a course
may request supplementary case studies by e-mailing
editionsmarketing@ala.org.

MANAGEMENT BASICS
FOR INFORMATION PROFESSIONALS

THIRD EDITION

G. EDWARD EVANS
AND CAMILA A. ALIRE

An imprint of the American Library Association

Chicago // 2013

DR. G. EDWARD EVANS is semiretired after a career of more than 50 years in academic librarianship. (Currently he consults at the Harold S. Colton Memorial Library and Archives at the Museum of Northern Arizona.) Academically, he holds graduate degrees in both anthropology and librarianship. He started his career as a high school student worker in the St. Paul Public Library System and spent the past 25 years as a library director. His last full-time position was as Associate Academic Vice President for Scholarly Resources at Loyola Marymount University. He has taught librarianship courses as a practicing librarian and completed the faculty "academic ladder" (moving from assistant professor to full professor) while at the University of California, Los Angeles. Evans's practical experience was in both public and private academic library environments. He has held both National Science Foundation and Fulbright fellowships during his career and has been active in statewide and national library associations. He currently has eight books in print, covering a range of library-related topics, including management, collection development, public services, and technical services.

DR. CAMILA A. ALIRE is Dean Emerita at the University of New Mexico and Colorado State University. Camila received her doctorate in Higher Education Administration from the University of Northern Colorado and her MLS from the University of Denver. She teaches in the PhD program in managerial leadership at Simmons College. Camila is Past President of the American Library Association (ALA) and ALA/APA (2009–2010). She is Past President (2005–2006) of the Association for College and Research Libraries (ACRL) and also Past President of national REFORMA, the National Association to Promote Library and Information Services to the Spanish-speaking.

© 2013 by the American Library Association. Any claim of copyright is subject to applicable limitations and exceptions, such as rights of fair use and library copying pursuant to Sections 107 and 108 of the U.S. Copyright Act. No copyright is claimed for content in the public domain, such as works of the U.S. government.

Printed in the United States of America

17 16 15 14 13   5 4 3 2 1

Extensive effort has gone into ensuring the reliability of the information in this book; however, the publisher makes no warranty, express or implied, with respect to the material contained herein.

ISBNs: 978-1-55570-909-9 (paper); 978-1-55570-925-9 (PDF); 978-1-55570-926-6 (ePub); 978-1-55570-927-3 (Kindle).

Library of Congress Cataloging-in-Publication Data
Evans, G. Edward, 1937.
    Management basics for information professionals / G. Edward Evans, Camila A. Alire.—Third edition.
      pages cm
    Includes bibliographical references and index.
    ISBN 978-1-55570-909-9 (alk. paper)
    1. Library administration—United States. 2. Information services—United States—Management.
  I. Alire, Camila A. II. Title.
  Z678.E9 2013
  025.1—dc23   2013010868

Cover design by Kimberly Thornton. Cover photography © pixelfabrik/Shutterstock, Inc.
Text design in Minion Pro and Gotham by Adrianna Sutton.

♾ This paper meets the requirements of ANSI/NISO Z39.48-1992 (Permanence of Paper).

CONTENTS

PART II MANAGERIAL SKILL SETS

CHAPTER 4. THE PLANNING PROCESS // 85

CHAPTER 5. POWER, ACCOUNTABILITY, AND RESPONSIBILITY // 109

CHAPTER 6. DELEGATING // 131

PART III MANAGING PEOPLE

CHAPTER 16. STAFFING // 389

PART IV MANAGING THINGS

CHAPTER 17. MANAGING MONEY // 425

ILLUSTRATIONS

FIGURES

TABLES

PREFACE

This edition, like its predecessors, covers the basics of management that you ought to understand as you begin your career as a librarian. As we discuss in Chapter 1, you are likely to be called upon to begin to manage one or more people more quickly than you might expect. Having basic management skills will benefit both yourself and those whom you are asked to manage. Although the basics themselves have not changed since the previous edition appeared, the thinking about their application has evolved, technology has changed, and, most significantly, the economic environment in which libraries must operate is very different. We address such developments throughout the text.

The material is presented in five parts. Part I looks at the context of managerial activities that influence what managers, in both for-profit and not-for-profit organizations, cannot, can, and should do; it includes three chapters, one of which is new—legal issues and library management. Part II includes eight chapters that discuss the skills required to be an effective manager. Part III addresses the essential people managerial skills that all great managers understand; it includes five chapters, one of which is new—building teams. Part IV's three chapters examine how to manage such things as money, technology, and facilities. Part V presents some insights into managing yourself and your career through two chapters, one of which is new—ethics in the workplace. While the material is presented in a sequential manner, it is important to understand that the practice of management and leadership involves complex activities that are intertwined. This fact is why management is an art as well as a science.

Perhaps the most significant change in this edition is that we had a team of six readers/advisors who reviewed each chapter as it was drafted. Their insightful comments provided invaluable improvements in the edition's content. As you will see in the following, they brought a wealth of experience from almost all types of libraries. Including the authors' library management experience, the team that developed this book has more than 175 years of management experience, not counting management teaching experience. If you include the experience of the past American Library Association (ALA) presidents who contributed material, the total library management experience exceeds 300 years.

Another new feature is the presence of sidebars featuring the Authors' Experience and Advisory Board Experience. As the titles suggest, these boxes present real-life managerial experiences of the authors and advisory board members. The content is not presented as "best practices" but instead is intended to illustrate what can and does happen in libraries. As you read the text you will note that we have mentioned a number of their articles and books that address management topics.

Here's a look at who our readers were and, in their own words, their experience:

Dr. Susan Carol Curzon, retired Dean, University Library, California State University, Northridge, from 1992 to 2010: I worked in academic, public, and corporate libraries. My doctorate is in Public Administration from the University of Southern California. My master's degree in librarianship was from the University of Washington. I was in management positions for 30 years—whew, really?

Dr. Joseph Mika, Professor Emeritus at the School of Library and Information Science, Wayne State University (Detroit, MI): Mika served as Director of the School twice (15 years) during his tenure of 25 years at the University. He was also Assistant Dean at the School of Library and Information Science, University of Southern Mississippi (Hattiesburg); Assistant Library Director at Johnson State College (Johnson, VT); and Assistant Library Director, Ohio State University, Mansfield Campus. His teaching areas included administration, customer service, personnel management, and collection development. He is co-owner of Hartzell-Mika Consulting, a firm that has been in business since 1999, providing assistance with library director searches, strategic planning facilitation, facility development and planning, and staff and board training sessions. Mika is a retired Colonel in the U.S. Army, having served 29 years in the Army Reserves.

Dr. Carol Sinwell, recently retired: Carol Sinwell's career has included leadership and management duties in both public and academic libraries. For 12 years she worked in one of the largest public library systems in the country, serving in management positions that included children's service, reference coordinator, branch manager, and staff development. During her 19 years in the academic arena her positions included Associate Dean and Dean of Learning and Technology Services, a division that included the library, six tutorial centers, a testing center, Faculty/Staff Professional Development Center, and technology services. While at the college, Dr. Sinwell completed her second master's and doctoral degrees and was recognized in 2003 as a "Mover and Shaker" by the American Library Association as part of their recognition of the 50 Most Innovative Librarians in the United States and Canada.

Dr. Glenda Thornton, Director of the Cleveland State University's Michael Schwartz Library: Glenda Thornton's career of four decades has included a variety of professional positions in four states. She has been the library director at Cleveland State University's Michael Schwartz Library for the past 14 years. Her experience as a library manager and supervisor began while she was in library school and managed a branch library at the University of Oklahoma. She is the author of numerous articles and has been Reviews Editor for *Technical Services Quarterly* since 1997.

Dr. Virginia Walter, retired from the University of California, Los Angeles, Department of Information Studies: Virginia Walter has had a number of managerial and leadership roles in her career: President of the Society of California Librarians, President of the Association for Library Service to Children, middle manager at Los Angeles Public Library, and Chair of the Information Studies Department at UCLA. Now she is retired and content to teach a little, write a little, consult, and train a little—everything in moderation!

Sachi Yagyu, Reference and Consulting Librarian, RAND Corporation: Sachi spent the first 18 years of her career at a private university. She started as an entry-level reference librarian and progressed to the position of Head of Reference and Circulation. Curious about other library environments, she is currently a reference librarian in a not-for-profit, public policy research organization.

In addition, we wanted to offer the words of wisdom of national library leaders noted for their expertise in and/or passion for specific chapter topics. These include ALA past presidents Richard M. Dougherty (1990), Pat Schuman (1991), Betty Turock (1995), Barbara Ford (1999), Sarah Long (1997), Nancy Kranich (2000), John W. Berry (2001), Carol Brey-Casiano (2004), Jim Rettig (2008), Camila A. Alire (2009), and Molly Raphael (2011). We also invited ALA leader James Neal (Treasurer, 2010) to share his wisdom. Their insights, which are reflected at the beginning of appropriate chapters, set the stage for those chapters. We want to thank each of them for their contributions.

G. Edward Evans, Flagstaff, Arizona
Camila A. Alire, Sedalia, Colorado

PART I

MANAGERIAL ENVIRONMENT

Many of us choose the library career path because we like books and information and we like people. We remember the libraries of our youth. These were happy days and we think that getting a MLIS will be the ticket to an idyllic career based on a self-evident good. Building partnerships, being a team player, dealing with the power structure, building a budget, devising and implementing assessment tools, strategic planning, effective reporting, etc., are just some of the topics every librarian will confront in the first two weeks on the job. These topics and more are covered in library management classes and for perhaps the first time confront the aspiring librarian with the hidden policy issues involved in library work. Put another way, think of a library management class as an invitation to look behind the curtain and see what makes a librarian successful—working at any level or in any type of library. Library specific knowledge is great. Library history is fascinating. Knowing about the latest and greatest technological advances impresses library colleagues. But library success is achieved by having insight into how the staff works together and how the library as an institution works with the community. Call it politics or call it library management. Without this sort of insight, success will be elusive. Don't take a library management class at your peril!

—Sarah Long, ALA President, 1999–2000 (2012)

I think the corruption of management as a word is partly the result of a 100-year period of trying to make sense of the big, industrial, hierarchical, bureaucratic, company. All of the words we use around management now are essentially words about how you manage dehumanized, standardized machines that pump out millions and millions of identical products.

—Julian Birkinshaw (2010)

The twenty-first century workforce has experienced tremendous changes due to advances in technology; consequently, the "old way" of doing things may be effective but not efficient. . . . [T]he best way to prepare potential employees for tomorrow's workforce is to develop not only technical but also human-relation abilities.

—Geanna W. Mitchell, Leane B. Skinner, and Bonnie J. White (2010)

Our recent economic turmoil has sparked widespread soul-searching about the approach of business school in educating managers. How is it that so many smart people made poor decisions? In the words of Henry Mintzberg, "The economic crisis is not a financial one. It is one of management, and management education has been a significant part of the problem."

—Peter Todd (2010)

1

INTRODUCTION

MITCHELL, SKINNER, AND WHITE'S quotation emphasizes the importance of people skills and abilities and that such skills should be at the center of libraries' operations and services. Todd's citation of Henry Mintzberg, a name you will see often in the following chapters, makes the point that organizations' problems are often traceable back to poor management education. Management education, or lack of, is something of an issue for librarianship, as 43.8 percent of American Library Association (ALA) accredited library school programs do not require any management course work (Mackenize, 2009, p. 140). Jeanne Cross (2005), writing about what the future may hold for libraries at a time when a large number of senior librarians have recently retired or soon will be retiring, noted, "This [lack of managerial experience] is particularly troubling in the area of library management where the problem is compounded by fewer librarians choosing library administration as a career path. . . . The problem is not only attracting people to the field but also finding avenues for individuals to gain the skills and experience necessary to become tomorrow's library administrators" (p. 193).

Some of you who are reading this material as part of a required management course may be thinking something like, "I do not expect, nor do I want, to be a manager. All I want to do is be a good _____ librarian." You fill in the blank. You are the not the first to have such thoughts, nor are you likely to be the last. Many of us do not think about or recognize the pervasiveness of the basic management elements (planning, budgeting, and decision making, for example) in our daily lives. And, it is surprising how fast we begin to have to manage when we become librarians. A recent article by Lynne Olver (2011) makes our point: "Some people are born to be library directors. Not me. In fact, that was the last thing on my mind when I entered library school at SUNY Albany in 1980. My entire goal was to be the best reference librarian I could possibly be" (p. 6). She is currently a public library director, although she was neither "born" into it nor officially trained in management techniques. Most of us who have been or are directors, middle managers, or even frontline supervisors did not enter or, in most cases, leave library school thinking our careers would be in management. It just hap-

AUTHORS' EXPERIENCE

On Evans's first day in his first full-time library position he was given an assistant. Had he not had some undergraduate course work in administration he probably would have made a mess of that responsibility. The library school program he graduated from had no management/administration course requirement. He had taken the academic library course, which had a very modest emphasis on basic management knowledge and much less on skills.

Alire, on the other hand, became the library director at a small college at age 24 immediately after receiving her MLS. If it hadn't been for the required management course she took in her MLS program, she also probably would have made a mess of that responsibility. It was her need for more management/administrative education that propelled her to pursue an advanced degree in higher education administration.

pens. This is why the quotation from Sarah Long, past president of ALA, leads this book.

Although several of the opening quotations are not from the library literature, they do apply to library management and library education as much as they do to business. Every organization is managed, successfully or not so successfully. All of us must manage our lives—also successfully or not. In a broad sense, management has been an aspect of human life since individuals started living with one another.

Some years ago, Yale economist Charles Lindblom (1959) described management as "the science of 'muddling' through." People have been muddling for tens of thousands of years. As we became better at working things out, the less muddled the process and outcomes have become. In today's world, the more you know about the process of accomplishing goals—organizational or personal— the less muddled and the more successful you will be.

There are those who claim management is just common sense. They are only marginally correct. What is "common sense" is something one learns to a greater or lesser degree over time. Some people believe that because management is "just common sense" there is nothing to be learned about the activity. However, even those who have such beliefs do receive an "education" through trial and error while they try to find that common sense. Also, it is safe to assume that these are the individuals who engage in the most muddling and, generally, the people who cause the most grief for those who work with them because they seem not to employ a system to their "managing."

Reading about management, taking a course, or attending some workshops on the subject improves your chances of being better at it. Poor managers can

ADVISORY BOARD EXPERIENCE

Joe Mika, who teaches the basic management course at Wayne State University (Detroit), also points out that students should take the management and administration course because they themselves will have managers. Such course work will help them to understand their managers and directors and how the different administrative styles will affect their careers.

and do hurt their organizations and the people they work with as well as themselves. Course work and workshops will not ensure you will be a good manager, but these tools can improve your managerial skills. Everyone engages in a little "muddling" regardless of training; however, the amount of muddling decreases as the amount of training increases.

Libraries, other not-for-profit (NFP) organizations, as well as government agencies have been rather slow to see the need for formal management training. In fact, such formal training as a core subject in educational programs for librarians is relatively recent. Note, although "type of library" courses do contain some administrative/management elements, their primary focus tends to be on services and programs relevant to the library type, not on basic management concepts.

Higher education programs in business and management schools focus on profit and loss as well as on precisely defined products and markets. Libraries lack both of these characteristics; their "products" vary from library to library, and their markets are highly diverse. That is, each library creates its own approach to providing services based on its assessment of local needs. Lacking precise goals and measures of achievement (such as profits), this meant that, in the past, librarians saw little need for general management training.

The notion that any librarian can be an effective manager shifted to recognition that there is a need for some formal training in management. The Mackenzie (2009) article cited earlier offers an in-depth look at the current status of management education in U.S.-accredited library schools. Formal training provides an understanding of the basic elements of managerial activities and about what tends to lead to successful organizational performance.

One reflection of the changing views regarding management education for information professionals occurred in 1983 at an international conference of educators from the International Federation of Library Associations and Institutions (IFLA), the Fédération Internationale d'Information et de Documentation, and the International Council on Archives. The purpose of the meeting was to explore the possibilities of identifying a universal "core" for the education of information professionals in management. By the end of the conference it

AUTHORS' EXPERIENCE

Evans was a presenter at the 1983 international conference mentioned and was not surprised by the rather rapid agreement reached by educators from around the world on what the core management concepts are for information service work.

was agreed that (1) it is essential to provide all information professionals with management training and (2) there is a core set of topics that the information professional should know (Evans, 1984). In this book we cover all of the core topics (such as planning, decision making, staffing, and budgeting) as well as several that were not part of the identified core (such as legal issues, technology, and career planning).

WHAT IS MANAGEMENT?

Perhaps the shortest definition of management is one attributed to Mary Parker Follett (1941): "management is the art of getting things done through people." This definition belies the complexity of management yet concisely sums up management. A longer and more complex definition is Daniel Wren's (1979): "management is an activity essential to organized endeavors that perform certain functions to obtain the effective acquisition, allocating, and utilization of human efforts and physical resources for the purpose of accomplishing some goal" (p. 3). There are literally hundreds of other definitions of the term. All contain two elements: they mention people and activities, and they reference organizations.

Managers direct and facilitate the work of others. There is generally something of a pyramid shape to any organization, with more people involved in working directly with customers than in performing solely managerial duties. Most organizations consist of a "top" (few people), a "middle" (several people), and a "bottom" (many people). This is despite recent efforts to flatten organizational structures. Certainly there has been significant flattening, but a person is hard pressed to identify an organization with less than three levels. Even in a fully team-based organization there is some type of team supervisor(s), team leader(s), and team members.

FOR FURTHER THOUGHT

Find two other definitions of "management." Now compare the four. What do they have in common? How do they differ?

AUTHORS' EXPERIENCE

Evans developed the first general management course that was not based on a library type at the University of California, Los Angeles library school. For the first several years it was an elective, and 20 to 25 students enrolled each time it was offered. When the school moved from a one-year to a two-year degree program the students voted to have the management course a requirement. As such, the level of student interest in the subject matter became highly varied. For several years after the change to a required course, the first day of the class was devoted to students' views about "management" and their expectations about what path their career would take. Evans offered to bet one month's salary against one dollar that, if the graduate worked in a library for more than 18 months, he or she would be engaged in some type of management activity—if nothing more than looking after a part-time student or volunteer. He never lost a bet.

Discussions were spirited, pointed, and not infrequently bitter. Comments such as "I will never manage anyone; management is manipulation"; "Managers are anti-people; they exploit people"; and "Never trust a manager" were rather common.

After several times teaching the course, Evans developed a definition of management based on the negative comments and used it to get the discussion going by asking how many thought the following was a reasonable definition: "management is getting others to do your work." Many thought it was an accurate statement; it certainly got the discussion going. The discussions also illustrated the fact that most of the individuals with negative views had had one or more bad experiences in the workplace.

The authors' philosophy of management is reflected throughout this text, and it is not that management is about how to get others to do our work. A short version of our philosophy is: "select good people, trust them, delegate authority while retaining responsibility, build true teams, and be supportive."

To support our point, *Library Journal*'s 2012 Librarian of the Year Luis Hererra, of the San Francisco Public Library, when interviewed, stated that the advice he received as a library administrator from his mentors was to surround himself with good people. "I have a great team. My mentors all said, 'Surround yourself with good people,' and I did" (Berry, 2012, p. 30).

We believe that supervisors and leaders should engage in team member activities from time to time. One of our professional mottos is "Everyone must get their hands dirty from time to time." This means that when a major task comes up, the entire staff does the work. Having everyone shelf reading, shifting materi-

---

ADVISORY BOARD EXPERIENCE

Joseph Mika was influenced in his management style by the U.S. Army, which had an approach much like that of Follet (1941)—get results through people—but over the years his approach mellowed to "get results with people."

---

als in the stacks, or whatever results in a sense of everyone feeling that they are part of a team and that there is mutual support when needed.

Such sharing of work activities provides supervisors and leaders with a first-hand sense of what frontline staff members face on a day-to-day basis. It also demonstrates they have the professional technical knowledge, experience, and skills to perform, as well as direct, team activities. We will discuss, in Chapter 13, that one element of leadership is the staff's belief in the technical abilities of their "leader."

WHAT DO MANAGERS DO?

Just what do managers do? There are many answers to this question, and the question actually contains two issues: function and behavior. Some managerial functions are planning, directing, and budgeting, while behavioral aspects involve the roles filled, such as negotiator or group spokesperson. Writers tend to emphasize one side or the other. This book is organized according to functions; however, we also explore behavioral aspects and place great emphasis on user needs.

Managers and supervisors often say, "I never get my real work done." This response usually relates to the functional aspects of management. The standard concepts of a manager's functional activities are outlined in a classic management paper by Gulick and Urwick (1937), in which they coined the acronym POSDCoRB, which stands for the following functions:

- Planning
- Organizing
- Staffing
- Directing
- Coordinating
- Reporting
- Budgeting

POSDCoRB functions underlie, in one form or another, all management behavior; however, they do not describe the work of a manager. They merely identify the objectives of a manager's work.

TRY THIS

Approach a person you know is a manager. Ask the individual to describe what she or he does. The response will likely be something like, "Well, I'm head of the reference department" or "I'm assistant director for technical services" or "I'm the director of the archives." These reflect the person's position rather than her or his work. Further probing is likely to get a response something along the lines of "I attend lots of meetings; I'm on the computer doing e-mail and writing reports, memos, and letters; and I listen to complaints. It seems like I never get anything done." Another common response is, "I spend most of my day solving problems and putting out brush fires" (behavioral response). Seldom will the answer be, "Oh, I direct, plan, control, delegate, budget, and hire and fire people" (functional context).

Henry Mintzberg (1973) suggested that because the functions fail to describe managerial behavior they are of little use. We believe this is too harsh a judgment, for if we do not know where we are going (that is, if we do not have objectives), how will we know when we get there? By studying POSDCoRB concepts, a person can gain an understanding of what good management attempts to accomplish.

A reasonable question to ask is, "Do all organizational levels engage in the same activities?" A short answer is "yes," but such an answer obscures many important differences, especially in terms of the skills employed (see Figure 1.1). Senior managers tend to devote more time to planning than do other managers, and planning calls for a major use of conceptual skills. They also tend to devote more time to interacting with a variety of people both internal and external to the library. Such interaction calls for strong interpersonal-relations skills. Finally, they engage in very little direct user service work, and thus they make limited use of the technical skills they once employed when they became a librarian.

A good discussion of differences in skill set usage by level of responsibility is Robert Katz's (1974) "Skills of an Effective Administrator." Mahoney, Jardee, and Carroll (1964) also discuss the concept of time spent on various activities, but

FOR FURTHER THOUGHT

POSDCoRB—think of an example of each of these functions. Remember that they are principles, not descriptions of the work of the manager.

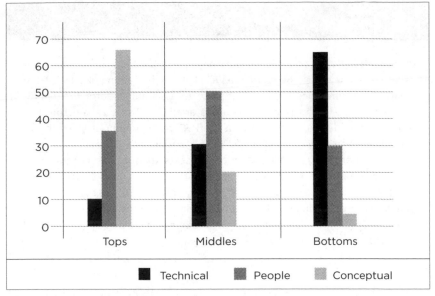

Figure 1.1 Organizational Skill Sets

they approached it from bottoms to tops. For bottoms, the emphasis is almost a mirror opposite of the tops: great emphasis on technical skills, a strong component of human-relations skills, and only limited use of conceptual skills. As always, middles are in between: less use of technical skills than bottoms but more than tops and a greater need for conceptual skills but less than for tops. You can envision these differences in terms of percentages. For a bottom, perhaps 60 to 70 percent of the emphasis is on technical skills, 20 to 30 percent on human relations, and the balance on conceptual abilities. Middles would perhaps be 20 to 30 percent technical, 10 to 50 percent human relations, and the balance conceptual. Conceptual abilities would be 40 to 50 percent for tops, with technical skills at 10 percent or less, and the balance involving human relations.

ORGANIZATIONAL SKILL SETS
Henry Mintzberg (1971, 1973, 1975) has had the greatest general influence in the area of how managers behave and how knowledge of behavior should change how management is taught. His critique of the functions approach led him to suggest that looking at the roles played would be more effective. He identified ten roles divided among three categories: interpersonal, informational, and decisional. Under interpersonal are three roles: figurehead, leader, and liaison. The informational category contains the roles of nerve center, disseminator, and spokesperson. Decisional activities include the roles of entrepreneur, disturbance handler, resource allocation, and negotiator. We suggest that there is a fourth role under informational: politician. To some extent such a role is part of being a figurehead, leader, negotiator, and spokesperson. However, given the

AUTHORS' EXPERIENCE

Alire team-teaches a course in a managerial leadership doctoral program on managing libraries in a political context. The idea for the course came from a national board of advisors who recommended such a course within the context of organizational culture and who thought it was one course that students in managerial leadership need to be successful as managerial leaders. The course is required in the PhD program. Invariably, students from each PhD cohort have mentioned that it was probably one of the most relevant courses in their program, especially when they became a head of a library.

social and political changes that have occurred since Mintzberg carried out his research (in the 1970s), the political role has become ever more important.

Without question, Mintzberg's work added substantially to our understanding of what managers actually do. For teaching and learning purposes, however, the approach does not work very well, because the research on which he based his concept focused on top managers and, to a lesser extent, on middle managers, and it focused on observable activities rather than on the reasons for the activities. Also, it does not represent a full picture of a manager's work; as we noted, the role of politician is not clearly delineated. Because of these deficiencies, the classic "functions" approach is still the most useful method for newcomers to conceptualize managerial responsibilities. We will, at various points in later chapters, note how Mintzberg's ideas come into play.

As in many fields, there is a question of whether management is an art or a science. Our belief is that, despite elements of science, management is an art. Although a person can learn the basic concepts, principles, functions, techniques, and roles, each management situation is unique. Two situations may appear similar, but the individuals involved will be different. Even similar situations that involve the same personnel are unique. Thus, what worked yesterday may or may not work today. Your ability to read the changes and make appropriate adjustments is the real art of management.

MANAGEMENT CONCEPTS

Many people have influenced how organizations were and are managed. It is important to understand that while organizations change and operate over time, the underlying basics of management functions remain in place.

Looking at management literature you quickly discover that, although people have managed organizations for thousands of years, it is only within the past 150 years that there has been serious interest in what it takes to have a successful operation. Furthermore, only in the past 60-plus years has there been widespread research into management operations and activities.

In this section we briefly explore the development of management thought and how the process is reflected in library operations. One reason for devoting space to such a discussion is to provide you with a sound base for assessing the latest management ideas (which often are only passing "fads"—think of total quality management, or TQM) put forward by consultants and others who make their living by churning out "secrets" to organizational success. The real secrets lie in understanding the fundamentals and applying them thoughtfully. Most of the "new" approaches are merely repackaged older ideas about the basic functions of management.

We cover eight approaches to thinking about management:

1. Scientific
2. Administrative
3. Behavioral
4. Management science/quantitative
5. Systems
6. Contingency
7. Quality
8. Composite

As you might guess, management practice and theories have evolved over time. You might also correctly suspect the approaches became ever more complex by taking into account more and more variables. They also became more focused.

Deciding where to begin the review was a challenge; we finally settled on covering some of the best-known individuals who published their thoughts on the subject. This is not to suggest that many others did not contribute to how we practice management today.

SCIENTIFIC MANAGEMENT

One of the first people to write about his ideas of "effective" management was Frederick W. Taylor (1856–1915). His book *Principles of Scientific Management* (Taylor, 1947) has appeared in many editions over the years. He focused on manufacturing organizations and how to make them as efficient as possible (time and motion studies) and on what would be a fair wage for the workers meeting the standards. Contrary to what you might read elsewhere, Taylor was not anti-worker—he believed that efficient operations made work less stressful or tiring and that workers should be paid for their efficiency.

Scientific management had a number of followers, some of whom you may recognize. For example, you would know Frank (1911–2001) and Lillian (1878–1972) Gilbreth if you have seen the film *Cheaper by the Dozen* (2003, 20th Century Fox). The Gilbreths' many refinements to work–motion study methodology were their major contribution to the field. They also were among the first to emphasize an organization's need to "develop" employees to improve employee morale and effectiveness. Lillian Gilbreth (1914) was one of the first people to write about industrial psychology that focused on employee issues.

> **KEY POINTS TO REMEMBER**
>
> **Scientific Management**
> - Economic issues are workers' primary motivation factor.
> - Organizations, because they control economic rewards, can direct worker behavior through those rewards.
> - The distrust between workers and management and the lack of understanding about what was a "fair day's work" could be removed by using scientific (rational) studies.
> - A rationalized work activity would lead to an acceptable basis of compensation (task plus bonus) that would be beneficial for both worker and management.

Another figure whose last name is widely known, if not much else about the man, is Henry Gantt (1861–1919). He was a protégé of Taylor's; they worked together early in Gantt's career. Gantt's task and bonus plan has led some people to view Gantt as more humanitarian than Taylor. Gantt's major contribution was developing charting techniques for projects and activities that still carry his name (Gantt, 1916, 1919). You will find his techniques useful throughout your managerial career.

Following World War II, libraries began applying a combination of scientific management ideas and some of the mathematical/operations-research techniques developed during that war. Richard Dougherty and Fred Heinritz's (1982) *Scientific Management of Library Operations* and Dougherty's (2008) more recent work *Streamlining Library Services: What We Do, How Much Time It Takes, What It Costs, and How We Can Do It Better* are representative of libraries' concern with efficient operation. As you move into greater managerial responsibility you learn that efficient and effective library operations are essential.

ADMINISTRATIVE APPROACH

Two of the proponents of this approach are Henri Fayol (1841–1925) and Max Weber (1864–1920). Other notable figures are Lyndall Urwick (1891–1983) and Chester Barnard (1886–1961).

Henri Fayol was both a practitioner/manager and a thinker about management. He believed his success was due to skills he developed over the years as well as his ideas about what it takes to be an effective manager. He published his "principles" in 1916 in *Administration Industrielle et Generale* (Fayol, 1962). Fayol's 14 principles of management, with the major points for each, follow:

1. Division of labor—workers perform best (are most productive) when they specialize.
2. Authority and responsibility—giving orders and being responsible must go together.

3. Discipline—this arises from having clearly defined policies and rules for staff.
4. Unity of command—employees must have only one supervisor.
5. Unity of direction—units must operate in a unified effort to achieve organizational goals.
6. Subordination of individual to general interest—employees must focus on organizational rather than personal interests while on the job.
7. Remuneration—wages for staff must be appropriate and fair.
8. Centralization—authority should be "reasonably" centralized to ensure overall organizational direction.
9. Scalar chain—an organization must have a formalized structure for authority and communication.
10. Order—relationships among units should be logical and ensure a timely flow of information and materials.
11. Equity—employee treatment should be fair and equitable.
12. Stability of tenure—high employee retention is a hallmark of a well-managed organization.
13. Initiative—managers should encourage employee initiative, especially in terms of how they might improve their work performance.
14. Esprit de corps—managers should strive to achieve high morale and team spirit in their units.

Lyndall Urwick was perhaps one of the first and strongest English-speaking supporters of Fayol's concepts. He was a British management consultant who emphasized a "Fayolian" approach. His book *Elements of Business Administration* attempted to integrate all the work of leading management thinkers and was his greatest contribution to the field (Urwick, 1943).

Max Weber, with his classic work on bureaucracy, became a key figure in management thinking. Although his study was of how governments operate, when you think about his concepts you will see how they apply to some degree to almost any large organization, including libraries.

Weber (1947, pp. 330–332) identified seven traits as characteristic of an "ideal" bureaucracy (e.g., organization):

1. It has continuous organization of official functions bound by rules.
2. It has a specific sphere of competence.
3. The organization of offices follows the principle of hierarchy; that is, each lower office is under the control and supervision of a higher one.
4. The rules that regulate the conduct of an office may be technical rules or "norms."
5. It is a matter of principle that the members of the administrative staff should be completely separated from ownership of the means of production or administration.

> **KEY POINTS TO REMEMBER**
>
> **Administrative Approach**
> - Worker motivation is a primary factor in effective productivity.
> - Social interaction factors are equally as important as, if not more important than, economic factors in employee motivation.
> - Self-actualization is a workplace issue because it motivates most people.
> - Research in the field of human behavior in search of concepts applicable in the workplace is important.

6. There is a complete absence of appropriation of official positions by incumbents.
7. Administrative acts, decisions, and rules are formulated and recorded in writing.

You may have a negative view of "bureaucracy" and think that libraries more or less fit his model. Whether an individual organization fits the positive or negative image of a bureaucracy depends on its managers and staff. When run properly, a classic bureaucratic organization provides effective, efficient, rational, and humane service. No organization is good or bad in itself. It is the staff operating an organization that determines its positive and negative characteristics.

Chester Barnard was the leading proponent of examining management in terms of twentieth-century profit organizations. His book *Functions of the Executive* is perhaps the most insightful of any written on the character of organizations (Barnard, 1938). He based his book on a combination of practical experience and extensive study of sociology, psychology, and philosophy.

BEHAVIORAL APPROACH

There is a connection between the scientific management and behavioral approaches. As we noted earlier, Lillian Gilbreth's book addressed industrial psychology, not scientific management and its importance to effective management. Hugo Munsterberg (1863–1916) is probably the best candidate for being the founder of the behavioral approach to management. His book *Psychology and Industrial Efficiency* makes the case for applying psychology to the workplace (Munsterberg, 1913). He proposed three major foci: identifying the person with the proper characteristics to perform the job (skills, attitudes, physical abilities), developing methods to identify the ideal psychological condition for engaging in a task, and creating optimal motivational influences on the worker. He drew on scientific methods, specifically conducting experiments to accomplish the field's goals. His work led to the development of preemployment skills testing.

KEY POINTS TO REMEMBER

Behavioral Approach
- The behavioral approach focuses on organizational issues in a holistic manner.
- It recognizes that managers, not just workers, need training and development.
- It focuses on activities that are still relevant in today's organizations.
- It provides a solid basis for thinking about organizational structure and its operational implications.

Most management textbooks in the United States devote some space to Elton Mayo (1880–1849). Mayo led a research team from Harvard's Graduate School of Business Administration that undertook a long-term study of worker fatigue and productivity at Western Electric's Hawthorne, Illinois, plant. The purpose of that study was to determine the validity of a suggestion (by the Gilbreths) that brief rest periods would improve production.

In 1927, his team began a series of experiments by making changes in such things as having rest periods and allowing a light lunch in the morning and afternoon. No matter what changes took place, production improved. Sick time and tardiness dropped to about one-third the level of the employees not in the study, and supervision time shrank to a minimum.

The study's important outcome is known as the "Hawthorne Effect," and it is common in all studies of human behavior. That is, an observer's presence and the subject's awareness of the observer result in atypical behavior. In the case of the Hawthorne workers, they saw themselves as a special group getting special attention and wanted to maintain that special status, so they always

IMPORTANT TO NOTE

From the mid-1960s to 1980, libraries and archives began shifting away from the director-controlled management approach to one involving the professional staff, if not the entire staff. Human relations management in libraries usually means democratic administration, staff participation in decision making, and use of committees.

By the mid-twentieth century, management thought began to focus on one element of the basic concepts discussed. Each of the following approaches plays some role in how today's organizations operate.

performed better regardless of the change. However, we cannot predict in any given case what the effect will be of observing staff: they may become nervous and perform very badly; they may work harder than normal; or they may see your presence as a threat and respond with the performance that will cancel the perceived danger.

Mayo's research confirmed the concept that an honest concern for workers pays dividends in terms of performance. He also highlighted the fact that a manager's style was an important factor in employee motivation and, ultimately, in productivity (Mayo, 1933).

MANAGEMENT SCIENCE/QUANTITATIVE APPROACH

There are a variety of subfields within management science or the quantitative approach. Operations research, decision analysis, simulation, forecasting, game theory, mathematical modeling, management information systems, project management, and data mining are but a few of the variations.

A major figure in management in general and in management science in particular was Herbert A. Simon (1916–2001). He was an early leader in the fields of quantitative modeling of human behavior, artificial intelligence, and problem-solving strategies (simulation). His book *Administrative Behavior* (Simon, 1947) focused on the behavioral and cognitive processes involved when people engage in rational decision making. Any decision involves a choice selected from a number of alternatives; through modeling the process and alternative choices, the organization can and should make a better decision.

Two other notable individuals, who to some degree collaborated with Simon, are Richard Cyert (1921–1998) and James G. March (1928–). Their seminal work, *A Behavioral Theory of the Firm* (Cyert and March, 1963), explored organizational decision making. They challenged the idea that organizations always operate "rationally" and in their own best interests. They concluded that although organizations intend to operate rationally, the real-

KEY POINTS TO REMEMBER

Management Science/Quantitative Approach
- Organizational issues can be approached rationally and logically.
- Employing mathematical modeling for the purpose of predicting alternative outcomes and results improves decision making.
- Modeling decisions and actions leads to better solutions.
- The approach is useful for both complex and unstructured problems/situations.
- Incorporating computing power is the key to successful modeling.

ity is rather different. The authors suggest a variety of variables, both internal and external, that cause decisions and actions to occur that are at odds with rationality.

SYSTEMS APPROACH

General systems theory draws on the concept that everything is part of a larger system. A system regardless of type (biological or social) consists of interdependent parts with four basic components—input, transformation, output, and feedback. Ludwig von Bertalanffy (1901–1972), a biologist, is the person most writers credit with founding this approach. His purpose was to develop a theoretical framework that would apply to any academic discipline. In its simplest form, the theory holds that all organizations exist in an environment; they take "inputs" (people, resources, money) from the environment, process ("transform") the inputs, and produce "outputs" that go back to the environment with constant "feedback" taking place (von Bertalanffy, 1950). Russell L. Ackoff (1919–2009) is another significant figure in the fields of operations research and systems theory. He coauthored with C. West Churchman and Leonard Arnoff (1957) *Introduction to Operations Research,* which helped define the field.

Perhaps one of today's best-known "systems approach" people is Peter M. Senge (1947–), who has promoted the concept of the "learning organization." His "cornerstone" discipline in *The Fifth Discipline* (Senge, 1990) is systems thinking, which leads to a holistic approach to organizations and the people who work in them. You will find his book and many others on learning organizations in new-book bookstores, and the idea is discussed in current library literature.

The five "component technologies" of a learning organization are:

1. Systems thinking
2. Personal mastery
3. Mental models
4. Building shared visions
5. Team learning

KEY POINTS TO REMEMBER

Systems Approach
- The interdependency of all the parts of an organization must be recognized.
- Interdependency thinking focuses attention on the fundamentals—input, transformation, output, and feedback.
- Systems thinking makes it clear that organizations are complex rather than simple in character and thus require complex thinking and planning.

Senge puts systems theory to work in a very practical manner. One of his key points is that much of what is done in the name of management is too simplistic and therefore fails to recognize organizations as complex systems (a focus on parts rather than on the whole).

CONTINGENCY THEORY

Contingency theory holds that there are no universal answers in management. Rather, the manager must view each situation as unique and determine what steps are appropriate on a situation-by-situation basis. In this approach, "size" encompasses more than the number of people; it includes outputs as well as resources (facilities and capital). Some of the ideas regarding size (the percentage of the organization involved in "overhead" activities, increased structuring, and decreased power concentrations) are being rethought in today's tendency toward maintaining flatter bureaucratic structures and smaller staff numbers.

Mary Parker Follett (1868–1933) was one of the first women to be recognized for her contributions to management theory. Recognition was a result of her explorations of a wide variety of management topics in the 1920s—leadership, power and authority, conflict management, empowerment, teams, and what she termed the "law of the situation." Her background was in philosophy and social work, and while most of her career occurred during the scientific management period and while she agreed with some of its principles, she believed there was undue emphasis on authority/control. One of her major contributions was developing the idea that management leadership should not, and cannot, come from the power of formal authority but rather from a person's knowledge and expertise.

Fred Luthans (1939–) suggested that you need to specify upon what and in what ways the situation depends in order to manage effectively (Luthans, 1973). For example, sometimes in one environment, tightly defined jobs with

KEY POINTS TO REMEMBER

Contingency Theory
- Managers need to employ a variety of strategies and techniques when dealing with people and activities—no one approach is always "right."
- Selecting the appropriate strategies and techniques calls for a solid knowledge of research into organizational theory as well as an assessment of the environment.
- Environmental scanning is a key component of this approach (see Chapter 2 for a detailed discussion of this topic).
- "Diagnosis" of situations is a skill managers should develop in order to select actions that fit the circumstances.

"close" authoritarian supervision can result in high productivity and employee satisfaction, while in another environment such an approach would be disastrous. He also placed a strong emphasis on leadership.

Two important researchers in this area are Tom Burns and George M. Stalker. They explored how the environment impacts an organization, its structure, and its operations. They identified two types of environment—stable and innovative (Burns and Stalker, 1961). Fred Emery and Eric Trist (1965) expanded Burns and Stalker's ideas into four such environments (see Chapter 2 for a discussion of their concepts).

QUALITY APPROACH

Quality as an approach began generating interest in libraries in the 1990s and early 2000s. It focused on customer satisfaction by providing high-quality goods and services. Some of the labels for this approach are quality control, quality assurance, quality circles, and total quality management. The concept went beyond "quality" to include "just-in-time" delivery of resources and services—the right equipment and technology for the job when needed—and eliminating waste.

Although many individuals worked in this area, two early figures are W. Edwards Deming (1900–1993) and Joseph Juran (1904–2008). Both spent much of their career in Japan and assisted in the transformation of Japanese methods of production and quality control. Their success in those endeavors turned Japan's economy around, and U.S. firms became interested in what some believed to be the Japanese "secrets to success." This was before it became widely known that Deming and Juran—both Americans—were the "secrets."

Deming was invited to Japan by industrial leaders and engineers to help counteract the negative perception of the quality of Japanese products. Rather quickly his "14 points" of management became a basis for operating many Japanese firms (Deming, 2000):

1. Maintain constancy of purpose.
2. Adopt a new philosophy—waste, delays, and poor quality are unacceptable.
3. Cease dependence on mass inspection.
4. Stop using lowest price as the sole factor in accepting bids from suppliers.
5. Improve every process.
6. Institute on-the-job training.
7. Eliminate arbitrary numerical goals.
8. Permit/encourage pride of workmanship.
9. Lead with the aim of helping people do the best possible job.
10. Drive out fear—solve the problem rather than look for someone to blame.
11. Break down barriers between units and people.
12. Encourage and support self-improvement and educational goals of staff.
13. Clearly define top management in terms of quality and productivity.

14. Eliminate slogans, exhortations, and targets asking for zero defects or new levels of productivity.

Joseph Juran went to Japan in the mid-1950s to conduct a series of executive seminars addressing such topics as planning, organizational issues, management's responsibility in maintaining quality goods and services, and goal setting. He published his ideas in *Managerial Breakthrough* (Juran, 1995). There are three key pieces to this approach—quality planning, quality improvement, and quality control. Another feature of his thinking is the importance of the internal customer (e.g., another library department) as well as the external consumer (e.g., users, other libraries, vendors) of the goods or services.

You can probably see why quality service to the "end user/customer" is important to library operations. Libraries' sole purpose is to provide service, and anything but quality service should be unacceptable. Certainly, limited funding and limited staffing create challenges and, all too often, make it impossible to do all we wish we could. However, such challenges should not deter us from thinking about and doing the very best we can.

KEY POINTS TO REMEMBER

Quality Approach
- Successful organizations have satisfied customers.
- Satisfied customers are developed and retained when they receive high-quality goods or services from an organization.
- Maintaining high-quality goods or services requires a staff that is committed to quality.
- Staff commitment is best achieved through staff involvement in teamwork, planning, and decision making.

COMPOSITE APPROACHES

We end this brief review of management approaches with a discussion of Peter Drucker (1909–2005) and Henry Mintzberg (1939–). Each has had a long and distinguished career as a scholar and a teacher of management. They are not associated with any particular management approach, but rather they draw from the vast array of options available to contemporary managers. If anything, they are closest to the contingency approach. Also, they draw on ideas, concepts, and theories from any academic discipline that offers something for managers to ponder and, in some cases, implement. Certainly you will find frequent references to these scholars throughout this book, as their wide-ranging approaches also reflect our views about management.

KEY POINTS TO REMEMBER

Composite Approaches
- Management is a multidimensional activity.
- Useful management concepts are found in almost every academic discipline.
- Effective managers do not restrict themselves to a single approach.
- Effective managers read on a regular basis about a wide variety of topics beyond management.

YOUR FUTURE AS A MANAGER

Earlier we mentioned that many library school students do not see themselves as ever becoming a manager. However, the fact is that you, more often than not, will quickly find yourself being a "manager." In today's tight economic conditions, libraries face staffing shortages, along with other financial concerns, that result in such things as vacant positions being unfilled and new positions impossible to secure. These in turn often mean newcomers are asked early on to assume some managerial duties. You are better served, as are those you first supervise, if you have thought about what to do when called upon to assume some supervisory duties before the call comes.

Today's effective managers employ the full range of options in the management tool kit, choosing which to use at any given time depending on the circumstances—a mix of the contingency and composite approaches. Almost everyone has a preferred managerial style; good managers are flexible and change approaches when it is necessary. Doing so is the art of management—drawing on the basics, developing the skills to assess situations quickly and accurately, and having a finely honed set of people skills.

If you accept the idea that management is an art, it goes without saying that there is a need to develop a personal style. Furthermore, in moving from one management role to another, slight variations will emerge in that style. Individuals do not respond to everyone in the same way. A management style must change as situations and the persons involved change. A corollary of the statement that management is an art is that there is no such thing as a "correct" style. Many of us have had the opportunity to observe two persons of differing personalities and styles effectively manage the same organization. Such an experience is the clearest demonstration that a variety of management styles can be effective in the same work situation.

You might well start the thinking process by assessing your personal strengths and weaknesses. Here are some sample questions to consider:

FOR FURTHER THOUGHT

Regularly scanning recent issues of two or three general management journals, such as *Harvard Business Review* or *Library Management*, is one easy method to keep current with trends and new approaches. We provide a list of some of our favorite titles for doing this in this chapter's Launching Pad section.

- What are the positive work experiences that I've had?
- What was it about those experiences that made them good?
- What were my worst work experiences? What made them so?
- What don't I like done to me?
- What type of direction or supervision do I like?
- What type of directions am I comfortable giving?
- Can I, and how do I, tell someone that he or she has done a good or a bad job?
- What management approaches do I find most comfortable?

As you develop answers to such questions, you are drafting your own management style.

AUTHORS' EXPERIENCE

The authors employed different management styles; however, each was successful in their own ways.

Evans's preferred method was a mix of management by objectives, maximum delegation, and trust in those he worked with. That was the starting point in each new work relationship and remained so for as long as the individuals were successful. When there were problems, he adjusted the style to better match the situation.

Alire, recognized as a change agent, preferred a humanistic management style, believing that a flatter organizational structure provided for more staff involvement and input. This in turn allowed more buy-in to the established strategic directions. With that structure came more responsibility and accountability on the part of staff. Coupled with effective communication and strong interpersonal relations skills, this style was key to her management success.

ADVISORY BOARD EXPERIENCE

Carol Sinwell's management style evolved over time. As she moved from K–12 classroom teacher/manager to public library manager to community college library/learning resources manager to college classroom/manager, she learned about and practiced many theories and faced many realities.

Key to Sinwell's development was quality mentoring by senior managers, and she tried to carry on that practice with her employees. She recognized the importance of genuine communication and personal interaction with staff, especially when working in a team environment. "Knowing yourself" and "knowing the organization culture" were critical if programs and staff development were to reach fruition. Learning to appreciate different personality styles, that is, the strengths and weaknesses individuals bring to the workplace, enhanced team productivity. Cross-training and using collaborative work teams are essential in libraries to provide quality, comprehensive services with reduced resources and to meet the emerging learning needs in the public and college environs.

Joseph Mika's preferred administrative style is based on the contingency theory, and he refers to it as "situational." He has been a library administrator and active in library and information science (LIS) programs for over 30 years, and he has also been influenced by education in management courses from business schools, LIS classes, and U.S. Army programs. Over the years what developed was a participative management style that considers the individual who is being managed and takes actions.

KEY POINTS TO REMEMBER

- Managing is a pervasive activity, and it has been part of humankind's environment for as long as people have lived together.
- Thinking you will never become a "manager" as a librarian is counterproductive, as almost all of us do manage to some degree and much sooner than expected.
- Learning about management concepts and practices does not ensure success, but that knowledge can assist in avoiding mistakes that hurt everyone involved.
- Studying the major approaches to management and some of the major thinkers is part of the learning process for successful managers.
- Understanding the options available as well as understanding yourself is important in developing your own style.
- Locking into a single style is not wise, as different people require different approaches.
- Being flexible is one of the cornerstones to being a successful manager.

References

Ackoff, Russell L., C. West Churchman, and Leonard Arnoff. 1957. *Introduction to Operations Research.* New York: Wiley.

Barnard, Chester. 1938. *Functions of the Executive.* Cambridge, MA: Harvard University Press.

Berry, John N. 2012. "Luis Herrera: Librarian of the Year 2012." *Library Journal* 137, no. 1: 28–30.

Birkinshaw, Julian. 2010. "Rethinking Management." *MIT Sloan Management Review* 51, no. 4: 14–15.

Burns, Thomas, and George M. Stalker. 1961. *The Management of Innovation.* London: Tavistock.

Cross, Jeanne. 2005. "Opportunities for Internships in Library Administration." *Library Administration and Management* 19, no. 4: 193–196.

Cyert, Richard M., and James G. March. 1963. *A Behavioral Theory of the Firm.* Englewood Cliffs, NJ: Prentice-Hall.

Deming, W. Edwards. 2000. *The New Economics for Industry, Government, Education.* 2nd ed. Cambridge, MA: MIT Press.

Dougherty, Richard M. 2008. *Streamlining Library Services: What We Do, How Much Time It Takes, What It Costs, and How We Can Do It Better.* Lanham, MD: Scarecrow Press.

Dougherty, Richard M., and Fred J. Heinritz. 1982. *Scientific Management of Library Operations.* 2nd ed. Metuchen, NJ: Scarecrow Press.

Emery, Fred, and Eric Trist. 1965. "Causal Texture of Organizational Environments." *Human Relations* 18, no. 1: 21–31.

Evans, G. Edward. 1984. "Management Education for Archivists, Information Managers and Librarians: Is There a Global Core?" *Education for Information* 2, no. 3: 295–307.

Fayol, Henri. 1962. *Administration Industrielle et Generale.* Paris: Dunnod.

Follett, Mary Parker. 1941. *Dynamic Administration.* London: Pitman.

Gantt, Henry. 1916. *Work, Wages, and Profits.* 2nd ed. New York: Engineering Magazine Co.

———. 1919. *Organizing for Work.* New York: Harcourt, Brace, and Howe.

Gilbreth, Lillian. 1914. *Psychology of Management.* New York: Sturgis and Walton.

Gulick, Luther, and Lyndall Urwick. 1937. *Papers on the Science of Administration.* New York: Institute of Public Administration, Columbia University.

Juran, Joseph. 1995. *Managerial Breakthrough.* New York: McGraw-Hill.

Katz, Robert. 1974. "Skills of an Effective Administrator." *Harvard Business Review* 52, no. 9: 90–102.

Lindblom, Charles. 1959. "The Science of 'Muddling Through.'" *Public Administration Review* 19: 78–88.

Long, Sarah. 2012. E-mail communication sent to Camila A. Alire, February 29.

Luthans, Fred. 1973. "Contingency Theory of Management: A Path Out of the Jungle." *Business Horizons* 16, no. 3: 62–72.

Mackenzie, Maureen L. 2009. "Management Education for Library Directors:

Are Graduate Library Programs Providing Future Library Directors with the Skills and Knowledge They Will Need?" *Journal of Education for Library and Information Science* 50, no. 3: 129–142.

Mahoney, Thomas, Thomas Jardee, and Stephen Carroll. 1964. "The Job(s) of Management." *Industrial Management* 4, no. 2: 97–110.

Mayo, Elton. 1933. *The Human Problems of an Industrial Civilization*. Salem, NH: Ayer.

Mintzberg, Henry. 1971. "Managerial Work: Analysis from Observation." *Management Science* 18, no. 2: B97–B110.

———. 1973. *The Nature of Managerial Work*. Englewood Cliffs, NJ: Prentice Hall.

———. 1975. "The Manager's Job: Folklore and Fact." *Harvard Business Review* 53, no. 5: 49–61.

Mitchell, Geanna W., Leane B. Skinner, and Bonnie J. White. 2010. "Essential Soft Skills for Success in the Twenty-First Century Workforce as Perceived by Business Educators." *Delta Pi Epsilon Journal* 52, no.1: 43–53.

Munsterberg, Hugo. 1913. *Psychology and Industrial Efficiency*. New York: Houghton Mifflin.

Olver, Lynne. 2011. "So You're the New Director? Twelve Points to Help You Survive the First Year." *Public Libraries* 50, no. 2: 6–7.

Senge, Peter. 1990. *The Fifth Discipline*. New York: Random House.

Simon, Herbert. 1947. *Administrative Behavior*. New York: Macmillan.

Taylor, Fredrick. 1947. *Principles of Scientific Management*. New York: Harper.

Todd, Peter. 2010. "Embracing New Mindsets." *BizEd* 9, no. 1: 28–32, 34, 36.

Urwick, Lyndall. 1943. *Elements of Business Administration*. New York: Harper and Bros.

von Bertalanffy, Ludwig. 1950. "Theory of Open Systems in Physics and Biology." *Science* 3, no. 1: 23–29.

Weber, Max. 1947. *The Theory of Social and Economic Organizations*. Translated by A. M. Henderson and Talcott H. Parsons. New York: Free Press of Glencoe.

Wren, Daniel. 1979. *The Evolution of Management Thought*. 2nd ed. New York: Wiley.

Launching Pad

Abbasi, Sami, Kenneth Hollman, and Robert D. Hayes. 2008. "Bad Bosses and How Not to Be One." *Information Management Journal* 42, no. 1: 52–56.

Christensen, Clayton M., and Michael E. Raynor. 2003. "Why Hard-Nosed Executives Should Care about Management Theory." *Harvard Business Review* 81, no. 9: 66–74.

Cox, Richard J. 2005. *Archives and Archivists in the Information Age*. New York: Neal-Schuman.

Daly, Gail M. 2011. "Earl C. Borgeson's Ten Rules for Law Library Management." *Law Library Journal* 103, no. 3: 515–519.

Fisher, Donna M. 2004. "Flying Solo." *Information Outlook* 8, no. 9: 23–24.

Hopp, Wallace J. 2008. "*Management Science* and the Science of Management." *Management Science* 54, no. 12: 1961–1962.

Hunter, Gregory S. 2007. *Records Management.* New York: Neal-Schuman.

Matheson, Heather. 2007. "Promoting (for) Change: New Academic Librarians in Managerial Roles." *Feliciter* 53, no. 2: 70–72.

Mintzberg, Henry. 2011. "Looking Forward to Development." *T + D* 65, no. 2: 50–55.

Roberts, Ken. 2009. "From Outgrown and Overmanaged to Resilient Organizations." *Feliciter* 55, no. 1: 37–38.

Roberts, Sue, and Jennifer Rowley. 2004. *Managing Information Services.* New York: Neal-Schuman.

Ryan, Marianne. 2010. "Catching On: Management Training in Depository Libraries." *Reference and User Services Quarterly* 50, no. 2: 119–121.

Simon, Carol. 2005. "How Can You Be a Manager? You're a Solo." *Information Outlook* 9, no. 3: 13–14.

Staley, T. L. 2008. "Wisdom Trumps the Latest Management Fad." *Supervision* 69, no. 6: 3–5.

Management Journals Well Worth Regular Reading

General Management

Academy of Management
Executive Association News
Harvard Business Review
Journal of Business Ethics
Journal of Management
Journal of Managerial Issues
Leadership and Organization Development Journal
Management Science
MIT Sloan Management Review
Organization Science
Performance Management and Metrics
Public Administration Review
Public Personnel Management
Strategic Change Supervision

Library Management

American Libraries
Bottom Line
College and Research Libraries
Computers in Libraries
Evidence Based Library and Information Practice
Feliciter

Information Management Journal
Information Outlook
Information Technology and Libraries
Journal of Academic Librarianship
Journal of Library Administration
Knowledge Quest
Library Administrator's Digest
Library and Archival Security
Library Leadership and Management
Library Trends
School Library Monthly

The journals listed are certainly not the only worthwhile ones to read on a fairly regular basis, but they are some we have found valuable during our careers as managers.

The business environment has become more turbulent and competitive because of advancement of information and communication technologies and globalization. Business organizations are pressured and challenged by these phenomena while striving for their business success or even their survival.

 —Ching Seng Yap and Md Zabid Abdul Rashid (2011)

Librarians should be consistently scanning the environment to look for signs of the changes that may come.

 —David J. Staley and Kara J. Malenfant (2010)

Organizations have identities. They are distinguishable; they have names, occupy space, and are accorded legal rights much the same as people.

 —Dennis Duchon and Brian Drake (2009)

Public service organizations (PSO) function in patterns that endure over time. Derived from the study of complex systems, the observation of patterns is important for public policy and organizational change. Although the notion of organizations having cultures is now well accepted, organizational patterns involve more than culture—they are the product of dynamic multidimensional factors at work in organizations.

 —Eleanor D. Glor (2008)

Most of the management literature on culture refers to its inclusive properties. It refers to the intangible part of an organization, which gives it its cohesiveness. Cultures embody systems of meaning and signification.

 —Sarah Rutherford (2001)

2

OPERATING ENVIRONMENT

This chapter focuses on the following:

- The pervasiveness of organizations and their impact on our lives
- What constitutes a formal organization
- The difference between for-profit and nonprofit organizations
- The impact of the external environment on organizations and their operations
- Why scanning the external environment is vital for organizations
- The nature of organizational culture and its importance

WE CANNOT AVOID organizations or management no matter how much we might wish we could. From birth to death, organizations play a role in our daily lives. In fact, some government organization will certify whether we are officially alive or dead. We are constantly interacting with organizations in some manner.

An organization is almost always where you earn a living. The workplace is often the most significant formal organization in our daily lives. We talk about work with workplace colleagues as well as with family and friends. We are likely to complain about how "that place" functions from time to time. Certainly most of the complaints relate to "management"; however, to some degree management practice is influenced by the organization and its environment, both internal and external. Organizational culture is a key component in the internal environment, as it impacts our view of "our workplace."

As our opening quotations suggest, organizations have a life and, like people, change over time. They are affected by outside factors, are created, and have a life span, and many die in time. Someone suggested there are no more than 63 organizations still in existence that were established before 1400—most of which are universities. Organizations die because of several factors, such as a changing environment and failure to adjust to those changes.

Like us, organizations face challenges over which they have little control. However, just like us, they can develop plans for how to address potential challenges.

Such planning may well reduce the negative consequences and, in some circumstances, even benefit organizations by having anticipated the event(s). Their success or failure in doing so will impact us as employees in some way.

Organizations come in a variety of forms. There are two broad categories—formal (voluntary and involuntary membership) and informal. Beyond these broad types there are a number of variations, such as formal for-profit and formal nonprofit and open/public membership and restricted/private membership. Libraries fall into what Eleanor Glor (2008) labeled public service organizations (PSOs). PSOs are government agencies that work directly with the public.

Individuals voluntarily join an organization, to some degree, because its mission and goals more or less match their personal and/or professional values and interests. As an organization grows and changes, so do its goals. Those goals change over time to such an extent sometimes that the founders would have difficulty recognizing "their" organization. Organizations are like people; once they attain a goal, they seek out new ones. Goals expand and contract as a result of successes and failures as well as from changes in the environment. Over time, an organization can change so much that some individuals leave because their personal goals/values no longer match the institution's goals.

People generally belong to several formal organizations beyond the workplace, such as community service organizations and personal hobby interest groups, as well as subgroups within the workplace (such as a staff association or advisory board). We are also involved in informal groups (such as a Thursday-night concert group or a book club). With so many organizations in our lives, we must handle conflicting goals and objectives.

FORMAL ORGANIZATIONS

Chester Barnard (1956), whom we mentioned in Chapter 1, studied organizations and how they develop, function, and change through time. Human organizations, according to Barnard, consist of five basic elements: *size, interdependence, input, throughput,* and *output.* Organizations vary in *size* from one as large as the U.S. federal government to one as small as two people. Sometimes people forget that two- and three-person operations, such as small school and public libraries, are in fact organizations. As such, they share most of the same organizational issues as large ones.

Interdependence means there is a recognition of shared common goals as well as recognition that by working together it will be easier to achieve the goals. Disagreement and tension will be present over the "hows" to achieve the goals, but the value of the shared benefits maintains organizational cohesion.

Established goals require a list of the *inputs* to achieve them, such as materials, energy, money, and information. After acquiring the resources, the organization uses the resources (*throughput*) effectively to achieve the desired results. The end product of that processing is the *output*. Output can be as tangible as an automobile or as intangible as the answer to a reference question.

For each of Barnard's five basic elements, try to provide two examples that relate to a library service you know.

As an organization becomes more complex, its goals and objectives may conflict with one another, with other organizations, as well as with at least some of its staff. Such conflict is counterproductive for all concerned. Handling such conflicts becomes a normal fact of managerial life.

One major source of organizational conflict is competition for resources. No matter how "well off" others may think an organization is, within the organization there is a finite pool of resources to distribute. During any given period, some resources may be more available than others; and the pattern of availability and demand fluctuates. In the 1950s, libraries worried about material resources, physical facilities, and funds to support intellectual freedom. During the 1960s, the big resource problem was personnel. In the 1970s and 1980s, it was financial support. In the 1990s, libraries faced the burden of having adequate funding for information communication technology (ICT) equipment and electronic resources. In the first decade of the twenty-first century, libraries became concerned about competitors such as Google, a very difficult economic situation, and the public's view about the value of library services and the bad economy. While the specifics vary, the conflict over resources remains a constant.

Competition for scarce resources takes place both inside and outside the organization, and competition among similar organizations can be very strong. Because most libraries are publicly supported, they find themselves in a yearly struggle for funds. Generally the process involves requesting an increase that will at least keep pace with inflation. All agencies in the jurisdiction compete for at least last year's allocation as well as request greater support. Each agency will attempt to seek support and justify all requested increases. The total money requested by all agencies usually far exceeds the available funds; therefore, conflict arises as each agency tries to prove that it is more worthy of support than the others. We explore this type of competition in more detail in Chapter 17 ("Managing Money").

Resource competition also takes place within the organization. For example, suppose the library secured only one of its six requested new positions. The six requesting department heads will, in all likelihood, attempt to show their staffing need as the primary one. Just as with interagency conflict, the ultimate decision maker must realize that the final decision will probably result in some lasting tension(s).

Whatever the source, managers must have a tolerance for conflict. Methods of dealing with conflict situations range from using personal judgment to negotiation. Management writers have addressed conflict control. They look at a series of interpersonal and interorganizational interactions that constantly occur:

- Individuals interact with the environment.
- Individuals interact with one another.
- Individuals interact with organizations.
- Organizations interact with other organizations.
- Organizations interact with the environment.

In the past, managers had a tendency to focus on internal issues, such as improving operations, to achieve organizational goals more efficiently and effectively. That focus usually meant looking at technology/equipment, people, tasks, and structure from within rather than looking at the external environment. Today, if their organizations are to succeed, managers must devote significant time to studying what is taking place in the world around them.

NONPROFIT ORGANIZATIONS

Before turning to the primary topic of this chapter, we must pause to discuss the nature of nonprofit organizations, such as libraries, as this discussion does matter when it comes to studying the surrounding environment. Almost all libraries are nonprofit or PSOs. The nonprofit status has several implications for managers. These are two of the most important:

- Financial resources are generally derived from outside funding sources (such as taxes, grants, and private benefactors) rather than from sales of services.
- Many nonprofit organizations are public rather than private and are therefore subject to public scrutiny in ways for-profits are not.

Profit-making organizations have a clear indicator of effectiveness—profit or loss—and a long period of loss leads to failure. For nonprofits, lacking such a clear indicator, poor performance may pass unnoticed for some time. Failing to secure adequate operating funds may be the first indication of a serious performance problem. However, as we all know, economic conditions and political decisions are also leading causes of low funding. Knowing what is taking place in the environment is the key to identifying the real cause of the funding problems.

What was a rather sharp line dividing for-profit and nonprofit organizations has been blurring since the late 1990s. There is also a blurring of the line between the types of nonprofit (donation based and publicly funded) organizations.

One factor driving the changes for nonprofits is "forced cooperation" or, to use the current term, "collaboration." Certainly there has always been some useful and productive cooperation/collaboration among various nonprofits on a voluntary basis. What is different today is that a large number of funding sources for nonprofits are more or less forcing cooperative ventures through funding preferences for collaborative projects. One such example is IMLS (Institute of Museum and Library Services), which indicates in its "Grant Eligibility" that "Additionally, ineligible organizations may still be able to participate in grant programs through partnerships with eligible organizations" (http://www.imls.gov/applicants/criteria .shtm). Many of the IMLS grants are for consortia or statewide activities. Single institutions can apply, and some do succeed; however, limited funds often mean the collaborative projects have a definite edge in the process. Such joint efforts over time begin to blur the organizational difference. Stretching limited funds through partnerships is important; however, when the organization's real goal is just to secure extra funding some strange bedfellows come about.

Another feature of today's nonprofits, regardless of type, is growing "commer- cialization." Almost all donation-based organizations face the issue of expanding its support base (you can think of this as increasing market share, a for-profit concept) as well as retaining its major donors (customer loyalty). Publicly funded organiza- tions, which include most libraries, are under pressure to "recover costs" for various services. To take a standard library service example—photocopy service—setting the cost of copies is very much like how for-profit organizations set their product prices (materials, labor, and equipment costs plus what the market will bear).

Faruggia Gianfranco (2007) summed up the changing world of nonprofits in a literature review article about them:

> Does all this sound like mission-driven stewardship or brazen commer- cialization for the sake of the nonprofit industry? . . . [T]he literature seems to offer very strong indications that the sector is more of an industry. . . . How can the sector possibly return to . . . the world in which commu- nity-oriented philanthropy in the pursuit of enlightened self-interest is no longer as compelling as ensuring short-term returns to stockholders and gaining market share? (p. 10)

He offers no answer to the last question beyond suggesting there should be broad-based community discussion of the issues.

With the exception of special libraries in the for-profit sector (such as law and corporate libraries), most libraries depend, to a greater or lesser degree, on tax funds derived from a government jurisdiction (community, county, state, or national) to cover operating expenses. Government funding always means that political issues are important factors in decisions about when, where, and if to spend money. A library manager who fails to recognize this fact will find herself or himself getting fewer and fewer dollars.

SOMETHING TO PONDER

Reflect on the differences between managing in the for-profit sector and in the nonprofit sector. For each, list three advantages and three disadvan- tages that the manager may encounter.

Politics (not partisan politics but the politics of decision making and organizational politics) and the political process is part of maintaining publicly funded libraries. The word "politics" has many definitions and connotations, most of which cover the following: the acquisition and maintenance of power, competition and conflict over scarce resources, allocation of resources, and determination of who gets what, when, why, and how. Aside from the first point, libraries constantly find themselves involved in these "political" areas. Taxpayer "revolts," a global trading environment, and varying economies demonstrate that politics can dramatically affect funding for library operations and underscore the need to constantly monitor the world around us.

Most libraries (with the exception of a few private libraries) are a part of a larger organization. As part of a larger organization, you must also be aware of what the "whole" does as well as recognize that the whole will have a say in what the library does.

Beverly Lynch (1974, p. 127) described four very important factors to consider when studying the library environment:

- The nature of the environment itself
- The relationship among the libraries within a set of organizations
- The characteristics of the exchanges that take place among libraries
- The impact that the environment has upon the libraries' internal structure and operations

What are the characteristics of library services that affect the management function? Try to identify six characteristics, drawing on this text and on your experience as a customer.

ENVIRONMENT AND THE ORGANIZATION

Libraries have a tripartite environment. As mentioned earlier, few libraries exist as independent entities; rather, they are part of a larger organization—a city, a university, a school district, or a corporation. As such, first, there is the internal library environment, over which managers have or should have reasonably good control. Second, there is the parent organizational environment, over which librarians may have some, if small, influence. Third, there is the environment beyond the parent institution, over which almost no one has control. All three environments require monitoring if the library is to be successful. A good article that explores the reason for examining the environment of a nonprofit organization is by Andrews, Boyne, and Walker (2006).

Almost 50 years ago, F. Emery and E. L. Trist (1965) identified four basic types of organizational environments regardless of type of organization: *placid-randomized, placid-clustered, disturbed-reactive,* and *turbulent.* Although Emery and Trist were not concerned with libraries as such, their four types of environments can be applied to library environments.

A *placid-randomized* environment is one in which the organization assumes that both the goals and the dangers are basically unchanging. (A danger is something that would adversely affect the viability of the organization.) Organizational goals are long term and seldom need adjustment. Such organizations assume that changes or dangers to their well-being occur randomly, and there is little or no predictability as to when such changes or dangers will be encountered. In such an environment, the organization collects information to meet long-term goals, and these goals are considered predictable. In the past, large research libraries and archives were typical examples of organizations that operated in a placid-randomized environment. Today, and for the foreseeable future, it seems unlikely that many libraries will be operating in a placid environment.

Many libraries operate in a *placid-clustered* environment, which is where goals are primarily long term but the organization must quickly adjust the goals when external factors warrant. In this environment, the organization assumes that dangers, and to some extent opportunities, will arise in clusters. Furthermore, the organization assumes that it will need to expend some effort in identifying and collecting information about the clusters. A library example from collection management is when the collection is relatively unchanging, but time, energy, and money are directed toward identifying changes in the parent (a new degree program/subject emphasis, for example) or external environment (changes in exchange rates or information delivery systems). Most educational institutions and public libraries operate in this type of environment. They set long-term goals and rarely change those goals, although they may change short-term objectives. However, they do recognize that dangers exist, such as changing public attitudes about the value of social services generally and library services specifically. Once the questioning starts, it generally expands in scope (clustering) and does not disappear quickly. Also, new service opportunities arise as new technologies become available. These opportunities may counteract some or all of the dangers (e.g., competition) arising from the new technologies.

Disturbed-reactive environments are those in which there are active organizational competitors. Two examples of library competitors are the Google Books

Library Project for academic libraries and handheld reading devices to accommodate e-books for public libraries. In the disturbed-reactive environment, having prompt, accurate information about what the competitors are doing—and, when possible, what they are planning to do—is important. One label for this type of information is "competitive intelligence." Jan Davis (2008) noted the importance of competitive intelligence for clients of special libraries: "The conference theme, Energize, Explore, Evolve, was exemplified by the popularity of the competitive intelligence (CI) sessions. Indeed, law librarians were energized and ready to explore their evolving role as CI professionals with law firms" (p. 14). For libraries there are two aspects of CI. First, it can assist the library's clients in learning about what their competitors are doing. Second, it can gather information that may assist the library itself to become ever more competitive.

Jan Schwarz (2007) also defined the concept: "Competitive intelligence (CI) has been perceived as an activity primarily concerned with analyzing the competitors of an organization and as an activity that considers the environment of that organization" (p. 55). For special libraries, CI has been used to assess what the parent organization's competitors are doing or may do. This type of CI is something in which for-profit organizations are interested in order to keep or increase their market share. All libraries can identify some useful techniques in CI to assist in effectively dealing with their competitors.

Although an organization in a disturbed-reactive environment has long-term goals, it revises its goals in light of information received about competitors' activities. Business and industrial (special) libraries operate in such an environment. Here, four or five years may represent a large time span for long-term goals.

Finally, there is the *turbulent* environment. Not only do competitors exist but also the level of competition necessitates focused efforts in order to survive. As a result of knowing what others are doing or planning to do, an organization may make a radical change in its basic purposes. Anyone who reads the business section of a newspaper encounters examples of organizations that made successful basic goal changes and those that failed because they did not change. On a slightly less extreme level, libraries serving research and development teams experience occasional abrupt shifts in service emphasis. Thus, the organizational environment is also an information environment, and the nature of the environment affects the nature of library activities.

Managers must develop methods to assist in effectively handling a changing environment. The external environment has several major dimensions: sociocultural, technological, political, legal, economic, and institutional. In addition, there exist many subvariables of the major dimensions that the manager must also consider, including dimensions on local, regional, national, and international levels. Other subvariables, such as customers, suppliers, competitors, and sources of funding, all become factors in developing an effective service organization.

Information and communication technologies (ICTs) are a major issue in today's environments. Governmental change (such as election outcomes) can produce policies and regulations that affect, for example, the management of staff. Political change can also produce the possibility of additional funding if governments can be persuaded of the benefits of investing in library services. Managers working in countries that have a volatile exchange rate should keep a close watch on economic developments that may benefit—or limit—their spending power. These are just some of the reasons why managers need to scan the environment for developments that may affect their services, seek opportunities and benefits, and watch for threats and impending problems.

Burns and Stalker (1961) identified two organizational systems that help match the organizational structure to the environment: "mechanistic" and "organic." Mechanistic systems emphasize specialization and a hierarchical organizational structure. This approach creates a stable organization that tends to change slowly, which is most suitable for placid environments. Organic systems typically emphasize work groups and a flat structure. Such systems work well in turbulent environments. Based on their research, Burns and Stalker suggested that some combination of mechanistic and organic systems was most effective in the disturbed environment. Lawrence and Lorsch (1967) further extended this work by looking at the relationship between departmental/unit values and goals and the environment. They found that organizations operating in changing environments had highly differentiated units and made use of committees, task forces, and a flat structure to achieve intraunit coordination.

There are several ways to apply the concepts of Burns and Stalker to today's organizations. Martin Harris (2006) drew upon their concepts in a paper exploring innovation and organizational structure. His finding suggested that a "bureaucratic" structure may not have as negative an impact as some writers, with a "post-bureaucratic organizational" view, have contended. Ingrid Bonn (2005) explored methods for improving strategic thinking and relationships between environmental issues and organizations. The concepts of Burns and Stalker played a significant role in her analysis.

SOMETHING TO PONDER

In terms of libraries, compare the differences and similarities between Emery and Trist's concepts and those of Burns and Stalker.

ENVIRONMENTAL SCANNING

Some management writers suggest that a manager can learn a great deal from reading Sun-Tzu's *The Art of War*. Although we don't fully agree that the book should be a basic management guide, it does explore some concepts that can be useful. Perhaps one of the most useful concepts comes from the opening of the first chapter: "Warfare is a great matter to a nation; . . . it is the way of survival and of destruction and must be examined" (http://www.sonshi.com/sun1.html). By substituting two words, one has the focus of this section: "Environment is a great matter to an organization. . . ."

Environmental scanning is the process of gathering information about activities, trends, relationships, competitors, potential dangers, and any other factors in the environment that can impact the organization. The data collected can inform a variety of management activities, but they are essential in planning and decision making. Other library activities include fiscal and collection management. With a formalized scanning process in place, you can avoid pitfalls or being blindsided. Lacking such a process, the chances for long-term viability decline (Albright, 2004). In today's rapidly changing world, monitoring the environment is important for any organization.

Most libraries ought to examine some basic environmental factors on a regular basis. These are some of the common variables:

- Customers—user behavior and needs are the foundation upon which one should build information services.
- Competitors/market—libraries face competition from one another as well as from other services.
- Funding sources—funding is crucial for effective library services, and knowing what factors are affecting the source(s) is the key to successful planning.
- Suppliers—two key categories of suppliers are firms that provide information materials services (jobbers and publishers, for example) and those that handle library/information service technologies. Factors impacting such firms will impact the library and end users and vice versa.
- Labor issues—an important ongoing concern is the availability of qualified people for positions in libraries, both professional and support staff.
- Legal/regulatory factors—legal, regulatory, and legislative factors impact managerial actions in many ways, from facilities to staffing. A worldwide example of a legal concern for libraries is copyright.
- Economic trends—economic factors affect information services in two

TIP

Keeping up with the economic, political, and social factors can be done easily by regularly scanning such weekly journals as *Newsweek, Time,* and *The Economist.* Naturally local, regional, and national newspapers should also be monitored.

primary ways: what one can buy with available funds and how much money is available to spend.

- Technology—technology is a critical variable for information services, as we will discuss in some depth in Chapter 18 ("Managing Technology").
- Political changes/trends –any library that derives a significant portion of its operating funds from public sources must monitor political trends. Thinking about the potential implications of a changing scene is useful when developing short-term and medium-term plans.
- Sociocultural factors—by sociocultural factors, we mean the values, attitudes, demographics, historic context, and customs of the society in which the organization operates. All of the factors have obvious implications for libraries.

FORECASTING THE ENVIRONMENT

Forecasting is one method for looking at societal changes and thinking about what future implications such changes may have. Jack Malgeri (2010) defined forecasting as "the ability to develop and maintain a forward-looking perspective and to anticipate emerging opportunities and problems by continually scanning the environment for trends and new developments" (p. 39). There is a saying about forecasts: "The only certainty is the forecast will be wrong." While this holds true more often than not, a forecast does not have to be 100 percent right to be useful. If nothing else, forecasting causes managers to consider possible changes in the environment and to think about how to respond if change does occur. Being proactive is almost always better than being reactive. In essence, scanning and forecasting provide highly valuable data for the planning process.

Normally, forecasting focuses on factors that are critical to the organization. Some factors may be controllable to an extent, while others are beyond the organization's control (e.g., population, birthrate, and high school graduation rate). Often, the data needed for forecasting are already available in the library; other data will be available from the parent organization or obtainable from government agencies. Forecasts can be qualitative or quantitative in character.

Like all methods intended to anticipate future events, environmental scanning/forecasting success is a function of what you look for/at and how you interpret what you see. Wayne Stewart, Ruth May, and Arvind Kalia (2008) noted that "Because environmental issues are often ambiguous and require interpretation for issue diagnosis, perceptions are critical in guiding decision making" (p. 86). Their main point is that the more ambiguous the situation, the more time and effort you should put into data gathering in order to reduce as much ambiguity as possible.

John Castiglione (2007) made a strong case for libraries to engage in efforts that help identify future trends, whether it is called scanning, forecasting, futuring, or some other term: "Libraries of every type and size are facing similar resource constraints and competitive pressures from corporate entities—external to the library—that are vying to provide service directly to stakeholders that libraries have traditionally served. . . . [O]ur professional associations need to understand and monitor—on a global basis—the shifting competitive landscape" (p. 528). We agree that our associations ought to assist in the scanning process and are perhaps best able to do so on a global basis. However, only the individual library can economically assess the future local trends and how those trends may impact the library's services.

ANTI-ENVIRONMENTAL VIEWS

Not all management writers agree that the external operating environment plays a significant role in managerial actions. Perhaps the most thoughtful "anti-environment" writer was John Child (1972). He raised three arguments against the idea that the environment plays a dominating role in how an organization operates. According to Child, the decision makers have more autonomy than expected even if you assume that the environment is a determining factor. His position was that decision makers may select from a range of viable alternatives and choose the type of operating environment that they consider most suitable for their organization. Thus, the environment does not unduly constrain actions. Although his point may be valid for profit-oriented organizations, few libraries are free to change their operating environment. However, we certainly agree there are usually a number of viable alternative courses of action.

Child's second point is that organizations are not always passive reactors to the environment. Certainly many influences are beyond the control of the organization, but there are also some that the organization can try to modify or influence. For example, one library environmental factor that you can influence is the funding authority's view of the importance of library services.

His third argument states that having an environmentally deterministic point of view blurs the distinction between real environmental characteristics and the perception and evaluation of these characteristics by management. We completely agree with this argument, as it is essential to base action on reality rather than on perception.

A relatively recent writer to suggest that scanning or forecasting can do little to help avoid unexpected nasty surprises is Nassim Taleb (2007). His book *Black Swan* is a detailed discussion of the role and impact of random events or developments on society and, to a degree, the futility of forecasting. "Our inability to predict in environments subjected to the Black Swan, coupled with a general lack of awareness of this state of affairs, means that certain professionals, while believing they are experts, are in fact not. . . . Black Swans being unpredictable, we need to adjust to their existence (rather than naively trying to predict them)" (Taleb, 2007, pp. xx–xxi). In the remainder of the book, Taleb does not suggest organizations should cease looking toward future developments but rather should be more realistic about the role randomness plays in what will happen.

ORGANIZATIONAL CULTURE

Organizational culture and the external environment may at first glance appear unrelated. They are related in that the external environment influences the internal organizational culture. To be effective, environmental scanning and assessing the implications of changes in the environment is a complex activity. It is something that some staff member is expected to do. If the organizational culture is

SOMETHING TO PONDER

Consider your current or most recent place of employment. Did you realize it had a special culture? If so, what elements or what experiences helped you learn and absorb that culture? Do you think that culture helped or hindered change?

such that everyone understands the importance of such scanning and they can assist in the process, the activity will be even more beneficial for the library.

Like societies, every organization has a culture that its members learn, or should learn, in order to be an effective member. That culture plays a significant role in how the organization operates. Unless someone acts in a manner contrary to the cultural norm, it is common for staff members to be unaware of the culture's influence on their actions—"learning" the culture is seldom a formalized process.

CHECK THIS OUT

Edgar Schein's 1990 article "Organizational Culture" (*American Psychologist* 45, no. 2: 109–119) offers a very good basic overview of the topic.

One key element in an organization's culture is the view of top leadership, which sets the tone for the rest of the staff. Supervisors and middle managers further set the tone in their areas of responsibility based on what they perceive to be top management views. There are other factors as well, as Sarah Rutherford (2001) noted: "An organization's culture is also heavily influenced by its past and its environment" (p. 374).

Just what is "organizational culture?" As Thomas Kell and Gregory Carrott (2005) noted, "Corporate culture, like personal character, is an amorphous quality that exerts a powerful influence" (p. 22). They go on to note both the positive and negative aspects of organizational culture. Although we acknowledge that the concept is rather amorphous, some elements are generally agreed upon. One such element is that members of the organization (consciously or not) share a set of values, assumptions, and expectations regarding what the organization is "about," how things should be done, and what is important,

FROM THE AUTHORS

Organizational culture also affects diversity in the organization. Organizational culture can lead to institutional racism where the beliefs and values are so embedded within the organization that when someone different shows up, they don't fit in. Managers should watch for and guard against this happening.

According to Geoffrey Bloor and Patrick Dawson (1994), organizational culture arises from interactions among these elements:

- Operating and cultural systems (dynamic/ongoing interaction)
- Historical factors (founders' vision, for example)
- Societal context (external to organization)
- External organizational environment (competition)
- Professional external environment (association values, practices)

Avan Jassawalla and Hemet Sashittal (2002) took a different tack and suggested that people learn organizational culture through these:

- Heroes (people past and present who made significant contributions to the organization)
- Stories (tales told about the good and bad of the past)
- Slogans ("the virtual library," "24/7 service")
- Symbols (name tags, pins, signs)
- Ceremonies (birthday parties, years of service)

It seems likely that all of the factors listed play some role in the learning process. What is significant is that culture does matter. In our view, organizational culture constitutes a major environmental situation for the staff and the organization. It is incumbent on managers to assess and understand that culture.

such as environmental scanning, and acceptable. Staff members act on these views even though the culture is rarely articulated, much less recorded. You learn it, as you learn social culture, through observation and through making mistakes. Although it is an internal environment, it can and does change as the result of changes in the external environment. Managers who ignore this internal environment do so at their peril—understanding the culture can make all the difference when it comes time for the organization to make adjustments because of external factors.

AUTHORS' EXPERIENCE

As we stated, organizational culture is unwritten and learned through experience. Top management's views about how things are done and what the general work attitude should be play a major role in determining the organization's culture. Evans worked at a Catholic university prior to his retirement from full-time employment. It had a culture that was open and people oriented and maintained a constant concern with learning. One picked up the values as one worked with others and learned that while it was a Catholic-based institution that fact, while important, was not dominant.

One example of that occurred one day when Evans and Fr. Ryan were having lunch in a crowded cafeteria. Fr. Ryan was in his "clerics," and Evans happened to be dressed all in black that day. A young lady asked if she could share their table because it was so busy. After indicating that was fine, the two men continued their conversation. The young lady looked at them several times and finally asked, "Are you priests?" Fr. Ryan quickly said, "I am; he certainly is not," pointing at Evans. "Why do you ask?"

After a moment, she replied, "If you were, I just wanted to thank you. I'm a freshman, and I'm Jewish. My family and I were rather worried about my coming to a Catholic university. We decided to take a chance because of your guaranteeing a four-year degree in four years. Everyone here is so friendly and open. No one seems to have a great interest in another person's faith. It's all about learning. I'm glad I came here. Thank you both, even if he isn't a priest."

PEOPLE-FRIENDLY ORGANIZATIONS

As long as the manager remains fully aware of the ramifications inherent in managing organizations and people, and as long as the manager tries to maintain a balance between the needs of the two, people control the organization. When the balance tips in favor of activities, people are no longer in control. An organizational threat to individual freedom and dignity cannot exist in a balanced situation. Saul Gellerman (1973) summed up the situation with the following:

> Thus we return to the dilemma that organizations have always faced, and always will, as long as they are comprised of individuals. The organization exists, thrives, and survives by harnessing the talents of individuals. Its problem is to do so without hobbling those talents or turning them against itself. This perpetual balancing act is the responsibility of management, especially those members of management in the lower echelons, whose influence upon employees is most direct. (p. 13)

ADVISORY BOARD EXPERIENCE

Joseph Mika has been fortunate to work in five different states and cities. He has enjoyed each location, while often hearing others complain about the same environment. What made the difference for him was his approach. Because he was the new professional, rather than expecting others to adapt to him, he adapted to the environment, adopting the business, academic, and cultural norms of the institution and the city in which he lived. Having grown up in Pittsburgh, Pennsylvania, there were certainly adjustments to be made as he worked and lived in the Midwest, New England, and the South over the course of his career.

Very few people deny that every formal organization has a few anti-people elements; nevertheless, when someone threatens the entire organizational structure, many others rush to the defense of the status quo. If, however, managers direct some of their attention toward correcting the anti-people elements and developing a balance between people and things, then almost everyone in an organization will help with the process.

KEY POINTS TO REMEMBER
- Organizations—formal and informal—play a key role in our working and personal lives.
- Organizations are pervasive.
- Organizations exist to accomplish specific objectives.
- Objectives evolve or change over the lifetime of the organization.
- Organizations try to be self-sustaining, changing objectives in response to a changing environment.
- Most libraries operate as nonprofit organizations (with public support and scrutiny).
- How organizations operate and survive are in large part determined by their highly complex environments.
- Library managers must recognize the need to assess three environments—one external and two internal (internal to the service itself and the internal environment of its parent organization).
- Managers who fail to monitor, assess, and adjust to the changing environments risk failure for themselves and their organizations (environmental scanning).
- Organizational culture plays a major role in an organization's internal environment.
- Understanding the organizational culture is essential for everyone on the staff.

References

Albright, Kendra. 2004. "Environmental Scanning: Radar for Success." *Information Management Journal* 38, no. 3: 38–42, 45.

Andrews, Rhys, George Boyne, and Richard Walker. 2006. "Strategy Content and Organizational Performance." *Public Administration Review* 66, no. 1: 52–64.

Barnard, Chester. 1956. *Organization and Management*. Cambridge, MA: Harvard University Press.

Bloor, Geoffrey, and Patrick Dawson. 1994. "Understanding Professional Culture in the Organizational Context." *Organization Studies* 15, no. 2: 241–275.

Bonn, Ingrid. 2005. "Improving Strategic Thinking: A Multilevel Approach." *Leadership and Organization Development Journal* 26, no. 5: 336–354.

Burns, Tom, and G. M. Stalker. 1961. *Management of Innovation*. London: Tavistock.

Castiglione, John. 2007. "Environmental Scanning: An Essential Tool for Twenty-First Century Librarianship." *Library Review* 57, no. 7: 528–536.

Child, John. 1972. "Organization Structure, Environment, and Performance— The Tale of Strategic Choice." *Sociology* 6, no. 1: 1–22.

Davis, Jan. 2008. "Competitive Intelligence at AALL's 2008 Annual Conference." *Searcher* 16, no. 10: 14–15.

Duchon, Dennis, and Brian Drake. 2009. "Organizational Narcissism and Virtuous Behavior." *Journal of Business Ethics* 85, no. 3:301–308.

Emery, Fred, and Eric Trist. 1965. "Causal Texture of Organizational Environments." *Human Relations* 18, no. 1: 21–31.

Gellerman, Saul. 1973. *Management of Human Resources*. Hinsdale, IL: Dryden Press.

Gianfranco, Faruggia. 2007. "How Is the Nonprofit Sector Changing?" *Futures Research Quarterly* 23, no. 1: 5–16.

Glor, Eleanor D. 2008. "Identifying Organizational Patterns: Normative and Empirical Criteria for Organizational Redesign." *Journal of Public Affairs Education* 14, no. 3: 311–333.

Harris, Martin. 2006. "Technology, Innovation, and Post-Bureaucracy: The Case of the British Library." *Journal of Organizational Change Management* 19, no. 1: 80–92.

Jassawalla, Avan, and Hemet Sashittal. 2002. "Cultures That Support Product Innovation Processes." *Academy of Management Executive* 16, no. 4: 42–54.

Johansen, Bob. 2007. *Get There Early: Sensing the Future to Compete in the Present*. San Francisco: Berrett-Koehler.

Kell, Thomas, and Gregory Carrott. 2005. "Culture Matters Most." *Harvard Business Review* 83, no. 5: 22.

Lawrence, Paul, and Jay Lorsch. 1967. *Organization and Environment*. Homewood, IL: Irwin.

Lynch, Beverly. 1974. "The Academic Library and Its Environment." *College and Research Libraries* 35, no. 2: 127.

Malgeri, Jack. 2010. "Organizational Foresight and Stewardship." *The Public Manager* 39, no. 4: 39–42.

Rutherford, Sarah. 2001. "Organizational Cultures, Women Managers, and Exclusion." *Women in Management Review* 16, nos. 7/8: 371–382.

Schwarz, Jan Oliver. 2007. "Competitive Intelligence: A Field for Futurists?" *Futures Research Quarterly* 21, no.1: 55–65.

Staley, David J., and Kara J. Malenfant. 2010. *Futures Thinking for Academic Librarians: Higher Education in 2015.* Chicago: Association of College and Research Libraries.

Stewart, Wayne H., Ruth C. May, and Arvind Kalia. 2008. "Environmental Perceptions and Scanning in the United States and India." *Entrepreneurship Theory and Practice* 32, no. 1: 83–106.

Sun-Tzu. 2012. *The Art of War.* Available: http://www.sonshi.com/sun1.html. Accessed October 9.

Taleb, Nassim Nicholas. 2007. *Black Swan: The Impact of the Highly Improbable.* New York: Random House.

Yap, Ching Seng, and Md Zabid Abdul Rashid. 2011. "Competitive Intelligence Practices and Firm Performance." *Libri* 61, no 3: 175–189.

Launching Pad

Association of College and Research Libraries. *ACRL Research Committee. Environmental Scan: 2007.* Chicago: American Library Association.

Calvert, Philip, Daniel Dorner, and G. E. Gorman. 2006. *Analyzing What Your Users Need.* New York: Neal-Schuman.

Day, George S., and Paul J. H. Schoemaker. 2005. "Scanning the Periphery." *Harvard Business Review* 83, no. 11: 135–148.

Hough, Jill R., and Margaret A. White. 2004. "Scanning Actions and Environmental Dynamism." *Management Decision* 42, no. 6: 781–793.

Kaczorowski, Monice. 2008. "Uniting in Competitive Intelligence." *AALL Spectrum* 12, no. 5: 26–28

Martin, Jason. 2012. "Symbols, Sagas, Rites, and Rituals: An Overview of Organizational Culture in Libraries." *College and Research Libraries News* 73, no. 6: 348–349.

Mehra, Bharat, and William C. Robinson. 2009. "The Community Engagement Model in Library and Information Science Education." *Journal of Education for Library and Information Science* 50, no. 1: 15–38.

Nastanski, Michael. 2004. "The Value of Active Scanning to Senior Executives." *Journal of Management Development* 23, no. 5: 426–436.

Stoffel, John D. 1994. *Strategic Issues Management: A Comprehensive Guide to Environmental Scanning.* Tarrytown, NY: Elsevier Science.

Westbrook, Lynn. 2000. *Identifying and Analyzing User Needs.* New York: Neal-Schuman.

As library managers we need to write policies for local libraries that recognize the broader information environment driven by the U.S. Constitution—particularly the First and Fourth Amendments, as well as the ethics, statutes and legal cases that shape library practice while protecting and promoting users' rights and responsibilities. In recent years, substantial legislation and litigation has focused on digital information and communication technologies related to such issues as copyright, privacy, filtering, gaming, Web 2.0, cyberbullying and the digital divide. An understanding of our constitutional legacy and ethical responsibilities is essential when we develop local policies related to digital technologies—policies not universally popular but reflective of our core values and legal constraints.

    —Nancy Kranich, ALA President, 2001–2002 (2012)

The focus . . . is on the most common events that working librarians on the frontline of public contact [are] likely to confront and on the guidelines for the successful navigation of difficult situations. Specifically, although we will touch on some of the legal defenses of libraries as institutions, our main concern here is what you, as a practicing professional, can do to keep you and your library from legal difficulties.

    —Spencer L. Simons (2005)

A well-written JSA [job safety analysis] cannot guarantee serious injury avoidance by itself. It can, however, be a tool for defining the expected behavior.

    —David D. Glenn (2011)

Comprehensive data repositories are an essential part of practically all research carried out in the digital humanities nowadays. . . . Hand in hand with this development goes a high degree of legal uncertainty.

    —Timm Lehmberg, Georg Rehm, Andreas Witt, and Felix Zimmermann (2008)

While the diverse implementations, effects, and levels of acceptance of CIPA across schools and libraries demonstrate the wide range of potential ramifications of the law, surprisingly little consideration is given to the major assumptions in the law.

    —Paul T. Jaeger and Zheng Yan (2009)

3

LEGAL ISSUES AND LIBRARY MANAGEMENT

This chapter focuses on the following:

- The importance of laws and regulations in the management and operation of libraries
- The legal basis of the creation and operation of libraries
- Legal factors related to services that a library offers
- The importance of privacy
- The legal difference between and implications of contracts and licenses
- The impact of copyright laws

LAWS, RULES, AND regulations play a role in many aspects of management in general and, our concern here, in the management of libraries. Some laws apply to both for-profit and nonprofit organizations. In order to exist, all formal organizations have some basis in law, such as papers of incorporation, a charter, or a legislative act. Other laws apply to for-profit or nonprofit organizations. Still other laws apply to a single type of organization such as libraries.

You may be a little surprised by how pervasive legal issues are in terms of library operations. Some legal matters will be addressed in later chapters within specific contexts, such as the hiring process and financial matters (Chapters 16 and 17). The best advice is: when in doubt, seek legal counsel. Doing so may cost some money on the front end, but it saves money in the long run by heading off any major legal issue that may result from not seeking such advice.

The David Glenn quotation is a reference to rules and regulations that apply to all types of organizations, in this case OSHA (Occupational Safety and Health Administration). The JSA reference in his statement denotes job safety analysis. One of the areas where OSHA impacts library operations is in terms of ergonomic standards for computer-based activities.

Copyright, the issue of interest to Lehmberg, Rehm, Witt, and Zimmermann, is a global concern. It has been and is of significant interest to libraries; and understanding those laws (there are several) affects what a library and its users may do with covered material.

The final quotation from Jaeger and Yan relates to a U.S. law that is specific to libraries and their services—CIPA, the Children's Internet Protection Act (http://www.fcc.gov/cgb/consumerfacts/cipa.html). This law, from one perspective, has First Amendment implications in terms of adult access to Internet information in public libraries. Some children's advocates raised similar concerns during the legislative debates and during the early stages of CIPA implementation.

ESTABLISHING A LIBRARY

As stated earlier, all libraries or their parent organizations have a legal basis. Some private academic institutions have state charters, and others are incorporated as nonprofit organizations. Publicly supported academic institutions are legislatively established and, to a degree, controlled by legislative action. A few such institutions are based in the state constitution—for example, the University of California, University of Michigan, and University of Colorado.

Public and school libraries can be created through legislative acts as well. A public library example from Arizona addresses funding levels for library support should a community decide to establish one:

> A city or town may levy annually, in addition to all other taxes, a tax not to exceed one and one-half mills on the assessed value of all property in the city or town, exclusive of the valuation of property exempt from taxation, for the purpose of establishing and maintaining therein free public libraries and reading rooms, for purchasing books, journals and other publications, and erecting and maintaining such buildings as may be necessary therefore. (Ariz. Rev. Stat. § 9-411, Tax levy for library purposes)

A school library law example from *Colorado Revised Statutes* relates to school districts:

> (1) In addition to any other power granted to a board of education of a school district by law, each board of education of a school district shall have the following specific powers, to be exercised in its judgment: . . .

(c) To provide furniture, equipment, library books, and everything needed to carry out the education program; . . .

(dd) To provide, in the discretion of the local board, out of federal grants made available specifically for this purpose, library resources which, for the purposes of this title, means books, periodicals, documents, magnetic tapes, films, phonograph records, and other related library materials and printed and published instructional materials for the use and benefit of all children in the district and the use of teachers to benefit all children in the district, both in the public and nonpublic schools, without charge and without discrimination on the ground of race, color, religion, sex, or national origin (Colo. Rev. Stat. 22-32-110 [2010]), Board of education—specific powers)

Consortia and other collaborative arrangements are a standard element today for most libraries. Such activities are also based in law. Consortia composed of public and private institutions usually have to have some type of authorization in order for the public institutions to expand funds outside their political jurisdiction. Some cooperative ventures cross state lines. An example of a law allowing cross-state library cooperation is New York State's Interstate Library Compact. It also, among many other things, mandates a governing board that would supervise the organization's operations:

Because the desire for the services provided by the libraries transcends governmental boundaries and can most effectively be satisfied by giving such services to communities and people regardless of jurisdictional lines, it is the policy of the states party to this compact to cooperate and share their responsibilities; to authorize cooperation and sharing with respect to those types of library facilities and services which can be more economically or efficiently developed and maintained on a cooperative basis, and to authorize cooperation and sharing among localities, states and others in providing joint or cooperative library services in areas where the distribution of population or of existing and potential library resources make the provision of library service on an interstate basis the most effective way of providing adequate and efficient service. . . .

Article IV. Interstate Library Districts, Governing Board
(a) An interstate library district which establishes, maintains or operates any facilities or services in its own right shall have a governing board which shall direct the affairs of the district and act for it in all matters relating to its business. Each participating public library agency in the district shall be represented on the governing board which shall be organized and conduct its business in accordance with provision therefore in the library agreement. But in no event shall a governing board meet less often than twice a year.

> ### TRY THIS
>
> Choose a state and investigate what laws it has related to libraries. If you have access to the LexisNexis Academic database, the search can be quick and informative.

(b) Any private library agency or agencies party to a library agreement establishing an interstate library district may be represented on or advise with the governing board of the district in such manner as the library agreement may provide. (NY CLS Unconsol Ch 111-B § 1 [2004])

The forgoing is a very small sampling of the many laws that have a bearing on the options available to library managers for carrying out library operations. All states have such laws that affect funding, cooperative activities, how and if fines are imposed, and where any such money is deposited.

LIBRARIES, USERS, SAFETY, AND THE LAW

Part of a library manager's responsibility, regardless at what level of management—senior, middle, or frontline—is to be a good steward of the resources and people involved in library services and activities. One aspect of that stewardship is safety. There are times when resources and people's safety conflict.

We cover the topic of managing physical facilities in Chapter 19; however, we need to mention the issue here. When resources and people's safety issues collide, naturally people take precedence. This can mean substantial loss of collection resources even when there is no direct threat to people. One example is the fire code–mandated ceiling sprinkler systems. In the case of fire, such systems are invaluable; however, such systems can and do spring leaks—it often seems as if the system about to leak waits until the weekend when the library is closed and has 48 hours to drip/spray on the collection. It is surprising how much damage can be done in just a few hours and how costly the clean up and recovery turn out to be. (Mold forms rather quickly in wet materials, creating yet another hazard for staff, users, and materials.) There are ways to avoid such problems and still comply with fire codes, but they almost always cost more than what is available.

Another fire code challenge involves the placement of emergency exits around the library. Few libraries have a facility in which all the emergency exits are under the visual control of staffed service points, or, if they do, their staffing costs are higher than average. Again the manager has to balance costs, safety, and preservation of collection and equipment resources.

HEALTH AND INJURY CONCERNS

As we will discuss in Chapter 19, conducting a library risk assessment is key to avoiding many health and safety dangers and OSHA site visits. OSHA rules and regulations present another set of issues for managers. "Congress created the OSHA to ensure safe and healthful working conditions for working men and women by setting and enforcing standards and by providing training, outreach, education, and assistance" (http://www.osha.gov/about.html). The agency's responsibilities cover almost all aspects of workplace health and safety concerns. It also makes an effort to inform workers of their rights. One example of the education focus is a wallet-sized card for workers that reads in part:

If you think your job is unsafe and you have questions, call OSHA.
It's confidential.
WE CAN HELP!
(http://www.osha.gov/Publications/3385magnet-english.pdf)

Many, if not the majority, of OSHA library site visits arise from employee calls.

Workplaces such as libraries are rarely in the top 50 or so of hazardous work environments. Even so, library managers must have an awareness of OSHA rules and regulations because OSHA issues do arise from time to time. The U.S. Department of Labor periodically issues *Nonfatal Occupational Injuries and Illnesses Requiring Days Away from Work* (http://www.bls.gov/news.release/osh2.nr0.htm). Different editions place libraries in one of two categories: "Education, training, and library occupations" or "Information." Not surprisingly, these categories are among the lowest in terms of cases reported.

In 2011, there were 14,030 instances of days lost by "information" occupations, while there were more than 129,030 cases for manufacturing. As you might expect, back, hand, and wrist issues were the common "information" injuries resulting in lost hours. These types of injuries are caused by repetitive motion and overextension while lifting. Clearly, both factors are potential problems in libraries where so much of the work is done by using a computer or by lifting, bending, and stretching while doing stack maintenance activities.

Libraries need to have proper equipment and furniture for the staff to prevent staff injury. However, just having the physical items is not enough; there also needs to be staff training in the proper use of the items. Although a workstation may have all the necessary ergonomic features, this does not mean the person working there will use them properly; therefore, training is a part of the library's due diligence. David Glenn's quotation makes the point regarding defining expected safety behavior. We are not aware of a library that was fined by OSHA for health or safety issues, but we do know of cases where the agency placed a time frame for correcting reported problem(s) with the possibility of a fine for failure to meet the deadline.

Long-established libraries face some challenges in terms of equipment and furniture—few have had the budget or resources to exchange all the old workstations and equipment at one time. It is a matter of making priority decisions based on available funds. This can mean some risk of injury will exist, prompting an OSHA site visit. Another challenge, in older buildings, is asbestos and the environmental health problems it can cause. Asbestos was a common fireproofing and insulating component used in older buildings. Left undisturbed, it poses little health risk. However, older libraries are modified from time to time to meet the needs of new technology, and the asbestos is disturbed. This creates the potential for health problems.

Removing hazardous materials is rather costly and requires trained personnel and clean-up operations. Senior library managers should know if their building contains any hazardous material—not just in its construction but also in the products used in operational activities. Something as innocuous as installing new carpet can lead to health concerns for some people (staff and/or the public), because fumes from the adhesive used with the carpeting can cause allergic reactions. Not knowing or thinking about such issues ahead of time can lead to a visit from OSHA inspectors should a staff member, or a member of the public, call them.

Although not a major issue, health and safety concerns for staff and the public is part of managing a library. As noted earlier, we will cover this topic in more detail in Chapter 19. Our point in addressing the topic here is that there are rules and regulations from agencies such as OSHA and local fire departments that

AUTHORS' EXPERIENCE

Evans once managed a university library in its original (1958) building with an addition built 20 years later. Needless to say, the older portion had asbestos throughout and was not designed for the needs of twenty-first-century technology. At one point extensive work was needed in the technical service area, located in the old building.

A hazardous material company was hired to carry out the necessary mitigation work and clean the area upon completion. Technical service staff were given paid time off for the duration of the work, and no staff was allowed in the work area.

Shortly after the staff returned to work, one person started complaining of health problems that she attributed to asbestos exposure. The university's OSHA compliance officer did an inspection and found no evidence for the claim. Not satisfied, the person called OSHA. That led to a site visit and resulted in another no-evidence decision; in fact, its report was complimentary of how the work was handled and for giving staff paid leave. Still not satisfied, the person filed a lawsuit against the university, including Evans as the library manager. The outcome of the suit was in favor of the university; however, for the better part of 18 months, the library staff was somewhat disrupted by the affair. The outcome could have been very different had the university not understood the need for great caution and proper procedures.

require compliance. There is also the potential for lawsuits against the library for failure to protect staff and users.

DISRUPTIVE USER BEHAVIOR

User behavior, and to some extent staff behavior, can create an unsafe situation, and you as manager will have only modest control. Certainly given daily contact with staff members, you have ample opportunities to observe any changes among them that have the potential to be disruptive. For the general public, however, you have to rely on proper policies and staff training to keep the inevitable problems to a minimum. There are two common user behavior concerns—situations when a person is upset regarding some library issue and situations when issues arise between users. Both types of challenging situations will occur from time to time. Being prepared is the key to keeping the situation to its lowest possible level in terms of disruption and to resolving it quickly.

Almost all libraries must address disruptive behavior. Special libraries are the least likely to have such situations arise on a regular basis. For-profit special libraries rarely have individuals in their space who do not belong to the organization, and nonprofit libraries usually have limited access and often require previsit vetting of the user. Their most likely situation will involve a staff person; regardless of the cause, failure to have procedures in place for handling the event will likely make a bad situation worse.

You might think that school libraries are also low on the scale for disruptive behavior. They are certainly lower than libraries open to the general public, but they do have to think about how to handle potential problems. When a kindergarten student can bring a loaded gun to school and discharge it (http://www .thedailybeast.com/cheat-sheet/item/6-year-old-brings-gun-to-school/terrible/#), you have to know that there is serious potential for unacceptable behavior even in an elementary school library. Middle and high schools have increasing levels of concern about confrontations among students (involving drugs, bullying, or weapons, for example) in the library.

Libraries that are open to the public have the greatest number of incidents. As Sarah Farrugia (2002) stated, "Public libraries are more susceptible to patron violence than academic and other special libraries, as their open door allows anyone to use the building. This can sometimes invite trouble from asocial citizens who can cause disruption and uneasiness amongst staff and patrons and even lead to acts of extreme violence" (p. 309).

Our opening quotation from Spencer Simons's (2005) article suggests that disruptive behavior is a problem that library staff will experience. It is disconcerting when it is a fellow staff member; however, with a colleague you have a baseline for judging what is wrong. With the public, there is almost no basis for knowing what is wrong and what to expect, unless it involves one of the regular visitors.

The following list presents some of the most common unacceptable behaviors that library staff will encounter:

- Drug/alcohol use (staff or users)
- Drug/alcohol sale
- Verbal abuse toward staff by a user
- Verbal abuse among users
- Assault on staff
- Assault among users
- Gang activity
- Indecent exposure
- User viewing/printing pornographic material
- Trespassing
- Arson (especially in book return boxes)
- Disorderly/menacing conduct

As we stated earlier, successful handling of any of the behaviors listed, as well as others not listed, depends on having sound legal policies in place and having the staff trained in what to do, and what not to do, when a circumstance arises. It is *essential* to work with legal counsel when developing appropriate policies. Additionally, legal counsel will be aware of the community and state laws, as well as court decisions, that will affect the policies.

When does unusual or strange behavior become disruptive? Every library must have an answer to this question. Once that is determined, the attorney may not always agree with library staff that the behavior can be controlled by the library. You cannot call security every time someone exhibits slightly strange behavior; doing so could lead to a lawsuit against the library. Libraries do face the possibility of litigation over staff action or inaction. Thus, you must have properly formulated policies and staff trained in their application. Workshops conducted by professionals specializing in human behavior/mental health and substance abuse can help prepare the staff to safely handle such behavior problems. These professionals can also help set reasonable guidelines for when to call for assistance. The staff should be trained on how to follow the guidelines, and the policies should be written down for later consultation when the inevitable need arises.

SOMETHING TO PONDER

An increasing percentage of homeless people in the United States are individuals who, in the past, would have been hospitalized and given medication. Most of them are harmless, but without their medication their behavior can be erratic and often disruptive. Some users are uncomfortable when homeless people are around them. They may ask you to have such individuals removed from the library. Remember, public buildings are indeed public. How would you handle the situation?

If the library posts reasonable rules regarding access, hours, and behavior, it may, without too much legal concern, remove anyone violating those rules. The two key considerations are reasonable rules and posting. The rules *must* reflect existing laws and should have been reviewed by legal counsel. Both conditions must be present for removal from the library to be legal. Repeat offenders can face legal action, if the library wishes to press charges.

In 2006, *American Libraries* reported on problems with the "reasonableness" of library access/behavior polices. In one instance, the Dallas Public Library's plan to ban persons "emitting odors (including bodily odors or perfumes) which interfere with services by other users or work staff" was challenged *(American Libraries*, 2006d, p. 11). Homeless advocates questioned the fairness of such a rule. In Massachusetts, the ACLU filed a lawsuit over a rule that limited a homeless person to checking out only two books at any one time when other users could have at least ten items *(American Libraries*, 2006b). These two incidents illustrate the fact that just having written rules regarding access/behavior does not end controversy.

Another type of disruptive situation is when a user becomes verbally abusive. Anyone who has worked in public services for any length of time will have experienced such abuse over some library issue (fines are among the top three issues that draw users' ire). How much verbal abuse must one tolerate? F. J. DeRosa (1980) commented:

> People in all areas of public service, and librarians in particular, seem resigned to the opinion that abuse from their public is inescapable and there is not much they can do about it. Much of this misconception is due to the fact that many people do not realize the point when disruptive behavior becomes antisocial behavior and when antisocial behavior becomes criminal behavior. (p. 35)

HANDLING THE HOMELESS

San Francisco Public Library System administrators thought that the homeless library user situation at their central library was extreme enough that they devoted a professional librarian salary line to hire a full-time social worker who was housed in the central library. This was after library staff complained repeatedly that they were not adequately trained to handle such a pervasive social circumstance. This has not only led to a much better work environment for the library employees but it also had led to the library social worker collaborating with other city/county agencies to help the homeless library users.

You cannot avoid some verbal abuse if you work in public services, but certainly there are limits to what you have to endure. Libraries should work with legal counsel to establish legally sound guidelines for when "enough is enough," although this does not guarantee that there will be no lawsuits from angry users. There are some techniques that you can employ during some circumstances to defuse anger and abuse. The following extended discussion illustrates how to try to calm down a situation as well as reduce the chances of litigation.

Defusing Anger

There are three types of abusive users that staff will encounter at some time: upset, angry, and disruptive. Some of the individuals will be upset about a library service concern, and others will be upset about a nonlibrary issue and direct their feelings toward the staff or other users or toward both.

The first, and most common, level is the confused or upset person. With these individuals, as is true for the other levels, attentive listening is the starting point. Asking for additional information is often helpful: "Tell me more." "I do not quite understand, please tell me about . . ." Paraphrasing the person's comments indicates that you are listening. It is not a good practice to make the response a personal choice (such as, "I wish I could . . ."); it is better to respond in terms of specific library policy and practice. Focus on determining what the situation is and keeping the event from escalating while maintaining library policy so that the event does not become a personal matter between the user and staff member.

Level two (anger) is more complex and less common. Angry people can exhibit one of three categories of anger: controlled, expressed, and irrational. Occasionally the person who appears confused is really in a state of controlled anger. A sensible approach is to assume that anyone with a complaint is at a controlled anger level. If you make this assumption and follow the appropriate steps, you have a better chance of keeping the situation under control. The best approach is to:

- rephrase/paraphrase the person's statement of concern;
- always treat the person with respect to show that her or his concern is important;
- clearly state the library's position on the concern once the nature of the concern is fully understood; and
- present firmly and clearly the possible consequences of actions contrary to the position of the library.

When you rephrase the person's statement, use your own words; do not "parrot" their comments. Key elements in restating are to treat the user as an equal, not use professional jargon, and mirror the user's vocabulary. By paraphrasing, the person has an opportunity to clarify any misunderstanding. It also indicates you are trying to understand the situation. Using phrases that equate the library to the "authority" and the person as "subordinate" is likely to escalate the situation. Use of jargon and/or complex terms and words may confuse and offend the person.

Another element in displaying respect for the person is to acknowledge the emotion(s) the person feels regarding the situation. This does not mean agreeing with the user regarding what the person wants; rather, it lets the individual know there is respect for the individual and the goal is to find a satisfactory solution.

If the matter is one of library policy, explain it from the library's perspective and identify what the limits are on what can be done immediately. Keep the explanations in the third person. Making it appear as if "I" can in fact do something or as if "I" am responsible for the problem often leads to greater confrontation. In many cases, less explanation is better.

An alternative approach, if the situation appears to be escalating, is to outline the possible consequences if the person persists; however, take care not to threaten. Telling a person what may or will happen is very different from delivering an ultimatum. What this does is allow the person to make a decision with a full awareness of the possible outcomes. While this step may make the person angrier, the demonstration of concern and respect for the person's rational decision-making capability more often than not leads to a successful resolution.

When the person is uncontrollably angry, begin by acknowledging the person's anger while being ready to call for backup help. As with controlled anger, the goal is validation and understanding of the anger and feelings. Identify the problem; rephrasing the concern allows the person to verify that there is or is not agreement concerning the nature of the problem. When it is not a library issue, get backup assistance.

If it is a library operation matter, explain how the person's behavior affects you and others in the area. By emphasizing the behavior and its effects, the focus is kept off the person. Saying "this behavior" rather than saying "you" may make the person less defensive and consequently easier to handle. When doing this, it is best to avoid sweeping generalities about the behavior's impact. Personalizing the effects leaves little room for the angry person to argue, especially if it has already been acknowledged that the anger is a justifiable feeling.

Allow the person to vent the emotions. If possible, have the "conversation" away from the public area but not isolated from other staff; you have no way of knowing what might happen. Although it is not enjoyable to listen to someone "rant and rave," there is a better chance of resolving the situation by first letting the person release some of the anger. People who are irrationally angry will not be very likely to hear anything until they have "had their say." Being patient and listening for clues as to what is the issue is difficult but essential. There is little point in giving a long explanation or apologizing unless it is clear there was an obvious library error. All too often it is necessary in such situations to use direct confrontation: "Your behavior is disruptive to our work (and perhaps to other people here). If you do not stop, then we must . . ." (call the security office/police, for example). Try to present the statement in an unemotional manner. The statement sets clear limits and identifies what the consequences will be and leaves it to the angry person to decide what to do. To summarize, this is how to deal with an upset user:

- Listen first, watching for nonverbal clues as to the emotional state of the person.
- Rephrase the person's concern in order to clarify the issue.
- Maintain an unemotional state, if possible.
- Acknowledge the emotions and do not try to calm the person just in order to be comfortable. The goal is to find a solution.
- Do not be defensive; that will usually not help resolve the situation.
- State clearly the options and consequences in institutional rather than personal terms, and, if possible, allow the user to decide which option to take.

We know that dealing with irate people is neither comfortable nor easy. It is something you get better at with training. Having an opportunity to practice conflict-management skills in a workshop environment is useful for frontline staff as well as supervisors and senior staff. Knowing what conflict-management skills are and using them are two very different things. Staff members who work shifts that have minimal staffing should be the first to receive training and practice; they have fewer backup resources available when disruptive behaviors arise.

Sometimes, no matter how carefully handled the circumstance was, the person will go to the media or to an attorney. This happens occasionally, and having proper policies in place and posted and staff trained in conflict control will help keep the "fallout" as small as possible.

CHECK THESE OUT

An excellent book to consult on handling problem behaviors of all types in libraries is Mark Willis's *Dealing with Difficult People in the Library* (Chicago: American Library Association, 1999). It addresses just about every type of "difficult person" category you can think of in a library setting.

Jan Thenell's *The Library's Crisis Communications Planner: A PR Guide for Handling Every Emergency* (Chicago: American Library Association, 2004) provides practical guidance for managing the situation if a complaint explodes beyond the library.

Two other good resources for handling "difficult people" are Karen Mannering's *Dealing with Difficult People* (London: Hodder Education, 2008) and Susan Benjamin's *Perfect Phrases for Dealing with Difficult People: Hundreds of Ready-to-Use Phrases for Handling Conflict, Confrontations, and Challenging Personalities* (New York: McGraw-Hill, 2008).

TORT LAW AND LIABILITY

We have mentioned liability several times. What is involved, and what does it mean? Liability is:

> *a comprehensive legal term that describes the condition of being actually or potentially subject to a legal obligation. . . . Primary liability* is an obligation for which a person is directly responsible; it is distinguished from *secondary liability* which is the responsibility of another if the party directly responsible fails or refuses to satisfy his or her obligation. (*The Free Dictionary*, http://legal-dictionary.thefreedictionary.com/liability)

Are libraries susceptible to being held liable for some action or failure to act? Sometimes the answer is yes, and sometimes it is no. In the past, tax-supported libraries had some form of governmental immunity from law suits and liability. Today many states have greatly reduced the available immunity.

One of the most common concerns for library liability is personal injury, which is governed by tort law. Tort law addresses injuries—physical, mental, or emotional—resulting from negligence or from intentional acts. Libraries have been involved in litigation arising from both causes. For libraries, it is the negligence category that is most significant.

Broadly thinking, there are three interrelated issues related to negligence regardless whether the resulting injury is mental, emotional, or physical in nature. Negligence requires the existence of three conditions:

- the cause of the injury is a person, not an act of God;
- the person causing the injury has a responsibility/duty to the injured party; and
- the duty is one of warning or one of action.

An example of possible library negligence would be the failure of the staff to put out signs warning of slippery entryway floors on a rainy or snowy day and a person falls and injures himself or herself.

Within the concept of personal injury law in the United States and England is a subsection that involves premises, such as the library's property. Premises include everything associated with a building—sidewalks, grounds, parking lot, and lighting, for example. The courts have divided the "controller" of the premises' duties into three broad categories: those involving invitees (users and staff in public areas), those involving licensees (users and staff in nonpublic areas, such as technical services and administrative offices), and those involving trespassers. There is a descending order of duty to the categories, from invitees down to trespassers. Beyond these basic categories, there are special duties to children and to persons who are mentally or physically challenged. We discuss the Americans with Disabilities Act (ADA; http://www.ada.gov/) later in the chapter.

ADVISORY BOARD EXPERIENCE

Carol Sinwell offered the following example that illustrates the potential liability issues for libraries:

> One year I had a patron slip on a snowy curb outside my public library. She told me she hurt her ankle and wanted to know what we would do regarding her need of medical attention. A mandatory accident form was completed.
>
> Our risk management guidelines are clear that "we are not to say we are responsible or liable in any way" when talking to a patron.
>
> The lady made a claim to the county and was told the county would be in touch with her about paying medical costs. A county risk management officer interviewed me and staff who worked that day to verify what had been said.
>
> Note: I had had her sit down and offered some ice for her ankle. As I was returning to the place where she was sitting, she didn't see me, but I saw her walking ably around to help her son with something. When I approached she started limping and complaining of pain.

One all too common situation for libraries (except special libraries and a few specialized research libraries such as the Huntington Library in San Marino, California) regarding potential liability is the presence of unattended children. Dealing with "latchkey children" has been a major challenge for public and academic libraries. Some parents have their child to go to the library (being considered a safe place to be) after school and wait to be picked up. A few parents even bring children to the library and leave them unsupervised while the parents attend to other business outside of the library. There is a question of just how much liability a library has for looking after unsupervised children. Can the parent(s) hold the library and its staff liable for an injury or health problem that occurs when the child is alone in the library?

Whatever steps the library takes to control such a problem, a first step is absolutely necessary to prevent even greater problems: have clear policies and a plan of action that have been reviewed by the library's or parent institution's legal counsel. Some of the options that exist in various jurisdictions are to:

- have libraries bar children without parental supervision;
- offer special programs designed for such children;

> **SOMETHING TO CONSIDER**
>
> A few public libraries in the United States have made arrangements with nearby schools to offer children the opportunity to come to a designated room in the library where they can get help with homework and/or be kept busy with activities until a parent can pick them up. The room is staffed by trained teachers and individuals experienced in summer camp programs. This type of cooperative activity is common in the Nordic countries. Such arrangements, of course, involve serious legal issues related to such things as who may pick up a child and how a health issue will be handled.

- have policies requiring staff to call child welfare services or police to pick up any unattended child at closing time; and
- have policies allowing staff to contact police/security when a child is left unattended for a specified period of time during normal school hours.

Libraries need to make it clear that they assume no child care responsibilities. Policies need to be posted in prominent locations, especially at public entrances, and provided to parents when a child is given a library card. The library's website is another location for posting such policies.

The list of potential problem areas for injury is long; some are ongoing such as stairways, carpets, and furniture, while others are intermittent or rare, for example, weather or construction related. To ensure reasonable safety in all areas, the library needs to have a security plan. Conducting a security audit is the first step in developing a plan that helps ensure the safety of the collections and of the people.

MALPRACTICE AND LIBRARIANS

A related liability concern is malpractice. The issue is complex because the librarian is almost always an employee, and as such the library/government jurisdiction is the legal party with the duty (*respondent superior*). Should a librarian be worried about malpractice?

Perhaps the article that first raised the issue of librarian malpractice was Allan Angoff's (1976) "Library Malpractice Suit: Could It Happen to You?" His fictional case involved the collapse of a deck built according to directions in a book borrowed from a library. In his story, the governing board, the library director, and the head of reference services were named as defendants. The basis of the lawsuit was that the librarian and the library should have known the book was faulty or the library and the librarian assumed the responsibility of the outcome of using a deck-building book that was in error.

Over the years the matter has remained an open question in the field. According to Paul Healey (2008), who holds both a JD and an MLS, neither basis would be a sound basis: "Reliance on the librarian such that liability would result is just

CHECK THIS OUT

Paul Healey's book *Professional Liability Issues for Librarians and Informa-tion Professionals* (New York: Neal-Schuman, 2008), mentioned in the text, covers a host of liability issues for librarians. His background as both a practicing attorney and a librarian gives his material credence. The chap-ters on the legal concepts are straightforward and provide a basis for understanding just how much legal issues can impact what you do as a manager, at least in terms of liability.

not reasonable" (p. 76). His point was that both tort and contract laws rely on reasonable expectations. Essentially, it is unreasonable to expect a librarian to be an expert in home construction much less deck building. It is reasonable to assume a librarian is expert in locating information about such an activity but not for the correctness of that information.

Although the chances are not great of your being included in a malpractice lawsuit, if you are at a service desk at the time an injury occurs, it is not totally out of the question that you will be named a defendant. Also, as you assume more senior management roles, the risk increases. Lawyers have a tendency in liability suits to name everyone they can identify as having even a slight "duty" involving the event. Obviously "the library" and its parent body will be the lead defendants, as they have the "deep pockets"; however, you may also be named. While the parent institution is likely to cover legal fees, there may be instances when other individuals will also be liable to cover legal costs as well as any legal "judgments." As a result, it is prudent for librarians to check their homeowners/renters insurance to determine if the liability coverage also applies to their work activities. If not, it may be wise to see what the cost of workplace liability may be. Some library associations offer such coverage to members.

LIBRARY SERVICES AND THE LAW

Many of the services libraries provide are circumscribed by a variety of laws. Accessibility to faculties and collections, what users may do with the resources available, and who has access to materials are but a few of the issues involved.

Access to library resources must comply with ADA (Americans with Disabili-ties Act), as we noted earlier. Title III of the act states that it is a violation to dis-criminate "on the basis of disability in the full and equal enjoyment of the goods, services, facilities, privileges, advantages, or accommodations of any place of public accommodation" (42 U.S.C. § 12182[a] 2000). Access includes such physi-cal factors as wheelchair ramps where needed from the front entrance to else-where in the building, drinking fountain height, restroom accommodations, and the aisle width in publicly accessible stacks. Many libraries built long before the act was passed face substantial remodeling renovation costs to become compliant. Most libraries have addressed the physical access issues; however, modifications to ADA or new legislation may bring about new requirements and costs. For example, ADA requirements changed in 2004 when new guidelines were issued (69 Fed. Reg. 44,084, et seq., July 23, 2004, http://blog.librarylaw.com/librarylaw/disability_access/).

On the service side, there were and are compliance concerns. For example, what percentages of your library's collections are accessible to the visually impaired users? Does the collection access meet the "full and equal" provision of ADA? Large-print books are one way to meet this need; however, only a small fraction of books are available in that format. Mary Anne Epp (2006) noted, "Experts estimate only 5 percent of the world's publishing output is made accessible in alternate formats for people who cannot use print" (p. 411). Her article discusses potential collaborative projects to help address the challenge of providing the visually impaired with access to print-based materials. There are options available to help meet the local need, such as reading machines and volunteers to assist those with vision limitations. Again, they come with budgetary as well as legal considerations to address.

E-resources and other types of media also need to be taken into account. Diane Murley (2008) provided some sound advice regarding improving accessibility for websites. Solutions are available, but you must think about the issues on an ongoing basis. We know from firsthand experience that failure to address these issues for just one user can lead to at least a visit from the user's lawyer and perhaps even a lawsuit.

An example of legislation that circumscribes what resources a library may make available to users is CIPA (the Children's Internet Protection Act). CIPA primarily impacts school and public libraries and to a lesser extent any library hoping to get federal funds for Internet access. CIPA is the outcome of an earlier effort to protect children from offensive Internet material that was ruled unconstitutional on First Amendment grounds. The issue was resolved by using access to federal funding; according to CIPA, a library wishing to secure federal E-Rate funding must employ filtering software on its computers.

Jaeger and Yan (2009) reported that, by 2005, 100 percent of U.S. public schools had implemented CIPA filtering and "safety policies." In terms of public libraries, however, by 2008 only 38.2 percent were filtering (pp. 9–10). Adults in public libraries that do filter may request the staff disable the filter while they use the computer. This option for adults appears to be a good one; however, Jaeger and Yan (2009) noted there are problems in its implementation, "including librarians not allowing the filter to be turned off, . . . librarians not knowing how to turn the filter off, the filtering software being too complicated to turn off without injuring the performance of workstations in other applications, or the filtering software being unable to be turned off in a reasonable amount of time" (p. 12). You have to wonder just how many librarians refuse to turn off a filter on the basis of personal values, or do they refuse because of how complicated/time-consuming the process is and don't communicate those facts? Also, once the person is finished using the unfiltered computer, the process must be reversed, taking yet more staff time. Another question for libraries that do filter is this: Do users know that when they sit down to a machine it might have filtering software and that, if it does, they have the right to request that it be turned off? We know a few public libraries where all computers are filtered, but there is no signage indicating adults may have unfiltered access to the Internet.

In between children and adults are young adults. What about CIPA's impact on them? Barbara A. Jansen (2010) wrote, "The landscape of Web 2.0 offers various viewpoints, original information from many sources, and a means to express ideas and share results with a wide audience" (p. 49). Jansen (2010) also noted, "In addition to blocking access to educationally valuable resources as described above, restricting access to social media sites in schools also calls into question the erosion of the principle of intellectual freedom for youth" (p. 48).

Some libraries, especially those open to the public, also face lawsuits unrelated to tort or even to any law at all. It appears at times that anyone, at any time, can file a lawsuit over something he or she dislikes. One long-standing reason that people have taken legal action against a library is that its collection contains something they object to (e.g., the subject matter of a book). These cases involve issues of censorship and intellectual freedom and are beyond the scope of this book.

How library public meeting spaces may or may not be used can also be governed by laws. Perhaps the most common situation, especially for public libraries, is when religious groups want to use the space. The underlying issue is the concept of separation of church and state. People on both sides of the issue have at one time or another filed lawsuits over granting or not granting such use.

For example, in Colorado Springs (*American Libraries*, 2005), the Rampart Library District had a board-approved policy that stated if the rooms were used by religious or political groups, the meeting must provide a balanced view. Early in 2005, a religious group asked to use a room, and the request was turned down because it would be a religious service. Shortly after the denial, the library received notice that a lawsuit was being filed by Liberty Counsel (a religious rights defense organization located in Florida) against the library district for denying use of the

CHECK THESE OUT

Two good books to consult about censorship and intellectual freedom are Helen R. Adams's *Ensuring Intellectual Freedom and Access to Information in the School Library Media Program* (Santa Barbara, CA: Libraries Unlimited, 2008) and the ALA Office for Intellectual Freedom's *Intellectual Freedom Manual,* 8th ed. (Chicago: American Library Association, 2010).

room for a religious service. The Rampart District decided to modify their use policy, because they did not have the funds to engage in a legal battle. Liberty Counsel
has filed at least seven such suits since 2000. It won some for the same reason that
Rampart conceded—lack of funds to engage in a legal battle.

A 2006 example occurred when the Montana State Library cancelled an ACLU
film screening that was critical of the USA PATRIOT Act because of complaints
that the program did not list a speaker who would support the act. Rather than file
a lawsuit, the ACLU booked a room in the Lewis and Clark Library (the local public library). The difference between the two libraries, according to *American Libraries* (2006c), was the presence and absence of room usage policies. Lewis and Clark
had a policy that stated as long as programs dealing with a controversial topic provide most, if not all, points of view on the topic, the meeting room could be booked.

A final example took several years to resolve (2004–2007). It started in 2004
when the Antioch branch of the Contra Costa County (Orinda, California)
Library system rejected a room request from the Faith Center Church Evange-
listic Ministries. The denial led to a lawsuit. The denial was based on the library
board's policy that stated that rooms cannot be used for religious services—
based on separation of church and state grounds. Library staff stated the denial
was made because the group indicated it would hold prayer services as part
of the program. The group had distributed flyers throughout the area inviting
people to attend a worship service at the library. Interestingly enough, the U.S.
Department of Justice took the position that Contra Costa County had to allow
the group to use the library room for the service, a somewhat strange twist on
the separation of church and state concept (*American Libraries*, 2006a). Contra
Costa County pushed the case forward, as it viewed this more than a matter of
library room use. It had no problem with the group using the space for non–
worship service purposes but not for a service. Each side appealed the case, and
each side won and lost in the lower courts. On the first day of the 2007–2008
term, the U.S. Supreme Court refused to hear the appeal of the Ninth Circuit
Court of Appeals ruling that the library and county had acted properly. (Note:
the ruling applies only to those libraries in the Ninth Circuit Court's jurisdiction.) *American Libraries* (2007) reported that the religious group said it would
revisit the case in lower courts using a new set of arguments.

USER PRIVACY

How is library user privacy a legal concern? In most states library user records
are legally confidential, for example, in California (Cal. Civ. Code § 1798.3,
2011), Colorado (Colo. Rev. Stat. 24-72-204, 2010), Illinois (75 Ill. Comp. Stat.
5/1-7, 2011), and New York (NY CLS CPLR § 4509, 2011). Just because there
is a legal basis for confidentiality does not mean that decisions regarding confidentiality are always simple for library staff to make. Librarians must release
information when there is a court order or subpoena. It is not uncommon for
law enforcement officers to request such information without such documentation and to present the request as a means of speeding up an investigation. Once

again, having a policy in place for handling such requests is important. As we will discuss later, often how to handle the request depends on what agency is asking—local enforcement or the FBI. These ALA webpages are good starting points for policy formulation:

- "Privacy: An Interpretation of the Library Bill of Rights" (http://www.ala.org/ala/issuesadvocacy/intfreedom/librarybill/interpretations/privacy.cfm)
- "Position Statement on the Confidentiality of Library Records" (http://www.ala.org/ala/mgrps/divs/aasl/aaslissues/positionstatements/confidentiality.cfm)
- "USA PATRIOT Act and Intellectual Freedom" (http://www.ala.org/offices/oif/ifissues/usapatriotact)

There are three broad categories of user information libraries must consider in terms of confidentiality: data collected from a person upon becoming a registered user, data about what a person uses (items checked out, online services, document delivery services, for example), and user data collected by library vendors as a result of a person using their services. Law enforcement officers are rarely concerned about the first category; however, other people may want that information and can and have presented their requests in seemingly innocent terms (trying to locate a family member—"just need the address"). A library should have good control over the data in the first category. It is having control of data in the other two categories that becomes less clear. A staff member receiving such a request should politely, but firmly, refuse to comply and immediately report the request to the supervisor and otherwise follow the library's confidentiality policy.

Libraries with ILS circulation systems are in a good position to ensure collection usage data confidentiality, as today's systems are able to break the link between the borrower and the items upon return and any associated fees that are paid. If the circulation system requires that the name of a borrower appear on a book card or some other traceable record, the staff should render the name illegible as part of the discharging process. Although circulation records are the usage data most often thought of in terms of confidentiality, there may well be other data, such as time reserved to use library computers and usage of document delivery services, that should be considered.

One type of usage data that the library has little control over is database usage. Angela Maycock (2010) noted, "Privacy, one of the foundations of intellectual freedom, is a compelling concern for school librarians. We live in an era when more and more personal information is available online" (p. 68). Many library database vendors, like almost all commercial web organizations, collect data about people using their services. Trina Magi (2010) stated the issue well: "The Web 2.0 environment, however, poses new challenges for librarians in their commitment to protect user privacy as vendors of online databases incorporate personalization features into their search–retrieval interfaces, thereby collecting personally identifiable user information not subject to library oversight" (p. 254). Most of the major online library product vendors have a prominently placed button on their opening search page that allows users to personalize their search; some examples are EBSCO's "My EBSCO*host*," Emerald's "Your Profile," and Wilson's "My Wilson Web."

What might vendors collect and do with such data? Many vendors also offer the option for e-mailing the requested file(s) to the person. That alone provides a vendor with two pieces of marketable information: what the person may be interested in and a means of contacting the person. The personalized profile can generate more marketable data. Magi (2010) reported that LexisNexis sells marketing lists such as "Homeowner" and "Relatives and Room Mates" (p. 268).

Is what others do regarding use of library services a concern for libraries and the issue of confidentiality? What can libraries do about vendor data collection activities? Should users be told that vendors are collecting personal information when they use a database? Do users care? We do not have the answers; however, we do believe that libraries ought to have a serious discussion of the matter and

---

CHECK THESE OUT

The following resources explore in more detail the issues of privacy, libraries, and digital environment:

Barnes, Susan B. 2006. "A Privacy Paradox: Social Networking in the United States." *First Monday* 11, no. 9. http://firstmonday.org/htbin/cgiwrap/bin/ojs/index.php/fm/article/view/1394/1312

Fernandez, Peter. 2009. "Online Social Networking Sites and Privacy: Revisiting Ethical Considerations for a New Generation of Technology." *Library Philosophy and Practice* March: 1–9. http://www.webpages.uidaho.edu/~mbolin/fernandez.htm

Hus, Julia (Chiung-wen). 2006. "Privacy Concerns, Privacy Practices, and Web Site Categories: Toward a Situational Paradigm." *Online Information Review* 30, no. 5: 569–586.

Litwin, Rory. 2003. "The Central Problem of Library 2.0: Privacy." In *Library Juice Connection*, edited by Rory Litwin, pp. 71–74. Duluth, MN: Library Juice Press.

Sturgess, Paul, Eric Davies, James Dearnley, Ursula Iliffe, Ursula Iliffe, Charles Oppenheim, et al. 2003. "User Privacy in the Digital Library Environment: An Investigation of the Policies and Preparedness." *Library Management* 24, no. 1: 44–50.

Woodward, Jennette. 2007. *What Every Librarian Should Know about Electronic Privacy.* Westport, CT: Libraries Unlimited.

develop a policy regarding how to address a complaint from a user who objects to personal information being collected.

After 9/11, there was a change regarding access to library records at least by federal law enforcement officers. The USA PATRIOT Act authorized warrantless searches and required that the library not communicate to anyone that such a search occurred or was underway. What data might law enforcement officials obtain from library records that they might more easily access elsewhere? Karl Gruben (2006) wrote, "In actuality, the Department of Justice does not have as much interest in what Johnny is reading as it does in what he is looking at or e-mailing or Instant Messaging on the Internet, particularly since there is suspicion that the 9/11 hijackers communicated through Internet terminals in public libraries" (p. 303).

Section 215 of the act allows the government to secure secret warrants to obtain "business records"—this includes library records and records from library database vendors for named individuals. The act also authorizes the issuance of National Security Letters (NSLs), which do not require a judge's review and which require organizations to secretly provide information. At least one library has been on the receiving end of such a letter. Between 2003 and 2006, the FBI issued over 140,000 NSLs (Pike, 2007).

FROM THE ADVISORY BOARD

Virginia Walter commented that the only thing she would add to this chapter is mention of the somewhat ambiguous nature of confidentiality of children's library records. Most libraries routinely allow parents to access their child's borrowing record, usually to see if there are any materials outstanding. However, a few libraries—Santa Clara County (Los Gatos, CA), for one—restrict access and require that an adult have the child's permission before accessing the record. There are some legal justifications for this; a few city and county attorneys have reasoned that the right to privacy should not be abrogated because of a person's age and that this right carries more weight than a parent's rights. Other child advocates have pointed to more nefarious uses that have been put to a child's library records, particularly in child custody cases.

RADIO FREQUENCY IDENTIFICATION TECHNOLOGY

Some libraries now use a radio frequency identification (RFID) technology that may present some challenges in terms of user privacy, at least as it has been presented in the press (for one such discussion, see Butters, 2007). Originally employed as an effective method for library inventory control, item identification, and self checkout, when its capabilities are extended outside the library building, an unlikely event, problems might arise.

An embedded RFID chip identifies a specific item and its location unlike the magnetic strips commonly used in libraries in conjunction with their exit control system. The magnetic strip is not item specific and indicates only if the item has or has not been properly checked out. An RFID tag can track locations over a substantial distance—in theory far beyond the library building. Some states have proposed banning or at least greatly limiting the use of RFID chips because of their tracking capabilities. The concern is not particularly directed toward libraries because the typical library RFID is capable of being read from only about 3 feet. The concern is over commercial interests that claim knowing where and when a consumer uses their products is essential. Commercial tags have far longer ranges than library tags.

What the long-term outcome will be for RFID tags is impossible to accurately predict. Used for their original purposes in a library, RFID tags should not cause major concerns beyond the high cost of the chips and the labor required to embed one in each item in the collection. That their tracking capabilities can be applied beyond the library proper does seem problematic. You can easily keep up on the topic of RFID in libraries by monitoring the ALA's RFID webpages:

- "RFID Resolution" (http://www.ala.org/ala/aboutala/offices/oif/statementspols/ifresolutions/rfidresolution.cfm)
- "RFID: A Brief Bibliography" (http://www.ala.org/ala/professionalresources/libfactsheets/alalibraryfactsheet25.cfm)

CONTRACTS AND LICENSES

People sign contracts every day. Probably several thousand car rental "agreements" (they are contracts) are made every few hours. If people had time to read the agreement and understand it, there would probably be many fewer cars rented every hour. Hasty signing usually has no adverse consequences until something as simple as a scratch or a chip from a stone comes up. Then you learn just what was in the agreement.

Organizations cannot afford a hasty contract signing. Even when attorneys have put in days, weeks, or months of work and everyone thought they understood the terms, interpretation problems can and do arise. This in turn often results in lawsuits being filed. As we noted earlier regarding lawsuits over meeting rooms, many times a library simply has no money for fighting a lawsuit, be it for something it wants or needs, to defend itself.

Libraries normally have several contracts in force at any time—contracts for integrated library system vendors, book vendors, equipment maintenance, and janitorial services, for example. There are also license agreements for the access/use of some services and products such as online databases. In the case of a contract, it is likely that the director signed the contract but may not be the person who implements the terms. The person doing the implementation must have a grasp of what the contract calls for in order to protect the library and avoid unexpected problems.

CHECK THIS OUT

Because licensing is a major legal issue for libraries, we suggest you look at the "Principles" for licensing electronic resources as proposed by the Association of Research Libraries (http://www.arl.org/sc/marketplace/license/licprinciples.shtml). Although they were formulated in 1997 and are for large research libraries, they remain just as valid today. They can provide useful ideas for all types of libraries when thinking about what they should seek in the way of license changes.

What is the difference between a contract and a license? They are certainly related; however, there are differences, and understanding the differences can help the library avoid legal entanglements. A contract is a "voluntary, deliberate, and legally enforceable (binding) agreement between two or more competent parties. . . . Each party to a contract acquires rights and duties relative to the rights and duties of the other parties" (*Business Dictionary*, http://www.businessdictionary.com/definition/contract.html). A license is a "revocable written (formal) or implied agreement by an authority or proprietor (the licensor) not to assert his or her right (for a specific period and under specified conditions) to prevent another party (the licensee) from engaging in certain activity that is normally forbidden (such as selling liquor or making copies of a copyrighted work)" (*Business Dictionary*, http://www.businessdictionary.com/definition/license.html). Essentially a license gives one the privilege to use something under certain conditions.

Typical library licensing agreements outline the library's (lessee's) responsibilities for such things as security, customer service, payment and delivery, limitations and warranties, termination, indemnification, and assignment. All of these factors can affect allowable use of a product or service. Although adding attorney fees to the cost of creating user-oriented services or collections is unappealing, the fact is that most of the vendors will negotiate changes, and librarians should demand changes, based on attorney input, that benefit or at least do not create unreasonable demands on the library and its end users.

Compliance is a key issue, and the library must do what it can to ensure compliance with contracts and licenses. Some database licensing agreements contain language that places responsibility on the library (subscriber) to monitor what users do with material after they leave the premises. Such clauses are beyond any library's ability to handle, and librarians should insist that they be deleted from the agreement.

The licensing agreement often comes with other products in the same way that it does with computer software, that is, after the purchase. It is sealed in a package with a warning message to the effect that opening the package constitutes accepting the terms of the agreement inside the package. When consid-

ART OF NEGOTIATION

Negotiation is a skill that is essential for being a successful manager. We discussed where to touch upon this topic within the book. Because it crosses into so many aspects of managerial activities, we decided to place small segments in each appropriate chapter. Here we will outline some of the negotiation basics because successfully negotiating database licenses impacts many of the library's staff.

In negotiation, the skills to influence people come into play. You want people to see your point of view and gain their support for it, or perhaps you want to persuade them to come around to your viewpoint. Danny Ertel's (2004) advice regarding shifting your mindset from concentrating on making a deal to focusing on implementation is helpful in gaining support. Given the range and size of the licenses and contracts that a library enters into today, his four approaches will be useful in your negotiations:

1. Start with the end in mind. Imagine the deal 12 months out: What has gone wrong? How do you know if it's a success? Who should have been involved earlier?
2. Help the other party prepare, too. Surprising the other side doesn't make sense, because if a vendor promises things it can't deliver, you both lose.
3. Treat alignment as a shared responsibility. If your counterpart's interests aren't aligned, it's your problem too.
4. Send one message.

ering a product from a new vendor, ask for a copy of the licensing agreement before making a final decision to purchase. This gives you an opportunity to review the document. It also provides an opportunity to request changes that the vendor may or may not be willing to make. In any event, it will give the library a chance to consider whether it can live with the conditions of the licensing agreement before committing to the purchase.

COPYRIGHT

Copyright is the most widely discussed legal issue in the profession's literature. It has been bedeviling librarians for a very long time. The term "copyright" comes from the law's original purpose—to protect against unauthorized copying and selling a printed work. Over time, the concept became more complex, going far beyond copying someone else's work and selling it. Today it is thought of as protecting "intellectual property" (IP)—a concept that relates to almost all formats that individuals and organizations produce. The complexity is a result of the variety of materials covered, and each new technology is viewed as a potential threat to the copyright holder's rights.

Adding yet more complexity is the fact that most countries have copyright laws based on their own varying definitions of coverage terms and so forth. For the better part of 80 years there has been an international effort to "harmonize" the laws. Today, the major international body trying to bring some standardization to the field is the World Intellectual Property Organization (WIPO). Its website states, "The World Intellectual Property Organization (WIPO) is a specialized agency of the United Nations. It is dedicated to developing a balanced and accessible international intellectual property (IP) system, which rewards creativity, stimulates innovation and contributes to economic development while safeguarding the public interest" (http://www.wipo.int/about-wipo/en/what_is_wipo.html).

WIPO consists of 185 member countries as of mid 2012. Earlier we mentioned that IP was a very broad concept in today's digital world. WIPO's definition of IP is reasonably comprehensive:

Intellectual property (IP) refers to creations of the mind: inventions, literary and artistic works, and symbols, names, images, and designs used in commerce.

IP is divided into two categories: Industrial property, which includes inventions (patents), trademarks, industrial designs, and geographic indications of source; and Copyright, which includes literary and artistic works such as novels, poems and plays, films, musical works, artistic works such as drawings, paintings, photographs and sculptures, and architectural designs. Rights related to copyright include those of performing artists in their performances, producers of phonograms in their recordings, and those of broadcasters in their radio and television programs. (http://www.wipo.int/about-ip/en/)

The website contains a number of useful explanations of how copyright laws vary around the world as well as a detailed discussion of copyright.

Copyright impacts what libraries can do in the way of services in at least five significant areas where the law and library services intersect: fair use (17 U.S.C. § 107), photocopying/scanning (17 U.S.C. § 107 and § 108), interlibrary loan (17 U.S.C. § 108(d)), performance (17 U.S.C. § 107), and out-of-print status (17 U.S.C. § 108).

Fair use and performance are probably the two areas that create the greatest challenges for libraries, especially those supporting educational programs. Although the concept of fair use appears in the current law, just what constitutes fair use is not defined. There are guidelines, but even they leave ample room for interpretation/misinterpretation. Users do, rather often, ask librarians to help them understand what is and is not fair. There are long books about copyright and libraries, such as Kenneth D. Crews's *Copyright Law for Librarians and Educators: Creative Strategies and Practical Solutions* (3rd ed. Chicago:

American Library Association, 2011) and Carol Simpson's *Copyright for Schools: A Practical Guide* (5th ed. Santa Barbara, CA: Linworth Publishing, 2010). Even they cannot provide more than guidance. The only safe answer is, "It depends."

Libraries with media collections and public stations for using the media must address performance rights. The issue also comes up in terms of a library program that uses such media. One means of dealing with the issue is to acquire use rights when you purchase the items.

Almost all libraries provide photocopy services. There are regulations regarding posting proper signage related to photocopying and copyright. Failure to have such signs could put the library in jeopardy of becoming a defendant in an alleged copyright violation lawsuit.

Interlibrary loan (ILL) has been a staple service for a very long time. There are copyright ground rules for how often a library may borrow articles from a single journal title before it risks a lawsuit for using ILL in place of subscribing to the title. Some online database vendors' licenses do not allow for the use of its materials for ILL purposes unless the library can negotiate that the clause be dropped.

The Digital Millennium Copyright Act of 1998 (DMCA) updated U.S. copyright law in terms of the digital formats and technology, as well as to conform to the 1996 WIPO treaties. The 1978 copyright law is still in force but dramatically changed as a result of amendments and the DMCA.

One aspect of the DMCA that is important to libraries is "Title II: Online Service Provider Liability." It is important because the DMCA defines "online service provider" (OSP) very broadly, and libraries that offer electronic resources or Internet access could be considered OSPs. The law creates some "safe harbors" for specified OSP activities. When an activity is within the safe harbor, the OSP qualifies for an exemption from liability. You should read the most current material available about this title (http://www.copyright.gov/legislation/dmca .pdf), as it is complex, and legal interpretation of it is likely to evolve.

Title IV of the DMCA provides some clarification about library and archival digitization activities for preservation purposes. It allows the creation of up to three digital preservation copies of an eligible copyrighted work and the electronic loan of those copies to qualifying institutions. An additional feature is that it permits preservation, including in a digital form, of an item in a format that has become obsolete.

Distance education activities are also addressed in Title IV. The Register of Copyrights (the director of the U.S. Copyright Office) provided Congress with a report on how to promote distance education through digital technologies (http://www.copyright.gov/docs/regstat52599.html). Part of the report addresses the value of having licenses available for use of copyrighted works in distance education programs.

Like all legal issues, copyright is modified through court decisions. Thus, what may or may not be legal can change in a matter of days. It is critical that you stay in touch with legal developments that may impact library operations. Sometimes a seemingly unrelated court decision can later become a library issue.

CHECK THESE OUT

These two Internet sites will assist you in tracking legal issues and laws that may impact your library:

- "Law of Libraries and Archives" (http://www.wku.edu/~bryan.carson/librarylaw/)
- "LibraryLaw Blog" (http://blog.librarylaw.com/librarylaw/disability_access/)

One example, from 2010, is a U.S. Supreme Court split decision (4 to 4, as the newest justice recused herself because of prior involvement in the case). That decision essentially changed the "first sale doctrine," which could impact library lending. As *Library Journal* (2010) noted, "Why is the Library Copyright Alliance (LCA) interested in a legal battle between watch manufacturer Omega and big box retailer Costco? Because a pending Supreme Court case may threaten the 'first sale doctrine' in the copyright Act, which allows libraries to lend freely copies of all the books it has bought" (p. 13). Omega's position, which was upheld, was that its watches are produced outside the United States and thus Omega had the right to set a U.S. price (higher than elsewhere in the world). Furthermore, Costco could not purchase watches elsewhere in the world (first sale) and resell them in the United States at the lower cost. Certainly there is much more to resolve before we know what, if any, impact this case will have on libraries. The worst-case scenario is that U.S. publishers will use the decision to move all their production activities outside the country.

A related factor is that some countries (e.g., Australia, Canada, and the United Kingdom) employ the concept of public lending right (PLR) for authors and libraries. PLR allows an author to be compensated for the circulated use of his or her copyrighted works from libraries. Given copyright owners' increasing attempts to charge a fee for various types of usage that are free, it may not be too long before the PLR will come to the United States. Certainly the Omega decision removes one of the issues that clouded the efforts to get a U.S. PLR program in place: what happens after the first sale? Nothing may change as a result of the decision, but *LJ* certainly deemed it important enough to bring attention to the potential threat to free lending.

DOCUMENTATION

No matter the incident or the event, we have three strong words of advice: document, document, document. This is something the head of any library, her or his management team, or any library manager must never forget. Documentation is essential in building or defending a case. You would like to think that not all actions would require this, but it is better to be on the safe side and document

> ### AUTHORS' EXPERIENCE
>
> Alire, while leading a disaster recovery project at a large university library, had instructed her disaster recovery team in their very first emergency response meeting to document every job-related interaction they had. Several years later, while still in the disaster recovery situation, a major contractor threatened to sue the library and the university over payment for services that the library maintained were not adequately completed (noncompliance). After a meeting with the university and the contractor's attorneys, Alire instructed her disaster response team to gather all the e-mail correspondence regarding the specific issue between the contractor, his staff, and the library. As a result of the documentation, Alire was able to produce a file two inches thick of e-mail correspondence to the attorneys on both sides; the threat to sue was quickly withdrawn, saving the university several millions of dollars in funds for services not rendered.

than not. Documentation can range from e-mail transactions to something written on paper—anything that records what transpired. When in doubt, check with your parent organization's attorney.

KEY POINTS TO REMEMBER

- A variety of legal issues constrain a library's freedom of action, from establishing the organization to specifying who, how, and what users and staff may do.
- It is important to get legal counsel involved early in any potential legal issue.
- Have counsel review polices regarding access and services.
- Training staff in the policies, such as user access and handling difficult users, is a key step in avoiding liability issues.
- Professional malpractice lawsuits are unlikely to impact library services, at least in the near term. Liability and negligence lawsuits, however, are a different matter, and libraries and some staff have been sued.
- Keeping up with current developments in the field is something you ought to do; however, following legal developments that impact the field is critical to avoid potential stressful and costly legal action.
- Document, document, document!

References

Angoff, Allan. 1976. "Library Malpractices Suit: Could It Happen to You?" *American Libraries* 7, no. 8: 489.

American Libraries. 2005. "Colorado Gets Meeting-Room Religion." *American Libraries* 36, no. 9: 28–29.

———. 2006a. "DOJ Supports Prayer Meets." *American Libraries* 37, no. 2: 18–19.

———. 2006b. "Homeless Residents Sue over Borrowing Limits." *American Libraries* 37, no. 7: 18.

———. 2006c. "Montana State Library Pulls ACLU Film Screening." *American Libraries* 37, no. 4: 12.

———. 2006d. "Stir Raised by Dallas Body Odor Rule." *American Libraries* 37, no. 2: 11.

———. 2007. "Supreme Court Won't Hear Meeting Room Appeal." *American Libraries* 38, no. 10: 18.

Butters, Alan. 2007. "RFID Systems, Standards and Privacy within Libraries." *Electronic Library* 25, no. 4: 430–439.

DeRosa, Frank J. 1980. "The Disruptive Patron." *Library and Archival Security* 3, no. 3/4: 29–37.

Epp, Mary Anne. 2006. "Closing the 95 Percent Gap: Library Resource Sharing for People with Print Disabilities." *Library Trends* 54, no. 3: 411–429.

Ertel, Danny. 2004. "Getting Past Yes: Negotiating as if Implementation Mattered." *Harvard Business Review* 82, no. 11: 60–68.

Farrugia, Sarah. 2002. "A Dangerous Occupation? Violence in Public Libraries." *New Library World* 103, no. 9: 309–319.

Glenn, David D. 2011. "Job Safety Analysis: Its Role Today." *Professional Safety* 56, no. 3: 48–57.

Gruben, Karl T. 2006. "What Is Johnny Doing in the Library? Libraries, the U.S.A. PATRIOT Act, and Its Amendments." *St. Thomas Law Review* 19, no. 2: 297–328.

Healey, Paul D. 2008. *Professional Liability Issues for Librarians and Information Professionals*. New York: Neal-Schuman.

Jaeger, Paul T., and Zheng Yan. 2009. "One Law with Two Outcomes: Comparing the Implementation of CIPA in Public Libraries and Schools." *Information Technology and Libraries* 28, no. 1: 6–14.

Jansen, Barbara A. 2010. "Internet Filtering 2.0: Checking Intellectual Freedom and Participative Practices at the Schoolhouse Door." *Knowledge Quest* 39, no. 1: 46–53.

Kranich, Nancy. 2012. E-mail communication sent to Camila A. Alire, March 23.

Lehmberg, Timm, Georg Rehm, Andreas Witt, and Felix Zimmermann. 2008. "Digital Text Collections, Linguistic Research Data, and Mashups: Notes on the Legal Situation." *Library Trends* 57, no. 1: 52–71.

Library Journal. 2010. "Copyright Case Could Threaten Library Lending." 135, no. 13: 13.

Magi, Trina. 2010. "A Content Analysis of Library Vendor Policies: Do They Meet Our Standards?" *College and Research Libraries* 71, no. 3: 254–272.

Maycock, Angela. 2010. "Choose Privacy Week and School Libraries." *Knowledge Quest* 39, no. 1: 68–72.

Murley, Diane. 2008. "Web Site Accessibility." *Law Library Journal* 100, no. 2: 401–406.

Pike, George. 2007. "The PATRIOT Act Illuminated." *Information Today* 24, no. 5: 17–18.

Simons, Spencer L. 2005. "Lawsuits and Legal Challenges: Librarians on the Frontline." *Texas Library Journal* 81, no. 1: 18–21.

Launching Pad

Airoldi, Joan. 2004. "One Book, One County, One Subpoena." *Alki* 20, no. 3: 19–20.

———. 2006. "A Grand Jury Subpoena in the PATRIOT Act Era." *Library Administration and Management* 20, no. 1: 26–29.

Allen, Susan. 2007. "Patron Abuse Prompts Trial of Social-Network Filter." *American Libraries* 38, no. 8: 41.

American Libraries. 2008. "Security Revisited after Child Is Assaulted." 39, no. 4: 24.

American Library Association Office for Intellectual Freedom. 2007. "Model Policy: Responding to Demands for Library Records." *American Libraries* 38, no. 8: four-page insert.

Anderson, Judy, and Lynne DeMont. 2001. "Treading Carefully through Murky Legalities of Electronic Reserves." *Computers in Libraries* 21, no. 6: 40–45.

Balas, Janet L. 2007. "I'm a Librarian, Not a Lawyer!" *Computers in Libraries* 27, no 6: 34–36.

Culler, David. 2010. "'Getting to Yes' through Negotiation." *Quill* 98, no. 1: 37.

Diamond, Randy, and Martha Dragich. 2001. "Professionalism in Librarianship: Shifting the Focus from Malpractice to Good Practice." *Library Trends* 49, no. 3: 395–414.

Dockens, Elaine B. 2010. "Vendor Pitfalls in Negotiating Large Multi-Year Contracts." *AALL Spectrum* 14, no. 4: 8–12.

Dougherty, William C. 2010. "The Copyright Quagmire." *Journal of Academic Librarianship* 36, no. 4: 351–353.

Gasaway, Laura N. 2010. "Libraries, Digital Content, and Copyright." *Vanderbilt Journal of Entertainment and Technology Law* 12, no. 4: 755–778.

Grogg, Jill E. 2008. "Negotiation for the Librarian." *Journal of Electronic Resources Librarianship* 20, no. 4: 210–212.

Grogg, Jill E., and Beth Ashmore. 2009. "The Art of the Deal: Negotiating in Times of Economic Stress." *Searcher* 17, no. 6: 42–49.

Harris, Lesley Ellen. 2009. "Licenses and Legalities." *American Libraries* 40, nos. 6/7: 58–59.

LeComte, Richard. 2009. "Writers Blocked: The Debate Over Public Lending Right in the United States During the 1980s." *Libraries and the Cultural Record* 44, no. 4: 395–417.

Liberman, Varda, Nicholas Anderson, and Lee Ross. 2010. "Achieving Difficult Agreements: Effects of Positive Expectations on Negotiation Process and Outcomes." *Journal of Experimental Social Psychology* 48, no. 4: 494–504.

Library Journal. 2007. "Report to UCLA Slams Campus Police: Taser Use in

Library Was Inappropriate Response to Uncooperative Student." *Library Journal* 132, no. 14:14–15.

McMenemy, David, and Paul F. Burton. 2005. "Managing Access: Legal and Policy Issues of ICT Use." In *Delivering Digital Services*, edited by Alan Paultez, 1–34. London: Facet Publishing.

Terry, Jenni. 2010. "Access to Copyrighted Works for Those with Disabilities." *College and Research Libraries News* 71, no. 1: 38.

Whitehouse, Guy. 2009. "A New Clash between Human Rights and Copyright: The Push for Enhanced Exceptions for the Print-Disabled." *Publishing Research Quarterly* 25, no. 4: 219–231.

PART II

MANAGERIAL SKILL SETS

Futurists begin with the assumption that the future is uncertain, because a combination of variables and unknowns could produce any number of results. Thus their goal is not to predict but rather to posit alternative futures, each of which aim to provide a plausible, internally consistent view of what might happen.

—**David J. Staley and Kara J. Malenfant (2010)**

An economic downturn can quickly expose the shortcomings of your business strategy. But can you identify weak points in good times as well? And can you focus on those weak points that really matter? . . . As Peter Drucker once warned, "The serious mistakes are not being made as a result of wrong answers. The truly dangerous thing is asking the wrong questions."

—**Robert Simons (2010)**

The strategic planning process is not only complex, but is complex in different ways for different types of institutions. For instance, the process for museums and even academic libraries is significantly different than the ideal strategic planning process for public libraries.

—**Lee Price (2010)**

Scenarios are instruments for ordering people's perceptions about alternative future environments in which today's decisions might play out. They are carefully constructed stories about the future.

—**Ruth Saurin and John Ratcliffe (2011)**

4

THE PLANNING PROCESS

This chapter focuses on the following:

- The importance of planning
- The nature of planning
- Types and variations in plans
- Strategic planning
- Mission, vision, and value statements and planning
- Sources of planning information such as SWOT
- Linking strategic plans and goals, objectives, policies, and procedures
- Scenario planning
- Project planning and management

PLANS COME IN all shapes and sizes. Personal plans range from what to do today to "my career plan." Organizational planning is also diverse—from strategic planning (grand strategies) to planning this afternoon's staff meeting. We all plan, and some of us are better at it than others. In part, the difference is how well and how far we look into the future and how flexible we are in adjusting plans to changing circumstances.

In today's rapidly changing world, library managers are challenged on just about every front—technology, demographics, funding, and so forth. Navigating the library through a highly uncertain world takes many skills and a great deal of thinking and planning. The plans are like charts setting forth where you are and where you want to go. They do not ensure that you will not run aground, but they do help you avoid some of the reefs, assuming the plans are thoughtfully developed.

Our opening quotation from Robert Simons suggests that part of thoughtful planning starts by asking the right questions. Asking the right questions brings to mind a passage in *Alice's Adventures in Wonderland* in which Alice asks the Cat, "Would you tell me, please, which way I ought to go from here?" "That depends a good deal on where you want to get to," said the Cat. "I don't much care where," said Alice. "Then it doesn't matter which way you go," said the Cat

A POINT OF REFLECTION

Think about an organization in which you have worked. Was there any evidence of planning? If so, how was it made evident to you? Was the plan made available to all staff? Was the staff involved in developing the plan?

(Carroll, p. 27, Project Gutenberg, 2008, http://www.gutenberg.org/files/11/11-pdf.pdf). Unlike Alice, organizations must have a clear idea of where they want to go. Certainly there are times when the "where" is rather vague; asking the right questions helps clarify the direction. Richard Wayne (2011), in writing about planning methods at the University of Texas Medical Center at Dallas Library, suggested that "The foundation of the methodology is the vision statement" (p.

SOMETHING TO PONDER

Contemplate the following statements, and keep your answers in mind as you explore the remainder of this chapter. When thinking about your answers, keep in mind the organizational context. You are thinking about your role as a manager, not about your personal planning process.

1. Usually when I start something I have a clear and detailed sense of what I want the outcome to be.
2. In a work setting, when I give a task to someone, I tell them only what the objective/outcome should be, not how to accomplish the task.
3. I set specific and measurable objectives for myself.
4. Most of the objectives I set for myself and others are challenging but doable.
5. Setting deadlines and schedules is easy for me, but keeping to them is difficult.
6. I set both long-term and short-term goals for myself, with some short-term goals intended to help achieve the long-term goals.
7. I tend to look at many options before I set a course of action.
8. At work I stick to my plans for the day and avoid changing course, except in an emergency.
9. I ask others for advice before setting goals and objectives.
10. I follow all organizational policies, procedures, and rules.
11. I devote some thought to "what if" actions and try to have some "contingency" actions in mind in case the unexpected happens.

13). Vision statements should be about where you want to go; we look at such statements later in this chapter.

Plans allow you to check on your progress toward defined goals. They assist in coordinating activities designed to achieve an outcome. Planning is forward-looking and should force you to look to the future. Plans indicate to people, both inside and outside the organization, where the organization hopes to go.

Maurice Line (2004) comments on long-term and short-term thinking and planning in the library: "There are very many examples of disastrous past failures to foresee effects . . . [and] there are few who can predict longer-term effects of short-term measures. . . . The ability of librarians to plan ahead is constrained by their parent body, and plans have to be made within more or less strict parameters" (pp. 62–63).

THE NATURE OF PLANNING

According to Nohria and Stewart (2006), twenty-first-century managers must devote more time and thought now than in the past to handling risk, uncertainty, and doubt. They make the point that planning is future looking in nature, but there is great uncertainty as to what will actually happen. This means more risk and doubt. They consider these three variables—risk, uncertainty, and doubt—to be distinct yet interrelated, and their potential for disrupting plans is always present.

Risk is something you can calculate ("I took a calculated risk") to some degree. Uncertainty is incalculable. With risk and uncertainty, there is the underlying assumption that you know what you want, if not how to achieve it. "Doubt comes into play when there is no right outcome, when one must choose between two evils, or when good outcomes have bad side effects. . . . How does one choose between valued objectives, for example, safety versus liberty, scientific discovery versus the sanctity of human life, individual versus group?" (Nohria and Stewart, 2006, p. 40). Although libraries do not face making such weighty plans or choosing between such complex issues, they still have to consider risk, uncertainty, and, at times, doubt.

Some years ago, Miles and Snow (1978) outlined four ways that organizations go about handling risk and uncertainty. There are the "defenders"—those who stay with what they do best and operate on the assumption that keeping to the narrow, welltrodden path will minimize risk and uncertainty. Such behavior, in the past, often worked well, especially for long-established organizations, such as libraries and archives. Today, that style is undoubtedly a much higher risk strategy. "Analyzers" are inclined to take on a moderate amount of risk and uncertainty. Their approach is to watch and analyze what others are doing and imitate what appears to be working ("Let's not be on the bleeding edge of the IT curve"). "Prospectors" see opportunities in risk taking and uncertainty. They want to be leading the way. Their plans devote little attention to "what if"—essentially they pay little attention to risk calculation. As a consequence, they experience a higher rate of failed plans. When they succeed, they create tremendous results, often forcing competitors out or causing major shifts in how all like organizations operate. Finally, there are the "reactors." These organizations are passive and change direction only when there is a crisis. Changing plans in a crisis is probably the riskiest of all options. As we noted earlier, effective planning requires time and careful thought—which are generally in short supply in a crisis. Although there is no way to avoid risk, uncertainty, and doubt in the planning process, some techniques will make them less intimidating and problematic. The balance of this chapter will explore these techniques and planning processes.

TYPES OF PLANS

Broadly thinking, there are three categories of plans. *Strategic plans* are long term (most often two to five years) and generally are initiated by senior managers, although the actual planning process may involve most, if not all, of the staff. *Tactical plans* are mid term in length (six months to two years) and are geared toward achieving the strategic plans. Middle managers and supervisors are the people who initiate work on tactical plans. *Operational plans* are short term (one day to one year) and are intended to guide staff in their day-to-day activities; these plans obviously need to be clearly linked to the tactical and strategic plans. Such plans are generated by individuals, teams, supervisors, and middle managers. Because, in the ideal world, all plans arise from and are linked to the organization's strategic plan, we begin with strategic planning.

STRATEGIC PLANNING

Three important concepts need clarification to underscore their interrelated character as well as their differences: strategy, strategic planning, and strategic management. A strategy identifies and sets the overall direction of an organization. Strategic planning is the process of creating action steps designed to achieve the overall strategy. Strategic management involves all the staff in formulating and implementing activities intended to move toward the desired outcome of the strategy and strategic plan.

Think of the planning process structure (as shown in Figure 4.1, p. 96) as starting with an environmental scan that provides the basic material for thinking about and formulating the strategy. Three key elements in strategic plans are the mission, vision, and value statements. These statements draw on environmental information and existing organizational capabilities, resources, and parent body limitations. All these factors are the context for developing a strategy and designing an action plan. Once the strategic plan is set, work begins on identifying a set of goals and objectives. With the goals and objectives in place, it is relatively easy to determine what tasks are necessary to address them.

Carter McNamara (http://managementhelp.org/plan_dec/str_plan/models .htm) suggests there are five models of strategic plans: basic, issue based, alignment, scenario, and organic. Basic is what most people think of as strategic planning. Issue based is a more detailed methodology; one of its components involves

CHECK THIS OUT

A good book on strategic planning is the Harvard Business School's *Strategy: Create and Implement the Strategy for Your Business* (Cambridge, MA: Harvard Business School Press, 2005).

the use of SWOT analysis (covered shortly) and similar techniques to assess various elements in the environment. Alignment is a further fine-tuning with a focus on internal organizational issues. Scenario plans (covered later in the chapter) develop alternative future possibilities (help deal with the uncertainty factor). McNamara's organic is similar to what many people label "rolling" plans—"on an ongoing basis, e.g., once every quarter, dialogue about the processes needed to arrive at the vision." We touch on rolling planning in this and later chapters. Realistically the ideal strategic plan incorporates all of the approaches. As you might expect, it is a highly labor-intensive and time-consuming process.

Mission Statements

Essentially a mission statement is the organization's very long-term strategy: What do we want to accomplish? Where do we want the organization to go? For a strategy to be useful there must be congruity between the organization's capabilities and its operating environment.

In most cases, the strategic activities of libraries occur within a larger organization or system, which sets the parameters for thinking and planning. Maurice Line (2004), quoted earlier in this chapter, also wrote:

> Few libraries operate on such a scale, and opportunities for long-term planning are limited. . . . Strategic planning was very popular in all types of libraries a few years ago, though I sense that its popularity has waned recently. . . . The best that can be done is to prepare a vision of what the library should aim to be like in the longer-term (ten years), a general strategy for moving towards that vision in the medium-term (five years say), and a one-year plan of action. Both vision and strategy should be revisited once a year. (p. 63)

There should be a dynamic interaction between assessing the organizational environment and reviewing the mission and vision statements. Although the mission and vision statements should have a long-term perspective, you must revisit them periodically. We addressed the basics of environmental scanning in Chapter 2. In the analysis and monitoring of the environment, it is important to focus on the degree of congruence between the mission and vision statements and the environmental factors.

FROM THE ADVISORY BOARD

Joseph Mika has been involved in approximately 100 strategic plans (as consultant, facilitator, and library school director). His preferred approach to vision and mission is to have minimal, meaningful statements. He interprets vision as an all-encompassing statement that needs to be brief and to the point. Vision examples: "Anchored in Excellence . . . Unlimited Horizons" (for a library with a waterfront); "World-Class Education in the Real World" (a university); "Treasured Past—Vibrant Future" (a library that prides itself on its community ties); and "Inspiration through Information." Mission examples: "The XXX Library provides information, resources, and quality service"; and "The mission of the XXX Library is to enrich our community with unlimited opportunities for learning and discovery through excellence in services, resources, and cultural programs." He likes it when the mission and/or vision statements can easily fit on the staff's business cards; the cards serve as a reminder for the staff and as a public relations tool when given to community members or visitors.

Most mission statements are relatively short and general in character, but not so general that they could apply to almost any other organization in the same field. Such statements vary in character; some are only a few hundred words long, while others may contain several paragraphs. As you would expect, the longer statements contain greater detail. Striking the correct balance between conciseness and detail can be a challenge. V. Kasturi Rangan (2004) provides sound advice for achieving a good balance. He states, "Most non-profits have broad, inspiring mission statements—and they should. But they also need a systematic method that connects their callings to their programs" (p. 112).

Valentinov and Larsen (2011) maintain that nonprofit managers, who are aware of the need for broad mission statements in order to maximize support from interested individuals and other stakeholders, are taking a risk with each broadening of the statement: "Non-profit managers are motivated to keep nonprofit missions sufficiently broad to make them legitimate; yet excessive mission breadth may be perceived as vagueness that would provide disincentives for the potential stakeholders to support" (p. 20). Being broad enough, succinct, memorable, but not vague is a true challenge.

Peter Gow (2009) in his article "Missions, Mantras, and Meaning" noted an all too common problem with mission, and we would add vision, statements: "Assembled by committees from a parts kit of hoary clichés and trendy buzzwords, many of today's school mission statements are so general and so alike that they fail to differentiate themselves and the schools they represent reducing even most noble aspirations to banalities" (p. 25). While his focus was private schools, libraries also face falling into banality; avoiding banality is not simple.

SOMETHING TO CONSIDER

The following is an example of how a library gathered data for a planning process, in this case a strategic plan. The text is courtesy of the Fairfax County Library in Fairfax, Virginia. The process started in 2011, and the text that follows was prepared in December of that year:

As part of our overhaul of the library's strategic plan, we are currently gathering information. We have conducted three public meetings with the title "Conversations with the Director." Each meeting was held in a library branch with an average attendance of about 45 people. We focused the discussion by asking the following questions:

- The Library Board's number one priority is "access." What does "access" mean to you?
- What do you feel the library's top three priorities should be?
- What should the public library look like in three years, in five years?
- If you could have the library make one change, provide one resource, or offer one service regardless of cost, what would it be?

We also are using three surveys that are either recently completed or to begin soon. There are a number of questions that each survey has in common as well as some different questions more tailored to the audience.

Library Website User Survey: ran Oct. 31–Nov. 8. We received 199 responses to questions ranging from whether respondents have a system library card, to satisfaction with the website, to what they think the library's greatest asset is, to whether they own some type of e-reader. Results are currently being analyzed.

Short In-Branch User Survey: ran Nov. 14–Dec. 2. We received 4,140 responses. This questionnaire included a number of demographic questions so we could better understand who our customers are and compare our users with the general makeup of the county. This questionnaire also asked if the respondents had visited our website or followed us through our presence on social media sites; what services they think we should provide or continue to provide in the future; if there are any essential services that we do *not* currently provide; what they think the library's top three priorities should be for the future; and about customer satisfaction. Results are currently being analyzed. *(continued)*

Staff Survey: ran Dec. 6–Jan. 9. We received 270 responses, about 60 percent of staff. This survey was made available online through our Infoweb. The survey asked for staff opinions on many of the questions already described as well as sought to gather input on staff development and training needs and staff knowledge and understanding of what they know customers are looking for the library to provide. There were also a number of questions that asked staff to indicate what they thought the value was of the library offering certain services/resources to the community.

Our hope is that, by gathering input using these different surveys, we can create a more coherent picture of what our customers are looking for from the library now and moving forward. We will be examining such issues as, do staff and customers differ in their views; if so, how? Are there differences based on such factors as age, branch location, whether usage is online or in-branch, and a host of demographic factors? Does one group point us in a wholly new direction or at least in a direction diverging from what our, for example, older, more traditional library customers may be telling us?

Fred David (1989) provided some insights into how to address the challenge of being short, general, and yet specific. He suggested thinking in terms of answering a series of questions. We modified the questions to better fit the library context:

- What is our primary service community?
- What are our key programs and services?
- Who are our competitors within the service area?
- What are our key technologies?
- What are our basic values and aspirations, and what are the philosophical priorities of our activities?
- What is our fiscal operating base?
- What are our major strengths and weaknesses?
- What is our operating philosophy regarding staff?

Vision Statements

A vision statement should also be concise while providing clear guidance for the more detailed thinking and planning that must follow. A good vision statement is articulate, compelling, exciting, and challenging. It paints a broad picture of how the library will or should operate at some point in the future. It should be appealing to the staff, the service community, and all other stakeholders. Burt

Nanus (1992) drew up a list of questions to ask about a vision statement (pp. 28–29). His view is that for a statement to be useful the answer to all of these questions should be "yes":

- Does the statement reflect the organization and its environment?
- Does it set forth a clear purpose?
- Is it forward-looking?
- Is it likely to inspire/motivate the staff?
- Is it challenging/ambitious but attainable?
- Will it require the staff to perform at high levels?
- Can it be easily understood?
- Does it communicate what is special about the services and programs that the organization hopes to achieve?

PRACTICAL EXAMPLES

The following examples are actual mission and vision statements of a public library, although we deliberately omitted the name of the city.

Mission Statement

The mission of the City Public Library is to promote the development of independent, self-confident, literate citizens through the provision of open access to cultural, intellectual, and information resources.

Vision Statement

The City Public Library Board of Trustees envisions a future in which the library's collections, programs, and leadership help ensure:

- That every city resident has the opportunity to enjoy an intellectually and culturally rich life.
- That every child enters school with the requisite developmental skills.
- That every child experiences the pleasure of reading and the joy of learning.
- That our community celebrates and appreciates diversity.
- That those in need find assistance and information with ease.

A web search for library management mission and vision statements generates hundreds of valid hits. Some are good in terms of Nanus's (1992) questions (see p. 93), some are fair, and a few seem to lack something. Test some of the statements you find against the questions.

One of the challenges for newcomers to writing mission and vision statements is determining what the difference is, if any, between them. Piet Levy (2011) provides one of the clearest distinctions: "A mission statement basically says who we are as a company and the vision statement says what we want to be in the future" (p. 10).

SWOT Analysis

Another source of data to assist in your thinking is the SWOT (strengths, weaknesses, opportunities, and threats) analysis. This analysis can facilitate thinking through the implications of environmental data and the capabilities of your organization. Although the process does take time, especially when done as a group endeavor, it can produce useful ideas. The process also feeds into the writing or revision of the mission and vision statements and of the strategic plan. In addition, it will help you identify what went right, went wrong, or changed since the last major planning effort. Two of the SWOT elements are outward looking (opportunities and threats), and two are inward in character (strengths and weaknesses). Such factors as staff skills, competencies, programs, service–community relations, and fiscal base can be either a strength or a weakness. When conducting a SWOT analysis, consider whether the factor will help or hinder the accomplishment of your strategy or plan. Likewise, opportunities and threats are anything that would hinder your plan.

SWOT is not without its critics, despite its widespread use (e.g., Armstrong, 2004; Hill and Westerbrook, 1997; and Valentin, 2005). Everett and Duval (2010, pp. 525–526) listed seven common concerns related to SWOT usage:

- It yields banal or misleading results.
- It has a weak theoretical basis.
- It implies the organization factors can be "neatly" categorized as positive or negative.
- It encourages "superficial scanning and impromptu categorization."
- It promotes list building as opposed to thoughtful consideration.
- It does not look at tradeoffs among factors.
- It promotes muddled conceptualizations, particularly between accomplishments and strengths.

We would add that it is not really a forward-looking activity. Typically it asks us to identify what our challenges are and what our strengths are—the current situation.

Despite its shortcomings, SWOT can add to the thinking process, especially if you add some other assessment techniques. One such technique is the PEST (political, economic, social, and technological) analysis or the extended version PESTEL, which adds environment and law to the mix. Other possibilities include the Ansoff matrix, which focuses on alternative growth strategies for an organization's present and potential products and markets (users), and the Boston Consulting Group matrix, which focuses on competition.

Value Statements

For a library, the preparation of a value statement can be a useful exercise when done with the staff. A value statement concisely expresses the operational priorities or values of the organization. Although this might at first appear to be an unnecessary activity, it can often lead to some rather surprising staff input regarding operational values (or at least their assumptions about what is "valued"). While there may be easy agreement that service to the user is a top priority, there are often strong differing views about how that goal translates into behavior and services. It is also likely that the discussion will raise ethical concerns. A value statement, while not essential for planning or for operational success, can be beneficial as long as the values are represented "on the floor and not just the wall."

GOALS

Once you have performed some analyses and written your statements, you still face some significant work to translate the ideas into action. Setting goals and objectives takes time and thought; in essence they are the tactical plans for achieving the strategy. It is now time to create operational plans—policies and procedures—to carry out the goals and objectives. Needless to say, you *must* link the policies and procedures to the broader plans. If they don't, revise them until they do. This is where, as they say, "the rubber meets the road"; they are the implementation of all the time and effort to developing grand plans.

A short definition of a strategic goal is an accomplishment that will aid in the achievement of a strategy. Most goals have a mid-term to long-term time frame. A library might divide its goals into the three broad categories suggested by Heather Johnson (1994, p. 9): "service goals, resource management goals, and administrative/directional goals."

Useful goals are SMARTER goals—specific, measurable, acceptable, realistic, time-framed, extending, and rewarding. An example of a SMARTER goal for an archive is, "By 2014, 80 percent of the archival electronic records will be accessioned within ten working days." The statement is specific and measurable. It also has two time frames. We do not know if the goal is acceptable, realistic, extending, or rewarding. We might well assume that there is some degree of staff acceptance of the goal as doable (realistic) if we know the staff was involved in writing it. It is unlikely that an organization would waste time formulating goals that do not, in some manner, stretch (extend) its capabilities. Just how rewarding its achievement may be is difficult to say; however, for libraries the achievement of a goal that serves the parent body will often translate into greater support in the future.

Jim Romeo (2011), in writing about goal setting, suggested, "Keep current circumstances and conditions in perspective and update your expectations accordingly. Review long-term goals and revise them to account for the current environment" (p. 93). Essentially, as is true for all plans, periodic assessment and possible revisions are key factors in long-term organizational success.

OBJECTIVES

To illustrate objectives, we again use an example from an academic library, with slight adjustments and omission of the institution's name. The institution took a

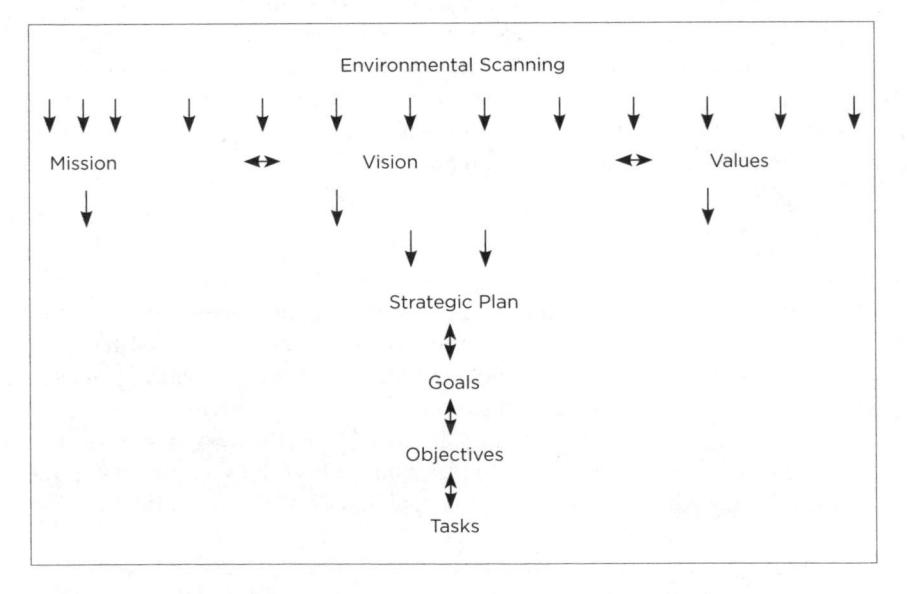

Figure 4.1   Strategic Planning Model

slightly more complex approach, in that it started by establishing strategic goals and then subgoals and objectives. One strategic goal is to "prepare an information-competent student." A subgoal is to "provide effective and sustainable instruction to 100 percent of a larger and more diverse student body and curricula by 2016." This particular subgoal has three objectives:

- Develop electronic tools and web tutorials as alternatives to face-to-face instruction by creating two or more modules each year.
- Provide faculty and student mentors with tools and methods to integrate information competency into 60 percent of classes by 2015.
- Remodel and increase the capacity of the bibliographic instruction classroom by 2013. Remodeling will improve interaction by reconfiguring space and allowing instructors to control all workstations from the instructor's station. Capacity will be increased by 20–25 percent.

Again you can see the SMARTER elements in the objectives and how the objectives become the basis for effective action.

Once you establish the goals and objectives, it becomes relatively easy to identify appropriate activities, policies, and procedures as well as the resources required to achieve the desired results.

POLICIES

Policies are statements that guide staff thinking in making decisions and handling work processes. Policies set the limits within which you may act. Policy implementation is an activity that almost all of the staff engages in from time to time. A library might have a policy that normally grants access to only specific categories of users but that also grants access to others under certain circumstances. The unit that controls access likely would generate some typical exceptions to the overall policy to ensure more consistent implementation/interpretation of the policy's intent.

There are several types of policies: originated, appealed, implied, and imposed. Libraries must deal with all four types. Originated policy is the ideal. Such a policy is created because the organization anticipates a situation will occur that requires one. The more policies that come about in this way, the better, because they originate from an understanding of the library's overall strategic plan. A danger for originated policy is structuring it so tightly that it becomes a rule rather than a guide to thinking.

Appealed policies arise when a situation occurs and there is no policy for how to resolve it. Lacking a policy, staff will create their own when the need comes up—often unaware they are doing so. When several people do this, several somewhat different "policies" come to exist. Appealed policies most commonly cause problems when a user becomes unhappy after experiencing variations in an assumed "policy" when interacting with different staff members; another situation is when a staff member complains about the lack of consistency. Often the frontline staff appeal to their supervisor to sort out the differences. If the supervisor believes the issue is too important to resolve, the problem moves up the hierarchy. As this happens, time passes; and differences of opinion become entrenched in the absence of a resolution, making it more difficult to resolve the matter. There is little hope of completely stopping appealed policy making, but you do have options for keeping it to a minimum. The best way to avoid appealed policy is to spend significant time and thought developing originated policies that are clear enough to preclude the need for appeal.

Implied policy is the most dangerous type for user relations. Such policy arises from staff or user perception of what a policy actually intends. Senior managers usually assume that staff members understand and employ policies as originally intended. At the operational level, however, people may well be acting on the basis of what they believe is the intent of a policy. One way to reduce the risk of this happening is to provide new staff with policy orientation sessions. It is also helpful to hold regular policy review sessions with all staff involved in implementing policies.

Imposed policy comes from outside agencies and groups. Some imposed policies in libraries come from the parent organization (examples are personnel, promotion, retirement, and budget policies). When the library operates with a union or a collective bargaining unit, policies covering such topics as work hours and conditions often are imposed through a contract. Such policies may well conflict with the library's strategic plans, goals, and objectives. Such policies should be addressed when developing strategic plans.

SOMETHING TO PONDER

Review the four types of policies described, and give two examples of each taken from a library you know. If you feel that you don't have this depth of knowledge, try using an academic department in which you currently study.

PROCEDURES

Procedures are guides to actions rather than to thoughts. They provide a chronological sequence of steps that staff use to carry out the activities necessary to achieve a specific policy, objective, or outcome. Procedure planning consists of a number of elements, including keeping procedures to a minimum. Long lists of procedures that detail every action stifle initiative and individuality and induce staff boredom. Failure to limit the number of procedures can lead to a morale problem, which often becomes a staffing problem. Because procedures are rather easy to generate, once you understand the process, some managers "procedure-ize" every activity they can. In the process, they create a deadly atmosphere for the people working with them.

Having basic procedures in place, especially for complex activities, is essential, because they provide the framework for training new staff as well as a baseline for evaluating unit outcomes. However, in those cases when it is possible to allow latitude, let the employees work out for themselves what is most effective. (Note: Allowing latitude does not mean "anything goes" in terms of performance. Instead, let the individual formulate how to achieve the goal.)

A key question to ask is, "Did I plan the procedure, or does it merely reflect existing practice?" Analyzing a procedure carefully (is it useful, is it still necessary, is it a plan?) is your responsibility as a manager. If the organization has clearly stated policies to guide (and promote) sound thinking and good procedures to guide actions (yet allow for individual initiative), then the work environment is usually pleasant and effective. Striking the best balance is a challenge but one that you can easily meet with some thought and staff input.

PROGRAMS

The term "program" is usually applied to a complex undertaking that involves several types of plans. Programs consist of policies, procedures, rules, job allocations, resource requirements, sources of resources, and other elements necessary to carry out a combination of objectives. Not every program includes all types of plans, but anything labeled as a program should outline actions to take (when, where, and by whom). They should also indicate the purpose of those actions and how the actions fit into the library's objectives. Programs need not be institutionwide; they can apply to a single department. For example, consider the preservation program of an archive to increase microfilming or digitizing of materials already in the collection. Such a program would indicate how to select materials for treatment, how to handle them, what processes to employ, and who would do the work.

SCENARIO PLANNING

As stated earlier, a scenario plan differs from the basic strategic plan in that it develops alternative future possibilities. David Axson (2011) defined the concept as "a way of understanding the forces at work today, such as demographics, globalization, technological change, and environmental sustainability, which will shape the future" (p. 22). Balfe and Tretheway (2010) observed, "Scenario analysis is not about predicting the future or identifying a 'most likely' scenario. Rather, it is about developing several plausible outcomes, monitoring them, and trying to influence the one(s) that are most desirable" (p. 31).

There is consensus that scenarios must be relevant, challenging, and plausible if they are to be an effective managerial tool. To create an effective tool, you need to take a number of steps. The obvious starting point is to define the question(s) you want to answer; the question(s) should be specific rather than broad in character. With the questions in mind, set a time frame for your future—five, eight, and ten years are most common. The further out you place the end time, the less plausible the scenario. As with any plan, you need to identify the stakeholders that may be affected by outcomes. One of the biggest challenges is to identify those factors (drivers of change) that could or will affect the outcomes. Next you need to assess the factors—are they totally uncertain or somewhat predictable? In addition, you have to prioritize the factors—most to least significant—as well as their possible interactions. One aspect of the power of scenarios is that they tell a story which people can understand and remember, so you must write those stories. Finally, you, and others, must assess the plausibility of each scenario.

O'Connor and Au (2009) wrote about the application of scenarios in an academic library setting. The library generated three scenarios—"Learning Hub," "Meeting Place," and "Wal-Mart." The final "preferred scenario" contained nine elements—everywhere, outreach, social space, digital lives, sustainable, research involvement, avatar librarians, print value, and integral value. The authors' concluded by stating that "the images were being turned into the path of reality. The aim was to achieve this scenario in three years time. . . . [F]ive working groups who were charged with creating the actions and accountabilities . . . focused on Learning and Teaching, Research Enhancement, Collection Re-design, Physical Space, and Communication and Promotion" (p. 63).

A 2010 library-orientated scenario article by Ludwig, Giesecke, and Walton describes the use of the process in terms of health sciences libraries. In this case, the planning was for the Association of Academic Health Sciences Libraries. The authors concluded their article with the following thought:

> Libraries face a real dilemma: how to guide the library through an uncertain, changing environment while agreeing to follow some sort of action plan. Managers have tried numerous techniques including strategic, long-range, and short-range planning, crisis management, reengineering, redesigning, and total quality management. . . . We have no oracle to tell us what kind of world will result from the interplay of forces impacting our libraries, but it is possible to envisage plausible futures. (p. 34)

CHECK THESE OUT

These books provide details and insights into scenario planning in the library setting:

Giesecke, Joan. 1998. *Scenario Planning for Libraries.* Chicago: American Library Association.

O'Connor, Steve, and Peter Sidorko. 2010. *Imagine Your Library's Future: Scenario Planning for Libraries and Information Organizations.* Oxford: Chandos Publishing.

PROJECT MANAGEMENT

Almost every librarian has to address some type of "project" during her or his career. No matter what label you use—assignment, task, or project— successfully handling the activity calls for thoughtful planning.

Although people often use the terms mentioned interchangeably, they mean rather different things. Along with program, these terms form a continuum, with a task at one end representing the smallest activity (such as loading software updates) and a program at the opposite end representing the whole effort. A number of tasks make up a work assignment (maintaining all the online data-bases would be an example). Projects are single-purpose plans (installing a wire-less network in public access areas, for example). A program is a combination of tasks, assignments, and projects (the library's information communication technology program, for example).

Projects have a four-stage life cycle—definition, planning, execution, and closing. Start by defining the "big picture" for the project: setting out specific goals, looking at how the project will impact other activities and programs, outlining the assumptions underlying the project, establishing a target completion date, and developing a cost/resource estimate. Once you have the big picture well-established, you can move on to creating plans to achieve the project goals. During the execution stage, you must monitor progress, and you might need to make some rapid adjustments to stay on schedule. (Bringing in a project on time is wonderful; even better is doing so and being under budget. This happens only with consistent monitoring, thinking ahead, and trying to anticipate possible problems and potential solutions to those problems.) Closing is normally a short stage, with a focus on ensuring that the results are as expected, resolving "bugs," and assessing what did and didn't work in the project.

FROM THE ADVISORY BOARD

Virginia Walter offered the following insight about planning:

I find that librarians—particularly middle managers such as Youth Services Coordinators—get more involved with project management than in the kinds of large-scale organizational planning that is the focus of this chapter. I particularly like the Outcome-Based Planning and Evaluation Model developed by Eliza Dresang, Melissa Gross, and Leslie Holt (*Dynamic Youth Services through Outcome-Based Planning and Evaluation,* American Library Association, 2006). It brings together the planning and evaluation processes in a way that makes sense to practitioners and lends itself particularly well to doing the kind of evaluation required for grant-funded projects.

John M. Bryson's *Strategic Planning for Public and Nonprofit Organizations* (San Francisco: Jossey-Bass, 2004) provides a good planning model for libraries, and Elizabeth Stephan's "Strategic Planning on the Fast Track (*Library Leadership and Management* 24, no. 4: 189–198, 2010) is an example of the Bryson model in a library setting. The latter includes example mission, value, and vision statements.

WHO SHOULD PLAN?

The obvious answer is that we all plan. However, in the workplace, who is and is not involved in organizational planning matters more than you might expect. Certainly every staff member as well as volunteers plan their daily activities. Supervisors and middle managers develop operational plans; if they are wise, they involve their staff in that process.

When it comes to tactical and strategic planning, the "who" becomes increasingly important. In the not too distant past, these types of planning were viewed as a solely senior management prerogative, perhaps with some assistance from an outside consultant. Woolridge, Schmid, and Floyd (2008), in writing about middle managers' perspectives on the strategy process, identified when this began to change: "The recognition in the research literature of middle management's relevance to strategy formulation began in the 1970s. Up to that point, conceptualization of management generally, and strategy in particular, assumed a top-down analytical process that separated decision making from action" (p. 1193). Today there is general agreement that effective long-term planning ought to involve people in some, if not most, of the staffing categories, to some degree, in planning activities.

There is also general agreement that doing so can present some challenges. The more staff involved in the process, the higher the productivity "costs" will be. Good planning takes a substantial amount of time, and that time comes from normal work time. Each person involved will either spend less time performing their job description duties or put in overtime. Then there is the morale factor. Those not involved may resent that they were not among "the chosen few." Others may resent having to pick up at least some of the duties of those who are selected. Mantere and Vaara (2008) summed up the challenges: "Participation is a key issue in strategy research and practice. While there is no consensus on the degree to which organizational members should participate in strategy formulation, most scholars agree that lack of participation easily leads to poorly developed strategies, dissatisfaction among those excluded, and consequential difficulties in implementation" (p. 341). Reading their paper is well worth the time and effort.

Regardless of the challenges, we firmly believe staff participation is essential for successful library planning. Melanie Schosser's (2011) article discusses staff participation and makes the point that "The process aims to create a long-term plan for the organization while fostering a more collaborative, innovative culture" (p. 152).

VALUE OF PLANNING

Almost everyone agrees that planning is important and that good plans are useful. This being said, a growing body of literature raises serious questions about strategic planning. Questions about what characterizes meaningful long-range planning are also being raised.

Kaplan and Norton (2006) started their essay on implementing strategy by saying, "Strategic dreams often turn into nightmares if companies start engaging in extensive and distracting restructuring. It's far more effective to choose a design that works reasonably well, rather than develop a strategic system to tune the structure to the strategy" (p. 100). They also note that, because of changing circumstances, it is rare to achieve all the stated goals and that adding restructuring to the plan creates more obstacles to that achievement.

Markins and Steele (2006) were rather direct in their article:

Is strategic planning completely useless? . . . In the fall of 2005, Markins Associates . . . surveyed senior executives from 156 large companies worldwide. . . . We asked these executives how their companies developed long range plans and how effectively they thought their planning drove strategic decisions. The results [indicated] . . . that timing and structure of strategic planning are obstacles to good decision-making. . . . No wonder only 11% of the executives are highly satisfied that strategic planning is worth the effort (pp. 76, 78, 81)

Much of the negative views regarding strategic planning arose from Henry Mintzberg's article "Crafting Strategy" in the July–August 1987 issue of *Harvard Business Review*. In that article, he took exception to the presumed rationality and detachment of strategic planning. Given his stature as a management thinker, the article had a more profound impact than he probably intended. He did not and does not believe strategic planning is a worthless activity. In 2008, Richard Whittington and Ludovic Cailluet edited a themed issue of *Long Range Planning* (41, no. 3) titled "The Craft of Strategy." The purpose was to "recall Mintzberg's classic study in formal strategy making and the plurality of forms such strategy activity can take in different contexts" (p. 241). The Whittington and Cailluet issue makes it clear that, done properly, strategic planning is worth the effort.

KEY POINTS TO REMEMBER
- Planning aids in achieving goals by measuring progress, coordinating activities, addressing the future, and coping with uncertainty.
- Effective planning requires time and careful thought.
- Planning is forward-looking and entails elements of risk, uncertainty, and doubt.

- Planning takes on three time aspects: long term (strategy), mid term (tactical), and short term (operational).
- There are five major models for long-term strategic planning: basic, issue based, alignment, scenario, and organic.
- Strategic plans build on mission, vision, and value statements.
- A mission statement sets overall organizational purpose (why we exist).
- A vision statement sets forth the long-term direction/goals.
- A value statement sets forth how the library expects to operate (service philosophy).
- Environmental scanning and SWOT analysis are key tools for effective long-term planning.
- Creating SMARTER goals and objectives is important to achieving the desired outcome(s) of any long-term plan.
- Plans come in several varieties: strategies, goals, objectives, policies, procedures, rules, programs, and budgets.
- Effective planning draws on input from all affected and interested parties.
- Successful project management requires careful and detailed planning.
- Staff involvement is a key element in achieving a successful strategic plan.

References

Armstrong, J. Scott. 2004. "Don't Do SWOT: A Note on Marketing Planning." ManyWorlds.com. August 8. http://www.manyworlds.com/logContent.aspx?to=coViewURLLink&coid=CO85041445304.

Axson, David A. J. 2011. "Scenario Planning: Navigating through Today's Uncertain World." *Journal of Accountancy* 211, no. 3: 22–27.

Balfe, Bruce E., and Barton G. Tretheway. 2010. "Scenario Planning Power for Unsettled Times." *Association News* 6, no. 2: 31–35.

David, Fred R. 1989. "How Companies Define Their Mission." *Long Range Planning* 22, no. 1: 90–97.

Everett, Robert F., and Catherine Rich Duval. 2010. "Some Considerations for the Use of Strategic Planning Models." *Northeast Decision Sciences Institute Proceedings* March: 525–530.

Gow, Peter. 2009. "Missions, Mantras, and Meaning." *Independent Schools* 69, no. 1: 24–30.

Hill, Terry, and Roy Westerbrook. 1997. "SWOT Analysis: It's Time for a Product Recall." *Long Range Planning* 30, no. 1: 46–52.

Johnson, Heather. 1994. "Strategic Planning for Modern Libraries." *Library Management* 15, no. 1: 7–18.

Kaplan, Robert S., and David P. Norton. 2006. "How to Implement a New Strategy without Disrupting Your Organization." *Harvard Business Review* 84, no. 3: 100–109.

Levy, Piet. 2011. "Mission vs. Vision." *Marketing News* 45, no. 2: 10.

Line, Maurice. 2004. "Management Musings 15: Looking Ahead: How Far?" *Library Management* 25, nos. 1/2: 62–63.

Ludwig, Logan, Joan Giesecke, and Linda Walton. 2010. "Scenario Planning: A Tool for Health Sciences Libraries." *Health Information and Libraries Journal* 27, no. 1: 28–36.

Mantere, Saku, and Eero Vaara. 2008. "On the Problem of Participation in Strategy: A Critical Discursive Perspective." *Organization Science* 19, no. 2: 341–358.

Markins, Michael, and Richard Steele. 2006. "Stop Making Plans; Start Making Decisions." *Harvard Business Review* 84, no. 1: 76–84.

Miles, Raymond, and Charles C. Snow. 1978. *Organizational Strategy, Structure, and Process.* New York: McGraw-Hill.

Mintzberg, Henry. 1987. "Crafting Strategy." *Harvard Business Review*, July–August: 66–74.

Nanus, Burt. 1992. *Visionary Leadership.* San Francisco: Jossey-Bass.

Nohria, Nitin, and Thomas A. Stewart. 2006. "Risk, Uncertainty, and Doubt." *Harvard Business Review* 84, no. 2: 39–40.

O'Connor, Steve, and Lai-chong Au. 2009. "Steering a Future through Scenarios: Into the Academic Library of the Future." *Journal of Academic Librarianship* 35, no. 1: 57–64.

Price, Lee. 2010. "On the Vital Importance of Strategic Planning." *Public Libraries* 49, no. 2: 25–27.

Rangan, V. Kasturi. 2004. "Lofty Missions, Down-to-Earth Plans." *Harvard Business Review* 82, no. 3: 112–119.

Romeo, Jim. 2011. "The Fine Art of Goal Setting." *Alaska Business Monthly* 27, no. 2: 92–94.

Saurin, Ruth, and John Ratcliffe. 2011. "Using an Adaptive Scenarios Approach to Establish Strategies for Tomorrow's Workplace." *Foresight* 13, no. 4: 46–63.

Schlosser, Melanie. 2011. "OSUL 2013: Fostering Organizational Change through a Grassroots Planning Process." *College and Research Libraries* 72, no. 2: 152–165.

Simons, Robert. 2010. "Stress-Test Your Strategy: The 7 Questions to Ask." *Harvard Business Review* 88, no. 11: 92–100.

Staley, David J., and Kara J. Malenfant. 2010. *Futures Thinking for Academic Librarians: Higher Education in 2025.* Chicago: Association of College and Research Libraries.

Valentin, Erhard K. 2005. "Away with SWOT Analysis: Use Defensive/Offensive Evaluation Instead." *Journal of Applied Business Research* 21, no. 2: 91–104.

Valentinov, Vladislav, and Karin Larsen. 2011. "The Meaning of Non-profit Mission Breadth." *Social Sciences Journal* 48, no. 1: 29–38.

Wayne, Richard. 2011. "The Academic Library Strategic Planning Puzzle: Putting the Pieces Together." *College and Research Libraries News* 72, no. 1: 12–15.

Woolridge, Bill, Torsten Schmid, and Steven W. Floyd. 2008. "The Middle Management Perspective on Strategy Process." *Journal of Management* 34, no. 6: 1190–1221.

Launching Pad

Capron, Laurence, and Will Mitchell. 2010. "Finding the Right Path." *Harvard Business Review* 88, nos. 7/8: 102–107.

Clemens, Russell. 2009. "Environmental Scanning and Scenario Planning." *Systemic Practice and Action Research* 22, no, 4: 249–274.

Eckel, Nathan, and Philip Witmer. 2010. "Strategic Planning Simplifies." *T+D* 64, no. 9: 32–35.

Edmondson, Amy C. 2011. "Strategies for Learning from Failure." *Harvard Business Review* 89, no. 4: 48–55.

Gavetti, Giovanni, and Jan W. Rivkin. 2005. "How Strategists Really Think." *Harvard Business Review* 83, no. 9: 152–153.

Maguire, Stuart, Udechukwu Ojiako, and Ian Robson. 2009. "The Intelligence Alchemy and the Twenty-First Century Organization." *Strategic Change* 18: 125–139.

McClamroach, Jo, Jacqueline Byrd, and Steven Sowell. 2001. "Strategic Planning: Politics, Leadership, and Learning." *Journal of Academic Librarianship* 27, no. 5: 372–378.

Nelson, Sandra. 2001. *The New Planning for Results: A Streamlined Approach.* Chicago: American Library Association.

Niebor, Nico. 2011. "Strategic Planning Process Models: A Step Further." *Property Management* 29, no. 4: 371–382.

Raman, S. Raghu. 2009. "Middle Managers' Involvement in Strategic Planning." *Journal of General Management* 34, no. 3: 57–74.

We all have some power in our work. At an entry level, power may not be obvious, and it may vary widely, depending on the workplace. We tend to be focused on the power of those above us within our organization. As a public library director, some staff would comment about how they had no power, while I had all the power. They failed to see that the power that they did have, they gave away because of their viewpoint.

Some people are afraid of power, probably because of two elements that go with power: responsibility and accountability. If responsibility and accountability come with power, then those who want neither feel that seeing themselves as having no power means that they do not have to be accountable or responsible. They are wrong.

In fact, responsibility and accountability are what makes power attractive. We learn how to improve what we do by making responsible decisions and having ways of being held accountable. These two factors are what allow us to continuously learn, to get better at what we do. As an urban public library director, I encouraged both staff and those from whom we "received" power (boards, elected officials, and ultimately taxpayers) to see accountability and responsibility as the foundation for using power wisely.

—Molly Raphael, ALA President, 2011–2012 (2012)

Power is part of leadership and is necessary to get things done—whether those things entail changing the U.S. health-care system, transforming organizations so they are more humane places, or affecting dimensions of social policy and human welfare.

—Jeffery Pfeffer (2010)

So, perhaps it is time to remember that making work interesting and creating the sort of jobs people want to do is a two-way street and that discretion and trust are key components of this.

—Irena Grugulis (2011)

When people are asked if they and others in their department are held accountable for results, a high percentage of the responses are favorable. However, ask them if other people in other departments are being held accountable and the percentage of favorable responses typically is low.

—Richard Lepsinger (2010)

5

POWER, ACCOUNTABILITY, AND RESPONSIBILITY

This chapter focuses on the following:

- The concepts of power, authority, accountability, and responsibility
- The interrelated nature of the concepts
- How these concepts impact library governance
- The formal and informal organization and authority and responsibility
- The role of "office politics" in power, influence, accountability, and responsibility

SOME YEARS AGO Charles Handy (1993), when making the point that organizations are people, not an entity, noted, "They are communities of people, and therefore behave like other communities. They compete amongst themselves for power and resources; there are differences of opinion and values, and conflicts of priorities and goals" (p. 291). We believe his comments in the last sentence apply to units within an organization as well as to the individuals who make up the organization.

Everyone has heard the phrase "office politics"; many of us have experienced those politics as well. Much of politics, regardless of setting, is about acquiring power, authority, and control of resources. Sometimes overlooked in the process of seeking power and authority is the fact that having gained them you also acquired accountability regarding their use. Our opening quotation from Richard Lepsinger makes the point that people generally believe they are held accountable but others are not. This belief can and does color work relationships. What you want as a manager is both the belief and the fact that everyone in the organization is accountable. Molly Raphael's quote is perfect in that she recognizes that power doesn't stand alone; it comes with responsibility and accountability. She also recognizes that staff do have power in the organization; they just have to recognize it and deal effectively with it.

There are times when accountability seems not to be in play (a recent example is the Deepwater Horizon or BP oil spill, with all the parties pointing the finger of blame at one another). This is never the case for libraries, which are almost always part of a larger organization and, as such, are always accountable to one or more bodies for how they handle their operations. For example, public libraries often have trustee boards; academic libraries have campus faculty governance "library committees." This structure can lead to questions about who has the power, authority, responsibility, and accountability for what.

All managerial activities involve elements of power, authority, accountability, responsibility, and influence. Understanding the differences among the concepts is important to being an effective manager. Having this understanding can make work relationships more efficient and pleasant and much less stressful.

The terms "power," "authority," and "influence" are often used interchangeably; however, they are very different concepts. Power is the ability to do something; authority is the right to do something; and influence (something charismatic leaders employ) is the ability to use words or actions to cause others to change their behavior.

POWER

Defining power has been difficult for management scholars. Dean Tjosvold and Barbara Wisse (2009) commented on the challenges of arriving at an acceptable definition: "power is such a pervasive phenomenon and involves many important issues, including moral ones, that agreeing on a definition of power has proved difficult; imposing a definition is impossible. Indeed, even holding a discussion about it is a challenge. Some researchers seem to assume that defining power is too obvious even to specify; others just give up" (p. 2). Tjosvold and Wisse (2009) go on to list six "assumptions" about power that create the difficulty:

1. Power as the potential to influence another's actions. . . .
2. Power as the potential to overcome resistance. . . .
3. Power as the potential to affect outcomes. . . .
4. Power as the potential to bring about desired change. . . .
5. Power as actual influence. . . .
6. Power as actually overcoming resistance. . . . (p. 3)

While defining power may be a challenge, the managerial importance of power lays in part in the sanctions available to the person holding power. A manager's sanctions include the ability to give, promise, and withdraw (or threaten to withdraw) rewards; inflict (or threaten to inflict) punishment; and fire (or threaten to fire) subordinates. These sanctions are common to all organizations and form the basis of power. From a positive point of view, power involves the right to give such things as praise, rewards, and public recognition. Good managers, who use power to achieve plans and goals, know that the less the negative sanctions come into play the more effective the work environment will be. All library managers are in turn influenced by the power exercised by their supervisors as well as by outside bodies such as governing boards.

A frequently overlooked aspect of power is its subjective nature. Opinions differ (between the office holder and a governing board, for example) as to how much power a position or person should or does have. There is also a reciprocal aspect of power that is unrecognized at times. That is, staff can impose sanctions as well, particularly when they believe abuses of managerial power exist. The weakness of subordinate sanctions is that, to be effective, they require the cooperation of most of the staff. While many libraries are a government unit and are therefore generally forbidden to strike, this sanction does exist. Groups outside the organization can also contribute to staff sanctions. Unions, professional associations, and special interest groups can bring pressure to bear on an institution and its administrators. One type of agency that can employ sanctions in many government-funded organizations is the body that handles the employment process (e.g., the U.S. Civil Service). The existence of independent bodies, therefore, acts as a strong sanction against blatantly prejudicial managerial actions.

To some degree, all sanctions act as psychological whips because they exist, and they impact workplace behaviors of both employees and employers. When it becomes necessary to apply a sanction, it is in a very real sense an admission of failure. No matter who imposed the sanctions, it is a managerial failure to a greater or lesser degree. Either the manager was unable to correct a problem or misused the powers available to her or him.

In 1965, Cartwright reviewed the literature on the nature of managerial power, providing one of the best brief conceptual summaries of the types of managerial power. Cartwright (1965, pp. 28–30) presented five sources of power:

- *Reward power* arises from a subordinate's belief that the supervisor has the ability to grant rewards. (Example: raises or promotions.)
- *Coercive power* arises from a subordinate's belief that the supervisor has the ability to impose punishments. (Example: transfers or demotions.)
- *Referent power* arises from a subordinate's desire to be identified with the supervisor and that person's power.
- *Legitimate power* arises from a subordinate's internalized belief that the supervisor has the right to direct that person's activities.

- *Expert power* arises from the subordinate's belief that the supervisor has special knowledge and skills that make it reasonable that the supervisor directs the person's activities.

Most managerial power is a combination of these categories, usually with one or two of them dominant. When a manager has strong expert and referent power, there is seldom a question in the staff's mind about the manager's right to power. When expert power is weak, there is usually a significant question about legitimate power. How often have you heard (or made) the statement that "X shouldn't have that job—he doesn't know anything about it"? When an individual becomes a senior manager, there is generally a testing period during which staff wait to see how much expert knowledge the person possesses. Should they find the person lacking, a power struggle may result.

George Graen (2009) identified six formal power bases:

- Ownership
- Managership
- Employment contracts
- Standard operating procedures
- Special operating procedures
- Court systems

In addition, he suggested there are seven informal sources of power:

- Social norms and roles
- Psychological employment contracts
- Social and work networks
- Education and training
- Personal charisma
- Family connections
- Religious connections

Graen (2009) further stated, "Considering behavior in organizations, formal bases of power account for perhaps 80–90 percent of observed behavior" (p. 105).

John Kotter (1977, pp. 135–136) identified six characteristics of managers who use power successfully for the good of the organization and its employees:

- Effective managers are sensitive to the source of their power and are careful to keep their actions consistent with people's expectations.
- Good managers understand—at least intuitively—the five bases of power and recognize which to draw on in different situations and with different people.
- Effective managers recognize that all bases of power have merit in certain circumstances.

> **REMEMBER**
>
> Power is latent; political behavior is the action.

- Successful managers have career goals that allow them to develop and use power.
- Effective managers temper power with maturity and self-control.
- Successful managers know that power is necessary to get things done.

David Mechanic (1962) identified several sources of informal power of subordinates. For him, a critical source of a subordinate's informal power is his or her knowledge of, and information about, daily operations and activities. Withholding such information can make supervisors look foolish or cause them to make bad decisions. Two other sources of a subordinate's informal power are the skills of the subordinate and how those skills impact the use of the organization's resources. Power is an important issue in an organization; it is "good" or "bad" depending on whether it is used for the benefit of the organization or against the organization/work unit. The goal should be to "use it, not abuse it" in furthering the organizational mission and goals.

INFLUENCE

The dividing line between "power" and "influence" can be blurry. Influence implies persuasion (Bierstedt, 1950) and can be exercised by using words, actions, or personality. Within a library, people can be influential but not hold a position of power—or they may hold a position of power but have little influence.

Clearly the greater the influence you have, within both the workplace and the wider organization, the more likely it is that the library will benefit. Managers who understand organizational politics can identify those who have influence within the library, the user community, and the profession.

> **CHECK THESE OUT**
>
> One of the classic works on the nature and role of power in organizations is Jeffrey Pfeffer's *Managing with Power: Politics and Influence in Organizations* (Cambridge, MA: Harvard Business School Press, 1992).
>
> A more recent book is *Power and Interdependence in Organizations*, edited by Dean Tjosvold and Barbara Wisse (Cambridge, England: Cambridge University Press, 2009).

Respect is a factor in gaining influence. You gain respect when you are straightforward: for example, knowing when to discuss an issue with a peer prior to raising it at an organizationwide meeting, or issuing an instruction within the library. Over time this ensures that you are seen as open and trustworthy. Developing good listening skills, understanding how to work effectively in committees, and thinking strategically all help you gain influence.

AUTHORITY

Authority is a necessary part of organizational life. Fayol indicated that authority is the right to give orders and to exact obedience. Max Weber, in his *Theory of Social and Economic Organization,* suggested that there are three types of authority: (1) traditional, (2) charismatic, and (3) legal (Weber, 1947). Traditional authority is found in monarchies, and it gains a level of legitimacy through the concept of "divine right." This type of authority is inherited. Charismatic authority is moral authority gained through an individual's special abilities, visions, or sense of destiny. Gandhi, Mohammed, and Castro are examples of charismatic individuals. This type of authority seldom passes on to others. Legal authority is a function of the position held by a person; it resides in the office rather than in a person. Legal authority derives from laws established by legislative bodies to govern the ways in which a society agrees to function.

All organizations, including libraries, must address the distribution of power and authority within the organization. Wrong's (1979) view of authority is widely held—the right to do something being associated with a position within an organization. R. V. Presthus (1962) provides a fuller definition in an excellent article on authority and organizational structure:

> Authority, power, and influence are usually interlaced in operating situations. However, the definitions attempt to focus on the conception of organizing as a system in which interpersonal relations are structured in terms of the prescribed authority of the actors. (p. 123)

In a library environment, a manager's authority consists of rights such as those related to making decisions, assigning work to subordinates, reviewing their work, and recommending their retention or release on the basis of performance.

Authority is made legitimate in part by the process of socialization. One element in the staffing process is integrating a new hire into the organization and

IN THE EXPERT'S WORDS

"Authority exists where one person has a formal right to command and another has a formal obligation to obey" (Wrong, 1979, cited in Drummond, 2001: 123).

work group. Every organization has individuals identified as having a degree of authority, and current employees accept this as being proper. A new employee is likely to accept that arrangement as well. Chester Barnard (1968) labeled this as the acceptance theory of authority.

While socialization is basic to the legitimization process, other factors are equally important for the acceptance of authority. There must be a constant validation process. A position may carry an accepted amount of authority, but the office holder must demonstrate an ability to retain that office and exercise its authority, usually through technical or professional skills and/or knowledge. Presthus (1962) calls this legitimation by expertise. Whenever subordinates begin to doubt a supervisor's ability or knowledge, that person loses authority and may resort to the use of sanctions. In so doing, the supervisor is admitting to a loss of authority by using whatever power is available. While the wielding of power may enforce conformity, that conformity will last for only a limited time.

Formal role and rank is another way to legitimate authority. For instance, if your position in the library is above mine, then you probably have more authority than I do. In libraries, especially in large archives and libraries, authority resides in small amounts in a number of positions, but each level in the structure has some authority. This results in a hierarchical pattern of authority; most bureaucratic organizations depend on this method of legitimating authority. As Presthus points out, however, both expertise and formal role methods of establishing the right to authority lead to conflict at the higher levels, where the office holder cannot be expert in all the fields in which authority has to be exercised.

As libraries suffer economic problems, particularly in the recent past, many libraries have reduced or done away with the typical hierarchical/authority chart and with it the ability to look at an organizational chart and recognize immediately legitimate authority. In assessing your new position in a library, it is important to know both your position in the organization/hierarchical/authority chart and who has legitimate authority above you.

Leadership that depends on personal qualities apart from technical expertise represents another method of legitimating authority. Presthus (1962) labeled this as legitimation by rapport, and it seems to have an element of Weber's ideas about charismatic authority. For many individuals, their real basis of authority lies not in position or professional skill but in an ability to work with people. Some can hold a great deal of authority in an institution solely on the basis of being "a real person with a genuine interest in people." Individuals of this type hold their positions because of the affection and loyalty that subordinates and superiors have for them. They also have to demonstrate an understanding of the area managed, or they will not be able to hold authority for very long.

Authority is an active process, both subjective and reciprocal. It flows in two directions: downward, through an organizational structure of positions, and upward, from staff to individuals holding superior positions. The bases for validating authority are traditional acceptance of authority, expertise, position, rank, and personal characteristics.

SOMETHING TO PONDER

Reflect on the concepts of "authority," "power," and "influence." Focus on a service in your library interest area, select a type of library, and identify the ways in which each of the concepts impacts on the service.

ACCOUNTABILITY

Accountability, authority, and power are interrelated yet different. The process of accountability includes three basic factors: legal, legislative, and administrative. Two of these (legal and legislative) are, for the most part, extrainstitutional. Administrative accountability is basically internal in nature, although it can be external.

Legal accountability relates to laws about actions both taken and not taken. Most frequently, the failures involve national laws or orders concerning such matters as equal employment, affirmative action requirements, and access to services (we provided some examples of legal accountability in Chapter 3).

Lawmaking bodies enforce legislative accountability in two main ways: through the courts and through hearings. Hearings are the most common approach. Investigative hearings, budgetary hearings, and new legislation hearings are some of the types you will frequently encounter. Lawmaking bodies also have the ability to reduce or increase an agency's authority and appropriations. Libraries in the public sector are especially vulnerable to such control.

Legislative control operates within limits. No legislative body has the time to oversee all operational details of all agencies accountable to it. Because details are left to the agencies, interpretations vary of what a legislative order means and what can be done. Usually, the legislative body's primary interest arises only during budget hearings, or when an agency makes a request, or when it receives a number of complaints about the agency.

Although legislative bodies require accountability, a library director usually discovers that there is a wide range of activities not determined by legislative mandates. For example, rarely does the legislative body look at who is hired for a vacant position (it may impose a time frame for when a position may be filled), what items should added to a collection (it may get involved when there is a "challenge" about a collection item), and what vendors the library may use (it may have some rules about how the contract selection takes place). These examples illustrate the sometimes complex processes of being accountable and having the authority to act.

Administrative accountability is common to all libraries. For government-associated libraries, the matter is somewhat more complex than it is for private institutions. Political factors enter the picture. Frequently there are doubts as to where real accountability lies, especially when legislative and administrative units clash over an issue in which political gain seems to be the dominant factor.

GOVERNANCE

Administrative accountability is a significant factor in library governance. There are few libraries, with the exception of those in the for-profit sector, that do not have some type of board or committee that has some oversight of their activities. For example, most academic libraries have some type of "library committee" composed of a mix of campus stakeholders. Public libraries generally have a board of trustees, and school libraries have school boards that take an interest in their operations. Boards almost always have legally based oversight responsibilities. Although most academic "library committees" are advisory in character and appointed or elected, there are times when the question arises of just how "advisory" advisory is.

Charlotte Gellert (2011) identified the key point about oversight bodies when she quoted from the *Georgia State Library Handbook* section regarding trustees: "Trustees represent citizen control and governance of the library as specified by state law. The library director represents the administration and management of the library" (p. 14). Words such as "control," "governance," administration," and "management" can be, and at times are, viewed differently depending on your perspective.

Achieving the proper balance between the board and the library director regarding these terms is a delicate matter, calling for skill and goodwill on everyone's part. Nanci Milone Hill (2008) highlighted the balancing issue when she opened her article regarding boards and library directors with, "The relationship between library boards and library directors is a fragile one, yet it need not be. Education and understanding of each other's unique roles and responsibilities can help smooth the path to a more fruitful relationship" (p. 26).

David C. Miller (2011), a long-time library trustee and on ALA's National Advocacy Honor Roll, wrote a short article about some of the "unique roles" mentioned in the Hill (2008) essay. He said, "To avoid micromanaging, library

AUTHORS' EXPERIENCE

Evans had only positive experiences with his oversight groups. They were instrumental in securing important library objectives. One such experience was at a university where libraries had an outside group known as "overseers." Evans's overseers were key to gaining approval for the library to switch to the Library of Congress Classification (to be an effective member of cooperative projects) from the local classification system that had a 150-year history. The objections to the switch were worldwide, not just on the campus. The overseers spent a substantial amount of time and effort in looking at the pros and cons of such a move before supporting the library's position that the switch was essential to the library's future.

CHECK THESE OUT

Howell, Donna W. 2004. "The Politics of Public Library Boards." *Rural Libraries* 24, no. 1: 15–24.

Moore, Mary Y. 2010. *The Successful Library Trustee Handbook*. 2nd ed. Chicago: American Library Association.

Reed, Sally Gardner, and Jillian Kalonick. 2010. *The Complete Library Trustee Handbook*. New York: Neal-Schuman.

Trustee Trouble. 2012. Video. Cheyenne: Wyoming State Library. Accessed October 18. http://www.wyominglibraries.org/trusteetrouble.html.

boards of trustees need to remain focused on the big picture and let the staff deal with details that make up the big picture" (p. 18). Table 5.1 presents some examples of the big picture and the details that Miller made reference to in his article.

Given the delicate balance among, and at times the differing views regarding the definitions of, concepts such as accountability, authority, control, management/administration, and power, it is not surprising that there are occasional head-to-head battles between trustees/committees and directors. Mary Wilkins Jordan (2008) wrote, "I'm sure the members of my board were actually human and not demons from hell, but at the time I was not so positive" (p. 270).

There are times when the differences of opinion lead to a director resigning or to the board dismissing the director. You will occasionally see a "news note" about such events in the professional journals. One such instance that gained national attention (*American Libraries*, 2007) was when the Boston Public Library Trustees voted not to renew the director's employment contract. Some people outside Boston viewed the decision to be a political firing (Robinson, 2007).

Certainly conflicts, some very serious, do arise; however, they are very much the exception. The vast majority of relationships between directors and boards/committees are highly positive. Such bodies can be among the most effective advocates for the library. The starting point for developing effective relationships is for everyone to review and understand any existing laws, regulations, and polices that relate to the functions and responsibilities of the parties. Keeping everyone informed is another key to having positive relationships. Having a few early sessions devoted to developing clear understandings regarding who is accountable for what is also beneficial.

RESPONSIBILITY

Although some people use the terms "accountability" and "responsibility" interchangeably, there is a significant difference between them. Responsibility is what you ought to do, whereas accountability is being answerable for an action. Thus,

TABLE 5.1   Division of Roles and Responsibilities

Trustee Areas	Staff Areas
When to seek additional funds for the library	When to pay invoices for services received
How to allocate funds to services, such as collection development	What items to buy for the collections
When to seek a new physical facility	How to lay out service points within the library
When to set official policies	When to draft proposed policies
What the average salary percentage increases are	Which employees get salary increases and how much they get within the set percentages
Whom to hire as a director	Whom to hire for other library positions

Source: Based on Miller, 2011.

accountability is important in the process of enforcing responsibility. As Simon Robinson (2009) noted, "Actions can be attributed to a person. Hence, the person can be seen to have been responsible for those actions and the decision that led to them" (p. 11).

As a manager you are always accountable for your actions as well as the actions of those you supervise. While you can make someone accountable, you retain responsibility. Responsibility is always shared. You must take responsibility for your supervisee's failures; your job is to monitor and assist in supporting the person's performance.

When you accept a task, you also accept responsibility, more often than not, without giving much thought to that fact. Someone unwilling to accept responsibility usually refuses the task. Everyone has worked at some time with an individual who did not accept responsibility for her or his work and performed just well enough to keep from being fired. No amount of talking or delegating responsibility

TRY THIS

Write down the differences between "accountability" and "responsibility," and give two examples of this in relation to a place where you have worked.

ADVISORY BOARD EXPERIENCE

Joseph Mika was informed early in his career, while serving in the U.S. Army Reserve, regarding the difference between responsibility and accountability. As a young unit commander, he made members of the unit responsible for specific tasks. Their failure was noted by his superior, who informed Mika that he could make individual soldiers responsible but that he never relinquished his accountability or responsibility. Similarly a library director may provide a librarian with the responsibility for collection development, but the director never surrenders responsibility for library purchases or for the collection development budget.

will change such a person's attitude. Acceptance must come from within. Responsibility is a person's obligation to himself or herself to perform given tasks.

STATUS

Status, power, and authority are linked. Changes in authority or responsibility usually bring about changes in status. When you are thinking about changing some workplace activities, devote some time to thinking about the potential impact of the change(s) on the involved staff members' status. What you may think of as a very minor change, your staff may view as significant. Knowing if the change will have a positive or a negative impact on someone's status requires your having had long-term work relationships with the staff. Thus, think things through carefully when you are the new person and are tempted to be the "new broom" that will quickly set something right in the unit.

The status that staff members assign to an individual is not entirely the result of formal authority and rank. Some individuals dislike taking orders from anyone they consider equal to themselves unless they believe the individual has earned the right to do so through demonstrated work performance. For example, a person may take orders from a peer in areas where that peer has more experience or skill.

The use of titles and other status symbols can be helpful but also dangerous. You should not use titles or status symbols as a substitute for real rewards for

TRY THIS

Check out the titles given to staff members in a library you know. Are they made known to users, and, if so, are they meaningful?

work performance. When using titles, be sure to use them for clearly defined activities and abilities. Many libraries do not make a clear distinction among the abilities, skills, and training required for top-grade support staff and beginning librarians. (We explore the importance of proper job descriptions in Chapter 15.) Some job descriptions are so confusing that you cannot readily determine whether the position requires, for example, the abilities of a paraprofessional or a professional. Confusion as to role, status, and authority often results in poor work performance, communication, and morale. There should be clear-cut distinctions among titles, and the titles should be applied consistently throughout the library.

THE VISIBLE AND INVISIBLE ORGANIZATION

All organizations have both a visible (formal) and an invisible (informal) structure. Most organizations have an organization chart, which is a way of describing the official governance structure—the visible structure. Usually it reflects a hierarchical structure to some degree. Each level on the chart reflects an increase in power, authority, and accountability from bottom to top. It also reflects the official lines of communication.

There is also the invisible organization. Often it is this informal side that reflects the actual flow of communication and the drivers of work performance. Organizational cultures, office politics, and personal influences are some of the factors that create and maintain the informal organization. Who has influence— referent power—within the organization? Who influences the decisions, and how is this achieved?

We will explore influence and informal leadership further in Chapter 13. Both are important in the way an organization actually operates. They are also central to organizational politics. Some people refer to organizational politics as "the game of office politics." If you took a poll of employees' attitudes about office politics, the results would likely be similar to the statements Paul Glen (2010) heard:

AUTHORS' EXPERIENCE

Alire, when assuming a new academic library deanship, spent the first several months determining the formal and informal leaders in the new organization. Finding the formal leaders was easy enough to do by reviewing the formal library structure—who had chairperson positions on key library committees, within the library faculty governance, on staff councils, and so forth. However, observing those chairs in terms of effectiveness in handling power and influence was critical. Determining the informal leaders required listening to and observing all that went on in the library. Her recognizing and working with the informal leaders was as important as with the formal ones.

- "I'd love my job if weren't for the politics."
- "This would be a great place to work if not for the politics."
- "Politics aren't my job. Why do I spend so much time on them?"

Most of us have said or thought similar things, yet we have engaged in the process. Often we don't even think of what we are doing as "political." Glen (2010) continued:

> Politics will never be expunged from professional life, and that is mainly because they play a very positive role. . . . Political astuteness is one of the most important tools you have for creating an environment in which people can develop and maintain great technology. . . . As managers move up the ladder, overseeing the actual provision becomes a smaller and smaller portion of the job, and politics become a bigger and bigger one. (p. 34)

Although his focus was on ICT professionals, his point applies to almost any type of organizational setting.

Politics enters into organizational life for a number of reasons. Even in the best of times, there are never enough resources. Disagreements can spring up between departments or teams down even to the level of individual staff members; and often the question of self-interest arises. Managers have a responsibility to try to get their unit its "rightful share" of scarce resources. Managers work to gain influence and control of major decisions and do this by building alliances and coalitions with other managers. This is one situation where networking, building good working relationships, and being visible within the organization and the user community all play an important role in effectively dealing with organizational politics.

It goes almost without saying, power and politics are interrelated. Jeffery Pfeffer (2009), in discussing why power makes people uncomfortable, suggested:

> There are a number of possible reasons for this ambivalence and the conflicted feelings people have about power and politics in organizations, although few of these explanations have been empirically explored. . . . Politics may be important for organizational success, but because people are often unskilled and unschooled in building and exercising influence, this discrepancy between their need to do something and their perceived

FROM THE AUTHORS

Alire, a strong proponent of Pfeffer, developed a working principle known as Alire's P2 Principle, which maintains that politics and power (and influence) are factors essential for transformational, managerial leaders.

CHECK THIS OUT

A useful guide to developing political skills is Peter Block's *The Empowered Manager: Positive Political Skills at Work* (San Francisco: Jossey-Bass, 1987).

ability to navigate organizational politics effectively could be a source of discomfort. (pp. 18–19)

Managers develop public relations skills in order to be better advocates and lobbyists for their services. In our experience, the smaller the library, the more important it is for the manager to be a skilled advocate and lobbyist. Senior managers have to devote time to having the library recognized as being essential and adding value to the parent organization as well as to its service community. A high profile and a positive image help to overcome many barriers.

In 2006, Catherine Green and Lillian Chaney identified the following as the "most important areas relating to office politics" (p. 3):

- Self-promotion
- Honesty and truth telling
- Flattery
- Gossip
- Favors
- Hidden motives
- Attire
- Grooming
- Etiquette
- Business socializing

Green and Chaney (2006) make the point that "office politics involves understanding how to get things accomplished. To get things done, it is necessary to build relationships with people with whom you work. The reality is that careers are built or destroyed based on relationships" (p. 3). They go on to discuss each of the areas they listed as important.

A contrary view of organizational politics was put forward by Marilyn Moats Kennedy (2008). Her view is that office politics are dead: "Today's 20- and 30-year-olds distain careers in large companies as 'so last century.' They have eviscerated organizational politics with one highly effective technique; nonparticipation. They don't share Boomer values, goals, or loyalties—so they won't play Boomer politics" (p. 18). Time will tell if her assessment is accurate. Perhaps the deep recession that followed the appearance of the article has changed some of the attitudes regarding work, values, and goals of the 20- and 30-year-olds.

CHECK THIS OUT

Danny Ertel (2004) in "Getting Past Yes: Negotiating as if Implementation Mattered" (*Harvard Business Review* 82, no. 11: 60–68) noted that effective negotiation requires:

- A carefully thought-through strategy
- The ability to sort out what is important from the less important
- Carefully considered tactics
- Flexibility, developed by weighing up the costs
- A clear decision on your approach
- Understanding your own strengths
- Knowing the weaknesses of the other party(ies)
- A face-to-face meeting, if possible
- Assertiveness but not aggressiveness
- Not expecting to win every time, because losing can bring benefits long term

Sometimes long-standing elements of the workplace, such as office politics, have surprising staying power. There is a chance that, like Mark Twain's comments about his death, the death knell of office politics was premature.

Negotiation plays a role in organizational politics. Information professionals develop good communication skills, including the art of listening—an important factor in negotiation.

Coalitions and alliances also play a role in organizational politics. Smaller departments can share their common interests in forming alliances when resources are allocated. Coalitions become important in sharing access to resources among units. One example is the way that libraries set up consortia to purchase electronic resources or ILS systems. In such situations, it is important that there is a high degree of trust and respect among the parties involved.

Our experience in organizational politics indicates the following:

- Everyone needs time to develop political skills.
- Managers who are skilled at politics understand the organizational culture and climate and the tacit aspects of power and influence.
- Networking and visibility matter.
- It is essential to take care with what you say and to whom—the grapevine is powerful.
- Managers should know who owes the service favors and call them in when necessary.

FROM THE AUTHORS

There is another type of workplace politics. That is the politics of elections and political beliefs. Every adult, in the United States, has some level of political values and beliefs as well as beliefs on a wide range of social issues. For many, these values and beliefs are low key and are in the background of their everyday activities. Others are very motivated by their values and from time to time try to convince others to accept their views. Another fact of U.S. life is that everyone has the right to free speech. From a management perspective, how much, if any, of this kind of political activity is appropriate in the workplace?

In terms of libraries that are part of government, it is forbidden to engage in political and social advocacy while on duty. The ban includes such passive things as wearing campaign pins or having a campaign sign on your desk.

Evans worked in a public academic library where all staff punched in and out of work. During a heated campaign, one staff member began arriving early and staying late and went about both public and nonpublic areas wearing a campaign pin and trying to engage people in conversations about the campaign. When confronted about this behavior the person claimed it was before and after she "was on duty" and therefore allowable. The behavior ceased a week before the election. The staff never learned what led to the change.

The issue of advocacy and appropriate staff behavior goes beyond political activity, although at times it is difficult to sort out what is political and what is social. Does wearing a cross, a Star of David, or a head scarf, at least in publicly supported libraries, constitute a violation of the separation of church and state? What about wearing a pin advocating a position on some social or religious issue? Unfortunately, we can provide no definitive answers, as state and local laws/regulations are too variable.

One article (Fox, Adrienne. 2008. "Politics in the Office." *HR Magazine* 53, no. 10: 38–42) provides some insight into the variables in terms of political campaigns.

- A willingness to compromise on small matters can increase influence and power.
- Behaving in an ethical manner is vital.
- It is beneficial to underpromise and overdeliver.
- The interests of users are paramount—without users the service would not exist.

Learning about organizational politics takes a little time. Again, it is important to remember that no two organizations play the game in exactly the same way.

KEY POINTS TO REMEMBER

- Power is not as powerful as many people think. There are very real limits in terms of workplace power.
- Authority is not identical to power, although the concepts are interrelated.
- You are always accountable and responsible for your use of power and authority.
- Senior management does not hold all the power or even all the authority.
- Staff have the power and ability to withhold recognition of the skills of the manager as well as withhold knowledge from the manager, which effectively reduce the manager's power and authority.
- Staff have the power to control the level and quality of their work, which places a control on the manager's actions.
- Managers should recognize that these concepts are reciprocal and act in a positive manner so that the work environment has a strong element of mutual respect and, perhaps, understanding.
- Libraries almost always have some type of oversight group in addition to the parent organization—trustees or a committee.
- Senior managers must devote considerable time and effort to developing and maintaining solid working relationships with oversight groups.
- Organizations are structured in different ways, and there is a visible and an invisible structure.
- All organizations are political, but political skills have to be learned before they are used.

References

American Libraries. 2007. "Boston Board Ousts Director Margolis." *American Libraries* 38, no. 11: 21–22.

Barnard, Chester I. 1968. *The Functions of the Executive*. 30th anniversary ed. Cambridge, MA: Harvard University Press.

Bierstedt, R. 1950. "An Analysis of Social Power." *American Sociological Review* 15, no. 6: 730–738.

Cartwright, Dorwin. 1965. "Influence, Leadership and Control." In *The Handbook of Organizations*, edited by James G. March. Chicago: Rand McNally.

Drummond, Helga. 2001. *Introduction to Organizational Behavior*. New York: Oxford University Press.

Gellert, Charlotte. 2011. "The Roles of Library Trustees, Directors and Friends." *Georgia Library Quarterly* 48, no. 4: 14.

Glen, Paul. 2010. "Think Politics Aren't Part of Your Job? Think Again." *Computer World* 44, no. 10: 34.

Graen, George E. 2009. "Growing Powerful Using Cherry-Picking." In *Power and Interdependence in Organizations,* edited by Dean Tjosvold and Barbara Wisse. Cambridge, England: Cambridge University Press.

Green, Catherine G., and Lillian H. Chaney. 2006. "The Game of Office Politics." *Supervision* 568, no. 8: 3–6.

Grugulis, Irena. 2011. "Show Staff Trust and They Will Respond." *Employee Benefits* March, Supplement: 21.

Handy, Charles B. 1993. *Understanding Organizations.* 4th rev. ed. New York: Oxford University Press.

Hill, Nanci Milone. 2008. "Whose Job Is It? The Relationship between Trustees and Directors. *Public Libraries* 47, no. 5: 26–27.

Jordan, Mary Wilkins. 2008. "Buyer Beware." *Public Libraries* 47, no. 3: 27–28.

Kanter, Rosabeth Moss. 1983. *The Change Masters: Innovations for Productivity in the American Corporation.* New York: Simon and Schuster.

Kennedy, Marilyn Moats. 2008. "The Death of Office Politics." *Conference Board* 45, no. 5: 18–23.

Kotter, John P. 1977. "Power, Dependence and Effective Management." *Harvard Business Review* 55, no. 4: 135–136.

Lepsinger, Richard. 2010. "Building Accountability and Commitment." *Industrial Management* 52, no. 6: 21–25.

Mechanic, David. 1962. "Sources of Power of Lower Participants in Complex Organizations." *Administrative Science Quarterly* 7 no. 12: 349–364.

Miller, David C.. 2011. "Avoid Micromanaging." *Library Administrator's Digest* 46, no. 3: 18.

Pfeffer, Jeffery. 2009. "Understanding Power in Organizations." In *Power and Interdependence in Organization,* edited by Dean Tjosvold and Barbara Wisse. Cambridge, England: Cambridge University Press.

———. 2010. *Power: Why Some People Have It and Others Don't.* New York: HarperCollins.

Presthus, R. V. 1962. "Authority in Organizations." In *Concepts and Issues in Administrative Behavior,* edited by S. Mailick and E. H. VanNess. Englewood Cliffs, NJ: Prentice-Hall.

Raphael, Molly. 2012. E-mail communication sent to Camila A. Alire, February 29.

Robinson, Charles W. 2007. "Politics in Boston." *Library Administrator's Digest* 42, no. 10: 77–78.

Robinson, Simon. 2009. "The Nature of Responsibility in a Professional Setting." *Journal of Business Ethics* 88, no. 1: 11–19.

Tjosvold, Dean, and Barbara Wisse. 2009. *Power and Interdependence in Organizations.* Cambridge, England: Cambridge University Press.

Weber, Max. 1947. *Theory of Social and Economic Organization.* Translated by A. M. Henderson and T. Parsons; edited by T. Parsons. New York: Free Press.

Wrong, Dennis Hume. 1979. *Power: Its Forms, Bases, and Uses.* Oxford: Basil Blackwell.

Launching Pad

Atinc, Guclu, Mahmoud Darrat, Bryan Fuller, and Barry W. Parker. 2010. "Perceptions of Organizational Politics: A Meta-Analysis of Theoretical Antecedents." *Journal of Managerial Issues* 22, no. 4: 494–513.

Chamberlain, Jane. 2009. "Trustees and Administers: These Are the Days for Advocacy." *Illinois Library Association Reporter* 27, no. 3:6–9.

Connor, Jim. 2010. "Public Library Trustee . . . What's That?" *Georgia Library Quarterly* 47, no. 3: 16.

Essex, Louellen, and Mitchell Kusy. 2008. "Playing the 'Office Politics' Game." *T+D* 62, no. 3: 776–779.

Ferris, Gerald R., James H. Dulebohn, Dwight D. Frink, Jane George-Falvy, Terence R. Mitchell, and Linda M. Matthews. 2009. "Job and Organizational Characteristics, Accountability, and Employee Influence." *Journal of Managerial Issues* 21, no. 4: 518–532.

Harris, Kenneth J., Martha C. Andrews, and K. Michele Kacmar. 2007. "The Moderating Effects of Justice on the Relationship between Organizational Politics and Workplace Attitudes." *Journal of Business Psychology* 22, no. 2: 135–144.

Henington, David M. 1994. "Public Library Directors: Hierarchical Roles and Proximity to Power." *Library Trends* 43, no. 1: 95–104.

HR Focus. 2007. "HR Must Handle Productivity Challenges from Office Politics." *HR Focus* 84, no. 5: 8–9.

Miller, E. 2001. "Getting the Most from Your Boards and Advisory Councils." *Library Administration and Management* 15, no. 4: 204–212.

Price, Lee. 2008. "Letter to a Newly Appointed Library Trustee." *Public Libraries* 47, no. 4: 27–29.

Royle, M. Todd, and Gavin Fox. 2011. "The Relationship between Psychological Strain, Self-Regulation, and Informal Accountability for Others." *International Journal of Management and Marketing Research* 4, no. 1: 1–18.

Snyder, Herbert. 2005. "Management Basics: Life as a Library Board Member." *Indiana Libraries* 24, no. 1: 52–53.

Thorsby, Mark O. 2011. "10 Things I Wish I'd Known about Governance." *Associations Now* (Volunteer Leadership issue) 7, no. 1: 46.

Zelenka, H. Dayle. 2008. "A Trustee for the Twenty-First Century." *Illinois Library Association Reporter* 26, no. 4: 3–6.

In a recent group coaching session, we were talking about the challenge of delegating actions and decisions to your team while keeping yourself informed of things that could put your organization or career at risk.

—Scott Eblin (2010)

Grasp the capabilities of each staff member. Who are those most capable of taking on responsibility for certain tasks and decisions?

—John Beeson (2010)

The benefit of involving the entire team in real-world issues also creates a sense of togetherness and stimulates continuous improvements and ongoing achievements. Involve your team in planning library services, creating a mission statement, and even developing a budget. Involve the entire staff in devising solutions to real library issues and improving library procedures.

—Carol Sheffer (2009)

As we think about the future, we have affirmed the overall strategic direction laid out in our strategic plan and added two more: (1) build and operate a responsible organization, and (2) develop a research agenda for the library. A major impetus for this has been the library's response to academic and administrative restructuring since we straddle both sides within the UCLA community.

—Gary E. Strong (2010)

6

DELEGATING

This chapter focuses on the following:

- How delegation and delegating assist in achieving organizational strategic plans and goals
- The value of delegation in assisting in directing the staff's energy most effectively to achieve appropriate performance levels and in reducing role ambiguity
- Traditional issues in delegating
- Team formation and the issues in delegating responsibilities
- How a "learning" environment assists in keeping the library vital and viable as well as providing growth and development opportunities to staff

DELEGATION IS THE process of creating an order or structure for handling the activities and tasks that the library wishes to accomplish. Two of our opening quotations mention planning. Delegation and planning are tightly linked. Perhaps in the distant past a manager might have been able to create an operational structure and never think about it again. Any manager today doing that will have a failure on her or his hands. Libraries must be flexible in their planning process to remain viable. Being flexible means adjusting what is done, how it is done, and where it is done. Thus, it becomes imperative to rethink and restructure the organization fairly often.

Today's environment is less stable and more complex than in the past. For libraries, some of the environmental factors creating pressure for more flexibility include the following:

- User demand is less and less predictable.
- Technology is constantly and rapidly changing.
- Competition for scarce resources is growing.
- Economic cycles are less and less predictable.
- Workforce expectations, especially those of younger workers, are changing quickly.
- Workforce lifestyle expectations are changing.

Bob Schoofs (2007) made a similar point about academic libraries: "On the one hand, technology is rapidly changing how we go about our work. On the other hand, competition among institutions of higher learning is such that only those who provide the best educational experience for their students will thrive. Faced with these challenges, college and university libraries have implemented a variety of reorganizational strategies" (p. 13). Judy Hunter (2002) rather concisely stated today's organizational needs:

The factors that most affect the design of an organization can be categorized into two segments. The first segment consists of contextual elements that include strategy, environment, business size/life cycle, and culture. The second segment consists of structural elements that include reporting relationships, decision-making processes, communication processes, coordination of work, forms of complexity, and distinguishing characteristics. The responsibility of managers is to design organizations that fit these elements. (p. 13)

The Economist (2006) also made the case that organizational structure must change. The editors suggested that restructuring is especially necessary for "knowledge workers." They acknowledged that professional firms (knowledge workers) have existed for years—accounting, legal, libraries, medical, and so forth—and have successfully employed some form of sharing to structure their activities. However, they suggest that this does not work in large firms and especially not in the nonprofit sector.

Traditional organizational structure came into being during an age when manufacturing/production was the major economic powerhouse and the vast majority of people were engaged in some form of physical labor. *The Economist* (2006) noted:

"Alas," writes Mr. Davenport, "there is no Fredrick Taylor equivalent for knowledge work. As a result we lack measures, methods, and rules of thumb for improvement. Exactly how to improve knowledge work productivity . . . is one of the most important economic issues of our time." (p. 10)

One approach for a new structure is what the editors called "disaggregated." A disaggregated organization is one in which responsibility (and its necessary authority) is pushed down to frontline staff, and more group processes and many more leadership roles are at lower levels. Essentially they were suggesting team formation. Interestingly, this is the type of restructuring that libraries have been undertaking for a number of years.

The 2005 article by Higa and colleagues describing the redesign of the University of Texas Southwestern Medical Center's library provides insight into the factors you need to consider when rethinking organizational structure: "The

ADVISORY BOARD EXPERIENCE

Carol Sinwell provided the following thoughts about delegation:

I also use delegation to grow potential new managers/leaders—to offer professional development for staff members. The big challenge, for me, is to "let it go" and not micromanage. Sometimes projects don't come out the way I had hoped when I step back, but I have to ask myself, Is the outcome what is needed even if it wasn't done exactly the way I might have done it?

A bigger issue is how to handle a situation when you have delegated and the project didn't work out at all.

Another challenge is when you delegate to a team and the team doesn't work well together or one person doesn't do his or her part.

project's goals were as follows: Have the right people in the right number of jobs (allocated to the right tasks) to best support our current environment and the Library's stated vision for the future" (p. 42). In it the authors identified three major factors/challenges that lead to the undertaking:

- A growing gap between the staffing needs for the new digital environment and adequate allocation of staff
- A problematic team approach that challenged traditional workloads
- The absence of a clear vision to unify staff efforts (p. 44)

The before and after organizational charts at the end of their article illustrate some of the ways you might go about restructuring a library. Also, their second factor highlights that just following the current trends in structuring does not automatically lead to success.

Effective delegation should ensure that the library's tasks and activities are structured to reflect its strategic plan and its goals. Delegating has several broad purposes—effective and efficient achievement of organizational goals and personal goals. The personal goals relate to avoiding micromanagement and accomplishing more by not trying to do everything yourself. There is another benefit of good delegation—reduction in staff stress; it clarifies who is expected to do what (reduces "role ambiguity"). Role ambiguity can occur when staff members face situations in which the role requirements are unclear, for example, whom they report to or what is expected of them. Role conflict emerges if there are conflicting role requirements.

TRUST AND DELEGATION

Trust and delegation go together; without trust, delegation will not be effective. Trust needs to be present between managers and their bosses and between managers and their staff. It is an essential part of teamwork, and it is vital to knowledge management, where every person needs to share information fully. Hurley (2006) developed a model to predict whether a person will choose to trust someone. He identifies ten factors that come into play during the decision-making process:

Decision-maker factors:

- The degree of risk tolerance of the truster
- The level of adjustment of the truster
- The amount of relative power held by the truster

Situational factors:

- The degree of security felt by the parties
- The number of similarities they have in common
- How well their interests are aligned
- The trustee demonstrates benevolent concern for the team
- The trustee is competent
- The trustee has demonstrated predictability and integrity
- The parties have good communication

Building trust is a precursor to delegating responsibilities.

Delegating responsibilities is one of the challenges you will face as a new manager. Learning how to delegate effectively comes with work experience. No two organizations operate identically, and it takes time for you to judge senior management's views on delegation. However, you will quickly understand that you can't do everything—there are not enough hours in the day, nor do you necessarily have all of the skills and experience held by the other staff.

AUTHORS' EXPERIENCE

Alire, as a new academic library director at a very small college at the age of 24, used to believe the old adage: "If you want the job done well, do it yourself." Only when she moved into much larger academic library environments as the dean did she realize how important delegating and teambuilding/teamwork were. This change in beliefs led to her developing a strong leadership philosophy combining transformational and emotional intelligence leadership skills.

TIP

When you confront the need to think about delegating something, ask yourself three questions to sort out important issues and concerns about when and when not to delegate:

1. Because of my special knowledge or skill, do I need to be involved in this?
   - Does this really fall within my sole responsibility, and/or will it affect the entire unit or its budget?
   - Is there a deadline, and would it negatively impact unit performance if I don't do this myself?
2. Is there someone on staff better equipped and/or with better knowledge for this particular task?
3. Is this something I could do but others could do if given the chance?

When the answer is "no" to one or more of the questions, delegation is probably not a good option. Things like paperwork and other "routine" activities are always prime candidates for delegation. Clearly anything confidential and/or personnel related should not be delegated. Often special projects and technical matters are most effectively handled on a shared basis.

Associations Now (2010), a journal for nonprofit organizations, asked four CEOs what they considered to be the most difficult part of delegating. The issues the CEOs identified were:

- Accurately communicating what the delegated task is and the expected outcome
- Letting go of authority while retaining responsibility
- Delegating but not remaining a constant presence—micromanaging
- Deciding what can be delegated

To their list we would add, having trust in others to carry out the task(s). There are some guidelines to help make delegating less difficult:

- Plan ahead and consider which tasks, responsibilities, or decisions can, and should, be delegated.
- Think about staff members—their strengths and weaknesses—and delegate to the person best suited; don't play favorites.
- Delegate complete tasks so that the outcomes can be built into the appraisal process; this is part of building the learning organization.

- Building outcomes into the appraisal process is one incentive that can motivate the person to whom the work is delegated. Other incentives may be identified, such as training.
- Give clear instructions—verbally and perhaps backed up by an e-mail—so that clear parameters are set for the individual. An ambitious person may end up treading on colleagues' toes as a result of misplaced enthusiasm.
- Follow up on your instructions to ensure that there are no misunderstandings and that the work is in hand.
- Extend the person's skills. Then let go. Don't micromanage—you have other tasks to do. Encourage staff members, and wait for feedback.
- As parameters change within the organization or the task(s), be sure to communicate those to the staff. Throughout, communicate, communicate, and communicate.
- Assess outcomes in a discussion with the person to whom the work was delegated—with their supervisor, if appropriate.
- Be sure to compliment staff on the success of the task(s), or, if not successful, provide information in a supportive manner on how the task(s) could have been done successfully.

CREATING A STRUCTURE OR RESTRUCTURING

Whether you are starting from scratch or thinking about restructuring, you have at least four broad areas to think about before you begin to consider your actual options. First, you need to understand the priorities of your unit's goals. Certainly all of them need to be accomplished; however, some are more important than others. Generally the more important a goal is, the more resources are assigned to it.

Second, you need to assess your "talent pool." What skills, background, and so forth does each staff member have for carrying out the required activities? When you are a newcomer to the unit you will need time to assess who has what skill, ability, and interest in the existing activities—another reason for restraining any desire to be the "new broom sweeping clean." If you have a person with both the skills and an interest in an activity, give that person the task. More often than not, you will find a mix of skills, abilities, and interests that are less than ideal for the required activities. Your goal is to try to get the best fit(s) and start thinking about what types of support and training might be possible to make the fit better.

Third is to asses what resources you have for restructuring. Two key resources are equipment/furniture and any support materials or staff training that may be needed. Equipment and furniture almost always exist in the unit; however, restructuring most often arises from new strategic goals that arose from a changing physical environment. Existing equipment and furniture may have been fine for former requirements but sadly inadequate for the new demands. Securing the funds to upgrade or replace the items generally takes more time than you'd like. Getting funding for staff development purposes can be a major challenge.

The fourth area is to address physical space issues, especially when the restructuring involves activities based on greater or new technology usage. More and more new libraries are being constructed and can meet the needs of the new technologies. However, of ALA's estimated 122,101 libraries only a small percentage have a facility built in the past 15 years (http://www.ala.org/ala/professionalresources/libfactsheets/alalibraryfactsheet01.cfm). Although libraries have been planned using a modular design process (see Chapter 19 for further information) since the 1950s, the older the building, the less capable it is for handling today's technological needs. Older buildings' infrastructure will need upgrading, redesigning, or replacement. In some cases, the building has been remodeled or added to over the years. Where your unit is located in the building may make your technological restructuring easier or harder.

Now you can begin to think about the options for structuring the tasks—creating logical groupings of the activities for an individual to perform (work assignments). There are a number ways to combine the activities as work units (departmentalization). You need to make certain the activities connect to one another in an effective manner (coordination and span of control). Last, but far from least, you must monitor the outcomes and be ready to adjust the structure in light of the outcomes (assessment/quality control).

You will also experience worries about "what if I don't get it right." This is common for everyone, not just first-timers. Getting it "right" is perhaps not the best way to think about the outcome, because it implies there is one best answer. Given a rapidly changing environment, "right" will probably have a relatively short time span. Creating something that makes a positive improvement should be your goal; and recognizing that you will repeat the process again and again as library goals adjust to the changing environment helps reduce the stress. As a first-timer, you will find that getting advice from more experienced people will also help.

In the broadest sense, you can think of delegation as a form of time management tool for both yourself and the organization. By developing clear reporting structures, assigning authority and responsibility, and so forth, you reduce the need for consultation as well as confusion about who does what and when. Making effective use of your time will make your work life less stressful. It is easy to slip into poor work habits that cost you valuable time; so, by providing

CHECK THESE OUT

The following are four very useful books on time management:

Allen, David. 2001. *Getting Things Done.* New York: Viking.
Covey, Stephen. 1989. *Seven Habits of Highly Successful People.* New York: Simon and Schuster.
——. 1994. *First Things First.* New York: Simon and Schuster.
Lencioni, Patrick. 2004. *Death by Meeting.* San Francisco: Jossey-Bass.

SOMETHING TO PONDER

Reflect on an organization in which you have worked and the person to whom you were responsible. Did the manager delegate tasks? If so, how did the manager ensure that the delegated tasks were completed satisfactorily? If the manager did not delegate, why do you think this was so? Was the manager's approach appropriate?

a structure for yourself and others, you have a start on managing your time. As Ted Pollock (2011) said: "Remember—delegating is the easiest way to get more done. The manager who neglects to use it fully is short-changing employees, the company, and—most of all—him/herself" (p. 26).

Years ago, Harvey Sherman (1966, pp. 83–84) outlined the degrees of delegation with which a manager has to work. These degrees of delegation still hold today. His scheme starts with the highest degree of delegation and progresses to the lowest:

- Take action—no further contact with me is needed.
- Take action—let me know what you did.
- Look into this problem—let me know what you intend to do; then do it, unless I say not to.
- Look into this problem—let me know what you intend to do; delay action until I give approval.
- Look into this problem—let me know alternative actions that are available with pros and cons and recommend one for my approval.
- Look into this problem—give me all the facts, I will decide what to do.

DELEGATION OPTIONS

There are a number of options available to you for organizing or restructuring work assignments. Each has some merits as well as demerits. Your choices may be circumscribed by parent organizational preferences. For example, the parent body may favor highly centralized structures, making it difficult to implement an empowered team approach. The major options are these:

- Functional/commonality
- Customer/user
- Territorial
- Equipment/process/use frequency
- Product
- Matrix
- Teams
- Committee

CHECK THESE OUT

To read about structural issues and the parent body's impact consult such articles as these:

Euster, Joanne. 1990. "The New Hierarchy: Where's the Boss?" *Library Journal* 115, no. 8: 41–44.

Shaughnessy, Thomas. 1996. "Lessons from Restructuring." *Journal of Academic Librarianship* 22, no. 4: 251–257.

You also need to think about such issues as these:

- Degree of centralization/decentralization
- Span of control
- Operational costs
- Accountability

It is important to keep in mind Joseph Boisse's (1996) point that "there is no 'best' way to organize a library" (p. 77)—tall, flat, matrix, team oriented, and so forth. Very often a mixed structure works well for handling the variety of services that libraries offer.

Functional/commonality often appears to be the simplest approach. It calls for grouping people who perform the same tasks into one unit or area. Determining what constitutes basis for choosing these people is not always as easy as it may seem. Consider word processing skills; commonality would suggest that a common pool of individuals to handle all the word processing for all units would be best. Would increased production result from combining the workload from senior managers with the work of preparing order forms? In some cases, perhaps it would; in others cases, probably not. The point to remember is that the application of this option is more complex than it first appears.

The functional option is also the oldest method; traditional "managerial functions" are production, sales, and finance. In terms of libraries, you need to think broadly about each function. When you define production as adding value to goods or services, then you can understand how an archive adds utility or value to the collections it acquires through processing, grouping of materials in a logical order, and creating "finding aids." Defining sales as attracting users who are willing to accept library goods or services, with their attendant rules and conditions, helps clarify how the public service areas of a library fit into sales. Defining finance as securing and controlling the expenditure of funds means that department heads and senior managers engage in finance functions.

The functional method has a long and successful history, especially as a method for broadly structuring an organization. For many years, libraries used this method for their overall structure—technical services (production), public services (sales), and administration (finance). The advantages of the functional method are that it is logical, it reflects the broad functions of any organization, and it ensures that staff members give proper attention to these basic functions. The major issue with the functional method is that it is hard to employ in an institution having units in different (and sometimes distant) locations. The method can, on occasion, result in deemphasizing institutional goals and objectives. Since the early 1990s, libraries have been moving away from this pattern as they adjust to a changing environment.

A *territorial* approach focuses on service points where distance is an issue. In theory, while all organizational functions (production, sales, and finance) can take place in each library branch, the result would be at best a loose federation. Branches would probably be competing for a finite pool of resources to support their activities with little or no regard for the larger picture. Typically, library branch operations carry out only a "sales" function, with a central unit handling all production and finance activities.

There are several situations in which you should not use the territorial approach. If there is a sense that there is a significant communication problem, dividing the organization into branches will do little to improve the perceived problem. Another situation is if there are complaints about slow delivery service to distant users. Delays usually are due to ineffective handling or routing, not the service point location.

The territorial approach is a good method for providing more personal service. Although service may be somewhat slower, the personal touch—usually because the user-to-staff ratio is better—results in increased client satisfaction. Having a large satisfied user base, especially if users are willing to speak out about the value received, can be a valuable asset when it comes time to ask for funding increases.

From management's viewpoint, there is another reason to use the territorial approach. Because branch managers and supervisors are on their own when it comes to such things as having to make quick decisions, they either develop or fail much more quickly than in a large centralized service. Branch supervisors become more confident in their managerial skills as they operate more or less independently. Thus, branches can serve as a testing ground for individuals who may do well in even more responsible positions.

You can employ the *product* (often libraries refer to this as form or format structuring) option to create little "organizations" within larger ones. Under this approach, a unit takes on all the activities of the parent institution (generally with limited financial responsibilities), but for only one product (e.g., archives, serials, maps, government documents, media collections). When using the territorial method, staff usually deal with all forms of materials but only one function (sales); with the product option, the staff specialize in one form and engage in all functions to some degree. This type of specialization allows staff to develop a high level of competence with all aspects of one format, gaining a depth of skills and knowledge that someone working with many formats has little opportunity to acquire. Another advantage is that the high knowledge level usually results in an equally high quality of client service. User confidence increases, as well as satisfaction with the materials and services received.

The *customer/user* option is useful in circumstances where the library wishes to address some special needs of a class of users. Some academic libraries have undergraduate libraries. The most obvious example of user-oriented work assignments is in public libraries that have a separate children's services unit and/or young adult services. Some libraries have special units for the visually impaired and handicapped or shut-ins, and still others have "institutionalized" service units (for hospital wards, prisons, and nursing homes). Often, such units require special skills (such as storytelling or very sophisticated database searching) and special equipment (such as children's furniture, reading machines, or other equipment to assist the visually impaired). This approach can also produce a very high quality of service and a high level of user satisfaction. Client-oriented service also increases staff skills because staff members develop in-depth expertise in one area.

Frequency of use (equipment/process) options come into play when one department accounts for the majority of use or when no unit has more than a small portion of the use. Libraries rarely employ this approach, except in areas such as photocopying and ICT support. Proper use of this method depends on two factors: money and space. For instance, it is costly to provide photocopy equipment for every library department. In addition, doing so would mean most of the machines would be idle most of the time. Therefore, it is usually cost-effective to set up one or perhaps two locations, depending on the physical facility, and have one or two staff members near those location(s) who can assist with problems when they arise. One of the benefits of this approach is that most of the staff do not need to devote much time to learning to effectively use the equipment.

Each of the options has advantages and disadvantages. Only through careful analysis of a library's goals and the local environment can you determine which form(s) are the best match. What works today may not be appropriate tomorrow. Functional and product approaches are most common at the higher levels of the organization, while the lower levels normally use territorial, customer, and equipment methods to organize the work.

Some other methods for organizing work groups are matrix, teams, and committees. As is true of other options, each has some strengths and weaknesses. Knowing when to use which approach takes time and thoughtful analysis of current circumstances.

The *matrix* approach is a combination of functional and product options. One major advantage of the matrix approach is its flexibility, especially in handling one-time projects. The simplest way to think of matrix organization is as a grid that addresses multiple activities and reporting structures. Interest in matrix structuring peaked in the late 1970s and early 1980s, although many large international

AUTHORS' EXPERIENCE

Alire inherited the matrix model in all three university libraries she led. The models were more hybrid and not necessarily interdepartmental but intradepartmental. That is, a librarian working in public services might have a matrix that included reference, information literacy, and collection development. The biggest challenge, not surprisingly, was reporting to three different supervisors.

organizations adopt it for special projects. Thomas Sy and Laura Sue D'Annunzio (2005) provide an excellent overview of the concept and its current use.

Pure matrix is a semi-to-permanent arrangement of staff. Under this approach, staff members may work for several supervisors. Many years ago, the University of Nebraska–Lincoln Library attempted an ambitious matrix organization. While retaining the traditional department heads of acquisitions, cataloging, and reference, as well as a support staff in each department, other librarians had duties in all three areas.

Table 6.1 will make it easier to visualize the structure of a matrix organization such as the one the University of Nebraska–Lincoln Library used. The time percentages are illustrative only. The chart shows that each librarian would work in three areas on a regular basis. It may also mean that they are working for three different supervisors. Clearly, this is a violation of Fayol's dictum of "unity of command." Multiple supervisors can create reporting problems and stress for those having to handle the expectations of two or more supervisors.

The University of Nebraska library effort failed, not because of the problems attendant with trying to meet the expectations of three supervisors, but rather most of those involved in the matrix did not always have an equal interest in each area of responsibility. As a result, they tended to neglect or at least put off doing the less-favored activities. The concept behind implementing this organizational structure for the library was, in theory, that matrix librarians would become better subject experts. Efforts were made to hire individuals with both a degree in librarianship and an advanced subject degree. They were then to work in that or a related subject area. By selecting, processing, and managing the collection they built, the idea was that they would provide more effective customer service. It was an interesting idea but one that did not prove workable in that situation at that time.

Using a matrix approach for projects can be an effective means of bringing together staff with the necessary skills to handle a special project; it also helps you create a unit that emphasizes multiple organizational concerns. By combining the skills in a single unit, a task can be accomplished effectively. These units give you the flexibility to respond to changing situations. Their major disadvantage is the one we mentioned earlier—multiple supervisors.

TABLE 6.1   Percentages of Staff Time in a Matrix Organization

	Acquisitions Department	Reference Department	Cataloging Department
Librarian 1	10%	40%	50%
Librarian 2	40%	50%	10%
Librarian 3	50%	10%	40%
Librarian 4	10%	40%	50%

The Sy and D'Annunzio (2005) article identified five areas of concern on the part of their respondents regarding the matrix structure. The most commonly mentioned concern should not come as a surprise—ambiguous authority. Two others—misaligned goals and unclear roles and responsibilities—are also issues that an organizing process is to resolve, not muddying the water as to who does what and when. The fourth—silo-focused employees—is a concern with almost any structure you might choose. In our view this is not a structural issue; however, you can correct this through training and team building with a focus on understanding the overall picture and needs. Their fifth concern is probably the key to the success or failure of the matrix form—a lack of a "matrix guardian," someone solely responsible for the matrix performance.

TEAMS

Management writers and people in general use the term *team* in a variety of ways when referring to workplace groups. This is one definition of a workplace team that appears to capture today's environment: "A work group is made up of individuals who see themselves and who are seen by others as a social entity, who are interdependent because of the tasks they perform as members of the group, who are embedded in one or more larger social systems, and who perform tasks that affect others" (Guzzo and Dickson, 1996, pp. 308–309). Perhaps two more elements ought to be part of the definition—teamwork groups develop a shared commitment to one another, and the group is empowered to make decisions regarding their work activities.

Teams in the workplace have been with us for a long time in one form or another. They are not a new concept despite what you might think from reading the management literature. They are, however, playing an ever-greater role in how organizations get things done. Over the past 20-some years, organizations including libraries have undergone a "flattening" of their structures, resulting in fewer layers of management. In many cases, they experienced downsizing or at least received no increase in staffing even with increased workloads (delegation). As a result of these events, the staff must be more productive, be flexible, learn new skills, and take on more responsibilities.

Diane Coutu (2011) wrote, in her introduction to an interview with J. Richard Hackman:

TIP

"Team members frequently discuss the information that they are all aware of and fail to share unique information with one another" (Max Bazerman and Dolly Chugh, "Decisions without Blinders," *Business Review* 84, no. 1: 94, 2006).

Over the past couple of decades, a cult has grown up around teams. Even in a society as fiercely independent as America, teams are considered almost sacrosanct. The belief that working in teams makes us more creative and productive is so widespread that when faced with a challenging new task, leaders are quick to assume that teams are the best way to get the job done.

Not so fast says J. Richard Hackman, the Edgar Pierce Professor of Social and Organizational Psychology at Harvard University and a leading expert on teams. . . . Most of the time, his research shows, team members don't even agree on what the team is supposed to be doing. (p. 1)

Some of the differences that exist between a true team environment and the traditional workplace are significant. Teams call for consensus rather than command and control. They require acceptance of the idea that conflict (both positive and negative) is a normal part of team operations, and those conflicts must be addressed in an open, honest manner. Reaching decisions in a team setting tends to be based more on the group's knowledge than on one person's opinion. In teams, the emphasis is on the "whys" more than on the "hows." Essentially, it requires a collaborative process within the team in order for the group to succeed.

The decision to employ teams—temporary or permanent—is not one to make lightly. Teams and time go together like bacon and eggs. They require thoughtful planning, a careful assessment of staff capabilities, and an assessment of the organization's ability to adjust to team operations *before* starting the selection of team members. Teams require careful, ongoing nurturing from the time they are created until they are disbanded. They also require a different, and rather complex, assessment process to ensure sound and proper accountability.

There are two broad categories of teams: integrated and self-managed. Integrated teams receive task(s) from a manager, and the team works out how and who will do what to achieve the desired outcome(s). Self-managed teams receive goals rather than tasks. They generally have a "contact" manager they cay turn to for guidance and assistance but overall operate very independently. Needless to say, the issue of coordination between teams is a major concern for successful team operations. Another challenge for team-based organizations is performance evaluation and issues of accountability.

CHECK THIS OUT

An excellent article describing the reorganization of a unit within a library is Barbara Brattin's "Reorganizing Reference" (*Public Libraries* 44, no. 6 [November–December]: 340–346, 2005).

Teamwork is effective when trust and delegation are present and when the staff understand the concepts of authority and responsibility. Given the flatter hierarchies and extended service hours of most libraries, teamwork is an effective way to organize staff. You can form teams to coordinate work across the service, to work on specific aspects of service, or to act as a facilitator to change management.

The team needs to have a mission—to know what is expected of it and whether there are "markers" that will measure progress and achievement. In addition to a mission, all team members have to understand the boundaries of the authority that the team has been delegated as well as who has the responsibility to ensure that the team works effectively and efficiently.

TRY THIS

Following are some questions to ponder regarding your approach to teams:

- When making decisions, do you consult with a few individuals whom you know and trust or with anyone who will be affected by the decisions?
  ☐ Rarely   ☐ Occasionally   ☐ Often
- How often do you fall back on rules, procedures, and policies to achieve goals?
  ☐ Rarely   ☐ Occasionally   ☐ Often
- How comfortable are you with group decision making?
  ☐ Not At All   ☐ Somewhat   ☐ Very
- How comfortable are you being accountable for the performance of other people?
  ☐ Not At All   ☐ Somewhat   ☐ Very
- How comfortable are you in work situations where you must trust people with whom you don't have a long history?
  ☐ Not At All   ☐ Somewhat   ☐ Very

Related to clear goals and directions and the "right" team environment are the tasks the team is to perform. A manager must be certain the tasks *require* teamwork. A common mistake, especially in first-time team environments, is creating a team in name only (tasks, yes, but not requiring teamwork). What happens is an appearance of teamwork, but in reality it is just individuals doing their own independent work. Making this mistake quickly leads to disillusionment. Another fairly common mistake is assigning tasks that only occasionally call for teamwork. Although there will likely be times when team members need to work independently to produce a product that is shared by or ultimately benefits the entire team, assigning too many individualized tasks to the team risks sending a mixed message and does not take advantage of the benefits of a team-based structure. This creates a pull on team members, making it difficult to build a team commitment.

An area where team-based work differs from the traditional workplace is accountability. At least in the United States, most workers are accustomed to being individually responsible for their work outcomes. Group accountability may be one of the most difficult concepts for team members to understand and accept. Teams *must* be accountable, and success or failure is a *team* responsibility. Having to accept that "my performance assessment" may be negatively affected

CHECK THESE OUT

Here are two good resources on team empowerment:

Christopher, Connie. 2003. *Empowering Your Library: A Guide to Improving Service, Productivity, and Participation.* Chicago: American Library Association.

Manville, Brook, and Josiah Ober. 2003. "Beyond Empowerment: Building a Company of Citizens." *Harvard Business Review* 81, no. 1: 48–53.

Perhaps the best-known team-based information service with the longest operational experience in the United States is the University of Arizona Library. It has received a substantial amount of publicity. The following are two good articles about the Arizona model:

Bender, Laura. 1997. "Team Organization—Learning Organization." *Information Outlook* 1, no. 9: 19–22.

Diaz, Joseph, and Chestalene Pintozzi. 1999. "Helping Teams Work." *Library Administration and Management,* 13, no. 1: 27–36.

This is an interesting article discussing the team concept in a public library setting:

Bernfeld, Betsy. 2004. "Developing a Team Management Structure in a Public Library." *Library Trends* 53, no. 1: 112–128.

by someone else's actions often does not sit well. (An important feature of self-managing teams and their accountability is that the teams must be allowed to address member performance on an ongoing basis rather than have the external leader handle any problems.) The question becomes: are there staff who already have a sense of team accountability or appear capable of accepting the concept?

Transitioning to teams requires everyone—managers and staff—to rethink roles and responsibilities. Ceasar Douglas (2002) noted that the transition period is critical to success and can take 24 months or more to complete satisfactorily. One of the first managerial shifts must be from a "command and control" mode of behavior to one of being an advisor, which is not always an easy transition for some people. Another issue for managers is their self-monitoring ability. (Self-monitoring is the ability to strategically adjust your "influencing behavior" to fit the situation.) For the staff, adapting team behaviors and accepting those behaviors is critical. One behavior some people have difficulty with is group decision making and the time that it takes. Related to group decision making is that conflict and its resolution are a part of the process. For some people conflict is something to avoid at almost any cost, including conflicts involving strongly held views. A few individuals have significant difficulty having their performance judged on the basis of the group's performance.

COMMITTEES

Committees are important to an organization in a number of ways. They can serve in an advisory/informational capacity (gathering material and making recommendations), promote coordination and cooperation (especially among disparate areas), improve communication (which, unfortunately, can backfire), handle short-term projects, and make decisions. Although rhetoric about committees is often negative, everyone continues to use them. The reality is that committees, although occasionally ineffective, are frequently the best means of accomplishing a specific goal.

The governing boards and other oversight groups for libraries operate as committees. Senior managers employ committees to handle special tasks or issues that cut across functional lines. Middle management can use them to coordinate existing operations, plan new programs and services, and evaluate work. "Floor" managers find committees useful in handling operational issues, unit decision making, and procedural change recommendations.

TRY THIS

Identifying all of the committees that exist in a service may not be easy. If you are working in a library, try to list all of them. If you are not, try talking with a senior person who is and see how many committees he or she can identify.

When setting up a committee, you must take time and thought to formulating an accurate statement of what the committee duties, responsibilities, and authority ("committee charge") will be. A sound charge clearly spells out each of these topics. Perhaps the greatest area of confusion, almost always due to a poorly prepared charge, is between an advisory and a decision-making role. It is rather common to read or hear about members of a committee being angered when their "advice" is not taken—members thought they were making decisions when the person establishing the committee only sought advice. The time used to prepare a formal charge can ultimately save a lot of time and, not infrequently, emotional energy.

One advantage of committees is that they can involve a number of people in a process that may impact most if not all of the staff. Another plus is that they can bring to bear a variety of viewpoints, skills, and experiences. They can help coordinate work among departments. They are effective in soliciting users' input regarding services.

There are also drawbacks to using committees: high cost, stalemate, inordinate delay, compromise, domination of the group by a single strong personality, and no true accountability. The high cost can be mitigated (in salary, time, and lost production) by closely monitoring the activities of committees. If they are proving wasteful and unproductive, they can be disbanded. The ease with which they can be disbanded depends on the status of the committee—a standing committee or a special committee. It can be difficult to disband a formal, or standing, committee. A good example of this type is a committee that is formed through some aspect of library governance (staff advisory committee, library faculty committee, etc.).

Another disadvantage involves the quality of the decisions reached by a committee. If all a committee can achieve is a compromise decision that would only worsen a situation if implemented, or a decision forced on the group by a dedicated minority, then the committee has failed in its function. If an unworkable compromise forces a manager to create his or her own solution, then feelings may be hurt and future cooperation endangered. If the manager rejects a minority recommendation, then that minority will probably be especially vocal in opposing any proposed solutions.

Perhaps the greatest disadvantage of committee work is that, because of the shared responsibility of the committee, a manager cannot hold one person, not even the committee head, accountable for a poor decision. Even if an idea began with one person, the group's acceptance of it makes it their work.

From a manager's point of view, it is important to distinguish between a committee and a task force. In a nutshell, committees are usually part of the formal organizational structure; they are charged to work for and/or represent the whole organization in some way. Many committees in libraries are standing committees. That is, no matter the committee charge, the committee stands until formally disbanded.

A task force, on the other hand, is more informal and usually consists of members who have a certain expertise to help accomplish the task (i.e., the charge). Once the

AUTHORS' EXPERIENCE

Alire used task forces throughout her career as a library administrator. Task forces could be more focused to accomplish the "task" in a timely manner in that they usually have a deadline date; they are more flexible in terms of membership in that staff are appointed to the task force, not elected; and they have a beginning and an end. Task forces also allowed her and others to involve library support staff who may have developed an expertise in certain areas but sans the LIS degree.

task force accomplishes that task/charge, it is disbanded. A task force can, however, be given another charge based on the work it accomplishes. What is important is to remember that a task force has a beginning and an end.

SPAN OF CONTROL

At some point in developing a structure, you must think about the question, "How many people or units can this position reasonably handle?" The issue was perhaps first brought out in a verse from the Bible; in Exodus 18: 17–18, Moses was told, "This thing is too heavy for thee. Thou are not able to perform it thyself all alone. Thou wilt surely wear away." Delegation is a sharing of responsibility and authority. No one is capable of making all the decisions required in our present complex social and institutional environment. Span of control denotes the degree of sharing.

A narrow span of control (few reports) results in a "tall" structure—multiple levels. A "flat" structure usually means a wide span of control. Use of teams flattens a structure when it is the sole method of structuring, but teams may add to the complexity when they supplement other structural forms.

The environmental rate of change is a factor in determining how many people/ teams constitute a workable span of control. Quickly changing situations call for a narrow span of control. Libraries have traditionally followed the classic rule of four to six full-time people as the best span of control.

There are cost factors associated with span of control. First, as the span widens, the system costs more in terms of salaries and benefits. A second cost is in terms of communication. As the span of control widens, communication becomes more complex and interaction time increases. Finally, coordination becomes more difficult as the number of supervisors increases; poor coordination carries with it a high performance cost.

There are arguments supporting wide spans of control. The primary argument maintains that subordinates assume more responsibility under a wide span of control because they have less supervision. In conjunction with this is the idea that staff begin to develop their managerial skills as they exercise more independent judgments regarding their daily work activities. Moreover, people respond positively, maintain higher morale, and frequently perform better when they have less supervision.

Through the careful use of personal contact, a manager can expand her or his span of control. By creating an atmosphere of availability, the supervisor lets subordinates know that they can get help when necessary. Knowing that such support is available when requested allows subordinates to work independently. Such situations tend to lead to high staff morale, but supervisors must maintain a balance among availability, personal concern, and socializing.

CENTRALIZATION/DECENTRALIZATION

When management writers discuss centralization/decentralization, they usually are addressing decision making, not physical location. Beginning librarians sometimes think that because a system has "branches" it is decentralized. They may be correct from an organizational theory point of view, if the branches have a high degree of decision-making autonomy. A system may be highly centralized in its decision making and yet have numerous branches. Some years ago, for example, a large metropolitan library system (with 63 branches) operated with the rule that a branch collection could contain only titles that were in the central library's collection. Branch librarians had to convince a collection development officer in "central" to order a title before a branch could do so. Thus, while having a widespread geographic distribution (physically highly decentralized), decision making regarding collection development was highly centralized.

Although decentralization has acquired something like hallowed status among employees by virtue of its association with phrases such as "more democratic" and "less authoritarian," it can lead to some very real problems. The following quotation from Ernest Dale (1952), a major researcher in this area, indicates some of the problems:

> I find myself just a little annoyed at the tendency of all of us to adopt certain clichés about decentralization and then glibly announce that we're for it. I've been somewhat amused at some of my colleagues who have been vocal at expounding the virtues of decentralization and yet quite unconsciously are apt to be busily engaged in developing their own personal control over activities for which they are responsible. (p. 18)

The lip service given to the concept of decentralization often belies the reality of day-to-day operations. Given a little thought, it becomes clear that pure centralization or decentralization is impossible in almost any organizational setting. A one-person enterprise is an example of pure centralization. As soon as a second person joins the enterprise, there will be some degree of decentralization, however slight. Pure decentralization is anarchy and therefore, by definition, not an organization.

Dale (1952, p. 105) developed four criteria for determining the degree of centralization within an organization. They are as valid today as they were in 1952, when he carried out the research:

FOR FURTHER THOUGHT

Using our example of the large metropolitan library (with 63 branches), consider if it was a decentralized service. Which factors affected the decision to operate a centralized or a decentralized service?

- The greater the number of decisions made lower down in the management hierarchy, the greater the degree of decentralization.
- The more important the decisions made lower down the management hierarchy (for example, the greater the sum of capital expenditure that can be approved by a plant manager without consulting anyone else), the greater the degree of decentralization.
- More functions are affected by decisions made at the lower levels (thus, companies which permit only operational decisions to be made at separate branch plants are less decentralized than those which permit financial and personnel decisions to be made at branch plants).
- The less checking required on the decision, the more decentralized the organization. Decentralization is greatest when no check at all is made, less when the supervisors have to consult before the decision is made. The fewer the people to be consulted and the lower they are in the management hierarchy, the greater the degree of decentralization.

Although such criteria make the examination and analysis of an organization's structure more objective, they also involve several subjective elements. Appearances do not always reflect reality, and what someone says often differs sharply from what takes place.

Many organizations, including libraries, decentralize some areas and not others. In our earlier example, the large metropolitan library decided to decentralize the "sales" decisions and centralize the "financial" decisions. Such an arrangement reflects senior management's desire to closely monitor the financial transactions of the organization. Other managers might have a different philosophy, such as allowing lower level managers to make financial decisions with the view that such responsibility assists junior managers in developing their managerial skills. Managerial interest, and/or the personal need to be "in control," plays a significant role in how the service handles decision making. Some individuals are very uncomfortable delegating decision making to junior staff. In such cases, they will retain as much decision making as possible, frequently more than they can effectively handle.

As noted in Chapter 2, environment is always a factor in how an organization manages its affairs. Rapidly changing environments (turbulent) tend to generate decentralized decision making within an overall strategic plan. That is, lower level managers have the power to make tactical decisions as long as they stay within the overall strategic plan. Placid environments tend to generate increasingly centralized decision making.

Another factor is the importance or cost of a decision. The correlation between the cost of a decision and how high up in the structure it is made is very positive: the more money involved, the higher the position of the person making the final decision. For instance, because most user fines and fees are small and involve or affect the service's long-term interests in minor ways, the decisions are in the hands of frontline staff. However, when it comes to determining who may use the service, instituting a new service, or planning a new facility, department heads or the director normally make these decisions. This is true, not because top-level administrators make fewer mistakes, but because one cannot fully delegate responsibility along with authority.

Finally, staff abilities influence the degree of decentralization. Decentralization requires a staff that has the knowledge to make decisions. If those elements are lacking, the manager should either postpone decentralization until staff with the requisite abilities are available or undertake staff development activities to improve skills.

LEARNING ORGANIZATIONS

Proper delegation not only helps achieve focused work activities and quality productivity but it will also provide staff with growth and development opportunities. Staff members who are learning new skills tend to be more motivated and committed to the organization and its well-being.

Peter Senge's book *The Fifth Discipline: The Art and Practice of the Learning Organization* (2006, revised edition) generated great interest in his concept of a learning organization when it first appeared in 1990. Learning organizations attempt to generate/acquire and pass on information/knowledge within themselves with the goal of adjusting their activities based on "new" knowledge to create a more effective organization.

Senge (2006) defined a learning organization as one "where people continually expand their capacity to create the results they truly desire" (p. 3). His five disciplines are personal mastery, mental models, shared visions, team learning, and systems thinking. "Personal mastery" is about your learning how to expand your ability to generate the best possible outcomes. It also helps create an environment where others seek to learn and develop their skills sets. "Mental models" is thinking about your mental images of the world and how those images influence your actions and behavior. "Shared visions" is about developing group commitment to current and future goals. "Team learning" is about building ever stronger trust and effective communication and accepting team members' ideas as possible solutions to challenges with the objective of achieving ever greater team results. "Systems think" is about understanding and describing interrelationships in existing behavior systems in order to be more effective in changing those systems when necessary.

ADVISORY BOARD EXPERIENCE

Sachi Yagyu mentioned another valuable organizational benefit arising from thoughtful delegation:

> Delegation and teamwork help spread critical knowledge throughout a group, which has long-term organizational benefits. As I get further along in my career, I try to share organizational information and to get others to do likewise, because I know if, for some reason, I can't continue a task, others will be able to pick up where I left off. This saves valuable time for the organization as well as for it users.

As a manager, you have important roles to play in a learning organizational environment. You need to actively bring new ideas to the staff and wider organization; the discussion of new ideas also will assist you when you need to institute change. Actively removing barriers to sharing new ideas is also something you should do. The sharing process is one technique for reducing the "silo" effect that often afflicts units in large organizations. Another role is to assist staff in modifying their behavior in light of the new information.

KEY POINTS TO REMEMBER
- Delegation is an important and complex process.
- Organizational structure plays a key role in an organization's effectiveness.
- Knowing yourself in terms of "trusting" others is especially important when it comes to delegation.
- Do not delegate responsibility without providing the necessary authority.
- Assessing tasks and designing jobs are essential steps in creating an effective organizational structure.
- Successful restructuring requires detailed planning and thinking.
- Recognizing both the abilities and the limitations of each staff member is basic to successful organizing.
- Team structures require special managerial skills.
- Width of span of control depends on factors such as the speed of change and the rate of growth.
- The concept of centralization/decentralization is more than an either/or issue; in most organizations both exist.
- Learning organizations tend to be more responsive to a changing environment because they value and act upon new ideas.

References

Associations Now. 2010. "What Is the Hardest Thing about Delegating?" *Associations Now* 56, no. 8: 61.

Beeson, Jon. 2010. "Micromanaging: Break the Deadly Cycle." *Sales and Service Excellence* 10, no. 9: 8.

Boisse, Joseph A. 1996. "Adjusting the Horizontal Hold: Flattening the Organization." *Library Administration and Management* 10, no. 2: 77–80.

Coutu, Diane. 2011. "Why Teams Don't Work." In *Harvard Business Review Building Better Teams*, 1–18. Cambridge, MA: Harvard Business Review Press.

Dale, Ernest. 1952. *Planning and Developing the Company Organization Structure. Research Report 20.* New York: American Management Association.

Douglas, Ceasar. 2002. "The Effects of Managerial Influence Behavior on the Transition to Self-Managed Teams." *Journal of Managerial Psychology* 17, nos. 7/8: 628–635.

Eblin, Scott. 2010. "Delegating While Managing Risk." *Executive Leadership* 25, no. 5: 7.

The Economist. 2006. "The New Organization." *The Economist*, Special Supplement, 378, no. 8461: 1–18.

Guzzo, Richard, and Marcus Dickson. 1996. "Teams in Organizations: Recent Research and Performance Effectiveness." In *Annual Review of Psychology*, edited by James Spence, 307–338. Palo Alto, CA: Annual Reviews.

Higa, Mori Lou, Brian Bunnett, Bill Maina, Jeff Perkins, Therona Ramos, Laurie Thompson, et al. 2005. "Redesigning a Library's Organizational Structure." *College and Research Libraries* 66, no. 1: 41–58.

Hunter, Judy. 2002. "Improving Organizational Performance through the Use of Effective Organizational Structure." *Leadership in Health Services* 15, no. 3: 12–21.

Hurley, Robert F. 2006. "The Decision to Trust." *Harvard Business Review* 84, no. 9: 55–62.

Pollock, Ted. 2011. "How Well Do You Delegate?" *Supervision* 72, no. 4: 26.

Schoofs, Bob. 2007. "Abolish the Periodicals Department: How One Library Restructured and Redistributed the Work." *College and Research Libraries News* 68, no. 1: 17–19.

Senge, Peter. 2006. *The Fifth Discipline: The Art and Practice of the Learning Organization.* Rev. ed. London: Random House Business.

Sheffer, Carol. 2009. "Team Building." *Public Libraries* 48, no. 2: 4–5, 24.

Sherman, Harvey. 1966. *It All Depends: A Pragmatic Approach to Organizations.* Tuscaloosa: University of Alabama Press.

Strong, Gary E. 2010. "Restructuring at UCLA Library." *Research Library Issues* 272: 16–22.

Sy, Thomas, and Laura Sue D'Annunzio. 2005. "Challenges and Strategies of the Matrix Organizations: Top-Level and Mid-Level Managers' Perspectives." *Human Resource Planning* 28, no. 1: 39–48.

Launching Pad

Bender, Laura. 1997. "Team Organization—Learning Organization: The University of Arizona Four Years into It." *Information Outlook* 1, no. 9: 19–22.

Bernfeld, Betsy. 2004. "Developing a Team Management Structure in a Public Library." *Library Trends* 53, no. 1: 112–128.

Bowen, John J. 2010. "Delegate It!" *Employee Benefit Advisor* 8, no. 6: 58–59.

Christopher, Connie. 2003. *Empowering Your Library*. Chicago: American Library Association.

Damon, Camille, and Annie Wu. 2010. "Strong Beginnings in Academic Libraries: Innovating Employee Orientations as a Start to a Learning Organization." *Texas Library Journal* 86, no. 2: 52–54.

Davis, Jason Lee, and Harley Davis. 2009. "The Learning Organization Implemented through Advisory Committees." *Education* 130, no. 1: 114–117.

Druskat, Vanessa, and Jane V. Wheeler. 2004. "How to Lead Self-Managing Teams." *MIT Sloan Management Review* 45, no. 4: 65–71.

Fabbi, Jennifer L. 2009. "Discovery Focus as Impetus for Organizational Learning." *Information Technology and Libraries* 28, no. 4: 164–171.

Hunter, Judy. 2002. "Improving Organizational Performance through the Use of Effective Elements of Organizational Structure." *Leadership in Health Services* 15, no. 3: 12–21.

Johnson, Lauren Keller. 2007. "Are You Delegating So It Sticks?" *Harvard Management Update* 12, no. 11: 3–5.

———. 2008. "Helping New Managers Succeed." *Harvard Management Update* 13, no. 2: 3–4.

Kelly, Darron. 2009. "From Senge to Habermas." In *Philosophy of Education Yearbook*, 104–112. Philosophy of Education Society. http://ojs.ed.uiuc.edu/index.php/pes/issue/view/24.

Kuhlthau, Carol C., and Leslie K. Maniotes. 2010. "Building Guided Inquiry Teams for 21st-Century Learners." *School Library Monthly* 26, no. 5: 18–21.

Lubans, John. 2003. "Teams in Libraries." *Library Administration and Management* 17, no. 3: 144–145.

Pan, Denise, and Zaana Howard. 2009. "Reorganizing a Technical Services Division Using Collaborative Evidenced Based Information Practice at Auraria Library." *Evidenced Based Library and Information Practice* 4, no. 4: 88–94.

Sheffer, Carol. 2009. "Team Building." *Public Libraries* 48, no. 2: 4–5, 24.

Signorelli, Paul, and Lori Reed. 2011. "Professional Growth through Learning Communities." *American Libraries* 42, nos. 5/6: 56–59.

Decisions are the coin of the realm. . . . Every success, every mishap; every opportunity seized or missed is the result of a decision someone made or failed to make.
   —Paul Rogers and Marcia Blenko (2006)

I think one of the single biggest challenges that organizations are going to face—and one of the biggest opportunities they face—is changing how they make important decisions.
   —Michael S. Hopkins (2011)

Individuals in organizations make decisions and take action every day, whether they are CEOs who are deciding on a hostile takeover or new frontline employees who may be deciding whether to follow the rules concerning safety.
   —Richard Priem, Bruce Walters, and Sali Li (2011)

Making decisions is the most important job of any executive. It is also the toughest and the riskiest. . . . So where do bad decisions come from?
   —John Hammond, Ralph Keeney, and Howard Raiffa (2011)

7

DECISION MAKING

This chapter focuses on the following:

- The decision-making environment
- Decisions and accountability
- Types of decisions
- Decision-making styles
- Aids for decision making
- The difference between decision making and problem solving
- Individual and group decision-making processes

WE ALL MAKE decisions every day. Some of us have more difficulty than others when it comes time to do so. Our opening quotations make the point that decision making is important and suggest they are not always easy to make. When it comes to our workplace decision making, the stakes can become much higher than with most of our personal decisions.

In a broad sense, decision making underlies all managerial action. Before you develop a plan, you must make a decision regarding the plan's goal(s). Libraries do not hire someone until there is a decision regarding the required and desired skills and abilities of the successful candidate. Managers monitor work performance based on decisions made about acceptable and unacceptable performance. The list could go on and on, but the point is that decision making is a part of daily work life. Staff members, no matter at what level, do make some decisions.

Napoleon is reputed to have said, "Nothing is more difficult and therefore more precious than the ability to decide." Whether he said this or not does not change the fact that the sentiment is accurate. A significant factor in your career is how well you handle decision making and problem solving. We each develop a personal style of decision making and problem solving. An obvious difference between personal and workplace decision making is the number of people impacted by the quality of your decision(s).

Herbert Simon (1976), in his classic study of organizational behavior, stated that behavior involves both unconscious and conscious selections of our actions. Furthermore, the conscious actions (such as in planning) are decisions that you can, and should, analyze. Henry Mintzberg (1976) described some of the complexities of decision making and elaborated on its dynamic factors:

> Decision-making processes are stopped by interruptions, delayed and speeded up by timing factors, and forced to branch and cycle. These processes are, therefore, dynamic ones of importance. Yet it is the dynamic factors that the ordered sequential techniques of analysis (problem-solving) are least able to handle. Thus, despite their important analysis, the dynamic factors go virtually without mention in the literature of management science. (p. 55)

Some management scholars, for example, Noel Tichy and Warren Bennis (2007), use the word "judgment" rather than "decision." Is there any difference in meaning between the two words? Not according to *Webster's Third New International Dictionary, Unabridged* (2002): "Decision, 1a: act of deciding; specif: the act of judgment" (p. 585). Tichy and Bennis (2007) suggested, "We believe we've made a start at picking apart the elements of judgment, but we know it's just that—a start. Judgment is a complex phenomenon, too intertwined with luck, and the vicissitudes of history, too influenced by personal style, to pin down entirely. . . . [I]f all problems were identical, judgment would be a science, not an art" (p. 102). Indeed, decision making is art and not one easily perfected.

DECISION-MAKING ENVIRONMENT

Hammond, Keeney, and Raiffa (2011), in one of our opening quotations, noted that decision making is risky. They are right. Every decision has some element of unpredictability, uncertainty, and risk. Thus, you have to assume not all of your decisions will turn out as planned—"a mistake" in the minds of some people—and that is why decision making is problematic.

Throughout life we develop a "risk tolerance," which varies according to past risk taking and decisions. Buchanan and O'Connell (2006) stated that "risk is an inescapable part of every decision. For most of the everyday choices people make, the risks are small. But on a corporate scale, the implications (both upside and downside) can be enormous" (p. 34). Thinking about risk taking, ambiguity, and conflict tolerance levels as a continuum helps you assess personal and workplace comfort levels with making decisions. At one end of the scale is "flight," at the opposite end is "fight," with a midpoint of "flow."

Individuals at the flight end avoid risk, confrontation, and change as much as they can. We all face a situation at times when flight is undoubtedly the best action. However, you should not become a Linus from the *Peanuts* cartoon in which he said, "This is a distinct philosophy of mine. No problem is so big or complicated that it can't be run away from."

In the organizational setting, as far as decision making is concerned, a typical "flight" behavior is procrastination. How often have you heard, "We are still waiting for a decision?" Although it is not always the case, all too frequently "the wait" is in fact decision avoidance in action. "Needing additional information" can also be an avoidance mechanism while not appearing to be. Occasionally a decision-making situation will pass without the need to decide; however, such a situation is very rare in an organization. More often than not some decision is better than no decision.

Fight-inclined individuals see opportunities and challenges in change and decision making. They have confidence in their skills, accept occasional mistakes as unfortunate but natural outcomes of the processes, and are quick to move on when mistakes happen. Risk taking and ambiguity are not things about which they worry. Working for such people can be rewarding and exciting as well as frustrating and unsettling. At its most extreme ("gut" decisions), the results can be spectacular—either smashing success or resounding failure.

Most people are somewhere in between the extremes of flight and fight. They move toward one end or the other based on recent experiences. They also tend to shift along the continuum more frequently than do individuals at the extremes. Essentially they flow with events. They assess risk, have a concern about ambiguity, know mistakes will happen, and do their best to balance all the factors.

TYPES OF DECISIONS

David Snowden and Mary Boone (2007) discussed four decision-making environments—simple, complicated, complex, and chaotic. The simple context is one with repetitive events and patterns, clear causes and effects, and almost total "knowns." A complicated situation requires "expert diagnosis," causes and effects are not clear but are "discoverable," and there is some knowledge of what unknowns may exist. The complex environment is filled with unpredictability, many unknowns, and many potential and competing options. Chaotic situations are very much like Emery and Trist's (1965) "turbulent" environment (see Chapter 2 for a discussion of their concepts), with high tension, pressure to quickly decide, no sense of what the causes and effects may be, and almost no knowns. Snowden and Boone (2007) concluded their article with this thought: "A deep understanding of context, the ability to embrace complexity and paradox, and willingness to flexibly change leadership style will be required for leaders who want to make things happen in a time of increasing uncertainty" (p. 76).

Some management writers suggest only two broad types of decision making—programmed (Snowden/Boone's simple) and nonprogrammed (complicated, complex, and chaotic). Programmed decisions are routine and occur on a regular basis (making a reference desk schedule, selecting items for the collection, determining who prepares an annual report, and determining who may use or check out a particular item are examples). Such decisions are the stuff of daily decision making at all levels in a library. People rarely think of them as "decisions"; they are low risk, outcomes are highly predictable, and few people have trouble making them.

Nonprogrammed decisions are another matter. They are rarer, risks are high, outcomes uncertain, and the decision environment is often unstructured.

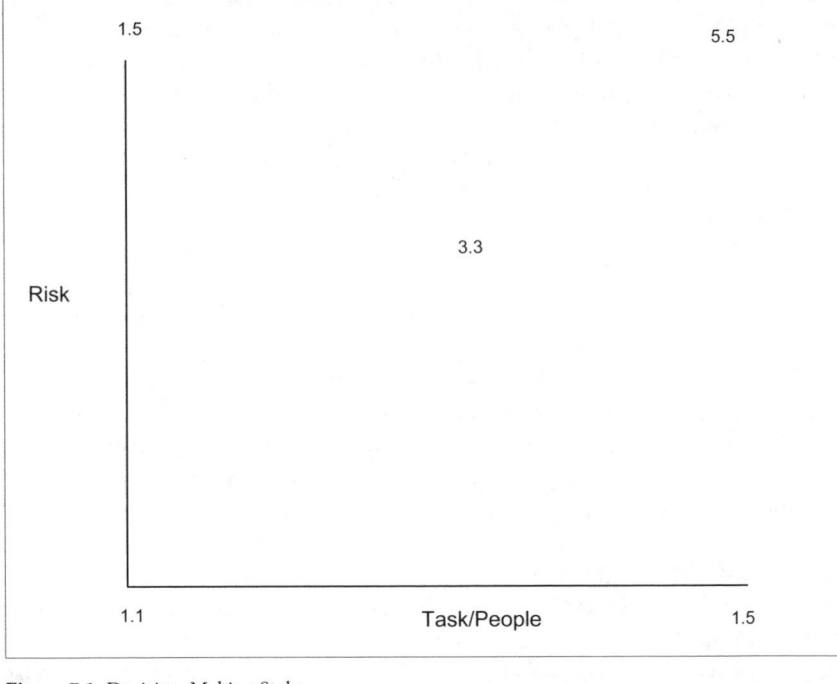

1.5   5.5

Risk   3.3

1.1   Task/People   1.5

Figure 7.1 Decision-Making Styles

They often have wide implications for the organization. They are also relatively uncommon at lower levels of an organization (probably the most common situation for lower level staff to confront a nonprogrammed decision is some type of emergency). Some examples of nonprogrammed library decisions are decisions regarding remodeling or planning a new facility, purchasing a new automaton system, and selecting a new senior manager. On a personal/professional level, the decision whether to accept a new position or promotion is nonprogrammed.

You should not think of decision making as an "event." The vast majority of decisions develop over time. Yes, there is the moment of choice, but generally there is an elapse of time between knowing a decision is necessary and reaching the decision point. Even quick gut decisions usually draw upon some knowl-

CHECK THIS OUT

A good article addressing crisis decision making is Ken Naglewski's "Are You Ready to Make Effective Decisions When Disaster Strikes?" *(Journal of Private Equity* 9, no. 2: 45–51, 2006).

edge base. Research suggests that people who view decision making as a process rather than an event are more effective (Garvin and Roberto, 2001).

Knowing who should make a decision is essential to keeping things flowing. "Even in companies respected for their decisiveness, however, there can be ambiguity over who is accountable for their decisions. As a result, the entire decision-making process can stall" (Rogers and Blenko, 2006, p. 52). Assigning nonprogrammed decisions, as much as possible, to certain offices/positions will help avoid delays. The Rogers and Blenko (2006) article outlines how one can begin this process. One category of nonprogrammed decisions that must have careful thought is crisis/disaster management. (We discuss disaster preparedness in Chapter 19.)

STYLES OF DECISION MAKING

Management writers use a number of labels for decision-making styles. One major influence on your organizational decision-making style is your risk tolerance. A second factor is your "value" orientation, that is, how much importance you place on task/technical issues versus people/social issues. As with risk tolerance, there is a value continuum. It is possible to think of the two factors as axes on a grid (see Figure 7.1). One axis of the grid would represent tolerance of risk, and the other axis would be task and people. The lower left corner of the grid would be low-task/low-risk (1.1), the lower right corner would be high-task/low-risk (5.1), the upper left corner would be high-risk/low-task (1.5), and the upper right corner would be high-risk/high-task (5.5). Most individuals employ several styles of decision making, adjusting the style to the circumstances; however, they usually have a favored approach based on their past experiences.

A "directive style" would fall somewhere in the lower right quadrant of the grid. It is a style with low risk tolerance and places a high value on tasks. The

TRY THIS

Examine your decision styles by answering the following questions:

- How comfortable are you with uncertainty?
- How much "risk" do you usually take?
- Do you think and assess options or "just" decide?
- When there is a deadline, do you wait as long as possible or do you make the decision well in advance?
- When confronted with a "people versus thing" decision, which do you favor?
- When making a decision, do you seek advice whenever possible or only when necessary?
- How often do you regret a decision?

CHECK THESE OUT

Hayashi, Alden M. 2001. "When to Trust Your Gut." *Harvard Business Review* 79, no. 2: 59–65.

Meyer, David G. 2002. *Intuition: Its Powers and Perils.* New Haven, CT: Yale University Press.

---

style is practical or systematic in character. Another label for this approach is "reflective," although this label usually carries with it the implication of taking ample, sometimes seen as excessive, time to decide.

The "analytical style" (upper right quadrant) is another high task value approach but with a high risk tolerance. It can also be reflective in character, with a slightly greater speed in decision time.

FROM THE AUTHORS

One challenge, when it comes to decisions, is not to quickly think of a couple of options and then pick one. There are times when this is a good approach, such as with many programmed decisions. However, even when making a first-time programmed decision, some extra time and thought may well be beneficial.

When Evans teaches management courses, he always uses case study reports as a course component. As part of the discussion of what he considers an ideal report, he uses a PowerPoint slide depicting a perplexed individual standing in front of a coffee vending machine. (What could be more simple/programmed than buying a cup of coffee?) The perplexity arises from the fact that the machine, dispensing only caffeinated coffee, offers 24 choices, from plain black to two creams with one artificial sweetener. If you added a decaffeinated option the possibilities are in the forties.

Evans's point is, don't assume three or four options are all you ought to consider, especially in the workplace. As Hammond, Keeney, and Raiffa (2011) suggested, bad decisions come about in part when "the alternatives were not clearly defined" (p. 1).

Typically, even with the discussion about the fact that many options exist, the first student reports rarely contain more than eight or ten possibilities. After the class discussion of the first case, students see, from one another, that 20 or more possibilities exist. By the end of the case studies almost every report contains 20 to 30 options.

The "behavioral style" falls in the lower left quadrant. Its low-task/low-risk orientation can lead to decisions that are less decisive than some might wish. Occasionally, the people/social values lead to decisions that avoid conflict but do not solve the problem.

The fourth style is "conceptual," and it falls in the upper left quadrant. For some people, conceptual decisions lack a degree of practicality or seem hard to implement. This is because they are low-task/high-risk options.

Realistically, most peoples' styles fall somewhere in the middle of the grid—some balancing of risk and tasks/people (perhaps 3.3). A label for this style would be "consistent."

Another "style" that received recent attention is what one might call "reflexive" or "reactive." Other labels are "shooting from the hip" and "gut decisions." These labels describe making a quick decision based on limited information and looking for few alternatives. Stewart Thomas (2006) suggested that "the contest between rationality and gut instinct pervades the research on decision-making" (p. 12). Eric Bonabeau (2003) indicated that while increasing numbers of decision makers are doing so, it is not a good idea to "trust one's gut" when making key decisions. He described what he considers three major factors causing people to make the mistake of thinking/deciding based on instinct rather than on fact and assessment. First, as decisions become more complex, so do the number of alternatives that potentially can address the situation; developing and assessing more and more possibilities takes precious time. Second, as we all know, the volume of information grows faster than we are fully capable of processing. Finally, and perhaps most significantly, the time frame for making the decision keeps shrinking. While acknowledging that intuition has its place in the process, just as does one's conscience, Bonabeau (2003) claimed that thinking intuition can replace reason "is indulging in a risky delusion" (p. 116).

RATIONAL DECISION MAKING

Hundreds of books and articles discuss various aspects and models of rational decision making. The concept has value and has a place in decision-making, but it does have limitations. Herbert Simon (1976) noted that managers could never be 100 percent logically rational in their decision because of what he called "bounded rationality." Constraints (boundaries) on rational decision making are numerous; some of the obvious ones are time, money, information/data, conflicting goals/objectives, complexity, and even intellectual capability.

Rational decision making rests on three basic assumptions. The first assumption is that the decision is, or can be, made with complete information (Snowden and Boone's simple context)—thus there is no uncertainty/risk. (However, there is almost always some small risk even with simple decisions.) The second assumption is that the decision maker will be without bias or emotion and thus logical. (Unfortunately, none of us is without biases and personal values.) However, more or less bias-free decisions are possible for many organizational situations—at least for thing choices. When people issues are part of the picture, the risk of bias or emotion becoming a factor increases. The third assumption is that the decider knows the organization's future directions—thus the decision will be the "best" one possible. Predicting the future with any degree of accuracy is unlikely; thus what is "best" for today may not be best tomorrow.

PROBLEM SOLVING AND RATIONAL DECISION MAKING

Problem solving is the first step in almost any decision-making situation. You need to know the purpose for the decision. In essence, it helps you identify the desired outcome. Nooraie (2008) noted that "managers are faced with a multitude of problems every day. In order to solve the problems, they have to make decisions. To make too many decisions, too fast, about too many strange and unfamiliar problems introduces a new element into management" (p. 641). How individuals go about solving the multitude of problems is highly varied, as Taatgen (2011) wrote: "One of the challenges of understanding problem-solving is the sheer variety of strategies that people employ to solve a particular problem. Anyone who has investigated problem-solving through methods like protocol analysis can attest, it often seems as if every subject employs a different strategy" (p. 152). The result of all the variations is that there are many models for the process.

The most commonly used model consists of six steps. First, start by defining the situation requiring a decision (e.g., a problem, opportunity, or challenge). Second, determine the objective(s) that the decision must address. Third, gather information about the issue, and generate as many alternatives as possible—even those that might initially seem foolish. Fourth, evaluate each of the alternatives in terms of the decision objectives, and consider what might be possible consequences or outcomes if you implement each alternative. Fifth, carefully consider how the alternative would be implemented (e.g., people, time, and resources). Sixth, implement and monitor the "best" alternative.

SOMETHING TO CONSIDER

Consider the following about what constitutes a "successful decision." In baseball, a batter is thought to be successful when making the right decision (getting a hit) between 30 and 40 percent of the time. The player becomes a superstar if, throughout a career, the right decision took place about 40 percent of the time. For a brain surgeon, anything less than 100 percent success is a major problem. The vast majority of organizational managers make successful choices somewhere between the two extremes, but in reality they rarely get beyond 75 percent. Given the "bounded rationality" issues, this is an admirable level. Mistakes and wrong choices are a fact of managerial life; the goal is to limit them as much as possible.

Kepner and Tregoe (1965), among many writers on decision making, identified seven factors in analyzing (solving) problems. The following is a summary of their approach to problem analysis:

1. Assume that a standard of performance exists against which one can compare real performance. For most libraries, this statement usually reads, "There should be a standard of performance against which one can compare real performance." A decision-making or problem-solving situation arises when there is a difference between the actual and the desired results.

2. Determine whether a deviation from the standards has occurred, and determine the degree of deviation. Once managers establish standards, it becomes possible to monitor if and how much deviation occurs. Without a standard, managers may only have a sense that deviation exists, and staff members may or may not agree. Thus, standards save time and conflict.

3. Locate the point of deviation in the sequence of activities or in the situation. Frequently, it is more difficult to establish such a point than it might seem, especially when the deviation appears only in the finished product. The deviation may have entered the system at the very beginning, come into the system with the material itself, entered with a person somewhere during the processing sequence, or intruded into the presentation of the final product. The important thing is to correctly identify the source of deviation (a common problem with intuitive problem solving). Failure to identify the source correctly can create additional problems in terms of staff morale and trust.

4. Ascertain what distinguishes the affected group from the unaffected group. What constitutes the deviation? Once the manager carefully reviews what distinguishes the affected group from the unaffected group, the problem is almost solved.

5. Look for a change in the system. The change may be minor, or it may be in a related system; however, some type of change is causing the problematic deviation. The only exception to this rule is when one is testing a new system.

6. Analyze all possible causes that can be deduced from the relevant system changes. First, identify all changes in the system. Then, examine each change to determine if it could be the cause of the problem or if it is, in fact, the actual problem.

7. Take the cause that most exactly explains the facts, correct that point in the system, and test the system to see whether deviation continues to occur. If the deviation disappears, the proposed solution was correct; if not, continue to search for other potential causes. Managers ignore this step too often, which usually results in even more problems.

These seven steps can be very useful in solving problems—both job related and personal. Beginning information professionals should practice them on some simple problems until they become second nature.

Clearly, not every decision involves a problem, except under the broadest definition of problem. For example, selecting a method for providing selective dissemination of information to users is a problem only in the sense that there may be several good alternatives. A decision about how to handle a specific complaint from a user, on the other hand, may indeed be a problem situation. Even a manager's values and beliefs influence the problem he or she chooses on which to work. Guth and Tagiuri's (1965) research showed that managers, primarily motivated by economic values, prefer to make decisions about practical issues. Managers with a theoretical orientation prefer to work on long-term issues, such as planning and strategy. When the individuals have more political values, they tend to focus on competitive issues and on those that will likely be career enhancing

TYPES OF SOLUTIONS

Once a problem is identified, managers have options for solving it. Five of the more common solution methods are interim, adaptive, corrective, preventive, and contingency.

Interim solutions buy you time while you search for the cause of the problem. They will also buy time to implement long-term solutions. All too often, interim solutions have a way of becoming permanent or at least becoming long-term bandages.

Adaptive solutions do not really solve the problem, but they allow the organization to continue to function (or appear to function) somewhat normally. If an interim solution is a bandage, an adaptive solution is a plaster cast. It is often chosen in the hope that, with the application of a few cosmetic changes, the problem will take care of itself. Most job situations, unlike broken bones, do not heal themselves. More often than not, someone who glosses over a problem will find it coming back as a larger problem later.

Corrective solutions actually resolve the problem. Such solutions require time, effort, and careful analysis of the problem. Resolution is the ideal, and, if a system is to be healthy, the corrective solution is the one to seek.

Preventive solutions go back to Kepner and Tregoe's (1965) idea of exploring decisions for adverse consequences. In this way, you solve not only the problem at hand but also potential problems arising from the planned solution. This method takes even more time than finding a corrective solution, but it could repay its costs by allowing you more time in the future to devote to other management functions.

Contingency solutions simply involve the establishment of standby or emergency procedures to help offset the effects of a serious problem. Effective libraries typically have contingency plans for disasters, such as fires, earthquakes, and floods. Unfortunately, some managers do not make time to prepare such contingency plans. The issue is not if a disaster will strike, but only a question of when. While a disaster plan will not forestall a disaster, it will help keep the damage to a minimum.

DECISIONS AND ACCOUNTABILITY

Because most decision-making situations involve risk and unpredictability, we make wrong decisions from time to time. People who are afraid of making a mistake try to avoid making decisions in hopes of avoiding accountability for decisions that go wrong. From an organizational point of view, decision making normally calls for clear-cut accountability on someone's part. Accountability is one reason that committee decision making may well be problematic.

Some years ago the *Los Angeles Times* published a news story about a controversial committee decision. The University of California, like many U.S. academic institutions, employs numerous committees; some have decision-making authority. In the situation in question, there was concern regarding what high school courses would count toward meeting the university's English language entrance requirement. The university established a systemwide committee to make a decision about which high school courses would satisfy the freshman entrance requirements. Eventually, the university sent letters to California high schools announcing that journalism, speech, and drama courses would no longer be acceptable. Not surprisingly, there were objections to the decision, especially from high school journalism teachers. In an attempt to learn when and how the decision came about, a *Los Angeles Times* reporter interviewed the committee members who presumably made the decision as well as university officials, all of whom could not remember making such a decision. The reporter concluded the article by saying, "the result: a circle of accused, bemused, and slightly embarrassed designated decision makers in search of an important decision that no one says he made. And yet a decision was made. Minutes of a June 3 committee meeting of the statewide Academic Senate say so!" (Speich, 1976, p. 34).

Problems such as this occur in most organizations from time to time. Certainly, they occur most often when the organization makes extensive use of committees. However, you will also encounter situations in which the only decision maker involved remembers neither how, when, nor whether he or she made the decision. Unfortunately, the issue of ultimate accountability does not disappear.

TRY THIS

Think back to a major decision in your personal life. Do you consider that you made a good decision for yourself? For others involved? Do you feel that you are a good decision maker? Try to identify the reasons for your responses.

INDIVIDUAL AND GROUP DECISION-MAKING PROCESSES

Up to this point we have primarily addressed individual decision making. Although much of the discussion thus far also applies to group decision making, there are some special group process issues. If anything, group decision making is even more complex than individual decision making.

Ana Shetach (2009) noted that, in team environments, "decision-making and decision implementation are the heart of all team management activity, at all levels of organizational life. . . . A cardinal dilemma regarding efficient implementation is, therefore, how to verify in advance that a decision, one is about to take, is a good one, in terms of quality and applicability" (pp. 7–8). While there are aids for assessing potential decisions, you can never be totally confident that your ultimate choice is in fact "a good one." When it comes to group decisions, the uncertainly is even greater.

One important aspect of group decision making (committees and teams) is how the group views the process. Is it searching for the best outcome, or is it making a case? While this aspect also affects individuals, it becomes critical in the group setting. When a group views its purpose is to advocate for a case, there is often competition to see if a personal view can prevail. This type of atmosphere does not lend itself well to sound (or at least rapid) decision making. Strong personal views and hidden agendas can get in the way of meaningful and open exchanges while limiting the number of alternatives that are developed and considered

Another issue is that vigorous debate about positions or alternatives can generate some conflict. Here the fight, flight, and flow scale can come into play. In a group setting, it is likely that two, if not all three, of these behaviors will be present and thus will impact the group process and the quality of the decision reached. Conflict, in and of itself, is not the problem. It can be beneficial when it is cognitive rather than emotional in character. The challenge is to achieve the highest possible level of cognitive conflict and the lowest level of emotional conflict. One way to meet the challenge is to carefully frame the decision goals for the group. Another technique is to monitor the group—when emotions are running high, call a time-out for the group.

Groups can easily fall into the trap of "groupthink." Two factors frequently play a role in groupthink. Perhaps the most common factor is the desire to get or

CHECK THIS OUT

A good article that provides guidance on group decision making in a library environment is H. Frank Cervone's "Making Decisions: Methods for Digital Library Project Teams" (*OCLC Systems and Services* 21, no. 1: 30–35, 2005).

keep things moving along. This desire often results in a too quick decision made without much effort and without assessing multiple options. The second common factor is the desire to be a "team player"; this desire, too, can reduce options and very likely will limit thoughtful critical assessment or idea generation.

An interesting article about impasses in team decision making is Bob Frisch's (2008) "When Teams Can't Decide." Although his focus was senior management teams, his points apply to most team as well as committee settings. "Reaching collective decisions based on individual preferences is an imperfect science. Majority wishes can clash when a group of three or more people attempt to set priorities among three or more items" (p. 122). What can happen is a "voting paradox." The paradox was first identified by a French mathematician in the eighteenth century; solving it once and for all has not yet happened. The paradox arises even with apparently simple yes/no voting—there is always the third option, abstain.

Consider this example of a three-person team of librarians—Al, Betty, and Carol—charged with selecting one of three online databases—DB-1, DB-2, and DB-3. They decide they should each list their first, second, and third choices. The results could be a voting paradox (see Table 7.1) because three different people can have three different preferences. Any outside person (supervisor, department head, director) breaking the impasse will offend two-thirds of the committee, no matter what selection is taken; thus "the 'boss' is always wrong," at least in terms of voting paradoxes.

You might think such occurrences are rare; unfortunately, they happen rather often. You can take some steps to reduce the chances of a paradox occurring. Start by having a crystal clear outcome the group is to achieve—one database. Provide some nuanced options—such as, use document delivery to supply items not in the selected database. Suggest the group start with an open, frank discussion of each person's preferences—pros and cons. Theses steps will help but not ensure there will be no impasse.

Libraries increasingly are part of another group that makes decisions—a consortium. While all the elements and issues discussed thus far are in play with this type of group, some other issues complicate the matter further. First and foremost, unlike internal group decisions, in consortial decision making there is rarely a single person "in charge" of the decision (in case of an impasse). Thus, accountability is very vague at best. Also, the choices for action, for a library concerned about a decision, are limited—accept and hope,

TABLE 7.1   Voting Paradox

	1st Choice	2nd Choice	3rd Choice
Al	DB-1	DB-2	DB-3
Betty	DB-2	DB-3	DB-1
Carol	DB-3	DB-1	DB-2

pull out of the group, or fight to reverse the decision and, perhaps, risk breaking up the group.

Generally within consortia and similar groups, decisions become a situation in which concessions and consensus are the keys to a resolution. Another "C" for such decision making is consideration—one may not always get what one would like—if the group is to succeed. A final "C," often the most significant, is coalitions. In many ways, coalitions assist in moving matters forward, as they normally reduce the number of variables in play with a large group.

A major challenge for consortia is determining what is "best." The number of bests is substantially greater in a consortial environment than for a single library. There are the bests for each institution, the bests for coalitions, and, of course, the bests for the group as a whole.

Building trust is always a factor in group decision making, but it becomes a significant challenge for consortial members because they spend less time together than internal groups. Time is a key factor in creating trust, and it is limited in consortial situations. A related factor is that, more often than not, institutional representatives at such meetings are senior, if not the senior manager. Generally such people are not used to having their views openly challenged, which they may be in a consortial setting.

Time together, trust, concessions, and consensus are the key elements for successful consortial decision making.

DECISION AIDS

Many techniques exist to aid the decision maker in selecting the best alternative. Some of these techniques are quantitative in nature; other methods are qualitative. Qualitative techniques are useful in assessing those elements in a decision-making situation that are value oriented. Almost all decision making has some value elements, but those that relate to customer service and/or involve ethical situations can benefit from qualitative techniques. "Thing" decisions benefit most from quantitative methods.

CHECK THIS OUT

An outstanding article, if complex for those uncomfortable with quantitative methods, is Robert M. Hayes's "Cooperative Game: Theoretic Models for Decision-Making in the Context of Library Cooperation" (*Library Trends* 51, no. 3: 441–461, 2003).

QUANTITATIVE TECHNIQUES

Libraries face ever-increasing pressure to be accountable. One very valuable tool to demonstrate accountability is hard data. Such hard data as percentage of

CHECK THIS OUT

Jeffrey Pfeffer and Robert Sutton (2011) wrote a good overview of what evidenced-based management is and is not: "Evidenced-Based Management." In *Harvard Business Review on Making Smart Decisions*, 75–107. Cambridge, MA: Harvard Business Review Press.

increased usage, number of reference questions answered, and number of documents delivered are also useful in making decisions. Without question, decisions informed with hard data (evidence based) carry greater credibility than those not so informed (anecdotal based). An integrated library system (ILS) can provide a wealth of data; but without a plan for how to use the information, the data can be overwhelming. As Caroline Cummins (2006) stated, "making sense of the data lurking in the ILS is crucial" (p. 14). Hiller and Self (2004) defined data as "records of observations, facts, or information collected for reference or analysis" (p. 129). ILSs are capable of providing an ocean of data; the good news is that most major vendors offer packages that make it possible for the decision maker to organize and analyze the data.

A somewhat new concept is data mining, sometimes labeled "bibliomining" in a library context (Nicholson, 2006). A short definition of data mining is the identification of new, useful patterns and trends in large quantities of data through the use of statistical and mathematical techniques. (Computing power is what has made this a cost-effective technique even for small institutions.) A common use of the methodology is pattern recognition/description and prediction. Koontz and Jue (2004) describe a form of data mining from the Public Library Geographic Database. They identify several possible "questions" that one might address using the database, such as the relationships among collection usage, community demographics, and the number/percentage of U.S. public

CHECK THESE OUT

A good overview of EBL (evidenced-based librarianship), along with an annotated bibliography on the concept, is Susan N. Lerdal's "Evidence-Based Librarianship: Opportunity for Law Librarians?" (*Law Library Journal* 98, no. 1: 33–60, 2006). Mari Davis, Concepcion Wilson, and Anne Horn's "Informing Decision-Making in Libraries: Information Research Input to LIS Education and Practice" (*Australian Academic and Research Libraries* 36, no. 4: 195–213, 2005) is a thoughtful article that relates to decision making, data, accountability, and libraries.

libraries that serve areas with more than a 25 percent poverty level. The article has some exercises for exploring the potential of the database and the concept of data mining.

Other quantitative aids are useful as well, including linear programming, simulation modeling, queuing theory, decision tree, matrix algebra, and linear mathematical equations—all forms of operational research techniques. To use linear programming, the circumstances must meet several conditions. First, there must be a definite objective, and the manager must be able to express the objective in a quantifiable way: money, time, or quantity. Second, the variables that will affect the outcome must have a linear relationship. Third, restrictions on variables must be present (otherwise, this approach would not be necessary). Linear programming is very mechanical; most library processes do not have a linear relationship. Even in the circulation of items in the collection—the most obvious place to apply the technique—there are enough variations in terms of work to make the application of quantifiable methods difficult.

Simulation model techniques attempt to carry out a solution in a controlled environment. The researcher or decision maker creates a model representing some aspects of the real-world situation and subjects the model to various changes, one at a time, to determine what might happen. The simulation model attempts to trace changes in activities as variables come into play. It attempts to quantify the behavioral and nonlogical attributes of a situation. The Monte Carlo technique is a simulation model in which the goal is to control chance. Random sampling helps to simulate natural events and to establish the probability of each of several outcomes. This type of simulation assists in answering a variety of questions: What are the chances of an event actually happening? Which of the alternative decisions appears to be best? What are the probabilities of a breakdown in a given unit or in a class of equipment? In the case of libraries, the use of this method can assist in decisions related to technology, new services, and changes in service.

Queuing theory deals with the length of time it takes to render a service or to process something. For instance, how long must staff, customers, and equipment remain idle because of an inefficient physical arrangement? Combining queuing theory and the Monte Carlo approach, a manager can determine expected arrival rates in a facility and the anticipated delay that arrival will generate. This approach could be quite valuable in a heavily used customer area (e.g., an academic library's reserve room or a public library's reference room) in determining staffing patterns in a way that will meet demands most efficiently.

A technique that any library manager can use is a decision tree, which presents a graphical representation of different alternative decisions. It helps the manager understand the consequences of implementing different decisions. Successful use of decision trees depends on the careful analysis of the situation and the examination of a variety of options.

An example of how a decision tree might apply to a library situation is the problem of how to increase access to a growing volume of serial publications in an environment of limited funding. A library might consider four broad options:

- Subscribe to all the desired journals in hard copy.
- Expand traditional interlibrary loan and document delivery services.
- Subscribe to online databases, and drop paper-based titles in the online resources.
- Subscribe to on-demand document delivery service for access to necessary articles with users ordering directly (perhaps paying the requisite fee).

Each option has consequences in terms of staffing, equipment, budget, customer satisfaction, and, perhaps, cost of services passed on to customers. By developing a decision tree and/or decision matrix (which incorporates the concept of probability of an event happening), the decision makers are provided with a picture of the outcomes.

Knowledge of basic statistics is one of the manager's tools that come into play rather often, especially when trying to keep current with the literature. If you do not think that your knowledge is up to par, make sure that you study basic statistics. Not all textbooks present statistical topics in the same way. Find one that you feel comfortable with, and purchase a copy to keep close at hand in your office.

QUALITATIVE TECHNIQUES

Because of the inability to validate ethical (value) judgments objectively, managers must ask a very basic question concerning the values employed: Whose standard of correctness should be employed? Another factor is that decision making often appears to be an unconscious activity because it is one that goes on continuously in everyone's life. The steps that we outlined earlier can help bring this process to a more conscious level and perhaps improve the quality of the decisions being made.

Consider the issue of whether to charge "outside" users a fee for accessing library online databases. (We are assuming the library knows that its license agreements would not preclude this if the fees are shared with the vendor.) An unlikely approach would be simply "to decide" to impose a fee. A more likely approach would be to attempt to use the quantitative methods previously outlined. Such an approach would help identify the major variables and assist in

CHECK THIS OUT

Decision aids often lead to the formulation of decision rules, such as how to allocate funds. Donald Conlon, Christopher D. Porter, and Judi McLean Parks's "The Fairness of Decision Rules" (*Journal of Management* 30, no. 3: 329–349, 2004) is an interesting article that explores the value of such rules.

weighing the alternatives. But neither approach will resolve the ethical (value) conflicts that will arise; and the ethical considerations often determine the final disposition of a matter. Thus, the hypothetical manager may have determined demands on the library's resources by "outsiders," the cost of providing the service, and an equitable fee (based on demand and cost). However, the basic question of deciding whether to charge a fee remains unanswered. Some of the qualitative questions to answer are: Would creation of a service fee hurt the library's relations with its users? Would it hurt the public relations of the institution of which the library is a part? Would continuing free service lead to greater support of the institution and the library? Would a service fee be contrary to public welfare? To whom is the library obligated (if publicly supported) to provide free service and under what circumstances? Every answer involves a value judgment.

KEY POINTS TO REMEMBER

- Careers are made or broken by the quality of decisions made.
- Decision outcomes are rarely completely certain or risk free.
- Decisions are either programmed or nonprogrammed.
- Programmed decision making takes place daily at all levels of the organization.
- Nonprogrammed decisions carry the greatest uncertainty and risk.
- Understanding decision-making and problem-solving processes is a managerial asset.
- Rational decision making, despite its limitations, is a useful tool.
- Decision making carries with it accountability.
- Group/team decision making is more complex than individual decision making.
- Consortial decisions involve the four Cs: concessions, consensus, consideration, and coalitions.
- Decision aids are both quantitative and qualitative in character.

References

Bonabeau, Eric. 2003. "Don't Trust Your Gut." *Harvard Business Review* 81, no. 5: 116–123.

Buchanan, Leigh, and Andrew O'Connell. 2006. "A Brief History of Decision Making." *Harvard Business Review* 84, no. 1: 32–41.

Cummins, Caroline. 2006. "Below the Surface." *Library Journal* (Net Connect Supplement), Winter: 12–14.

Emery, Fred, and Eric Trist. 1965. "The Causal Texture of Organizational Environments." *Human Relations* 18, no. 1: 21–31.

Frisch, Bob. 2008. "When Teams Can't Decide." *Harvard Business Review* 86, no. 11: 121–126.

Garvin, David A., and Michael A. Roberto. 2001. "What You Don't Know about Making Decisions." *Harvard Business Review* 79, no. 8: 108–116.

Guth, William, and Rento Tagiuri. 1965. "Personal Values and Corporate Strategy." *Harvard Business Review* 37 (September–October): 123–132.

Hammond, John S., Ralph L. Keeney, and Howard Raiffa. 2011. "The Hidden Traps in Decision-Making." In *Harvard Business Review on Making Smart Decisions*, 1–27. Cambridge, MA: Harvard Business Review Press.

Hiller, Steve, and James Self. 2004. "From Measurement to Management: Using Data Wisely for Planning and Decision-Making." *Library Trends* 53, no. 1: 129–155.

Hopkins, Michael S. 2010. "Putting the Science in Management Science?" *MIT Sloan Management Review* 51, no. 3: 1–4.

Kepner, Charles H., and Benjamin B. Tregoe. 1965. *The Rational Manager*. New York: McGraw-Hill.

Koontz, Christie, and Dean K. Jue. 2004. "Customer Data 24/7 Aids Library Planning and Decision-Making." *Florida Libraries* 47, no. 1: 17–19.

Mintzberg, Henry. 1976. "Planning on the Left Side and Managing on the Right." *Harvard Business Review* 54, no. 4: 49–58.

Nicholson, Scott. 2006. "Proof in the Pattern." *Library Journal* 131 (Supplement January): 2–4, 6.

Nooraie, Mahmood. 2008. "Decision Magnitude of Impact and Strategic Decision-Making Process Output." *Management Decisions* 46, no. 4: 640–655.

Priem, Richard L., Bruce A. Walters, and Sali Li. 2011. "Decisions, Decisions!" *Journal of Management* 37, no. 2: 553–580.

Rogers, Paul, and Marcia Blenko. 2006. "Who Has the D?" *Harvard Business Review* 84, no. 1: 52–61.

Shetach, Ana. 2009. "The Revised Decision-Square Model (RDSM): A Tool for Effective Decision Implementation in Teams." *Team Performance Management* 15, nos. 1/2: 2–17.

Simon, Herbert. 1976. *Administrative Behavior*. 3rd ed. New York: Free Press.

Snowden, David J., and Mary E. Boone. 2007. "A Leader's Framework for Decision-Making." *Harvard Business Review* 85, no. 11: 68–76.

Speich, Daniel. 1976. "English Ruling: UC Decisions Sometimes Just Seem to Happen." *Los Angeles Times*, November 14 (pt. 1): 34.

Taatgen, Niels. 2011. "The Minimal Control Principle Predicts Strategy Shifts in the Abstract Decision-Making Task." *Journal of Problem Solving* 3, no. 2: 151–166.

Thomas, Stewart. 2006. "Did You Ever Have to Make Up Your Mind?" *Harvard Business Review* 84, no. 1: 12.

Tichy, Noel M., and Warren G. Bennis. 2007. "Making Judgment Calls: The Ultimate Act of Leadership." *Harvard Business Review* 85, no. 10: 94–102.

Launching Pad

Bazerman, Max H. 2006. *Judgment in Managerial Decision-Making*. 6th ed. New York: Wiley.

Beghtol, Carol. 2005. "Ethical Decision-Making for Knowledge Representation and Organization Systems for Global Use." *Journal of the Society for Information Science and Technology* 56, no. 9: 903–912.

Foudy, Gerri, and Alesia McManus. 2005. "Using a Decision Grid Process to Build Consensus in Electronic Resources Cancellation Decisions." *Journal of Academic Librarianship* 31, no. 6: 533–538.

Koontz, Scott. 2003. "The Bibliomining Process: Data Warehousing and Data Mining for Library Decision-Making." *Information Technology and Libraries* 22, no. 4: 146–151.

Mankins, Michael C., and Richard Steele. 2006. "Stop Making Plans: Start Making Decisions." *Harvard Business Review* 84, no. 1: 76–84.

Paul, Souren, Carol Stoak Saunders, and William David Haseman. 2005. "A Question of Timing: The Impact of Information Acquisition on Group Decision-Making." *Information Resources Management Journal* 18, no. 4: 81–100.

Schachter, Debbie. 2006. "The Importance of Good Decision-Making." *Information Outlook* 10, no. 4: 12–13.

Smith, Jim, Ray Wyatt, and Peter E. D. Love. 2008. "Key Decision-Making Attributes for Project Inception." *Facilities* 26, nos. 7/8: 289–309.

Welch, David A. 2001. *Decisions, Decisions: The Art of Effective Decision-Making.* Amherst, NY: Prometheus Books.

Before I became a librarian, I studied music—classical flute, to be exact. And, I learned the value of practicing anything that was important enough to play for others. In fact, it was all those hours in the practice room that made me realize I wanted to be a librarian!

Today, I still practice anything I want to share with others. I practice speeches in front of the mirror; I review talking points for the media; and I even go over important conversations I want to have with others—in my mind, beforehand.

I have learned that effective communication must contain at least 4 key elements: 1) Clarity, 2) Conciseness, 3) Advance preparation, and 4) Respect for the person receiving the message.

In my library career, I have had the opportunity to communicate with colleagues, friends, employees, superiors, government officials, the media, and the general public—at all levels, and in several languages. Knowing the message that I want to convey beforehand—and how I want to present it—has helped me become a more effective communicator in almost any setting.

And, if all else fails—I can still play a tune on the flute!

—Carol Brey-Casiano, ALA President, 2004–2005 (2012)

Talk is easy. Everybody talks. The question is, how can you make your words count? How can you *really* communicate with others?

—John C. Maxwell (2010)

Communication is the foundation for successful human interaction regardless of the setting in which it occurs. As we advance in an increasingly complex work environment, the importance of organizational communication as a driver of success becomes profound as well.

—Joan F. Marques (2010)

Our society has perhaps degraded communication to some extent by lessening the value of face to face contact and simultaneously putting technology utilized for communications on a pedestal. What do we lose when we don't communicate face to face any more?

—Richard Moniz (2011)

8

COMMUNICATING

This chapter focuses on the following:

- The importance of communication skills for effective managers
- The communication process/model
- Organizational communication issues
- Generational communication preferences
- What people need to know to do their jobs
- Principles of effective communication
- Technology issues in communication
- Listening as a key skill

PICKING THE RIGHT CHANNEL FOR YOUR MESSAGE

Almost everyone can talk and hear; with all due respect to John Maxwell (2010), some people are mute and some are deaf, and they also find ways to communicate. Most of us talk, listen, and read every day. Because these activities are second nature to us, we rarely think much about how well we perform them. The reality is, in most cases, we could do better with one or more of them if we knew how to improve them. As John Maxwell (2010) suggested, "Connecting is something anyone can learn to do, but one must study communication to improve it" (p. 96).

In our personal lives, it may not matter too much how good we are at communicating—things might be more pleasant if we could communicate better, but this is not critical to our well-being. However, in the workplace it matters very much. It is something of a toss up whether your decision making or your communication skills are more important to your long-term career success. Both are significant; probably for a new manager/supervisor, the communication skills or lack thereof are most quickly apparent. When a manager is lacking something in his or her communication skills, workplace colleagues quickly notice and begin to doubt other abilities.

Richard Moniz's opening quotation suggests that today there is a lessening concern about face-to-face communication, much less how effective it is when we do do it. Certainly among today's young people, the focus is on keeping in touch technologically. It is also true we are increasingly dependent on technology for workplace communication. However, we engage in face-to-face interactions with both our work colleagues as well as our users, and we must be effective in these interactions

Years ago, David Berlo (1960) estimated that more than 70 percent of the average person's time was spent in listening, speaking, reading, and writing. Considering the messages that are occasionally sent and received solely by nonverbal means and adding in a person's nonverbal (observation) time, the total time is much greater. In 2005, Elway Research (http://elwayresearch.com) claimed each of us experiences more than 30,000 "messages" a day. Its count included everything, such as ads on television, in the newspaper, on the radio, on billboards and other signs, and so forth. Of that gross number, we probably don't need to pay attention to more than 10 to 20 percent. Whatever the percentage may actually be, it is likely a large number. The remaining balance is very large, and the point is that we do not pay any attention to them. Getting and holding attention to organizational messages as well as workplace efforts to communicate are important. Knowing how to create attention-getting messages requires an understanding of the communication process.

During your career, three communication skills will stand out and impact your progress—oral, written, and listening. The first two skills get attention much more frequently than does the last one. In many ways, it is the last one that separates the great manager from the good manager. There is a significant difference between hearing and listening. Listening is a skill that you must practice to develop it effectively. We address this issue later in the chapter.

Ralph Waldo Emerson supposedly said, "Communication is like a piece of driftwood in a sea of conflicting currents. Sometimes the shore will be littered with debris; sometimes it will be bare. The amount and direction of movement is neither aimless nor nondirectional at all, but is a response to all the forces, winds, and tides or currents that come into play." Library staff must think about both internal and external communication. The "currents and tides" can become obstacles to effective communication. Library communication activities should not be pieces of driftwood; rather, they should be targeted and appropriate for the intended audience.

Despite the attention, energy, and time devoted to the communication process, it sometimes ends in failure—if success means complete agreement on the intended and perceived meanings of the message. Certainly, more often

---

TRY THIS

Keep a diary for the next few days, and jot down the time you spend in communicating and the methods used. Separate the time for study or work and other activities. See how study/work activities take place in "free time" and vice versa.

ADVISORY BOARD EXPERIENCE

Carol Sinwell shared the following general thoughts about communication:

> Library administrators have to communicate in so many directions, and I would say that public and community colleges experience the greatest challenges as their service communities are the most diverse in almost all demographic categories. One challenge is in identifying and understanding "how to get your message across" to different people, both within and outside of the library.
>
> An example of the internal issue is, I had a colleague completely lose staff support or even to listen to her because she was insistent she was always right and they just had to do it her way. I tried to teach her that her message may have been factually correct but that was not what her message was conveying and she needed to rethink her approach. There was some improvement; however, she really saw little point in taking it seriously as the staff should "understand."

than not the general sense gets through, but not its precise meaning. Given all the potential problems in communicating, it is perhaps surprising that people are able to communicate and work together as well as they do.

COMMUNICATION PROCESS

To understand the challenges in communication, it helps to have knowledge of the basic communication model and the issues associated with that model. When individuals understand the effects of their communication habits, they become better at getting their intentions through to others and having them understood.

Figure 8.1 (p. 182) provides a visual representation of the communication process as well as some of the factors that create difficulties for effective communication. At its simplest level, a "message" has a source and a receiver. There may be times in our personal lives that communication is as simple as this—I say dinner is ready, and you come and sit down at the table. In the workplace, it is never this simple.

For the vast majority of all our communication efforts, the center line of boxes in Figure 8.1 represents the fundamental process. Think of yourself as the "source"—you select the words (encoding) that create your "message." You pick a "channel" (face-to-face, memo, e-mail, texting, etc.). Your receiver(s) decode the message and give it a meaning. It is a surprisingly complex process, as a host of factors can interact at each step that can result in the sender's

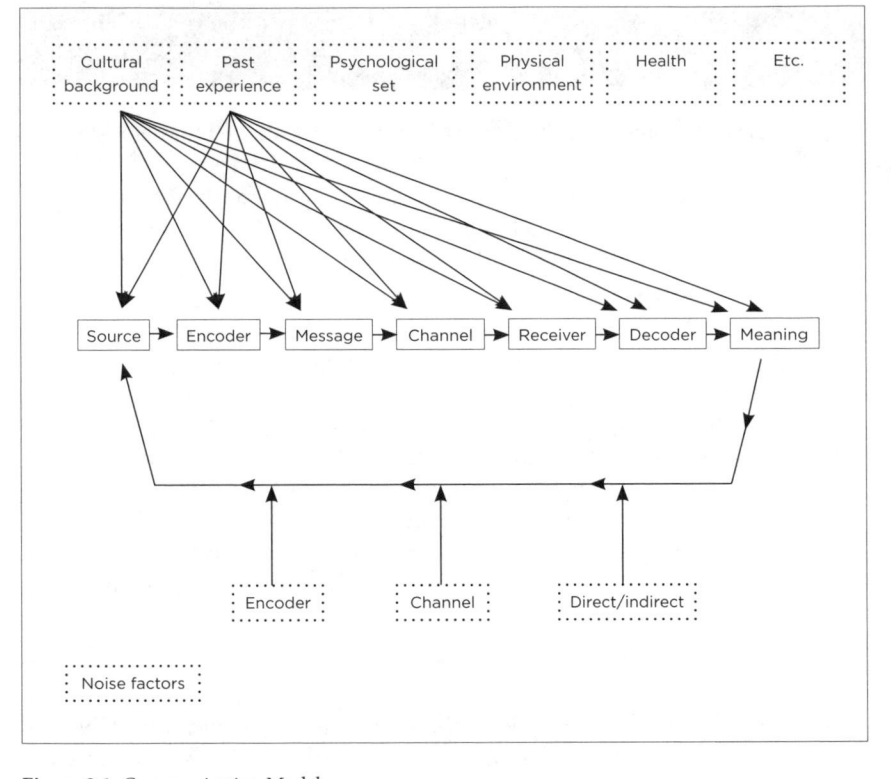

Figure 8.1 Communication Model

intended meaning being rather different from the receiver's interpretation of the meaning.

Above and below the boxes in Figure 8.1 are "noise factors" that can lead to different intended and perceived meanings. (Note that there are many more factors than we could put into the figure and still have it readable; we included enough to make it clear that the factors can cause problems throughout the process.) Feedback is a critical element for there to be effective communication. In our simple statement, "dinner is ready," your coming and sitting down is feedback. I know you heard and understood the message. Had you not done

TRY THIS

Drawing on your own experience, list four or five barriers to understanding in a library. Can you identify three experiences that have shaped your ideas and values?

TIP

Keep in mind that people from different cultures may have varying approaches to authority. Some may feel it is inappropriate to question a statement made by someone whom they perceive is in an "authority role," which affects meaning and how the message is understood. The extra time spent verifying messages results in better performance and better relations and, in the long run, saves the library time and money.

so the feedback would let me know something failed in the process. For managers and supervisors, feedback is essential in knowing if the message arrived and how it was interpreted. All of the "noise factors" shown in the Figure 8.1 can impact the feedback loop, not just the three we have in the bottom row. Any one of them can distort the intended meaning. Certainly most messages are more or less understood at least well enough to move on; however, the danger of misinterpretation is always lurking in the background. The more complex the message, the greater the danger is.

Returning to the center line of boxes in Figure 8.1, there are many semantic issues that further complicate our efforts to communicate effectively. These are three key ones that impact our word choices for encoding: words are not the thing they represent; words never cover everything about anything; we use words about words with ever-growing abstraction.

We learn the meaning of words through life experiences. When we encounter a new word, some of us look it up in a dictionary; however, many more of us just ignore it. Usually no great harm comes from not knowing the word's meaning, but not always. The more abstract the word, the greater the chances are some people will not understand the message. Using jargon—unless you *know* the receiver will understand—is a good way to have the message misunderstood. Will the user really know what to do when you say, "you can look it up in the OPAC?"

REMEMBER

The English language exists in very many different versions—what may be clear to a person in the United States may not be clear to colleagues in Canada, the United Kingdom, or Australia. A "redundant" job in the United States may be boring but it is a job; in the other countries it means becoming unemployed.

BULLETIN 79-12

SUBJECT: Summer comfort

REMARKS:

1. Because of the necessity for energy conservation measures, temperatures must be maintained at somewhat higher levels during the summer months than has been the practice in the past. Accordingly, in the interests of good health and on-the-job effectiveness, employees should dress comfortably within the limits of good taste.

2. For male employees, neat-looking, open-neck short-sleeve dress shirts are appropriate. Of course, there will be occasions or situations when coats and neckties would be more suitable and should be worn. Similarly, female employees should feel free to wear neat, comfortable clothes.

3. This attention to added comfort does not diminish the responsibility of every employee to dress in a manner that is considerate of fellow employees and suitable for a government facility, nor does it modify existing requirements with respect to the wearing of uniforms.

4. Those employees who have questions concerning the appropriateness of clothing should discuss them with their immediate supervisors. Supervisors are responsible for ensuring that employees dress appropriately and should not allow inappropriate attire in areas they supervise.

5. You are reminded that we can minimize the impact of higher summer temperatures by observing and controlling our work environment through measures such as:

   a. Closing blinds.

   b. Keeping corridor doors closed.

   c. Turning off lights in rooms with adequate natural light.

   d. Turning off lights in unoccupied areas.

   e. Turning off electrical equipment when it is not being used.

6. Authority: Director's letter IL 4-6-12

Figure 8.2 Example of a Vague Staff Memo

An important part of our learning word meanings comes from our upbringing and attitudes about word choices—an example is someone using "fancy" words (many syllables). Depending on our cultural and/or past experiences, we may perceive a person who uses "fancy" words as, for example, untrustworthy, highly educated, or a show-off. Early learning experiences do carry forward and color our interpretations of messages received.

Bartlett (1951) suggested that the mind constantly tries to link new materials into the existing mental patterns in order to make the new material meaningful. The relating of new information to old, unstated preconceptions can create major psychological stumbling blocks to effective communication.

DATE: 1 May 2012
TO: Reference Librarians
FROM: JKL
SUBJECT: Night Work

REMARKS: At present Circulation is minus aides; so is Serials. Therefore it will be necessary for the Reference Librarians to be more active in the closing routine. If there is not an aide available and even if there is, please be helpful and place the current issues of the magazines on the slant shelves. Do not pile them up in the microfilm area. Do not put information file material in the microfilm area. Be responsible and do your part. You are lucky to be employed the way things are. Read and initial.

Figure 8.3 Example of a Blunt Staff Memo

Many common words have multiple meanings, and their intended meaning depends on their context. For example, a word employed many times in the workplace, "fair," has 34 meanings according to *Webster's Third New International Dictionary*. Will your staff know just what you intend to convey when you use a particular word? Chances are they will not know the first few times you do so; in time, with shared experiences, they will have a basis for knowing. Shared workplace experiences are an important element in gaining better and better communication. Thus, when you are new to the group, take more time and give deeper thought to what you wish to convey before you start.

Figure 8.2 (p. 184) is an example of a memo that was subject to wide interpretation because of word choice (encoding). Just what did the writer intend by such words and phrases as "comfortable," "appropriate," "good taste," and "neat"? Shorts are comfortable; in hot weather they are appropriate; they can be "designer shorts," which surely are in good taste; and they can be neat. Even when the writer made an effort to be specific—"open-neck short-sleeve dress shirts"; what is a "dress shirt"?—the memo generated several weeks of staff discussion and debate about what was and was not allowable.

Another example of a problematically encoded memo is Figure 8.3. In this case, the intended and perceived meanings were worlds apart. According to the memo writer, his intent was to be funny. Not surprisingly, the staff not only failed to see any humor but felt threatened. This is an example of where "noise" played a major role in how the staff interpreted the content. At the time, the economy was in deep recession, unemployment near all-time highs, and many government agencies were laying off personnel.

The emotional state of the individual is a factor as well. Staff members who are anxious or worried about something can be extra-sensitive to what they

---

ADVISORY BOARD EXPERIENCE

Carol Sinwell shared the following general thoughts about communication challenges:

> Library administrators have to communicate in so many directions. In both my public and community college experiences I have found one of the greatest challenges to be "how to get your message across" to different populations (age, culture) both within as well as outside of the library. Managers need to finesse conversations with senior management when addressing library issues; at the same time they need to be able to converse with staff about operational issues. The most important conversations are those that show a personal interest in each staff person.
>
> An example of a miscommunication scenario: I had a management colleague completely lose staff support because she insisted she was always right; i.e., staff just had to do it her way. She asked for my advice. I explained that while she may have all the academic or factual knowledge needed to accomplish a task, she needed to have her staff on board to implement programs. I suggested she rethink her approach to include having conversations with staff that showed respect for their expertise and input. At the same time, her direct supervisor required her to attend "effective communication" seminars/training. She attended several sessions but saw little point in taking it seriously. She continued to say staff should just accept what she said and do it. Senior management finally moved her out of a personnel supervisory role and finally out of the organization.

---

perceive as a hidden meaning in a chance statement you might make—oral or written. An effective communicator takes into consideration expectations and anxieties (especially if they are at a high level) when preparing any message.

The way in which you say something—emphasis, lack of emphasis, omissions, and order of presentation—also influences meaning. Only when you have had some experience working with the same people will the meanings of their word order, tone of voice, facial expressions, and other nonverbal characteristics be clear. This understanding is not always possible to achieve; so it is best to remain constantly alert to these points, no matter how well the parties involved think they know one another. It is an essential factor to consider in team settings.

AUTHORS' EXPERIENCE

Alire, in each library deanship she held, made it a practice, upon her arrival as the new dean, to communicate immediately her personal philosophy about professionalism to all library employees. That is, she explained that professionalism was a state of mind. It did not depend on whether one had a professional degree (MLS or higher) but on how employees handled themselves with library customers/users and with each other. She made it clear that she expected all employees to be professional. With that in mind, she ensured that paraprofessionals were included on task forces, committees, special projects, and so forth, based on their expertise or as a representative of the support staff, as appropriate.

ORGANIZATIONAL BARRIERS TO COMMUNICATION

The organizational structure of the library can influence the way in which staff interpret messages. A large archive or library is a series of overlapping and interdependent units, each with its own immediate and long-range objectives and managers. Each manager has her or his preferred managerial style. So members in each unit first interpret messages in light of their shared experiences; only after they finish that assessment do they take a broader view.

Bartels and colleagues (2010) noted, "Insight into the existence of different identities within an organisation is critical to managing communication therein. Identifying with one's profession is not the same as identifying with the entire organisation; encouraging participation in decision-making and supplying adequate information can contribute to making employees identify more strongly with the organisation as a whole" (p. 221). Too strong a professional identification in libraries can lead to tensions between librarians and the rest of the staff, which in turn hinder effective communication and cooperation.

Work relationships, authority structure, and status also impact the communication process by influencing people's expectations regarding who should communicate with whom, about what, and in what way. We have found that varying interpretations of relationships within an organization also cause communication failures. These are then magnified by the continuous flux of personal as well as professional relationships within the library; you cannot even count on consistent misinterpretation.

GENERATIONAL COMMUNICATION PREFERENCES

Today's workplace is perhaps the most diverse in terms of number of generations working together. Older staff members, who might well have retired in the past by this time, are staying on the job as a result of the recent deep recession and

FROM THE AUTHORS

Early in his career Evans worked with an academic vice president who used a method for communicating with his "reports" (the individuals who reported directly to him)—it worked well then, and Evans used it during the rest of his career.

The approach Evans always took with his direct reports consisted of having a discussion with each person about her or his information needs from Evans as early as possible in the working relationship. There was always a significant difference among the individuals regarding what they thought was necessary and what was "information overload." Some were of the "just give me the facts" type, and others wanted great detail. The approach allowed Evans to tailor his style for each person. Ninety-nine percent of the time there were no surprises, and communication flowed smoothly. Evans also made it clear in those sessions what he expected in the way of information from them. Evans's first priority was not to get "blindsided."

slow economic recovery. Retirement funds were reduced by huge amounts, and one of the mainstays of retirement support—a person's home—lost major value. Thus, it is common for libraries to have three and sometimes four generations on the staff. The different generations have different views about communication and how to carry out such efforts. Having an understanding of the preferences will improve library communication. Hammill (2005) described generational differences in managing four generations; Table 8.1 (p. 189) draws on his observations concerning workplace communication. There is also a question of language. The "new" language, texting, can be confusing to the older generations or to anyone not actively using that channel.

COMMUNICATION NEEDS

One ongoing communication challenge for managers, at all levels, is being able to strike the appropriate balance between providing too much and not enough information. In medium-sized and large library staffs, a manager will never be

TRY THIS

Reflect on the communication needs of library users, drawing on your experience of using a university library. Write down six needs that are important to you.

TABLE 8.1   Workplace Communication across the Generations

	Veterans (1922–1945)	Baby Boomers (1946–1964)	Generation X (1965–1980)	Generation Y (1981–2000)
Communication media	Rotary phone One-on-one Written memo	Touch-tone phones "Call me anytime"	Cell phones "Call me only at work"	Internet Picture phones E-mail
Communications	Formal memo	In person	Direct Immediate	E-mail Voice mail Social media Social networks

able to satisfy everyone; some people will want more, and others will want less. This is similar to staff meetings; some individuals think there too many, and some think there are too few. You try for the middle ground and see what the results are and then adjust with more or less information.

Both time and feedback are necessary for effective communication on the job. People need time to get to know one another and to start building a base of shared experiences and meanings. Staff need to understand "the way we do it here." Different organizational cultures produce their own accepted practices. Knowing when a written message is expected and whether it should be paper or electronic or when a phone message is sufficient are some examples of the value that time and shared experiences bring to organizational communication. Each library has its practices, and they are often not explicitly described.

Time is important in another way. You should always provide sufficient time for the staff to assimilate messages. This can be challenging given the way that communication has speeded up in today's workplace. Needless to say, this is critical when changes are involved. There needs to be adequate time for feedback from the staff. Certainly there are urgent situations when time is of the essence and feedback is not possible. However, those are, or should be, rare instances, and planning and thinking about how and when to communicate should almost always have feedback time factored in.

PRINCIPLES OF EFFECTIVE ORGANIZATIONAL COMMUNICATION

Table 8.2 (p. 190) demonstrates how almost any management issue (budget, staffing, decision making, organization policy and procedures, customers, and so on) may generate a communication problem. It also illustrates the importance of communication to good management. This table was compiled from the input of working librarians, not academic researchers—people reporting their real frustrations

TABLE 8.2 Principles of Effective Organizational Communication

General Principles	Basic Organizational Communication Needs	Specific Communication Needs of Staff
• Get information out before the fact rather than during or after the fact. • Identify and communicate problem areas in order to provide guidance and assistance in resolving problems before they reach the crisis stage. • Define what is confidential. • Overcome "personality" blocks in communication. • Coach staff members in interpersonal communication. • Provide information without creating a verbal, electronic, or paper overload. • Develop communication skills and techniques in all staff. • Select an appropriate method of communication, and use technology effectively.	• Encourage all levels of staff to speak out without fear of rebuke or reprisal. • Provide a clear picture of each staff member's place in the organizational structure, and clarify the chain of command. • Establish links with communication systems outside the organizational hierarchy. • Ensure that administrators are visible. • Establish personal contact between administrators and staff. • Provide effective leadership and communication. • Supply administrative feedback to upward communication. • Keep open input and response channels in all directions, primarily upward. • Ensure that the system is interested in communicating with the individual. • Reduce communication barriers between groups of staff, for example, between support and professional staff. • Overcome communication problems caused by geographic locations of units, flex working schedules, telecommuting, differing shifts, and so forth. • Define who needs to know what and when. • Establish a systemwide rapid communication mechanism for pressing matters. • Know the people with whom you interface in other units. • Maintain lateral communication between and among units, sections, teams, and staff performing dissimilar functions. • Create a mechanism that will provide opportunity for ongoing consultation and understanding between units.	• Tell the staff how and where they can obtain information. • Clarify the goals of the library. • Generate and encourage an interest in system and organizational goals at the beginning. • Ensure that supervisors, including unit heads, obtain training and orientation from those to whom they report. • Provide consistent orientation. • Provide procedure information and a grievance policy. • Publicize staff development opportunities. • Provide a clear description of the criteria for the evaluation and promotion of all levels of staff. • Publicize salary schedules.

and needs regarding on-the-job communication. The following sections explore some steps that can be taken to meet the needs identified in the table.

Conroy and Jones (1986) outlined the major purposes for managerial communication. It is a good list to keep in mind:

- To inform: convey both information and understanding.
- To gather information: collect input from others to help make decisions and solve problems.
- To motivate: change or reinforce behavior and prompt specific action.
- To instruct and/or train: enable another to carry out instructions, tasks, or procedures appropriately.
- To coach and/or discipline: encourage faster growth, prevent disciplinary action, help another learn how to do a specific task better, and improve attitudes or behavior.
- To counsel: help someone with a personal problem that affects work productivity or morale.
- To mentor: help another succeed, usually by imparting better understanding of organizational policies, practices, or politics.
- To develop staff: guide staff progress and growth with performance appraisals and goal-setting sessions.
- To build teams: help work groups establish interpersonal rapport, build esprit de corps, and develop cohesion.

Graham and Valentine (1973) point out one of the important facts a supervisor must remember about the communication process:

> The communication problem is even more complex when the "established" or "official" channels are involved. These are in themselves seen as manipulative and therefore, received if at all, with considerable cynicism.
>
> But the fundamental problem is even more serious; the act of communicating at all is inherently manipulative. Attempts at communication are often evaluated in terms of observed change in behavior on the part of the receivers of the message. (pp. 963–964)

There are times when the staff may interpret a message as manipulative (such as in Figure 8.3), but there are ways you can counteract the possible hostility. First, try to establish authenticity by gaining rapport with the staff, engendering an atmosphere wherein staff realize that they can freely discuss problems without fear of reprisal or rebuke. Also, by shortening the time between work activities and their evaluation, you can improve trust. Job evaluation is less threatening when it involves the immediate situation rather than a review of a person's annual performance. A third step that you can take is to involve the staff in all processes of the unit that are not sensitive or confidential in character, giving each person an opportunity to see that each job is important to the unit's success.

WRITTEN AND ORAL COMMUNICATIONS

Deciding when to write or when to talk is a matter of fine judgment and an understanding of accepted organizational practices. You need to decide on the channel to use—face-to-face, paper memo, e-mail, text message, and so forth. Communication in the workplace is both informal and formal, and there are situations when one may be more appropriate than another.

ICT technologies can either facilitate or, if policies and procedures are not in place to overcome a growing problem, act as barriers to communication. The ways computers, e-mail, voice mail, and cell phones are used are personalized by their users. The computer has a password; e-mails have unique addresses, as do voice mail and cell phones. In the days when communications were written on paper, telephones lacked voice mail, and someone was absent, a secretary or colleague handled the absentee's mail or phone calls. Today this does not always happen. It can be frustrating for someone who wants to make contact with the library and who uses a specific phone extension or e-mail address but does not receive a prompt response. You need to ensure that there is a policy and procedure in place to overcome this potential problem.

There is also the question of the work and life balance—work communication can be carried over into personal time, and personal messages can be received at work. Getting the balance right and getting an acceptable practice followed by staff needs sensitive handling and clear guidelines.

WRITTEN COMMUNICATION

Every letter and memo, whether electronic or paper, should be a "sales" letter in some sense, even if it attempts to sell a point of view on a minor matter. Persuasion results from fine directional hinting, not from overtly blunt or offensive statements. It is vital that memos are carefully worded; some managers spend as little time on memos as they do on casual oral presentations. Just because something is written down does not necessarily mean that it is clear.

Robert Cialdini (2011) noted, "research shows that persuasion works by appealing to a limited set of deeply rooted human drives and needs, and does so in predictable ways" (p. 30). By understanding the predictable elements, you can become more persuasive. Many of the elements are things that come about prior to the actual message that is intended to be persuasive—such as the persuader being seen as very similar to those who are to be persuaded (a team member in fact or more generally—"we are in this together"). The persuader is liked and the persuader treats others fairly are elements in creating an environment where greater persuasion is possible. Perhaps the most important element is as Jay Conger (2011) stated: "persuasion, in other words, often invokes—indeed, demands—compromise" (p. 88).

One problem with the two illustrated memos (Figures 8.2 and 8.3) lies in inadequate planning. Taking a few moments to review some of the following questions can improve any written or oral communication:

- What am I trying to convey?
- With whom am I communicating?
- When is the best time to do this?
- Where is the best place?
- What is the best channel?
- Why am I communicating?

When you add to these questions the four elements that Carol Brey-Casiano shared in her opening quote at the beginning of this chapter—clarity, conciseness, advance preparation, and respect for the person receiving the message—you will be on the road to communicating effectively.

One of the most important aspects of organizational communication is readability. The communication should include a frame of reference (established at the beginning); a clear, well-thought-out statement of what is meant or desired; and an explanation of how, when, and where the staff are to meet the expectations.

ELECTRONIC COMMUNICATIONS

Guidelines and procedures for electronic communication are needed. First, for the use of e-mail, what are legitimate work uses? Second, what type, if any, surfing is allowable? Third, from a records management perspective, what is to be archived, by whom, where, and for how long? The guidelines will need to be clear to all members of staff within the organization. It is essential that a member of staff leaving the organization does not purge files without consultation and that his or her replacement has access to nonconfidential messages to enable work to flow smoothly. Paper records present fewer problems.

Intranet
An intranet has benefits and potential pitfalls. It can provide quick access to basic organizational information. It can become *the* means of communicating for staff,

---

CHECK THESE OUT

Anandarajan, Murugan, and Claire Simmers, eds. 2004. *Personal Web Usage in the Workplace: A Guide to Effective Human Resource Management.* Hershey, PA: Information Science Publications.

———. 2006. *The Internet and Workplace Transformation.* Armonk, NY: M. E. Sharpe.

Flynn, Nancy L. 2009. *The E-policy Handbook: Rules and Best Practices to Safely Manage Your Company's E-mail, Blogs, Social Networking, and Other Electronic Communication Tools.* New York: American Management Association.

but staff can forget that perhaps not everyone has access to the intranet. Two common groups not given access are volunteers and interns. Sometimes part-time staff are slow to be given an account. This can lead to some people, perhaps people significant in terms of the message's content, failing to "get the word." These are some advantages of intranet communications:

- They can be quickly updated.
- Managers can be sure that staff members have access to the most recent information.
- Internal details can be broadcast quickly—such as dates, times, and agendas for meetings.
- General information can be quickly disseminated—such as the success of a staff member.
- Internal discussion groups can be established.
- The volume of paper circulated can be greatly reduced—and a few trees saved!
- The work of secretarial staff can be examined to produce a more interesting workload.

These are some of the potential pitfalls:

- Not every staff member (part-time, volunteers, interns, etc.) may have equal access—for example, to a computer, to a password, or to training.
- There is a real danger of information overload.
- One person must have responsibility for managing the intranet or else chaos may reign and information will not be updated systematically.

The design and layout of the intranet needs care and attention so that it is visually attractive and easy to navigate and locate information. You can add links to useful external information sources that can make the work of staff easier. For personnel staff, this may be links to relevant legislation available online. The aim of the intranet is to provide easy access to up-to-date information required by the library staff in their daily work. In a library where the staff work shifts, or where telecommuting makes it difficult to get everyone together, an intranet will ensure that everyone has access to needed information. An intranet design is not effective forever and needs periodic updating.

E-mail

Electronic communication is both a great blessing and a headache. One of the blessings is the quick and easy communication we now enjoy around the globe. One headache is the widespread expectation of a speedy response from the recipient.

Information overload can also become a problem. It can be difficult to keep up with e-mail, for example. E-mails can be collected at home and during holidays, making it difficult to get away from the office. There can be a perceived sense of urgency about attending to e-mail, but sometimes the library e-mail goes down. And, even with the best filters, there is the constant issue of spam messages.

Here are some basic points about using e-mail:

- Make sure that you add your name, mailing address, phone, and fax number so that you can be identified and a reply sent in a different format if the recipient prefers one.
- Is your message really necessary, or is it a form of "chat"? Never use it for gossip—you could be breaking a law.
- Think before you write, and think before you send. It is easy to write in haste and later have regrets (perhaps over style, the content of the message itself, or words that reflected your emotions at the time).
- Indicate the subject, to allow the receiver to prioritize the opening of messages.
- Make sure the receiver will understand the content. Avoid using an abbreviation unless you know it will be understood.
- Do a spell check before sending.
- Remember legal constraints, because a message sent outside the library may be taken to represent the view of your employer.
- Observe the organizational policies and procedures for filing electronic mail.
- Select the discussion lists that you join carefully—they can be very time-consuming—and observe the same courtesies you would in joining a discussion around a table.

Social Media

Libraries are making ever-increasing use of social media to connect with their users. The media range from blogs to interactive sites. Blogs are the successor to the bulletin boards and electronic discussion lists of the 1980s and 1990s. They

---

CHECK THESE OUT

Choate, Mark. 2008. *Professional Wikis.* Indianapolis, IN: Wiley.

Pressley, Lauren. 2010. *Wikis for Libraries.* New York: Neal-Schuman.

Stephens, Michael. 2006. *Web 2.0 and Libraries: Best Practices for Social Software.* Library Technology Reports. Chicago: American Library Association.

West, James A., and Margaret L. West. 2009. *Using Wikis for Online Collaboration: The Power of the Read–Write Web.* San Francisco: Jossey-Bass.

are a powerful way for people to make their views known. You can employ a library blog to communicate with and among users. Children's and young adult services in public libraries are examples of where blogs can make effective connections with the intended target of communication.

Blogs have a downside, too, because they are a democratic means of communicating; an unpopular decision or action on the part of the library may give rise to unwelcome public attention. Conversely, a blog in which the user community contributes may be of help if the library comes under threat. This has happened when public libraries have faced closure. In this case, blogs became a tool to express public opinion.

If a manager is considering an official blog, then decisions about servers and software policies need to be made, covering the purpose of the blog, the nomination of a person to be the focal point for the blog, who can make a posting to the blog, and whether the blog is to be password protected. If in any doubt, then follow parent organization guidelines. Guidelines are essential so that staff know and respect the purpose of the blog.

Wikis offer a more open means of communication, because they are websites that allow people to add, edit, or remove content, often without the need to register. *Wikipedia* is the largest example of a wiki; it acts as an online encyclopedia. The advantages of wikis are that they are usually up to date and can bring information and knowledge together on very specialized topics. The downside is that the information can be inaccurate because the updating feature is not always used by those best informed on the topic. Within a library, they can be used for staff to exchange information.

ORAL COMMUNICATIONS

Our experience suggests that managers and supervisors need to keep the following points in mind regarding oral communication:

- Do not take the managerial position too seriously.
- Do let other people talk.
- Do listen carefully.
- Do not become overcommitted to an idea.
- Do try to keep the discussion from wandering aimlessly.
- Do keep it simple and straightforward.
- Do try to get to know the level of understanding of the person to whom you are talking.
- Do not argue.

A speaker's position within the organization naturally affects the ways in which people listen and respond to that person. If someone holding a superior position acts in a superior manner, that person will have problems talking with subordinates. One danger for the new manager (as well as for the experienced manager) is becoming an instant expert on everything. An instant expert rarely hears anything that others say, unless it provides her or him with a springboard. Subordinates of such a person stop listening. Total commitment to one idea—to the exclusion of entertaining a discussion of the idea's possible defects—is another way to lose an audience. When the manager believes that there is only one right way, and the workers know from experience that this way is not working, the workers usually remain quiet until the system collapses.

Sticking with the topic of the conversation is essential from two points of view: internal and external. It is important to provide only the details that are necessary for people to adequately get their jobs done. Remember that users may not warm to someone who consistently gives more information than necessary (or information that has only slight relevance). Keep messages short and simple. This allows for greater clarity, and it saves time. Knowing the audience is essential for a speaker, as is selecting the appropriate level of presentation. Word choice and the manner of delivery are important in effective oral communication. Overly complicated messages cloud issues; likewise, simplistic approaches can insult an audience and/or reduce matters of complexity to clichés. If you spend time considering the level of understanding of an audience, then you'll achieve better communication.

SOMETHING TO PONDER

Which is your preferred method of communication and why? Do you need to brush up your skills in using any method?

LISTENING

As we stated earlier in the chapter, careful listening is one of the hallmarks of great leaders/managers. It is a skill you must work at developing despite the fact that most of us hear and think we are listening. Effective listening is harder than most people realize.

A major challenge is that we can process what we hear about four times faster than most people speak. This leaves about three-quarters of our listening time free for our minds to wander, and they will unless we work at not letting that happen. Think back to your most recent class session. Did you think about the next class with a test scheduled? Were you thinking about something you wanted to tell your best friend in the class? Perhaps you started wondering where the instructor came up with *that* idea. Did you doodle? Were you checking your BlackBerry? Our list could go on and on, but you get the point; all of those thoughts meant you were not actually listening. We all do such things all the time while we think we are in fact listening.

In addition to having substantial amounts of time available for our minds to wander while listening, we also "filter" what we do hear. Communication process researchers identify three major types of filtering: leveling, sharpening, and assimilating.

Leveling occurs when the recipient of a message omits certain elements of the original message, thereby essentially changing its meaning. For example, assume a children's librarian is told a vacant position will not be filled until the level of usage of children's library services or programs increases. (There has been a decline in the number of children getting library cards and attending storyhours.) The department head, in a leveling situation, might report to the staff that the position was withdrawn because of a declining number of children, not that it was a result of declining use by children. While part of the original content comes through the filtering process, the meaning has been changed through significant omissions.

Sharpening is a process in which a part of a message receives greater emphasis than the original message intended. Assume during a staff development review that a supervisor tells a staff member, "Your performance is excellent. If you continue at the present rate of development, you may be considered for a new position that we expect to have in the next year or so." What the staff member tells others is, "I have been chosen for the new position the department will get next year." In essence, the person emphasizes what she or he wants to hear and plays down, or filters out, the qualifying elements.

Assimilation retains the entire original message and adds elements to it, thereby expanding the original meaning. Suppose a university president told the university librarian, "I am talking with a potential donor who is interested in making a major contribution to the new library building fund. I expect we will have an answer soon." The university librarian reports to the staff that "the president is very supportive of a new library building—it is a priority. The president is working with a prospective donor at present and a new building will be started very soon, as soon as the donor makes the major contribution." All of the elements of the original message are present, but there are many added elements that essentially change the meaning.

Some other common problems in "hearing" a message are assuming you already know the content, assuming the content is uninteresting or of no concern, or thinking the topic is unimportant. Listening with such thoughts in mind almost ensures that the message's purpose is lost. Not only is the "extra" listening time wasted but so is the one-quarter time needed to take in the message. The best way to overcome this problem is to make a conscious effort to suspend judgment. From the outset, keep an open mind; the message may not be what you think it will be.

A related issue is assessing or criticizing the speaker's method of presentation. People who make presentations are particularly prone to criticizing others' presentations. When you do that, you cease listening to the content. How often do we hear, "Oh, it was a good talk, but she had a horrible PowerPoint presentation," or "there were too many pauses and asides"? The person making such comments had ceased to listen and transferred his or her attention to the delivery of the message. Keeping an open mind helps, but the real issue is to stop focusing on the "how" and switch to the "what" is being said. Think, off and on, during the presentation, "Am I thinking about the what or the how of the message?" Failing to concentrate on the "what" erects barriers to effective communication.

Jumping to conclusions is something most people do, at least occasionally. Once you think, assume, or feel you know where the speaker is going with her or his talk, your listening tends to fall off, if not cease. Again, suspending judgment until the message is complete is an effective way to keep communication open. Another technique that helps slow conclusion jumping is to consciously reflect on what is being said.

A less common but nonetheless significant barrier to effective listening is wanting only the "big picture" or general information. This barrier often takes the form of not wasting time on details—"spare me the details." Certainly the big picture/overview is essential, but often the details of how the speaker has arrived at the big picture are critical to understanding the message or situation. Thinking about how the details interconnect, and how the speaker is making the connections, helps to concentrate on the "what" of the message.

A related barrier is an overreaction to certain words or phrases. Each of us has a set of phrases and words we really do not like hearing. These phrases and words carry special meanings based on a past experience—when someone used them in a manner that caused us discomfort, harm, or emotional distress. Frequently these are relatively common words and phrases that have no special meaning for other people. In the workplace we must be cautious about overreacting to any message, especially when we hear words or phrases from our personal "hot button" list. One step to take is to spend time thinking about the words and phrases that tend to upset us. Thinking about what those are and why they cause us discomfort can help us control our reactions in the workplace. Another obvious step is to always wait before responding. An angry or confrontational response seldom leads to a discussion in which the people listen to one another. Rather, such a response, more often than not, leads to a situation of talking at one another. Thoughtful, unemotional responses are much more likely to lead to real communication.

OTHER ISSUES IN COMMUNICATION

Some people appear attentive when their minds are far, far away. The nonverbal cues suggest to the speaker that the listener is listening. If there is no feedback when the speaker finishes, a normal assumption is that the message was understood when in fact nothing came through. Body language and the other signs we give, often unconsciously, can impede communication. Arms akimbo, running our hands through our hair, and other idiosyncrasies that we all possess can be very off-putting to someone who doesn't know us well.

CHECK THESE OUT

The following journal articles give you a starting point for further exploring nonverbal communication:

Collett, Peter. 2004. "Show and Tell: Think You Can See When Someone Is Lying?" *People Management* 10, no. 8: 34–35.

Page, Daniel. 2004. "The Importance of Nonverbal Communication in Library Service." *Library Mosaics* 15, no. 6: 11.

Whipple, Robert. 2006. "E-body Language: Decoded." *T+D* 60, no. 2: 20–22.

Xu, Yu, and Ruth Davidhizar. 2004. "Intercultural Communication in Nursing Education." *Journal of Nursing Education* 44, no. 5: 209–215.

The following books provide in-depth information:

Lawton, Eunice. 2006. *Body Language and the First Line Manager.* Oxford: Chandos.

Pease, Allan, and Barbara Pease. 2006. *The Definitive Book of Body Language.* New York: Bantam Books.

Ribbens, Geof, and Greg Whitear. 2007. *Body Language.* London: Hodder.

This is a very informative DVD:

Dresser, Norine, and Joel Asher. 2007. *Body Language: Cultural Differences.* New York: Insight Media.

Face-to-face communication entails more than the words said and how they are said. Everyone in a conversation sends a variety of "messages" through nonverbal actions. Your emphasis, lack of tone, speed, and so forth are factors in nonverbal communication. Other elements in the process are facial expressions (frowns, smiles, eye contact, and the like); gestures (head nodding, hand movements, method of pointing, etc.); and body posture (arms and legs folded, angle of the body, and such). You may also send intended or unintended messages by the color of your clothes, the way you arrange your office furniture, and seating arrangements for meetings. Just to add to the complexity of the process, cultural background plays a major role in nonverbal communication.

Is it important to understand the nonverbal communication cues? In our opinion, absolutely! An estimated 60 percent of the real message comes from the nonverbal side of the communication process (Arthur, 1995).

Trust in the workplace is essential for many reasons. We sometimes forget that people judge our trustworthiness all the time, especially if they believe we misled them in the past. Christian L. Hart, Derek Fillmore, and James Griffith (2010) wrote about how people often judge another person's veracity:

The cues that many people report using to detect deception in everyday situations are non-verbal behaviors, verbal cues, and paraverbal cues. Nonverbal cues are the movement of limbs, torso, head, and face that might yield some indication of lying or truthfulness. . . . [V]erbal cues of deception can be defined as the content of speech that may provide evidence of deception. . . . Paraverbal cues can be defined as those that accompany speech behavior such as voice pitch, response latencies, filled and unfilled pauses, message duration, speech errors, and repetitions. (pp. 176–177)

When working in a culturally diverse library or one that serves a diverse population, as so many of us do today, having a sound grasp of the nonverbal side of things is very important. Even in what may seem to be a homogenous group, there are likely to be some unexpected interpretations of what you might think of as unimportant actions or gestures.

Just two examples will illustrate the point. If you come from a Western European background, your "comfort zone" for conversation is at least three feet away from the others—in fact, a wider spacing is often preferred. People from Latin America or Asia prefer to be much closer (one foot on average). Learning what is or is not the comfort range (interpersonal space) in a diverse group can take some time.

Eye contact is another area where culture matters. Most children with a Western European background learn early on to look at their parents. A common phrase is, "look me in the eye when I'm talking to you." English language novels are filled with nasty characters with "shifty eyes." For most Native American groups and most Asian peoples, on the other hand, direct eye contact is thought to be impolite at best and rude at worst—an attempt to gain control of another's spirit. Not understanding such differences can play havoc with work-related activities, from job interviews, throughout your working life, all the way to retirement. Devoting a little time to learning about, and perhaps gaining some understanding of, the variations within your work group can pay dividends over time.

A related problem is conveying disagreement, either verbally or nonverbally, before the speaker has finished. Doing so effectively cuts off further communication. Such a response conveys to the speaker the sense the listener has reached a conclusion without hearing everything. Even when you disagree with what is said, not showing those feelings or thoughts until after the speaker finishes will improve your chances of having a meaningful discussion about the topic or issue.

There are two other communication challenges. First, avoid the use of technical words or professional jargon in sending either messages or feedback unless you are certain the other person understands the jargon. Asking for feedback after delivering a message helps ensure the intended and interpreted message meanings are sufficiently close to one another. Never be embarrassed to ask for clarification of a word, phrase, or the entire message—especially in work situations. Managers and supervisors should welcome such requests. Reacting in a negative manner will cut off essential feedback, which in some circumstances leads to serious problems.

A second challenge is to know if the listener has a problem with the physical aspect of hearing. If you have a hearing impairment, saying so allows speakers to adjust their presentation to help ensure better communication. Likewise, if the speaker's voice does not carry well enough for you to hear, let the speaker know this. People frequently do this in formal presentation settings and neglect it in less formal situations. Failing to do so may result in important information being missed.

CHANNELS, DIRECTION, AND LEGITIMACY OF COMMUNICATION

Channels of communication run up, down, and across an organization. In cases of upward communication, tact and diplomacy are very important. Also, sensitive topics, such as disagreements with a supervisor's actions, probably should be discussed orally (with considerable supporting detail). Distinguish clearly between fact and opinion, being neither subservient nor argumentative.

Communication with senior management and/or the governing board requires careful handling. Giving too many messages may present a picture of insecurity on the part of the manager. Giving too little often means the board/senior managers are not fully informed about what is happening—they may start to feel insecure. Seeing a problem coming down the track and failing to inform senior management is a managerial disaster waiting to happen. So, judge how much information should be passed upward, how frequently this should be done, and using which channel. Discover how much communication should take place in social settings. Two golden rules in upward communication—never be evasive, and keep senior management informed.

When you are planning on sending "important" information, especially if it is a complex message, it is wise to have at least one other pair of eyes review the message. For significant messages to the user community, governing board, and senior managers of the parent organization, you really need to have more than one extra pair of eyes. Almost everyone has difficulty seeing errors in their written work—they know what they mean to say and that is what they often see when reviewing the message. Spell checkers are helpful, but they do nothing in terms of catching a properly spelled word that is the wrong word. There are similar issues with grammatical software packages. Essentially the rule is that the eyes (not the software packages alone) should review an important message before it is sent to the intended recipient(s).

In downward communication, diplomacy and tact are also the keys to success. Avoid carelessness in communications, as it indicates a lack of respect for the person receiving the message. In union contract talks, careless speech has been known to lead to strikes. A manager must give explanations for actions rather than allow the workers' imaginations to fill in the gaps. Managers should always encourage staff to ask questions and to contribute ideas. Only in such ways can the manager know whether communication is effective and to what degree. If management encourages such behavior on all levels, the result is likely to be more buy-in and greater appreciation and loyalty throughout the library.

ADVISORY BOARD EXPERIENCE

Joseph Mika was drafted back as director from faculty in a situation which had a number of administrative problems. He prepared the following "Mika Missives" and informed all staff that these would be the "rules" under which the administrative team would operate:

1. STUDENTS ARE WHY WE ARE HERE. Our focus, and reason for being, are the students of the Library and Information Science Program. CUSTOMER SERVICE is everyone's responsibility.
2. THE GOLDEN RULE. After students, the faculty, the library staff, and ourselves are customers—Internal Customers. Treat them like you would like to be treated. Their requests and needs are important too.
3. LOYALTY—to your job, the LISP, your coworkers, the University, the Library System, and to me—is required.
4. IF YOU CAN'T SAY SOMETHING NICE, don't say anything at all. Reserve your criticisms for me. I will not tolerate hearing your concerns secondhand.
5. YOU ARE THE SOLUTION. When you bring me a problem, bring me your suggestions for solutions. This goes for problems that we identify in each other's areas as well.
6. REACCREDITATION is important to the University, the Program, students, alumni, faculty, and you. We all MUST work toward ensuring we receive the full 7 years reaccreditation.
7. CONFIDENTIALITY is Key! What we say among ourselves at meetings, what we learn about students, faculty, etc., stays among ourselves. WHAT IS SAID HERE STAYS HERE!
8. THERE IS TIME FOR FUN. I enjoy my job, and I like to have fun at it. I want us all to enjoy our jobs, have fun, and like what we do!
9. CHANGE IS A GIVEN. We don't do things because we have always done them that way—we'll do them better, smarter, and more effectively.
10. DO YOUR JOB! I work hard; I expect you to work hard too! I have my job to do; I don't want or expect to do your job too.

Although the classic functions of the manager are to make decisions and to give orders, the reality is that they occupy only a small proportion of the time spent in communicating. In a library, a vast amount of communicating takes place among peers in order to get tasks done. This type of communication in a collective enterprise involves not only the formal structures but also the informal structures (status structure, friendship structure, prestige structure, etc.)

of the library. All of these are in constant flux, contradicting the notion that all communication in an organization is downward and horizontal.

People communicate in order to achieve a goal, to satisfy a personal need, or to improve their immediate situation with respect to their personal desires. People need to communicate with those of higher status than themselves, which means that managers need to spend time with their subordinates. The effectiveness of this will depend on the individual relationships between supervisors and subordinates and the degree to which each subordinate's needs are satisfied by upward communication.

Picking the proper channel for your message takes some experience. It is important to remember that what was the proper channel in your last library may not be in your new library.

There is a "dark side" to communication. Some individuals, for a variety of reasons, deliberately miscommunicate. We have encountered such instances in both our personal and work lives. Sometimes it is a matter of unconscious filtering (we covered filtering issues earlier in the chapter). Misinterpreting a message happens for numerous reasons; however, there are occasions when it is deliberate and intended to cause problems in or for the organization. In the workplace when you receive a message that seems unbelievable, be sure to check the legitimacy of the source. Even letterhead paper can be misused.

KEY POINTS TO REMEMBER
- Effective and clear communication is vital in decision making, planning, organizing, staffing, and budgeting.
- Improved understanding leads to better working conditions, higher morale, and greater staff commitment.
- Supervisors have the responsibility to provide these benefits by ensuring that communications are as honest, clear, and open to discussion as possible.
- Avoid information overload, particularly in electronic formats, because it can create stress for staff members—and supervisors—and impede communication.
- Personality—for example, being out going or reserved—influences communication practices.
- Develop a sense of humor, and learn how to lighten situations when this will aid the communication process.
- Learn how to use the various channels of communication efficiently and effectively, especially as new channels emerge.
- Observing the strengths and weaknesses of staff identifies training needs.
- All staff members, at all levels, need to have excellent communication skills if quality library service is to be provided.
- Adhere to these five key points for clear and effective communication:
  1. Know what to communicate.

2. Know who needs to know what.
3. Know who should communicate with whom.
4. Know how to time messages.
5. Know how to listen and read nonverbal cues such as body language.

References

Arthur, Diane. 1995. "Importance of Body Language." *HRFocus* 72 (June): 22–23.

Bartels, Jos, Oscar Peters, Menno de Jong, Ad Pruyn, and Marjolijn van der Molen. 2010. "Horizontal and Vertical Communication as Determinants of Professional and Organisational Identification." *Personnel Review* 39, no. 2: 210–226.

Bartlett, Frederic C. 1951. *The Mind at Work and Play*. London: Allen and Unwin.

Berlo, David K. 1960. *The Process of Communication*. New York: Holt.

Brey-Casiano, Carol. 2012. E-mail communication sent to Camila A. Alire, February 29.

Cialdini, Robert E. 2011. "Harnessing the Science of Persuasion." In *Harvard Business Review on Communicating Effectively*, pp. 29–51. Cambridge, MA: Harvard Business School Press.

Conger, Jay A. 2011. "The Necessary Art of Persuasion." In *Harvard Business Review on Communicating Effectively*, pp. 83–112. Cambridge, MA: Harvard Business School Press.

Conroy, Barbara, and Barbara S. Jones. 1986. *Improving Communication in Libraries*. Phoenix, AZ: Oryx Press.

Graham, Roderick, and M. Valentine. 1973. "Management, Communication and the Destandardized Man." *Personnel Journal* 52, November: 962–979.

Hammill, Greg. 2005. "Mixing and Managing Four Generations of Employees." *FduMagazine Online* (Winter/Spring). http://www.fdu.edu/newspubs/magazine/05ws/generations.htm.

Hart, Christian L., Derek Fillmore, and James Griffith. 2010. "Deceptive Communication in the Workplace: An Examination of Beliefs about Verbal and Paraverbal Cues." *Individual Difference Research* 8, no. 3: 176–183.

Marques, Joan F. 2010. "Enhancing the Quality of Organizational Communication." *Journal of Communication Management* 14, no. 1: 47–58.

Maxwell, John C. 2010. *Everyone Communicates, Few Connect*. Nashville, TN: Thomas Nelson.

Moniz, Richard. 2011. "Communicating Who We Are: The Theory of Organizational Culture in the Workplace." *Library Leadership and Management* 25, no. 1: 1–4.

Launching Pad

Andres, Hayward P. 2006. "The Impact of Communication Medium on Virtual Team Group Process." *Information Resources Management Journal* 19, no. 2: 1–17.

Bekmeier-Feurhahn, Sigrid, and Angelika Eichenlaub. 2009. "What Makes for Trusting Relationships in Online Communication?" *Journal of Communication* 14, no. 4: 337–355.

Chalmers, Mardi, Theresa Liedtka, and Carol Bednar. 2006. "A Library Communication Audit for the Twenty-First Century." *portal: Libraries and the Academy* 6, no. 2: 185–195.

Gordon, Rachel Singer, and Michael Stephens. 2006. "How and Why to Try a Blog for Staff Communication." *Computers in Libraries* 26, no. 2: 50–51.

Hannan, Adrienne. 2011. "Communication 101: We Have Made Contact with Teens." *Aplis* 24, no. 1: 32–38.

Krishnan, Yvonne. 2011. "Libraries and the Mobile Rev." *Computers in Libraries* 31, no. 3: 6–9.

Macaluso, Stephen J., and Barbara Whitney Petruzzelli. 2005. "The Library Liaison Toolkit: Learning to Bridge the Communication Gap." *Reference Librarian*, 43, no. 89/90: 163–177.

Mazzei, Alessandra. 2009. "Promoting Active Communication Behaviors through Internal Communication." *Corporate Communications* 15, no. 3: 221–234.

Sabol, Byron. 2011. "Adjusting Your Style Improves Communication with Difficult and Challenging Personalities." *Business Credit* 113, no. 4: 8, 10–11.

Tannen, Deborah. 2001. *Talking from 9 to 5: Women and Men at Work*. New York: Quill.

Yarwood, Dean L. 1995. "Humor and Administration: A Serious Inquiry into Unofficial Organizational Communication." *Public Journal Administration Review* 55, no. 1: 81–91.

Change. Here is a word that causes some to shudder, while others welcome it as an opportunity to make things better. But have no doubt—without change, industries and individuals for that matter will stagnate, putting their future at risk.

   —Richard A. Roberts (2011)

We see a picture of considerable pressures on existing resources, demands for new services, and a workforce ill-equipped for change. It is clear we not only need to do more, but do differently, and that we need to cultivate a culture that is not only tolerant of change but one that embraces the opportunity for transformation.

   —Merrilee Proffitt (2011)

Many organizations commit large amounts of resources to maintain their competitiveness through innovative activities. How do they ensure that those resources are allocated to the uses that are most likely to yield innovations?

   —Daniel Tzabbar (2009)

The adoption of innovations in organizations is complex and varies according to the type of innovation, whether administrative, technological or process. . . . Before initiating an innovation process within an organization, it is essential to understand the types of innovation and the factors related to each type.

   —Kristina Jaskyte (2011)

9

CHANGING
AND INNOVATING

This chapter focuses on the following:

- Why change and innovation are essential
- The nature of change
- Managing change
- Resistance to change
- Implementing change
- Stress and the organization
- Generating new approaches to services and operational activities

EVER SINCE THE "Big Bang" occurred, change has been a constant in the universe. When humans began creating societies hundreds of thousands of years ago, the pace of social change was very slow. With the start of the industrial revolution, the pace accelerated. Today the pace of change is almost mind-boggling, especially for organizations. You get a sense of that when you see some companies offering packages that allow you to upgrade your purchase if a new model comes on the market—the time frame for most of those agreements is 24 months.

People handle change in different ways, as suggested by Richard Roberts in our first opening quotation. Some fear it, and others embrace it. In our personal lives, we more often than not accept change in part because we have some control over its pace. When it comes to the workplace, we tend to resist change and cling to the status quo, partially because it is imposed and we have little control over its speed.

One truth about today's organizational environment is that change is ubiquitous and constant. Another truth is that successful organizations address change proactively. We made the point in Chapter 2 that monitoring the operating environment is a key to long-term organizational viability. That process provides clues to and assists in anticipating developments in the environment that may call for organizational adjustments. One of your responsibilities is to assist the staff in effectively handling change.

Change and innovation are tightly linked for organizations. To implement innovative ideas or practices the staff must make changes. There are times when developments in the environment (in a turbulent environment, for example) call for change, sometimes radical in nature. The two concepts are drivers of one another many times. Tomalee Doan and Mary Lee Kennedy (2009) noted in their article "Innovation, Creativity, and Meaning":

> Librarians today have come to view change as the means of accomplishing significant goals, recognizing that our organizations must keep pace with user needs, acknowledging that we do indeed have information competitors and that we are part of organizations and therefore must align with larger objectives than our own. It is essential to innovate in order to continue to be meaningful. (p. 349)

Ester Baldwin, in an interview with Michael Hopkins (2010), made an important point when she said, "Traditionally, people think innovation is just about creativity, about being able to create ideas. In fact, it's a very disciplined area. Companies really can manage innovation in the ways they manage quality" (p. 1). Baldwin was not suggesting that innovation does not involve creativity—it does—but rather that it is possible to manage it. Also, the type of innovation she was referring to, and what is of interest to us in this chapter, is *not* artistic creativity and innovation. We explore organizational creativity and innovation later in this chapter.

It is as Lourdes Munduate and Francis Media (2009) stated: "Organizations will only survive if they have the flexibility to react to the constantly changing demands and if they are adept enough at redirecting, orientating, and exploiting their resources efficiently" (p. 299). We know change is inevitable in both our personal and workplace lives. How we handle workplace change may well have an impact on our private lives. Managing change is central to organizational viability, and innovation may be especially important to long-term well-being. To manage change well and to be innovative, you must understand the change process and the techniques that help staff accept and embrace change.

NATURE OF CHANGE

"There is nothing more difficult to take in hand, more perilous to conduct, or more uncertain in its success than to take the lead in the introduction of a new order of things" (Machiavelli, 1952, p. 52). Organizational change takes place across a continuum from incremental to radical. "New order of things" (radical change) may be required when there are crisis conditions in the organization's environment. On the other hand, every day there are small changes both externally and internally. Staff members deal with change on a daily basis without realizing it. The vast majority of the changes are so small as to be almost unnoticeable.

Leslie Szamosi and Linda Duxbury (2002, p. 186) discussed change as a continuum—incremental to radical. They defined radical change as something that:

- interrupts the status quo
- happens quickly or abruptly
- is fundamental and all encompassing

Virginia Walter offered this insight regarding library organizational structure and workforces and change:

> Some academic and public libraries, at least the larger ones, tend to be bureaucratic in structure and often unionized. Both issues greatly restrict a library's ability to respond with any kind of flexibility to external changes. Bureaucracies are, after all, designed for permanence. This is their strength, as well as an ironic weakness. Civil Service rules and union contracts further tie the hands of managers who want to respond creatively to environmental changes or to simply streamline or improve operations. The recent budget shortfalls have shaken things up a little for some libraries; they have been forced to change. This is another dimension of change. It is one thing to change because it will improve the way one does business. It is quite another when change is dictated by outside forces. How can managers put a positive spin on a budget cut that will mean decreased pay and increased workload?

- brings something that is dramatically different from what used to be.

Radical change of the type they describe is difficult for any staff, even those who are accustomed to change and are generally positive about its value. However, usually they are used to making "adjustments." Clearly a change that has the features Szamosi and Duxbury outlined is much more than an "adjustment." Nevertheless, organizations with staff with a positive attitude about change are better positioned to successfully navigate what will be turbulent times than those that do not have such staff.

At the opposite end of the continuum, incremental change may not be the best approach either. Michael W. McLaughlin (2011) identified two potential flaws beginning with the tortoise approach in the tortoise and hare change race. He suggests that "many people respond negatively to incremental change. . . . When stakes are low, some people cling to entrenched positions until forced to change. . . . Second, starting small is often an invitation to push issues that really matter to the back burner" (p. 12).

Kate Hawker and Melissa Garcia (2010) made a case for a tortoise approach: "One of the great misconceptions about making incremental change is that doing nothing translates into passivity. This is not true. While an organization may 'wait' to take a specific action until the right pieces are in place, progress

> ### SOMETHING TO PONDER
>
> What are some of the change areas in technology, structure, and strategy for information services? Thinking about your current or recent work experience, what forces of change did you observe?

should be a constant. If you relentlessly nudge many projects forward by small amounts, significant achievements can occur quickly" (p. 27). They go on to describe how their organization made slow but steady progress by following five practices (p. 28):

- Be self aware—know when the organization is ready to change.
- Have good information—gather data aggressively.
- Be nimble—don't be unwilling to adjust if there are problems.
- Develop goals and budgets from the bottom up.
- Exert pressure from the top to create incentives for staff to change.

Hawker and Garcia describe something nearer the middle of the change continuum. Essentially it is a state of constant small changes being made that all lead toward larger change goals. They indicated that they drew on the Chinese saying, "The sage does not attempt anything very big and thus achieves great things." Seeking the middle ground is often the best approach to change. In today's environment you may find that something similar to their approach—almost constant change—is what you will have to engage in.

CHANGE PROCESS MODELS

In terms of helping staff address change, it is useful to have some knowledge of the two widely discussed models for planned change: Lewin's model and Kotter's model, both of which are discussed in more detail later in this section. Kurt Lewin's (1951) change model was one of the first to be described, and it is certainly the most commonly thought of one when it comes to discussing the change process and management. His force-field analysis has become a classic model for thinking about organizational change.

How change occurs is a factor in how staff will react to a proposed change. The earlier comment from Virginia Walter mentions imposed change, that is, change mandated by outside agencies such as the library's parent organization. Recently there seems to be too much change imposed on libraries. The economic downturn has caused almost every organization to look at ways to reduce expenses. For libraries, this has often meant reduced hiring or hiring freezes, reduced service hours, and fewer programs. Clearly such requirements mean change for the staff. Mandated changes almost always present you with the challenge of broader based and stronger resistance to the proposed/required change.

Oreg and Sverdlik (2011) emphasized the importance of understanding the different types of change, stating:

> An important factor that distinguishes between the various types of change . . . is the amount of discretion that individuals have in adopting change. Whereas some changes are voluntary, others are imposed, and whereas reactions to any change are influenced by how the individual feels about the notion of change, reactions to imposed (vs. voluntary) change are also influenced by how the individual feels about the imposition. (p. 338)

Presenting a change to the staff as "an experiment" is a good way to cause it to fail. "Why bother with an experiment? Doesn't management know what they're doing?" are very common reactions to this approach. Lewin, a sociologist, noted in many cases in his research that change often lasted only a brief time before people reverted, as much as possible, to their former ways. Lewin suggested that if a person's behavior is to change, three interrelated conditions must occur: unfreezing, changing, and refreezing.

Lewin (1951) developed his three-step model from his force-field analysis concept. The concept involves a person, unit, or organization and how he/she/it must overcome the status quo or the state of equilibrium in order to change. He suggested that two sets of forces are at work to maintain the equilibrium: driving forces and restraining forces (see Figure 9.1, p. 214). For changes to occur, the driving forces must be greater than the restraining forces.

"Unfreezing" is a process for creating a readiness to acquire or learn new behaviors. This means assisting staff in recognizing the ineffectiveness of the current behavior in terms of the area of the planned change. It also means pointing out how the change will benefit the staff and the organization (e.g., a task will take less time, a task will be less stressful, the organization will stay viable in a changing environment). Unfreezing staff may be a time-consuming process, and without their active participation it will be difficult. Not only do people need to adjust to change but also, in many cases, the organizational culture needs to adjust as well. Without successfully completing this process, you are not likely to achieve long-lasting change.

"Changing" is the period when staff begin to work with the new behavior pattern. More often than not, there will be a testing period first while staff members make up their mind about the new situation. You should be watchful during the changing period, as staff may begin to slip back into the old pattern. You should be even more supportive than usual during this period.

"Refreezing" takes place when the staff internalize the change and it becomes part of the organizational culture. Rewards for implementing the new pattern are a key factor in achieving refreezing.

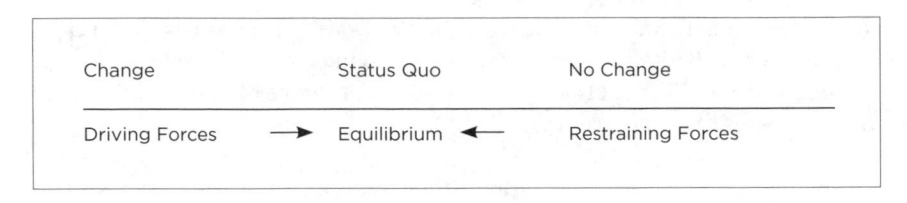

Figure 9.1 Lewin's Force-Field Concept

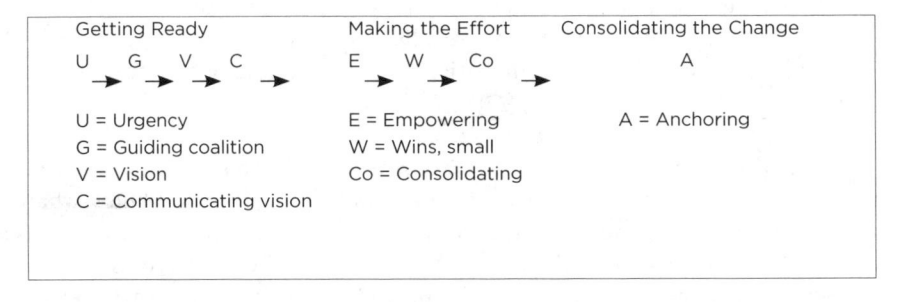

Figure 9.2 Kotter's Eight-Stage Change Model

John Kotter (1990) expanded Lewin's three-phase model by breaking down Lewin's steps into eight smaller components (see Figure 9.2). During the unfreezing process he suggested that managers should establish a sense of urgency, create a "guiding" coalition, develop a vision and strategy for the change, and finally communicate the change vision.

His components for the change phase are empower staff for action, generate some short-term "wins," and consolidate gains (don't declare victory too soon). The only difference between Lewin's refreezing stage and Kotter's "anchoring" stage is that Kotter points out that it may take years for change(s) to be anchored and become a part of the organizational culture.

Kotter's (1990) model is successfully used today. He made this point about change (anywhere on the continuum): "It is because such [change] is so difficult to bring about that the transformation process has eight stages instead of two or three, that it often takes so much time, and that it requires so much leadership from so many people" (p. 158). His book provides a number of cases illustrating how the process works in the real world.

Change models have a long history of use and are generally viewed as having value, within limits. Perhaps the most significant limit is that they focus on the incremental to the upper middle range of the change continuum. When you are near the radical end of the scale you have much less time for engaging in the steps suggested in the models. Another limitation is the assumption that the organization's operational environment is relatively stable and therefore would make a smooth transition from one stable state to another. Such an assumption seems less and less valid in today's world. Third, the models do not apply well, if at all, to crisis situations where consultation, widespread involvement, and the like are neither possible nor appropriate. Finally, critics suggest that the models do not give adequate weight to staff resistance and instead give too much to the notion of staff agreement/acceptance.

Research into organizational change has shown that almost 70 percent of change efforts fail to achieve all or most of their objectives (e.g., Kotter, 1990; Higgs and Rowland, 2000). That figure is surprising at first glance and almost unbelievable; however, when you think about it, how many times does one read about failures compared to announcements of success? Few of us like to announce a failed effort. Also, remember that the statistic covers "all or most" of the objectives; thus a partial success counts as a failure. Regardless of what the count of failures should or should not include, why is total success difficult to achieve?

One significant factor lies in the traditional way managers are taught to think about change. Recent research suggests that long-standing models may no longer be fully sufficient for managing change (e.g., Higgs and Rowland, 2000; Burnes, 2004a; Black, 2000; Fitzgerald, 2002). The sense is that, at best, managers have an understanding of how to address complicated change as opposed to radical change.

Senior (2006) outlined three categories of change—rate of occurrence, what triggers it, and its scale. These categories can help you assess the complexity of a change you are considering for your library. In the past, there was a view that successful organizations were highly stable (infrequent change). Clearly, in today's world just the opposite is the case. Success comes from ongoing monitoring of the operating environment and making appropriate adjustments.

One newer approach is "emergent change." The essential point in the emergent model is that you should not think of change as a linear process through

AUTHORS' EXPERIENCE

Alire, in two of her three university library deanships, was hired specifically to be a change agent by the provosts. One of the libraries was constantly referred to by users and campus administrators as the most "dysfunctional and unhealthy organization" on campus, which was affecting its service to the campus community. The other university library system was described internally and externally as a "rat's nest." Blame was flying around the innards of both libraries. Alire's change process was basically emergent, and her modus operandi in both situations was to immediately invalidate the blame mentality and approach change using a service philosophy of "doing what's best for our customers." She did not come into the new situations immediately demanding and implementing change, because the first hurdle she had to deal with was the staff's distrust of "management."

Her modus operandi in concert with her management team was more systematic, focusing on gathering hard data and on implementing an input process to engage staff and library customers/users. Alire's position was: "Everyone had the opportunity to provide input at the department level during discussions about what the library should be focusing on in the strategic plan(s)." Because this process was more systematic, evidence based, and less emotional, it helped to develop more trust, which was critical.

Using the information gathered, the management team worked to develop a vision, mission, and strategic plan. One of the strategic planning goals was transforming the library to better serve the customers. In the meantime, efforts to prepare the staff for change were ongoing. New organizational models were introduced, again based on the need to better serve the libraries' customers.

Although constant communication was used, some staff were still fearful of and resistant to change. The road was definitely rockier at one university library than the other. Over time and as the new organizational models started to be used, more staff adopted the change. The change was by no means perfect, but it did start the library on the road to recovery and to better customer service. Goals and objectives were reviewed and evaluated every year and tweaked as necessary to stay focused on service.

time. Rather, you should think of it in terms of being an open-ended process in which unexpected turns and events are normal (something very similar to what Hawker and Garcia [2010] wrote about). Thinking this way, advocates believe, allows you to cope more effectively with complexity and uncertainty (for details, see Burnes, 2004b; Bamford and Forrester, 2003). Another aspect of the emergent change concept is the need to have staff members who are open to learning.

Returning to the last of Senior's three categories of change, scale, there is less difference of opinion. Scale is the variation along the change continuum. A commonly accepted way to think about scale is as five distinct points: fine-tuning, adjustments, modular unit/department, organizational transformation, and radical. Rune Todnem (2005) summed up the case regarding the high failure rate for change efforts:

> This may indicate a basic lack of a valid framework of how to successfully implement and manage organizational change since what is currently available is a wide range of contradictory and confusing theories and approaches. (p. 378)

Moran and Brightman (2001) defined change management as "the process of continually renewing the organization's direction, structure, and capabilities to serve the ever-changing needs of external and internal customers" (p. 111). An interesting article by Brown and Mark (2005), reporting on focus group sessions with librarians regarding organizational change, suggests librarians are well aware of the need to manage change: "It is particularly interesting to note that the study's participants spoke consistently in positive terms about successful change mechanisms" (p. 73). It takes little thought to understand how McWilliam and Ward-Griffin's (2006) opening statement applies to libraries: "Declining resources and organizational restructuring distract attention from efforts to develop more client-centered, empowering partnership approaches to health and social services" (p. 119).

RESISTANCE TO CHANGE

One fact you must keep in mind is that, while resistance to change is inevitable, there is no definitive means of knowing who will resist and how strong that resistance will be. Some people seem to thrive on change, and some prefer never to change. Occasionally, people switch reactions, creating an unexpected challenge. Knowing exactly what circumstances and what types of change will trigger acceptance or resistance is difficult at best.

What are some of the issues in resistance? When faced with a greater than incremental change, people normally go through a four-stage process: denial, resistance, exploration, and commitment. Denial may take the form of "It will not impact me" or "Why is this necessary?" or "This is unnecessary." When people realize that change will occur, some will actively resist, some will unknowingly resist, and a few will move on to the next stage on their own. Exploration is the first phase of actively accepting the need to change and starting to look at how it will impact personal activities. The final phase is actively working toward making the process a success.

A few people resist change based on some type of fear. One obvious fear relates to job or wage security ("What will happen to my job?"). Change generally brings uncertainty that goes well beyond one's job. Today's status quo is known and is, to a greater or lesser degree, comfortable (the unknown is worrisome). "What will happen to my work relationships?" is a common issue.

SOMETHING TO PONDER

Think about the ways that people demonstrate resistance to change; then consider a change situation you experienced. What, if any, forms of resistance did you feel and/or engage in?

Possible loss of control regarding one's status, power, and future prospects, for example, may play a role for some people.

Change often calls for new duties that may require learning new skills. Learning anxiety is a very real issue for many people ("Can I learn what is required?" "Will I look incompetent in front of my peers?"). The anxiety can lead to serious resistance when something like a new software package is introduced.

Kegan and Lahey (2001) describe a form of resistance that is frequently unrecognized because it occurs with people who appear to be committed to change: "Many people are unwittingly applying productive energy toward a hidden *competing commitment*" (p. 85, emphasis in original). One example Kegan and Lahey give is a project manager who is "dragging his feet" on a project because of a stronger and unrecognized competing commitment (avoidance)—the fear that the next project will be beyond his capabilities. Kegan and Lahey (2001) acknowledge that overcoming such hidden commitments is difficult because "it challenges the very psychological foundation upon which people function" (p. 86). Their article is well worth reading before you undertake a major change.

Lack of information and poor communication are other causes of resistance. The more you explain the exact nature of change and listen to staff concerns, the less likely the staff are to actively resist. Open and honest communication is a key component to achieving a successful change. People who understand the change and its necessity are more accepting of change than are those who do not understand.

BASIC STEPS FOR ADDRESSING RESISTANCE TO CHANGE

- Develop a plan.
- Communicate the need to change, and communicate the plan.
- Build trust (use existing trust).
- Identify potential benefits.
- Openly acknowledge any potential drawbacks.
- Empower people by securing their input and modifications to the plan.
- Provide active encouragement, training, and resources to ensure success.

TABLE 9.1   Common Resistance-to-Change Variables

Personal	Work Situation
Age	Organizational position (level)
Disposition to resist	Tenure in position
Ambivalence to change	Employment status (full, part-time)
Trust in change agent	Support provided for change process
Trust in management	

Related to that understanding is the sense of having a say about the change. Managers must realize that some valid resistance develops when people identify flaws in the proposed change. Pointing out potential or perceived problem areas is not always a method for passively resisting or delaying a change. It may identify an important but overlooked problem area.

John Kotter and Leonard Schlesinger (1979) provided four realistic suggestions for managing resistance to change. In fact, the four points are good management tools for almost any purpose:

- Education plus communication
- Participation plus involvement
- Facilitation plus support
- Negotiation and agreement

You can never predict with 100 percent accuracy who will or will not resist a change, because a host of variables interact with one another. Over the years, researchers interested in change management have studied dozens of variables (see the references listed in the Oreg and Sverdlik [2011] article for many such studies). Table 9.1 lists nine of the most common variables. Not only does each variable manifest itself differently over time and according to the nature of a proposed change, but they also interact with one or more of the other variables. When you consider the range of possibilities from just the nine variables (there are many others as well) you can understand why you can never be 100 percent certain about how much and from whom resistance is likely to arise.

One of the best means for overcoming resistance to change is creating an environment in which people become more accepting of change and its steps. There are at least six broad long-term processes for creating such an environment: generating an acceptance that change is necessary and positive, building a willingness and ability to change, cultivating a support structure for change, providing necessary resources for change, creating an organizational culture that assists staff in changing, and rewarding efforts to change. These are some of the steps you can take to carry out the processes:

- Offer coaching and training in the change process and its value.
- Form diverse staff member teams to assist in planning change.
- Have frequent meetings to discuss and think about potential changes.
- Encourage staff to discuss with users their perceptions of service enhancements.
- Emphasize the importance of thinking about the changing external environment and what, if any, implications it might have for the library.
- Listen to and reward staff suggestions for change, even if the suggestions are not implemented and/or the rewards are modest.

TRY THIS

The list of possible steps you could take can go on for several pages; spend some time thinking about other possibilities, and share your ideas with classmates.

IMPLEMENTING CHANGE

One useful managerial concept is organizational development (OD). This is a method for generating both individual and organizational changes. The approach has been used since the end of World War II. Over the years the focus has shifted in emphasis from its initial concern with creating a "mechanistic" (scientific management) method of managing organizations to today's need to manage change. OD's primary focus is on people who are or will be undergoing an organizational change process. Some of the most frequent uses of OD are assisting with mergers, managing conflict, and revitalizing organizations.

Karen Holloway (2004) outlined 12 elements of OD as applied to libraries. The people elements were letting the people doing the work make as many of the decisions related to their activities as possible; focusing on user community needs and wants; having a focus on group/team dynamics and organizational culture; improving collaborative work efforts and processes; and understanding and accepting shared responsibility/accountability. The organizational elements were creating trust through the organization; focusing on being an agile organization; constantly looking to improve processes; thinking in terms of improvements in "service" for both internal and external customers; employing evidenced-based data in decision making; generating performance-based managerial tools; and linking all activities to mission, vision, values, and organizational goals.

In looking at these elements, you can probably see how you might employ OD for managing change, innovation, team building, and a many other activities.

CHECK THESE OUT

A classic text on organizational development is Richard Beckhard's *Organization Development: Strategies and Models* (Reading, MA: Addison-Wesley, 1969).

The *Library Trends* issue "Organizational Development and Leadership" (2004, 53, no. 1) is a good resource. Of particular interest is Shelly Phipps' essay relating the 10-year experience of the University of Arizona library in using OD.

One reason that OD has lasted as long as it has is its many uses and flexibility. How one organization makes use of OD is often very different from what you will see in another OD-oriented entity.

David Payne (2010) suggested that some conflict may be beneficial:

A recently overheard criticism of a work colleague was surprising—"she makes her employees too comfortable." This appeared to fly in the face of much that librarians have been taught about management, such as fostering team spirit, encouraging openness, and making employees feel valued. In this case, however, the issue was that the manager's employees were not growing. . . . They were not being taken outside their comfort zone; they are never challenged. (p. 6)

He goes on to review the value of conflict within the organization and how to manage it for the organization's benefit. Another good article about this topic in relation to libraries is Jane McGrun Kathman and Michael D. Kathman's (1990) "Conflict Management in Academic Libraries."

Technology can be a disruptive force at times in the workplace, and conflicts often arise when you introduce a new technology or software package. When an information service decides to shift to a new integrated library system, change is organizationwide, and, if all goes well, the organization is revitalized. Organizational development techniques can assist with such challenges.

STRESS AND THE ORGANIZATION

Workplace stress is very common. It can and does arise from many causes. Without too much debate, it seems clear that organizational change is one of the leading causes of stress for many employees. One question is, is workplace stress always a bad thing? The answer is, not always.

In 1946, Hans Selye introduced his concept of general adaptation syndrome. He defined stress as a bodily reaction to any positive or negative stimuli. A more detailed definition of the concept by Charles Bunge (1989) is "a person's psychological and physiological response to the perception of a demand or challenge. The nature and intensity of this response depends on the meaning one gives to that demand or challenge and on one's assessment of the resources that are available for meeting it" (p. 93).

Excessive stress, personal or organizational, can diminish health and thereby adversely affect work productivity; however, "less agreement exists regarding the effects of stress on organizational effectiveness" (Zaccaro and Riley, 1987, p. 1). Some management researchers, such as James Quick (1992), suggest that organizational and staff stress are not necessarily bad. J. E. McGrath (1976) showed that in the workplace there is an inverted-U relationship between stress and performance. That is, when there is little or no stress, staff are in a state of boredom and performance/productivity is low as well. As stress increases, so does performance up to a point (after which it falls). Using a scale of 0 to 100 to indicate the level of stress, when stress is somewhere near the midpoint performance begins to fall off and drop back to the low point, indicating boredom. The issue for managers is to find the right level and type of stress to achieve maximum performance and not go beyond that point.

CHECK THESE OUT

A must-read for anyone going into management is Richard Boyatzis and Annie McKee's *Resonant Leadership: Renewing Yourself and Connecting with Others through Mindfulness, Hope and Compassion* (Cambridge, MA: Harvard Business School Press, 2005), which covers dealing with power stress and recovery.

Maria Vakola and Ioannis Nikolaou's excellent article "Attitudes towards Organizational Change" (*Employee Relations* 27, no. 2: 160–174, 2005) addresses change, stress, and commitment.

Karen Brown and Kate Marek's "Librarianship and Change" (*Library Administration and Management* 19, no. 2: 68–74, 2005) is a fine piece examining change and librarians.

For many people, the response to too much stress is physiological, often taking the form of illness. Undoubtedly, stress contributes to mental illness, alcoholism, and drug and other substance abuse, as well as to other dysfunctional conditions that lead to poor job performance. It is also clear that stress is not just work related. People can usually cope effectively when either personal or workplace stress is low, but problems develop when both are high. When coping strategies fail, burnout is often the result. Stress, distress, strain, and burnout are a continuum of a condition wherein:

- on the whole, challenges are sources of happiness and productive responses;
- perceived imbalances between demands and resources are painful, but coping strategies restore the balance and reduce the pain;
- inappropriate coping strategies are out of control (i.e., are contributing to the problem); and the person's physical and mental resources are depleted (Bunge, 1990, p. 94).

One of the challenges for you as a manager comes from the fact that what is stressful for one person may not be stressful for someone else. There is no way to know what will or will not be stressful for any staff member, nor is there a single "cure" for resolving the stress once you identify it. Some methods of coping can be taught, such as relaxation, meditation, and biofeedback. While these techniques are individualized and no organizational support is necessary, some large organizations do offer training courses in these techniques to interested staff.

David Fisher (1990) claimed, based on critical analysis of stress and burnout studies in the library profession published up to 1989, that there is no empirical evidence that stress and burnout are any higher in library services than in similar professions. As you might expect, stress can be a significant factor in the change process and a major contributor to workplace burnout.

INNOVATION AND LIBRARIES

Is there a difference between creativity and innovation? The most straightforward answer is that creativity is the process of producing/generating new ideas, while innovation is about implementing a new idea in an organization. Thus it is possible to be "innovative" through the introduction of a new idea for your organization even if the idea itself has existed for some time and/or has been used in other organizations.

Something to keep in mind about innovation and libraries is this: "Historically, most managers equated innovation with the development of new products and new technologies. But increasingly, innovation is seen as applying to the development of new service offerings, business models, pricing plans and routes to market, as well as new management practices" (Birkinshaw, Bouquet, and Barsoux, 2011, p. 43).

CHECK THIS OUT

A good article about innovation and libraries is Jennifer Rowley's "Should Your Library Have an Innovation Strategy?" (*Library Manage*ment 32, nos. 4/5: 251–256, 2011).

Catherine Wang and Prevaiz Ahmed (2004) conducted a literature review and identified five areas of typical organizational innovativeness: product, market/service, process, behavioral, and strategic. In an academic library, an example of product innovation might be developing the concept of an electronic "institutional repository" for the parent institution. In terms of market/service innovation, it might be to offer faculty members office delivery (in person or electronic) of documents. From a process point of view, ceasing to check in serials (we do know of at least one case) might qualify as innovative. A behavioral example might be greeting everyone when they enter the library or archives and perhaps offering jelly beans or mints. A strategic innovation might be to shift from an institutionwide service focus to a tailored service focus—including staffing—aimed at a college, school, institute, and so forth.

Voelpel, Leibold, and Streb (2005) concluded that "recent academic and business evidence indicates that innovation is the key factor for companies' success and sustained fitness in a rapidly evolving, knowledge-networked economy" (p. 57). They described how 3M, known for its innovations, fosters innovative thinking and actions. Although libraries may not be able to set as clear a target for innovations as does 3M (30 percent of future sales should come from products that did not exist four years earlier), the principle is relevant to their situation—thinking about and acting innovatively. The idea that top management can foster, or not foster, innovative ideas is true. The point to remember is that you will demonstrate your support of innovative ideas whether you are aware of that fact or not; your values and beliefs are the key to whether your unit/library is innovative.

You should give some thought to innovation as part of the change process. If you seek input from staff regarding how to change and let them know

TEST YOUR INNOVATIVENESS

Think of additional innovative ideas for an academic library with which you are familiar. Pick another type of information service, and try to come up with some ideas for each of the five areas identified by Wang and Ahmed (2004).

> ### CHECK THIS OUT
>
> An older but still very informative resource on innovation and information services is Carmel Maguire, Edward Kazlauskas, and Anthony Weir's *Information Services for Innovative Organizations* (San Diego: Academic Press, 1994).

that "crazy ideas" are welcome, you will cultivate an environment where staff members see themselves as part of the process of making things better, where change is less frightening, and where new approaches are encouraged. Do you want to be on the incremental end of the continuum—adopting ideas that are successfully and widely used in other libraries? Do you want to move toward the center by using an idea that has a successful track record in other types of organizations but has not yet been tried in a library? Or do you want to be the innovator (on the radical end of the change continuum) by applying new knowledge to your unit or library? Only you can answer these questions.

We suggested earlier that organizational culture plays a significant role in the success or failure of organizational change. Organizational culture influences creativity and innovation in at least two ways:

- Through shared values and norms, people make judgments and assumptions regarding the acceptability of creative/innovative behavior within the organization.
- Established forms of behavior and activity, especially as reflected in practices and procedures, lead people to develop perceptions about valued and non-valued behaviors and activities. (Martins and Terblanche, 2003, p. 68)

Other factors that encourage organizational innovation include the following:

- Socialization regarding acceptable work behavior
- Values related to acceptability of risk taking

> ### CHECK THIS OUT
>
> Charles O'Reilly and Michael Tushman wrote an informative article, "The Ambidextrous Organization" (*Harvard Business Review* 82, no. 4: 74–81, 2004), on the subject of innovation and organizational culture.

AUTHORS' EXPERIENCE

Evans uses an exercise with students when discussing change and innovation that seems to stay with them for years. It is also a technique he used with the staff in the libraries he administered.

Participants are asked to list as "many uses for a brick" as they can. After five minutes there is a discussion of the lists. As is true of possible solutions for cases, the total of potential uses surpasses any one person's list. If there are less than 30 participants, it is rare for a person to list "break the brick," that is, think of a way to modify the brick's form. When this does occur, several participants will get upset; when no one makes a suggestion to modify the brick, Evans suggests one additional possible use—cut the brick in half to make a pair of book ends. Either way, others in the group say, in some variation, "You didn't say we could change the form of the brick." Evans's response is, "I didn't say you couldn't. You imposed that constraint on yourself, not me. When faced with a difficult situation, you must try to "break the brick."

Over the years Evans has received numerous notes from people with anecdotes regarding additional uses of a brick. Most also say they have used the technique with their staff to promote innovative thinking.

- Flexibility in actions and thinking
- Freedom and encouragement to explore new ideas
- Cooperative, empowered work teams
- Support from management
- Treatment of mistakes as opportunities for learning rather than punishment
- Tolerance of conflict as natural and useful in developing new ideas
- Open and honest communication

What can a small library do to encourage innovative thinking? The typical small public or school library is staffed by one or two professionals, with perhaps a few paraprofessionals or volunteers. Sometimes a person is the only staff. Certainly this situation can encourage stagnation, because the stimulation of working with professional peers is lacking. In such cases, material about new ideas and their managerial applications is of the utmost importance.

It takes considerable mental stimulation to keep current with professional developments and to continue professional growth. You should try keep up with the profession through reading journals and attending conferences to avoid settling into a dull, unimaginative routine, even though finding the time for these activities can be difficult given your workload and need to have a personal life.

Perhaps you could delegate one or two of your tasks to a coworker or a good volunteer to gain a few minutes for professional reading during work time.

Within a library (regardless of size), managers need to make special efforts to encourage innovation. Although overcontrol (micromanagement) does provide a stable environment, it is not the best method for generating new ideas, independent thinking, and responsibility on the staff's part. The more they see they are a part of decisions, planning, and so forth, the more willing they will be to explore and accept possible changes in their work environment.

You shape library services and programs based on user needs, or you should. Getting the users involved in planning changes and even for generating "innovative" ideas can pay dividends when you have time to do so. Sara D. Smith and Quinn Galbraith (2011) provide an example of user involvement when they describe how a Student Advisory Board had an impact: "These groups have lead to changes in their respective libraries. . . . One of the most significant and innovative changes has been the creation of a music zone" (p. 395). The authors report that this innovation in a low-use area increased student use there by 20 percent. Users often think outside the library/professional box when asked to be involved.

INNOVATION TECHNIQUES

Some techniques can assist an individual in generating new ideas about ways of behaving or doing things. These operational techniques help people to overcome their fear of using their imaginations by enabling them to move back to the childhood pattern of asking "why," "what if," and "how." They then explore their environment to find the answers. Table 9.2 (p. 228) provides some suggestions for how to encourage staff to think in new ways. Table 9.3 (p. 229) outlines some of the basic "rules" for helping to ensure that the techniques are as successful as possible.

The successful management of innovation and change builds on an understanding of how the service developed over time. We can comprehend the present only by examining the past. In addition, an awareness of the environment in which the service operates is necessary, together with data and information derived from a marketing program.

Here is a final thought about creativity and innovation. Perhaps we can take some comfort regarding the recent "Great Recession" from Steve Jobs (Gallo,

AUTHORS' EXPERIENCE

Another catalyst for creativity and innovation is a disaster! Alire, in her role leading a major disaster recovery at Colorado State University, was constantly in awe of a library staff that employed creativity and innovation, from developing never-before-used cost models for insurance claims to systems designs of recovery processes never used in disaster recovery.

TABLE 9.2   Techniques to Foster New Thinking

Method	Process
Logical/problem-solving approach	1. Start with a defined situation/activity. 2. Identify all elements of the situation/activity. 3. List all possible changes/options. 4. Consider each change/option against others. 5. Assess consequences.
Input/output	1. Identify desired outcome in broad terms. 2. List all possible changes/options that could lead to desired outcome. 3. Assess consequences.
Free association/brainstorming	1. Provide a very general frame of reference for discussion (do not define the problem). 2. Encourage any and all thoughts even tangentially related to the topic under consideration. 3. Assess ideas after the flow of ideas/thoughts ceases.

Note: These methods work best with small groups.

2011, p. viii): "The good news is that recessions often act as catalysts for innovation. . . . History shows that the greatest innovations have been introduced in periods of severe economic stress. . . . Indeed stress, conflict, and necessity seem to be nature's way of saying, 'Find a new way.'" Libraries and you must find those "new ways" using your creative thinking.

KEY POINTS TO REMEMBER
- Change is inevitable.
- Change is essential.
- Change is a managerial challenge.
- Change is either reactive or proactive.
- Change takes place along a continuum—incremental to radical.
- Change most often happens in terms of people, technology, structure, and/or strategy.
- Change will generate resistance.
- Change process models assist but do not completely solve organizational issues.

TABLE 9.3   Basic "Rules" to Encourage New Thinking

Element to Consider	Action to Take
Duration	Treat group sessions as ongoing rather than one-time events. Staff members need time to adjust and realize that the purpose, value, and intent of management are serious.
Size	Keep group size small to encourage wide participation (five to seven people seems to work best).
Feedback	Provide serious, thoughtful, honest feedback to group about their ideas. Lack of such response tends to raise doubts about management's intent.
Monitoring	Monitor early group discussions to ensure that no "judgments" are made during the idea-generation phase of the process. Negative/judgmental reactions will kill the process.

- Change management is an important managerial activity.
- Innovation may lead to uncertain outcomes, but those often are rewarding.
- Innovation and change are complex processes.
- Innovation is knowledge intensive.
- Innovative/new ways of staff thinking can be developed.
- Innovation can be controversial (benefit or boondoggle).
- Innovation requires risk taking.
- Innovation and effective change flourish in flexible, open, learning-oriented, empowered organizations.

References

Bamford, David, and Paul Forrester. 2003. "Managing Planned and Emergent Change within an Operations Management Environment." *International Journal of Operations and Production Management* 23, no. 5/6: 546–564.

Birkinshaw, Julian, Cyril Bouquet, and J. L. Barsoux. 2011. "The 5 Myths of Innovation." *MIT Sloan Management Review* 52, no. 2: 43–50.

Black, Janice A. 2000. "Fermenting Change." *Journal of Organizational Change Management* 13, no. 6: 520–525.

Brown, Karen, and Kate Mark. 2005. "Librarianship and Change: A Consideration of Weick's 'Drop Your Tools' Metaphor." *Library Administration and Management* 19, no. 2: 68–74.

Bunge, Charles. 1989. "Stress in the Library Workplace." *Library Trends* 38, no. 1: 93–102.

Burnes, Bernard. 2004a. "Kurt Lewin and Complexity Theories." *Journal of Change Management* 4, no. 4: 309–325.

———. 2004b. *Managing Change.* 4th ed. New York: Prentice-Hall.

Doan, Tomalee, and Mary Lee Kennedy. 2009. "Innovation, Creativity, and Meaning: Leading in the Information Age." *Journal of Business and Finance Librarianship* 14, no. 4: 348–358.

Fisher, David. 1990. "Are Librarians Burning Out?" *Journal of Librarianship* 22, no. 4: 216–235.

Fitzgerald, Laurie A. 2002. "Chaos: The Lens That Transcends." *Journal of Organizational Change Management* 15, no. 4: 339–358.

Gallo, Carmine. 2011. *The Innovation Secrets of Steve Jobs: Insanely Different Principles for Breakthrough Success.* New York: McGraw Hill.

Hawker, Kate, and Melissa Garcia. 2010. "Radical Change One Step at a Time." *Associations Now* 6, no. 11: 27–30.

Higgs, Malcom, and Deborah Rowland. 2000. "Building Change Capability." *Journal of Change Management* 1, no. 2: 116–131.

Holloway, Karen. 2004. "The Significance of Organizational Development in Academic Research Libraries." *Library Trends* 53, no. 1: 5–16.

Hopkins, Michael S. 2010. "Innovation Isn't 'Creativity,' It's a Discipline You Manage: An Interview with Esther Baldwin." *MIT Sloan Management Review* February, 51, no. 3: 1–7.

Jaskyte, Kristina. 2011. "Predictors of Administrative and Technological Innovations on Nonprofit Organizations." *Public Administration Review* 71, no. 1: 77–86.

Kathman, Jane McGrun, and Michael D. Kathman. 1990. "Conflict Management in Academic Libraries." *Journal of Academic Librarianship* 16, no. 3: 145–149.

Kegan, Robert, and Lisa Laskow Lahey. 2001. "The Real Reason People Won't Change." *Harvard Business Review* 79, no. 10: 85–92.

Kotter, John. 1990. *A Force for Change: How Leadership Differs from Management.* New York: Simon and Schuster.

Kotter, John, and Leonard Schlesinger. 1979. "Choosing Strategies for Change." *Harvard Business Review* 57, no. 2: 106–114.

Lewin, Kurt. 1951. *Field Theory in Social Sciences.* New York: Harper and Row.

Machiavelli, Niccolo. 1952. *The Prince.* New York: New American Library.

Martins, E. C., and F. Terblanche. 2003. "Building Organizational Culture That Stimulates Creativity and Innovation." *European Journal of Innovation Management* 6, no. 1: 64–74.

McGrath, Joseph E. 1976. "Stress and Behavior in Organizations." In *Handbook of Industrial and Organizational Psychology,* edited by Marvin D. Dunnette. Chicago: Rand McNally.

McLaughlin, Michael W. 2011. "The Trouble with Incremental Change." *The Conference Board Review* 48, no. 1: 12–13.

McWilliam, Carol L., and Catherine Ward-Griffin. 2006. "Implementing Organizational Change in Health and Social Services." *Journal of Organizational Change Management* 19, no. 2: 119–135.

Moran, John, and Baird Brightman. 2001. "Leading Organizational Change." *Career Development International* 6, no. 2: 111–119.

Munduate, Lourdes, and Francis Media. 2009. "Organizational Change." In *Power and Interdependence in Organizations*, edited by Dean Tjosvold and Barbara Wisse. Cambridge, England: Cambridge University Press.

Oreg, Shaul, and Noga Sverdlik. 2011. "Ambivalence toward Imposed Change." *Journal of Applied Psychology* 96, no. 2: 337–349.

Payne, David. 2010. "Harnessing Conflict." *Library Leadership and Management* 24, no. 1: 6–11.

Proffitt, Merrilee. 2011. "Something's Got to Give: What Can We Stop Doing in a Time of Reduced Resources?" *RBM: A Journal of Rare Books, Manuscripts, and Cultural Heritage* 12, no. 2: 89–91.

Quick, James. 1992. *Stress and Well-Being in the Workplace*. Washington, DC: American Psychological Association.

Roberts, Richard A. 2011. "You Want to Improve? First You Must Change." *Supervision* 72, no. 1: 11–13.

Selye, Hans. 1946. "The General Adaptation Syndrome and the Diseases of Adaptation." *Journal of Clinical Endocrinology* 6: 117–231.

Senior, Barbara. 2006. *Organizational Change*. 3rd ed. New York: Prentice-Hall.

Smith, Sara D., and Quinn Galbraith. 2011. "Shopping Carts and Student Employees: How Student Committees Can Bring Innovative Ideas to Academic Libraries." *College and Research Libraries News* 72, no. 7: 395–397.

Szamosi, Leslie, and Linda Duxbury. 2002. "Development of a Measure to Assess Organizational Change." *Journal of Organizational Change Management* 15, no. 2: 184–201.

Todnem, Rune. 2005. "Organizational Change Management." *Journal of Change Management* 5, no. 4: 369–380.

Tzabbar, Daniel. 2009. "What Helps and Hinders Innovation? *MIT Sloan Management Review* 51, no. 1: 17.

Voelpel, Sven C., Marius Leibold, and Christoph K. Streb. 2005. "The Innovation Meme: Managing Innovation Replicators for Organizational Fitness." *Journal of Change Management* 5, no. 1: 57–69.

Wang, Catherine, and Pervaiz Ahmed. 2004. "The Development and Validation of the Organizational Innovativeness Construct Using Confirmatory Factor Analysis." *European Journal of Innovation Management* 7, no. 4: 303–313.

Zaccaro, Stephen, and Ann Riley. 1987. "Stress, Coping, and Organizational Effectiveness." In *Occupational Stress and Organizational Effectiveness*, edited by Stephen Zaccaro and Ann Riley, 1–18. New York: Praeger.

Launching Pad

Buono, Anthony F., and Kenneth W. Kerber. 2010. "Creating a Sustainable Approach to Change: Building Organizational Change Capacity." *Advanced Management Journal* 75, no. 2: 1–14, 21.

Cervone, H. Frank. 2011. "Overcoming Resistance to Change in Digital Library Projects." *OCLC Systems and Services* 27, no. 2: 95–98.

Garrow, Valerie, and Sharon Varney. 2009. "What Does OD Do?" *People Management* June 4: 28–30.

Heath, Chip, and Dan Heath. 2011. "Overcoming Resistance to Change." *School Administrator* 68, no. 3: 28–32.

Konings, Kees, and Ronald Dekker. 2005. "Strategy and Change Management in Delft University of Technology." *New Review of Information Networking* 11, no. 1: 109–121.

Kotter, John P. 2002. *The Heart of Change: Real-Life Stories of How People Change Their Organizations.* Boston: Harvard Business School Press.

Latham, Scott F., and Michael Braun. 2009. "Managerial Risk, Innovation, and Organizational Decline." *Journal of Management* 35, no. 2: 258–281.

Library Technology Reports. 2010. "Lesson for Library Innovation" *Library Technology Reports* July: 38–43.

Miller, Nick. 2010. "Leading Workplace Innovation and Change: Brave New Role." *T+D* 64, no. 6: 545–558.

MIT Sloan Management Review. 2008. "Learning to Innovate." *MIT Sloan Management Review* 49, no. 3: 12–13.

Rothaermel, Frank, and Andrew M. Hess. 2010. "Innovation Strategies Combined." *MIT Sloan Management Review* 51, no. 3: 13–15.

Russell, Keith. 2008. "Evidenced-Based Practice and Organizational Development in Libraries." *Library Trends* 56, no. 4: 910–930.

Schachter, Debbie. 2005. "Creative Chaos: Innovation in Special Libraries." *Information Outlook* 9, 12 December: 10–11.

Schwirtlich, Anne-Marie. 2010. "Public Libraries and Change: A Perspective from Victoria." *Aplis* 23, no. 1: 22–27.

Smedley, Tim. 2010. "It Is Possible to Manage Disruptive Change and Take the Staff with You." *People Management* 3, June: 16–19.

Travis, Tiffini A. 2008. "Librarians as Agents of Change: Working with Curriculum Committees Using Change Agency Theory." *New Direction in Teaching and Learning*, no. 114: 17–33.

Tupper, Cawsey, and Gene Deszca. 2007. *Toolkit for Organizational Change.* London: Sage.

Over the years I assisted a number of libraries and library-related organizations to develop change strategies, but during that time I rarely encountered a library administrator who placed a high priority on analysis of either existing workflows or activities. There were a few who talked the talk but rarely walked the walk.

I was really disappointed at the reception to *Streamlining Library Services*. I thought that librarians would find it to be a valuable resource, but I was dead wrong; it didn't make a whit of an impact. As I said, library administrators weren't interested or didn't appreciate the potential benefits. In part this lack of interest might be explained by the absence of professionals equipped to conduct analyses of library activities. I believe I'm correct when I say that there is no LIS school that currently offers a course on analysis using the type of tools presented in *Streamlining*. . . . One or two classes in an Administration course doesn't get the job done.

Many years ago Ralph R. Shaw (a library giant and the founder of Scarecrow Press) once reminded me that doing something efficiently that didn't need to be done at all was pretty foolish. (Stupid is the word that Ralph probably used. Dr. Shaw didn't suffer fools lightly.) The same is true today. There are all sorts of activities that libraries perform today that could be either streamlined or entirely eliminated.

Librarians increasingly are going to be expected to demonstrate that their contributions to their parent institution or community justify the current level of funding they enjoy. Effectiveness and relevancy of core activities should be an essential ingredient of an assessment environment.

—Richard M. Dougherty, ALA President, 1990–1991 (2012)

Assessment is a cycle; its purpose is improvement; its application is local. The cycle of assessment can be described simply as listening to the patron (collecting information), analyzing the implications of what we hear, and improving based on the input.

—Jeanne M. Brown (2010)

Librarians sometimes have difficulty quantifying the value of the services and resources we provide our constituencies.

—Virginia L. Cairns (2006)

Library administrators have been faced with many difficult and painful choices in recent years as budgets have remained persistently tight, and society and governments demand greater accountability among social institutions such as libraries. . . . . One way to free up staff time and dollar resources is to streamline process and procedures or, better yet, get rid of existing operations that are redundant or unnecessary.

—Richard M. Dougherty (2008)

10

ASSESSMENT, QUALITY CONTROL, AND OPERATIONS

This chapter focuses on the following:

- Assessment and accountability
- Why assess quality library service
- Measuring performance and quality
- Basic questions before you start
- Assessment tools (standards, surveys such as LibQUAL+, benchmarking, balanced scorecard, focus groups)
- Quality control
- Methods for controlling operations (cost accounting, systems approach, time and motion, work flow analysis)

ASSESSMENT, QUALITY CONTROL, and operations management may appear to be an odd combination of topics for a chapter. In one sense they are, yet in another sense they are in fact intertwined. Assessment is a vital tool in a manager's tool kit as are quality and operations control.

Quality is a significant issue for libraries; they ought to always be looking at what and how they are performing their services. This said, in difficult economic times, libraries must redouble their focus on quality, effectiveness, and efficiency. As Richard Dougherty stated in his first opening quotation, maintaining the status quo was, is, and probably will be a major challenge for many U.S. libraries, at least until the economy is healthy again. Assessment, quality control, and operations management activities are tools you can use to stretch limited funds as well as gather value data/facts to support your requests for funding.

In Chapter 5, we discussed accountability; in this chapter we look at a related concept—assessment. On one level the concepts are interrelated; both can, and at times do, look at what the libraries have done and do now. Both can, and at times do, lead to significant changes in what, how, when, and where we carry out library activities. Both can be conducted internally and externally to the library. One useful way to differentiate the two concepts

ADVISORY BOARD EXPERIENCE

Virginia Walter commented on public libraries' approaches to evaluation and assessment:

> Evaluation as a component of accountability has been a big deal in the public library community since at least the 1990s when the first manuals on output measures were published by the Public Library Association. They helped librarians learn to collect quantitative data that would accurately reflect the outputs of their services and then communicate them to decision makers. More recently, outcomes assessment is on everybody's radar. Outcomes evaluation requires a somewhat more sophisticated methodology, and many libraries with big grant-funded projects hire consultants to do the work for them. Some of us have been encouraging librarians to do-it-themselves with what might be called "outcomes evaluation light," using methods that are a compromise between academic rigor and practicality. The book that I refer to for this approach is *Dynamic Youth Services through Outcome-Based Planning and Evaluation* by Eliza T. Dresang, Melissa Gross, and Leslie E. Holt (ALA, 2006).

is that accountability is usually performed by someone from the outside, while assessment is something we do, or should do, ourselves. The goal in either case is most often to improve the quality of our operations, services, and programs.

Chapter 8 (on communication) made the point that common words usually carry multiple meanings. Assess is one such word. Using a standard thesaurus you can identify 18 or more synonyms for the word—to audit, to check up, to judge, to review, to scrutinize, and many more. All of the words apply to the topics in this chapter—that is, looking at a behavior or service and making a quality determination. Effective managers are almost always rating, ranking, grading, gauging, estimating, valuing, and so forth what takes place in their unit, department, or library.

ASSESSMENT AND ACCOUNTABILITY

Today, parent organization administrators; federal, state, and local governmental authorities; and users and the general public are demanding that institutions be accountable. They want evidence of value for monies provided. Libraries are attempting to address the accountability challenge through new and more purposeful assessments that go beyond quantifying inputs and outputs. For much of the twentieth century large libraries, and academic libraries in general, were often

SOMETHING TO PONDER

Can you give four examples of accountability as they apply to any type of library? We have suggested that greater emphasis is being placed on accountability. Does this agree with your experience?

viewed by funders as "black holes," absorbing ever greater quantities of money and little evidence of positive outcomes. What funders now want is evidence or, to use a business term, ROI (return on investment).

The trend calling for increased accountability is driven by economic pressures on all funding agencies. This in turn has led to greater concern about the outcomes of all expenditures. The federal Government Performance and Results Act of 1993 required annual progress reports from every government agency toward achieving performance goals and being accountable. This has affected publicly funded state and local libraries. Major foundations are also requiring greater accountability for how their funds are used. Some state libraries, for example, Florida, expect libraries submitting grant proposals to use outcomes assessment as a measure of accountability. The Institute of Museums and Library Services (IMLS), through grants and awards, encourages the adoption of outcome-based evaluation in both libraries and museums.

Many libraries are moving toward more user-centered assessments that measure how a library affects its users. Most notable in this change is the growing popularity of assessing the quality of library services. To do this many libraries are moving toward assessing outcomes, especially in the context of how the library program affects users. In higher education, for example, the regional accrediting associations have modified their standards to include requirements to document learning outcomes as evidence of student learning, and libraries are called on to provide evidence of their contribution to the teaching and learning mission of the parent institution.

WHY ANALYZE PERFORMANCE?

The impression a newcomer to the field might get from looking at the professional literature is that assessment/evaluation is new to the profession; this view would be incorrect. Libraries have been evaluating their activities for at least 100 years by collecting statistics on the inputs and outputs related to services delivered. Librarians have used the statistics for planning, justifying budget requests, and improving services. Inputs and outputs have been mainstays in library management for a long time. Perhaps without a firm grasp on what is actually being achieved from the outputs, such as the number of reference questions answered, the number of items checked out, the number of information literacy lectures delivered, and the number of ILLs obtained for library users and loaned to other

CHECK THIS OUT

Cole, Bryan R., and John B. Harer. 2005. "The Importance of the Stakeholder in Performance Measurement: Critical Processes and Performance Measures for Assessing and Improving Academic Library Services and Programs." *College and Research Libraries* 66, no. 2: 149–170.

libraries, the statistics do not tell you much about library value, outcomes, benefits, or quality in terms of users.

Assessment was defined, in terms of academic libraries, by Hernon, Dugan, and Schwartz (2006) as documenting "observed, reported, or otherwise quantified changes in attitudes and skills of students on an individual basis because of contact with library services, programs, or instruction" (p. 4). Substitute the word "users" for "students," and this definition applies to all types of libraries.

Certainly two of the key reasons for conducting assessment are to address accountability issues and to support budget requests. However, there are several other reasons that are at least equally important. Libraries have stakeholders beyond those who provide the operating funds. Two obvious groups are the users and the staff. Another group is the general community, members of which either directly or indirectly support the library. One group that is sometimes overlooked is other libraries, especially members of consortia to which the library belongs. All of these groups have an interest in the library's performance.

In terms of outcomes, Catherine Haras (2010) wrote about efforts at California State University–Los Angeles (CSULA) to assess the outcomes of its information literacy program. Like all universities in California, CSULA has to address the assessment/outcome expectations of the WASC (Western Association of Schools and Colleges) accreditation requirements. Although assessment is important for accreditation, it is also valuable in terms of planning, assigning resources, improving services, and so forth. Haras (2010) noted, in her discussion of starting an assessment effort for the information literacy program, that "The library involved all campus stakeholders early in the process, including students, faculty, and administration. To this end, we used measures that were by turns homegrown and standardized, direct and indirect, and qualitative and quantitative, on the basis of type, need, and stakeholder" (p. 92). Her concluding comment is worth remembering: "The program is successful precisely because the library has continued working with and involving stakeholders directly. . . . Depending upon your library and your culture, you may identify new stakeholders who will ultimately drive your program" (p. 94). Her thoughts are worth remembering for several reasons. First, it makes the point that assessment is, or should be, ongoing. Second, getting and keeping stakeholders involved in the process helps ensure that they buy into the results. And third, you should always keep an eye open for potential new stakeholders.

Users are why libraries exist, and involving them in your assessment program will pay dividends. However, before going too far in that direction, you might spend some time thinking about the performance factors that they view as important. People take a keen interest in the quality of service they receive regardless of organization, not just libraries. Generally, people have four criteria by which they judge service. They expect to get what they want, when they want it, at a cost that is acceptable to them, and delivered in a way that meets their expectations. Organizations that provide services work hard to ensure that the consumers' criteria are met so as to retain user loyalty. This is as important for libraries as it is for supermarkets. You probably have been on the receiving end of poor service more than once in your life. Thus, you can understand how easy it is to walk away and become an ex-customer. Libraries need to keep all its existing users and, as well, expand that pool. Assessment data can help in both of these efforts.

We sometimes forget that library staff members also have expectations regarding quality. They expect/hope to work in a high-performing organization where they are valued by the other stakeholders. Knowing that they are performing well enhances their job satisfaction. In turn, this creates and sustains an organizational climate in which quality service is paramount. The better the library performs, the more likely the users are to return; conversely, staff members who realize they are not achieving a high level of performance lose motivation, and service quality slides.

We operate today's libraries in an environment filled with competitors. One way libraries attempt to meet the challenges is by having a rich collection of online resources available 24/7. Very few libraries can provide such access on their own. We are increasingly dependent on consortia to achieve some "economy of scale" in terms of database costs. Many libraries are members of several such groups, and all the members of those groups are at least indirect stakeholders in your library. How is that possible? Most database vendor pricing models are based either on the number of participating libraries or on the total number of users in the combined libraries taking part in the "deal." As those numbers increase, the cost per library usually declines. That means that if your library runs into serious assessment/accountability issues and must pull out of a deal, the remaining libraries may face increased costs.

There are times when libraries, especially special libraries, have to address some form of the request/requirement: "Prove the worth of your library." The statement may not be that sharp (perhaps "What benefits are we getting from the

Educational libraries have another critical stakeholder—accreditation agencies. Both schools and academic institutions, if they wish to have a label the general public views as evidence of quality, must address the expectations of regional accreditation bodies on a regular basis.

Evans served on a number of accreditation "visiting teams" during the years he was a library director. Over those years, the issue of accountability and assessment shifted from input/output statistics to one of demanding evidence of ongoing review of quality and outcomes. The questions the visiting teams ask also changed to reflect the new focus. During the shift both the institution and its library scrambled to think of ways to show outcomes as well as methods to employ to collect the appropriate data/evidence.

Accrediting agencies take an interest in how institutions plan and the processes they employ to carry out an activity. Traditional ways of looking at planning revolved around resources—looking at inputs, processes, and outputs. In that setting, the typical questions were "Does the institution have strategic and financial plans?" "Are the plans current, and do they involve all groups in the institution?" or "Do plans set clear goals and priorities?" Today the questions are "Do plans draw upon institutional data?" "In what ways do strategic and academic plans include learning goals and priorities?" "What ongoing data collection (qualitative and quantitative) and analysis are used to assess the effectiveness of planning?" "How does the planning process include the assessment of learning?" "How is evidence of outcomes and effectiveness used in planning?" and "To what extent is learning an integral and embedded part of planning discussions?"

Turning to some specific library questions, it is possible to see more clearly the shift in thinking. Typical resource-type questions used to be "What is the size and currency of collections, budget, staff, and physical facilities?" "Does the library engage in periodic planning and program review processes?" or "Are the collections, and access to them, adequate?" The new questions are harder to answer from statistics alone. For example, "How does the library collect and analyze data on its collections, staff, budget, and so forth?" "Does the library identify learning goals for itself, and are they linked to institutional learning goals?" "Are satisfaction surveys regularly conducted and used?" "How does the library assess the accomplishment of its learning goals?" "How are library assessment results incorporated into planning and improvements?" and "How are library learning goals linked with institutional learning goals?"

library?"); however stated, the message is the same—"We want evidence of ROI from our funding your library." Often what is being asked for is financial justification. That can be challenging.

When you face the "prove it" question for the first time, you may well feel as though you and your library are under fire and are not sure what to do next. There are resources available to assist you in answering the question. This is especially true if you have been engaging in assessment/evaluation activities on an ongoing basis. All you need do is to pull the data together in a thoughtful manner. Virginia Cairns's (2006) article provides many useful ideas for generating an effective answer.

Cairns (2006) put the issue succinctly, principally in terms of the special library environment:

> Much of what librarians do are considered "soft" costs and difficult to quantify in the current business climate that stresses hard numbers, return on investment, and cost-benefit to the organization. Since the majority of special library funding is dependent on budget allocations from executive administration, the development of sound strategies for demonstrating the worth of our services becomes crucial to our continued success. (p. 1)

Questions such as the ones posed earlier, while broad in concept, ought not to be responded to in general terms. The best way, if perhaps difficult to do, is to provide hard data and, as much possible, with dollars and cents evidence. Jeanne Brown (2011) provided some solid examples of techniques that can help generate such data/evidence. One example from her article is from the University of Hawai'i–Mānoa (UH), which collects "value" information from users.

Students, faculty, or anyone using the library's services can go to UH's library use calculator webpage to learn about the value of the services they are receiving (http://library.manoa.hawaii.edu/about/calculator/library_calculator.html). The page lists 15 services the library offers. The user can then enter the number of times he or she used a particular service in the past month. The "calculator" then automatically generates a dollar value. For example, one category is books bor-

CHECK THIS OUT

ALA has a bibliography of library ROI studies and articles at http://www
.ala.org/ala/research/librarystats/roi/index.cfm.

rowed during a month. If a person indicates two books were borrowed, the value
that would appear is $120 (2 × $60, the average cost of an academic book and
circulation labor costs). Just how detailed the library's cost analysis is is not made
clear; however, the concept is good and allows you to modify the costs when
necessary. The library cost is not shown on the calculator page; however, there
is a link to another page that spells out the cost basis of each category (http://
library.manoa.hawaii.edu/about/calculator/UHcalexplanation.html). Some of
the categories employ library cost figures, while others use retail firms' charges
for the dollar value (e.g., DVD rental fees and retail hourly charges for computer/
Internet access). We explore how you do cost analysis later in this chapter.

Since the mid-1990s, public libraries have worked on demonstrating their
ROI. A 2010 example of such an effort is a report from the Fels Institute of Government at the University of Pennsylvania titled *The Economic Value of the Free
Library of Philadelphia* (http://www.freelibrary.org/about/Fels_Report.pdf). The
major findings were that the library generated:

- $21.8 million in benefits from its literacy program
- $6 million in terms of workforce development
- $3.8 million in benefits from its services to business
- $698 million increased home value

Almost all studies of public library value to its community, in terms of dollars and
cents, have shown very positive ROIs. Studies done by independent agencies are
particularly useful in illustrating the dollar value of a library or library system.

Related to assessment and proving one's worth is a relatively new approach—
evidence-based practice. The concept is not really new; using research results
to improve practice has probably been around since research activities started.
What is new is the idea/philosophy that almost all practice should be based
on research evidence and provide approaches to speed the implementation of
research results. Perhaps the driving force in the development of the concept
came from a study released early in this century from the Institute of Medicine indicating that it was taking more than 17 years for research results to find
their way into accepted clinical practice. That generated a movement to greatly
increase the speed of implementation. EBP (evidence-based practice) has developed a library and information science following, albeit a small one. (The journal

Evidence Based Library and Information Practice is available at http://ejournals. library.ualberta.ca/index.php/EBLIP.) Both the Medical Library and Special Library Associations promote the development and implementation of EBP.

Doug Suarez (2010) wrote a good article about how you might engage in assessing research studies and reports for useful evidence for practice. As Suarez (2010) stated in his closing sentence: "By employing an assessment framework such as the one offered here, and by combining its use with personal work experience and common sense, librarians will be able to judge the inherent value of published library research and to use it as evidence for practice" (p. 84).

Prudence Dalrymple (2010), in writing about the implementation aspect of EDP, noted that "barriers to conducting research, such as the lack of time, knowledge, and skill, and the absence of a culture of inquiry and incentives from leadership all affect research productivity" (p. 45). Obviously these are the factors limiting the utility of this approach. Nevertheless, the more you can do to provide solid evidence to stakeholders, the stronger their support will be. Dalrymple's position about leadership lacking the culture of inquiry supports Dougherty's frustration in his first quotation at the beginning of this chapter.

This brief discussion suggests that there are a variety of reasons why a variety of stakeholders have an interest in your library's assessment outcomes. We explore assessment techniques later in this chapter.

WHAT IS QUALITY?

How to define and how to measure library quality have been debated over the years. Some critics argue that library "performance" and "quality" are elusive concepts that are difficult, or even impossible, to measure. Critics are correct that both are difficult to measure but are wrong about the possibility of doing so.

We can count most of our library activities (outputs) and, as noted earlier in this chapter, those numbers fail to tell us anything about quality or very much about performance. Here's a short exercise to do; ask yourself the following questions:

CHECK THESE OUT

Two seminal papers discussed the complexity of measurement, and, although they were written some years ago, they still have value today:

Gore, Daniel. 1978. "The Mischief in Measurement: A Caveat on the Hazards of Using Faulty Instruments to Measure Library Performance." *Library Journal* 103, no. 9: 933–937.

Orr, Richard. 1973. "Measuring the Goodness of Library Services: A General Framework for Considering Quantitative Measures." *Journal of Documentation* 29, no. 3: 315–332.

1. What do the terms "performance," "quality," "effectiveness," "impact," and "outcomes" mean to you? Can you define them? How do they differ from other measures you can think of? Consider the terms "goals," "needs," and "satisfaction"; can you write down lucid definitions? Do the definitions match your philosophy concerning the library?

2. Where does the demand for the measures originate? From policy makers, funding agencies, the parent organization, users, nonusers, ex-users, the staff?

3. What is the purpose behind the request for measures? To continue or discontinue a service; improve practices or processes; add or drop specific service strategies; allocate resources among competing services; accept or reject a service approach or theory; justify existing activities; justify a new activity; or as a public relations exercise?

4. What other information is needed to achieve measures? Assessment of costs, efficiency, professional opinion, policy makers or users' opinions; comparison with standards or with similar services?

5. Before you measure—Have you specified what you want to measure and why you want to measure it? Have you designed the investigation; ascertained what sources to use; decided what method to use and designed a sample; decided how to analyze the data/information and present the findings? Have you calculated the cost of this exercise in terms of visible and invisible costs (e.g., staff time, including your own)?

6. Who is to do the measuring? Are you making the best use of available resources; would it be cost-effective to bring in outside assistance; do you have the skills required; could there be a benefit in terms of staff development for the project? Have you discussed the exercise with stakeholders and obtained feedback?

7. After you measure—Have you collected all the data/information required; is it in a suitable form and reliable and valid for the purpose; is it sufficient to base decisions on? Is other data/information needed; in the course of collecting information/data has the problem area been altered; are your objectives still relevant and feasible? Have the outcomes been reviewed with the staff? What is their response?

8. What action is now required? Returning to the purpose of the investigation, do you need to institute change, no change, deploy resources, communicate the outcomes and to whom? Who should carry out this action; how and when should this be done; how will you assess the effect of the action taken?

By answering this set of questions, the purpose of the exercise will be clarified—you will perform a cost/benefit analysis of a project undertaken and consider the possible implications of the findings determined.

Effective assessment looks at more than outcomes such as quality, effectiveness, and efficiency. "Quality" is another of those "little" words with multiple meanings and personal interpretations. "Effectiveness" is also subject to personal interpretations. Both often fall into that realm of "I don't know how to define it, but I know it when I see it." At least "efficiency" is reasonably clear-cut. A key to useful assessment is to establish the intended meanings for the effort.

One way to handle "quality" interpretations is to break the concept down into small components. This both gives you a better basis for selecting the best assessment technique(s) and reduces debates in how to interpret the data generated. These are some components of quality:

- Reliability (consistency in performance)
- Currency (age of resources to provide service)
- Accessibility (ease of use—both services and facility)
- Courtesy/responsiveness (adjusting style to user, friendly service)
- Speed (response time)
- Service variety (broad based, user focused)

You can probably think of additional components; you can see how breaking quality into components helps focus on the significant quality issues for your library and reduces interpretations of what you mean by quality. You can use the same approach to breaking down effectiveness.

Perceptions of quality will vary from person to person and even by geographic region. There are also generational differences in attitudes as well. Table 10.1 (p. 246) lists some general attributes regarding quality and how younger people often view those elements, especially in terms of technology. Given that young people comprise an ever-growing segment of a library's service population, considering how they perceive quality is useful.

ASSESSMENT TOOLS

Selecting which data collecting approach to adopt depends to a great extent on the reason for the assessment. For example, is it intended to:

- meet the requirements of an external body (e.g., government or accreditation);
- examine how well the library meets one or more professional standards;
- examine performance in a holistic way;
- examine the efficiency of service delivery;
- gather the users' views of the service; or
- be an ongoing data gathering exercise?

You have to stay well-informed about the current objectives, policies, and procedures of the agencies that take an interest in library operations. The data/information collected for addressing outside interests also forms part of the internal management information system.

TABLE 10.1   Points to Ponder Regarding Quality Service and Millennials

Service Quality Attributes	Millennials' View
Service exists only at the point of delivery.	Expect instantaneous results
Quality exists during the delivery process; it cannot be ensured prior to that time.	Expect consistent performance
If it is of poor quality, it cannot be called back.	Are used to "what you see is what you get" and make judgments accordingly
Quality service is a one-on-one process.	High touch rather than high tech
Quality is not something you can put on display like a book or a video; it does or does not happen during the service delivery process.	Have high expectations and don't revisit disappointing sites very often
Quality is intangible; it is an experience.	Are comfortable with virtuality
Quality cannot be traded, sold, shared, or experienced by anyone but the recipient.	Are fans of trading and sharing
Quality cannot be stored for future use.	Expect to come back to a service time and time again and experience the same results
Quality is highly subjective, "in the eye of the beholder."	Are into sharing their views on matters with the world (using social networking websites)
Service quality declines as additional people become involved in its delivery.	Are no more fond of being shifted from one person to another when seeking service than any other generation

STANDARDS

In a sense, professional standards are not directly linked to assessment activities, and they do not carry the same weight as funding authorities or accreditation agencies. Nevertheless, they can be useful yardsticks for looking at your operations and services. While voluntary, standards can generate some broad-based quality levels across library types. They can, and do, save libraries large sums of money when they are implemented locally. Perhaps the most striking example of such savings is the MARC (Machine Readable Cataloging) standard and its role in shared cataloging. There are professional association standards, such as the Association of College and Research Libraries'

(ACRL) *Standards for Libraries in Higher Education* (http://www.ala.org/acrl/standards/standardslibraries) and the American Association of School Librarians' (AASL) *Standards for the 21st-Century Learner* (http://www.ala.org/aasl/guidelinesandstandards/learningstandards/standards), that establish baselines for types of libraries.

The National Information Standards Organization (NISO) develops Z39 standards (which relate to library, vendor, and publisher activities) that are technical and intended to make work more efficient. An example is Z39.9, which is the International Standard Serial Number standard that helps publishers, vendors, and libraries handle serials more efficiently. OCLC's development and support of the Dublin Core Metadata Initiative (DCMI) is another example of an organization helping to create a standard, in this case for handling e-materials.

Standards, especially from professional groups such as ALA, have a way of changing through time and occasionally shifting back and forth between an emphasis on general and specific factors as new versions appear. Two examples of changing versions make this point. In 2010, Pat Franklin and Clara Gatrell Stephens wrote about some concerns about the 2009 AASL standard mentioned earlier, *Standards for the 21st-Century Learner.* Franklin and Stephens (2010) reported that "many school librarians thought they were vague" and that many other "school librarians had trouble visualizing how the program would be applied in their school and work with state standards" (p. 36). Keep this in mind when thinking about doing any standards assessment project—competing standards can pose a challenge for libraries.

Also in 2010, Patricia Innuzzi and Jeanne M. Brown summarized the results of a survey given to academic library directors (988 responses) regarding what should be included in the replacement version of ACRL's existing standards. One clear desire was to have better linkage between the standards and accreditation expectations (competing standards). Perhaps the most interesting finding was that 47 percent of the directors know of the standards and had used them. Somewhat fewer, 38 percent, know of the standards but made no use of them. A surprising 17 percent admitted to not knowing of the standards. You can find the ALA standards manual at http://www.ala.org/ala/professionalresources/ guidelines/standardsmanual/manual.cfm and many of the standards themselves at http://www.ala.org/ala/professionalresources/guidelines/standardsguidelines/ index.cfm.

Some standards, such as the AASL and ACRL, do in general look at a library holistically. Depending on the overall focus of the standards—qualitative or quantitative—you may or may not have a total picture of service quality. Libraries, by their nature, provide many services that are rather intangible. Thomas Shaughnessy (1987) identified three points that help to explain "service intangibility." First, services are often performances or processes rather than products, and unspecified (unarticulated) user expectations are the typical criteria by which a service is evaluated. Second, most services are heterogeneous. Performance varies from producer to producer, from user to user, and from day to day. Many libraries are open long hours each day and every day of the week. Staffing varies because of the need to cover all the service hours, so uniform quality becomes more difficult to ensure. And third, frequently production and consumption of services are inseparable. Judgments of quality ought to involve evaluations of the delivery process and a comparison to consumer expectations, not just outcomes.

A number of approaches to quality management that take a holistic view have elements that require careful consideration. First, the process is often facilitated by a consultant and should not be undertaken by an untrained and inexperienced

CHECK THESE OUT

Coyle, Karen. 2005. "Libraries and Standards." *Journal of Academic Librarianship* 31, no. 4 (July): 373–376. Coyle discusses the main U.S. organizations and the problems and issues involved in library standards.

Pember, Margaret. 2006. "Sorting Out the Standards: What Every Records and Information Professional Should Know." *Records Management Journal* 16, no. 1: 21–33. Pember considers the types of standards and how they are used in practice.

person. Second, there will be visible costs—for example, the hiring of a consultant—and invisible costs in terms of staff time. Third, the process will result in change, and this may give rise to staff concern. The reasons for and against trying the process must be carefully considered. We discuss several approaches in the following sections.

TOTAL QUALITY MANAGEMENT

Total quality management (TQM) is an approach that had currency in the 1980s and 1990s in U.S. libraries. It started in the United States in the for-profit sector and slowly moved into the public sector. We mention two of the major TQM writers in Chapter 1, W. Edwards Deming (1986) and Joseph M. Juran (1995); two other important writers are Kaoru Ishikawa (1985) and A. Blanton Godfrey, who with Juran published an important work in 1999. A related concept is quality circles—both Deming and Ishikawa promoted their use in conjunction with TQM.

The TQM model developed by the Association of Research Libraries' Office of Management Services illustrates the complexity of implementing the concept in a library. The model involved a 10-step process (Barnard, 1993). A few academic libraries implemented some modified versions during the 1990s. We are unaware of any U.S. library doing so in late 2012.

An element of TQM is its customer focus, something that fits the LIS environment well. Also useful is the idea that you always have two "customers"—an external customer and an internal customer. The external customer is the end user. Your internal customer is the direct recipient of your work output. It is essential that both customer types be satisfied for TQM to work properly.

LIBQUAL⁺

LibQUAL⁺ (http://www.libqual.org/) grew out of interest in TQM and now takes the form of an annual survey completed by subscribing libraries in a number of countries. The instrument measures user perceptions and expectations of library service quality in three dimensions: Affect of Service, Information Control, and Library as Place. Users are asked for their judgments on three scales for each question: the desired level of service they would like to receive, the minimum they are willing to accept, and the actual level of service they perceive to have been provided.

Few libraries participate in the survey every year. In 2010, over 200 libraries participated; in 2009, 161 took part. The survey is not inexpensive—$3,200 (per year) to participate in the 2011 and 2012 surveys. Each year ARL creates norm tables based on that year's responses, so a library can compare its data with a broader base. The participating libraries, of course, receive both a summary of their data and the raw data so that they can engage in further analysis. Thus, a library gains insights into its service quality both locally and nationally (a form of benchmarking). Although some people, for example, William Edgar (2006), have raised questions about the adequacy of LibQUAL⁺ as the sole assessment method, it is useful.

Alire encountered LibQUAL⁺ at both of the ARL libraries she led. Using LibQUAL⁺ was instrumental in developing objectives to adjust and improve services for the next fiscal and academic year(s) and was tied directly to the strategic plans in place. However, the LibQUAL⁺ data was coupled with data gathered from focus groups and other instruments. Each year LibQUAL⁺ was used to evaluate whether services identified the previous year and adjusted had actually improved in the eyes of the specific group of users who were identified the previous year.

Alire used the LibQUAL⁺ data to demonstrate to campus decision makers and stakeholders (i.e., faculty and student governance) that the library was using quantitative methodology to identify areas of service concern, to improve those service areas, and then to show results in improvement.

Some libraries use another service, similar to LIBQUAL⁺, for assessment purposes—Counting Opinions (http://www.countingopinions.com/). The organization's statement of purpose/service is to provide "comprehensive, cost-effective, real-time solutions designed for libraries, in support of customer insight, operational improvements and advocacy efforts." Their list of customers includes both

CHECK THESE OUT

Here are four examples of the use of LibQUAL⁺ in a variety of academic library settings:

Kayongo, Jessica, and Sherri Jones. 2008. "Faculty Perception of Information Control Using LibQUAL+ Indicators." *Journal of Academic Librarianship* 34, no. 2: 130–138.

Ladhari, Riadh, and Miguel Morales. 2008. "Perceived Service Quality, Perceived Value, and Recommendation: A Study among Canadian Public Library Users." *Library Management* 29, nos. 4/5: 352–366.

Thompson, Bruce, Martha Kyrillidou, and Colleen Cook. 2008. "How You Can Evaluate the Integrity of Your Library Service Quality Assessment Data: Intercontinental LibQUAL+ Analyses Used as Concrete Heuristic Examples." *Performance Measurement and Metrics* 9, no. 3: 202–215.

Wolf, Dominique. 2008. "LibQUAL+ en France: Un Outil pour L'Evaluation de la Qualité de Services en Bibliothèque." *Bulletin des Bibliothèques de France* 53, no. 3: 39–47.

academic and public libraries. Two of the company's products are LibSat ("the means to measure customer satisfaction") and LibPAS (library performance assessment).

BENCHMARKING

To some degree, LibQUAL+ offers a limited form of benchmarking; however, the technique is generally a stand-alone process. Benchmarking, at least in U.S. libraries, is a relatively recent phenomenon, as jurisdictions and parent organizations have become increasingly concerned about operating costs. Benchmarking is basically a tool for either internal or external comparisons.

The goal of benchmarking is to provide data that can help managers answer the following questions:

- How well are we doing compared to others?
- How good do we want to be?
- Who is doing the best?
- How do the best do it?
- How can we adapt what the best do to our organization?
- How can we be better than the best?

There are four basic types of benchmarking—internal, competitive, industry, and best-in-class. As the label suggests, *internal benchmarking* looks at internal practices within an organization. An example is what it costs to create a purchase order in various departments across a campus. A *competitive benchmarking* project might collect data on the cost of creating purchase orders in various departments in a number of institutions. *Industry benchmarking* would collect data from all or a representative sample of all organizations within an "industry." *Best-in-class benchmarking* collects information across industries, essentially seeking the most effective practices.

Internal benchmarking may also vary between vertical and horizontal projects. A vertical project seeks to quantify the costs, workloads, and productivity of a defined functional area, for example, handling accounts payable. A horizontal study analyzes the cost and productivity of a single process that crosses two or more functional areas; an example is database searching in acquisitions, cataloging, and document delivery.

The National Association of College and University Business Officers has been conducting benchmarking studies of various areas in academic institutions, including libraries, since the mid-1990s. These are large-scale efforts involving various member institutions in the United States and Canada (http://www.nacubo.org/Research/NACUBO_Benchmarking_Tool.html). In 2011, the Urban Libraries Council (http://urbanlibraries.org/displaycommon.cfm?an=1&subarticlenbr=669) joined with the International City/County Management Association and several other city and county management organizations to begin developing benchmarks for public library technology access. The goal is to provide public libraries with information about technology practices in order to create more effective policies regarding access.

SIX SIGMA

Based on the statistical tools and techniques of quality management developed by Joseph M. Juran, the Six Sigma approach was adopted by Motorola in the 1980s and has been implemented in some U.S. public libraries. It is both a philosophy and a technique designed to eliminate waste and improve performance. Using statistical analysis, it aims to bring down defects in processes and services to near zero. At the same time, it fosters a culture that focuses on creating value for the user and eliminating any redundant processes. Thomsett (2005) wrote an introductory book about the technique that can be applied to libraries. Brett and Queen (2005) described the application of Lean Six Sigma to streamline a records management service. Improving self-service using Six Sigma has been reported by Kumi and Morrow (2006).

Sarah Murphy (2009) provides one example of an academic library employing the Lean Six Sigma method. She discussed the applicability of the concept to one service element at the Ohio State University (OSU) libraries. Library service is a fleeting event and presents challenges as to when and how often to assess such transactions. As Murphy (2009) stated, "Services are both intangible and heterogeneous, inviting variability in processes as customers and providers contribute to the inputs and outputs of the service product" (p. 216). The focus of her project was the OSU libraries' process for managing and answering users' e-mail questions. Murphy (2009) concluded her article with this statement:

> Libraries can customize and borrow a number of quality management systems and tools from the business community to both assess their service process and continuously improve their operations. By adopting an approach like Lean Six Sigma, a library can respond better to changing customer needs and desires by creating an infrastructure that supports, nurtures, and sustains a culture of assessment and change. (p. 224)

BALANCED SCORECARD

The balanced scorecard was developed by Robert Kaplan and David Norton as an approach to strategic management based on a measurement system. It provides feedback on the internal operations and the external outcomes to assist organizations to continuously improve strategic performance (Kaplan and Norton, 2006). The approach views the organization from four perspectives for which metrics are developed and data is collected and analyzed. The perspectives are the learning and growth perspective, the business process perspective, the customer perspective, and the financial perspective (http://www.balancedscorecard.org/).

Alfred Willis (2004) published an article based on interviews with two key University of Virginia library administrators who were lead figures in using the balanced scorecard at the library. Jim Self, in responding to a question regard-

CHECK THIS OUT

An outstanding book that provides a wealth of detail on assessment and quality control is Peter Hernon and Ellen Altman's *Assessing Service Quality: Satisfying the Expectations of Library Customers* (Chicago: American Library Association, 1998).

ing the value of the technique, said that "It can focus the library. It makes the library as an organization decide what is important. It can be used to improve organizational performance. It broadens our perspective in a structured way, and gives us a more balanced view of our work" (Willis, 2004, p. 66). Lynda White's response to the question was that "Our balanced scorecard is so user-oriented, it fits really well with what we value. Many of our metrics focus on the results for our users whether or not they are technically in the user perspective" (Willis, 2004, p. 66). Tom Bielavitz's article provides a detailed assessment of the method in the library context. Bielavitz's (2010) final statement was, "The example illustrates that the balanced scorecard can serve as a typical systems planning model to evaluate and assess an academic library's learning outcomes" (p. 45).

USER DATA COLLECTING METHODS

Libraries' service communities' views regarding library quality are essential to understand for several reasons. Obviously those views play, or should play, a key role in making adjustments in programs and services. Perhaps even more important is the impact those views may have on library funding levels and funding authorities. Such views, whether positive or negative, can and do impact library usage levels, which will in turn influence library support.

Individual and group interviews and mailed and telephone surveys have a long history of use by libraries for gathering service community data. To a large extent the assessment tools discussed earlier have superseded these methodologies. One more recent technique for more targeted local information is focus groups.

Focus groups are intended to elicit information about individuals' thoughts and views about some topic or issue. The technique involves a small group of individuals and a researcher/moderator. The researcher serves as moderator, listener, observer, and ultimately analyst. As the name suggests, the topic under discussion is narrow/focused (such as the usefulness of the library's web presence). To have some assurance of valid results, at least three groups should make up your sample. In general, the usefulness and validity of the collected data depend on the groups' comfort in sharing views that may not be thought popular. A moderator/researcher must have some skill in assessing an individual's comfort level as well as the group's and make the environment as nonthreatening as possible.

CHECK THESE OUT

For more details about the focus group methodology and its values and limitations, see Richard A. Krueger and Mary Anne Casey's *Focus Groups: A Practical Guide,* 4th ed. (Thousand Oaks, CA: Sage, 2009) and Thomas L. Greenbaum's *The Handbook for Focus Group Research,* 2nd rev. ed (Thousand Oaks, CA: Sage, 2002).

A useful bibliography on the use of focus groups for art and humanities and social science research (including librarianship) is Graham R. Walden's *Focus Groups Volume 1: A Selective Annotated Bibliography* (Lanham, MD: Scarecrow Press, 2008).

Researchers employ three types of approaches—full groups, mini groups, and telephone groups. Each type has an impact on group and individual comfort levels. Full groups consist of eight to ten people, with the discussion lasting 90 to 120 minutes. Mini groups have four to six individuals and last 60 to 90 minutes. Telephone conferencing arrangement groups rarely have more than nine to ten members and last 30 to 90 minutes.

Comparing focus groups to other approaches, you will find focus groups are an economical method for identifying group norms. They are not that useful for gathering data about attitudes and behaviors—interviews and surveys are better for this type of information. One special aspect of focus groups is that they extend public participation in assessment and planning activities.

QUALITY CONTROL

One of your responsibilities as a manager is to monitor and control the performance of your unit. What this means is that you must coordinate activities, ensure performance quality, and control operating costs—no small task. The control process has four components: establishing standards, measuring performance, comparing/evaluating performance against standards, and correcting deviations from the standards. Elements in these components are typically quality, quantity, time, and cost.

Standards assist in monitoring organizational performance. A key point is how they are established: historical, comparative, engineered, or subjective. Historical data, or past performance, can assist in establishing a standard if the component elements remain constant and serve as the initial standard until more scientific data is available. A problem is that there is no assurance that in the past the activity was done efficiently, effectively, or perhaps even very well. "We've always done it this way" does not always translate to being the best, or only, way. There may be implications for related activities that cause overall organizational performance to suffer. (Remember, part of the control/operations function is to coordinate activities and view the whole.) Another source is comparison with the same activities in a number of like organizations, and benchmarking is one approach. Unless a systematic approach is taken and the information and data obtained from another service is robust, the outcomes may not be reliable. Also, no two institutions are totally identical, but the best use of comparative data is to establish standards.

"Engineered standards" is just a different label for "scientific management." Engineered standards use hard data collected from work analysis. There are times when subjective estimates and assessments of what is realistic as a standard must be used, such as morale, public relations, image, and staff development. Such areas are almost impossible to directly measure in an objective manner. An attempt to measure some aspect of these issues can be made through questionnaires and surveys, but these are at best indirect. The questions asked would reflect subjective assessments about what is important. Having subjective standards is better than not having them, but recognize them for what they are.

By applying work-analysis techniques, managers can improve the climate of the work environment for everyone while establishing performance standards. Work analysis can also assist in solving layout problems in physical spaces, choosing a sequence for doing work, and finding ways of performing tasks more efficiently so as to achieve coordination. The relationship between work analysis and budgeting becomes clear when it is recognized that most work-analysis techniques relate in one way or another to time or money. As a result, they provide much of the quality data needed for budgeting and planning.

Work sampling is a component of any work-analysis project and requires an understanding of basic statistics. A typical application would be in the acquisitions department, when establishing performance standards for the many tasks carried out in the unit. The process consists of two parts: establishing realistic workloads (standards) and comparing them to the staff's performance. The current workload represents in statistical terms the study universe, or population. If you wanted to know with almost complete certainty what is being done within a unit, you would have to study all steps in the acquisitions unit for one year. Even then you could not be absolutely confident that some unusual characteristics made the year atypical. Fortunately, a reasonably small, properly selected sample of the work will provide results that will supply almost as much confidence as if you had studied the entire year's operation.

The sampling technique rests on certain assumptions regarding the nature of the phenomenon under study. One basic assumption is the distribution of the collected data (e.g., responding to e-reference questions) will resemble a normal distribution (bell-shaped curve). Normal distributions are ones in which the characteristics under study cluster around a central point. As you move away from the central point, there are fewer instances of those characteristics.

Not all work-analysis techniques relate directly to establishing standards. They may help improve the work flow so that standards can be set, or aid visualization of the interrelated nature of a set of activities to improve coordination, or establish that the present system is the best method. All assist in controlling and monitoring organizational work activities.

Block diagrams are the most elementary form of work analysis, providing a simple overview of the relationships among various units or activities and identifying possible problem areas. The *flow diagram* introduces a finer level of analysis, as it gives a graphic view of both the work area and the movement of personnel or materials within that area—for example, a scale drawing of the facility with all activities clearly identified.

A *flow process chart* indicates the movement of an object but does not relate the movement to a physical space. It answers questions such as "Is this the best sequence?" "What would happen if . . . ?" or "Could we combine steps X and Y?" It ensures that a step is not missed in the process.

The *decision flow chart*—typically used in systems analysis for computer applications—analyzes work flows in which numerous decisions occur. *Operations analysis* studies the motions of the hands, eyes, and feet of an individual who is working on a particular activity in one location. This is the classic activity of Taylor's scientific management. It is most effective when used sparingly and on jobs that involve high levels of repetition; this is where the classic time-and-motion study is important. The goal is always the best, most effective arrangement.

Another useful type of analysis is *form analysis.* Paper, electronic forms, and files seem to multiply rapidly. Too often they remain in use because "we've always done it that way." The result is often unnecessary work for a department. An annual review should determine which forms still serve a useful function.

Man–machine charts allow studies of the relationship between people and machines. When people or machines are idle for long periods, the organization's investment is not optimal. *Gantt charts* emphasize the importance of time values and people or things. When developing a complex schedule, a Gantt chart can help plan the workload in terms of overall objectives.

Linear programming can help determine the best use of scarce resources to achieve a specified goal by:

- improving the use of all organizational work resources,
- keeping the costs of an operation or activity to a minimum,
- determining volume–cost relationships, and
- selecting the optimum mix of customer services.

Queuing theory deals with waiting lines and provides models for operations. You can apply the concept to people or things, and it is especially effective in determining the optimum number of service points. Users who have to wait too long become frustrated, angry, and, ultimately, ex-users. *Game theory* is useful when allocating resources among competing demands. *Search theory* is for the optimization of locating information, and the *Monte Carlo method* addresses issues of chance occurrences. These are the most prominent techniques from

---

CHECK THIS OUT

For a comprehensive resource for quality and performance control methods, see Richard M. Dougherty's *Streamlining Library Services: What We Do, How Much Time It Takes, What It Costs, and How We Can Do It Better* (Lanham, MD: Scarecrow Press, 2008).

---

among the many available. The appropriate application of these techniques enhances the image of a library as being effective and cost-conscious.

Cost accounting is the process of comparing costs (expenses) with results (products or services). The purpose is to ascertain the actual cost of a single product or service (processing a document or answering a telephone inquiry, for example). When done properly, cost accounting is a powerful tool for preparing a budget, determining staffing needs, planning new services, or arranging new service locations. It is essential in making decisions about outsourcing. Only by having data on the unit costs for a process can reasonable decisions be made about whether or not to use an outside agency.

A common way is to divide costs into three categories: labor, supplies, and overhead. Supplies such as pens, paper, and computer printer ink cartridges are easy to identify. How do you handle such things as computers, desks, and chairs, as well as the maintenance of these items? Are they supplies or overhead? Does it really matter what category they are in if you include them somewhere? (It may, depending on the overall goal of the cost accounting project.) Do you depreciate equipment cost over a fixed period and use only a given year's cost? Do you use the original purchase price or the cost of replacing the item? Various methods and rationales are used to decide these issues. If you overlook a cost, you may ignore the real expense of whatever activity is under study.

Overhead (indirect) costs are those not directly attributable to the production of a particular product or service. Administrative salaries, building maintenance, utilities, travel expenses, and insurance are common overhead items. Because publicly funded activities usually take place in public buildings that are tax and rent free, some writers suggest that cost figures that do not take these factors into account are unrealistic. They suggest treating the building as a private one for accounting purposes, but this would require a great deal of time, effort, and money to establish realistic "rent" and tax figures. Would it be worth it? In today's culture of privatization, it may become necessary regardless of the time and effort required.

An expert should assist in establishing a proper cost accounting system. However, for "down and dirty" purposes, rough cost accounting is not that difficult. Use staff salaries (not forgetting benefits) as labor costs, the annual supplies budget as supplies cost, and administrative salary as overhead. This provides the total cost to divide by the number of units of service or products produced in a year by a unit. The figure will probably be surprisingly high for unit costs.

Engaging in assessment is now a fact of library management. There is a reasonably large body of literature on how-to-do-it. However, there is very little on what, if anything, came about as a result of the work. Yes, if the activity was the result of a request from some outside agency, that body saw the results. Did it see what was done with the results? Perhaps, perhaps not, depending on the time frame. An accreditation agency may say something needs to be done about perceived shortcomings but is unlikely to revisit the issue for at least a while.

Most shortcomings identified by an assessment likely will require money, people, and/or other resources. The reality of today's economic conditions is that all of these resources will be difficult to secure. The result is often that nothing is done. Given these facts, it is not too surprising that most libraries do not "broadcast" the results of their assessment activities. Another reality is that a library with superlative assessment results is unlikely to see much, if any, increases in its support as a result. Often the best that happens is that during the next round of reductions the library takes a smaller hit.

Assessing library programs, activities, and so forth is both essential and complex. Assessment is essential for addressing accountability externally and internally. It is complex based on the number of variables involved and, at times, conflicting expectations/requirements for conducting an assessment. The good news is that the more often you engage in assessment activities, the easier it becomes.

Because assessment is so important, as well as complex, it is wise to have at least one person on the staff who becomes the "assessment guru." This person should be key in planning, or assist in planning, any assessment program as well as in suggesting additional activities that would help the library prove its worth to whoever asks.

KEY POINTS TO REMEMBER
- Determining the effectiveness and efficiency of a service is of growing importance; there are a variety of approaches.
- Those who provide budgets for information services keep an eye on the bottom line and the extent to which the services satisfy the community served.
- Decision makers on governing boards are likely to be drawn from the business sector and expect to see familiar approaches to performance measurement.
- Managers need to have some basic mathematical and statistical skills but also understand that data and information do not necessarily provide the sole answers about library efficiency and effectiveness—experience and judgment play a role.

References

Barnard, Susan B. 1993. "Implementing Total Quality Management: A Model for Research Libraries." In *Integrating Total Quality Management in a Library Setting*, edited by Susan Jurow and Susan B. Barnard, 57–70. Binghamton, NY: Haworth Press.

Bielavitz, Tom. 2010. "The Balanced Scorecard: A Systematic Model for Evaluation and Assessment of Learning Outcomes." *Evidence Based Library and Information Practice* 5, no. 2: 35–46.

Brett, Charles, and Patrick Queen. 2005. "Streamlining Enterprise Records Management with Lean Six Sigma." *Information Management Journal* 39, no. 6: 58, 60–62.

Brown, Jeanne M. 2011. "Demonstrating Library Value: Examples and Applications." *Art Documentation* 30, no. 1: 48–53.

Cairns, Virginia L. 2006. "Demonstrating Your Worth to Administration." *Tennessee Libraries* 56, no. 2: 1–11. http://www.tnla.org/displaycommon .cfm?an=1&subarticlenbr=38.

Dalrymple, Prudence W. 2010. "Applying Evidence in Practice: What We Can Learn from Healthcare." *Evidence Based Library and Information Practice* 5, no. 1: 43–47.

Deming, W. Edwards. 1986. *Out of Crisis*. Cambridge: Massachusetts Institute of Technology Press.

Dougherty, Richard M. 2008. *Streamlining Library Services: What We Do, How Much Time It Takes, What It Costs, and How We Can Do It Better*. Lanham, MD: Scarecrow Press.

———. 2012. E-mail communication sent to Camila A. Alire, February 10.

Edgar, William B. 2006. "Questioning LibQual⁺: Expanding Its Assessment of Academic Library Effectiveness." *portal: Libraries and the Academy* 6, no. 4: 445–465.

Franklin, Pat, and Claire Gatrell Stephens. 2010. "Learning for Life: Applying the AASL Standards." *School Library Monthly* 26, no. 5: 36–37.

Haras, Catherine. 2010. "Listening to the Customer." *Library Leadership and Management* 24, no. 2: 91–94.

Hernon, Peter, Robert E. Dugan, and Candy Schwartz. 2006. *Revisiting Outcomes Assessement in Higher Education*. Westport, CT: Libraries Unlimited.

Innuzzi, Patricia, and Jeanne M. Brown. 2010. "ACRL's Standards for Libraries in Higher Education: Academic Library Directors Weigh In." *College and Research Libraries News* 71, no. 9: 486–487.

Ishikawa, Kaoru. 1985. *What Is Total Quality?* Englewood Cliffs, NJ: Prentice-Hall.

Juran, Joseph M. 1995. *Managerial Breakthrough*. New York: McGraw-Hill.

Juran, Joseph M., and A. Blanton Godfrey. 1999. *Juran's Quality Handbook*. 5th ed. New York: McGraw-Hill.

Kaplan, Robert S., and David P. Norton. 2006. "The Balanced Scorecard: Measures That Drive Performance." *Harvard Business Review* 83, no. 7: 172, 174–180.

Kumi, Susan, and John Morrow. 2006. "Improving Self Service the Six Sigma Way at Newcastle University Library." *Program* 40, no. 2: 123–136.

Murphy, Sarah Anne. 2009. "Leveraging Lean Six Sigma to Culture, Nurture, and Sustain Assessment and Change in the Academic Library Environment." *College and Research Libraries* 70, no. 3: 215–225.

Shaughnessy, Thomas W. 1987. "Search for Quality." *Journal of Library Administration* 8, no. 1: 5–10.

Suarez, Doug. 2010. "Evaluating Qualitative Research Studies for Evidence Based Library and Information Practice." *Evidence Based Library and Information Practice* 5, no. 2: 75–85.

Thomsett, Michael C. 2005. *Getting Started in Six Sigma.* Hoboken, NJ: Wiley.

Willis, Alfred. 2004. "Using the Balanced Scorecard at the University of Virginia Library." *Library Administration and Management* 18, no. 2: 64–67.

Launching Pad

Americans for Libraries Council. 2007. *Worth Their Weight: An Assessment of the Evolving Field of Library Valuation.* http://www.ila.org/advocacy/pdf/WorthTheirWeight.pdf.

Ammons, David N. 1995. "Overcoming the Inadequacies of Performance Measurement in Local Government: The Case of Libraries and Leisure Services." *Public Administration Review* 55, no. 1:37–47.

Chen, Andrew N. K., and Theresa M. Edginton. 2005. "Assessing Value in Organizational Knowledge Creation: Considerations for Knowledge Workers." *MIS Quarterly* 29, no. 2: 279–309.

Cook, Colleen, and Michael Maciel. 2010. "A Decade of Assessment at a Research-Extensive University Library Using LibQUAL+." *Research Library Issues* no. 271: 4–12.

Crawford, Gregory A., and Glenn S. McGuigan. 2011. "An Exploratory Quantitative Analysis of Academic Library Services." *Library Leadership and Management* 25, no. 3: 1–18.

Dugan, Robert E. 2002. "Managing Technology in an Assessment Environment." *Journal of Academic Librarianship* 28, no. 1: 56–58.

Durrance, Joan C., Karen E. Fisher, and Marin Bouch. 2005. *How Libraries and Librarians Help: A Guide to Identifying User-Centered Outcomes.* Chicago: American Library Association.

Garry, Candi Pierce. 2010. "The Revised National Board Library Media Standards and You." *School Library Monthly* 27, no. 3: 9–11.

Gordon, Carol A., and Ross J. Todd. 2009. "Editorial: Weaving Evidence, Reflection, and Action into the Fabric of School Librarianship." *Evidence Based Library and Information Practice* 4, no. 2: 4–7. http://ejournals.library.ualberta.ca/index.php/EBLIP/article/view/6281/5412.

Hallberg, Anette, and Katarine Sipos-Zackrisson. 2008. "Improvements of Public Library Service Quality." *TQM Journal* 22, no. 1: 89–100.

Harada, Violet H. 2005. "Working Smarter: Being Strategic about Assessment and Accountability." *Teacher Librarian* 33, no. 1: 8–15.

Hiller, Steve, Martha Kyrillidou, and Jim Self. 2008. "When Evidence Is Not Enough." *Performance Management and Metrics* 9, no. 3: 223–230.

Holt, Glenn E., and Donald Elliott. 2003. "Measuring Outcomes: Applying Cost–Benefit Analysis to Middle-Sized and Smaller Public Libraries." *Library Trends* 51, no. 3: 424–440.

Kaske, Neal K. 2008. "Turning Data into Information: Details Behind Telling the Library Valuation Story." http://libraryassessment.org/bm~doc/tdi_handout.pdf.

Killick, Selena. 2010. "Service Quality Assessment with LibQUAL⁺ in Challenging Times: LibQUAL⁺ at Cranfield University." *Research Library Issues* no. 271: 21–24.

Kramer, Pamela K., and Linda Diekman. 2010. "Evidence = Assessment = Advocacy." *Teacher Librarian* 27, no. 3: 27–10.

McKnight, Susan, and Andrew Booth. 2010. "Identifying Customer Expectations Is Key to Evidence Based Library Service." *Evidence Based Library and Information Practice* 5, no. 1: 26–31.

Miller, Rebecca, Francine Fialkoff, and Michael Kelley. 2012. "Moving from Outputs to Outcomes." *Library Journal* 137, no. 1: 34–36.

Nagata, Haruki, and Lisa Klopfer. 2011. "Public Library Assessment in Customer Perspective: To Which Customer Group Should the Library Listen?" *Library Management* 32, nos. 4/5: 336–345.

Robison, Rex R., Mary E. Ryan, and I. Diane Cooper. 2009. "Inquiring Informationists: A Qualitative Exploration of Our Role." *Evidence Based Library and Information Practice* 4, no. 1: 4–18.

Sarli, Cathy C., and Kristi K. Holmes. 2012. "Beyond Citation Analysis: A Model for Assessment of Research Impact." *Journal of the Medical Library Association* 100, no. 2: 82.

Saunders, E. Stewart. 2008. "Drilling the LibQUAL+ Data for Strategic Planning." *Performance Management and Metrics* 9, no. 3: 160–170.

Simon, Carol. 2011. "An Examination of Best Practices and Benchmarking in Corporate Libraries." *Journal of Management Development* 30, no. 1: 134–141.

Symons, Ann K., and Carla Stoffle. 1998. "When Values Conflict." *American Libraries* 29, no. 5: 56–58

Walter, Virginia A. 1992. *Output Measures for Public Library Service to Children: A Manual of Standardized Procedures.* Chicago: American Library Association.

———. 1995. *Output Measures and More: Planning and Evaluating Public Library Services for Young Adults.* Chicago: American Library Association.

We have a compelling mission. The library message is powerful, and I am willing to work with others to make sure it is heard. I am committed to speaking out and recruiting others to do the same. Library advocacy's purpose is to make sure that the library point of view is heard. Whether they are at a cocktail party, or giving a formal speech, the ADVOCATES tell the library story wherever and whenever they can. What defines a library advocate is passion and commitment.

Many people say they love their libraries; library advocacy means we are willing to fight for all libraries—and to enlist and train others to do the same. The real task is to mobilize library advocates to speak out, loudly, clearly, and with a unified voice because it is in THEIR interest. Library advocacy means telling the library story by turning dedicated library users into active and articulate allies.

—Pat Schuman, ALA President, 1991–1992 (2012)

As libraries continue to move their resources from print to electronic formats, the challenge of effective marketing has become apparent. . . . How, then, do libraries best connect their patrons to appropriate electronic resources?

—Marie Kennedy (2011)

Conventional marketing wisdom holds that marketing adds value by creating an understanding of the value that customers seek, which in turn influences organizations to create and communicate value. Therefore, marketing skills appear to be critical for understanding customer needs and competitors' offerings, and for creating and communicating organizations' superior offerings.

—Rajesh Singh (2009)

By learning what clients really want you can avoid wasting time and money on things they won't use.

—Kathy Dempsey (2010)

The frontline library advocacy program is timelier than ever before, given our nation's economy and the funding challenges libraries are facing.

—Camila A. Alire (2010)

11

MARKETING
AND ADVOCACY

This chapter focuses on the following:

- Why libraries market
- What marketing is
- The marketing process
- Internal and external marketing issues
- Branding
- Public relations
- Promotion
- Advocacy

ESSENTIALLY MARKETING is a simple process of making potential "customers" know you exist and providing them, and existing customers, with information on what products and services you have available. It also lets you define the services you offer to better meet "customer" needs. This may appear straightforward and simple; however, doing it effectively is surprisingly complex. It requires a mix of information and persuasion. Striking the correct balance between the two elements is delicate. Today's competitive world of librarianship makes the persuasive side more and more important, yet going too far that way may be a major "turn off" for many people.

You can think of marketing as a social process, as well as managerial, in that it is about communication between your library and its service community. It is, or should be, a two-way process of exchanging information between the library and its community—what the community wants and what the library can provide. It is also a means for developing better relations between the library and its community. Good collection development officers have been engaged in key marketing steps for years without thinking of it as "marketing."

A related concept, advocacy, can assist you in striking a good balance in your marketing program. Susan DiMattia (2011) defined the concept: "Advocacy is neither marketing nor public relations. Simply put, it is the art of persuading or arguing in favor of something" (p. 14). Advocacy is a process for attempting to influence public policy and resource allocations; it differs from lobbying in that the focus is on policy and allocation issues, not on legislation. National PTA clarifies the difference between lobbying and advocacy:

When nonprofit organizations advocate on their own behalf, they seek to affect some aspect of society, whether they appeal to individuals about their behavior, employers about their rules, or the government about its laws. Lobbying refers specifically to advocacy efforts that attempt to influence legislation. This distinction is helpful to keep in mind because it means that laws limiting the lobbying done by nonprofit organizations do not govern other advocacy activities. (http://www.pta.org/1755.htm)

We also distinguish between marketing, advocacy, promotion, and public relations. In the broadest sense, all are processes that focus on "selling" something. However, they differ in significant ways. Marketing is finding out what your customers want and/or need and figuring out how to deliver those services. Promotion is telling your customers what the library is now doing that is meeting their "wants and needs." Public relations build relationships between a library and customers based on successful marketing and promotional efforts. Advocacy focuses on telling a broad story of the value of libraries and why the customers, other stakeholders, and decision makers need to support them.

WHY MARKET LIBRARIES?

Marketing and libraries, do they actually go together? Is marketing libraries appropriate? Jennifer Rowley (2003) noted that for many information professionals in the past, "marketing was regarded as an alien commercial process, inconsistent with the values of public service" (p. 13). In 2004, Shontz, Parker, and Parker published the results of an attitude survey of U.S. public librarians regarding the concept of marketing. Overall they found there were generally favorable views regarding marketing and a recognition of a need for the activity to some degree. Shontz, Parker, and Parker (2004) did note that "administrators and public service librarians had more positive attitudes than did reference and technical service librarians" (p. 74). An interesting finding was the more library experience one had, the more positive the view held. Unsurprisingly, those who had attended a workshop or taken formal coursework in marketing were the most positive about the process.

Lisa Smith-Butler (2010) wrote, "As a new librarian many years ago, I found the concept of marketing a library to be anathema. I was certain that sensible and intelligent patrons immediately understood the value and the necessity of a library. Marketing, in my opinion, was a dirty word, something done by MBAs marketing a product. Now, 15 years later, I think my younger self naïve" (pp. 7–8). She was not alone in her thinking at the time; perhaps newcomers to the field may hold similar beliefs. We firmly believe that in today's highly competitive information world, libraries must market themselves.

Smith-Butler's theory that intelligent people understand the value of libraries was and still is probably valid. However, even such people know that in tough economic times, tough decisions are necessary when it comes to expending limited funds. Priorities must be set, and everyone wants the maximum ROI (return on investment) for those limited funds. In the last chapter we discussed the importance of assessment and proving your library's worth—marketing can assist in that process.

There is strong evidence that almost all libraries have a positive ROI; however, this fact is not widely known outside the profession. Marketing, advocacy, and sound public relations efforts can be effective tools in getting the message out— libraries do provide good returns on the funds invested in them.

Successful library service depends on accurately determining population demographics (such as those mentioned in Chapter 3), community information wants and needs, and how people use the information supplied. Knowing these and other characteristics assists managers in a variety of activities, such as planning, programming, and allocating funds. A comprehensive marketing program can provide some of the requisite data that help create desired services and community support.

For many years, libraries and archives in general did not see much, if any, need to market their products and services. They expected users to know about the services, but they took little action to create awareness and persuade the community that their services were valuable. It was a perception issue rather than a lack of information on how to market libraries. Starting in the 1980s a number of texts on marketing appeared that focused on libraries (Cronin, 1992; Kies, 1987; McNeal, 1992; Rowley, 2001; Savard, 2000; Walters, 1992; Weingand, 1998; Wood and Young, 1988). We agree with Richard Leventhal's (2005) view that in today's environment "an effective marketing effort is based upon information which can be used in terms of developing sound business strategies, . . . allow[s] for more successful innovation, lead[s] to better branding efforts, increase[s] the effectiveness of your promotional efforts and strengthen[s] your web marketing" (p. 3).

There are four key reasons why you should consider developing a marketing program. First and foremost, almost all archives and libraries face either a decreasing resource base or stronger competition for existing resources while needing to provide an increasing range of services. Second, as a result, user convenience usually decreases—shorter service hours, fewer public service staff, and reductions in the number of locally owned information resources are some examples. Third, frequently libraries reach a smaller and smaller percentage of

SOMETHING TO PONDER

Consider a marketing program for a library of your choice. Target three activities that would be part of your program, identify the type of data that would be needed, and indicate how it could be obtained, noting the sources.

the total service population. (Actual numbers of interactions and customers may increase over the previous year, but when the overall service population increases sharply there can be a drop in the percentage served.) Finally, all libraries face stiff competition in the role of transferring information from the creators/producers to the end consumer.

One question to consider when creating a marketing program is, "Why is a nonuser a nonuser?" The following eight statements about noncustomers of for-profit organizations apply equally to libraries:

- The person does not know your product. Many surveys ask, "Does your community or organization have an archive or library?" and it is surprising how often the response is "no" when one does exist.
- The person cannot find your product, or it is not available when needed. Service location and hours are always an issue. There is always a "cost" to a person even when there is no monetary exchange required. There are at least four types of "social price" in using nonprofit service organizations: time, effort, lifestyle, and psyche. The first two are the ones that managers normally consider in their planning activities. Lifestyle is, in part, related to effort in that service hours or locations may require people to adjust the way they live in order to use the library. Too much adjustment usually results in potential users becoming nonusers. Psyche "price" is one of the areas where, for many individuals, the library's price is too high. Although our online catalogs and databases are substantially easier to use than those that existed just 20 years ago, people must still learn how the system functions and face changes as the system is upgraded. Many people find libraries to be intimidating or have difficulty asking for assistance. Very often, these potential users become nonusers because of such factors as self-esteem, pride, fear of loss of privacy, or the need to depend on others for assistance.
- The person does not need your product. In the case of libraries, this statement may not apply, because everyone needs some information to carry out life's activities. Nevertheless, libraries may not have the specific information that the user needs or wants.
- The person prefers a different brand of product. In many ways, this is probably the fastest growing factor for all types of libraries. Increased home and office access to high-speed Internet services has demonstrated that people prefer convenience when it comes to finding and using information. Also the psyche price is very low—no one else will know you could not spell this or that word or did not know this or that fact. Control, self-esteem, privacy, and so forth cease being issues.
- The person does not understand what your product can do. For archives and libraries, this is frequently the case—many people perceive them as offering at best a limited range of documents or print materials. The idea that an archive or library is a full-service organization is

> **TIP**
>
> It can be expensive and time-consuming to collect the data needed for a marketing plan. Libraries are not always good at estimating internal costs, principally staff time, of carrying out projects. It is worthwhile checking with a market research organization to get a quote for its services. It has experience to bring to the task and may be able to meet your information needs by piggybacking your survey with other data-collection exercises. Its fees might not be as high as you would expect.

only just becoming appreciated and understood by some individuals outside the field.

- The person believes the cost of your product is too high or the value for the cost is too low. For this to be a factor, the nonuser should have used your product at least once in order to form an opinion. Many people generalize about libraries and archives based on one or two experiences, often in their youth rather than a recent experience. Learning the basis for the nonuser's judgment is important when planning a marketing program.
- The person has had difficulty using your product. In the past, libraries and archives were not people friendly. In the days of card catalogs and complex filing rules, it was difficult to gain access to materials in the collection. If a user did not understand the rules, he or she was completely dependent on staff assistance. Someone who has not gone to a library or an archive since the arrival of online catalogs may well have memories of it being a difficult place to use.
- The person does not expect good service. While it is impossible to please everyone all the time, displeasing too many people is disastrous. The goal is to reduce the problems as much as possible to retain existing customers; it is not to create a cadre of dissatisfied former users who may discourage potential others from becoming users.

A sound marketing program provides the staff with data (market intelligence) that help them address these issues and develop a plan to increase both the number of customers and the percentage of total target population (market share).

WHAT IS MARKETING?

There are several ways to view marketing. One definition that dates from 1991, from the Chartered Institute of Marketing, is "the management process for identifying, anticipating, and satisfying customer requirements profitably" (http://www.cim.co.uk/marketingplanningtool/intro.asp). Darlene Weingand (1995) related the topic to the field of library science by defining marketing as "a process of exchange and a way to foster the partnership between the library and its community" (p. 296). More recently the definition has included the concept of exchange, which is the transfer of a service in return for something of value, and this is incorporated in Philip Kotler's (1980) definition of marketing as being the process of planning and executing the conception, pricing, promotion, and distribution of ideas, goods, and services to create exchanges that satisfy individual and organizational goals.

Ellyn Ruhlmann (2011) highlighted an important point regarding how library marketing differs from many other types of organizational marketing:

> Isn't it strange that *people* isn't one of the four Ps of marketing? Whoever came up with that list decided to lead with product then analyze how to *place, price,* and *promote* it. That approach doesn't apply all that handily to libraries, at least not ours. Our place, save the bookmobile and a few other exceptions, is already set. So is our price (free). Our products and promotions change, but only as the people they're targeting change. At Waukegan (Illinois) Public Library (WPL) the marketing mix *begins* [emphasis added] with another P—our patrons. (p. 14)

We should note that Ruhlmann's comments are valid up to a point. Marketing data does assist in thinking long-term about place and price. Indeed, the main library is almost always fixed. We also know that people nearly always employ the Law of Least Effort when it comes to satisfying their information/reading needs. Marketing data about user information-seeking behavior can help us think about where and what we might do to better meet the "when and where." Also, while most libraries do not charge fees for their services, they do impose a "cost"—limited service hours and complex search systems to master, for example. Again, marketing feedback can assist us in thinking about ways to reduce such costs.

Almost all definitions of library marketing mention the customer/user as being a key element in the process. They also suggest that people's needs are the focal point of marketing. When employing some form of user-oriented marketing, success will come to the organization that best determines the perceptions, needs, and wants of its target markets and that satisfies these needs through the

---

CHECK THESE OUT

A good resource on library marketing is Kathy Dempsey's *The Accidental Library Marketer* (Medford, NJ: Information Today, 2009).

A journal from the same publisher is *Marketing Library Services* (http://www.infotoday.com/MLS/default.shtml).

design, communication, pricing, and delivery of appropriate and competitively viable offerings (Andreasen and Kotler, 2008). If this sounds familiar in terms of libraries, it should; they have been engaging in such activities for many years, just not always thinking of it as marketing.

One marketing approach is strategic marketing. This approach is an excellent example of the integration of management activities that we view as critical for a successful manager. Essentially, the approach draws on methods of strategic planning (see Chapter 4) and combines them with marketing methods. Over the past 30 years, Phillip Kotler developed the idea that nonprofit marketing differs from for-profit marketing in important ways. He has published seven editions of his text on nonprofit marketing (Andreasen and Kotler, 2008). The first three editions emphasized the methods of marketing nonprofit organizations. Starting with his fourth edition, he added strategic planning aspects to the approach. With the fifth edition, the authors added a strong international component as well as social marketing.

Market analysis, and some of the related methods for assessing needs that employ similar techniques, can provide managers with vital data about a variety of topics, such as:

- when and how services are used,
- who does and does not use the services,
- what new services are desired,
- what information is desired,
- what formats are desired, and
- what image of the library is held in the minds of the community served.

Some libraries, particularly those that are publicly funded, need to emphasize the sales aspect and employ social marketing. Social marketing grew out of efforts by Kotler and others at a time when a number of nonprofit groups with relatively narrow interests began to engage in sales-oriented marketing. Some examples of such nonprofit groups are health-care and environmental or consumer protection organizations. Frequently, these organizations have a special aspect, or "cause," that they want to sell to the general public. Take the example of public libraries, which often have programs and activities that are social in the

SOMETHING TO PONDER

The term "marketing" is interpreted in a number of ways. Check dictionaries and websites for more examples. Scan the definitions; which one do you think best describes what you understand as "marketing?" Note the source, and put the definition in a safe place for future reference.

sense of social marketing—adult literacy programs, after-school storytelling, or programs for "latchkey" children.

In a sense, social marketing employs techniques that generate support for and perhaps move forward certain social causes or agendas. Social marketing for libraries is difficult to differentiate from advocacy activities. The difference, as stated by Andreasen and Kotler (2008), is that "social marketing seeks to influence social behavior not to benefit the marketer *but to benefit the target audience and the general society*" (emphasis in the original, p. 46).

Some of the marketing data require collection directly from the source. Direct collecting is often expensive and time-consuming. Building some of the collecting into normal operational routines will reduce overall costs. When the data collecting becomes part of the operational routine, it is almost cost-free. For instance, organizations often already collect a wealth of data about existing users (registration data, collection usage reports, and data from document delivery services). Such data provide the staff with profiles of what are, at the very least, semi-satisfied users. This information can be beneficial in choosing the most cost-effective services to offer to people with similar profiles. Another example would be deciding how to reach out to a very different segment of the population. When developing a marketing plan, managers would draw heavily on such data.

Market intelligence is data that are secured from four broad areas: environment, activity type, customers, and competitors. Data from the operating environment are essential in planning and goal setting, so the manager should have much of these data already collected for use in other management activities. All of the environmental factors we discussed earlier (see Chapter 2) apply to any marketing program. Activity data are really subsets of information about the operational environment, such as vendor activities, technological developments, and competitors. Users are a logical source of demographic data—level of use, age, and major responsibilities (researcher, teacher, and administrator) are some examples. Likewise, competitors provide more useful data when thought of in terms of subsets, such as market share, distribution methods, and price.

So far we have focused on external marketing (marketing to users and funding bodies, for example). There are, however, other stakeholders who together form the internal market—senior management and, most important, the staff of the library—and we will return to this point later.

CHECK THIS OUT

The January/February 2011 issue of *Public Libraries* (50, no. 1) is completely devoted to marketing ideas from a variety of public libraries. Almost any type of library will find one or more interesting ideas to explore in its environment.

MARKETING PROCESS

Philip Kotler's strategic marketing process for not-for-profit organizations has three major elements: analysis, strategy, and implementation (Andreasen and Kotler, 2008). Much of the process involves the steps of strategic planning. The steps are:

1. Generic product definition
2. Target group definition
3. Differential marketing analysis
4. Customer behavior analysis
5. Differential advantages analysis
6. Multiple marketing approaches
7. Integrated market planning
8. Continuous market feedback
9. Marketing audit

GENERIC PRODUCT DEFINITION

A key to the long-term success of any organization is a realistic answer to the question, "What is our business?" Every organization produces at least one of the following: physical products (tangible), services (intangible), persons (press agents), the organization itself (political parties or professional organizations), or ideas (population control or human rights, for example). Often, the answer to the question is product oriented rather than customer oriented. When that happens, the outcome limits the organization's growth potential. Thinking about the organization in terms of the user tends to broaden the scope of possible activities. Rather than being in the railroad business, think in terms of transportation—soap becomes cleaning, movies become entertainment, and documents become information.

TARGET GROUP DEFINITION

The generic or user-based product definition usually results in identifying a wide market. Looking at such a market can lead to the creation of a marketing program so broad that it fails to produce the desired results. Dividing the large market into smaller units usually produces more cost-effective marketing. A market "segment" comprises units with similar or related characteristics, units with common needs and wants, and units with similar responses to like motivations, and it accepts a service/product that fulfills these needs at a reasonable price. For years libraries have developed different services for different types of users (children/young adult/adult, undergraduate/graduate, literacy development, and English as a second language users, for example).

Market segmenting takes time and effort but pays off in a better response from a particular market segment. For example, for an academic library, what might its segments be? The most obvious segments are the faculty and students; however, even those groups are probably too large to fit our definition of a mar-

> ## CHECK THESE OUT
>
> Debra Lee's article "Market Segmentation and Libraries" (*Library Administration and Management* 18, no. 1: 47–48, 2004) explores segmenting in more depth.
>
> Another useful article is Charles Forrest's "Segmenting the Library Market" (*Georgia Library Quarterly* 42, no. 1: 4–7, 2005). The principles can be translated into other information settings.

ket segment. There are likely to be more useful segments if you think in terms of subject interest or major. A segment might group doctoral students with faculty instead of with the broader category—graduate students. Another way to divide students would be into undeclared-major lower-division undergraduates, declared-major lower-division undergraduates, undeclared upper-division, undergraduates, declared upper-division undergraduates, master's degree students, and doctoral-level students. This provides you with the sense of the many ways to approach segmentation as well as the need to think outside the box.

All types of libraries have equally diverse markets when you think carefully about the possibilities. The goal is to analyze the service population and divide it into small homogenous units. There is never enough money to address all the potential marketing areas; however, having smaller homogenous segments helps you make the decision(s) of where to expend the available marketing funds. Thinking about each segment and asking questions such as the following will help:

- What are the common needs/wants of this group?
- Which, if any, of those needs do we now serve?
- What do we know about the group's behavior patterns?
- How much benefit does the group currently receive from our services?
- What is the potential gain from meeting more of this group's needs and wants?
- What type of message is the most effective for reaching this group?
- What do we know about the group's perceptions of the service?
- Compared to other market segments, how important is this group for the service?
- Who is our competition?

The answer to the last question should facilitate the ranking of the various market segments by the library. (These rankings will vary over time as the situation and the operating environment change.) Some of the other questions may indicate the need to collect more data before a final decision is reasonable. All of the answers will help determine which group(s) will be the target(s).

DIFFERENTIAL MARKETING ANALYSIS

Different segments require different approaches and thus differentiated marketing. While most libraries have three basic product lines—collections, services, and programs—the mix in emphasis or importance for a particular market segment will vary. Using the for-profit terminology, each product line consists of several different, specific products. To take the example of a university library, specific collection products might be defined by dividing the collection into instructional, secondary, and primary research materials. Services might be document delivery and online searching. Program products might be electronic search methods instruction and dissertation format assistance. As you examine specific products, it becomes apparent how different packages would have greater or lesser interest to various market segments. For-profit organizations learned long ago that when serving more than one target population, differentiating products and communications about the products produces the maximum results. Thinking about the packages in terms of what costs and benefits a person accrues from using the package gives you two useful perspectives. First, it offers a complete picture of what the package consists of and the interrelationship between the component parts. Second, it gives you some sense of how the person perceives, or will perceive, the package. This latter element is very important because nonprofit organizations tend to believe that their service or package is vital.

CUSTOMER BEHAVIOR ANALYSIS

For many years, collection development officers knew that it was vital to understand the service community's information needs, wants, and lifestyles. Asking questions about what topics are of interest, "product" usage, when and where people use information, and when and where they would prefer to use it allows staff to structure services and programs more effectively. Such information is helpful in determining the most effective approaches to marketing existing services as well as in promoting new services. Focus groups can be a highly effective method for gathering answers to such questions.

A major issue for any organization, profit or nonprofit, is changing customer behavior and interests. Patrick Barwise and Sean Meehan (2010) asked the question, "How do managers ensure that their products and services are, and remain, relevant to customers?" (p. 63). They suggest the key to knowing this requires unsanitized information from frontline staff about what they hear and observe regarding users when it comes to the organization's products and services. Certainly marketing data helps with this; however, marketing programs do cost substantial amounts of money, especially for libraries. This means there may be several years between full market assessments, thus the importance of frontline staff feedback.

Barwise and Meehan (2010) provided some important questions to ask regarding the quality of staff feedback; we have paraphrased the questions to better reflect the library environment:

- Can your middle managers accurately describe what the library promises its service community? (Mission, values, vision, goals for a start.)

- Can senior and middle managers identify the four or five major issues that most undermine trust and/or satisfaction of users regarding the library's services?
- Are your services, for the targeted segments, the best option for them? Now, next year, in two years? If not, what can be done with the existing services to better fit user needs now and in the future?
- What innovations have you tried recently? In the past 12 months? What was user feedback if you did?
- Has frontline staff passed on any "uncomfortable" information about usage patterns or user comments recently? In the past 3 months, 6 months?

Barwise and Meehan (2010) concluded their article with the following: "Quality pioneer W. Edwards Deming is widely credited with the comment 'In God we trust, all others must bring data.' For those who are prepared to ask tough questions and *willing to hear* the answers, the potential benefits to the business are significant" (p. 68; emphasis added).

DIFFERENTIAL ADVANTAGES ANALYSIS
Once you understand the behaviors and needs of the various segments, it is possible to identify differential advantages for each segment. A differential advantage is one that exploits the reputation, services, or programs by creating or enhancing a special value in the minds of potential users. A public library example is having services for the visually impaired, such as large-print collections and "reading machines." For service organizations such as libraries and archives, it is essential to reinforce the values and/or needs of the service community and the parent organization.

MULTIPLE MARKETING APPROACHES
In planning a marketing effort, it is advantageous, if not essential, to employ several different marketing tools. The selected tools (such as websites, newslet-

---

TIP

Do not forget to take into consideration the senior managers of your parent organization when thinking about market segments. A good ongoing marketing public relations method is to underpromise and overdeliver. This almost always generates positive thoughts about you and your library. When you know one of the managers has a major project that requires research, offer the library's help; the offer may not be accepted but will generate positive thoughts.

ters, flyers, advertisements, and annual reports) should be those that best fit the lifestyle of the target segment. Receptions or open houses can be effective promotional tools, especially when there is a new service or product to demonstrate. In the case of a public library attempting to reach new immigrants, using the native languages of the target population is essential. One caution when preparing material in another language: it is imperative to have the material reviewed by a native speaker who understands both formal and colloquial usage.

INTEGRATED MARKET PLANNING AND CONTINUOUS FEEDBACK

When an organization implements an ongoing marketing program, there is the chance that, over time, different components of the program will be working at cross-purposes. An integrated program is the best insurance against ineffective use of marketing funds. One element in achieving an integrated plan is to have one person responsible for coordinating all marketing and promotional activities. Only the very largest libraries have the resources to allocate one or more full-time persons to work solely on marketing or promotional activities. In the past, such positions often carried the title "public relations officer." Today, more often than not the title is "marketing director." Even when the level of staffing will not allow for a full-time marketing position, only one person (or, a lesser second choice, a committee) should be responsible for coordinating all marketing and promotional activities. To make the work manageable, there must be a strategic marketing plan for the managers to review and update on a regular basis.

INTERNAL MARKETING

Internal marketing is not a set of separate processes: the processes are interrelated and overlap with external ones. Internal marketing along with performance or service quality monitoring provides an example of the effect of one activity upon another. Experience indicates that we remember poor service more often than good service, and the staff is the factor that can make the difference. Ensuring that staff members are well informed about the library should increase user satisfaction. After managers have prepared mission statements, strategic plans, and goals and objectives, these efforts may not be effectively conveyed to the frontline staff. They have to know and understand changes in policy. If, for example, a policy change includes "good news," informed staff members can convey the news to users. Updates and changes to the library's website also need to be conveyed to all staff. If they are not, staff at any level may be told by an outsider of an internal change.

One technique to judge the effectiveness of internal marketing is to conduct an employee satisfaction survey. The results will indicate the state of staff satisfaction and the organizational climate within the library.

Internal marketing to senior managers keeps them in touch with service developments. They need to be aware of both the "good news" and the "less good news." The "less good news" might be an incident (such as an influential user being upset by what he or she considered to be poor service) and service disruptions. Be sure

AUTHORS' EXPERIENCE

When dean of an ARL library, Alire's vision to change the negative reputation of the academic library included a strong marketing component.
The library knew that it provided good services and resources, but no one
believed it. As part of the new strategic plan, one of the library's strategic
goals was "To tell the library's story."

First, the library staff systematically researched what its users—students,
faculty, and staff—wanted; what they knew about existing services and
resources; and how they rated those services and resources (i.e., LibQUAL⁺).
Once that information was available, the library was able to strategically
determine what new services/resources were needed, which existing ones
needed attention, and which existing ones needed expanding.

Also, to help meet the marketing strategic goal of telling the library's
story, an aggressive marketing campaign ensued. First, Alire sent two librarians to a national ACRL all-day "train the trainers" workshop on academic
library marketing. (See http://www.ala.org/ala/mgrps/divs/acrl/issues/
marketing/. Go to: *Strategic Marketing for Academic and Research Libraries Participant Manual* or to *Strategic Marketing for Academic and Research
Libraries Facilitation Guide*. Note: There are similar ALA marketing toolkits
for public libraries and school libraries.)

Those two individuals then returned to the library and provided several workshops, which over 70 percent of the library staff attended. It was
important for the library staff to understand why a marketing campaign was
critical to changing the negative perception of the university community of
the library and to get staff buy-in for marketing. Also in those workshops,
the library staff developed the library's branding statement.

Once this marketing process was completed and existing services and
resources were refined and new services and resources were introduced, the
library then formed a marketing team that proceeded with the systematic
promotion of the library's services and resources by developing and following the library's marketing plan. The marketing team was headed by Alire's
executive assistant. Upon integration of the marketing/promotion goal (and
the marketing team) into the library's work, the next step was to design and
implement effective advocacy efforts.

to deliver such news with care, emphasizing how the situation is being positively
addressed.

MARKETING AUDIT

A marketing audit draws on feedback from the service community, library staff,
and governing boards. Looking at what worked and why, what did not work and

why, how the environment and community base has or has not changed, and what changes have taken place within the organization (staff, services, resources, facilities) all become important aspects in adjusting and maintaining a viable marketing program. Other elements include assessing the resources available to carry out the program, how well the people responsible for carrying out the program have performed, and how effective the program is in achieving long-term organizational mission goals and objectives. Darlene Weingand (1995) suggested:

> The audit should also develop a "futures screen" that identifies trends and projections in both external and internal environments in order to develop contingency plans that will relate to alternative future scenarios. The futures screen places considerable emphasis on securing data on what "may be" in the next five years (and beyond); objectives can then be developed to reflect that informed projection. (p. 303)

Additional issues for an audit involve how certain factors have or have not changed since the program's inception. For instance, if the time frame is five years, staff members probably will have changed. Another factor is that small variations in organizational resources over the years may, in totality, be significant. A careful review of the operating environment may reveal that new or different competitors exist for the library. In essence, one should examine all relevant changes, both internal and external.

Such an analysis often helps to increase library usage (quantitatively or qualitatively), to increase attendance at important events, or to build a following for a valued program. The problem is that managers may be tempted to initiate promotional efforts on an ad hoc basis to meet a particular need independent of larger or competing priorities. If such efforts succeed, they may become annual activities; the cumulative effect is a hodgepodge of disparate marketing efforts, which can consume massive amounts of time and energy but in total bear little resemblance to the strategic agenda of the institution as a whole.

BRANDING

Between marketing and promotion is the concept of branding. At its simplest, branding is the process of developing a symbol (often a logo) that embodies the essence of a product, service, or organization. Deborah Lee (2006) defined

CHECK THIS OUT

The American Library Association's @ your library logo is a registered trademark. Visit the ALA website to see the different ways the logo can be used (http://www.ala.org/advocacy/advleg/publicawareness/campaign@ yourlibrary/prtools/downloadlogos/download_logos).

CHECK THESE OUT

The following are useful for addressing branding concepts:

De Mesa, Alycia. 2009. *Brand Avatar: Translating Virtual World Branding into Real World Success.* Basingstoke, UK: Palgrave Macmillan.

Hammond, James. 2008. *Branding Your Business: Promoting Your Business, Attracting Customers, and Standing Out in the Market Place.* Philadelphia: Kogan Page.

Miller, Jon, and David Muir. 2004. *The Business of Branding.* Hoboken, NJ: Wiley.

Olins, Wally. 2004. *On Brand.* London: Thames and Hudson.

branding as "a marketing concept that identifies a good or service through the use of a name, phrase, design, or symbol" (p. 94). Libraries have a generic logo, originally developed by the American Library Association, to draw upon when thinking about developing a brand: @ your library. This logo has been translated into many languages.

Branding is not always just a matter of a single library, as evidenced by the headline of a story in *American Libraries* (2006b): "Britain Launches Campaign to Transform Libraries' Image." In 2011, Subnum Hariff and Jennifer Rowley, in writing about U.K. public library branding, noted, "There is increasing recognition that the future for public libraries is bleak, and that a major contributing factor is their failure to change the image or their 'brand' as their identity. This problem is not just prevalent in U.K. libraries but emblematic across the sector globally" (p. 347). They make the point that branding is more complex than "name, logo, strap-lines, and color schemes" (p. 347). They conclude the article with "branding can be used successfully to drive up borrowing and visits to libraries, and arguably to change brand image and perceptions of the library service" (p. 357).

Corporations spend large sums of money each year to maintain a brand they have created. Libraries may not have much, if any, money to maintain their brands. Two websites on branding that can be useful are What Makes a Great Logo (http://www.code-interactive.com/thinker/a112.html) and Logo Design Services Directory (http://www.logoterra.com/).

Brands invoke both a physical and a psychological experience. When a powerful sense of service is developed in the staff, a manager can be confident that users will experience a positive psychological experience in almost every case and ensure as good a physical experience as the facilities allow. Both will be significant assets in establishing and maintaining a library's brand.

PROMOTION

Promotion should be part of any marketing mix. Kotler (1980, p. 89) defines the marketing mix as consisting of price, promotion, and product. Promotion refers to a cluster of techniques to communicate, inform, persuade, stimulate, and remind the service community of the merits of the services and programs available. The goal of promotion is to modify or reinforce existing behavior. The successful approach will blend selective activities to reach and recruit potential users.

The basic forms of promotion, according to McDaniel (1996), are advertising, personal selling, sales promotion, and publicity. Relatively few libraries employ a wholehearted advertising approach—partly because of cost but also because, traditionally, advertising was thought to be somewhat inappropriate and too impersonal for the type of services offered. Another reason for its low use has been the thought that advertising was unnecessary. Today, we know that this is wishful thinking.

Some of the efforts that libraries call promotion are referred to in the profit sector as "sales promotion." Alexander (1961) defined sales promotion as consisting of "activities other than personal selling, advertising, and publicity that stimulate consumer purchasing and dealer effectiveness such as displays, shows, exhibitions, demonstrations, and various non-recruitment efforts not in the ordinary routine" (p. 20).

Looking at libraries as if they were a company, sales promotion can consist of discounts (such as volume discounts on copying), coupons, samples (e.g., limited free access to a fee-based service), toll-free numbers, films/videos (self-paced bibliographic instruction), catalogs and guides, decals, calendars, and other tactics normally used in the commercial world. Public libraries can and do make use of decals and posters prepared by state or national professional associations as well as locally developed items.

There are additional options to consider when building your marketing mix. Certainly the library's webpages are a powerful tool. They not only convey basic information about the services offered but also reflect the library's image and culture. The library may have a free-standing website, or it may have pages within the website of the parent organization. Naturally you must carefully consider what to cover (putting too much information on a page is as bad as having too little). Think about such issues as page indexing, links to other relevant sites, design, and layout—users should be able to navigate the site quickly to find the information they are seeking. Remember that the information provided needs to be updated regularly—a site that is not updated gives a very bad impression of the library. Pictures, video, and sound can enhance the site, but they can be expensive, and they can cause frustration for the visitor with a low-end computer. Maintain a balance between ease and speed of access and the use of such enhancements as images and sound.

Preprinted advertising inserts and circulars can be used to publish service offerings, schedules, or a calendar of events. A library can have these inserted into weekly community newspapers or mailed to home and work addresses. Some libraries have a weekly column in the local newspaper. Canvassing is the marketing category for a technique better known in public libraries as "outreach activities." If used discriminatingly—choosing events and locations where real prospects are likely to be concentrated—this tactic has its place in most strategies. If overused, it will drain resources from more cost-efficient alternatives.

Brochures can be a keystone element in a well-orchestrated sequence of varied communications efforts—if they are written, designed, and distributed at the right time in the cycle and if they are aimed at carefully targeted populations.

Billboards and print advertising are mass-media options that typically are expensive choices for trying to reach thousands of nonusers. On occasion, however, these tactics can lend key support. For example, such options are an appropriate means to promote a special event by identifying the time, the place, and the specific benefit to the target population. One obvious occasion to consider using this approach is during a bond issue campaign. Signs are often considered too humdrum a subject for creative marketers. For prospective users, however, effective signs and clear directions can make the difference between a positive experience with the library or extreme frustration. Libraries, especially public libraries, are often surprised to discover, after a survey of community members, how many people do not know that there is a library in their region or how many people cannot identify the nearest branch. Newspaper, magazine, television, and radio are all mass-media formats well-suited to targeting or segmentation, but they must be used with care. Certain sections of newspapers in targeted zip codes and certain radio or television programs may or may not fit the profile of the targeted population. If so, these media should be evaluated on the basis of cost per contact. This may be one of the few ways to effectively reach noncustomers. In the end, regardless of which tactics are chosen, the institution must "decide what it wants to say and how (by what media) it wants the message delivered" (McDaniel, 1996, p. 377).

In Chapter 9, on change and innovation, we mentioned there are times when you need to "break the brick." Library brick breaking is always worth considering when it comes to promotion. Jennings and Tvarzka (2010) provide on example of thinking outside the box for library promotion. They describe how their academic library employed fortune cookies (yes, the fortune cookies you get in Chinese restaurants) for promotional purposes. The library ordered customized fortune cookies (less than $200 for 1,000) to distribute at freshman orientation—two of the five custom messages in the freshmen cookies were "Right now your parents are remodeling your room" and "Worse things are to come, befriend a librarian." The cookies were such a success that the library used the idea during finals' week for students and faculty with a different set of messages for each

---

FOR FURTHER THOUGHT

Think about your local public library. Which tactics could it employ? Rank them in the order of their likely cost and effectiveness.

> **TIP**
>
> Most national library associations have awards for various categories of promotional activities. In the United States, one set of awards are the John Dana Cotton Awards. Look at the prize-winning entries each year (http://www.ebscohost.com/academic/john-cotton-dana). Some good examples can stimulate thinking about how to promote your library. At the ALA midwinter meeting, many libraries offer copies of their promotional materials. Sharing these materials among colleagues can lead to some creative thinking.

group. Jennings and Tvarzka concluded their article with: "Overall, the library produced a lot of good will by doing this simple, quick, and inexpensive promotion with faculty and students" (p. 13).

PUBLIC RELATIONS

Public relations is a profession with its own set of core values and ethics. The core values of the Public Relations Society of America are advocacy, honesty, expertise, independence, loyalty, and fairness. Its ethical code provisions address free flow of information, competition, disclosure of information, safeguarding confidences, conflicts of interest, and enhancing the profession. These are sound principles to follow in undertaking any public relations project.

Few libraries are able to employ a professional communications manager or publicist. Within larger or for-profit organizations, internal expertise may be available. Support in the library sector is provided by the American Library Association. Larger libraries may retain a public relations consultant on an as-needed basis.

Public relations is concerned with building relationships. One vital relationship is that between the library and either the public relations professional within the organization or the external consultant. A specialist's expertise may be needed to maintain a high profile in the user community, lobby for improvements in funding or facilities, launch a new building, promote a new service, introduce a new senior staff member, or publicize a success story. Public relations specialists aim to keep their clients in the public eye and present a positive image.

A frequently used public relations communication tool is the media release. If it concerns a major event, a media conference can be arranged with the local press, radio stations, and television stations, and a media release can be distributed by mail, fax, e-mail, or the Internet. This is a form of indirect promotion, and it is in many ways the most powerful. From the promotion or marketing communications mix point of view, it is also the least controllable of all the techniques. To paraphrase Kotler, publicity is nonpaid communication about a company or its products appearing in the media as news. As a result, "the seller pays

CHECK THIS OUT

Claudia O'Keefe provides excellent guidance on how to create an effective press release in her 2005 article "Publicity 101" (*American Libraries* 36, no. 6: 52–54).

nothing for the news coverage" (Kotler, 1980, p. 469). Communications about staff, services, or a special category of customer can be legitimate news, but they also serves as a form of promotion—as long as the news is good.

Unfortunately, negative publicity seems easier to get than positive press. Based on experience, we know that academic libraries can expect to see a negative story once or twice a year in the student-run newspaper. Any allegation of fiscal mismanagement or labor problems easily makes the local evening news, the morning newspaper, or some website. What is unfortunate, but typical, is that none of the major publications ever publishes anything on the resolution of the problems. This was the fate for the Boston Public Library, when the news story "Boston PL Defends Reputation in Wake of Scathing Report" (*American Libraries,* 2006a) was picked up in national publications and later developments were not covered. When negative stories hit the media, fast action is necessary, and a good relationship with a public relations expert is essential. Such an expert will have contacts and the experience to counteract the bad news.

Timing of your marketing and public relations efforts is always important but becomes critical during crises and bad news periods. Knowing how, when, what, and to whom to communicate is essential during a crisis. Flexibility is a key component of this activity as the event develops. Social media is useful for speed, but being too swift to communicate may create a bigger problem.

Public relations advisors will have the expertise to target segments of the stakeholders, tailor messages to specific groups, and perhaps arrange events to broadcast a message about a new service or development. By identifying influ-

CHECK THIS OUT

In her 2005 "Sensemaking a Public Library's Internet Policy Crisis," Mary Cavanagh (*Library Management* 26, nos. 6/7: 351–360) describes how a library board and library management resolved a public controversy led by staff and a community newspaper. The controversy centered on the right of the library staff to be protected from viewing Internet pornography and the community's reaction to the issue of protecting children's Internet access versus the library's commitment to intellectual freedom online.

TIP

When facing a major crisis situation it may be wise to turn to a professional for advice on what and how to communicate with your stakeholders and general public. The approach may well differ for the two categories. Two good resources to consult are W. Timothy Coombs's *Ongoing Crisis Communication: Planning, Managing, and Responding,* 3rd ed. (Thousand Oaks, CA: Sage, 2012) and Robert L. Heath and W. Timothy Coombs's *Today's Public Relations: An Introduction* (Thousand Oaks, CA: Sage, 2006).

ential people in the user community and organizing an event in which they are likely to be interested, both the users and the library may benefit. For example, an exhibition is organized for a migrant group within the community, and representatives from that group are invited to an opening. The opening receives publicity in the media tailored both for the group and the community at large. This event will incur a cost, but a public relations professional probably has contacts who would consider sponsoring such an event. The sponsor and the library could be in a win–win situation. Businesses within local communities know that they benefit from demonstrating community involvement, and the senior management of organizations recognize that obtaining sponsorship is beneficial. Other forms of sponsorship can include donated prizes for events organized for young people. In turn, a library may be able to offer sponsorship, incurring a small, visible cost, by making a room available for a one-time community event.

Public relations support is probably most needed when the library lobbies politicians and funding agencies about funding issues. Because politicians and agencies receive a large volume of mail and phone calls, skill and experience are necessary to catch their attention and make a convincing case. The American Library Association's website provides templates for letters (http://www.ala.org/acrl/issues/marketing), which can be very useful for small libraries with limited funding. In addition, it is always useful to know a friendly public relations person who might at times offer some pro bono advice.

Positive publicity requires patient cultivation and serious efforts to package, which cost time and money. Publicity may not be paid for, but it's not free. Large

CHECK THIS OUT

Elsie Finch's *Advocating Archives: An Introduction to Public Relations for Archivists* (Lanham, MD: Scarecrow Press and American Society of Archivists, 2006) is a good resource for dealing with archives and public relations.

public relations budgets do not always produce better results unless the outcomes are monitored and evaluated. Ideally, everyone on the staff acts as a salesperson or a press agent by being positive and highlighting the many worthwhile and fascinating activities that, after all, are characteristic of the library's operations. This is the essence of internal marketing, and it precedes external marketing.

A library's website serves as both a marketing and a public relations tool. Keeping the webpages "fresh" is important to retaining young people's attention. You have a variety of other social media tools as well. As we will discuss in more detail in Chapter 18 on technology, there are both technical and people issues to consider when you decide to move into such activities. Performing such activities well makes for wonderful marketing and public relations. Performing them not so well will send negative messages about the library and its services.

ADVOCACY

We noted earlier in this chapter that marketing and advocacy, while related, are different in purpose and practice. John Moorman (2009) wrote:

> Advocacy is a matter of perennial concern for today's librarians and library community as a whole. . . . As one who has been actively involved in library advocacy in four states for over thirty years and a registered lobbyist with the Commonwealth of Virginia, I know that without ongoing advocacy, libraries have no hope of receiving the resources they need to provide quality services to their user community. (p. 15)

Because advocacy is in general about supporting a cause or course of action, it is important that the library advocacy process become an integral part of a manager's responsibilities. It needs to be more than a recognized part of the marketing and promotion processes; it needs to be a "must do" for all library administrators. To become a successful library administrator, it is critical to develop advocacy skills. Pat Schuman in her quote at the beginning of the chapter emphasized that part of all library administrators' jobs was to rally and organize library advocates to speak out for their libraries because they are the ones who lose when libraries are cut or closed. This is also supported in the ALA's (2010) *Library Advocate's Handbook*: "Library administrators are responsible for developing and coordinating an ongoing advocacy effort, one with well-defined roles for staff, trustees, and friends" (p. 3).

Because of the ever-increasing financial strain on public-supported organizations and agencies, now more than ever library advocacy is critical. In the past, advocacy efforts were focused on the stakeholders—community users, students, and faculty. These grassroots efforts have been effective when applied systematically. Engaging library employees—librarians and support staff—to become frontline advocates has added another layer of personal involvement. Who better than the frontline staff to influence users whom they see regularly and probably know on a first-name basis? When referring to empowering frontline staff, Alire noted one frontline staff skill as the "[a]bility to advance the . . . library agenda

CHECK THESE OUT

The ALA's Advocacy, Legislation and Issues website is extremely helpful to becoming advocacy proficient (http://www.ala.org/ala/issuesadvocacy/index.cfm). Two other ALA websites to take a look at are Advocacy University (http://www.ala.org/advocacy/advleg/advocacyuniversity) and Advocacy Clearinghouse (http://www.ala.org/advocacy/advleg/advocacyuniversity/advclearinghouse). They provide tool kits, packets, webinars, and online tutorials for your use.

by helping them to reflect on their personal circles of influence and the strategies that would be most persuasive" (ACRL, 2006, p. i).

Carl A. Harvey (2010) in writing about school library advocacy suggested you need to be "tactical" in your efforts. We have paraphrased his "tactical" concept into the following format to fit almost any type of library (read his article for the school perspective):

T = Target (know who and what your target people and issues are)
A = Action (have actions, not just words, to share)
C = Communication (choose the proper channels and approaches)
T = Time (timing is critical to getting your message heard)
I = Involvement (become active in the target group[s], if possible. It makes your message[s] more meaningful)
C = Change (talk about how your library has and is changing)
A = Attitude (be positive, upbeat, excited about your topic—it becomes contagious)
L = Leadership (demonstrate your and your library's leadership in providing effective and efficient services)

AUTHORS' EXPERIENCE

As a follow-up to Alire's earlier example of successful internal marketing, the next step after "Telling the library's story" was to develop a frontline library advocacy process. Frontline librarians at the academic library were empowered and engaged in reaching out to faculty and students who they knew best to become involved in grassroots library advocacy. They followed the steps outlined in the ALA's Action Plan (American Library Association, 2010, p. 7). The goal was to have $700,000 added to the library materials' base budget; and, through those frontline advocacy efforts, they successfully achieved the goal.

KEY POINTS TO REMEMBER

- Marketing is an essential element in the strategic plan of a successful library.
- Marketing, in common with all managerial activities, requires time and careful thought.
- A sound marketing plan is based on generic product definition, target group definition, differential analysis, user behavior analysis, differential advantage analysis, multiple approaches, integration, feedback, and auditing.
- Internal marketing is essential.
- Branding a library is an important activity for projecting quality service.
- Public relations and communications management are related to, but different from, marketing activities.
- All marketing, promotion, and public relations activities should be monitored and evaluated.
- The library advocacy stage is set by the successful work completed through effective marketing, promotion, and public relations.

References

Alexander, Ralph S. 1961. *Marketing Definitions*. Chicago: American Marketing Association.

Alire, Camila. 2010. "Sustaining Advocacy." *American Libraries* 41, nos. 6/7: 8.

American Libraries. 2006a. "Boston PL Defends Reputation in Wake of Scathing Report." *American Libraries* 37, no. 5: 19.

American Libraries. 2006b. "Britain Launches Campaign to Transform Libraries' Image." *American Libraries* 37, no. 5: 22.

American Library Association. 2010. *Library Advocate's Handbook*. 3rd ed. Chicago: American Library Association.

Andreasen, Allen, and Philip Kotler. 2008. *Strategic Marketing for Nonprofit Organizations*. 7th ed. Englewood Cliffs, NJ: Prentice-Hall.

Association of College and Research Libraries. 2006. *The Power of Personal Persuasion: Advancing the Academic Library Agenda from the Front Line*. Chicago: American Library Association.

Barwise, Patrick, and Sean Meehan. 2010. "Is Your Company as Customer Focused as You Think?" *MIT Sloan Management Review* 51, no. 3: 63–68.

Cavanagh, Mary. 2005. "Sensemaking a Public Library's Internet Policy Crisis." *Library Management* 26, nos. 6/7: 351–360.

Cronin, Blaise, ed. 1992. *Marketing of Library and Libraries*. 2nd ed. London: Aslib.

Dempsey, Kathy. 2010. "The Key to Marketing Success." *Information Outlook* 14, no. 8: 6–9.

DiMattia, Susan. 2011. "Advocacy and Image: Partners in Creating a Value Proposition." *Information Outlook* 15, no. 2: 14–16.

Hariff, Subnum, and Jennifer Rowley. 2011. "Branding UK Public Libraries." *Library Management* 32, no. 4/5: 346–360.

Harvey, Carl A. 2010. "Being Tactical with Advocacy." *Teacher Librarian* 37, no. 4: 80–90.

Jennings, Eric, and Kathryn Tvaruzka. 2010. "Quick and Dirty Library Promotions That Really Work." *Journal of Library Innovation* 1, no. 2: 6–14.

Kennedy, Marie. 2011. "What Are We Really Doing to Market Electronic Resources?" *Library Management* 32, no. 3: 144–158.

Kies, Cosette. 1987. *Marketing and Public Relations for Libraries.* Metuchen, NJ: Scarecrow Press.

Kotler, Philip. 1980. *Marketing Management Analysis: Planning and Control.* 4th ed. Englewood Cliffs, NJ: Prentice-Hall.

Lee, Deborah. 2006. "Checking Out the Competition: Marketing Lesson from Google." *Library Administration and Management* 20, no. 2: 94–95.

Leventhal, Richard. 2005. "The Importance of Marketing." *Strategic Directions* 21, no. 6: 3–4.

McDaniel, Carl D. 1996. *Contemporary Marketing Research.* 3rd ed. St. Paul, MN: West Publishing.

McNeal, James U. 1992. *Kids as Customers: A Handbook of Marketing to Children.* New York: Macmillan.

Moorman, John. 2009. "Advocacy Today, Advocacy Tomorrow, Advocacy Forever!" *Virginia Libraries* 55, no. 4: 15–16.

O'Keefe, Claudia. 2005. "Publicity 101." *American Libraries* 36, no. 6: 52–54.

Rowley, Jennifer. 2001. *Information Marketing.* Ashgate, UK: Aldershot.

———. 2003. "Information Marketing: Seven Questions." *Library Management* 24, nos. 1/2: 13–19.

Ruhlmann, Ellyn. 2011. "Stirring Up the Marketing Mix." *Public Libraries* 50, no. 1: 14–16.

Savard, Rejean. 2000. *Adapting Marketing to Libraries in a Changing and World-Wide Environment.* Munich: K. G. Sauer.

Schuman, Pat. 2012. E-mail communication sent to Camila A. Alire, April 3.

Shontz, Marilyn, Jon C. Parker, and Richard Parker. 2004. "What Do Librarians Think about Marketing?" *Library Quarterly* 74, no. 1: 63–84.

Singh, Rajesh. 2009. "Does Your Library Have a Marketing Culture?" *Library Management* 30, no. 3: 117–137.

Smith-Butler, Lisa. 2010. "Overcoming Your Aversion to the 'M' Word." *AALL Spectrum* 14, no. 5: 7–8, 23.

Walters, Suzanne. 1992. *Marketing: A How-To-Do-It Manual for Librarians.* New York: Neal-Schuman.

Weingand, Darlene. 1995. "Preparing for the New Millennium: The Case for Using Market Strategies." *Library Trends* 43, no. 3: 296.

———. 1998. *Future-Driven Library Marketing.* Chicago: American Library Association.

Wood, Elizabeth J., and Victoria L. Young. 1988. *Strategic Marketing for Libraries.* New York: Greenwood Press.

Launching Pad

Dasu, Sriram, and Richard B. Chase. 2010. "Designing the Soft Side of Customer Service." *MIT Sloan Management Review* 52, no. 1: 33–39.

Dougherty, Richard M. 2011. "Library Advocacy: One Message, One Voice." *American Libraries* 42, nos. 5/6: 46–50.

Dunenhoffer, Cynthia. 2012. "Pin It! Pinterest as a Library Marketing and Information Literacy Tool." *College and Research Libraries News* 73, no. 6: 328–332.

Fisher, Patricia H., and Marseille M. Pride. 2005. *Blueprint for Our Library Marketing Plan: A Guide to Help You Survive and Thrive.* Chicago: American Library Association.

Graham, Jamie M. 2008. "Successful Liaison Marketing Strategies for Library Instruction: The Proof Is in the Pudding." *Southeastern Librarian* 56, no. 1: 4–8.

Gupta, Dinesh, Christie Koontz, Angela Massisimo, and Réjean Savard, eds. 2006. *Marketing the Library and Libraries.* Munich: K. G. Saur.

Hoffman, Donna L., and Marek Fodor. 2010. "Can You Measure the ROI of Your Social Marketing?" *MIT Sloan Management Review* 52, no. 1:41–49.

Jarret, Joseph. 2009. "Communicating the Plan." *Public Management* 91, no. 10: 18–22.

Kim, Sora, Elizabeth Johnson Avery, and Ruthann W. Laiscy. 2009. "Are Crisis Communicators Practicing What They Preach?" *Public Relations Review* 35, no. 4: 446–448.

Osif, Bonnie. 2006. "Branding, Marketing, and Fundraising." *Library Administration and Management* 20, no. 1: 39–43.

Porter, Michael, and David Lee King. 2011. "Marketing and the Web." *Public Libraries* 50, no. 1: 21–23.

Sweetser, Kaye D., and Emily Metzgar. 2007. "Communicating During a Crisis: Use of Blogs as a Relationship Management Tool." *Public Relations Review* 33, no. 7: 340–342.

Thenell, Jan. 2004. *Library's Crisis Communications Planner: A PR Guide for Handling Every Emergency.* Chicago: American Library Association.

Thomas, Tina. 2011. "Building the Brand from the Inside Out." *Feliciter* 57, no. 3: 110–113.

Welch, Jeanie M. 2005. "The Electronic Welcome Mat: The Academic Library Web Site as a Marketing and Public Relations Tool." *Journal of Academic Librarianship* 31, no. 3: 225–228.

Yankelovich, Daniel, and David Meer. 2006. "Rediscovering Market Segmentation." *Harvard Business Review* 84, no. 2: 122–131.

PART III

MANAGING PEOPLE

When managers work to motivate their work force to create a sense of ownership and accountability for desired outcomes the job of getting better results gets easier.

—Clinton O. Longnecker (2011)

It is clear that employees [being] satisfied with their work does not necessarily mean they are highly motivated employees and vice versa. However one cannot rule out the fact that the satisfaction of workers and their will to work are linked to some extent by how enriched their jobs are, the job design, level of empowerment, training, performance appraisal, incentives, and flexible working hours among others.

—Anonymous (2010a)

Although academia includes numerous motivational theories, in general, the three theories of motivation are Theory X, which does not trust workers, Theory Y, which trusts workers, and Theory Z, a Japanese holistic management approach.

—J. J. Haener (2011)

So here's a reminder for managers. Take an active, genuine interest in the lives of your employees.

—Anonymous (2010b)

12

MOTIVATING

This chapter focuses on the following:

- Performance and motivation
- Motivation theories
- Motivation and behavior
- Content theories
- Process theories
- Reinforcement theories
- Team building
- Public service motivation

THERE ARE MANY AREAS of management where theorists and practitioners are in less than full agreement. The importance of motivation in the workplace is *not* such an area. They also agree that employee motivation is personal in nature. All of our behavior— workplace and personal—is based on motivation. A good definition of motivation is a person's inner drive to satisfy a need. What a short definition for something that so complicates our personal and work lives. Most of us struggle to understand what motivated this or that behavior, even with people we think we know. When it comes to the workplace the challenge is even greater; and as you become a more senior manager and the number of people you work with increases, so do the challenges of understanding what did and did not drive the behaviors of your colleagues. The second anonymous quotation about managers taking an interest in their staff is true up to a point. You need to be interested in each person as a person, but there is a need to keep some distance or rather a balance between "an interest" and acting like a friend. Achieving that balance can be more difficult than you might expect.

PERFORMANCE AND MOTIVATION

In difficult economic times, it is hard to motivate one's self and even harder to provide a positive leadership image to help your staff stay positive. The second anonymous article opened with the following:

> "Now listen to me, all of you. You are all condemned men. We keep you alive to serve this ship. So row well, and live." These were the words of Quintus Arrius in the movie *Ben-Hur*. And while he was speaking to Roman slaves, one can almost imagine a modern version coming from

a manager today. "Okay, people, you all know that unemployment is at a fifty-year high. You are lucky to have jobs. So, work hard, and no more complaining." (Anonymous, 2010b, p. 2)

This speech might well remind you of the poorly written memo we described in Chapter 8 (Figure 8.3). Our point in bringing it up is that motivation is personal. Thus, such a speech might generate harder work from a few individuals, frustrate others who might work no harder, and anger a few who might work less hard. What motivates you may not motivate me. All this means is you must tailor your approach to the individual. The following discussion of motivation theories and approaches to workplace motivation will give you a base for engaging in such tailoring. Clinton Longnecker (2011), in reporting on an investigation he conducted on employee motivation, noted, "Seventy-six percent of the managers believed that they must adjust their approach to motivating each individual employee" (p. 10).

We know motivation is a key element in work performance, from the most senior manager to the newest hire. People often think motivation is about top management motivating workers. That is certainly true; however, senior staff's motivation will impact the rest of the staff. No amount of effort on the part of an unmotivated manager to motivate his or her staff will produce much in the way of positive results. Verrill and Wilkins (1986) provided research evidence that employees have difficulty remaining motivated when their manager does not exhibit highly motivated behavior. Certainly a manager's motivation may not instill similar motivation in employees, but the absence of motivation on a manager's part has a negative influence on employees.

One challenge for every employee is to try not to let work issues impact home life and vice versa. That is simple to say but often very difficult to achieve, no matter what work role you have—newest hire or CEO. How often have you heard some variation of "Avoid Mr. Smith; he is having a bad day"? That "bad day" may or may not be the result of some work issue. Nevertheless, the bad day, whatever is driving it, impacts the work performance of more people than just the person having the bad day.

Consider the management concept of emotional intelligence (EI). Although the EI literature tends to focus on leadership, the fact is that it is related to workplace motivation, and we do explore EI in more depth in the next chapter (on leadership). As a manager, you must make serious efforts to control your emotions in the workplace. Peter Salovey and John Mayer (1990) broadly defined EI as a "subset of social intelligence that involves the ability to monitor one's own and others' feelings and emotions, to discriminate among them, and to use this information to guide one's thinking and actions" (p. 189). You can well imagine how useful this skill would be for you as a manager.

Many managers think about motivation in terms of a "formula": ability + support + effort = performance. This view emphasizes the interdependent relationship between managers and employees when it comes to productivity. An employee with all the necessary abilities making the highest effort will not perform well if the organization (manager) fails to provide proper support. It is equally true that all the support in the world will not generate high performance if the employee lacks either the skill or the willingness to make the effort. The idea of teamwork in the workplace is more than just an abstract concept; it is essential for successful performance.

Over the past 50 years, management researchers have explored the factors that motivate and satisfy people in their work environment. There is still no single answer to the following question: How can employees be most effectively motivated to achieve high productivity and quality of work without creating human-relations problems? There are a number of ideas, concepts, and theories that assist in motivating staff and understanding where sources of satisfaction and dissatisfaction may exist in the workplace.

We explore some of the main theories and concepts in the following pages. Much of the research was carried out in industrial settings where issues of productivity and quality were paramount before they became issues in the public sector. Management theories are closely related to the social and economic conditions at the times they were formulated. Because these conditions are cyclic, they may well return; and being aware of the different theories will help you understand generational differences in the workplace. Some findings continue to influence management practices today.

MOTIVATION AND BEHAVIOR

Motivation has its roots in the personal beliefs, attitudes, and experiences that induce a particular behavior pattern in a person. Motives arise partly from physiologically based needs (hunger, thirst, sleep, etc.) that cause a person to seek to satisfy these needs. In 1943, Abraham Maslow, a founder of content theory, published a paper on the hierarchy of needs.

Beyond the basic behaviors related to survival—satisfying thirst and hunger and having shelter—are behaviors that result from learned or conditioned behavior, environmental circumstances, and life experiences. Even the methods for "acceptably" satisfying the basic needs result from social and cultural conditioning. Culturally based conditioning can result in some values that are diametrically opposed to certain types of work environments (e.g., competitive, team, or individual). Consider work teams having members from different cultures and generations: in a diverse society motives can, and will, differ. It follows

SOMETHING TO PONDER

Reflect on the cultural setting in which you are working or studying, and identify four factors that shape the work or study environment.

that managers should not expect that all the staff members will share the same motives for performing their work.

Motives and needs are internal; goals are external. Goals (incentives) are the rewards the individual expects to receive as a result of his or her activities. Many managers are successful in providing incentives to motivate their staff but must avoid making an incentive the focus. Incentives can be tangible (e.g., pay increases, better working conditions, or new staff facilities) or intangible (e.g., praise, empathy, or recognition of achievement in front of peers). Each employee will respond to combinations of incentives.

Expectancy affects motives and needs; availability affects the perception of goals and incentives. Expectancy arises from a person's experience and perceived probability of satisfying the need; availability is the person's assessment of how accessible certain goals and incentives actually are. People act on their needs according to their perceptions of the world around them—in a sense, a personal worldview. Managers should always remain aware that their worldview may differ substantially from those of their staff and peers.

Similar actions do not necessarily reflect similar desires or wants. For example, a person might agree to take responsibility for the library's young adult blog as an added duty. This may be motivated by a desire to interact more directly with young people, an interest in social media in general, a belief that this is an opportunity to learn new skills or demonstrate existing skills that could lead to advancement, or a host of other reasons.

A corollary is that different actions may reflect similar desires. In the preceding example, someone interested in advancement might accept the new responsibility, but that same desire for advancement and recognition could lead someone else to turn down such a task in order to devote more attention to current responsibilities. (This would imply a belief that "shining" in one area will lead to advancement just as well as acquiring a "dull gloss" in several areas.)

MOTIVATION THEORIES
Motivation theories fall into three broad categories: content, process, and reinforcement:

- Content theories provide methods for profiling or analyzing staff in terms of "needs."
- Process theories provide insights into how people think about, and give meaning to, organizational "rewards."
- Reinforcement theories provide guidance about the way that people learn patterns of behavior when that behavior is the result of environmental (workplace) "reinforcements."

These theories and the research upon which the theories rest are complementary rather than contradictory. The following sections examine the different categories of theories in more detail.

CONTENT THEORIES

Maslow's (1943) article "A Preface to Motivational Theory" became the basis for almost all research on employee motivation. The theory has three propositions about human behavior. First, humans are "wanting beings"; they always want, and those wants are unending. When a strong need is satisfied, that need's strength will diminish, but it is immediately replaced with another need. Second, a satisfied need is not a motivator of behavior. Unsatisfied needs are the only motivators. Third, human needs present themselves in a series of levels. When a person meets all the needs on one level, needs at the next highest level will demand attention and satisfaction. The hierarchical order of Maslow's five levels of need is illustrated in Figure 12.1:

1. Physiological
2. Security
3. Social
4. Esteem
5. Self-actualization

Physiological needs, the most basic, are relatively independent of one another (e.g., hunger, thirst, and sleep). In an affluent society, physiological needs are not usually effective motivators of work behavior, because a person can satisfy them in

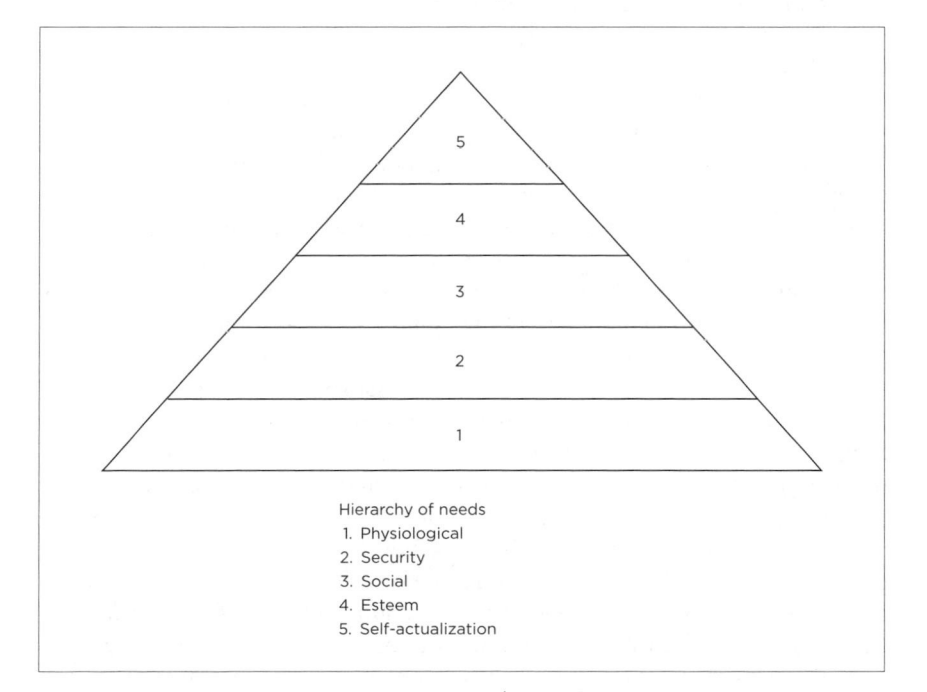

Figure 12.1 Maslow's Hierarchy of Needs

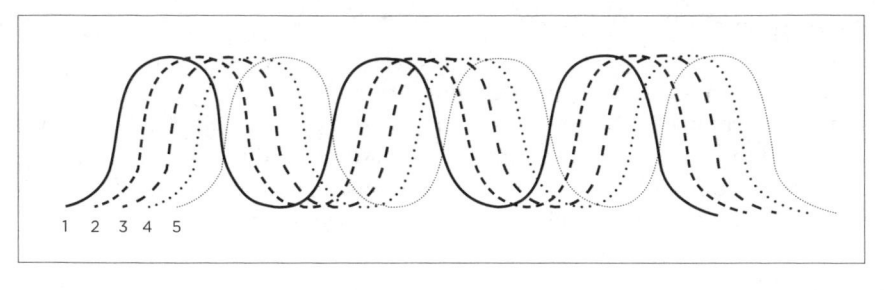

Figure 12.2 The "Wave Theory" of Needs

a variety of ways and with little effort. However, levels of expectation rise in an affluent society, resulting in the definition of "satisfactory fulfillment" changing. There are always people who for some reason(s) have trouble fulfilling these needs to their satisfaction, no matter how affluent they are.

Security or safety needs reflect the need for protection against danger and deprivation. This extends beyond self-preservation to some fundamental economic needs. Money is necessary in order to have shelter and protection, which means having some form of work. Safety needs often manifest themselves in the workplace in the preference for the status quo. Most factors relating to job security, promotions, and salary fall under safety needs.

Social needs include acceptance by coworkers, a friendly relationship with at least a few individuals, and the opportunity to associate with them and discuss problems. Most people are gregarious and want to belong to a group. Within every organization the informal organization helps meet this need.

Satisfying esteem needs includes gaining both self-esteem and the esteem of others. Self-confidence, achievement, self-respect, and independence are aspects of esteem needs that affect a person's reputation and need for recognition and appreciation. If work is not challenging, esteem satisfaction will be sought elsewhere.

A competitive drive enters into satisfying esteem needs for some people: "I won" or "I was the best employee of the month" are expressions of competition and esteem. A competitive drive is not part of every culture, but it is certainly strong in U.S. society. It is rare to completely satisfy self-esteem needs, partly because new goals for self-esteem emerge all the time. Fulfilling an esteem need can be a useful incentive when attempting to motivate work behavior. If you can tie in tangible incentives, work performance often increases dramatically.

The highest level of need is self-actualization or self-fulfillment—the need for self-development, creativity, and job satisfaction. It assumes a person has a clear perception of her or his potential and limitations. People rarely satisfy this need mainly because they do not have a clear perception of their abilities. Even those who reach the highest positions seldom believe that they have achieved their potential, but perhaps they are simply unable to see that they achieved their own level of incompetence—the Peter Principle (Peter and Hull, 1969).

While the conceptualization of needs as a series of steps in a hierarchy is probably accurate, it is more useful to think of them as a series of waves—that is, as a wave rising to a peak, being satisfied, then tapering off, with yet another need-wave building behind the tapering wave. Figure 12.2 illustrates this approach, which resembles a biorhythm chart. Maslow believed that extended existence at any of the lower levels tends to deaden and eliminate any higher aspirations. People living at the physiological and security levels have very little need, if any, for self-esteem and self-actualization. They simply do not have the time and energy left after securing food and shelter to worry about higher level needs.

The belief that need stimulus automatically elicits a certain behavior is not completely accurate. Maslow suggested that an individual deprived of two needs normally tends to seek to fulfill the more basic one. However, enculturation factors or experience can influence the choice, causing the person to select the option that fills the higher need.

Many researchers, in particular Clayton Alderfer, have questioned the value of Maslow's theory. Alderfer, on the basis of one experiment in one organization, suggested that a modified form of the Maslow theory would provide a more promising approach to the study of human motivation and its effects in the workplace. He retained the concept of a need hierarchy without the requirement that "it be strictly ordered" (Alderfer, 1969, p. 154). Alderfer's research supports what he called the ERG theory: Existence, Relatedness, and Growth. His existence needs are similar to Maslow's physiological and safety needs. Relatedness draws on the needs that Maslow labeled "social and esteem needs," and Alderfer's growth needs are a combination of esteem and self-actualization. The primary difference between the two theories is that Alderfer does not assume a hierarchy in meeting the needs. There are no higher or lower levels, just needs. The concept of growth needs is especially useful in the workplace.

David McClelland and associates also developed a need theory drawing on Maslow's work to provide managers with better guidance when motivating employees, labeling their theory "acquired needs" (McClelland, 1961). The theory was derived from data collected using the Thematic Apperception Test in which the person taking the test is shown pictures and then writes a short story about what he or she sees in each picture. The stories were analyzed for themes representing three types of need:

- need for Achievement (nAch)
- need for Power (nPower)
- need for Affiliation (nAff)

The concept behind the theory is that these needs are acquired as a result of life experiences; the amount acquired varies over time according to circumstances. As with other need-based theories, the notion is that needs motivate behavior.

> ### TRY THIS
>
> Take the content theories of Maslow, Alderfer, and McClelland and draw up a table to compare the ways in which they are similar and dissimilar. Do you agree with their ideas?

McClelland believed that managers can learn to recognize the three need profiles and then modify the work environment to encourage and promote better work performance. These are some examples of how this theory can be applied:

- High need for achievement—work in an area with high individual responsibility, with challenging but achievable goals, for example, cataloging, appraising documents, and database or systems management.
- High need for affiliation—work in an area where there is strong interpersonal interaction and communication, for example, any of the public service functions.
- High need for power—work in areas that entail directing the activities of others or controlling significant financial or equipment resources, for example, collection development or database management.

Content theories examine how understanding human needs assists in predicting employee attitudes and behavior. Almost all assume that managers are responsible for determining and allocating work-related rewards and should allocate the rewards so that all employees have the opportunity to realize some degree of work-related need satisfaction.

PROCESS THEORIES

Process theories examine the ways people think about work and which goals motivate them to perform to their maximum potential. Needs are just one of several factors that come together to generate work behavior. One aspect of process theories is the idea that people anticipate what is likely to occur given a particular behavior pattern (expectancy). One example is that while meeting deadlines is a normal part of the work environment, sometimes a manager must shorten the time frame for accomplishing an activity. Most employees would anticipate that, if they meet the changed deadline, the manager will at least praise them for a job well done, if not provide a more tangible reward. There may also be some expectancy on the part of the manager that comes into play, as we shall soon see in McGregor's theory.

Another factor in process theories is valence. Valence is the strength of an employee's desire or preference for a particular outcome. The stronger the preference, when combined with a positive expectancy, the more likely it is that the individual will exceed established goals.

Douglas McGregor (1960) formulated the now classic Theory X and Theory Y. To some extent his theory falls into both process and reinforcement approaches. According to McGregor, the traditional organization (centralized decision making, superior–employee pyramid, and external control of work) operates on a set of assumptions (expectations) about human nature and motivation. He proposed a continuum of assumptions with the end points, X and Y, representing opposite views of what motivates a worker.

Theory X assumes the following:
- Work is inherently distasteful to most people, and they will avoid it if they can.
- Because they dislike work, most people are not ambitious and have little desire for responsibility, preferring direction from above.
- Most people have little capacity for creativity and for solving organizational problems.
- Motivation occurs only at the physiological and security levels.
- Most people must be closely controlled and often coerced to achieve organizational objectives.

Theory Y assumes the following:
- The expenditure of physical and mental effort in work is as natural as play or rest. Depending on controllable conditions, work can be a source of satisfaction (and will be voluntarily performed) or a source of punishment (and will be avoided, if possible).
- External control and the threat of punishment are not the only ways to make people work.
- Commitment to objectives is a function of rewards associated with their achievement.
- The average human being learns, under proper conditions, not only to accept but also to seek responsibility.
- The capacity to exercise a relatively high degree of creativity in the solution of organizational problems is widely, not narrowly, distributed in a population.
- Under the conditions of modern industrial life, the intellectual potential of the average human being is only partially utilized.

Theory X assumes that employees' personal goals are incompatible with organizational objectives and that authority is the instrument of command and control. Theory Y asserts that people have much to offer an organization if they can fully accept its objectives. Managers using Theory Y believe the use of authority impedes the development of acceptance. The difference between the two theories is that Theory X precludes the use of motivational techniques (because of its assumptions regarding human nature), while Theory Y opens the door to their use. Managers who accept Theory X set up closely supervised

INTERDEPARTMENTAL COMMUNICATION

DATE: 17 January 2007

TO: Division heads; branch librarians

FROM: Library Director

SUBJECT: Vacation

The budget situation for the remainder of the fiscal year is touch-and-go. We want to be sure we have a positive balance as of the end of June.

To this end, we want to reduce all possible expenditures without adversely affecting public service. One way we can save some money is by asking everyone to postpone vacations until July or later if this will not cause a hardship. This will not only save vacation pay but also eliminate the need for additional part-time hours to cover vacation absences.

We are facing a year-end deficit. We cannot have a year-end deficit. This is one way a year-end deficit can be avoided.

Please explain this to the people in your division. If they have not made long-range plans, and if they can just as well take vacation after July 1, please urge them to do so. Review any vacation requests submitted to you, with postponement in mind.

GEE:ROL:dl

Note:
X-Y rating scale

X _____ Y

| 1 | 2 | 3 | 4 | 5 | 6 | 7 | 8 | 9 | 10 |

This is a Theory Y memo. It is based on the assumption that the staff will cooperate.

Figure 12.3 Example of Theory Y Misused in a Memo

and rigid structures because they believe that this is the appropriate method for handling unreliable, irresponsible, and immature people.

McGregor believed that work is as natural, and often as satisfying, for people as is play. Because both are mental and physical activities, there appears to be no difference. However, according to Theory X, people make a distinction between the two on the basis of need satisfaction: an individual controls her or his play, while managers and management control work. Again, Theory X holds this assumption, which actually causes people to think of work as a necessary evil, not as a source of personal challenge and potential source of satisfaction. Persons who feel their work is "stifling" usually look for, and find, a reason for spending more and more time away from work.

Libraries are generally closer to Theory Y than to Theory X, especially in terms of the professional staff. Donald Sager's (1979) research in libraries documented that management and managers treating staff as if Theory Y were operative tended to have higher productivity than those who operated on the Theory X premise.

Our opening quotation from J. J. Haener mentions Theory Z, which was developed during the peak of Japanese business success during the latter part of the twentieth century. It quickly faded when Japan went into a deep recession from which it has yet to fully recover. One element of the Z approach was that employees had lifetime employment once hired. Clearly this is not a fact of work life anywhere in the world today. The "iron rice bowl" employment concept is long gone, along with most of the elements of Theory Z.

In the late 1950s and early 1960s, a number of people built on the work of Maslow, McGregor, and others. These include Chris Argyris, Frederick Herzberg, and Rensis Likert, who have been placed in the process category because their findings relate to how people develop according to the manager's expectations of employees.

Argyris examined the effects of management practices on individual behavior and personal growth within an industrial work environment. Argyris (1965, 1973) identified seven changes taking place in the personality of an individual as she or he develops into a mature person:

- An individual moves from a passive state as an infant to a state of increasing activity as an adult.
- An individual develops from a state of dependency to a state of related independence as an adult.
- An individual behaves in only a few ways as an infant but is capable of behaving in many ways as an adult.
- As an infant, the individual has erratic, casual, and shallow interests but develops deeper, stronger interests as an adult.
- The child's time perspective is very short, involving only the present, but with maturity the time perspective involves both past and future.
- An infant is an employee to everyone but moves to an equal or a superior position as an adult.
- The child lacks self-awareness, but an adult is not only aware of the self but also able to control this awareness.

Argyris postulated that these changes exist as a continuum and that the healthy personality develops along the continuum from immaturity to maturity (see Table 12.1).

According to Argyris, the formal organization has a built-in need to keep people in an immature state; he argued that the formal organization often reflects its founder's conception of how the institution should achieve its objectives. Managers first design the tasks, often based on scientific management concepts of task specialization, chain of command, unity of direction, and span of control. In these situations, management views employees as interchangeable elements in the organizational machine.

TABLE 12.1   The Argyris Continuum

Immaturity	Maturity
Passivity	Increased activity
Dependence	Independence
Limited behavior patterns	Multiple behavior patterns
Erratic, shallow interests	Deeper and stronger interests
Short-time perspective	Long-time perspective
Subordinate position	Equal or superior position
Lack of awareness of self	Awareness and control of self

One of Argyris's consulting jobs involved a plant where top management was willing to allow employees to assemble the product in whatever way they thought best (Argyris, 1973). They had to inspect the product, sign it, and handle any complaints. Initially, production dropped 70 percent and morale fell quickly. Two months after its implementation, production rose. After four months, production was at an all-time high—all without managers having to inject their opinions about how to resolve production issues. Most impressive were the 94 percent decrease in waste and production errors and the 96 percent drop in complaints. Clearly, employee control over how they performed their work improved product quality. The experiment was repeated in several other firms with consistent results. Several large corporations implemented variations of his method. The primary problem is that some managers cannot understand that large numbers of employees experience an increase in motivation when they receive proper incentives and responsibility.

Frederick Herzberg and his colleagues conducted a number of experiments in the late 1950s and early 1960s, concluding that the job itself was the most important motivator in the work environment (Herzberg, 1959). They interviewed engineers and accountants concerning the good or bad points about their jobs. They found that positive thoughts were highest when managers indicated to the employees they were doing a good job or when they were considered to be an expert in their job or field. Fringe benefits did not produce positive feelings, as benefits generally produced negative thoughts when employees viewed them as inadequate. The same was true of salary. Negative thoughts and feelings resulted from the physiological and security aspects of the job; positive thoughts resulted from self-actualization, self-esteem, and social needs.

Job attitudes directly affect the quality of work. When people have a positive attitude toward their jobs, they use more creativity, are more careful, and try harder to achieve excellence. When they are unhappy, they are most likely to perform at the minimum acceptable level.

Herzberg (1959) proposed two sets of stimuli that produce job satisfaction or dissatisfaction: motivators and hygienic (environmental) factors. Motivators produced improvement in performance and attitudes. Hygienic factors merely maintained morale and efficiency. For the interviewees, motivators were chances to become more expert and to handle more demanding assignments. These conclusions are compatible with Maslow's hierarchy in that the hygienic (environmental) factors and the motivators (the job itself) concern the various levels in the hierarchy. Esteem needs are more complex. Recognition is an earned personal quality, whereas status usually is a function of the job itself. Consequently, status is a self-esteem need, whereas recognition is a motivator.

Prior to Herzberg's work, managers placed an emphasis on the concept of job enlargement, that is, increasing the number of tasks an individual performs. Herzberg suggested that doing a little of this and a little of that was no way to motivate people because variety of this sort does not alleviate boredom. He proposed job enrichment: a deliberate upgrading of the scope, challenge, and responsibility of a person's work. Applying this concept in libraries could prove useful, as Herzberg identified (his critics notwithstanding) the key workplace motivator is the job itself.

One criticism of Herzberg's work is that the methodology, asking employees what they did or did not like, motivated them to misrepresent their true thoughts. Later work by numerous researchers, using different data-collecting techniques, demonstrated there were flaws in the concept (House and Wigdor, 1967). Then there is a third factor to consider—the job/work situation.

Most researchers divide the work situation into three categories: the immediate work environment, the organizational culture, and work climate as a whole. Many of the immediate situation factors are similar to those identified with Maslow's self-esteem. The organization-wide culture sets the tone for how middle managers handle their units.

One of the questions about the two-factor (hygiene and motivators) approach is, "Does a "satisfied" employee translate into a high performer?" In part, the answer to the question depends on three alternative assumptions:

- Satisfaction causes performance (S > P).
- Performance causes satisfaction (P > S).
- Rewards cause both performance and satisfaction (R > P and R > S).

Each assumption has implications for managers. "Satisfaction causes performance" means that the focus should be on improving job satisfaction, but research does not indicate whether satisfaction is a good predictor of individual work performance. In the case of the second assumption, the manager should emphasize performance. The only way this can work is to have adequate rewards for high performance. Often the middle and lower level managers have little power to change or increase rewards. The third assumption has two managerial implications. If the manager's concern is just about satisfaction, she or he should provide high rewards. If the concern is with both performance and satisfaction, the manager should provide high rewards for

> **TIP**
>
> Remember:
> - Improvements in hygiene factors can prevent and/or help eliminate job dissatisfaction; they will not improve job satisfaction.
> - Improvements in motivator factors can increase job satisfaction; they will not prevent job dissatisfaction.

high performance and lower rewards for low performers. Most U.S. managers in both profit and nonprofit organizations operate on the basis of the third assumption. Table 12.2 reflects the consequences of high and low satisfaction, drawing on materials in Edwin A. Locke's (1970) "Job Satisfaction and Job Performance."

Rensis Likert (1958) indicated that managers fell into one of two categories of manager: production centered or employee centered. Production-centered managers advocate strict control of the work environment and view employees as instruments for getting the job done. They actively monitor the work at all stages, giving directions and correcting mistakes, and they are very hard drivers with the highest possible production as their primary goal. Employee-centered managers consider supervision rather than production to be their primary task, providing information about production goals and general guidelines for doing the work. They then allow the employees to determine individual work patterns, as long as those patterns fit into the overall process, and to ask for assistance as necessary. Likert concluded that high-production groups had employee-centered managers, while low-production groups had production-centered managers. He then described a number of management styles in organizations that fall along a continuum, as shown in Table 12.3.

System 1 prevails when management has no confidence in employees and does not involve them in decision making at any level. Fear, threats of punishment, and very occasional rewards characterize the motivation system managers employ. Top management retains most of the control, and an informal organization usually develops that opposes the formal organization's goals.

System 2 is a moderately good "master–servant" relationship. Although there is more trust involved than in System 1, condescension usually characterizes top management. Major decisions and goal setting occur at the top, but middle and lower level managers make many decisions. Punishments and rewards make up the motivation system. Employees tend to be fearful of punishment and are seldom open with their managers. The informal organization resists the formal organizational goals but does not oppose them outright.

System 3 managers have substantial but not complete confidence in employees. Broad policy and general decisions take place at the top, but many decisions occur at all levels because top management delegates responsibility. Communi-

TABLE 12.2 Consequences of High and Low Job Satisfaction

Job Facets	High Satisfaction	Low Satisfaction
Work itself	Come early; stay late; stay on job	Seek transfer; be absent or late; quit
Supervision	Approach supervisors; accept advice; stay on the job	Avoid; complain and argue with; reject advice; quit
Coworkers	Approach; conform to peer values; socialize; stay on the job	Avoid; argue with; complain about; be absent; quit
Promotion	Increase effort; raise aspirations; suggest new ideas; stay on the job	Decrease effort; lower aspirations; less willing to contribute; quit
Pay	Increase effort; stay on the job	Complain; solicit competing offer; decrease effort; quit

Source: Based on Locke, 1970.

TABLE 12.3 Likert's Continuum of Management Styles

Organizational Variable	System 1	System 2	System 3	System 4
Supervisors' confidence in subordinates	No confidence in subordinates	Condescending confidence such as master/servant	Substantial, but not complete; controls decisions	Complete confidence
Motivational system	Fear and threats, frequent punishment; little staff involvement in decisions	Some rewards; some staff involvement in decisions	Rewards; frequent heavy staff involvement in decisions	Many rewards
Supervisors' interaction with staff and its character	Little and always with fear and distrust	Little, with condescension	Moderate	Extensive and with full trust

cation flows up and down, and rewards are common. Superiors and employees interact, often with a strong degree of confidence. The informal organization may either support or partially resist the formal organization's goals.

System 4 exists when management has complete confidence in employees. Decision making exists throughout, and top management works to ensure integrated decision making occurs. Communication flows upward, downward, and laterally. Motivation takes place in part through participation in developing economic rewards, setting goals, improving methods, and appraising progress toward goals. Superiors and employees interact in a friendly, confident manner. The informal and formal organizations are the same, because the social forces support the organization's goals.

Libraries tend to be either System 2 or System 3, although a very few are System 1 and some employ System 4. The size of the library is a factor, and a collaborative or team environment will employ System 4. Larger libraries are moving toward System 4. However, as discussion of participative management (later in this chapter) will indicate, this system also has challenges.

Later studies, particularly by Vroom and Mann (1960), contradicted Likert's conclusion that employee-centered managers are responsible for high production. One study found a higher production figure for a production-centered manager's group than for a group with an employee-centered manager. Another study concluded that the nature of the job determined the type of supervision that would work best. For instance, in situations that demand a high degree of worker confidence (when employees know the manager's goals for them), a firm, no-nonsense attitude on the part of the manager is most effective.

TRY THIS

Using the process theories of McGregor, Argyris, Herzberg, and Likert, draw up a table to compare the ways in which they are similar and dissimilar. Do you agree with their ideas?

REINFORCEMENT THEORIES

Perhaps the individual most associated with reinforcement theories as applied to human behavior is B. F. Skinner. Reinforcement theories look at what the outcomes are of past actions when it comes to human behavior rather than at motives or needs. The basic notion is that people learn from experiences and tend to want to repeat experiences that were good and avoid those that were bad. In the workplace, managerial behavior and actions serve as the stimulus for conditioning employee behaviors and activities. One of Skinner's terms is *operant conditioning*, which refers to the process of controlling or modifying behavior by manipulating the consequences of that behavior. In an organizational setting, the concept is better known as *organizational behavior modification.* There are four strategies associated with operant conditioning:

- Positive reinforcement results in increased frequency or strengthens behavior by providing a desirable (from the employee's point of view) consequence whenever the behavior occurs.
- Negative reinforcement results in increased frequency or strengthens behavior by providing an undesirable (from the employee's point of view) consequence whenever unwanted behavior occurs.
- Punishment results in decreased frequency or eliminates undesirable behavior by providing unpleasant consequences whenever such behavior occurs.
- Extinction results in decreased frequency or eliminates undesirable behavior by removing a desirable consequence whenever such behavior occurs.

Positive reinforcement calls for immediate reward when the desired be-havior takes place. To use positive reinforcement successfully, you must perform the following actions:

- Identify desired behaviors for employees.
- Maintain a variety of incentives/rewards.
- Recognize employee differences in what is an incentive/reward.
- Ensure that employees know what they must do to receive a reward/incentive.
- Provide the reward/incentive immediately after the desired behavior is manifest.

Negative reinforcement is most effective when used selectively—selectively in the sense that it is not the primary method of reinforcement. When using negative reinforcement, you should do the following:

- Tell the person what is wrong with what he or she did or is doing.
- Tell the person how to correct what is wrong.
- Implement the negative reinforcement in private.
- Implement the negative reinforcement immediately after the undesirable behavior occurs.
- Ensure that the negative reinforcement is appropriate to the behavior.

Managing by results is a reinforcement motivation method. When an employee behaves compatibly with organizational goals, that behavior usually results in the person receiving some form of reward (reinforcement). When the behavior is antiorganizational, the manager chooses from among three alternatives:

- Use negative reinforcement (punishment) to achieve goals (although other alternatives avoid some negative aspects of punishment).
- Reevaluate both the stimulus and the person, as a different approach might well be effective.

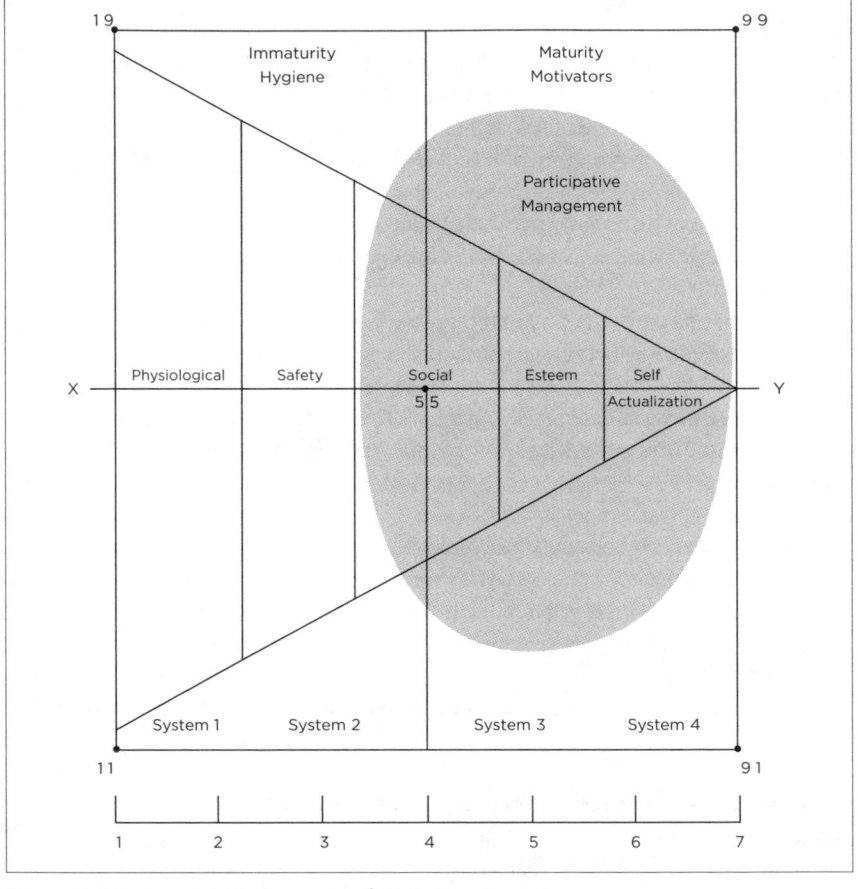

Figure 12.4 Participative Management and Motivation Concepts

- Fire the person, which is a last resort and an indication of failure on both sides.

The manager establishes job content and performance standards for the employee, but the individual can vary the pattern as long as she or he achieves the required result. (The difference from managing by objectives [MBO] is that in managing by results the manager sets goals and standards alone rather than with the employee.) Managing by results requires initiative on the part of the employee, but that can result only as part of a gradual process; expecting overnight maturity is unrealistic as well as unfair.

This approach also demands that the employees know that performance evaluation will be in terms of production and know the method of evaluation. The ground rules for making any value judgment must be clear prior to when the manager makes a judgment.

Careful definition of the boundaries of acceptable employee behavior is always essential, and it is vital in this approach. The levels at which decisions may, and may not, be made must be clear. Yet freedom to act within those boundaries must be present because the result is what matters, not the performance of activities leading to the result. The great temptation is to judge the activities, but this can do more harm than good.

Both the manager and the employees must realize that this system requires a great deal of interdependence. Moving in this direction is risky for the manager, because ultimate responsibility remains with the manager. Trust is absolutely necessary on both sides, and the employees must realize that both parties are vulnerable.

Participative management was a catchphrase among information professionals for many years. In fact, reading and listening to discussions might convince someone that this was the solution for all management problems, but participative management has not always produced the solution to management problems; in fact, it may create some new ones.

The participative management concept is Likert's Style 4 of management, with ideas drawn from various researchers in the field of motivation. Figure 12.4 depicts the way in which all the motivation concepts in this chapter relate to one another and where participative management fits into the picture.

As the term *participative management* implies, the entire staff should participate in the management of the organization. Also implied, but seldom practiced, is full participation by users. Ultimately, this process relies on group decision making, and, in order to achieve results, there must be group discussions. In 1976, Maurice Marchant, author of *Participative Management in Academic Libraries*, wrote:

> Participative management requires group discussion, and each group should be small enough that all may take part. The group is concerned with issues of mutual concern. Thus, the director would not discuss cataloging changes without involving public services personnel. Nor would he allow the discussion to center on personalities but would hold it to resolution of the mutual problem. (p. 39)

One important factor stands out in this statement—people need to meet together in small groups. However, this can quickly translate into costs of staff time. An alternative is to use e-mail, but this is not always sufficient and therefore committee meetings are needed. Committee meetings can also take up large quantities of time, especially if there is a need to reach a majority opinion or a consensus on an important issue. Libraries are public-service oriented, and time is a precious commodity. Hours spent in committee meetings do not serve the public well. One research library in the United States estimated that committee decisions on major issues cost approximately $5,000 per decision in staff salaries alone. Over time, extensive use of committees can also generate hostility.

As we noted in earlier chapters, committees can present significant accountability concerns. How to handle accountability needs in a participative management environment is also a problem you must address. Decisions require accountability in precisely those areas in which the staff generally want the most input. Given the authority relationships for agencies that receive government and public sector funding, accountability must be present. So, how can both accountability and staff input be achieved at the levels desired?

If a manager first determines staff views and then reserves the actual decision making for herself or himself or a small group of staff members, this is not participative management. A better label for this approach is *consultative management.* Misuse of the label *participative management* by top management when they really mean *consultative management* has probably caused more anger and frustration than people realize.

Manville and Ober (2003) outlined an approach that recognizes that motivating in a knowledge economy rather than in an industrial economy is different. They suggest that people should be motivated by building organizations on an Athenian model: "underpinning all the achievements was a system of governance based on personal freedom, collective action, and an open democratic culture" (p. 50). "People with expertise came forward whenever their skills were needed, without becoming part of any standing bureaucracy" (p. 51). Also, there are generational differences when it comes to workplace expectations and motivation. Joanne Sujansky and Jan Ferri-Reed (2010) made this point:

> Without question the culture clash between Millennials and earlier generations has already ignited. Veteran employees from the Mature, Boomers, and Gen X generations frequently complain about different attitudes and workplace expectations of Millennials. . . . Yet—writing off your Millennial employees before they have a chance to prove themselves is a big mistake! Generation Y is already one of the best-educated generations in American history; they are technologically savvy, embrace diversity, and have a strong preference for collaboration to solve problems and seize opportunities. (p. 14)

We discuss generational issues in some detail in Chapter 15 (on diversity).

Teresa Amabile and Steven Kramer conducted a survey with 600 managers regarding the managers' opinions about what motivated their knowledge workers. A companion multiyear survey looked at the workers' daily activities (including productivity), emotions, and motivation. Amabile and Kramer (2010) reported:

> Ask leaders what they think makes employees enthusiastic about work, and they'll tell you in no uncertain terms. . . . "Recognition for good work" (either public or private) came out number one. Unfortunately, those man-

agers are wrong. . . . On days when workers have the sense they're making headway in their jobs, or when they receive support that helps them overcome obstacles, their emotions are most positive and their drive to succeed is at its peak. (p. 44)

This finding helps illustrate just how complex motivating others can be. Often what really works is not what we think works.

MOTIVATING TEAMS

Although much of the research into motivation has been carried out in large for-profit organizations, some of the basic concepts are relevant for motivating teams. As organizations adopted a flatter hierarchy and technology was applied to administrative and certain professional tasks, there was a reduction in staff size. "Teams" were introduced at a time when there was a change in the way that organizations viewed their staff. Today's knowledge workers are not just labor—they are capital. And what differentiates outstanding companies is the productivity of their capital. "In a traditional workforce, the worker serves the system; in the knowledge sector, the system must serve the worker" (Drucker, 2002, p. 77). This statement applies as much to the nonprofit sector as it does to the private sector. Most public libraries have a governing board with some if its membership drawn from the business sector. Business believes that retaining skilled staff is a sign of good management because staff turnover adds to overhead costs such as training expenses.

There are other good reasons for the increase in teamwork: involving people who would be affected by decisions more readily achieves acceptance and implementation; as tasks become more complex, expertise can be brought into the group; and, when creating ideas or needing to retain information and experience, a group shares and retains that knowledge. So an emphasis is now placed on valuing a smaller staff working in teams, where self-motivation is important.

O'Connor (2006) reviewed the factors affecting individual performance in the team environment and their implications for library management. He identified two categories of performance factors—extrinsic and intrinsic—which combine motivating factors, theoretical models, and practical evidence that attempt to measure an individual's input performance. The extrinsic factors are collective efficacy or group buy-in; social rewards and sanctions or group acceptance or nonacceptance of an individual member; social dilemmas or disagreements within a team; social loafing or freeloading, where a person is removed from individual accountability; future interdependence or the potential for future collaboration; and social identity or the need shared with other members of the in-group but not with an out-group. The intrinsic factors affecting performance in teams are individual identity, desire to achieve, member role differences, team size, status attainment, and member commitment. The factors are not mutually exclusive, but they help to understand how best to organize teams.

O'Connor (2006) also identified three trends that demonstrated effective or ineffective management of teams. Outstanding was team composition and the importance of planning before implementing a team structure, followed by respect and communication within teams, and, finally, the need for clearly defined and articulated goals. Motivating teams to give optimum performance requires that they share enthusiasm, commitment, and values with their manager and have her or his trust. The manager should make a regular assessment of the team's output and way of working. In this working environment, the team can be empowered to take decisions to a prescribed level, having received initial training and continuing coaching to meet the goals set by the manager.

Virtual teams are increasingly part of the workplace, particularly in libraries that operate over extended hours, have staff working across the organization or off-site or off-shore, and have flexible hours. They communicate by telephone or video conferences, webcams, and simple group e-mails. Their challenges may be greater than a team working regular hours in one location, particularly if they do not have the opportunity to meet socially at regular intervals. To work effectively, the virtual team needs well-developed communication skills, especially if they are working across cultures. We explore other issues of team formation and management in Chapter 14.

PUBLIC SERVICE MOTIVATION

An area of motivation research that has received little attention by librarians and the profession is *public service motivation* (PSM). The vast majority of employee motivation research was and is conducted in the for-profit sector; a small percentage has focused on nonprofit organizations and even less specifically on libraries. However, PSM has a history of more than 20 years work. The research focus is on why people choose to work in "public service" positions. Although the initial focus was on government employees, researchers have expanded their interest to most "helping" professions.

Perry and Wise (1990) defined PSM as an "individual's predisposition to respond to motives grounded primarily or uniquely in public institutions and organizations" (p. 363). They suggested that the occupation choice (service work/helping others) and the relatively low salaries for such work indicate that what motivates "service-oriented" people might well be different from what motivates people in other job categories.

Leonard Bright (2011) noted that "Public Service Motivation has the potential of transforming the way employees are recruited, motivated, and retained in public

---

TRY THIS

Think about what motivates you as an employee. Make a list of those factors. Then talk to a friend, colleague, and/or fellow student and ask the person to list the factors that motivate her or him as an employee. Compare and contrast the lists.

organizations. For example, one potential benefit of PSM is its connection to the occupation choices of public employees. Scholars have hypothesized that an ethic to serve the community and help others eventually drives individuals into public service careers" (p. 11). Anyone who has talked to prospective library school students has heard on many occasions some variation of "I love books and like working with people." (The first part of such responses tells us we still have a long way to go to change the library image of being in the book business. The second part about service/helping is very important.) We believe it is important that our field explore the possibilities of PSM for recruiting, motivating, and retaining individuals in librarianship.

In 2010, Perry, Hondeghem, and Wise wrote an article reviewing 20 years of PSM research and the degree to which the three propositions they put forward in their seminal 1990 article stood up to research. The propositions were:

- "The greater an individual's public service motivation, the more likely the individual will seek membership in a public organization" (p. 683).
- "In public organizations, PSM is positively related to individual performance" (p. 684).
- "Public organizations that attract members with high levels of public service motivation are likely to be less dependent on utilitarian incentives to manage individual performance effectively" (p. 686).

They found that research strongly supported the first two propositions. The results for the third proposition, while positive, were mixed. They suggest the reason for the mixed results was because their original concept was based on U.S. culture; the idea has been picked up and studied in other societies. If they are correct in their assessment, this makes the point that when you have a culturally diverse workforce your motivation challenges are even more complex.

KEY POINTS TO REMEMBER
- There are three types of motivation theories: content, process, and reinforcement.
- The theories should be considered in relation to both staff and the user community.
- Motivation is inseparable from an individual's goals, values, psychic needs, and life experiences.
- What motivates one person may completely fail to strike a responsive chord in another.
- Most people modify their personal goals as they go through life.
- Salary can be a powerful motivator. Managers should treat employees equitably and provide recognition and rewards for superior achievement.
- Praise is a good motivator; be specific, and note how individuals are performing well.

- Keeping communication channels open can often resolve an issue before it becomes a problem.
- Listen to the staff—they need to know that their ideas count and that you hear them.
- Flexibility is a key word in a good motivation system.
- Make sure everyone—from the most senior professional to the junior support staff person—knows what is expected of them; check that they understand.
- Give people the tools they need to do the job well.
- Provide opportunities for learning and extending skills, and let people shine.
- Motivators can be generation specific.
- A number of factors affect the performance of individuals working in a team environment.
- Motivating users encourages use of the service provided for them.

References

Alderfer, Clayton P. 1969. "An Empirical Test of a New Theory of Human Needs." *Organizational Behavior and Human Performance* 4: 142–175.

Amabile, Teresa, and Steven J. Kramer. 2010. "What Really Motivates Workers?" *Harvard Business Review* 88, no. 1: 44–45.

Anonymous. 2010a. "Job Satisfaction and Motivation: Understanding the Impact on Employee Commitment and Organizational Performance." *Academic Leadership: The Online Journal* 8, no. 4. http://www.academicleadership.org/article/job-satisfaction-and-motivation-understanding-its-impact-on-employee-commitment-and-organisational-performance.

Anonymous. 2010b. "The No-Cost Way to Motivate." *Library Administrator's Digest* 45, no. 1: 2.

Argyris, Chris. 1965. *Integrating the Individual and the Organization*. New York: Wiley.

———. 1973. "Personality and Organization Theory Revisited." *Administrative Science Quarterly* 18, no. 2: 747–767.

Bright, Leonard. 2011. "Does Public Service Motivation Affect Occupation Choices of Public Employees?" *Public Personnel Management* 40, no. 1: 11–24.

Drucker, Peter. 2002. "They're Not Employees, They're People." *Harvard Business Review* 80, no. 2: 70–77.

Haener, J. J. 2011. "The Fourth Theory of Worker Motivation." *Industrial Management* 53, no. 2: 17–21.

Herzberg, Frederick. 1959. *Motivation to Work*. 2nd ed. New York: Wiley.

House, Robert J., and Lawrence Wigdor. 1967. "Herzberg's Dual-Factor Theory of Job Satisfaction and Motivation." *Personnel Psychology* 20, no. 4: 369–389.

Likert, Rensis. 1958. "Measuring Organizational Performance." *Harvard Business Review* 36, no. 2: 41–50.

Locke, Edwin A. 1970. "Job Satisfaction and Job Performance: A Theoretical Analysis." *Organizational Behavior and Human Performance* 5, no. 5: 496.

Longnecker, Clinton O. 2011. "How to Best Motivate Workers." *Industrial Management* 53, no. 1: 8–13.

Manville, Brook, and Josiah Ober. 2003. "Beyond Empowerment: Building a Company of Citizens." *Harvard Business Review* 81, no. 1: 48–53.

Marchant, Maurice P. 1976. *Participative Management in Academic Libraries.* Westport, CT: Greenwood.

Maslow, Abraham H. 1943. "A Preface to Motivational Theory." *Psychosomatic Medicine* 23: 85–99.

McClelland, David. 1961. *Achieving Society.* New York: Van Nostrand.

McGregor, Douglas. 1960. *The Human Side of Enterprise.* New York: McGraw-Hill.

O'Connor, Matthew. 2006. "A Review of Factors Affecting Individual Performance in Team Environments. Theories and Implications for Library Management." *Library Management* 27, no. 3: 135–143.

Perry, James L., Annie Hondeghem, and Lois Recascino Wise. 2010. "Revisiting the Motivational Basis of Public Service: Twenty Years of Research and an Agenda for the Future." *Public Administration Review* 70, no. 5: 681–690.

Perry, James L., and Lois Recascino Wise. 1990. "The Motivational Basis of Public Service." *Public Administration Review* 50, no. 3: 367–373.

Peter, Laurence, and Raymond Hull. 1969. *The Peter Principle.* New York: Morrow.

Sager, Donald J. 1979. "Leadership and Employee Motivation." In *Supervision of Employees in Libraries*, edited by R. E. Stevens. Urbana, IL: University of Illinois Graduate School of Library Science.

Salovey, Peter, and John D. Mayer. 1990. "Emotional Intelligence." *Imagination, Cognition, and Personality* 9, no. 3: 185–211.

Sujansky, Joanne G., and Jan Ferri-Reed. 2010. "Motivate Your Millennial Employee." *Supervision* 71, no. 4: 13–15.

Verrill, Phil, and Val Wilkins. 1986. "People Who Need People—Thoughts on Motivation." *Outlook on Research Libraries* 8: 7–11.

Vroom, Victor H., and Floyd C. Mann. 1960. "Leader Authoritarianism and Employee Attitudes." *Personnel Psychology* 13, no. 2: 125–140.

Launching Pad

Herzberg, Frederick. 2003. "One More Time: How Do You Motivate Employees?" *Harvard Business Review* 81, no. 1: 87–96.

Jay, Joelle. 2010. "Lead and Motivate." *Supervision* 71, no. 6: 11–13.

Karp, Hank, Connie Fuller, and Danilo Sirias. 2002. *Bridging the Boomer Xer Gap: Creating Authentic Teams for High Performance at Work.* Palo Alto, CA: Davies-Black Publishing.

Maslow, Abraham H. 1954. *Motivation and Personality*. New York: Harper.

Rowley, Jennifer. 1996. "Motivation of Staff in Libraries." *Library Management* 17, no. 5: 31–35.

Savage, Rhonda R. 2010. "No Raises This Year? Secrets to Employee Retention in Difficult Times." *Supervision* 71, no. 7: 25–26.

Squire, Jan S. 1991. "Job Satisfaction and the Ethnic Minority Librarian." *Library Administration and Management* 5, no. 4: 194–203.

Witt, Chris. 2009. "Motivating and Inspiring Your People in Difficult Times." *Supervision* 70, no. 9: 11–12.

I'll ask: why would you *not* want to develop as a leader?

—Dana C. Rooks (2011)

Relatively new library graduates (within five years or less) are moving into management positions much faster. The first day in a new leadership position arrives, and a new manager can experience a sense of excitement, anticipation and perhaps a few reservations.

—Ken Roberts and Daphne Wood (2011)

A visionary leader has a clear picture of what is important. A visionary leader knows he or she may lose a battle today, but the ultimate goal may still be attainable. Giving up is not an option for the visionary leader.

—Sharon Coatney (2011)

Leadership in an e-environment calls for some new skills.

—G. Edward Evans and Patricia Layzell Ward (2007)

Because leadership makes a difference, sometimes even a big difference, those of us who desire to make the world a better place must do what Tutu [Archbishop Desmond Tutu] did. We must come to grips with leadership as two contradictory things: good and bad.

—Barbara Kellerman (2004)

13

LEADING

This chapter focuses on the following:

- What leadership is
- Approaches to leadership
- Developing leadership skills
- Emotional intelligence
- Whether e-leadership is different
- Whether gender differences matter

CAN YOU BE A manager and not a leader? The answer is, of course, yes. Can you be a leader and not a manager? The answer to that question is not straightforward. Some of the time, the answer is yes. Some of the time, the answer is no. And, sometimes it is yes and no. Perhaps the more important question is, can you be both a leader and a manager? We firmly believe the answer is a loud *yes*! You can fill both roles in an organization/library. The roles are not mutually exclusive. You can have a vision of where you would like your work unit to go, get your work colleagues to share that vision (leadership), and implement that vision with the help of your colleagues (management).

Too often leadership literature can leave a reader with the impression that it is an either-or proposition. Many of the writers do not say that directly; they give that impression through a long list of traits and activities that contrast the two roles. Bennis and Goldsmith (2003) have a section that illustrates the duality issue in the first chapter of their book *Learning to Lead*. (Warren Bennis is considered one of the leading scholars and researchers in the field of leadership.) Table 13.1 provides a summary of the present differences between leaders and managers. These are stark differences, but they are not that clear-cut, and Bennis and Goldsmith's extended discussion makes it clear that effective managers and leaders in organizations carry out both roles. Such lists are often taken out of context and presented as either-or behaviors. A typical pattern is to be a manager early in your career and then develop your leadership skills while still managing.

Abraham Zaleznik leaves you in no doubt regarding his view of the differences. His 1992 article "Managers and Leaders: Are They Different?" was viewed a classic when *Harvard Business Review* reprinted it in 2010. In the article, Zaleznik (2010) stated: "But just as managerial culture differs from the entrepreneurial culture that develops when leaders appear in organizations, managers

TABLE 13.1 Characteristics of Managers Compared to Leaders

Manager	Leader
Administers	Innovates
Is a copy	Is original
Maintains	Develops
Accepts reality	Investigates reality
Systems/structure focus	People focus
Relies on control	Inspires trust
Short-term view	Long-range view
Asks how and when	Asks what and why
Eye on bottom line	Eye on the horizon
Imitates	Originates
Accepts status quo	Challenges status quo
Classic good solider	Own person
Does things right	Does the right thing

and leaders are very different kinds of people. They differ in motivation, personal history, and in how they think and act" (p. 16).

We don't fully agree with Zaleznik's position; yes, it can be true, but the differences are not always as clear-cut as he would make them. We do completely agree with the opening quotation from Dana Rooks suggesting that you can be both a manager and a leader, and probably you should be.

There is another aspect of leadership literature we should note; almost all of it gives the impression that leadership is "good." We agree that leadership can bring about good things for an individual, workplace colleagues, and the organization. However, as our opening quotation from Barbara Kellerman states, leadership can be good or bad. Later in the book from which we quoted, Kellerman (2004) relates a story about her giving a speech in which she said that Hitler was a bad leader and immediately someone in the audience shouted—"ethically he was bad, but he was a good leader. There is a difference." Indeed there is; leadership outcomes are not always good.

Related to the "goodness" of leadership is an underlying tone in the literature that leadership is positive and management is negative. We agree with Gary Yukl (another major researcher in the field) that both skills are necessary in order to have a successful organization: "To be effective, a leader must influence people to carry out requests, support proposals, and implement decisions.

In large organizations, the effectiveness of most managers depends on influence over superiors and peers as well as influence over subordinates" (Yukl, 2009, p. 207). We would suggest that his statement applies to any size organization, not just large ones.

WHAT IS LEADERSHIP?

Leadership is about convincing people that there is an organizational direction (vision) that is exciting, realistic, and doable. It is about inspiring people and getting them committed to the organization. It is about giving them confidence so that they can achieve the organizational goals and coaching and mentoring them in their career development activities.

What do we mean by "leadership"? It isn't easy to define, and some writers have compared it with love, saying leadership is easier to recognize than to define. We developed a working definition of leadership as being a collaborative activity generating the opportunity for all members of an organization to engage in the visioning and motivation of one another to meet the challenges of a continually changing operating environment. The outcome is that the organization moves forward to achieve its goal of fulfilling the information needs of the community it serves.

It's a long definition, but it contains some significant words and phrases: collaborative, opportunity, all members of an organization, visioning, motivating one another, challenges, continually changing environment, achieve, and goal. These terms are important for potential leaders. They indicate that leadership involves other people—followers who accept direction from the leader, which makes it possible for the leader to exercise leadership. A leader without followers leads nothing.

Moving into a leadership role tests any individual. Think about the descriptions of the two roles (manager and leader) listed in Table 13.1 (p. 320) and you'll see that they are, in some ways, diametrically opposed. From having the responsibility for ensuring the smooth operation of part of an organization and focusing on the bottom line, leaders take a wider, forward-looking perspective.

TRY THIS

It is difficult to define "leadership." Think of someone whom you consider is a successful leader. Now try to identify the qualities that make her or him a successful leader.

APPROACHES TO LEADERSHIP

The literature of leadership in general is extensive and ranges from research-based theories to gurus' philosophies. All have value in understanding what it takes to become a leader. The writings that form the theoretical base can be grouped into seven traditional approaches that draw from a number of disciplines, including psychology, management, sociology, and political science. The trait approach was followed by most writers from the early twentieth century until the late 1950s. It assumes that a person is born either a leader or a follower. However, as is the case with so many other personality trait studies (of the creative person, the successful writer, or the famous singer), the list of traits became very long, general in character, and sometimes contradictory. Hernon, Powell, and Young (2003) likewise produced an interesting list as a result of their contemporary research into the "qualities" or traits of library directors.

The behavioral approach was influenced by a classic paper in which Lewin, Lippitt, and White (1939) reported an experiment that examined three leadership styles: autocratic, democratic, and laissez-faire. Probably stimulated by world events in the 1940s, researchers moved on to examine how people act when operating as a leader. One outcome was the development of a questionnaire at Ohio State University in the late 1950s that is still used today in leadership surveys—the Leader Behavior Description Questionnaire (LBDQ). Originally it was a two-factor instrument measuring task-oriented and people-oriented behavior. Efforts to develop a more complex format have met with limited success.

In the 1960s, the focus shifted from personality traits and behavior to the environment in which leadership exists—the situational approach. Researchers began to study such factors as the interactions between the manager (leader) and the staff (followers), the organization's needs at any given time, the type of work that the organization performs, and/or the group's values, ethics, experiences, and so forth. Both experience and research studies indicate that the operating environment is an important factor in the success or failure of a leader, but it is not the sole issue.

One of the best situational models is Fiedler's (1978) contingency theory. Believing that there was no single best way to lead, his model contains three main variables: leader–member relationship, task structure, and leader's power position. Each variable has two subcomponents: good or bad relationships, structured or unstructured tasks, and strong or weak power position. Two other factors indicate whether the leader was/is relationship or task oriented. Research suggests that task-oriented leaders generally do better in situations that have good relationships, structured tasks, and either a weak or a strong power position. When relationships are good, the task unstructured, and the power posi-

CHECK THIS OUT

View the user documentation and try the Leader Behavior Description Questionnaire for yourself: http://fisher.osu.edu/research/lbdq/.

CHECK THIS OUT

Castiglione, James. 2006. "Organizational Learning and Transformational Leadership in the Library Environment." *Library Management* 27, nos. 4/5:

tion strong, they do equally well. The other situation in which task-oriented leaders perform well is in poor to moderate relationships, unstructured tasks, and a strong power position. Relationship-oriented leaders tend to do better in all the other situations.

In terms of libraries, the leader's power position in relation to outside agencies may be low because the library is normally part of a larger organization. So when the library needs strong leadership in its relationship with other agencies and organizations, there may be a problem; the staff often fail to remember this constraint on their leader when assessing that person's success with outside groups. Within the library, an individual has a clearly defined position of power resulting from the hierarchical structure that is typical of most libraries. Again, the more structured the work environment, the less room there is for maneuvering in order to obtain a desired result for the group.

Of the three factors identified by Fiedler, the one over which the leader has the most control is personal relations. By working on this aspect of leadership, an individual can achieve a certain degree of success even if the other two factors are not as favorable as they might be.

Transformational leadership emerged in the 1970s from the work of James McGregor Burns (1978), who blended the trait and behavioral concepts. A key element is influence, with both the leader and followers influencing one another. Burns distinguished two interrelated types of influence: transforming and transactional. Both charismatic and transformational leaders have vision, self-confidence, and the ability to arouse strong follower support, but transformational leaders possess two other factors—intellectual stimulation and individual consideration. Transactional leadership takes place when there is an exchange of valued "things" between leaders and followers, such as economic rewards and support.

CHECK THIS OUT

The Greenleaf Center for Servant-Leadership (http://www.greenleaf.org/) is an international nonprofit organization that supports and promotes servant-leadership.

One approach that has been adopted in a number of libraries is servant-leadership, introduced by Robert Greenleaf (1977). He considered that people who are viewed as great leaders first feel the need to serve, followed by making a conscious choice to lead. Greenleaf felt that servant-leaders are more likely to be trusted, to use initiative, to be thoughtful listeners, to have an active imagination, to feel empathy, to be persuasive, to have foresight, and to become a builder of communities.

Adaptive leadership thinks about today and what is likely to happen in the near future, and this is important for libraries. Fulmer (2000), writing about adaptive organizations, describes the volatile and complex landscape in which organizations operate in the twenty-first century, and libraries form part of that landscape. There will be increasing need to anticipate the nature and speed of change that will take place in the social, political, economic, and technological systems within which libraries operate and to determine how they can best adapt to change. Melding the situational, transformational, and servant-leadership approaches could create adaptive leadership, but it will call for smart footwork.

The changes taking place in the public sector have prompted research into leadership in the library sector. Pors and Johannsen (2003) carried out a comprehensive survey into leadership and management in Danish libraries, one aspect of which focused on leadership roles. They analyzed the data in relation to the new public management and value-based management. The library leaders perceive their future roles as being oriented toward people and toward values.

Mullins and Linehan (2006a) carried out a wider investigation into leadership, examining the views of 30 top-level public librarians from Ireland, Britain, and the east coast of the United States. One finding explored senior library leaders' perceptions of leadership: whether they distinguished classic leadership from management and administrative practices, both conceptually and in their daily work. They found that in all three countries leadership and management were confused and that leadership is a scarce quality (Mullins and Linehan, 2006a). A second finding was that there was no universal behavior, even within national boundaries, for effective leadership, but two-thirds of the respondents prioritized the implementation of vision as being the most essential element of library leadership (Mullins and Linehan, 2006b).

When questioned about their five-year vision, half of the respondents indicated it would include the maintenance and development of the current core services together with the introduction of innovative expansion of these services. Some 90 percent were optimistic that public libraries would survive into the middle of the century. One point that was stressed was that managers in public libraries are very different from managers in the private sector and other public sector areas. They believe they and their libraries are major catalysts of change in the social environments (Mullins and Linehan, 2006c). The respondents see the role played by followers as being the foundation of public library service. A partnership approach between leaders and followers is needed to develop and implement strategies and courses of action to meet organizational purposes and goals (Mullins and Linehan, 2005b).

The perceptions of the senior public library leaders indicated that they supported the centrality of leadership for optimal strategic and operational practices in librarianship. However, there is a challenge to identify and consider the leadership skills and personal attributes needed for success (Mullins and Linehan, 2005a.) Taken together, the findings of this transnational study appear to indicate that there is a need for leadership development programs to be provided for those at middle management levels in the three countries in order to ensure the health of public libraries at a time of major changes in their operating environments.

FUNCTIONS OF LEADERSHIP

So what do leaders do? The most important function is to drive the library forward and manage change, so the leader develops the vision for the library. The vision sets the direction for the library, enthusing and motivating staff. To achieve this, a leader needs to understand top management's thinking (both internal and external to the library), the emerging needs of the community served, and what is happening in the outside world (scanning). Using this information, the leader works with her or his team to anticipate changes, develop new ideas, and propose adjustments in the group's activities. The leader is a planner, working with the staff to turn the vision into reality and prepare concrete plans that can be implemented. These form the benchmarks or targets against which managers monitor performance, feeding the resulting data and information back into the planning process.

A manager operates on authority, receiving policy guidelines from above, but a leader derives the power as a policy maker both from above and from their subordinates as a result of gaining the trust of their subordinates by formulating policy with them. After consultation and taking advice, the leader has to be the ultimate decision maker.

A leader is more effective if she or he is an expert in the field in which she or he operates. Being an expert facilitates communication, because a common language will be used with senior management and the team; and the leader is able to use the full capabilities of the parent organization and resources within the profession.

AUTHORS' EXPERIENCE

Alire has had the opportunity to teach, as a professor of practice and part-time faculty, in two programs that focused on "managerial leadership." Those programs were the Simmons College Graduate School of Library and Information Science's PhD program in Managerial Leadership and the San José State University School of Librarianship and Information Science's Executive MLIS in Managerial Leadership. Both programs focus on preparing mid-level library managers for leadership roles.

A leader shares knowledge and skills willingly and in a manner suggesting an equal relationship, not a superior–subordinate relationship. This is the area that causes challenges for a leader recruited from outside the information sector.

Increasingly a leader has to be an example setter. In attitude and performance, the leader sets the tone and pace for the group, particularly in the field of ethical behavior. Sometimes a staff member emulates a leader's methods of working, attitudes, and, occasionally, even style of dress. One important function is for the leader to be the controller of internal relations. In a library supervised by a leader, the formal and informal structures are usually very similar (a situation that is rare for the nonleader). The leader ensures that these structures are the hub around which all activities revolve. In this way the leader has responsibility for the organizational climate. In carrying out this function, the leader also functions as a team builder. Although managers share part of this function, the leader is the ultimate arbitrator and mediator. When the staff have respect for and trust in their leader, they bring some of the tricky problems to that person for resolution.

Library managers and leaders are the library's spokespeople to outsiders. Although other people may be capable of assuming this role, the staff "know" that the leader will not only present the library's position but also do everything possible to protect their interests.

Leaders expect that sometimes they will receive the blame for actions over which they have no control. They know they can be a scapegoat and accept this as readily as they accept the accountability that accompanies their position. The phrase "The buck stops here," used by President Harry Truman in the 1950s, still holds now in terms of leadership accountability.

DEVELOPING LEADERSHIP SKILLS

Given the broad range of functions, what should a person do to become a leader? First, check back to the characteristics of a leader presented in Table 13.1. (p. 320) Consider whether you possess the attributes and skills and can achieve a healthy work/life balance—and then think about your motivation. Getting honest feedback from a mentor and colleagues can help a prospective leader identify her or his strengths and weakness. This is one way to evaluate your self-assessment. There are many instruments you can use in the assessment process.

The assessment results are meaningful only to the degree that the process is undertaken with the goal of gaining self-understanding. What follows is but a sampling of what one can find on the Internet searching for "leadership assessment." One starting point for online leadership assessment sites is the Leadership Learning Community's website (http://www.leadershiplearning.org/). This site also supplies links to other sites that have assessment instruments. Another resource is R. E. Brown and Associates' site (http://rebrown.com/). One of the resources offered is a 40-question instrument that assesses both managerial and leadership behaviors. The firm recommends that the manager-leadership scale be used in conjunction with two other instruments it offers.

The goal of the assessments is to create a personal development program that the firm also offers.

The Learning Center offers a 30-point "Leadership Assessment—Personal Satisfaction Survey" (http://www.learningcenter.net/library/leadership.shtml). Some of the areas covered include "making and communicating decisions promptly," "involving others in planning actions," and "believing in and providing training that teaches leadership, teamwork, and technical skills." One responds on a five-point scale from very satisfied to very dissatisfied with a "neutral" midpoint.

Having secured information from the self-assessment activity, you can make decisions about what areas to concentrate on in your development program—assuming you still wish to be a leader. (Even if you find you have no desire to become a leader, it is still worthwhile to work on those areas identified for improvement, as some individuals find leadership "thrust upon them" or becomes leaders "by default.") As is so often the case, Warren Bennis provides some sage advice about how to start a self-assessment process (Bennis and Goldsmith, 2003). He suggests there are four key areas to think about—self-motivation, taking responsibility, having self-confidence in the ability to learn, and thinking about your experiences. He, like almost every other writer on the topic

---

ADVISORY BOARD EXPERIENCE

Joseph Mika also successfully uses assessment tools in his management and leadership courses and workshops. He is partial to a self-survey set of instruments by Teleometrics International, namely, the "Blake and Mouton's Managerial and Leadership Style Grids" and particularly the "Styles of Management Inventory (SMI)," which identifies the individual's management style and indicates areas to be changed. Teleometrics also offers a "Management Appraisal Survey" designed to be taken by coworkers and that can be used by a manager to measure employee assessment against her or his own SMI; a "Styles of Leadership Survey (SLS)" that ascertains the individual's leadership style and suggests its affects on staff; and a "Leadership Appraisal Survey" that provides the leader with his or her associates' assessments of his or her leadership behavior as identified in the SLS (available at: http://www.teleometrics.com/programs/leadership_style_grid_blake_and_mouton.html)

Mika also is fond of using Taylor Hartman's *The People Code* (New York: Scribner, 2007; formerly titled *The Color Code*), which utilizes a very simple questionnaire (45 total questions) called "The Hartman Personality Profile." This is a straightforward assessment tool that helps managers and leaders in classifying their personality and behavior (according to the colors Red, Blue, White, and Yellow) and aids in improving relationships with others—including coworkers and family members.

of leadership, believes a key factor in long-term success is a commitment to life-long learning.

Leaders keep up-to-date with changes in approaches to management and leadership issues, and, of course, information and communications technologies. By maintaining currency in professional practice and issues, leaders help staff with their informal learning.

EMOTIONAL INTELLIGENCE

Two concepts have been described by Goleman (1995, 2006)—emotional intelligence (EI), which creates awareness of our own feelings and those of others, and social intelligence, which explores our relationships with others. Understanding these concepts is important to developing the behavior patterns essential for working effectively with staff, colleagues in the wider organization, the ultimate boss, and the community served.

Perhaps the most widely used definition of what EI is appeared in 1990 (Mayer and Salovey, 1990). EI is "the ability to monitor one's own and others' emotions, to discriminate among them, and to use the information to guide one's thinking and actions" (p. 189). This definition is fairly broad and encompasses most of the elements various authors and researchers include in their work regardless of the label they use for the concept. It is also one of the first efforts at defining the concept.

There are two primary models of what constitutes EI—mental ability and mixed (Zeidner, Matthews, and Roberts, 2004). The *mental ability* approach is led by John Mayer, while Daniel Goleman has led the popularized *mixed* approach. Mayer and Salovey divided EI into four broad areas—accurately perceiving emotions, using emotions to assist in thinking, understanding emotional meanings, and managing emotions. Meanwhile, Goleman and his followers employ a five-category approach—identifying one's emotional states and the links among emotion, thought, and action; managing one's emotions; entering emotional states related to the drive to achieve and succeed; reading, sensitivity to, and influenc-

AUTHORS' EXPERIENCE

Alire was hired in several of her university library deanships specifically as a change agent by the respective provosts. Using transformational leadership as her base, she adapted EI leadership qualities to help her and her management teams to effect major change in those libraries. Emotional intelligence leadership was critical to team building within the management teams. Change was not easy because many staff members feared change. Recognizing and managing that emotion and other emotions were key to their success.

CHECK THESE OUT

Compare and contrast the two models of EI by visiting John Mayer's website (http://www.unh.edu/emotional_intelligence/) and Daniel Goleman's website (http://www.eiconsortium.org/).

ing others' emotions; and entering into and sustaining satisfactory interpersonal relationships. Both approaches clearly relate to the earlier definition—knowing your and others' emotions, understanding those emotions, and employing that information in a positive manner.

You can see the potential value of understanding workplace emotions, especially one's own, along with the ability to control and use those feelings in a positive manner. Being able to effectively (positively) influence others based on an understanding of their emotions is a major plus. Both models provide guidance for developing such abilities. Emotionally intelligent leaders usually have a greater sense of well-being, stronger relationships, high morale employees, and overall greater success.

ONE-ON-ONE LEARNING

One-on-one learning can take several forms; however, we will cover three of the most common—coaching, mentoring, and modeling. Coaching, mentoring, and modeling are interrelated to some degree. A coach is often modeling while engaged in coaching and thus has an influence beyond the one-on-one coaching activity. A mentor can be, and often is, both a model and a coach. As Frederic Hudson (1999) says, coaching is not about advising, nor is it about fixing things or solving problems. Rather, it is about establishing a trust relationship with the goal of improving or developing a skill or ability. Likewise, mentoring is also about trust and respect. Modeling is not directed at a particular individual but rather demonstrates a behavior, value, and so forth that others can copy. Nevertheless, only a person who is trusted or respected is likely to have her or his actions and values modeled by others.

Coaching ought to play an ongoing role in the management of any library as a normal part of the control process and/or performance appraisal program. However, the type of coaching of interest here is not the "corrective" type, but, rather, it is developmental in character. As such, the coach for a leader may not necessarily be a member of the organization. Many of the firms that offer leadership development programs make available one-on-one coaching services. (Coaching at the senior level in both for- and not-for-profit sectors has become a small growth industry.)

Coaching for "success" is what the leader's goal should be. Most people have a desire to succeed, and activities directed toward improving (faster, easier, etc.)

CHECK THESE OUT

Goleman, Daniel. 2004. "What Makes a Leader?" *Harvard Business Review* 82 (1 January): 82–91. (Goleman's seminal paper on emotional intelligence)

Hernon, Peter, Joan Giesecke, and Camila Alire. 2007. *Academic Librarians as Emotionally Intelligent Leaders.* Westport, CT: Libraries Unlimited.

Hernon, Peter, and Nancy Rossiter. 2006. "Emotional Intelligence: Which Traits Are Most Prized?" *College and Research Libraries* 67, no. 3: 260–275.

Kihlstrom, John F., and Nancy Cantor. 2012. "Social Intelligence." Accessed November 8. http://socrates.berkeley.edu/~kihlstrm/social_intelligence. htm. (A discussion of the development and definition of social intelligence)

Mills, John. 2006. "Affect, Emotional Intelligence and Librarian–User Interaction." *Library Review* 55, no. 9: 587–597.

Richer, Lisa. 2006. "Emotional Intelligence at Work: An Interview with Daniel Goleman." *Public Libraries* 45, no. 1: 24–28.

success are welcomed, especially when the source is trusted and/or respected. Building/striving for ever-greater success means coaching is not a one-time event. The process should be a "philosophy" rather than a job for the leader. These are the underlying values of such a philosophy:

- Respect for the existing knowledge, skills, and abilities of all the members of the work group
- Belief that individuals should be free from controls that limits group members' initiatives and innovative behaviors
- Recognition that coaching is a partnership in which both partners have responsibilities
- Knowledge that the process is more about motivation and relationships than it is about power and control
- Recognition that listening more and talking less can be powerful elements in successful coaching
- Knowledge that feedback, especially positive comments, is a key to successful coaching

Because coaching as well as mentoring is one-on-one, it should be clear that the "one size fits all" approach is not very effective. Tailoring the approach to the individual being coached is what works best, but it calls for the coach to have a high degree of "people sensitivity." Working on developing or improving one's "people sense" is a worthwhile activity. One area where it should be clear a different approach would be more appropriate is when the work group has a range of generations. A tailored approach also requires the coach to keep in mind that the coaching process in itself will not change the person being coached. What coaching can and should do is motivate the person being coached to want to change (a personal "transformation").

DO GENDER DIFFERENCES MATTER IN LEADERSHIP?

As women moved into higher level managerial positions, the number of studies of the relationship between leadership and gender also increased. This is of interest to librarians because an increasing number of women occupy leadership positions. At one time the literature of management indicated that decisions were said to be made in men's locker rooms, but, given the rising numbers of women in senior positions, especially in the civil service and the public sector, more decisions are made today in the women's restrooms.

Is there a gender difference in leadership styles? The question has interested researchers. Valentine and Godkin (2000) explored the relationship between supervisor gender and perceived job design. They found that a supervisor's gender did influence a subordinate's perceptions of his or her job with the difference being attributed to different leadership styles. Those who had a woman supervisor perceived greater interpersonal aspects in their work, and those who were supervised by a man perceived greater structure in their work. A review of the literature reported by Trinidad and Normore (2005) indicated that women adopt democratic and participative leadership styles, with transformational leadership being the style most preferred by women. Manning (2002) argues that transformational leadership enables women to simultaneously carry out leadership and gender roles. The question of whether women's leadership styles are less effective than men's is derived from socialization (Appelbaum, Audet, and Miller, 2003). Women's styles are likely to be more effective in the context of team-based, consensually driven organizational structures, but both men and women can learn from each other.

There is a lesson here for new leaders who are appointed to positions held by someone of the opposite gender and for their staff. Knowing the style of the previous incumbent isn't immediately possible for a newcomer. Having to make a

CHECK THESE OUT

Virginia Walter recommended Sally Helgesen's *Female Advantage: Women's Ways of Leadership* (New York: Doubleday/Currency, 1995) as a very informative work. Helgesen's latest work, in 2010, coauthored with Julie Johnson, *The Female Vision: Women's Real Power at Work* (San Francisco: Berrett-Koehler Publishers), is also a good resource.

mark—and at the same time tread carefully—isn't easy. It is a challenge for both the new leader and the staff, and it can be difficult to meet.

E-LEADERSHIP

Technology-mediated environments require some adjustments in leadership behavior. We believe the underlying leadership basics remain valid, but there are changes in emphasis. Leadership in an e-environment calls for meeting the challenges posed by several paradoxes (some new and some old ones in new guises), accepting greater ambiguity, and understanding peoples' complex behavior.

Pulley and Sessa (2001) described five sets of paradoxes and complex challenges for e-organizations and their leaders:

- Swift and mindful
- Individual and community
- Top-down and grassroots
- Details and big picture
- Flexible and steady

These paradoxes will exist, to some degree, for all organizations, regardless of size or profit orientation.

Is it possible to make *swift and mindful* decisions, responses, and so forth, in today's e-environment? While it may be possible, it also becomes increasingly a challenge. E-mail, cell phones, instant messaging, faxes, and the like make it possible to communicate quickly and, in some cases, to places not possible in the past. The communications technologies also make it more difficult to get away from work pressures. Senders of messages know their message will arrive in a matter of seconds, and they very often have the expectation/hope of getting back a quick response whatever the time zone or location of the recipient. A recognized problem with quick responses is regret—"I hit 'send' too quickly."

Rapid decisions usually require drawing on past experiences with little or no opportunity to assess the current situation to even determine to what degree the current environment matches the past environment(s) of decision making. They also depend on quick and easy access to current management information. Collecting and locating and using additional data or information is not very compatible with speedy decision making unless appropriate systems are in place. Unless there are well-designed and robust information systems in place, technology's speed and capabilities may drive a behavior that may not always be beneficial in the e-world.

In terms of the *individual and community,* there may be greater freedom and autonomy when communicating with each other and the "outside" world as an outcome of ICT (information and communication technology). E-mail and the cell phone have generally replaced the landline telephone. (These modes of communication are preferred by Gen Xers and even more so for the millennials, and it is quickly extending to the boomers and veterans). As noted earlier, while technology facilitates *individual* autonomy and connectivity, it can also lead to a sense of isolation. Virtual teams and individuals working from home or elsewhere may not have the same opportunities to meet face-to-face and build the same "*community*" as those who are in the traditional workplace. Certainly, almost all the research on employee motivation and job satisfaction in the twentieth century shows that social interaction in the workplace was an important issue. Dependency on face-to-face communication and meeting at the water cooler will change significantly when the boomers start to retire over the next two decades.

Interaction with users who do not visit the library in person requires developing user-friendly Internet sites and having well-trained staff who can handle problems that concern issues of both technology and information access.

The third paradox, *top-down and grassroots*, has existed for a great many years. What makes it more important today is the impact of technology and the relatively recent changes in management practices. Empowering staff and the flattening of the organizational structure have been occurring for some years driven largely by economic conditions and technological developments. Both empowering and flattening (grassroots) means staff have a much greater influence on operations than in the past. Technology makes it possible for any or all "voices" to speak to an issue, invited or not. Those voices can be heard both within and outside the library. It is the unthinking leader who does not recognize the potential impact of one or more voices being heard by the outside world. Another factor favoring grassroots is the fact that change is occurring so rapidly that it is almost impossible for one person (the leader) to absorb it all; thus, input from the frontline people becomes very valuable. Leaders must grapple with the task of maintaining control and accountability while engaging in collaborative activities and empowering behavior.

The fourth paradox, *details and big picture*, also is also not a new phenomenon. Leader-managers have had to address this issue for a long time. Some individuals are prone to see only details (can't see the forest for tress) while others can't seem to get beyond the big picture. Either single perspective will cause some issues in the workplace.

In today's e-world vast amounts of detail are available at the drop of a hat. One example of the data overload is performing an Internet search, which can overwhelm you with millions of "hits." Some hits may be accurate and relevant but buried far down the list; others are useless for your purposes but high on the list. It takes time to sort the good from the bad. Within libraries, just the volume of infor-

CHECK THIS OUT

An article written with law librarians in mind, but which includes suggestions and insights applicable to any library setting, is Kathryn Hensiack's "Too Much of a Good Thing: Information Overload and Law Librarians" (*Legal Reference Services Quarterly* 22, no. 2/3: 85–98, 2003).

mation (*details*) generated every day by the ILS can be beyond one person's ability to handle and still maintain some sense of the big picture.

You ought to maintain some focus on the overall direction (*big picture*) of the library, its progress toward achieving desired goals, while keeping a sharp eye out for factors (*details*) that may indicate some adjustments are needed. One goal should be to ensure that all staff members understand the importance of both details and long-term goals and know to share their observations when they notice something out of the ordinary. Many staff members may have access to the information, but if no one has the responsibility for monitoring changes, critical information may fall through the cracks.

Pulley and Sessa's final paradox is *flexible and steady.* Again, this is not a new paradox for organizations. What have changed are its pervasive implications for all types of organizations. In the past, there were a number of organizational types—including a great many research libraries—that operated in what you might call a "placid" environment (limited threats, little change; think about the discussion regarding Emery and Trist in Chapter 1) and only a few in a "turbulent" one (many threats and high level of change). Today most organizations must be aware of changing circumstances and recognize there may be serious threats. Stability, as long as it did not endanger long-term viability, was highly desired, as it allowed for a clear focus and momentum toward well-established goals. For most of today's organizations, the requirement for flexibility and the associated changes make it difficult to discern how much, if any, progress is taking place. For today's leader, a major challenge is keeping everyone focused on long-term directions while responding to a rapidly changing environment.

Paradoxes like these, along with other challenges, make it less and less likely a successful organization will be led by a "Great Person" or "Lone Ranger." The "I am the boss, and I am in control" leadership style is probably a thing of the past. Yes, there are almost always one or more senior persons with ultimate accountability for the organization's success or failure. However, in many organizations, there is a growing use of multiple leaders/managers sharing most of the responsibility. This is particularly challenging when the staff is roughly proportional in terms of generations. Gen Xers and millennials are usually the ones who see the need for self-leadership and who are frustrated by the fact that not everyone shares this view.

An e-leader should not treat e-mail and other electronic communication as something between a telephone call and a formal letter. Treating it in the casual way that so many of us do, especially when one adds in the need, real or imagined, for a speedy response, often leads to ineffective or, worse, damaging communication. We also tend to forget that in some ways it is a more permanent form of communication than hard copy. It is also extraordinarily easy to forward messages, not to mention routing them, to the wrong person(s). As the saying goes, "Don't say anything in an e-message that you wouldn't want to appear on the front page of the newspaper." We believe this should be the motto of the e-leader.

A real challenge is when the leader has some followers interacting with her or him face-to-face and others primarily through technology. Often the e-group members believe (sense) that the face-to-face group, because of the collocation with the leader, has greater influence than they do. Naturally, this can influence their attitudes and morale in a somewhat negative way. The leader with such groups must work especially hard to create a balance between them.

Avolio and Kahai (2003, p. 333) summarized what they saw as the major issues for e-leadership in the early twenty-first century:

- Leaders and followers have more access to information which changes their interactions.
- Leadership is migrating to lower organizational levels and through the boundaries of the organization.
- Leadership creates and exists in networks that cross traditional organizational and community boundaries.
- Followers know more at an earlier point in the decision-making process, and this is potentially affecting the credibility and influence of leaders.
- Unethical leaders with limited resources can now impact negatively a much broader audience.
- The amount of time the most senior leaders can have with their followers has increased.

We would add, although it could be subsumed under their first point, that written communication and trust have become increasingly important in the virtual workplace.

E-TEAM ISSUES

There are two broad categories of e-teams—internal and external (multiorganizational)—with which libraries deal. A major difference in both is that a leader seldom has as much control over the basic issues, especially in the case of external teams. The primary reason for using virtual teams is to overcome time and/or space (geography) issues.

Cascio and Shurygailo (2003) suggest a four-cell matrix for thinking about variation issues with virtual teams. One axis is for either a single or a multiple leader situation, and the other axis represents either a single or multiple locations. The least complex situation is the single leader/single location variation. We would suggest that this is the place to start any migration to virtual teams or telecommuters, as it gives everyone a chance to work out problems and issues. One can then follow up with more complex arrangements.

Internal library teams, especially those created for a special project, usually consist of people from several departments who often engage in the team activities along with some or all of their "normal" duties. This creates the multiple leader-manager and, most commonly, the one location situation, although, where there are branch operations, it could be a multiple location situation. We mentioned earlier some of the problems that can arise from cross-departmental teams when "normal" duties exist alongside team responsibilities. While the use of technology makes it easier to shift work activities to "off hours," it cannot reduce the pressure of performance expectations for team members with additional duties.

When leading a virtual team tasked to handle a project, whether an internal or external team, there are several significant areas to address if the team is to succeed. In the case of a multiorganizational team, such as one working on a nationwide 24/7 reference service, the challenges are more complex than for the internal team. Based on our experience, the first key activity is to ensure that senior leaders are committed to the project and are willing to devote the necessary resources to see it through. Senior leaders must work out several important details, such as selecting one person to be the liaison/contact point between the team and the senior leaders. Establishing reporting and communication responsibilities should also be done before the team is created. A significant amount of time should go into discussing team mileposts, timelines, assessments, and the types of skills and abilities team members need to bring to the table. The last item regarding skills and abilities is very important to selecting a staff person based on capability of making a contribution to team activities rather than on local politics or personal feelings. Without such discussions it is almost inevitable that the team will have performance problems; the project could be delayed; and a growing sense of frustration will occur among the libraries.

We have noted from time to time in earlier chapters and will do so in later chapters that some libraries are unionized. Most public libraries operate under some type of public employee/civil service system. Both unions and civil service contracts and regulations limit your leadership options. You may have a wonderful vision, and the correct one, of what direction the library should move in. As one of our advisory board members commented, changing library direction in the foregoing environment can be akin to steering a mega tanker in a new direction rather than turning a row boat. Contract provisions and civil service regulations will slow your progress. It can be done but not quickly—take your time, actively engage in advocacy, be political, and think both tactically and strategically. If you do so, you will likely succeed; just know it may take longer than you'd like.

LEADERS OF THE FUTURE

Conger and Benjamin (1999, pp. 250–251) believe that workforce trends will demand that leaders of the future be all of the following:

- Sensitive to the issues of diversity
- Interpersonally competent
- Skillful communicators and motivators
- Community builders

- Capable of building well-aligned organizational architectures
- Developers of leaders

Note: In the remaining chapters we will employ manager-leader, leader-manager, managerial leader, leader, and manager interchangeably. In part we do it to provide some variation but more importantly to emphasize the fact that to be effective in today's work environment you need to be both a leader and a manager.

KEY POINTS TO REMEMBER

- The most successful people in organizations are both leaders and managers.
- Leaders can be found at every level in a library.
- Leadership is difficult to define but easier to recognize.
- There are significant differences between managing and leading.
- Seven traditional approaches to leadership can be identified.
- Leadership functions are enduring.
- It is never too soon to start learning how to be a leader.
- Leaders need to have many different skills.
- Communication, political, and team-building skills are very important.
- Appropriate structures are needed for employee-centered services.

References

Appelbaum, Steven H., Lynda Audet, and Joanne C. Miller. 2003. "Gender and Leadership? Leadership and Gender? A Journey through the Landscape of Theories." *Leadership and Organizational Development* 24, no. 1: 43–51.

Avolio, Bruce, and Surinder Kahai. 2003. "Adding 'E' to E-leadership: How It May Impact Your Leadership." *Organizational Dynamics* 31, no. 4: 325–338.

Bennis, Warren, and Joan Goldsmith. 2003. *Learning to Lead: A Workbook on Becoming a Leader*. New York: Basic Books.

Burns, James McGregor. 1978. *Leadership*. New York: Harper Collins.

Cascio, Wayne, and Stan Shurygailo. 2003. "E-leadership and Virtual Teams." *Organizational Dynamics* 31, no. 4: 362–376.

Coatney, Sharon. 2011. "Leadership in Hard Times." *School Library Monthly* 27, no. 6: 38–39.

Conger, Jay A., and Beth Benjamin. 1999. *Building Leaders: How Successful Companies Develop the Next Generation*. San Francisco: Jossey-Bass.

Evans, G. Edward, and Patricia Layzell Ward. 2007. *Leadership Basics for Librarians and Information Professionals*. Lanham, MD: Scarecrow Press.

Fiedler, Fred E. 1978. "The Contingency Model and the Dynamics of the Leadership Process." In *Advances in Experimental Social Psychology*, edited by L. Berkowitz, 60–112. New York: Academic Press.

Fulmer, William E. 2000. *Shaping the Adaptive Organization: Landscapes, Learning, and Leadership in Volatile Times*. New York: AMACOM.

Goleman, Daniel. 1995. *Emotional Intelligence*. New York: Bantam Books.

———. 2006. *Social Intelligence: The New Science of Human Relationships*. New York: Bantam Books.

Greenleaf, Robert K. 1977. *Servant Leadership: A Journey into the Nature of Legitimate Power and Greatness*. New York: Paulist Press.

Hernon, Peter, Ronald Powell, and Arthur Young. 2003. *The Next Library Leadership: Attributes of Academic and Public Library Directors*. Westport, CT: Libraries Unlimited.

Hudson, Frederic. 1999. *The Handbook of Coaching*. San Francisco: Jossey-Bass.

Kellerman, Barbara. 2004. *Bad Leadership: What It Is, How It Happens, Why It Happens*. Cambridge, MA: Harvard Business School Press.

Lewin, Kurt, Ronald Lippitt, and Ralph White. 1939. "Patterns of Aggressive Behavior in Experimentally Created Social Climates." *Journal of Social Psychology* 10: 271–299.

Manning, Tracey T. 2002. "Gender, Managerial Level, Transformational Leadership and Work Satisfaction." *Women in Management Review* 17, no. 5: 207–216.

Mayer, John, and Peter Salovey. 1990. "Emotional Intelligence." *Imagination, Cognition, and Personality* 9, no. 3: 185–211.

Mullins, John, and Margaret Linehan. 2005a. "The Central Role of Leaders in Public Libraries." *Library Management* 26, nos. 6/7: 386–396.

———. 2005b. "Leadership and Followership in Public Services: Transnational Perspectives." *International Journal of Public Sector Management* 18, no. 7: 641–647.

———. 2006a. "Are Public Libraries Led or Managed?" *Library Review* 55, no. 4: 237–248.

———. 2006b. "Desired Qualities of Public Library Leaders." *Leadership and Organizational Development Journal* 27, no. 2: 133–143.

———. 2006c. "Senior Public Librarians Looking to the Future." *New Library World* 107, nos. 3/4: 105–115.

Pors, Niels Ole, and Carl Gustav Johannsen. 2003. "Library Directors under Cross Pressure between New Public Management and Value-Based Management." *Library Management* 24, nos. 1/2: 51–60

Pulley, Mary Lynn, and Valerie Sessa. 2001. "E-leadership: Tackling Complex Challenges." *Industrial and Commercial Training* 33, no. 6: 225–230.

Roberts, Ken, and Daphne Wood. 2011. "Managers in the Making." *Feliciter* 57, no. 1: 8.

Rooks, Dana C. 2011. "Leadership: Some Personal Thoughts." *Texas Library Journal* 87, no. 1:14–16.

Trinidad, Cristina, and Anthony H. Normore. 2005. "Leadership and Gender: A Dangerous Liaison?" *Leadership and Organization Development Journal* 26, no. 7: 574–590.

Valentine, Sean, and Lynn Godkin. 2000. "Supervisor Gender, Leadership Style, and Perceived Job Design." *Women in Management Review* 15, no. 3: 117–129.

Yukl, Gary. 2009. "Power and the Interpersonal Influence of Leaders." In *Power and Interdependence in Organizations*, edited by Dean Tjosvold and Barbara Wisse, 207–223. Cambridge: Cambridge University Press.

Zaleznik, Abraham. 2010. "Managers and Leaders: Are They Different?" Reprint of 1992 article in *Leadership Insights: 15 Unique Perspectives on Effective Leadership* (*Harvard Business Review*). Cambridge, MA: Harvard Business School Publishing.

Zeidner, Moshe, Gerald Matthews, and Richard Roberts. 2004. "Emotional Intelligence in the Workplace: A Critical Review." *Applied Psychology* 53, no. 3: 371–399.

Launching Pad

Alire, Camila. 2001. "Diversity and Leadership: The Color of Leadership." *Journal of Library Administration* 32, nos. 3/4: 95–109.

Applegarth, Mike. 2006. *Leading Empowerment: A Practical Guide to Change*. Oxford: Chandos.

Bennis, Warren. 1998. *On Becoming a Leader*. London: Arrow Books.

Bossidy, Larry. 2007. "What Your Leader Expects of You and What You Should Expect in Return." *Harvard Business Review* 85, no. 3: 58–65.

Coatney, Sharon. 2010. "The Blind Side of Leadership, or Seeing It All." *School Library Monthly* 27, no. 2: 38–40.

Foster, Connie. 2010. "Fishing for Leadership: A Service Philosophy in Library Technical Services." *College and Research Libraries News* 71, no. 11: 603–605.

Gottfedson, Mark, Steve Schaubert, and Herman Saenz. 2008. "The New Leader's Guide to Diagnosing the Business." *Harvard Business Review* 86, no. 2: 62–73.

How to Lead in Uncertain Times. 2010. Cambridge, MA: Harvard Business School Publishing.

Kouzes, James M., and Barry Z. Posner. 2003. *The Leadership Challenge*. San Francisco: Jossey-Bass.

Kreitz, Patricia A. 2009. "Leadership and Emotional Intelligence: A Study of University Library Directors and Their Senior Management Teams." *College and Research Libraries* 70, no. 6: 531–554.

Leadership Insights: 15 Unique Perspectives on Effective Leadership. 1990–2002. Cambridge, MA: Harvard Business School Publishing.

Mavrinac, Mary Ann. 2005. "Transformational Leadership: Peer Mentoring as a Values-Based Learning Process." *portal: Libraries and the Academy* 5, no. 3: 391–404.

Mosley, Pixie Anne. 2005. "Mentoring Gen X Managers: Tomorrow's Library Leadership Is Already Here." *Library Administration and Management* 19, no. 4: 185–192.

Roberts, Ken, and Daphne Wood. 2011. "Thought Leadership." *Feliciter* 57, no. 4: 156.

Stueart, Robert D., and Maureen Sullivan. 2010. *Developing Library Leaders*. New York: Neal-Schuman.

It's hard to imagine managing contemporary organizations without the active coop-eration and collaboration of many individuals who bring unique abilities and skills to the enterprise. When a leadership team seeks ideas and builds consensus across an entire organization, including key external stakeholders, the creative, innovative think-ing that follows nearly always leads to great results.

    —John W. Berry, ALA President, 2001–2002 (2012)

Twenty-first century students are not passive consumers of information; rather, their learning experiences must involve active participation. Current pedagogies call for creative partnerships that engage students in a participatory culture.

    —Margeaux Johnson, Melissa Clapp, Stacy Ewing, and Amy Butler (2011)

When we looked at complex collaborative teams that were performing in a produc-tive and innovative manner, we found in every case the company's top executives had invested significantly in building and maintaining social relationships throughout the organization.

    —Lynda Gratton and Tamara J. Erickson (2011)

A supported team is a happy team, and that support would flow to and from volun-teers, pages, library assistants, librarians, managers, supervisors, directors and trust-ees, all reinforcing one another. This would assure that each team member's contribu-tion would be valued with equal importance.

    —Abby Preschel Kalan (2010)

14

BUILDING TEAMS

This chapter focuses on the following:

- What teams are
- Value of teams for a library
- How to build and support teams
- How to avoid some common pitfalls in team usage
- Role of negotiation in teamwork

OUR SECOND OPENING quotation regarding twenty-first-century students' learning and participative culture has major significance for all managers regardless of organizational type. Young people entering today's workforce have grown up in an environment that emphasizes working and playing together as well as sharing electronically large amounts of personal information. Many girls and boys have also engaged in team sports during their childhood—Little League baseball and softball, youth soccer, football and basketball, and the like. In school, team projects were typical in which a grade depended on each participant doing his or her share. They are comfortable teaming up and generally expect their work lives to be very similar in character.

Managers, especially those of older generations, now have to rethink some of their experiences, long-held workplace values, and performance expectations (at least in terms of how the work processes are done). Today's managers/leaders must build, support, and maintain effective and productive teams if their organizations are to succeed. This takes time and experience to do effectively, especially when having to integrate young and older workers into a team. (We explore generational workplace attitudes and expectations throughout the book.)

Workplace teams are not exactly "new" despite what the current literature might lead you to believe. Libraries did, do, and will continue to succeed only when the entire staff functions as a single team (sharing common goals, linking of work activities, and understanding the "big picture," for example). Successful departments have always been the ones that function as subteams of the whole team. Teams have been with us for a long time in one form or another.

What is new is how both team members and management expect "the team" to perform and how much independence the team may have. Teams, in the current sense, are playing an ever greater role in how organizations get things done. Over the past 20-some years, organizations including libraries have undergone a "flattening" of their structures (fewer layers); they have downsized (increasing workloads) and required existing staff to learn new skills. As a result, employees must be more productive, flexible, willing to learn, and generally must be willing to accept more responsibilities. All of these factors place a premium on flexibility and on having a knowledgeable workforce that is more capable of working independently than in the past.

Managers must get the best possible performance from their existing staff. They must depend on the staff to function and problem solve, often on their own. There are fewer managers available. If work is to progress in a timely fashion, team members must act without waiting for assistance from higher level personnel. While the management fundamentals—decision making, planning, organizing, and so forth—remain unchanged, there is a shift in who engages in these activities when true teams exist.

Some of the differences between a true team environment and the traditional workplace are significant. Teams call for consensus rather than command and control. They require that you accept the idea that conflict (both positive and negative) is a normal part of team operations and that those conflicts must be addressed in an open and honest manner. Although not every difference of opinion that occurs in a team will result in negative conflict, time will still need to be spent in meetings resolving problems or reaching decisions. Reaching decisions in a team setting tends to be more knowledge and technically based than when it is done on the basis of one person's opinion. In teams, you need to place more emphasis on the "whys" rather than on the "hows." Essentially, you must engage in a collaborative process with the team members in order for the team to succeed.

In a 2011 article in the *Harvard Business Review,* Paul Adler, Charles Hecksher, and Laurence Prusak addressed a new trend that may impact the spread of team-based structures, and we do know of some libraries that had a team-based structure that have now dropped that approach. Adler and colleagues discussed creating the collaborative organization, stating, "At many leading-edge enterprises, a new form of organization is emerging—one that is simultaneously innovative and efficient, agile and scalable. It is a way of working which focuses on knowledge production" (p. 97). It may be a growing trend as teams must be very collaborative in nature and operation.

What Adler, Hecksher, and Prusak (2011) suggest is slowly happening is the creation of organizational "collaborative communities." The communities are essentially a single team, as you will sense from what the authors identify as the key elements in developing such group:

- Clearly define and create a shared purpose.
- Encourage and enable individual contributions.
- Develop an infrastructure that encourages and rewards collaboration.
- Construct a means/process for coordinating people's contributions effectively.

Adler and colleagues had some concluding thoughts about the process: "We do not wish to downplay the undeniable challenges of building collaborative communities. . . . Indeed we found that patience and skill required to create and maintain a sense of common purpose rare in corporate hierarchies, particularly given it is not a set-it-forget-it process" (p. 101).

The type of organization these authors discuss may overcome some of the challenges in team-based operations that we discuss later in this chapter. We hope, with good leadership, this approach will replace what is now the "team concept." Essentially it is about creating a single organizational team with all the staff actively participating in the "community." We also wonder if it reflects what most of the great library leaders/managers did in the past before the idea of teams arose. For academic libraries with faculty status for librarians, this type of organization might well be beneficial. Faculty status is very much an "I" matter rather than "we."

VALUE OF TEAMS

You well might wonder if the team concept of today really is better than traditional work groups, at least in terms of performance and productivity. In 2009, Natalie Waters and Mario Beruvides reported on one such study. They asked: "Organizations are hoping that switching from a control paradigm will sharpen their competitive edge; however, does teamwork philosophy really change business for the better? Does processing work in a teamwork setting rather than a traditional assembly line setting allow for flexibility and adaptability?" (p. 36). Although their question mentions assembly lines, their research was broader in scope.

Waters and Beruvides (2009) drew on Beruvides's earlier work in which he and others (Beruvides, Omachonu, and Sumanth, 1989) identified three broad categories of work—blue collar, white collar, and knowledge work. Waters and Beruvides studied all three categories. Their view is that every position in the organization does, or should, involve all three elements from time to time. (We believe, and practice, the idea that everyone, including ourselves, must "get their hands dirty" from time to time if there is to be good library morale.) Waters and Beruvides (2009) listed eight categories of work and the different levels of involvement among blue collar, white collar, and knowledge workers. The categories were outputs, inputs, work type, degree of discretion, pursuits, level of endeavors, decision structure, and maturity level. For example, the differences by "work type" are that blue collar work is manual or physical, white collar work is part manual, and knowledge work is mainly mental. Another category, "decision structure," identified the differences as blue collar work is structured, white collar work is structured and semi-structured, and knowledge work is semi-structured and unstructured.

Waters and Beruvides's (2009) study conclusion was: "This research revealed a strong indication that work teams and traditional work schemes differed statistically along seven of the eight work characteristics. The results support the general main hypothesis of this research that a difference does exist between work team work and traditional blue-collar schemes" (p. 42). They go on to indicate that work teams are more effective and "can assist in today's competitive work environment" (p. 43).

An interesting counterpoint to this discussion and the emphasis on teams appeared in the September 24, 2011, issue of *The Economist* about corporate culture and the differences in the views of senior management and their employees. The research was done by the Boston Research Group. It surveyed several thousand employees, at all levels, in U.S. organizations. The survey indicated that 43 percent operated on the basis of "command-and-control, top-down management or leadership by coercion" and that only 3 percent fell into the category of self-governance (*The Economist,* 2011, p. 76). "Tragicomically, the study found that bosses often believe their own guff, even if their underlings do not. Bosses are eight times more likely than average to believe that their organization is self-governing" (p. 76). As we will discuss later in this chapter, top management's views play a critical role in how effective teams can be. *The Economist* (2011) puts a sharp point on the fact that there are often significant differences between talking the talk and walking the walk.

WHAT ARE TEAMS?

There are several types of teams; empowered, project, and working are three of the most common. Empowered teams have a high degree of autonomy in some activities and are more or less permanent in character. Such a group might be a retrospective cataloging team, if it has great latitude to determine its work activities. Project teams are assembled to carry out a specific task usually with a target completion date. Such a team might be a 24/7 reference service implementation group. You can create working teams to improve work coordination within your areas of responsibility; you can also use such teams to involve the staff in unit-planning and decision-making activities.

One definition of a workplace team that appears to capture today's environment is: "A work group [that] is made up of individuals who see themselves and who are seen by others as a social entity, who are interdependent because of the tasks they perform as members of the group, who are embedded in one or more larger social systems, and who perform tasks that affect others" (Guzzo and Dickson, 1996, pp. 308–309). Perhaps two more elements ought to be part of the definition—teamwork groups develop a shared commitment to one another, and the group is empowered to make decisions regarding its work activities.

Keep in mind that there are important differences between teams and committees. John Lubans (2003, p. 144) identified five significant differences:

- Team members are equals, while committees may have an implicit pecking order or hierarchy.
- Conflict in teams is normal and addressed, while committees may labor under unresolved, often historic, conflict.
- Teams seek high trust, while committee members may have turf issues and hidden agendas.

- Teams strive for open communication, while committee members may be overly cautious in discussions.
- Team members are mutually supportive, while committee members may work independently and represent factions.

When creating teams, essentially you must be certain it is a team and not a committee by another name. Doing so is not as easy as you might think; we have both experienced teams that were in reality a committee. Just calling it a team will not make it so nor will it really demonstrate how "up-to-date" you are managerially.

When an organization employs teams, especially self-managing teams, it should be beneficial in several ways. First, overall performance ought to improve, especially when teams work directly with users. Being able to make a decision on the spot, beyond enforcing rules and regulations, generally results in service(s) that better meet the user's needs and time frame. Second, there ought to be more "learning" and greater flexibility for both the organization and the staff. This occurs, in part, because teams can and do experiment as well as engage in new or innovative approaches to challenging situations. Third, staff commitment to the organization and its goals tends to be higher. Greater commitment results in higher retention of staff, which in turn reduces personnel costs (recruitment and training). Finally, more committed and motivated people are more productive as well as more willing to change as circumstances change.

BEFORE YOU START TEAM BUILDING

Teams require thoughtful leadership and support in order to realize all their benefits. Thus, implementing teams does not reduce an organization's need for leaders/managers. What follows are some thoughts for making teams a key component of library operations.

Deciding to employ teams—temporary or permanent—is not to be done lightly. Teams and time go together like bacon and eggs. They require thoughtful planning, a careful assessment of staff capabilities, and an assessment of the organization's ability to adjust to the team concept *before* you start. Teams require careful, ongoing nurturing from their creation to their disbandment. They also require a different and rather complex assessment process to ensure sound and proper accountability.

Time spent in preparing and thinking about creating teams will pay off in better long-term performance. You should think through some basic issues that fall into three broad areas—organizational, team, and team membership. Taken together, the assessment indicates how ready the organization is to implementing true teams.

ORGANIZATIONAL ISSUES

Perhaps the most basic issue is the organization's commitment to using teams. This may be one of the weakest links in team usage. The "Let's try it and see how it works" approach contains the seeds of trouble; there is no real complete commitment in this case. The level of commitment increases in importance when thinking about implementing self-managed teams. Being committed to this endeavor will entail modifying some or many of the existing underlying organizational structures and systems.

One example of the fundamental organizational issues necessary for team success is determining how to assess and reward team performance. Team assessment is very different from individual performance appraisal. Although teams are becoming increasingly common in libraries, the performance appraisal and reward systems for teams are still in their developmental stages. Another area that might require change(s) is access to information by staff. Teams often need more in-depth management information to function properly than the level the organization currently shares with personnel.

A related issue is how committed the senior staff are to shifting toward being a team-based organization. (Our earlier discussion of *The Economist* [2011] article suggests there may be a rather large disconnect between what senior managers believe and how the staff sees the commitment.) Successful team implementation seldom occurs in organizations where you or more senior staff have doubts about the concept. Such individuals can, even without thinking about their concerns, cause delays or otherwise impede a team's progress or activities. A more subtle factor can be a modeling behavior on the part of doubters that suggests, or makes clear, that they do not support the concept.

Resources are always an organizational issue, as they are almost never as plentiful as everyone would like. It is the rare case when the decision to move to a team structure also brings with it additional resources for implementation. This implementation naturally results in a reallocation process with some unit(s) losing something—people, equipment, funds, and so forth—to provide team resources. Because the usual process requires finding the necessary resources from what already exists, the question is, does the organization have sufficient resources to implement teams without undue loss of productivity, and is there agreement from where they will come?

Another resource the organization must allocate is time, which some people may view as expended partially on nonproductive activities. Forming teams for the first time in an organization calls for staff training and development in just what the team concept is and means. Both team members and the other staff will require this orientation.

Traditional workplace behavior, at least in the United States, has a strong element of competition and a low emphasis on cooperation/collaboration. Team-based work calls for just the opposite behavior; it takes time for team members to develop the change in focus. Taking time to develop needed team skills usually limits productivity during the developmental period; this in turn can cause resentment among non–team member staff because of a lack of understanding about team processes. Regardless of the extent to which teams are to be implemented, a critical question to ask is, does the organization have the necessary time and training capability to develop a proper team environment?

Some other issues exist: are team goals and anticipated results clearly articulated, have the team–management information-sharing systems been thought through, and has a team monitoring and support structure been developed? As you can see, the issues are substantial in character, and the decision to go with teams requires thought and planning; and beyond this there are team and team member concerns to consider.

TEAM ISSUES

There are fewer team issues to address. These issues are significant nonetheless. An obvious issue is the team's time frame—temporary or permanent? Certainly the answer may have an impact on the ease of getting agreement on resource realloca- tion. Often forming a temporary team creates more challenges than does a perma- nent team, because the "disruptions" may be twofold, once during the formation of the team and again during the reintegration of the team members into their former units. Another issue is whether the temporary team will in fact truly be a team or just another committee by a different name.

Identifying the appropriate team resources should be part of the planning process rather than finding them as needed, as there will be enough unexpected needs to keep the organization "on its toes." Preplanning in this area may identify one or two resources that are not readily available from existing sources. Know- ing what those sources may be gives you some lead time for securing them, or, if the resources are not available, rethinking team goals.

Effective teams exhibit a high degree of coordination and communication between team members as well as with nonteamwork units. Knowing what those activities are and what skills and abilities are required will help ensure success. This knowledge will also play a major role in selecting people for the team. A factor to keep in mind is that while there is a relationship between team goals and requisite skills, empowered teams can and do often come up with approaches to achieving the desired goal(s) that call for unanticipated skills.

TEAM MEMBER ISSUES

At the team member level, there are several topics to ponder before starting the selection process. A common feature of teams is cross-training of members. Although cross-training does take place in nonteam environments, it is not that common. Thus, few individuals have experience with the process and its pur- poses. Gaining acceptance of the value of cross-training on the part of indi- viduals new to the idea can take some time. Two rather common suspicions are that the idea is just a management ploy to "give me more work without any benefit" or a way to offload some of the work of low performers without man- agement addressing the nonperformers' behavior(s). The question to consider is, will the staff be receptive to cross-training, if needed? If the answer is that there may be resistance, are there resources available to help change the staff attitudes?

A key issue is, do the prospective team members have team membership personality characteristics? What are some of those characteristics? One is the

CHECK THIS OUT

For more information about team performance appraisal, see G. Edward Evans's book *Performance Management and Appraisal* (New York: Neal-Schuman, 2004).

preference for and ability to handle a high degree of autonomy. Another desirable characteristic is a preference for social interaction as opposed to solitary activities. Being receptive to new ideas, concepts, and approaches to problem situations is also necessary. A desire to grow and develop in your work is something good team members have. Additionally, having a willingness to address differences of opinion in an open, straightforward manner (negotiation) is essential for team members. They also have to accept the idea that differences and conflict are natural parts of the team environment and that resolving the issue(s) is a must for successful team operations.

An area where teamwork differs from the traditional workplace is accountability. As noted earlier, in the United States, most workers are accustomed to being individually accountable for their work outcomes. Group accountability may be the most difficult concept for team members to understand and accept. Teams *must* be accountable, and success or failure is a *team* responsibility. Accepting that "my performance assessment" may be negatively impacted by someone else's actions often does not sit well with some individuals. An important feature of self-managing teams and their accountability is that the team must be allowed to address team member performance on an ongoing basis rather than have an external person handle any problems. Do prospective team members have the maturity levels to engage in meaningful peer evaluation? For a great many employees, experience of peer evaluation is nonexistent or exceedingly limited. Peer evaluation in libraries is rather uncommon, especially for the support staff. There is some use of peer evaluations for professionals, primarily in academic settings. Lack of experience with the process as well as concerns, doubts, and fears about the fairness of the process and its impact on interpersonal relationships usually create a situation for which some serious training and development of staff are required.

CREATING AND MAINTAINING TEAMS

Your first steps, assuming it is a go for forming a team, are determining the team composition and size, creating the right environment (empowerment and support), establishing the initial activities and processes (interdependence and goals), and creating a plan for training and development. John Maxwell (1993) suggested some principles upon which you can base a staff development program. First, you must value people. Part of valuing is having a *commitment* to people. Commitment involves developing an individual's skills and abilities. In most successful organizations, that process goes beyond the skills and abilities required for the person's immediate job responsibilities. Basing a development program on clear and well-understood *standards* as well as on the vision for the future also helps create a successful organization. Two interrelated principles are *integrity* and *influence.* You must have influence over people in order to motivate their desire to learn and develop. Although most people have the desire to grow, even in the workplace, they take their cues from your positive attitude. A key factor in influencing behavior is your integrity. Without integrity, which builds trust, a leader's behavior is more likely to be viewed as negative rather than positive.

One means of building self-esteem is to give feedback and encouragement on a regular basis. Too often the manager waits for some especially noteworthy performance or idea before giving feedback. Certainly such occasions call for feedback; however, providing ongoing positive support and encouragement generally creates a more productive environment and committed staff. This applies to all staff, not just team members.

A related assumption about employees is that everyone can use assistance in their work activities, at least occasionally. Very few of us are perfect in everything we do, nor do we have all the desirable work skills and abilities. At the very least, we have some skills that could use improvement. We are not talking about corrective assistance but rather the coaching that develops a person's work attributes. Good coaching draws on a person's desire to succeed; it also can effectively build self-esteem. Employees who view the leader as actively assisting them to grow become more committed.

Remember, development takes time, especially when it comes to team building. Modeling appropriate behaviors, values, and goals is essential for successful leadership whether or not you in a team setting. Caring for people and developing their abilities will build strong work groups. With all this in mind, you can commence building the team(s).

CREATING THE TEAM CHARGE

The *charge* is the purpose of the group as assigned by the team's sponsor, coach, or external leader. The charge outlines the expectation for the team's performance. Although not every organization uses charges when creating teams, it can be useful to give the team a sense of its parameters, responsibilities, and resources. Scholtes, Joiner, and Striebel (2003, pp. 2–12) noted that a well-crafted charter can be useful in helping the team to understand the following:

- What the problem is
- Why it is important to customers and the organization at this time
- Any boundaries or limitations, including time and money
- The beginning and ending dates of the project, and key milestones for review

- The key measures related to the problem or process under study
- The scope of their authority, for example, to call in co-workers or out-side experts, request information normally inaccessible to them, and make changes to the process
- Who the core team members are and the amount of time allocated to the project

When discussing its charge, the group can then create its mission. Scholtes, Joiner, and Striebel (2003) include a *Charter Worksheet* that provides useful guidelines for creating a charter or charge.

TEAM SELECTION

Three critical factors in team selection are skills, abilities, and personal characteristics of the members. Some examples of necessary competencies for a database management team are knowledge of databases, knowledge of networking, knowledge of database contracts and licensing, and knowledge of fiscal management. On the personal characteristics side, such things as self-direction, social ability, being comfortable with group processes, being trustful of others, and having strong communication skills are desirable.

In many ways, identifying desirable abilities and characteristics is the easy step. Finding the right people is generally the big challenge. As noted earlier, it is the rare case when moving to a team-oriented environment brings with it additional resources—be they human, equipment, or funding. Even when everyone on the staff is in the selection pool, the process is complex. Some suitable members may be in positions that are critical to other operations, and moving them to a team would be highly problematic. A common circumstance is the necessity to select team members who lack one or more of the desired abilities or characteristics, which in turn means finding training opportunities in the lacking area(s). Another challenge is assessing the personal characteristics of potential team members, as some of the desired capabilities may not be apparent in the current working environment. The process is less challenging as the organization has more and more experience with teams and collaborative work projects.

Team size is a variable that you decide on a case-by-case basis. A team must be large enough to handle the assignment(s) but not so large as to create problems of coordination. If there is a team size rule, it is to not make the team any larger than absolutely necessary to accomplish the established goals.

TEAM ENVIRONMENT

Creating the best possible team environment is easier than putting the team together, but it is easier only when senior management fully supports the concept. One critical element in the environment is to ensure that the team and the entire staff receive the requisite training; this is particularly true when first moving into a team environment and staff has little or no experience with team processes. As noted earlier, when an organization shifts from a traditional to a team-oriented workplace, everyone must understand how teamwork differs. One of the most common causes for resentment of team members is that teams do spend significant time in meetings (gaining consensus, resolving conflicts, establishing priorities, etc.), especially during the startup period. Nonteam staff members often view such meetings as not constituting "real" work and think the team is getting paid for doing nothing.

The person selected to monitor the team—the external manager-leader—is another very important element in the team environment. Wageman (1997) suggests that leaders/managers who understand team design factors (goals, resources, personnel, size, etc.) most strongly impact team performance. They are also skillful in assessing team weakness and taking prompt steps to correct the problem(s).

A team has a much greater chance of success when it starts with a clear set of directions; if these can be inspiring, then it is even better. Keeping the focus on the whys rather than the hows, especially in the directions, improves the chances for successful team outcomes. If the manager-leader thinks of the charge as akin to a team's mission statement, this helps to focus on broad issues rather than on details that limit the team's initiative.

Related to clear goals and directions and to the "right" team environment are the tasks the team is to perform. You must be certain the task(s) *require* teamwork. A common mistake, especially in first-time team environments, is creating a team in name only (tasks, yes, but not requiring teamwork). What happens is that there is the appearance of teamwork, but in reality it is just individuals doing their own independent work. Making this mistake quickly leads to disillusionment. Another fairly common mistake is assigning tasks that only occasionally call for teamwork. While there will likely be times that team members will need to work independently in order to produce a product that is shared with the team, assigning too many individualized tasks risks sending a mixed message and does not take advantage of the benefits of a team-based structure. This creates a pull on team members, making it difficult to build a team commitment.

One element of the environment where you may not have as much influence as might be desirable is team rewards. The library will need to work closely with the HR department to develop a true team reward orientation. Such a system will ensure the vast majority of rewards are equally shared by team members. Although you can employ some individual rewards in a team system, they should be a very small percentage of the total available and then clearly related to the team's activities. Another approach is to allow the team to decide how, if, and when differential rewards should be distributed. A system that bases distribution of rewards as low as 50 percent on an individual basis sends a mixed message about the importance of teamwork.

EMPOWERING TEAMS

"Empowerment" is a word that is widely used, and it is apparent that many people want to be "empowered" in the workplace. Just what does empowerment entail? Empowerment is a form of delegation or sharing of power, but with you retaining most of the responsibility. Perhaps *the* key element to empowerment is an environment of high trust. This means trust that goes in both directions. You must trust the team, and the team must trust you.

You have to think about several personal barriers when it comes to empowering others. One such barrier is a concern about your position—if I empower, what may happen to my position? Will my position no longer be needed? When empowerment results in positive results, it actually enhances the empowerer's position. Managerial leaders of high-performing groups have little to fear when it comes to their position and the fact that they empower others. Another barrier is a dislike of change, especially when there are no apparent problems with what is taking place. In an empowered environment, change is common especially during the early days of the team when it is working out its operations. Individuals with low self-confidence, or whose self-worth arises largely from having a power position, have substantial problems with empowerment activities. Such individuals often talk about empowering and even think they have engaged in doing so, but what they don't do is relinquish any real power to act.

There are organizational barriers to empowerment as well. It is easy to talk about and to suggest that a person should empower her or his staff; however, it often proves to be more difficult than you might expect. Senior management can also be a barrier. One reason this comes about is because empowerment is not seen as important enough to devote adequate time, effort, and money to make the process meaningful. Sometimes empowerment requires that the organization provide training for staff members, training that requires both time and funding in most cases. Perhaps the greatest senior management barrier to empowerment is a lack of commitment to the concept. The lack of commitment is not so much a function of the age of the senior managers as it is a matter of management philosophy. Assessing senior management's views and commitment to empowering activities is something a person at lower levels in the organization should undertake. Just because you are committed and willing to engage in an empowering process does not mean you will succeed without top management support.

At the operational level, frontline personnel can also be a barrier, at least during the early phases of the process. Past negative experience with manag-

---

CHECK THIS OUT

For a number of suggestions for how to recognize and reward employees, consult Bob Nelson's *1001 Ways to Reward Employees,* rev. ed. (New York: Workman, 2005).

ers/leaders who only talked about empowerment can create a situation of "prove to us you mean it." Particularly in this case you will need to walk the walk, not just talk the talk. Beyond wanting proof, some staff members will have concerns about their skill and knowledge sets that may be required if they are empowered, as empowerment usually means some change(s).

Senior managers, if they truly desire effective leadership at all levels of their organization, ought to think about the following areas. First, undertake some self-study or training in empowering activities. Second, go beyond self-education and provide this training to all managers. Third, create an environment in which everyone can be a leader. Finally, reward high performance in the new activities—remember that rewards can be other than financial in character.

What are some common areas for empowering others? Underlying all empowerment is the authority and responsibility to succeed or fail because of your own efforts, actions, and behaviors. This is a fact that is often not fully understood by a newly empowered person, especially when it is the first experience with the process.

First and foremost, teams must be able to make *decisions* about its activities. Certainly you should be available to support the team's efforts (providing information or making suggestions, for example), but you must be careful not to make the decision for them. While you must set the overall goal(s) for the team, the team should have the power to *set internal goal(s) and targets* for how to achieve the ultimate goal(s). Related to setting goals and targets, teams need to *set work standards* if they are to be self-managing. Having the freedom to *experiment* with work processes goes with establishing standards. It also follows that the team should have the power to make member *assignments* as it sees fit. An area of shared power is *monitoring performance*—team monitoring of members' performance and your monitoring the team's progress. Another area where the team needs freedom to operate is in *allocating team resources* as appropriate. Effective empowerment managers/leaders are careful about when they intervene in team activities, especially when it comes to problem solving; having the latitude to *resolve problems* on their own is something effective teams have. Perhaps an area where leaders have the greatest difficulty timing their intervention is with regard to *conflict resolution*. Jumping in too quickly when team conflict develops, or at least before the team requests assistance, is something to avoid. When a team works through a conflict on its own, it tends

CHECK THIS OUT

A good book on empowering library staff is Connie Christopher's *Empowering Your Library* (Chicago: American Library Association, 2003).

to create a stronger team. A team that has all the powers mentioned is indeed empowered to succeed or fail.

TEAM RESOURCES

An obvious factor in a proper team environment is having the necessary resources to achieve the ultimate goal(s). It goes without saying that, lacking the required resources, a team cannot act in a timely manner, be proactive, or even be semi-functional. There is more to this than just receiving the resources; it is a matter of receiving them when needed. This can be a problem for both you and the team, particularly when senior management is not fully committed to team processes.

TEAM TRUST

Trust is a key element in effective team environments. There are three areas of trust to think about—your trust in the team, the team's trust in you, and team members' trust in one another. Trust underlies effective collaboration, and collaboration is a keystone in effective team performance. It is clear that without trust and collaboration in all three areas, the chances for the desired outcomes diminish.

Trust is built on some interpersonal skills that apply equally to both team and nonteam environments. One essential skill is listening and doing so with empathy. (There is a difference between listening and listening effectively.) *Effective listening* is a developed skill and one upon which most of us need to actively work. (See Chapter 8 for a discussion of listening.)

Finally, accurate feedback is critical to effective listening and ensuring the sender's and receiver's understandings are the same. Feedback is also related to building trust in that group processes require people to engage in "give and take." Accurate feedback must, at least occasionally, reflect the fact that we do not agree with something. Timing of such feedback is very important in building trust. Just hearing "negative" feedback, such as "That is a bad idea" or "What in the world makes you think that?," will create distrust in the group. Using less evaluative terms and phrases tends to encourage people to continue to contribute. Trustful team environments have people who are:

- open to ideas and feelings,
- committed to a shared set of goals,
- willing to explore alternatives, and
- satisfied with teamwork.

COACHING TEAMS

Group discussions about team goals are likely to elicit information about concerns about the team concept as it relates to both the team and the individual members. Many of those concerns will relate to resources and skills required. For first-time teams, there will be worries about team processes, whether or not they are articulated.

With the input from group discussions as well as independent judgment, you can begin to plan what training and development activities are appropriate. One challenge may be finding the resources for conducting the training, at least in a timely fashion. Some of the typical areas where coaching and development will be required are:

- group decision making,
- group problem solving,
- meeting management skills,
- conflict resolution, and
- peer performance assessment.

MAINTAINING THE TEAM

Having created the team(s) and the best possible team environment, you must now turn to the activities that support and maintain them. Remember, all of the elements that went into creating the environment remain as ongoing issues. However, in addition to these elements, you must address motivation, communication, feedback, and accountability.

The basics of team motivation do not vary that much from the basics of motivating individual employees. An underlying factor in everyone's motivation to work is self-interest—if nothing more than working as a legal means of securing the money on which to live. It is of course far more complex than that, but self-interest is a factor. Thus, the first difference in the team environment is the need to keep self-interest(s) to a minimum. Another difference is that the team is likely to have members from different "generations" who may be more or less inclined toward teamwork.

Monitoring team activities is essential. When a team exhibits morale or productivity problems, you must intervene. If the poor morale is arising from some performance problem as a team, start by assisting the team with its problem solving. This will not resolve the poor morale by itself, but it will stop the problem from "feeding" the morale issue. It may be as simple as the timing of resources for teamwork. On the other hand, it may be a nonperforming team member. When this is the case, the team may be hard pressed to resolve the matter on its own.

One weak member can and will create significant problems for the team. There are really only two options when it comes to a weak team member—train or replace. In the best of circumstances, it is just a matter of the team member needing the requisite training rather than unwillingness to learn on their part. When it is not a training-resolvable issue, often the team is not empowered to replace the person, which is something you must undertake. Failure to take action will

CHECK THIS OUT

One resource to consult for suggestions on how to support team activities is Michael West's *Motivate Teams, Maximize Success: Effective Strategies for Realizing Your Goals* (San Francisco: Chronicle Books, 2004).

AUTHORS' EXPERIENCE

Alire, hired as a new dean to turn an "unhealthy and dysfunctional" academic library into a healthier, more customer-oriented one, flattened the administrative structure to bring midlevel managers into the top level management team. One of the new members on the management team was not a big picture person, could not see beyond that person's department, and was not functioning as a team member, which was affecting the rest of the team's trust and morale. After the supervisor tried working with this person to no avail and it was clear that the person's attitude was detrimental to building the new team, Alire had to act. She knew that she needed a strong, united team in order to start the change management process. The midlevel manager was reassigned and removed from the management team. Immediately the management team bonded; trust developed and matured; and the team moved forward.

have disastrous consequences for the team. Poor morale will increase as other team members' resentments fester and grow. Resentment and poor morale almost always translate into exceedingly poor team performance. Another negative outcome of failing to act is that the team will begin to doubt and distrust you.

When morale is just starting to decline (moderate to low morale) there are several things you can do. One step is to be certain to model behavior that is positively geared toward success. It is also probably a good time for some serious coaching. Assisting the team in finding one or two small and quick successes almost always helps boost morale. Having a team meeting and discussing the vision and its beneficial values may also make a positive difference. Demonstrating your commitment to the vision and modeling that commitment will help team members buy into that vision. Such discussions may also lead to discussions about what may be causing a decline in morale.

TEAM COMMUNICATION

Effective communication—speaking, writing, and listening—is the glue of successful team functionality. Group commitment, decision making, problem solving, conflict resolution, accountability, and so forth all rest on the quality of the communication that occurs in the team.

Team members who understand and follow four communication rules find themselves, more often than not, on great teams. Rule one is to be open and honest with one another even though it can lead to vulnerability. This almost always leads to greater commitment to one another. Rule two is to be clear and concise. Trying to "show off" your vocabulary tends to turn off listeners as well as makes the real message harder to identify. Being "long winded" does little but eat up valuable team time. Rule three is to maintain consistency. Maintaining consistency does not mean being unwilling to compromise or admitting to be wrong about something. However, constantly changing views, positions, and so forth raises doubts about a person and may lead to less trust. Rule four is to be civil and courteous as well as reflecting a respect for others and their views. Teams that follow these rules in their communication with one another, with the leader, with other units and teams, and with the public are likely to achieve great things.

TEAM FEEDBACK

As location is to real estate, so timing is to feedback. At the right time it can work wonders; at the wrong time it can cause a surprising amount of damage. As noted earlier, feedback is crucial for establishing trust within a team. Establishing proper feedback timing takes a good deal of practice and careful thought on your part. One aspect of managerial/leader feedback that seldom receives enough attention is that it can be positive as well as corrective in character.

For feedback to be useful it must rest on accurate information. Leaders/managers collect their data from several sources—reports, documents, observations, thoughtful listening to staff comments, comments from the public, and comments from other units. Some things to bear in mind about feedback, particularly in a team setting, are the folloiwing:

- Ideally, it should be face-to-face, not in a memo or e-mail.
- It should be specific, which is essential when it is corrective in nature.
- It should allow for a response from the recipient.
- It should occur as close to the time of the event as possible.
- It should focus on behavior rather than on personality.
- It should be carefully thought through before being given.
- It should be based on your information, not secondhand data.
- It should be honest.

TEAM ACCOUNTABILITY

Developing a sense of group accountability in the team is absolutely essential for the organization. This will take some time, particularly in cases where teams and their accountability is a new concept. Once the team internalizes accountability, it is relatively easy to maintain, as peer pressure to achieve the best becomes high. Individual members become resolved to not let their teammates down. The team will be quick to respond to a member who slacks off and even make up for the lapses for a time, if the team believes there is a good reason for the lapse and it will not be a long-term issue.

One area of concern for you is the organizational reward system. As we mentioned earlier, when the parent organization's personnel system is individually focused, problems can arise for team usage. Even small rewards such as "employee of the month" can be detrimental to team functioning. Reviewing the organization's reward system is a worthwhile activity very early on in developing a team environment. Although it is not exhaustive, Robert Crow (1995) listed 10 potential "problem areas" for maintaining effective teamwork and a sense of group accountability:

- Institutional performance appraisal systems that rate individuals numerically and are used for ranking people
- Institutional performance appraisal systems that employ forced distributions (a system wherein a certain percentage of apprises must fall into a "needs improvement" category, and only a small percentage can receive high ratings)
- Pay for performance (individually based)
- Employee of the month/year programs
- Contests between units, individuals, and departments
- Internal promotion policies based solely on individual achievements
- Ranking of units from best to worst
- Use of individual quotas, piece rates, and so forth, as the basis for rewards
- Identifying units as profit or loss centers
- Managing "by the numbers"

Working with the organization to address practices such as these, or any others that emphasize individual work rather than teamwork, is vital to the long-term team.

You must engage in some level of individual appraisal. How do you go about doing that without damaging the group? Frank LaFasto and Carl Larson (2001) provide some useful guidance. They suggest that there are two categories of factors that distinguish the successful from the less successful team member— working knowledge and teamwork. They include two factors in the working knowledge—experience and problem solving. Within teamwork they have four factors—openness, supportiveness, personal style, and action orientation. Collecting information about the teamwork aspect takes observation, and when the observation has some structure it produces better, more accurate assessments. One way to structure the observation is to use the team evaluation form described by Laird Mealiea and Ramon Baltazar (2005). Other useful ideas about the process of evaluating group contributions are given by Phipps (1999) and Zigon (1998).

TEAM NEGOTIATION

A key element in team effectiveness is how well the team members negotiate with one another as well as the team's ability to negotiate with its outside manager-leader. We all negotiate every day, even if we don't think of it as negotiation. If nothing else, we interact with family members and coworkers about all manner of "minor" matters, be it whose turn it is to go to the post office or who should make the coffee for the staff association meeting. Such interactions are negotiation in action. Jill Grogg (2008) wrote that there are a "myriad of negotiations that each of us conducts every day—in both our professional and our personal lives" (p. 210). She also noted that, for many librarians, formal negotiations fall into the category of "business activities" in which they would rather not have to engage. Team negotiation is rather formal, although the team members may think of it as resolving differences of opinion about a team issue.

Negotiation is about resolving a matter in such a way that all parties involved achieve some gain rather than all or nothing. The "I Win! You Lose!" approach (also known as "zero sum" outcomes) is not what is needed in any negotiation but will be deadly in the case of a team.

In order to have a mutually beneficial negotiation, certain elements must be present on both sides of the negotiation table. First and foremost, there should be no hidden agendas. There must be open and honest exchanges of information regarding the party's positions. Everyone must be willing to listen and learn what the other side's views are and make serious efforts to understand those positions. If everyone can maintain control of their reactions to their "hot button" statements and words, the prospect for a good resolution is greatly improved. Finally, there must be a willingness to compromise; having a set of "never change" positions may well lead to an impasse.

Although he was writing about the corporate world's acquisitions, joint ventures, and "deals," Danny Ertel (2011) made a point that team members might well bear in mind during their negotiating activities: "People who view the contract as the conclusion and see themselves as solely responsible for getting there behave differently from those who see the agreement as just the beginning and believe their role is to ensure that the parties involved actually realize the value they are trying to create" (pp. 88–89). Indeed, if the team members view the process as aiding in the team's long-term success, the negotiating will move forward more quickly and have a positive outcome for the team.

TEAM-BASED LIBRARIES

Libraries currently do make some use of teams, and it seems highly likely the usage will increase over time. However, there are not a significant number of libraries where teams are the primary organizational pattern. Some academic libraries tried the approach and have ceased the practice; one such example is the University of Maryland Libraries. Most of the libraries employ teams in a few key areas (such as technical services) rather than as the only organizational structure.

Perhaps one of the best known team-based libraries with the longest operational experience in the United States is the University of Arizona Library. It has received a substantial amount of publicity since its first foray into becoming a team-based organization in the early 1990s. Two good articles about the Arizona model are Shelley Phipps's (2004) work "The System Design Approach to Organizational Development: The University of Arizona Model" and Carla J. Stoffle and Cheryl Cuillier's (2011) piece "From Surviving to Thriving." (Note: Stoffle and Cuillier were lead individuals in moving to a team-based structure in academic libraries.) An interesting article discussing the team concept in a public library setting is Betsy Bernfeld's (2004) "Developing a Team Management Structure in a Public Library." For an overview of teams in a technical services setting, see Lihong Zhu's 2011 piece "Use of Teams in Technical Services in Academic Libraries." For additional library-focused articles about teams, see the Launching Pad section at the end of this chapter.

KEY POINTS TO REMEMBER

- Workplace teams are not new.
- Empowered long-standing teams are relatively new.
- A shift to watch for is from team-based to "collaborative" work structures.
- Research suggests that teams do have a positive impact on productivity compared to traditional approaches.
- Creating a team is a complex process that involves both internal and external organizational issues, staff suitability and acceptance of team-based work, and your own views about teams.
- Several issues require very careful thought—how to address team accountability, evaluate performance, and implement rewards and salary adjustments.
- Moving to team-based approaches will bring with it the need to provide training for all the staff, not just potential team members, regarding the team concept and its operations and assessment.

References

Adler, Paul, Charles Hecksher, and Laurence Prusak. 2011. "Building a Collaborative Enterprise." *Harvard Business Review* 89, nos. 7/8: 94–101.

Bernfeld, Betsy. 2004. "Developing a Team Management Structure in a Public Library." *Library Trends* 53, no. 1: 112–128.

Berry, John W. 2012. E-mail communication sent to Camila A. Alire, March 1.

Beruvides, Mario, Vincent Omachonu, and David Sumanth. 1989. "The Measurement of White-Collar Knowledge Work Productivity." In *Productivity Management Frontiers II*, 39–46. Refereed papers presented at the Second International Conference on Productivity Research, February 22–24, 1989, Miami, Florida.

Crow, Robert. 1995. "Institutional Competition and Its Effect on Teamwork." *Journal of Quality and Participation* 18, no. 3: 46–53.

The Economist. 2011. "Corporate Culture: The View from the Top and Bottom." *The Economist* 400, no. 8757: 76.

Ertel, Danny. 2011. "Getting Past Yes." In *Harvard Business Review on Winning Negotiations*, 86–110. Cambridge, MA: Harvard Business Review Press.

Gratton, Lynda, and Tamara J. Erickson. 2011. "Eight Ways to Build Collaborative Teams." In *Harvard Business Review on Building Better Teams*, 45–71. Cambridge, MA: Harvard Business Review Press.

Grogg, Jill E. 2008. "Negotiation for the Librarian." *Journal of Electronic Resources Librarianship* 20, no. 4: 210–212.

Guzzo, Richard, and Marcus Dickson. 1996. "Teams in Organizations: Recent Research and Performance Effectiveness." In *Annual Review of Psychology*, edited by James Spence, 307–338. Palo Alto, CA: Annual Reviews.

Johnson, Margeaux, Melissa Clapp, Stacy Ewing, and Amy Butler. 2011. "Building a Participatory Culture: Collaborating with Student Organizations for Twenty-First Century Library Instruction." *Collaborative Librarianship* 3, no. 1: 2–15.

Kalan, Abby Preschel. 2010. "One Team: A Brave New World." *Public Libraries* 49, no. 3: 7–8.

LaFasto, Frank, and Carl Larson. 2001. *When Teams Work Best*. Thousand Oaks, CA: Sage Publications.

Lubans, John. 2003. "Teams in Libraries." *Library Administration and Management* 17, no. 3: 144–145.

Maxwell, John. 1993. *Developing the Leader within You*. Nashville: Franklin Nelson Publishers.

Mealiea, Laird, and Ramon Baltazar. 2005. "A Strategic Guide for Building Effective Teams." *Public Personnel Management* 34, no. 2: 141–160.

Phipps, Shelley E. 1999. "Performance Measurement as a Methodology for Assessing Team and Individual Performance." In *Proceedings of the 3rd Northumbria International Conference on Performance Assessment in Libraries and Information Services*, 113–117. Newcastle upon Tyne: Information North.

———. 2004. "The System Design Approach to Organizational Development: The University of Arizona Model." *Library Trends* 52, no. 1: 68–111.

Scholtes, Peter R., Brian L. Joiner, and Barbara J. Striebel. 2003. *The Team Handbook*. 3rd ed. Madison, WI: Oriel.

Stoffle, Carla J., and Cheryl Cuillier. 2011. "From Surviving to Thriving." *Journal of Library Administration* 51, no. 1: 130–155.

Wageman, Ruth. 1997. "Critical Factors in Creating Superb Self-Managing Teams." *Organizational Dynamics* 26, no. 1: 49–60.

Waters, Natalie, and Mario Beruvides. 2009. "An Empirical Study Analyzing Traditional Work Schemes versus Work Teams." *Engineering Management Journal* 21, no. 4: 36–43.

Zhu, Lihong. 2011. "Use of Teams in Technical Services in Academic Libraries." *Library Collections, Acquisitions, and Technical Services* 35, nos. 2–3: 69–82.

Zigon, Jack. 1998. "Team Performance Measurement." *Journal for Quality and Participation* 21, no. 3: 48–54.

Launching Pad

Abram, Stephen. 2012. "Ten Ways to Make Yourself Indispensable." *Information Outlook* 16, no. 1: 30–31.

Bazirjian, Rosann, and Rebecca Mugridge 2006. *Teams in Library Technical Services*. Lanham, MD: Scarecrow Press.

Bear, Julia B., and Anita Williams Woolley. 2011. "The Role of Gender in Team Collaboration and Performance." *Interdisciplinary Science Review* 36, no. 2: 146–153.

Boule, Michelle. 2008. "Best Practices for Working in a Virtual Team Environment." *Library Technology Reports* 44, no. 1: 28–31.

Cross, Rob, Peter Gray, Shirley Cunningham, Mark Showers, and Robert J. Thomas. 2010. "The Collaborative Organization: How to Make Employee Networks Really Work." *MIT Sloan Management Review* 52, no. 1: 83–90.

Fosmire, Michael. 2008. "Teams: What Are They Good For, and How Do You Get Them to Work?" *Science and Technology Libraries* 28, nos. 1/2: 123–132.

Nicholas, Jane, Alison M. Bobal, and Susan McEvoy. 2009. "Using a Permanent Usability Team to Advance User-Centered Design in Libraries." *Electronic Journal of Academic and Special Librarianship* 10, no. 2: 1–8.

O'Brien, Jill L., Donald R. Martin, Judith Heyworth, and Nancy R. Myer. 2008. "Negotiating Transformational Leadership: A Key to Effective Collaboration." *Nursing and Health Sciences* 10, no. 2: 137–143.

Senge, Peter M. 2006. *The Fifth Discipline: The Art and Practice of the Learning Organization.* Rev. ed. New York: Doubleday.

Shivers, Cassandra. 2012. "Shaking Up Expectations." *Computers in Libraries* 32, no. 2: 14–17.

Among the 21st century issues confronting our nation reside the seeds of a major challenge facing library managers. The demographic ballasts of our country are shifting, even as our professional moorings remain static. No matter the type of library or information agency, all will provide service to populations within an entirely new order of pluralism. In this future, greater workforce diversity is a necessity for the continued vitality and progress of the nation's libraries. A diverse workforce not only captures unique talents, it also yields innovation and creativity that arise as a result of seldom tapped perspectives brought to library problems from differing life experiences. Creating such workforces through a commitment to the recruitment and retention of a new generation of librarians responsive to the communities libraries serve must be a cornerstone in the strategic plan of today's transformational managerial leaders. Without that focus it is not clear that libraries can support diverse populations or understand their experiences, their needs, their languages, or their perspectives. And if libraries can't support the nation's Emerging Majority populations, how can we expect the nation's Emerging Majority populations to support libraries?

—Betty Turock, ALA President, 1995–1996 (2012)

The discussion of diversity as an organizational issue requires the consideration of the societal context in which libraries and library managers operate. In this regard, the societal context includes the political, policy, and legal context in which organizations operate as well as the social and cultural context.

—Mark Winston (2010)

A new Pew research study, "Millennials: Confident, Concerned, Open to Change," found that young adults and their elders agree: baby boomers and members of generation X have better work ethic and moral values than those in their 20s.

—Ian Shapira (2010)

15

ADDRESSING
DIVERSITY

This chapter focuses on the following:

- Defining diversity—cultural and generational
- How you view cultural diversity
- Legal framework
- Managerial responsibility
- Individual responsibility
- Role of professional associations
- Planning for diversity
- Generational issues
- Providing service to a diverse community

CERTAINLY THE 2010 U.S. census confirmed Betty Turock's statement about increased diversity in the country. The first decade of this century has seen an ever-increasing concern among people about diversity (of all types), immigration (legal and illegal), language skills and single-language desirability, and the long-standing notion that the United States is a "melting pot" in a positive sense. Groups of people appear to be taking increasingly hard positions on the various issues, and compromise seems harder and harder to achieve.

Managerial leaders and their organizations must navigate their ways through the diversity controversies while trying to remain effective in meeting their missions and goals. All organizations must address workforce diversity, such as meeting legal requirements that often change and working with a diverse staff. Some have to think about providing services or products to a diverse market. Publicly funded academic, public, and school libraries have special issues when it comes to diversity issues. We provide an example of this later in this section.

Needless to say, a diverse workplace requires managers who are sensitive to the diversity issues that surface from time to time. As Mark Winston noted in his 2010 quotation, there are many factors in play. Legislation brought some positive benefits in terms of diversity, but cultural experiences influence the way that we, as individuals, approach diversity. The politics of diversity are complex, contentious, and challenging. Culture influences the ways that people interact—sometimes consciously, sometimes subconsciously. Diversity touches on many managerial responsibilities relating to both the workforce and the community served.

From a library perspective the matter might seem cut and dried—service to all. What seems straightforward becomes challenging when, at least for publicly funded libraries, the community providing the funding for the libraries is deeply split about diversity. The ALA Office for Diversity (http://www.ala.org/ala/aboutala/offices/diversity/index.cfm) offers a wealth of information about dealing with diversity issues. The ALA has also produced some basic foundation documents regarding library service, which can be reviewed at http://www.ala.org/ala/professionalresources/guidelines/standardsguidelines/index.cfm.

The following is a small example of the types of diversity issues that create challenges for library managerial leaders. The *American Libraries* November 2007 issue devoted much of its text to discussions of bilingual collections. Although the topic was bilingual collections in general, the two feature articles focused on English and Spanish. Such a focus seems reasonable in light of U.S. demographics. However, the issue of bilingual collections is much broader than English–Spanish.

Leonard Kniffel (2007), in his editorial for the issue, stated, "Debate over bilingual education and companion library collections is healthy, but we should be asking ourselves why so many children grow up in America speaking only one language. We should all be learning English—and Spanish and Chinese and Arabic as well" (p. 3). Some people would agree with his thoughts, while others would strongly disagree, both within and outside our profession.

Todd Douglas Quesada (2007) wrote an essay in favor of bilingual library collections. His concluding comments were, "politically manipulating a library's collection development policy to alienate any portion of a community served is a marginalizing act, rendering the community's library as no longer truly 'public.' This is the underlying issue that we library professionals, as providers of free and open information accessibility for a community's enlightenment, must always be conscious of" (p. 44).

Julia Stephens's (2007) article against such collections end with, "By creating bilingual libraries, librarians are undermining the American democracy that has created one nation for all. Librarians have a duty to uphold the American way of life and save their English book and journal collections for Americans in the future" (p. 44).

The articles did, and probably still do, reflect the rather deep division in U.S. society regarding cultural diversity. There are equally strong views regarding other diversity areas, such as race, gender, age, and sexual orientation. Certainly ALA's positions regarding service and collections for everyone in a service community are clear. Nevertheless, librarians are no better than anyone else when it comes to suppressing one's life experiences, values, and beliefs. Librarians can and do try to be neutral when it comes to collection building and services. We believe they do a remarkably good job of this, too; however, it can be difficult, and there are slip-ups from time to time.

The Quesada and Stephens articles generated a large response from readers (published in the *American Libraries* January–February 2008 issue). Most of the letters supported Quesada's bilingual view—a side bar, in reference to the Stephens article, reads: "The article only helps spread fear, hatred, and divisiveness within our profession" (p. 8). However, like society at large, not everyone disliked the Stephens piece, "Julia Stephens is spot-on in her defense of predominately English-language collections in U.S. libraries. Before our current diversity cult and infatuation with multicultural mush, libraries played critical instructional roles in helping immigrants adapt to American cultural mores and assimilate into the mainstream of American life" (p. 11).

Why so much text about bilingual collections? Our reason is that it helps illustrate how complex and contentious the concept of diversity is for society and organizations. Almost every aspect of library operations carries with it the potential for raising a diversity issue. Library managerial leaders face challenging situations where strong community differences exist, and diversity is one such issue. There are times when the divide is between the majority community values and professional values. Decision making in such situations is difficult. We believe there are good reasons for engaging in activities that support diversity:

- First, there is the very human reason that it affects everyone who interacts with the library, the staff, and the service community. Everyone has a need to achieve their individual goals. For staff, the goals may relate to their career or personal life. For the users, they need to gain the greatest possible benefit from the service.
- Second, it makes good sense to create a collegial environment in which people are viewed as individuals. This encourages staff to become members of a team, and users are welcomed as valued members of the community. It optimizes both the potential of individuals and their productivity.
- Third, diversity is a factor in attracting and retaining the best talent among the staff. Staff turnover carries both visible and invisible costs.
- Fourth, when staff members know they are valued and take pride in the quality of their work, it influences how they interact with the community, which, in turn, increases the comfort level of users and raises the overall performance of the service. As business discovered, investing in good practice brings benefits for everyone and makes good sense.

CHECK THIS OUT

Dewey, Barbara I., and Loretta Parham, eds. 2006. *Achieving Diversity: A How-To-Do-It Manual for Librarians.* New York: Neal-Schuman.

DEFINING DIVERSITY

Diversity has been defined in a number of ways. Some writers and organizations take a narrow view, relating diversity mainly to racial or sexual identification. We believe diversity encompasses far more than these two important areas. It can involve cultural, religious, language, age, disability, and sexual orientation in addition to racial and gender concerns. We also believe generational differences can be a diversity issue. You can probably understand how all these issues make defining diversity difficult and certainly not in a few short sentences.

We prefer the broader view as described by Geert Hofstede (1991) in his book *Cultures and Organizations: Software of the Mind*:

> Every person carries within him or herself patterns of thinking, feeling, and potential acting which were learned throughout their lifetime. Much of it has been acquired in early childhood. . . . As soon as certain patterns . . . have established themselves . . . he [*sic*] must unlearn these before being able to learn something different, and unlearning is more difficult than learning for the first time. (p. 4)

By thinking about the way in which beliefs, such as diversity, are formed and the crucial issue of "unlearning," it becomes easier to understand why diversity is complex and sensitive. The range of issues influenced by diversity is easier to identify by considering the several layers of culture that Hofstede identifies that people carry within their "mental programming." His levels are, in summary:

- A national level, according to one's country of birth and early years
- A regional, ethnic, religious, and/or linguistic affiliation level
- A gender level, according to whether a person is female or male
- A generation level, which separates grandparents from parents from children
- A social class level, associated with educational opportunities and with a person's occupation or profession
- An organizational level for those who are employed (employees also become socialized by their work organization's culture)

Each country develops its own unique immigration policies. Some encourage assimilation, while others encourage integration. Either policy will, or should, influence library services, particularly those in the public sector.

CHECK THIS OUT

Geert Hofstede's website (http://www.geert-hofstede.com/) is worth looking at.

CONSIDER THIS

In the Nordic countries, there are strong differences of opinion concerning the role of the public library in the integration of immigrants (Skot-Hansen, 2002). Should libraries follow the political and social integration government policies or encourage cultural and artistic diversity? You can see the strength of the differences in recent 2010 and 2011 elections where anti-immigrate parties won a substantial number of parliamentary seats. Those results may place even greater pressure on libraries.

The United States has experienced high levels of immigration as well as population growth within ethnic communities. The 2010 census illustrated just how much demographics have changed over the preceding 10 years. Libraries must decide how to respond to the changes.

Regional differences often exist within national boundaries, for example, Latino and Spanish-speaking communities are widespread within the United States while Hmong are only in a few communities; Singapore has five official languages (Mandarin, Chinese, Malay, Tamil, and English); Canada has two official languages (French and English); and Wales also has two official languages (Welsh and English). Even moving within national boundaries can produce culture shock, even if the same language is used, for there may be a strong local dialect. All these factors come into play when planning library services.

Hofstede considered gender as male and female, but there are other gender-based groups that are included in the charge of the Diversity Council of the American Library Association (http://www.ala.org/ala/mgrps/committees/ala/ala-divcon.cfm) —the gay, lesbian, bisexual, and transgender communities.

Generational issues arise from life experiences that shape the values and attitudes of an individual, and, in turn, this process affects an individual's thoughts and behavior patterns. Today's workplace is likely to consist of several generations working side by side, with workers ranging from older volunteers to young interns. Ensuring that the different generations work together effectively calls for a greater understanding on the part of both individuals and managerial leaders.

Economic class can affect a person's potential use of a library, particularly in the public sector; so can educational level. Individuals with low income and educational levels are less likely to use libraries. Although they may need information, they are hesitant to ask for help. They may be intimidated by the prospect of entering an unfamiliar, imposing building. A potential user may not speak the common community language or not speak it well.

Another disadvantaged group that is not in any of Hofstede's categories but can face discrimination in the workplace and in using libraries is people with disabilities. While a physical disability may present challenges, society does not always recognize when it is unintentionally discriminating against employment or the use of services by disabled people.

All of these relate in some manner to diversity. Thus, we expect you can see why developing a short, comprehensive definition of diversity is not easy. Miriam Brewer (2011) provided an interesting way of defining diversity:

> Diversity is all of these elements and more:
> D—different styles, disabilities
> I —individuals, intelligence
> V—variety, veteran status
> E —education, economic status, ethnicity
> R—race, religion
> S —sexual orientation, social class
> I —immigration status
> T—thought processes, traits
> Y—youth, years (p. 28)

HOW DO YOU VIEW CULTURAL DIVERSITY?

One way to begin to understand the complexity of cultural diversity is to discover your own viewpoint by examining the concept through 10 lenses proposed by Williams (2001). He identified the ways people may approach race, culture, nationality, and ethnicity. The approach was validated in a large-scale Gallup poll. Williams's (2001) categories are the following:

- Assimilationist favors nationalistic and patriotic ideals.
- Colorblind views people as individuals (ignoring race and color has an equalizing effect).
- Culturalcentrist improves welfare by accentuating history and identity.
- Elitist believes in the superiority of the upper class (keeps advantages through social ties).
- Integrationist believes in breaking down barriers by having people live and work together.
- Meritocratist believes dreams will come true if you have the abilities and work hard.
- Multiculturalist celebrates diversity and its contribution to national character and history.
- Seclusionist wants to protect oneself (different groups should live and work apart).
- Transcendent focuses on the human spirit (diversity contributes to the richness of humanity).
- Victim/caretaker feels one is suffering from oppression and deserves compensation.

In which of the categories do you see yourself? Self-awareness is a building block in emotional intelligence. While attention has been focused on political correct-

CHECK THIS OUT

Alire, Camila. 2001. "Diversity and Leadership: The Color of Leadership." *Journal of Library Administration* 32, nos. 3/4: 95–109.

ness, there is a certain level of recognition that it may inhibit the development of cultural diversity.

MANAGERIAL RESPONSIBILITY

As a managerial leader, your responsibilities with regard to diversity are to:

- create an organizational culture that values diversity in all its manifestations;
- ensure that everyone has and demonstrates respect for the views and experiences of others; and
- implement practices based on sound policies so that diversity brings benefits to the library—for both staff members and users.

The key to success is to make flexibility a central component that will both support and retain staff and users.

There is a considerable body of legislation related to diversity, such as equal employment opportunity, equal pay, and antidiscrimination. Sometimes, in addition to federal laws, each state has a slightly different approach to such issues. Knowing the details of every change in the laws is not realistic for general managerial leaders. Keeping up-to-date on such matters is the responsibility of human resources and legal staff. It is also their responsibility to advise general managerial leaders of the changes that may impact them. We explore some of these concerns in more detail in the next chapter.

You often read about organizations having to defend their staffing practices, such as hiring, promotion, and salaries. For example, many women have experienced sex discrimination in both the nonprofit and private sectors. Institutional discrimination resulted in barriers to promotion if top management preferred to promote men to senior posts. Legal cases were pursued by women, and some paid a price, finding themselves labeled "troublemakers," and, if promoted, subtle ways were found to ensure that their work role was limited.

Carlson, Kacmar, and Whitten (2006) followed up with research carried out in 1965, finding that female respondents indicated steady support for the concept of women in management; and a favorable attitude on the part of men had increased from 35 percent to 88 percent. Despite attempts to level the playing field when it came to abilities, however, only 32 percent of men thought women had to be exceptional to succeed in contrast to 70 percent of women feeling that way. The researchers were unsure whether men actually were not seeing the barriers for women's advancement anymore or simply were providing politically correct responses. In the academic library sector, women hold the majority of directorships, and in some cases their compensation exceeds that of men in similar posts (Deyrup, 2004).

INDIVIDUAL RESPONSIBILITY

Every staff member has a personal responsibility to recognize and value differing attitudes and patterns of behavior of the people with whom they interact. Earlier we noted that individual values will differ, which creates different expectations when it comes to interactions. Unlike language, some differences are more subtle. For example, attitudes toward time vary; some people are relaxed about time, while others are rigid, which can cause conflicts. The rituals in meeting another person may vary from the warm smile, friendly handshake, and use of first names to great formality and using titles rather than names.

If you have lived in a different culture, it helps you to understand the degree of shock that a newcomer colleague or user experiences in a new society. For a newcomer, the challenge lies in identifying and understanding the values of the community. Often these values are not obvious or stated, and the newcomer has much to learn before adaptation takes place.

We mention culture shock because every staff member needs to understand how newcomers and new users feel during the process of acculturation. Everyone can experience frustration, helplessness, and perhaps hostility when faced with a new environment, as they compare the old and familiar life or organization with the new one. Remember that you don't have to move from one geographic location to another—the shock can happen simply in changing jobs. Wynn (1992) outlined steps that assist in working through the process of understanding:

- Becoming aware of the commonalties and differences among and between various cultures—taking a look
- Recognizing that yours may not be the "right or only" way—taking a perspective
- Investing yourself—Taking a part
- Developing positive relationships with people of different cultures—taking a hand
- Confronting the prejudice in others and ourselves—taking a stand
- Evolving bridge-building projects—taking a step
- Sharing the cultural bridges vision—sharing the dream

Although the steps were designed to bridge national cultural differences, we believe they apply equally well to other areas of diversity.

ROLE OF PROFESSIONAL ASSOCIATIONS

The ALA vigorously pursues programs to increase equal opportunities in the library workforce. Starting with a conference on women in the early 1970s,

ALA recognized that people of color were under-represented in the profession at large and adopted a leadership role to recruit and retain staff. Meetings and training sessions have been held at the national, regional, and state levels to exchange ideas and experiences about ways to improve the situation. ALA's Spectrum Initiative offers scholarships, mentoring, and leadership training (http://www.ala.org/ala/aboutala/offices/diversity/spectrum/scholarship information.cfm).

ALA's Office of Diversity updates Diversity Counts (a comprehensive study of gender, age, and race within the library profession) from time to time. The latest data available, in late 2011, is still based on the 2000 census data. Nevertheless, it probably still paints a reasonably accurate picture of the profession's diversity or lack thereof (http://www.ala.org/ala/aboutala/offices/diversity/diversity-counts/divcounts.cfm). Of 109,958 librarians, 97,827 identified as white, 5,244 as African American, 3,516 as Asian Pacific Islanders, 2,137 as Latino, and 310 as Native American. Gender was 80 percent women and 20 percent male. In terms of age, 97, 877 were over 35 years old. Less than 4 percent reported a disability. The projection of potential retirements, based on the revised 2006 data, was that 34 percent of the librarians reaching 65 were likely to retire between 2005 and 2014. It seems highly probable that the economic crisis the country has recently endured has affected the number of retirements.

ALA provides data regarding diversity as well as ideas for improving and maintaining a focus on diversity, but it is up to managerial leaders to make the library a more diverse workplace and one that serves all of the people.

PLANNING FOR DIVERSITY
The majority of libraries have a parent organization that holds the responsibility for developing a mission statement and policies to ensure that it meets statutory diversity requirements. The responsibility of library managerial leaders is to ensure that these organizational policies become part of the library's planning process and to work with staff to ensure that good practice is observed. Two other responsibilities of the parent body are to commit funding to implement diversity policies and to monitor goals. Royse, Conner, and Miller (2006) discussed the design, methodology, and outcomes of a diversity climate assessment survey that produced benchmarks for measuring the progress and success of diversity programs. The ALA provides examples of plans from large and small services that can be adapted to other types of information services (http://www.ala.org/advocacy/diversity/workplace/diversityplanning).

Kendall (1994) made a number of useful points about making a successful transition to a hospitable working environment, including the following:

- Top management must genuinely and seriously commit to an ongoing examination of its attitudes as well as its policies and procedures.
- The organization must view diversity as a long-term, multifaceted, continual process, not as an event or a quick fix.
- The organization must expect and be willing to deal with discomfort and resistance.
- The organization must not avoid discussions on institutional racism when addressing diversity and multicultural environments.
- The organization must develop a core staff willing to commit time and energy to bringing about a hospitable work environment for all people.
- The organization must know that its diversity activities will mirror its other activities.

And there will be challenges in evaluating the process of making a successful transition to a hospitable working environment. As Kendall (1994) stresses, difficulties can arise when:

- measuring changes in attitude,
- a lack of a discrete beginning and ending to the task exists, or
- stress caused by other events in the library manifests itself as resistance to diversity.

We stress the importance of monitoring performance. Data on recruitment, promotion, and retention is available. Adding qualitative information gathered from exit interviews, appraisal interviews, or surveys also helps you monitor progress toward diversity goals.

SOMETHING TO CONSIDER

Alire, when talking about ethnic and racial diversity, will share that most of her colleagues would claim that they are not personally racist. She believes them. However, she makes a distinction between personal and institutional racism. Institutional racism is when the values, beliefs, and attitudes are so embedded in the institution (or library organization) that when someone who joins the institution has a different set of values, beliefs, and/or attitudes, he or she is discriminated against, either overtly or subtly. And, many of the well-established coworkers don't even realize they are doing it. Can you think of any situation where you have experienced this within an organization or library with which you are or were affiliated?

R. Roosevelt Thomas (2011, pp. 22–25) identified five "factors" in creating a sound diversity plan that he labeled diversity and diversity management (D&DM):

- Identify and adopt contextual definitions.
- Identify and develop their organization's mission, vision, and strategy.
- Address three key strategic decisions—type of diversity to address, using a "fish or teach to fish" approach with staff, in what areas to apply the plan.
- Plan for transition and application.
- Audit organizational culture to determine whether it supports the enterprise's D&DM aspirations.

He also suggested that you build an infrastructure to support implementation of D&DM.

LIBRARY GOVERNANCE AND DIVERSITY

Appointments to governing boards or advisory groups should reflect the composition of the community served. It may sound like a statement of the obvious, but it can be tricky to achieve a balanced membership. It is often easy to identify regular users or those known to be supporters of the service, but it is essential also to have representatives from groups who make little use of the services or who do not use them at all. This is one facet of the managerial leader's role that benefits from by being visible and known within the whole community, ensuring that recruitment to the board or group is well-publicized. Political and social skills and networking help to achieve the vital balance.

Alire and Ayala (2007, pp. 184–185) when writing about recruiting Latino public library trustees (which could also be applied to any minority group) stated that the Latino trustee could be the liaison who could assist the library in the following:

- Identifying potential Latino staffing prospects
- Recommending effective programs to attract your underserved Latino community

CHECK THIS OUT

Donna Howell, in "The Politics of Public Library Boards" (*Rural Libraries* 24, no. 1: 15–24, 2004), suggests that the type of people who become trustees may not reflect the diversity of the population as a whole. She holds that this tendency can create a fertile ground for power games.

- Working on good public relations between the library and the Latino community
- Developing library and Latino partnerships/networking with individuals and organizations

STAFFING ISSUES

In an ideal situation, a library's staffing pattern reflects the diversity in the service community. The reality, however, is that it's likely to be a goal rather than an achievement. As a result of past recruitment to the professional schools, the profile of graduates is generally not representative of the community at large. Our earlier discussion of data from ALA's Diversity Counts illustrated the difference between the goal and the reality. Certainly there are fewer minority graduates in the pool of potential recruits. It also extends to the question of identifying staff for promotion if there are, for example, fewer members of minority groups ready for the next step. It takes time to achieve diversity goals, and tokenism is a risk.

RECRUITMENT

Tokenism presents challenges both for a person who may be seen as a "token" appointment and for his or her colleagues. Careful managing is necessary. In the past, women promoted to senior posts could be unpopular with male colleagues who believed they were unjustly passed over for promotion. A token appointment can present challenges beyond resentment, because there may not be ready acceptance into a peer group within the organization.

Position or job descriptions can discriminate in a way that may not be obvious, and so it is essential that they be written with care. The requirements for the post must not disadvantage any one group. Advertisements for vacancies require wide distribution in order to attract people from a diverse community. The local media and the organization's website can draw attention to the positive diversity work that is taking place, thereby attracting the attention of potential candidates.

AUTHORS' EXPERIENCE

One of the first "battles" Alire fought in all three academic libraries she led was starting the process to change the search committee policies and procedures. This included changing the composition of every search committee to include a minority staff member. It also included lessening the required years of experience so that it allowed more candidates of color to compete. Additionally, at one library, she initiated a residency program that encouraged candidates of color to apply and that made "experience working directly with minority groups" a requirement.

In selecting the short list of candidates, you must avoid any discrimination. Having a diverse selection committee will also assist you in achieving the library's diversity goals.

TRAINING

Regular training programs help ensure that existing staff—both paid and volunteer—are receptive to cultural diversity. Everyone must understand the code of acceptable behavior and that breaking the code will have consequences.

For newcomers from minority groups, you might consider having an extra in-service program designed to meet their needs. Most libraries have new hires go through the parent organization's orientation program, which usually covers matters such as the goals of the organization, its values, operating policies and practices, and expectations of new staff members. Offering an in-service program for minority hires can provide additional support and assist in networking.

CHECK THESE OUT

Bonnette, Ashley E. 2004. "Mentoring Minority Librarians up the Career Ladder." *Library Administration and Management* 18, no. 3: 134–139.
Thomas, David A. 2001. "The Truth about Mentoring Minorities: Race Matters." *Harvard Business Review* 79, no. 4: 98–107.

COMMUNICATION

Communication differs among cultures in a number of ways. Using the skills of observation helps one assess the comfort level of colleagues and users. Consider the contrasts between the Japanese and the American approaches to communication. The Japanese may communicate by not stating matters directly, while Americans communicate in a very direct way. In some cultures, it is not usual to question the words of a "superior" person, even for trivial matters. If a person fails to question a request she or he has not fully understood, mistakes may occur, which may affect both parties, whether they are staff or users. It can be particularly challenging for frontline staff who are unsure whether a user has received the right answer to a request. Making assumptions about the level of awareness of local practices and customs is not the wisest course of action.

CHECK THIS OUT

Beamer, Linda, and Iris Varner. 2005. *Intercultural Communication in the Global Workplace.* 3rd ed. New York: McGraw-Hill.

RELIGIOUS BELIEFS

Family obligations of some staff members can cause resentment among those who do not have such responsibilities. A similar issue is that of religious observances and national holidays. The organization may prefer that everyone conform to the holidays and dominant religious festivals of the country, but this practice can be a hardship for those having other religious beliefs or who observe other holidays. A positive approach that allows flexibility often works in services open to the public. For example, within multicultural communities, some staff may be quite willing to trade holidays, thus allowing for more flexible service hours. It can be a win–win situation. The process of achieving diversity is often slower than anyone would like; it is complex and requires sensitivity, patience, time, and monitoring by management.

CHECK THESE OUT

Montgomery, Jack G. 2002. "A Most Delicate Matter: Religious Issues and Conflict in the U.S. Library Workplace." *Library Management* 23, nos. 8/9: 422–434.

Montgomery, Jack G., and Eleanor I. Cook. 2005. *Conflict Management for Libraries: Strategies for a Positive, Productive Workplace.* Chicago: American Library Association.

GENERATIONAL DIFFERENCES

Managing a team of paid and volunteer staff composed of the different generations is challenging. Managerial leaders have the responsibility to ensure that everyone understands and respects the views of others to avoid potential tension.

Today's libraries very likely have paid staff and volunteers. That staffing pattern almost always consists of several generations—veterans, baby boomers, Gen X, and Gen Y. These generations have rather different general approaches to work such as employment expectations and work versus personal time. Often such differences create some tension.

There are now five generations that most writers on generational differences recognize. They don't always agree on the label for each generation, nor do they agree on the beginning and ending dates for the generations.

Those born before 1946 (*veterans* and *traditionals* are two common labels for this group) are almost all retired from full-time work but make up many of the volunteers who have library expertise that can benefit almost any library. Generally, these individuals are disciplined, with a strong respect for orderly processes and a stable organization. Most were inclined toward maintaining stability and are probably less likely to see the environment as posing serious threats to the organization. Those who are still in the workforce or are recently retired were probably exceptions rather than the rule for their generation. Going against type, they did, and still do, see the need to change (not committed to the status quo). However, the younger generations still view the veterans as past-oriented and overly concerned with history. For the younger generations, veterans, while perhaps willing to consider change, are too inclined to want to move slowly.

Baby boomers, born between 1946 and 1964, are the largest of the generations and represent a large number of senior managers today. In their youth, they were considered "rebellious," experimenting with many things as well as questioning operations and authority. However, by middle age they had become rather conservative in their approach to work. They are optimistic, ambitious, and highly loyal and view job status and symbols as important. They are more likely to focus on workplace process and output rather than on implications and outcomes. They do monitor the environment and see change as a necessary part of organizational life; however, again, the younger generations do not see changes implemented by this group as taking place fast enough.

Gen Xers ("latchkey children") were born between 1965 and 1979. Very often, they grew up in a home where both parents worked and thus were on their own sooner than the earlier generations. They tend to be very self-confident, individualistic, self-reliant, and often irreverent, especially about the older generations. In terms of work, they tend to focus on relationships and outcomes rather than on processes and organizational structure. As a result, they need a managerial leadership style that is inclusive, collaborative, and empowering. They can be very loyal to and work hard for a vision they share. They embrace change and are reasonably comfortable with uncertainty.

Gen Y (the "millennium generation," born between 1980 and 1999) is just like Gen X in terms of numbers; the birth rate was substantially lower for both generations than for the baby boomers. They are considered a technology generation; they grew up with the web and all the other information technology we take for granted today. They are more than adept at multitasking. For them, talking on their cell phones while doing something else or listening to music off the Internet while working on the computer is second nature. They are a now-oriented generation, and they are not used to waiting long for anything (even

CHECK THIS OUT

Pixey Anne Mosley published a good article on mentoring Gen Xers in a 2005 issue of *Library Administration and Management,* titled "Mentoring Gen X Managers: Tomorrow's Library Leadership Is Already Here" (19, no. 4: 185–192).

responses from supervisors). Patience is not seen as a virtue. Rapid change lies at the heart of their lifestyle; if nothing else, it is part of their technology-based approach to life. They are highly tolerant of diversity. They have a great tolerance for variation, and they expect they will receive the same type of tolerance toward themselves.

What motivates Gen Y? First and foremost, they want to know how they fit into the "big picture" and how they can make a difference. Coaching is a preferred method for gaining new skills. Continuous learning is something with which they are very comfortable. Respecting their creativity and diversity is very important. They respond better to informal and electronic communication than they do to formal written material. Above all, they expect state-of-the-art technology to be available in the workplace and that staff will make effective use of the technology's capabilities.

The newest generation, sometimes labeled *Linksters, Gen Z,* the *Digital Generation,* or *Gen Next,* will be in the workforce in a few years and add more variation to the managerial leader's mix. Depending on how long the slow economic recovery takes, they may have orientations that reflect the values of both Gen Y and the veterans who grew up during and after the Great Depression of the 1930s and early 1940s.

With increasing numbers of volunteers and no age set for retirement as well as the recession, age variations among staff members can be wide, representing specific motivators for different generations.

Veteran (1929–1946) motivators:
- Prefer formality rather than informality
- Communicate face-to-face and by phone, not e-mail or voice mail
- Need an explanation of the logic of actions
- Appreciate traditional recognition—plaques, photos, and so forth

Baby boomer (1946–1966) motivators:
- Need to see clear steps toward defined goals
- Want stated objectives and desired results in people-centered teams
- Love pep talks

CHECK THIS OUT

Richard Sweeney's article "Reinventing Library Buildings and Services for the Millennial Generation" (*Library Administration and Management* 19, no. 4: 165–175, 2005) provides useful insights for thinking about generational differences for the newest group to join the workforce.

CHECK THESE OUT

Two good books on managing/leading multigenerational staff are these:

Megan and Larry Johnston's *Generations, Inc.: From Boomers to Link-sters—Managing Friction between Generations at Work* (New York: American Management Association, 2010)

Chip Espinoza, Mick Uklja, and Graig Rush's *Managing the Millennials* (Hoboken, NJ: John Wiley and Sons, 2010)

A good article is Gail Munde's "Considerations for Managing an Increasingly Intergenerational Workforce in Libraries" (*Library Trends* 59, no. 2: 88–108, 2010).

- Prefer recognition with wide public profile (e.g., in an organization's newsletter)

Gen X (1966–1979) motivators:
- Tell them what needs to be done, but not how
- Give multiple tasks, but allow them to set priorities
- Avoid platitudes and buzzwords
- Ask for their reactions and opinions
- Allow time for fun
- Don't give pep talks
- Offer regular honest feedback and mentoring/coaching

Gen Y (1980–1999) motivators:
- Provide opportunities for continuous learning and building skills
- Know their goals and explain how they fit into the "big picture"
- Emphasize the positive
- Be more of a coach, less of a boss
- Communicate informally through e-mail and hallway conversations

PROVIDING SERVICE TO A DIVERSE COMMUNITY

Liu and Redfern (1997) surveyed students at San José State University, where the minorities accounted for 51 percent of the total student population. They found that for 60 percent of minorities English was their second language, over half coming from an Asian country. Statistical analyses indicated that a student's level of success in using the library was related to English-language proficiency, frequency of library use, and the frequency of reference desk inquiries. Among those who were less successful, the reasons for not asking for help at the reference desk were as follows (Liu and Redfern, 1997):

- Afraid of asking stupid questions
- Afraid that their English was not good enough
- Afraid of not understanding the answers well enough
- Did not think of asking questions
- Did not understand the role of the reference librarian

These findings are likely to be common in any culturally diverse community.

Users have to overcome difficulties if they are to gain the information they need; students, for example, are highly motivated to succeed with their education. However, the barriers to use can be greater in the case of a public library where the degree of motivation for use may be less. Public libraries may be forbidding to those who do not speak the language of the community, especially if they are first-time users. Instruction and coaching are likely to be needed in using computers and accessing catalogs and databases.

AUTHORS' EXPERIENCE

You never can be certain what or why cultural conflicts will arise in the workplace. Sometimes the underlying issue is personal, and cultural views just magnify the animosity. At one time Evans had a secretary who was a Mexican citizen and was married to a U.S. diplomat, and he also had a budget officer in the administrative office who believed the secretary was "gaining too much power." In addition, the office had work-study students who were selected primarily by the secretary. Often when the student was Hispanic the secretary discussed work in Spanish. This only increased the budget officer's irritation because the officer did not speak Spanish.

Things came to a head when flyers started appearing in the staff lounge and on tables in public areas saying, "The U.S. is an English ONLY country—USE IT." When another staff member saw and reported that the budget officer was distributing the flyers, Evans had a sound basis for having a meeting with the woman. Meetings like that are painful, contentious, stressful, heated, and so forth, but they *must* take place.

Evans never was certain what aspect of the session had an impact but the flyers stopped, and there was slightly less visible tension between the two women. Was it the suggestion that distribution of the flyers might be considered the basis for a lawsuit? Was it the suggestion that disciplinary action would follow if the problem persisted? Was it that the budget officer should have more respect for other languages as she was originally from Canada and had learned French (why not learn Spanish if she really wanted to know what was being said)? Perhaps all played a part. What Evans is certain of was that the person's feelings about the matter had not changed.

Having respect for people and culture as well as modeling that respect is an important element in managing diversity. Your big challenge is in terms of your staff, especially those in public service activities. When there is a lack of respect by one or more staff members toward certain categories of users, there can be substantial damage done to the library's reputation in some segments of the service community—not just within the group that experiences the lack of respect.

It is a fact of life that individuals hold views, sometimes extremely negative, about those they consider "other." It is also a fact of life that such individuals have the right to hold whatever views they wish and, within certain legal limits, the right to express their views. Your challenge, as a managerial leader, is how to control such expressions and conflicts in the workplace. You will have some laws on your side, but you are neither a lawyer nor a law officer. Certainly you can and should, when necessary, make the legal issue(s) clear to the staff. You can model expected behavior and provide sensitivity workshops (be certain you attend these, as this also models their importance). You may be able to get help from the human relations department; you might even begin progressive discipline in egregious cases (we cover progressive discipline in the next chapter). One or more of these options may work with this or that individual but not with everyone. As one member of our advisory board commented, "Good Luck" when it comes to managing cultural conflict. We agree that there is more than a modicum of luck when it comes to this challenge. We also believe that by following the ideas in this chapter you can reduce the amount of luck you'll need.

COLLECTIONS AND CULTURAL DIVERSITY

Alire and Ayala (2007, p. 154) identified management issues that could have a considerable impact on collection development:

- Reviewing collection development policies and practices
- Linking collections to the results of a needs assessment of the minority group(s)
- Establishing an advisory group
- Dealing with the lack of a second language skill among collection development staff
- Encouraging the development of a support system for collection development staff

CHECK THIS OUT

Neely, Teresa Y., and Kuang-Hwei Lee-Smeltzer. 2001. "Diversity Now: People, Collections and Services in Academic Libraries." *Journal of Library Administration* 33, nos. 1/2: 1–3.

CHECK THESE OUT

Mason, Karen M. 2002. "Fostering Diversity in Archival Collections: The Iowa Women's Archives."*Collection Management* 27, no. 2: 23–31.
Neal, Kathryn M. 2002. "Cultivating Diversity." *Collection Management* 27, no. 2: 33–42.

The majority of libraries will have an acquisitions policy, but not all may have fully addressed the question of diversity. Our earlier discussion on bilingual collections at the beginning of this chapter highlighted the fact that strong differences of opinion exist about the concept both in and out of the profession. Public and school libraries may find it difficult to gain consensus on the issue, especially when community input is part of the policy development process.

AUTHORS' EXPERIENCE

Some years ago, Evans wrote about creating collections to serve a diverse population. In his article, he illustrated just a few possible purposes for such collections. You could develop a collection that reflects:

- The root culture, to help it maintain its heritage and social values
- The experiences of the ethnic group in the United States
- Survival skills and general information about life in the United States
- The changing nature of society, emphasizing social changes in the root culture
- Relations with other ethnic groups
- The current situation of the group in the United States
- The future of the group in American society
- Educational needs of adults and children in various formal and informal educational programs

You can probably think of still other purposes for such collections and can understand how complicated getting agreement might be for one or two purposes. Even in the best of times there is not enough funding to meet all the above and still address other necessary aspects of collection development.

For a more complete discussion of items in the list, see G. Edward Evans's "Needs Analysis and Collection Development Polices for Culturally Diverse Populations" (*Collection Building* 11, no. 4: 167, 1992).

Making the collections accessible through appropriate subject headings and signage, in more than one language, will also help some segments of the service community be more comfortable using the library. Multilingual OPACs allow users to work in the language in which they are most comfortable. The use of different languages to describe how to search the catalog and the collections helps users to increase their skills in retrieving documents and information.

Exhibitions and displays are effective ways to create awareness of the range of resources available to users. They make a visual statement about the scope of the collection, drawing attention to its multicultural nature and providing a talking point between users and staff. Displays also can draw community groups into the archives or library. Offering a display facility in a public place brings out community pride, provides information to the community at large, and increases the awareness of available services.

KEY POINTS TO REMEMBER

- Cultural diversity touches on many of the manager's responsibilities.
- Cultural diversity affects everyone who interacts with the library.
- We each have a lens through which we view diversity.
- There are laws and regulations to be observed.
- Everyone has the responsibility to value and recognize differences in society.
- An acknowledgment of cultural diversity must be embedded in planning.
- Developing and supervising a diverse staff presents challenges.
- Cultural diversity should affect service to users in a positive manner.

References

Alire, Camila, and Jacqueline Ayala. 2007. *Serving Latino Communities: A How-To-Do-It Manual for Librarians*. 2nd ed. New York: Neal-Schuman.

American Libraries. 2008. "Opinion/Readers Forum: Letters and Comments." *American Libraries* 39, nos. 1/2: 8–11.

Brewer, Miriam L. 2011. "Diversity and Cultural Taboos: What Your Recruitment Practices Say about You." *Franchising World* 43, no. 6: 28–30.

Carlson, Dawn S., K. Michele Kacmar, and Dwayne Whitten. 2006. "What Men Think They Know about Executive Women." *Harvard Business Review* 84, no. 9: 28–29.

Deyrup, Marta Mestrovic. 2004. "Is the Revolution Over? Gender, Economic, and Professional Parity in Academic Library Leadership Positions." *College and Research Libraries* 65, no. 3: 242–250.

Hofstede, Geert. 1991. *Cultures and Organizations: Software of the Mind*. New York: McGraw-Hill.

Kendall, Frances E. 1994. "Creating a Multicultural Environment in the Library." In *Cultural Diversity in Libraries*, edited by Donald E. Riggs and Patricia A. Tarin, 76–91. New York: Neal-Schuman.

Kniffel, Leonard. 2007. "English Only Is English Lonely." *American Libraries* 38, no. 10: 3.

Liu, Mengxiong, and Bernice Redfern. 1997. "Information-Seeking Behavior of Multicultural Students: A Case Study at San Jose State University." *College and Research Libraries* 58, no. 4: 348–354.

Quesada, Todd Douglas. 2007. "Spanish Spoken Here." *American Libraries* 38, no. 10: 41–42, 44.

Royse, Molly, Tiffani Conner, and Tamara Miller. 2006. "Charting a Course for Diversity: An Experience in Climate Assessment." *portal: Libraries and the Academy* 6, no. 1: 23–45.

Shapira, Ian. 2010. "Study: Gen Y Not Defined by Drive." *Arizona Republic,* Sunday April 4: A18.

Skot-Hansen, D. 2002. "The Public Library between Immigration and Cultural Diversity." *Scandinavian Public Library Quarterly* 35, no. 1: 12–13.

Stephens, Julia. 2007. "English Spoken Here." *American Libraries* 38, no. 10: 42–43, 44.

Thomas, R. Roosevelt. 2011. "Developing and Implementing a Diversity Plan." *Franchising World* 43, no. 6: 22–25.

Turock, Betty. 2012. E-mail communication sent to Camila A. Alire, 2012.

Williams, Mark. 2001. *The Ten Lenses: Your Guide to Living and Working in a Multicultural World.* Sterling, VA: Capital Books.

Winston, Mark. 2010. "Managing Diversity." *Library Leadership and Management* 24, no. 3: 58–63.

Wynn, Michael. 1992. *Don't Quit.* South Pasadena, CA: Rising Sun Publishing.

Launching Pad

Al-Qallaf, Charlene L., and Joseph J. Mika. 2009. "Library and Information Services to the Arabic-Speaking Community: A Survey of Michigan Public Libraries." *Public Library Quarterly* 28, no. 2: 127–161.

American Libraries. 2006. "Retired and Inspired: After Leaving Their Jobs These Librarians Find Themselves Busier—and Happier—Than Ever." *American Libraries* 37, no.10: 32–37.

Angell, Kate, Beth Evans, and Barnaby Nichols. 2012. "Reflecting Our Communities: Brooklyn College Library's Internship Program Opens Doors and Minds." *American Libraries* 43, nos. 1/2: 45–47.

Behrens, William. 2009. "Managing Millennials." *Marketing Health Services* 29, no. 1: 10–21.

Darby, Lakeshia. 2005. "Abolishing Stereotypes: Recruitment and Retention of Minorities in the Library Profession." *Rural Libraries* 25, no. 1: 7–17.

Fontenot, Mitch. 2010. "Diversity: A Task Force—Survey of the Literature and Some Possible Trends for Academic Libraries." *Louisiana Libraries* 73, no, 1: 8–11.

Hankins, Rebecca, Michele Saunders, and Ping Situ. 2003. "Diversity Initiatives vs. Residency Programs." *College and Research Libraries News* 64, no. 5: 308–310, 315.

Howland, J. S. 2001. "Challenges of Working in a Multicultural Environment." *Journal of Library Administration* 33, nos. 1/2: 105–123.

Knapp, Jeffrey, Loanne Snavely, and Linda Kliczyk. 2012. "Speaking Up: Empowering Individuals to Promote Tolerance in the Academic Library." *Library Leadership and Management* 26, no. 1: 1–17.

Morgan, Jennifer Craft, Brandy Farrar, and Irene Owens. 2009. "Documenting Diversity among Working LIS Graduates" *Library Trends* 58, 2: 192–214.

Shachaff, Pnina, and Mary Snyder. 2007. "The Relationship between Cultural Diversity and User Needs in Virtual Reference Services." *Journal of Academic Librarianship* 33, no. 3: 361–367.

Strack, Rainer, Jens Baier, and Anders Fahlander. 2008. "Managing Demographic Risk." *Harvard Business Review* 86, no. 2: 119–128.

Tannen, Deborah. 1996. *Gender and Discourse*. New York: Oxford University Press.

Voelck, Julie. 2003. "Directive and Connective: Gender-Based Differences in the Management Styles of Academic Library Managers." *portal: Libraries and the Academy* 3, no. 3: 393–418.

Zemon, Mickey, and Alice Harrison Bahr. 2005. "Career and/or Children: Do Female Academic Librarians Pay a Price for Motherhood?" *College and Research Libraries* 66, no. 5: 394–405.

In many local governments, there are at least three groups or organizational units that share responsibility for human resource functions: managers and supervisors, human resource professionals and attorneys.

    —Amy M. McDowell and William M. Leavitt (2011)

Succession planning is active planning that ensures an organization will have the right people in the right place at the right time for the right job.

    —Pat Hawthorne (2011)

The twenty-first century workforce has experienced tremendous changes due to advances in technology; the "old way" of doing things may be effective but not efficient. The best way to prepare potential employees for tomorrow's workforce is to develop not only technical but also human-relation abilities.

    —Geana W. Mitchell, Leane B. Skinner, and Bonnie J. White (2010)

Performance appraisal (PA) is a fixture in management and a fact of life in the majority of libraries in the United States. Unfortunately, it is a part of library life that most people dread, no matter on which side of the appraisal they find themselves.

    —G. Edward Evans (2004)

16

STAFFING

This chapter focuses on the following:

- People make the difference
- Legal concerns in human resource management
- Planning staffing needs
- Staffing procedure
- Recruitment
- New employee orientation
- Developing and retaining staff
- Performance appraisal
- Volunteers

A RATHER COMMON statement, or some variation, from managerial leaders is "managing things is easy, managing people is the challenge." Indeed, things are much more predictable than people. However, the bottom line is that the staff are what make a great library regardless of how challenging they are. Staff, paid and volunteers, translate a library's strategic plan into services and collections for the community. They determine how the users and community view the library. All the other resources, no matter how rich they may be, can't, in the long term, overcome poor staffing—poor in the sense of skills and attitudes about one small word: service.

Every library would like to have a staff of the best and brightest people with a strong service orientation. Achieving that goal takes time, effort, and planning. Two elements in securing the people with that service focus are hiring individuals who are happy and hiring people who really do like people. "Hire happy people" may seem trite; however, there is research that shows ("Service with a Very Big Smile," 2007) that doing so does make a positive difference in customer service and satisfaction.

Hiring the right people is part of the mix for achieving quality service to users. There is also your opinion about what is needed. David Drickhamer (2006) opened his article on managing staff with the following statement: "Many operations managers believe as a matter of faith that if they take care of their employees—offer continuous training, regularly assess their performance, and treat them with the same respect with which they would like to be treated—those employees will help deliver superior performance. Lo and behold, it's true" (p. 42).

Most of the preceding chapters address people issues in one way or another and what you can do to carry out Drickhamer's points. In this chapter, we look at how you go about securing the best possible people, retaining those employees, and assessing their performance. Essentially this is a chapter on what organizations usually label human resource management (HR or HRM).

Staffing has never been simple, but in the past 25 years it has become even more complex. Increasing government regulations regarding employment practices (from recruitment to dismissal, resignation, and retirement) have created challenges for anyone involved in HR; look back at our opening quotation from McDowell and Leavitt, noting especially their mention of attorneys. Other factors complicating staffing are stagnant or diminishing budgets that often require staff adjustments, changing expectations of staff regarding the workplace, and employees' concerns about compensation and benefits. Recruitment and retention have become major concerns in most organizations, not just libraries. Finding and keeping people with the requisite skill sets is a challenge that grows more problematic.

Getting the best and brightest does not magically occur. You need to expend a significant amount of time on thoughtful planning. Effective HR programs utilize a series of steps, all of which require a thorough understanding of the country's employment laws and regulations. Once that understanding exists, the staffing procedure normally consists of eight steps:

1. Determining needs
2. Designing each job
3. Recruiting
4. Selecting
5. Providing orientation and training
6. Giving appropriate evaluations
7. Coaching and disciplining
8. Handling resignations and terminations

LEGAL CONCERNS IN HUMAN RESOURCE MANAGEMENT

Before exploring the eight HR steps, we start by looking at legal issues that impact those steps and how attorneys play an increasing role in the staffing process. There are four primary areas where legal concerns come into play in HR. First are the laws related to recruitment and selection. Second are factors related to equal opportunities such as promotions and training. Third, when it comes to retention, are laws and legislation that impact what you can and can't do in terms of compensation and benefits as well as health and safety factors. Fourth, for many public sector libraries, are issues about labor contracts (unions) and other aspects of labor relations.

Over the past 20 years, in the United States, it seems that every few months there is a new law, court decision, regulation, or guideline that impacts personnel matters. Monitoring the social, political, and legal dimensions of personnel or HR can be a full-time job.

Many of the legal issues in HR trace their roots back to the U.S. Constitution and the right of equal opportunity. As is often the case, national legislation follows after state action has led the way. The first federal legislation regarding employment equal opportunity was the 1964 Civil Rights Act.

Fair or equal employment opportunity (EEO) refers to an individual's right to employment and promotion without regard to race, color, religion, sex, age, health, or national origin. Any employer who does take such factors into consideration is practicing either overt or covert discrimination. Today, few employers purposefully fail to follow the various EEO laws. More often than not, the problem is covert—the outcome of procedures or processes that, while not intending to discriminate, have an outcome that is discriminatory (unlawful). The concept applies to all phases of employment—not just hiring but also promotion, training opportunities, and so forth.

Many seemingly "fair" procedures, such as pre-employment tests, can be discriminatory if certain categories of applicants fail the test at a higher rate than the average for the test (covert discrimination). Testing, evaluation, and selection of new employees must be done in terms of real job-related criteria or bona fide occupational qualifications (BFOQs), to use the U.S. legal phrase. Generally, race, color, religion, age, sex, ethnic background, disability, and marital status are not valid criteria—"generally" because there may be circumstances when one or more of them may be legal requirements, for example, when selecting models for advertising or actors for a play or a movie. However, in the case of libraries, we are unaware of a circumstance in which any of these would be a BFOQ for a position.

Another employment law phrase that is important to understand is affirmative action. Until very recently, affirmative action required employers to make an extra effort to hire and promote people in one of the "protected minorities." Under federal law, using current terminology, the protected groups are women, Latino/Latina, Asian and Pacific Islanders, African Americans, and American Indians. The goal of affirmative action is to counteract the effects of past discrimination, even though the current employer may not have had any role in creating past inequalities. In essence, the goal is to have the workforce more or less mirror the composition of the population in the local job market.

By the mid-1980s, affirmative action plans were legally complex, and some employers and nonprotected groups believed they were too complex. A 1987 U.S. Supreme Court decision in *Johnson v. Transportation Agency, Santa Clara County,* started a process that has reduced legal complexity but made it more confusing in practical terms. Table 16.1 presents a small sample of federal laws that influence your staffing activities. There will be state regulations as well and in some cases local government interests too, such as merit systems (we discuss merit systems and unions later in this chapter).

As noted earlier, employment legislation and regulation touches on all aspects of HR, from recruitment to retirement. Library managerial leaders must draw on the assistance of and depend on their human resources/person-

TABLE 16.1   Examples of Major Employment Legislation in the United States

Year Enacted	Legislation
1963	Equal Pay Act
1964	Civil Rights Act
1967	Age Discrimination Act
1970	Occupational Safety and Health Act
1974	Privacy Act
1978	Pregnancy Discrimination Act, Mandatory Retirement Act
1986	U.S. Supreme Court Ruling on Sexual Harassment
1986	Immigration and Control Act
1988	Worker Adjustment and Retraining Act
1990	Americans with Disabilities Act
1991	Civil Rights Act
1993	Family and Medical Leave Act

nel offices to avoid making mistakes that can lead to legal problems for the organization.

Legislation may set a national minimum wage, which is a factor for many libraries that frequently depend on part-time hourly workers. Government regulations may also set the hours that an employee should work per day or per pay period. Requiring someone to work beyond the legal amount requires paying a higher rate, such as "time and a half" or "double time." In some cases, the regulations may limit the options of either or both the employer and the employee as to the form of extra compensation—time off or money.

EEO and affirmative action certainly play a role in how and where you recruit for a position. They influence the types of information and questions that you can and cannot collect or ask during the recruitment/selection phase.

Workplace health and safety issues are frequently part of state or national employment laws and regulations. The Occupational Safety and Health Administration (OSHA) in the United States handles many of the issues, such as workplace air quality, exposure to and handling of materials that may pose a long-term health threat, and the required safety equipment. In the United States there are laws—local, state, or national—that relate to issues such as smoking and passive smoke in the workplace, AIDS in the workplace, and substance abuse. All of these issues involve dual rights or concerns; for example, the person who smokes and feels he or she has the right to smoke at work and the nonsmokers who think they have a right to a smoke-free workplace. These tend to be highly complex issues and a challenge to resolve.

You may encounter a variety of situations where libraries must work with unions or collective bargaining units. Many libraries have no unions, some have only staff unions, others have all nonsupervisory staff in a collective bargaining unit, and a small number have all but a very few of the top administrative staff in such groups. Regardless of what or how many staff are part of such groups, the contract or agreement adds another layer to HR activities.

Finally, there are regulations that impact the benefits of the employees. These range from retirement program contributions to paid and unpaid leaves for maternity or paternity or other family reasons.

By this point you can understand that there are indeed legal complexities to HR work. Also, it is why McDowell and Leavitt (2011) wrote:

> There is no question that the quantity and complexity of federal and state laws impacting the work of local government human resource departments has increased dramatically in the last few decades. . . . It would be fool-hardy for managers, supervisors, and human resource department personnel to set out through the minefield of employment laws and regulations without the competent guidance of attorneys who regularly practice in this area of law. (p. 240)

DETERMINING STAFFING NEEDS

"Workforce planning is a broad and more comprehensive approach to planning for overall workforce needs, not just for leadership or specific skills and knowledge, and it may involve extraordinary growth in workforce needs or significant downsizing" (Hawthorne, 2011, p. 8). Spending time to plan staffing needs is something effective managerial leaders do on a regular basis. An unfortunate fact of library managerial life is the major challenge of getting and keeping staff positions. It is rare to receive a new FTE (full-time equivalent) position the first time you ask for one. You may have trouble keeping a vacant position during economic downturns. Planning for staffing needs provides you some lead time and should include well-formulated reasons for keeping or increasing the staff size.

Assessing staffing needs starts with an assessment of existing staff. The purpose of this is to help identify what type and how many staff you will need in the future. Doing an inventory of current staff in terms of years of experience (perhaps grouped into categories of 5, 10, and 15 years of experience), skill sets (linguistic, technical, professional, customer relations), and potential for advancement helps start the process.

When it comes to estimating losses, you should consider four factors: retirements (relatively easy to project), promotions, transfers, and terminations (voluntary and nonvoluntary). One way to project a number for these factors is to assume past rates will probably continue at the same level in the future. Today, more and more organizations are asking about retirement time frames (Fisher,

2006) to assist both in planning for needs as well as in thinking about how to address institutional memory loss.

Unfortunately for many libraries, estimating the number of positions lost (nonreplacement) is a significant issue. Budget cuts are a major factor in losing positions; all too often a "temporary hiring freeze" becomes a permanent reduction in staff. New technologies may result in the loss of one type of position but will add a new type. Changes in service emphasis can cause a reduction in or phasing out of one type of position and an increase in another type. Reorganizations also result in changing skill set needs.

For most libraries, it is easier to secure additional funding for things than it is to get authorization to add new staff. Thus, estimates of changing types of staff for existing positions (usually referred to as FTE) are usually more accurate than estimates of new FTEs. New programs, new buildings, and increased workloads are the normal basis for requesting additional FTEs.

Assessing the "labor market" is part of the staffing process. As Bridges and Johnson (2006) noted, the root causes of both a skilled staff shortage and an aging workforce are related and include the following:

- Demographic trends affecting the size of the available workforce
- Demographic trends affecting the age of the available workforce
- Attraction of both industry and position available
- Hiring freezes and tenure based retention (p. 8)

We believe that the last two points are particularly important for libraries.

AUTHORS' EXPERIENCE

In two of the three university libraries Alire led, the information technology infrastructure was supported not by new funds but by salary savings (holding positions open) that were applied to build the necessary ITC infrastructure—personnel as well as state-of-the-art technology. This was basically "robbing Peter to pay Paul"—taking the funds from unfilled positions and putting them into ITC. This was common practice among academic libraries in the 1980s+ when they began building the ITC infrastructure for supporting OPACs. In most cases, the funds to purchase an OPAC were granted on a one-time basis with no additional funds added to the base budget to sustain ongoing technology infrastructure costs.

Evans's experience was more fortunate, as he was allowed to include any personnel requirements into the cost of the ILS systems. One important reason for this was that the total cost of the "projects" was funded by grants and donations.

Knowing how many FTEs to assign to a job type is part of the process of assessing staffing needs. Making this judgment calls for hard data. If the library has some existing workload standards, the process is somewhat easier; often union or collective bargaining agreements address this issue. In the absence of standards or data, the process is more difficult. Almost any unit head would like to have additional staff and can give several sound reasons why such an addition is justifiable. Lacking time to collect accurate in-house data, libraries can secure some measure of objectivity by making comparisons with units of similar size.

STAFFING PROCESS

Earlier we mentioned that staffing is an eight-step process—defining needs; designing each job; recruiting candidates for positions; selecting the right person; providing sound orientation, training, and development opportunities; giving appropriate assessments of job performance; coaching and furnishing fair discipline when necessary; and handling resignations and terminations. We will now look at these in depth.

JOB DESIGN AND DESCRIPTIONS

We will use a model that the U.S. Department of Labor suggests for designing and preparing job descriptions and deciding on the proper selection instruments. Figure 16.1 illustrates the model.

The analysis of staffing needs obviously must take organizational goals (OG) and long-term plans into consideration, just as decisions regarding staffing patterns do. All of the elements become factors in the writing of a sound job description.

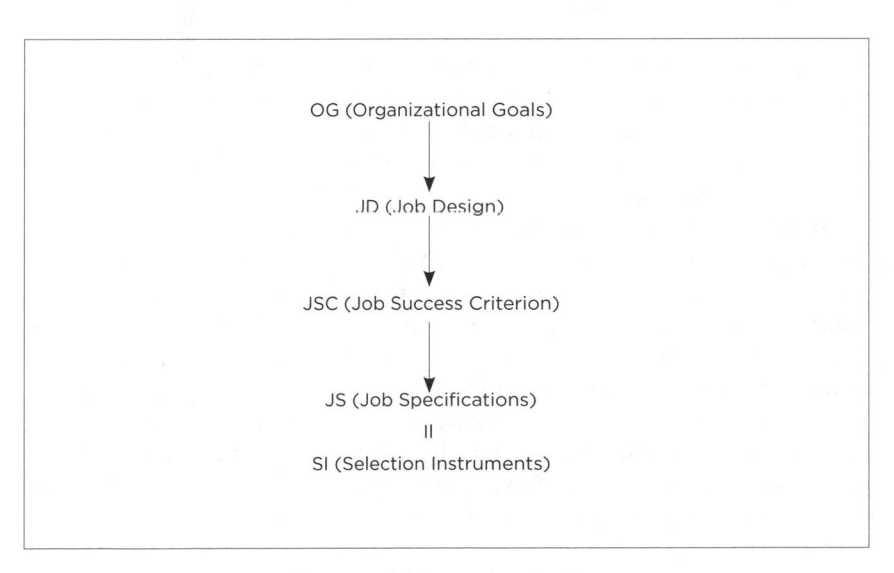

Figure 16.1 U.S. Department of Labor Model for Developing Job Descriptions

Job design (JD) asks the question, "What activities are necessary to accomplish organizational goals?" Answers to this apparently simple question are multiple and complex at times. The goal should be to have a comprehensive list of all tasks, not merely a few broad phrases. For example, a task for a reference service desk work should be more than "answer questions." It should cover all aspects of the work, such as providing answers to in-person questions, handling telephone questions, processing e-mail queries, and assisting users in finding information. Such detail is essential for developing sound job descriptions.

Once you have a list of tasks, it is possible to group them into logically related activities. To assist in the analysis, divide the activities into smaller units, called *elements*. An element is one action, such as opening incoming mail or reading e-mail messages. It is at this point that you may realize the person doing the action is either at a higher or lower level of skill set than is appropriate. Sometimes regrouping actions allows you to improve the unit's cost-effectiveness.

The grouping or regrouping of elements into related actions results in what HR officers refer to as *tasks*. The following would be a set of elements grouped into the task "sort e-mail reference questions":

- Log in to e-mail account
- Read e-mail questions
- Decide who can best answer the question(s)
- Forward question(s) to appropriate person
- Log off

Your next step is to group related tasks into a position—a grouping of tasks performed by one person; a cataloger might constitute a position. Everyone in the library occupies a position, and a position is not necessarily full-time.

A group of similar positions constitutes a job, such as an archivist. Only in the smallest organizations will there be a one-to-one relationship of positions and jobs. In most cases there will be several people in a job category. The elements, tasks, positions, and job become the basis for the job and position description used to recruit and select personnel.

For HR officers there is another step, that of developing a classification system. The purposes of a classification system are to group jobs that require the same skill sets and to provide similar compensation to people in a given class. Because most libraries are part of larger a organization and other units within the larger organization are likely to have jobs calling for similar if not identical skills, HR creates a system that helps to ensure equal pay for equal work. An example is a library IT staff member who maintains the server(s) probably has a skill set similar to that of a person working in a computer center who is responsible for maintaining its servers. Classification systems establish a salary *range*, which means salary differences may exist for individuals in the same classification category.

There are several aspects to job design: job depth, job scope, and work characteristics. Job depth is the degree to which the individual is able to control her or his work. A job that requires close adherence to standards, has detailed procedures for every step, or requires close supervision lacks depth. Depth occurs when there are established outcomes but the means of achieving the outcomes is in the hands of the individual. For a few people, low-depth jobs are what they want, as there is little responsibility beyond following established procedures. For others, only jobs with great depth are satisfactory.

Job scope relates to how many different activities or operations a person performs and how often. As you might expect, a job with few activities and with a high rate of repetition has little scope; the reverse is true for wide-scope jobs. There is also a strong relationship between job scope and where the job appears on an organization chart. Low-scope jobs tend to be first line and near the lower part of the chart.

Job characteristics relate to what it will take to perform the job. These characteristics include which skills are necessary, the knowledge needed, experience, independent judgment required, who the users are, and the importance of the job to the overall well-being of the library. Obviously there is an interconnection between job depth, scope, and characteristics; jobs of high depth and wide scope call for more knowledge, skill, and experience than do jobs with lower degrees of these factors. You should keep all three in mind as you engage in organizing.

JOB SUCCESS CRITERIA

Another step is establishing job success criteria (JSC). JSC are the key to selecting the right person for the right position. Establishing JSC is the most difficult and subjective of the steps in the model. While the goal is simple to state, what distinguishes successful from unsuccessful performance in the position is difficult to determine. What constitutes success will vary from library to library and, from time to time, within the same library. Many professionals would agree that these items could or should be on any list of JSC for a reference position:

- Accurately determine the nature of questions
- Provide accurate answers to questions

However, they might modify their view if any of the following were to occur:

- Accurate, but the person is abrasive to user
- Accurate but is "talkative" with selected users and handles fewer questions
- Accurate, quick, and pleasant with users but abrasive with colleagues

Before starting to interview candidates, you and the search committee should understand what JSC are appropriate and sought for the vacancy. Also, it is essential that JSC are the result of agreement among those currently performing the work, senior management, and the parent body's HR office.

TRY THIS

Look at four advertisements for library positions. What information is provided about (a) the organization placing the advertisement; (b) the position; and (c) the criteria for appointment? Compare the amount of information provided in the advertisements.

JOB SPECIFICATIONS

Job specifications (JS) are the skills, traits, knowledge, and experience that should
result in successful performance. JS frequently appear in job descriptions and
advertisements such as education required, years of experience, and a list of the
specific skills sought. From a legal point of view, you should be certain that the
items listed are in fact BFOQs (bona fide occupational qualifications). Merely saying that it is so will not satisfy a court; you must be able to prove it is true. Thus you
should not specify a master's degree in library or information science is required
unless you are ready to prove that the degree is *necessarily a prerequisite for success.*

SELECTION INSTRUMENTS

After completing the job description, which draws on the JSC and JS, you should
be able to identify the appropriate selection instruments (SI). During the 50-plus
years of legislation regarding equal employment and affirmative action, there have
been numerous U.S. court cases that in one way or another impact the selection
process. Often the cases grew out of requirements that were not clearly associated
with successful job performance. An example of an imprecise statement is "the
successful applicant will have a lively personality." We don't know which would
be more difficult to prove: (a) that a lively personality was essential for successful
job performance or (b) what factors are present in a "lively" personality. A better
way of getting at what the writers of such statements are looking for would be to
seek individuals with a "demonstrated ability to work effectively with customers
and staff in a highly service-oriented environment." Although more "wordy," it is
much clearer about what the library is seeking and less open to question. Another
example would be: instead of using the phrase "good speaking ability," use something like "make oral presentations of technical material in such a manner as to be
easily understood by a nontechnical audience."

Both of the suggested wordings could lead to appropriate selection instruments. For the first statement, evidence of demonstrated success could take the
form of letters from previous supervisors and/or coworkers that specifically
address the issue. Or, members of the search committee might ask the referees
a question about the issue. Whichever method you and the selection committee
decide on, the applicant(s) should know there will be inquiries about the issue.

Written testing is usually done only in positions that have modest to low-
level responsibilities, although some civil service libraries have written tests for
all positions—professional and nonprofessional. Oral presentations and the use

of an interview question, such as "What would you do in the following situation . . . ?," are both forms of testing. While it may appear self-evident that all applicants should go through an identical screening process, this is not always the case. (Asking slightly different questions or adding or omitting an activity to a candidate's interview would constitute a different screening process.) Today, identical screening is essential to be legal.

RECRUITMENT

Once you know the position needs, the search begins for suitable applicants. Large libraries often conduct national searches for their professional positions while drawing the majority of their nonprofessionals from the local area.

Advertisements for openings should provide the basic job description information and indicate where and when a person should apply. Recruitment takes time; a national search will probably require four to six months. This estimate covers the time from the development of the position description to the time the successful applicant begins work.

The search could begin as an internal process; that is, an announcement of a vacancy goes to the library's staff. In some organizations, the policy is to interview any internal candidates before going outside. More often, the search is both internal and external—with the internal applicants having the advantage of knowing more about the organization's issues. You must place advertisements or recruit in places where persons in the "protected categories" are likely to see the announcements.

Once there is a pool of applicants, the review or screening process begins. The process involves several elements: the application form, letters or statements of interest, the pre-employment test results (if required), a personal interview, and verification of qualifications and past work experience. Normally, you select only a few individuals for in-person interviews. The screening process relies on the applicant to supply the requisite information regarding her or his qualifications.

APPLICATION FORMS

The application can provide a great deal of information about the person not only from the data provided but also from its presentation. It can reveal a good deal about the individual's motivation, writing skills, maturity, and ability to understand and follow directions. Such forms usually provide the following information:

- The applicant's work history, including tenure in each position listed
- The applicant's educational background
- Names of persons to contact regarding the applicant's suitability for the position

There are certain questions you may not ask on the application or during the interview. These questions are those that could lead to discriminatory practices. Obvious questions about the applicant's race, religion, and age are not acceptable. Some forms have a space to indicate sex but often indicate this is "optional" information. There are times when the information about the applicant's sex would be useful. For example, not everyone's given name clearly identifies her or his gender. When writing to an applicant prior to meeting, a person with a gender-neutral name should be addressed as "Dear Applicant."

When using the phrase "or equivalent" for a skill or background, you must be ready to clearly state what is and is not equivalent. Because the application form normally provides the basis for the initial screening of applicants to determine interview invitees, the form should provide space to list information regarding equivalent training and experience. Having a space on the form or requesting a written statement regarding any "or equivalents" will usually satisfy legal requirements.

National searches as opposed to local ones present several challenges. Two significant challenges are costs and time. Few organizations have enough money to pay the travel and lodging expenses of every potential candidate. It is also unreasonable to expect candidates to pay their own way unless they have a very good chance of being selected. Professional association meetings, such as ALA, are a partial means of reducing costs. A limiting factor to using such occasions is that setting up a meeting time can be a challenge, because both the interviewer and interviewee will probably have program interests and obligations. Also, when using a search committee, it is likely only one person from the committee will be making a judgment about a person's potential for the position.

COVER LETTERS AND STATEMENTS OF INTEREST

Institution-based application forms usually are very general; they seldom provide the applicant with an opportunity to demonstrate why she or he is suitable for the position. Requesting a cover letter stating the applicant's interest in the position and what special skills and experience she or he has helps bridge the gap between an institutionwide application blank and an in-person interview.

Letters of interest are useful, especially if the person has the full job description, not merely the advertisement text. Advertisements tend to be short because of cost concerns, and they seldom provide enough information for preparing meaningful statements. Posting the full description on the web gives the applicant a better understanding of the job's duties and what her or his chances are as well as what to include in a statement. Most applicants and screeners believe such documents are very helpful, as they provide a fuller and fairer picture of the applicant.

TESTS

If a vacant position calls for "testable" skills, it is very useful to have preinterview tests. Testing has been criticized on several grounds: invalidity, invasion of privacy, or discrimination against certain classes of applicants. The only pre-employment tests that are legal in library settings are those that assess a common skill: typing, alphabetizing, numerical computation, or similar measurable traits. A number of such tests exist, and they are valid. If a JSC is the requirement to type 70 words a minute error-free, there is no reason to interview a person who manages to achieve only 30 error-free words per minute. This, of course, assumes the 70-word error-free requirement is a valid JSC.

INTERVIEWS

The interview provides the opportunity to explore in-depth the applicant's background, experience, knowledge, and expertise, as well as oral and social skills. From the applicant's point of view, the interview provides an opportunity to assess the position, potential coworkers, and the institution. Interviews and how you handle them is a key component in hiring the best and brightest people. You should plan the interview process to secure the most useful information from the interview time.

There are six aspects that ought to be part of any interview process—first is planning it. Beyond the obvious—such as when to conduct the interview—some of the key planning issues are where to interview, who should do the interview, what questions to ask, what the candidate ought to see, and how much time to build into the process for responding to candidate interests.

The second, and perhaps the most critical, aspect of the interview process is the set of interview questions. This part is crucial for ensuring that the library satisfies EEO requirements. Having a structured format is one of the best ways to ensure compliance as well as consistency and comparability of information about each candidate. It is also helpful in maintaining control of the interview and, at times, keeping an overly talkative candidate "on track."

Third, your questions must be job related. You should be able to link each question to the job description. Lacking such a linkage, it would be best not to ask the question. At the same time you link questions to a job description, asking some open-ended questions can be beneficial. Open-ended questions give candidates an opportunity to respond more fully and demonstrate some of their skills. They also allow the interviewers to learn about oral skills and to assess a candidate's ability to respond to an unexpected situation. The following are sample open-ended legal questions that could apply to a variety of vacancies:

- What would your (current or former) supervisor tell a friend about you?

CHECK THIS OUT

Susan Carol Curzon's *Managing the Interview: A How-To-Do-It Manual for Librarians* (New York: Neal-Schuman, 1995) provides in-depth information about this important aspect of the staffing process.

- What special skills do you think you would bring to this job?
- Who and what has motivated you in the past?
- When did you last perform the duties of our vacant position?
- How would you handle the following situation? (Give some typical "problem" a person performing the job might face.)
- What did/do you most like and dislike about your prior/present position?
- What do you consider one of your major accomplishments in your present position?
- What goals did you set for yourself in your current/last position?
- What does the term "service" mean to you?
- How might you improve your job skills?
- Where do you see yourself a year from now? In three years? Five years? Ten years?
- What would you like to ask me/us about the job, the library, and/or the community?

The fourth consideration is the "personal impact" of both the candidate and the interviewers. Taking a few minutes at the start to create a friendly atmosphere helps candidates relax and be more effective during the formal interview. Things such as tone of voice, eye contact, personal appearance and grooming, posture, and gestures on the part of both candidate and interviewers influence both parties.

Related to impact is how the interviewers respond to the applicant (the fifth aspect). One trait interviewers must be careful to control is nonverbal behavior that may encourage or discourage an applicant in an inappropriate way. Another is to reflect interest in what the candidate is saying. Anyone with extensive experience with the interview process understands just how difficult controlling those two behaviors can be at times.

The final consideration is assessing the applicants' information equitably. These are some of the issues that can cause unfair assessment:

- Overemphasis on negative information for one or two candidates
- Stereotyping the "right" person for the position
- Imprecise job information that leads to looking for irrelevant attributes in the candidates
- Use of different weights for various attributes by different members of a search committee
- Overuse of visual clues about the candidate that are not job related
- Placing too much emphasis on the candidate's similarity—such as sex, race, values—to the interviewer
- Not recognizing "contrast effects" (that is, when a strong candidate follows a very weak candidate, the contrast makes the stronger applicant look even stronger than she or he may be)

SOMETHING TO CONSIDER

The library and information services profession is a relatively small one with a robust network of colleagues working in the various multitype libraries. Before you consider giving a problematic employee an undeserved good recommendation full of inaccuracies, remember that your professional integrity and reputation is on the line. That recommendation could come back and bite you later on.

VERIFICATION AND EVALUATION

One of the more difficult and sensitive areas in any hiring procedure is verification of an applicant's education and work history. Letters of recommendation from former teachers and employers are often of questionable value because of the passage of time since the writer had direct contact with the applicant. It is not unheard of for present employers to write a glowing recommendation for a person they wish would leave. Dismissing an employee may lead to legal action, so some organizations "help" the person find employment elsewhere by giving less than accurate assessments.

Confidentiality issues may arise with references. Some public institutions allow candidates to see letters of recommendation. From the applicant's standpoint, it is unfortunate to keep using a person who is providing less than positive comments. On the other hand, it is almost impossible to secure an honest opinion in writing if the writer knows that the subject of a letter may see the recommendation. Some states (California and Colorado, for example) have open records laws that allow such examination, so use of letters may become even more of a rarity. Another problem is fraudulent education or work history. Some people overstate their previous salaries. Only by checking can you determine whether the candidate has the claimed skills and background. An easy method for verifying a person's educational background is to require certified transcripts mailed directly to the library. Likewise, any professional certification should be verified directly through the certifying agency.

FINAL DECISION

Once all the verification work is in, the final decision takes place. Who is involved in the job offer and salary negotiations may differ, particularly among types of libraries. Academic library administrators tend to be more involved in working with HR. In places where unions are not involved, academic library directors and deans have more leeway in offering and negotiating salary.

In other libraries, particularly public libraries, HR might make the call to the selected candidate to determine if the person is still available and interested in the position. HR is also usually the office that makes the decision on what salary and benefits to offer. Salary-level decisions are a mix of assessing the skills and background of the selectee, that person's prior salary history, and "equity" within the organization's and the work unit's salary structure. One of the most damaging events, in terms of morale, is to have a newcomer receive a higher salary than existing employees with similar skills, background, and experience.

When thinking about a salary offer, people, especially younger people, often consider only what appears on paychecks. Even here, they often fail to think about the impact of taxes and other reductions in "take home" pay. A more accurate way to think about the offer is the total compensation. Beginning people often think only of hourly or annual pay rates, forgetting the benefits package and leave time. Both of these are part of the compensation package. Good wages can be motivators. However, wages have lost some of their attraction and power. When wages are more than enough to ensure survival or a decent standard of living, they begin to be less and less a motivating factor. This is not to say that money becomes unimportant. However, factors such as more challenging work, more meaningful activities, and time off play an equally important role.

In addition to wages, there can be all or some of the following "costs" in retaining employees:

- Fully/partially paid health insurance
- Fully/partially paid dental insurance
- Fully/partially paid life insurance
- Fully/partially paid disability insurance
- Contribution to one or more retirement programs/pension schemes
- Paid vacation and holidays
- Paid sick leave
- Paid family leave
- Fully/partially paid educational expenses
- Paid travel expenses for job-related training

SOMETHING TO CONSIDER

Salary compression is a fact of life and an issue in colleges and universities among faculty new hires. Salary compression occurs when newly hired library faculty are offered a higher salary based on what the current market will bear. This salary is more than the salary of the librarians who are already working in the library. This is perceived by current librarians as unfair as the newly hired librarian may have less seniority and/or less experience. Salary compression in higher education institutions occurs in faculty hires across all schools and disciplines.

- Paid study leave
- Subsidized mortgage
- Relocation costs
- Access to or provision of a maintained vehicle for travel between branches of the library
- Bonuses/awards for service or useful ideas

HR staff know how to present the total compensation package so that a person may accept a position at a wage that is lower than the person originally thought was necessary. That office also works out a starting date for the new employee.

THE NEW EMPLOYEE

A new employee's first few days on the job set the tone for what follows. "Glad to see you; go to work" is not the best method for getting a new person to become a productive employee. By planning a formal orientation process, you create a solid beginning for both the person and the library.

The first day for the new person should be a combination of orientation and some training in the job and time with HR to take care of all the new employee paperwork. Possible events for the first day might include:

- Sending an e-mail to the staff letting them know a new person is starting today and asking them to please welcome the individual
- Starting at the HR office to complete the hiring and payroll process
- Escorting the new employee to the work area and reintroducing the person to her or his supervisor
- Supervisor introducing the person to other members of the department and giving the new employee a few minutes to put away personal items in a desk or workstation
- Supervisor providing a tour of the library, introducing the new person to staff members, and giving a short summary of what the person will be doing
- Returning to the department for an overview of its activities
- Demonstrating duties and activities the person is to perform

FOR FURTHER THOUGHT

Review the events for the first day for a new employee. What information does a new employee need to be given on the first day? Try to list three points that would help to make a new employee feel welcome during the orientation process.

- Providing a period of supervised practice
- Following with a private practice period
- Ending with a review session

During this orientation and training time, which may last for some time when the tasks or duties are complex, the new hire should receive information about the significance of her or his duties. Early and frequent praise helps to develop a good working relationship.

New employees often find the first several days confusing and unsettling. Spreading orientation out over several days helps make the new information, people, and duties less overwhelming. The training also should be flexible in order to adapt to various learning speeds as well as to the person's prior experience.

A new employee's past work experience may influence the way in which the person reacts to training. Experienced professional or supervisory personnel may require only an explanation of objectives, policies, practices, and potential problems. Beginning professionals should know the fundamentals of any starting position, although they will need to understand the local variations from standard practice. In any event, some monitoring will be necessary during the first month or two for beginners.

Most clerical jobs demand careful, specific instruction, as do manual and unskilled jobs. Group training programs are very efficient for such positions, but turnover seldom allows for such training. Libraries that hire a significant number of part-time workers may be able to take advantage of group training.

TIP

Linking a new hire to someone at her or his level in the work group will provide a point of reference for any matters that require clarification—without the new employee feeling that she or he might be asking a supervisor a silly question. It helps the mentor by giving recognition and the motivation to check over those points that are often taken for granted.

DEVELOPING AND RETAINING STAFF

For most of today's libraries, retention of their best people is a concern. The concern is due to hiring freezes and often the loss of a vacant position because of budgetary restraints. Certainly since 2008 employers have been quick to let staff go. In many ways this has caused some of the best and brightest to think, "Why should I have any loyalty to the organization if it has none for me?" For others, all it takes is a hint of staffing changes, real or imagined, or something else perceived as a threat to get them started looking for other employment. They have experienced or heard of organizations that announce a staff reduction and say to the staff, "We don't need you but fully expect you to give a 100 percent work effort until the day you are terminated." The outcome was what you would expect; performance declined, and people left as fast as possible.

With underlying "loyalty" weak at best, having programs that give ample opportunities to grow and develop is an important factor in long-term retention of the best and brightest people. You have two basic training and development areas to consider: specific job-related skills and career development competencies and opportunities.

Libraries today face a rapidly changing technological environment. Keeping staff current with the changes related to their activities is a major challenge, especially in times of "steady state" or declining budgets. Failure to maintain staff skills results in users receiving poorer service, which in turn leads to dissatisfaction with the library. You face a dual technological challenge: acquiring and upgrading the technology and finding training funds. We will cover technology management in some detail in Chapter 18.

Sometimes the HR office offers institutionwide training that the library finds beneficial: basic supervision, improving writing skills, or communicating with customers. One of the drawbacks to these programs is that, except for the very largest organizations, such programs seldom are available more than once a year and may not cover a topic any library staff need. The major drawback of such programs is that they are very general in order to draw enough participants to make the program successful for the organizers. Professional associations are an excellent source of training opportunities. Unfortunately, there are very few such organizational opportunities for support staff. The primary reason is that support staff members have few opportunities for paid travel, and their salaries are substantially lower, making it almost impossible for them to pay for such

---

CHECK THIS OUT

Louis Uchitelle, a *New York Times* reporter, published an interesting book in 2006 about the loyalty question: *The Disposable American: Layoffs and Their Consequences* (New York: Knopf).

AUTHORS' EXPERIENCE

Alire worked hard to engage support staff in training and development. She not only encouraged them to join their respective paraprofessionals' interest group within the respective library associations locally, statewide, and/or nationally but she also provided funds for travel, registration fees, and administrative leave for the library paraprofessionals to be involved. Her philosophy was that the more the support staff get out and network with other paraprofessionals, the more the library benefits in terms of morale, updated skills, and "our library isn't so bad after all" attitudes.

Evans was fortunate to have enough training funds to allow for each support staff member to have up to $500 for attendance at work-related workshops, seminars, and so forth, in addition to funds for the professional staff.

programs on their own. As more educational institutions and professional bodies extend the range of distance education programs, training opportunities will increase.

In addition to funding concerns, you face the problem of limited staffing, at least in most libraries. With limited staff, it becomes difficult to have staff out for training programs for any length of time. Some jurisdictions are so shortsighted that they refuse to give time off to attend training programs even when the staff member is willing to pay for the program—shortsighted because in time the libraries become less and less effective.

PERFORMANCE APPRAISAL

Management theory in the United States holds that performance appraisals are essential to the successful operation of any organization. In theory, it should help the worker to improve performance. There is a substantial list of beliefs about the appraisal process:

- Essential to good management
- Natural, normal part of human activity
- Ensures minimum performance at least
- Only valid method for granting or withholding economic benefits
- Means of maintaining control of production/service
- Essential for employee growth and development
- Essential for motivating employees
- Assesses quality/success of orientation and training programs
- Means of objectively assessing an individual's work-related strengths and weaknesses
- Reflects a continuous analysis of a person's daily work performance

> ### CHECK THESE OUT
>
> You can find an in-depth discussion of performance appraisal in general and in the context of libraries in G. Edward Evans's book *Performance Management and Appraisal: A How-To-Do-It Manual* (New York: Neal-Schuman, 2004). In 2006, Corey E. Miller and Carl Thornton explored the challenges of how to achieve reasonably accurate appraisals in "How Accurate Are Your Performance Appraisals?" (*Public Personnel Management* 35, no. 2: 153–162).

- Reflects an assessment of total performance, not just assigned duties
- Reflects staff members' future and potential for advancement
- Essential for planning library personnel needs
- Key to successful counseling of staff members

This is an impressive list of objectives for a single process, but all writers on management and practitioners know that the process has many land mines. They also know that only sometimes does the actual procedure match the ideal. In reality, the process has two goals that are seldom completely congruent. As you might guess from the list, one goal is administrative in character and the other is behavioral. Administrative goals relate to the employee, while the behavioral goals relate to the actions the employee takes.

Aspects of the administrative goals are highly subjective despite beliefs to the contrary. One aspect in the process is that it becomes the basis for defending the decisions managers make about salary increases, promotions, and dismissals. Another aspect is attempting to create "comparable data" from a series of subjective judgments by a number of supervisors/managers.

Confidential or secret aspects of the administrative process, where very few people know the results, are part of the need to have data to defend a judgment. Related to the preceding aspect is the fact that unless a person files a grievance, at least in the United States, the person seldom is fully informed about what and why certain judgments occurred.

Behavioral goals should help the individual identify areas where improvement is possible or necessary. These goals also identify areas where personal development might be desirable from the organization's point of view. Identifying exceptional performance is also part of the process. Statisticians will tell anyone who will listen that the "bell-shaped" curve is the normal distribution of data; that is, the vast majority of cases will fall into the middle-average part of the curve. On the other hand, anyone who reviews a significant number of appraisal forms knows that most organizations consist of primarily above-average or exceptional employees—mathematically impossible but managerially possible once a year.

Saul Gellerman (1976) identified the features of appraisal that achieve the "best" results:

Administrative purposes:
- Secretive
- Fixed
- Bureaucratic

Behavioral purposes:
- Candid
- Flexible
- Individualized

Attempting to achieve both sets of purposes in a single process is almost ludicrous. It would be better to utilize two separate systems, one for each purpose. Many organizations claim they do this by calling the annual process an "annual development review" and asserting that there is no connection between that process and any later salary adjustments; few employees believe this.

To gather the "comparable" data, organizations usually have an "appraisal form" that uses one of three formats: rating system, ranking system, and written performance criteria system. Ranking systems require a supervisor to rank each subordinate from 1 to "n"—for example, a supervisor with seven subordinates would rank them from 1 to 7. Such systems require each person to have an individual rank—no ties. Some supervisors who must use this system believe it can generate an environment in which teamwork becomes difficult, as there are no equals when it comes to performance assessment. The written system is the least comparable across the organization, even when there is a list of work-related factors managers are to address.

Most rating systems use a five-level approach, with average in the middle and with two above and two below average. When it is time to conduct the appraisal process, there are some steps you can take to make it as positive as possible. One step is to make certain everyone has a shared understanding of the terms and categories used on the appraisal form. To say, "you are a little below (or a little above) average but not enough to warrant disciplinary action or to receive an award" will generate anger, arguments, tension, and frustra-

FOR FURTHER THOUGHT

Write down three reasons why you think that performance appraisal is important. List six points that you would wish to see covered in an appraisal interview.

AUTHORS' EXPERIENCE

Evans worked for one university that required every department to have one employee in the unacceptable category every year. Needless to say, this was difficult, unpleasant, and, in reality, inappropriate. One year he dismissed a staff member and thought that would count for that year's "unacceptable" requirement but received a surprise when told that did not count because the person was gone! The way Evans dealt with the system was to get staff to agree that each person, including himself, would take a turn at being "unacceptable." A drawing of numbers set up the order. The result was an improvement in morale because everyone agreed it made the best of a bad situation.

tion. The individuals receiving slightly below average are not likely to change their performance, because they know the rater is wrong. For those slightly above but not rewarded, the most likely outcome is a drop in performance.

When you say to a person, "you did an average job this year," it usually results in the ratee thinking the rater cannot recognize excellence when it is sitting right in front of him or her. It generates anger and will not reinforce the person's good work habits.

The end result is a steady escalation of ratings until it appears as if all employees "walk on water" all year. This, in turn, leads to the organization imposing quotas that force supervisors to have a bell-curve result.

Performance appraisal is not a universally accepted practice. W. Edwards Deming (1993) listed evaluation by performance, merit rating, or annual review of performance as one of the seven deadly diseases of an organization. In many countries, the practice does not exist. For example, in 1982, Evans and Rugaas published an article that looked at variations in appraisal practices in several countries. In the United States, there is a heavy emphasis on performance appraisals; in the United Kingdom, a moderate emphasis is placed on such appraisals; and in Nordic countries, there is no emphasis. In examining library performance in these countries, it was difficult to determine how the presence or absence of the practice influenced service.

Regardless of what you may think about the process, it does exist as a managerial fact of life in many countries. In such cases, you must learn to make the process as useful as possible. A key factor is that you must make certain there are no surprises for subordinates. Daily feedback—both immediate praise and correction—is the best way to ensure good work performance. It will also provide some assurance there will be few, if any, surprises at performance appraisal time.

CORRECTIVE ACTION

Normally there is an organizationwide annual formal performance appraisal process. If you want good performance, you should make it an ongoing process. This avoids surprises during the annual review. It also avoids many of the administrative aspects and focuses on the behavioral issues. What you have will be a system that is corrective in character and should produce effective performance from the staff.

Despite the contentions of some human-relations school advocates, you should be willing to show concern when an individual performs in an unacceptable manner—especially when it is a matter of willfulness or neglect. The idea that the superior–subordinate relationship is a delicate, fragile thing that can be easily destroyed by a hasty word or an ill-timed move on the part of the supervisor receives too much emphasis in the human-relations school.

A healthy system provides for a two-way exchange between the managerial leader and the staff member. Each should be free to voice satisfaction or dissatisfaction. Attempts to avoid stress or other issues will solve nothing. When it is necessary to take corrective action—for example, counseling sessions—there are some steps you can follow to make the time as productive as possible. Start by stating the purpose of the session. Even if the situation has the potential for confrontation, speak quietly and plan on letting the employee talk as much as possible. Listen to the person; do not spend time planning a rebuttal. Periods of silence, even long ones, can serve a good purpose—letting the parties think about what is taking place. Setting a time limit for the session often defeats the goal of the session, as it may take a long time to get to the central issue(s).

Expect the employee to be unhappy, probably argumentative, and, occasionally, ready to initiate a "personal" attack. It is difficult but important not to take this behavior personally and not to respond in kind. Total resolution is not the only indication of a successful session. Sometimes it takes a series of sessions to reach a complete resolution. Try to end the session on a positive note and, if appropriate, schedule a follow-up session.

We subscribe to the "Five Rs" of performance counseling:

- Right purpose
- Right approach
- Right time
- Right technique
- Right place

We touched on some of the approach factors in the preceding paragraph: little advance notice, start the session quickly and come to the point immediately, state the facts and do not accuse, and keep calm. Some of the right purposes are to strengthen, maintain, or restore a working relationship. Right times include only when necessary, not when you are upset, during low activity times, and not too far in advance. In terms of place, it should be private—at a table, not at

FOR FURTHER THOUGHT

Can you suggest four occasions when it might be necessary to take corrective action? What skills are needed to counsel a staff member?

a desk—and do not allow telephone calls or other intrusions to interrupt the process. After the initial statement, devote more time to listening rather than talking, and do not push the session. Finally, use one of two basic techniques, directive or nondirective. Directive sessions address issues such as rule or policy violations, correction of mistakes, and control of hostility. Nondirective meetings work best for concerns such as restoring a positive attitude or productivity, strengthening or restoring relationships, and motivating for greater teamwork.

Another step is to think about personal biases you have when it comes to judging people and their performance. Review prior appraisals, think about the next appraisal (keeping in mind any personal biases), and be ready to take further action if a person has a negative review for two years in succession.

Despite your best efforts, there will be times when disciplinary action must occur. Needless to say, such action follows only after one or more counseling sessions have failed to resolve the issue. HR units label the process "progressive discipline." What the process consists of is a series of steps that become progressively more severe and end with termination. Most of the time the process never reaches the termination stage as the parties resolve the issue earlier.

First-time managerial leaders often make the mistake of not addressing a problem early. Frequently, it is because they think taking corrective action will lead to conflict. Then, when they do take action, it is to "get tough," "crack down," and "show who is boss." More often than not, the result is a greater confrontation than would have occurred earlier. The action taken is too severe, and some or all of the trust that developed earlier disappears.

PROGRESSIVE DISCIPLINE

A progressive discipline system provides managerial leaders and employees a fair way to slowly address performance issues and to take progressively sterner steps if performance does not improve. Normally, the process starts with oral counseling followed by one or more written warnings that ultimately lead to termination if worse comes to worst. This does not mean that there are not circumstances that will warrant immediate termination. A library requires order and discipline to succeed. Most organizations and HR departments reason that it is helpful to identify types of conduct that are impermissible and that may lead to disciplinary action, possibly including immediate discharge. Although it is impossible to provide an exhaustive list of all types of impermissible conduct and performance, the following are some examples:

- Being insubordinate, including acting improperly toward a supervisor or refusing to perform tasks assigned by a supervisor in the appropriate manner
- Possessing, distributing, selling, using, or being under the influence of alcoholic beverages or illegal drugs while on library property, while on duty, or while operating a vehicle or potentially dangerous equipment leased or owned by the library
- Releasing confidential information
- Stealing or otherwise removing or possessing without authorization property from the library, fellow employees, students, visitors, or anyone on library property
- Altering or falsifying any time-keeping record, intentionally punching another employee's time card, allowing someone else to punch one's own time card, removing any time-keeping record from the designated area without proper authorization, or destroying such a record
- Falsifying or making a material omission on an employment application or any other library record
- Misusing, defacing, destroying, or damaging property of the library, a fellow employee, or a visitor
- Fighting on the property
- Bringing on the property dangerous or unauthorized materials, such as explosives, firearms, or other similar items
- Using force or threatening force

GRIEVANCES

At some point in your career, the chances are a situation will arise in which a formal reprimand or dismissal is the only choice. When this happens you might anticipate the employee will file a grievance. Grievances can also arise out of a situation in which there is a union contract. It is important for you to maintain a solid paper record documenting what was done. Such a "paper trail" may include just a note on the desk calendar recording a discussion with Employee X about Situation Y that took place, or it may include memos or formal depositions.

Some writers liken a grievance to various stages of a river, where the goal is to stop the flow of water as quickly as possible. At its source, it is a small trickle from a spring that is very easy to block. If not checked, it can become a small stream as additional issues accumulate and resolution becomes more complex, just as damming the stream is more difficult. As time passes without resolution, more and more baggage becomes attached to the original small issue. The grievance takes on a force of its own (a number of tributaries creating a river). Ultimately, it becomes a major river that is almost impossible to slow or stop.

The river analogy goes further in that a grievance takes many forms. It will follow existing channels—if they exist—or it will cut its own channels. You can dam it up for a while (not resolving the issue), but this only applies constant pressure on the dam and eventually will cause a weak point to collapse. Once the dam breaks, it is impossible to stop the flood; it must run its course. After the course is run, many things will have changed. Having a grievance procedure helps control "the river" by providing a channel for addressing the issue. Most large organizations have a procedure in place to handle such situations when they arise.

A "grievable" issue means it is work related, and it can be resolved through existing procedures. Very often the first formal step in the grievance process, after the appropriateness of an issue is determined, is for a person from HR or a grievance committee/board to meet with the parties, including the supervisor's supervisor, to attempt to resolve the matter without further delay. Failure to resolve things at that time usually results in a formal "hearing" of the case by a group of individuals who have no association with the parties involved.

Another step can be taken after the committee/board action, which is to bring in an arbitrator or mediator from outside the organization. Arbitrators/mediators will look for most of the same issues as the grievance committee.

Even the objective outsider's judgment may not be acceptable to the grieving party. That situation is very likely to lead to a lawsuit. The following list notes some of the topics that can (and have) led to lawsuits, illustrating just how complex personnel management has become:

- Sexual harassment
- Downsizing/reducing the workforce
- Discrimination
- Wrongful termination
- Breach of commercial contracts
- Sexual assault
- Accidental injury/vehicular injury
- AIDS

UNIONS AND MERIT SYSTEMS

The previous discussion covers the typical staffing process activities. As we have mentioned from time to time in various chapters, unions and civil/merit/public employee systems may influence many of your managerial activities, especially staffing.

Both unions and merit systems focus primarily on employee rights and benefits, although they cover other employment issues as well. In the case of unions, there may be contract provisions that impact how you handle promotion opportunities and layoffs (seniority). Grievance processes are a concern for both unions and merit systems. Union contracts almost always cover "working conditions"; just what is covered under that heading varies from contract to contract, even within the same organization. The phrase in many job descriptions "other duties as assigned" is usually missing in a union contract; all duties will be clearly assigned. A major challenge in a union situation is when a staff member can elect to join or not join the union. You must remember who is and is not a member when it comes to tasks, and you may have to deal with staff tension between union and nonunion members. That dual situation can also complicate your salary administration responsibilities. Clearly these few examples indicate the added complexity when a union and/or merit system is in place. You will need to quickly learn the ins and outs of what is and is not possible.

Merit/civil service/public employee systems are a special situation and apply in many government jurisdictions. Again, the details will vary from jurisdiction to jurisdiction, from the highly structured to relatively loose forms. Also, today there is a growing trend to make the merit system more like what you see in the for-profit sector. The concept of a government employee system based on merit (ability to perform the work) rather than on political connections goes back to the late nineteenth century. It also was thought to provide equal employment opportunity. The idea of merit led to the testing of a person's abil-

AUTHORS' EXPERIENCE

Over the years Evans served on a number of merit system examiners' panels for librarian promotion opportunities. The panels would meet ahead of time and prepare a list of questions to ask and decide who on the panel would ask the questions. This information was then given to the merit system office—the panel had to follow the pattern laid out in that document. If the panel did not include something like "Could you tell us more about . . . ," then the panel could not ask that. The interviews were recorded so as to ensure all interviewee experiences were identical. If the process seems restrictive, it was; the effort was to try to ensure fair treatment for each candidate.

ity to perform the work, and this is still a key component for such systems—tests for getting the position and tests for promotions. As you might guess, or know, the notion of testing and equal opportunity are not always comfortable bedfellows.

One issue for both unions and merit systems is employment security (tenure is another label). The issue is also a factor in efforts to "reform" employment practices, especially in governmental environments. Most organizations, including for-profits, have a probation period for the new hire, often including those accepting a promotion. During that period, in theory, the employer can terminate the person for almost any reason. After "passing probation" the employee has greater job security. Under the merit system most employees are "classified"—they can be dismissed only "for cause," with cause clearly spelled out. The other employment category is "at-will"—in such cases the employer has much more freedom to decide who to dismiss and when. Many government jurisdictions are shifting away from classified to at-will. New hires, after a certain date, are at-will, and older employees retain their classified status.

VOLUNTEERS

Why do we include volunteers in a basic management text? There are at least three reasons. First, a large number of libraries are very dependent on volunteer workers. Second, volunteers and paid part-time staff are the most likely people a beginning librarian will be asked to manage/lead. Third, there is some tendency to think of volunteers as beyond normal management practices, which is a serious mistake.

Volunteerism is a major source of assistance for all types of organizations. Some corporations encourage, if not require, their employees to engage in some type of volunteer work outside the workplace. In 2009, U.S. volunteers contributed 8.1 billion hours of service to nonprofit organizations. The value of the work, based on a $21.36 per hour rate, was estimated to be $75 billion (http://independentsector.org/economic_role).

There is some concern about being able to retain volunteers. Daniel Kadlec (2006) reported there was a significant challenge for organizations that depend on volunteers: "Nearly 38 million Americans who had volunteered in a nonprofit in the past didn't show up last year. . . . That is a waste of talent and desire" (p. 76). The "last year" in the quote was 2005.

There is a vast pool of talented, energetic, and motivated volunteers, especially retired librarians, to tap and retain. They also can become highly committed to a library's organizational goals, given the proper environment. Part of that environment is thinking about volunteers as just as important to quality service as paid staff members. Creating the proper environment calls for careful thought and planning.

A good starting point for thinking about volunteers is to consider a few basic questions:

- Should we use volunteers? (a very key question to ponder)
- Where would we use volunteers?
- How would we use volunteers?
- Would the tasks be meaningful for volunteers?
- Who would supervise the volunteers?
- Do we have or can we create meaningful volunteer rewards?

Dale Freund (2005) explored the use of volunteers in libraries in terms of should you do it. On balance, he believed that, properly done and in the right circumstances, the answer is yes. Many libraries can benefit from using volunteers, but this should not be undertaken lightly; as Freund suggests, a volunteer program needs to be in the correct circumstances and properly designed.

Another important point to keep in mind during the early stages of your planning is that there are three major volunteer categories, at least in the United States. One type is the "short-term" volunteer—someone who will work on special projects, events, or activities but has little or no interest in a regular or ongoing commitment. Some examples are an annual book sale, disaster recovery efforts, or a capital fund-raising campaign. A second type is the "commitment volunteer." These volunteers have a strong personal interest in the subject or area they seek volunteer opportunities in, and they expect to gain gratification, knowledge, useful skills, as well as a sense of accomplishment from the work they perform. Gaining and retaining such volunteers is a goal of any long-term volunteer program; it is also a major challenge. The third variety of volunteer, in many ways, almost does not deserve the label volunteer. These are individuals who engage in the activity primarily because of outside pressure to do so. There are two significant sources of such pressure: the workplace and schools. Many for-profit organizations, while not making volunteering mandatory, make it very clear they expect employees to engage in some form of volunteer work, although such organizations use a very broad definition of what constitutes "volunteer" activity.

Once you have decided you can make effective use of volunteers for work activities you should employ most of the staffing concepts outlined earlier in this chapter. Rather too often libraries just decide some volunteers would be nice and think about what to have the person do after a volunteer agrees to come onboard. That approach works sometimes but is not recommended if you want a long-term committed volunteer.

Start with volunteer job descriptions for each type of activity just as you would for paid staff positions. Doing so provides a solid base for both parties regarding the whats and hows of the position. Surprises, such as "I don't want to make photocopies," are much less likely if the person reviewed a job description indicating photocopying was part of the expected job performance. As with paid positions, the job description should outline duties and experience/skills sought. After preparing the descriptions, it is wise to consult with the HR department to explore insurance issues, such as injury and liability coverage for volunteers.

If motivation is important for paid staff, it is critical for volunteers, if you expect to keep them. Some years ago William M. Marston (1979) suggested there are four basic personality types. The concept has taken on a number of labels over the years; for our purposes we will use Marston's original labels: dominance (D), influencing (I), steadiness (S), and conscientiousness (C). People of type D personality are action oriented—get something done, seek quick results, solve the problem now. Those who are type I are people oriented; they are verbal and enjoy interacting with people, and being liked is important to them. Type S people are dependable; they prefer to focus on one task at time, and whenever possible they want a workplace where they can concentrate on the task at hand. Type C people are focused on standards and procedures and are detail oriented. Think about yourself and your volunteers and recognize the importance of using different behaviors with each volunteer personality. No matter what "type" you or the volunteer may be, providing lots of positive feedback is essential. This does not mean you shouldn't correct problems, but it must be done in as positive a manner as you can use. Checking on volunteer job satisfaction is a key to keeping long-term volunteers—even with accurate job descriptions, the reality of the work, its location, or its colleagues can make what appeared to be an attractive activity less than satisfying.

Volunteers probably require more training and development than do paid staff. This is particularly true when the volunteer has retired from a somewhat similar paid position elsewhere. Such people may have to unlearn years of past practices and/or modify beliefs about "how things should be done." Often the managerial leader's assumption is that the person did this before and needs very little training, which sometimes also translates into limited orientation.

There are some areas where tension can arise between volunteers and paid staff. One obvious area is some fear or concern on the paid staff's part about their job security, especially when funding is tight or hiring freezes are in place. We are not aware of any documented case of paid staff losing positions because volunteers were available. However, we do know of instances where layoffs took place because of funding problems, with the library restarting based solely on volunteer help. Thus the concern is real and should be addressed openly and honestly.

A particular challenge is when volunteers and paid staff perform the same task(s). Whenever possible, you should avoid this situation. Performance assessment becomes a significant factor. Paid staff may resent the volunteer's apparent

CHECK THESE OUT

Driggers, Preston, and Eileen Duma. 2002. *Managing Library Volunteers.* Chicago: American Library Association.
Reed, Sally G. 1994. *Library Volunteers—Worth the Effort: A Program Manager's Guide.* Jefferson, NC: McFarland.
Volunteer Match. http://www.volunteermatch.org/.

freedom to come and go with little or no notice. They may also think or observe that a volunteer receives encouragement or praise for work the staff believes is less than standard or at least at a lower standard than they are expected to deliver. Your managerial creativity and ingenuity will face great challenges when you try to provide that extra level of encouragement to volunteers and retain their services while not undermining paid staff morale.

One last point to make about volunteers concerns a union environment. In some unionized libraries, volunteer programs do not exist.

KEY POINTS TO REMEMBER

- People—the staff—are the essential element in having a successful library.
- Attracting and retaining the "best and brightest" is a complex undertaking.
- Legal aspects impact all personnel activities, from recruitment to retirement.
- Assessing staffing needs involves position reviews and looking at labor force demographics.
- Recruiting and selecting the best person requires care and thought, including an understanding of legal issues.
- Tools for the selection process must be chosen with an eye on legal concerns.
- Selecting and "landing" a candidate can be a complex activity involving the library staff and the parent body's HR office.
- Proper orientation of new staff (during the first few days or weeks) is critical to good long-term work performance.
- Performance appraisal is a process that few people like and one that can have as many negative as positive outcomes unless handled thoughtfully.
- Discipline is a delicate activity that takes practice and skill to keep personnel views at bay and objective data in the forefront.
- Unions contracts and merit systems can and do influence what you can and cannot do in terms of staffing.

References

Bridges, Mark, and Heather Johnson. 2006. "The Aging Workforce: The Facts, the Fiction, the Future." *ASHRAE Journal* 48, no. 1: 6–9.

Deming, W. Edwards. 1993. *Out of Crisis.* Cambridge: Massachusetts Institute of Technology Press.

Drickhamer, David. 2006. "Putting People First Pays Off." *Material Handing Management* 61, no. 6: 42, 44–45.

Evans, G. Edward. 2004. *Performance Management.* New York: Neal-Schuman.

Evans, G. Edward, and Bendik Rugaas. 1982. "Another Look at Performance Appraisal in Libraries." *Journal of Library Administration* 3, no. 2: 61–69.

Fisher, Anne. 2006. "Retain Your Brains." *Fortune* 154, no. 2 (July 10): 49–50.

Freund, Dale. 2005. "Do Volunteers Belong in the Library?" *Rural Libraries* 25, no. 1: 19–41.

Gellerman, Saul. 1976. *Management of Human Resources.* New York: Holt, Rinehart.

Hawthorne, Pat. 2011. "Succession Planning and Management: A Key Leadership Responsibility Emerges." *Texas Library Journal* 87, no. 1: 10–12.

Kadlec, Daniel. 2006. "The Right Way to Volunteer." *Time* 168, no. 10: 76.

Marston, William Moulton. 1979. *Emotions of Normal People.* Minneapolis: Personal Press.

McDowell, Amy M., and William M. Leavitt. 2011. "Human Resources Issues in Local Government: Yesterday's Headlines Remain Today's 'Hot Topics.'" *Public Personnel Management* 40, no. 3: 239–249.

Mitchell, Geana W., Leane B. Skinner, and Bonnie J. White. 2011. "Essential Soft Skills for Success in the Twenty-First Century Workforce as Perceived by Business Educators." *Delta Pi Epsilon Journal* 52, no. 1: 43–53.

"Service with a Very Big Smile." 2007. *Harvard Business Review* 85, no. 5: 24.

Launching Pad

Brencic, Vera, and John B. Norris. 2012. "Employers' On-Line Recruitment and Screening Practices." *Economic Inquiry* 50, no. 1: 94–111.

Busi, Don. 2011. "The Position Description." *Supervision* 72, no. 9: 6–8.

Damasco, Ione T., and Dracine Hodges. 2012. "Tenure and Promotion Experiences of Academic Librarians of Color." *College and Research Libraries* 73, no. 3: 279–301.

Dineen, Brian R., and Ian Williamson. 2012. "Screening-Oriented Recruitment Messages: Antecedents and Relationships with Applicant Pool Quality." *Human Resource Management* 51, no. 3: 343–360.

Fitsimmons, Gary. 2010. "Directing the Personnel Search Part I." *Bottom Line* 23, no. 4: 205–207.

———. 2011a. "Directing the Personnel Search Part II." *Bottom Line* 24, no. 1: 38–40.

———. 2011b. "Directing the Personnel Search Part III." *Bottom Line* 24, no. 2: 110–112.

———. 2011c. "Directing the Personnel Search Part IV." *Bottom Line* 24, no. 3: 157–159.

Garcha, Rajinder, and John C. Phillips. 2001. "U.S. Academic Librarians: Their Involvement in Union Activities." *Library Review* 50, no. 3: 122–127.

"HR Can Play Crucial Role in Minimizing Exposure to Lawsuits." 2011. *HR Focus* 88, no. 8: 7.

Kellough, J. Edward, and Lloyd G. Nogro. 2006. "Dramatic Reform in the Public Service: At-Will Employment and the Creation of a New Public Workforce." *Journal of Public Administration Research and Theory* 16, no. 3: 447–466.

Latham, Joyce M., and Wyatt E. Ditzler. 2010. "Collective Effort: The American Union and the American Public Library." *Library Trends* 59, nos. 1/2: 237–255.

Matarazzo, James M., and Joseph J. Mika. 2004. "Workforce Planning for Library and Information Science." *Library and Information Science Research* 26, no. 2: 115–120.

Mesch, Debra J. 2010. "Management of Human Resources in 2020." *Public Administration Review* 70, no. 1: 173–174.

Munde, Gail. 2010. "Considerations for Managing an Increasingly Intergenerational Workforce in Libraries." *Library Trends* 59, nos. 1–2: 88–108.

Phillips, Laura C., and Mark H. Phillips. 2010. "Volunteer Motivation and Reward Preference: An Empirical Study of Volunteerism in a Large Not-For-Profit Organization." *SAM Advanced Management Journal* 75, no. 4: 12–19, 39.

"Putting the Job Review Out of Its Misery." 2010. *Executive Leadership* 25, no. 9: 2.

Solomon, Paul, and Susan Rathbun-Grubb. 2009. "Workforce Planning and the School Library Specialist." *Library Trends* 58, no. 2: 246–262.

Steffen, Nicolle, and Zeth Lietzau. 2009. "Retirement, Retention, and Recruitment in Colorado Libraries: The 3Rs Study Revisited." *Library Trends* 58, no. 2: 179–191.

PART IV

MANAGING THINGS

Library managers must make an effective transition from resource allocation to resource attraction. Identifying and securing new sources of funding are critical to library success in this challenged economic context. Fundraising requires the investment of staff and budget to identify priorities and opportunities, to cultivate sources and donor prospects, and to celebrate and recognize external support. Income generation needs to be advanced beyond traditional fundraising, like annual giving, major gifts, bequests and gifts-in-kind. It must also embrace new approaches to cost efficiencies, operating budget reallocation, and thoughtful budget reduction. It includes competition for government and foundation grants. It means co-investment with allied organizations, public–private partnerships, and new business development. Libraries must be agile, entrepreneurial, market-sensitive and focused on quality if new income generation is to be advanced successfully.

—Jim Neal, ALA Treasurer, 2010–2013 (2012)

Generally, the most important decisions a library administrator makes concern what to do with scarce resources. This usually comes down to people, money, or both because these are typically what are needed to accomplish what one wants to do.

—Mott Linn (2010)

When conscientious librarians try to absorb budget cuts without any fuss or disruption, they provide a disservice to their community. They hide the real costs of operation and suggest that there is no real consequence for inadequate funding.

—*American Libraries* (2010)

Fundraisers have patience. We take time to get to know potential donors. We share ideas and information with them. We develop relationships. And, if all goes smoothly, after months or years of cultivation, pledges or actual gifts are made to our libraries.

—Emily Silverman (2010)

17

MANAGING MONEY

This chapter focuses on the following:

- Budgeting's role in library performance
- Budget as a control device
- Budget cycle
- Budget preparation
- Defending the request
- Budget types
- Fund accounting
- Audits and auditors
- Income generation

WE MADE THE POINT in the last chapter that having the best and brightest people should be the top library goal if the library wishes to provide excellent service to its community. Coming in a very close second is securing adequate funding. Money is the underlying resource upon which everything else in the library depends. Your role as a managerial leader is to utilize all the resources effectively. To be successful in that activity, you must understand managerial and financial accounting, develop skills in raising funds from sources outside the library's primary funding source, and master the politics of the budgetary process, as well as other fiscal matters we address in this chapter.

Tight economic times call for very creative thinking to maintain quality library services. Meg Hartmann (2011), although writing about public libraries and their privatization, makes a point that applies to all of today's libraries:

> The success and survival of public libraries is due to the heroism of everyday librarians that continue serving the common good, despite the vagaries of a capitalist marketplace. Government administrators or library boards may believe cutbacks required by restricted funds are not only justified by economic downturn, but are desirable because they lead to a more streamlined library. . . . Whoever defines a good library and what model to use, defines where the budget is spent. (pp. 4, 7)

Managing today's library budget is a challenge on several fronts. Currently "the 800 pound gorilla in the room" is the severe economic condition. This has led, and probably will lead to, decreasing or, at best, stable library resources for some time to come. The economic conditions have not decreased user expectations or demands for quality service; if anything, they have increased the pressure on libraries. Technology's pace of change has not diminished, and the pressure of maintaining a networked information environment adds further demands on a library's limited resource base.

Finally, the slumping economy has not kept the costs of the services and products that libraries must have from escalating. Perhaps the only major library expense category that has not increased is staff salaries. The rapid increase in health-care insurance costs passed on, at least in part, to the employees means some staff may have experienced a decrease in take-home pay. Keeping those best and brightest people you worked so diligently to hire is frustrating in such conditions. As Terry Cottrell (2011) noted, "In this time of economic restructuring, a key reason why librarians leave their current position is salary" (p. 188).

Securing adequate, or as close as possible to adequate, funding is challenging and calls upon all your managerial and political skills. You must realize that at times you'll not succeed through no fault of your own. Economic conditions may make it impossible for any library to receive funding at "normal" levels, and budget reductions may occur. However, by preparing solid requests, having a track record of careful and thoughtful stewardship of funds granted, providing high-quality service to the user community, and having realistic but forward-looking plans you will, more often than not, secure the maximum possible funding. Fiscal management consists of three broad activities: identifying and securing funds, expending the funds, and accounting for and reporting on how you spent the funds.

Being an effective steward of funds is complex regardless of the size of your library. It begins by assessing what needs doing (especially user needs) and the cost of the requisite activities, establishing priorities (with stakeholder input), creating a plan (the budget), reflecting the costs and priorities, and presenting the plan to the appropriate funding bodies. We know of few, if any, cases where the costs of desired activities were below the realistic amount of money likely to be received. Thus setting priorities is a key element in fiscal planning.

No matter where you seek funding, you must have a well-crafted request. Preparing such documents takes time, effort, and a fair amount of creativity, as you will be in competition with other agencies and departments.

BUDGET AS A CONTROL DEVICE

A budget is a plan that serves three interrelated purposes: planning, coordinating, and control. It represents choices made about alternative possible expenditures. Furthermore, it assists in coordinating work. Funding authorities use budget requests and expenditures as a means of comparing what the library proposes and what the outcomes are. It is one of the parent body's most powerful tools for holding the library accountable.

These purposes apply to all levels of the library. Senior staff members use budgets to monitor departments' performance; frontline budget managers use the budget to track day-to-day performance. An example of the frontline use of the budget would be an acquisitions unit that develops plans on how much money needs to be expended each day to ensure a reasonable work flow throughout the fiscal year. Checking on actual performance against the planned expenditure provides useful information for control and coordination purposes.

While for-profit organizations begin budgeting by estimating sales and income, libraries start by estimating what income it will receive from the parent organization. If there is a shortfall in what is deemed to be the minimum level needed, the library must seek support from outside sources. There are few relatively predictable library-generated funds (user fees, endowment income, and other internally generated cash), while other sources are unpredictable (grant proposals and cooperative ventures, for example). All budgeting is essentially forecasting—how much will you get and how much will it cost to operate over the budget cycle. Overly optimistic predictions lead to problems when funding falls short and/or there are unexpected costs.

You rarely know what you will receive much before the start of the budgetary year (fiscal year). Often, the actual funding is an unknown until near the beginning of the fiscal year. We know of cases where publicly funded libraries had to start a cycle without an approved budget because the politicians could not agree on how much to approve. This can create some serious scrambling when there are shortfalls. There have been a number of times when all agencies except emergency departments had to close until the legislature or city council reached a compromise. Our experience has been that a conservative forecast is the safest and least disruptive to operations. Having a contingency plan also helps make managerial life somewhat easier for times when the politicians quibble over what and how much to fund.

Because budgets are estimates, to be effective you must make expenditure adjustments as circumstances change. Budgets need to be flexible in order to meet rapid shifts in needs, but any major alteration requires careful thought and caution. Too many rapid changes can damage the integrity and stability of a budget as well as the organization. In most libraries, there is only a limited authority to make budget adjustments; asking before doing is the best approach when it comes to budgets.

Financial planning and control consists of several steps:

1. Determine ongoing and desirable programs, and establish priorities.
2. Estimate the costs of plans for each unit in monetary terms.
3. Combine all estimates into a well-balanced program. This will require investigation of each plan's financial feasibility and a comparison of the program with institutional goals.
4. Compare, for a given time, the estimates derived from Step 3 with the actual results, making corrections for any significant differences.

A library's size does not materially affect the budgeting process, although in larger libraries each step is more complex. As a library grows, it may employ separate budgets for each department, division, or work unit. Because these units are somewhat independent, different performance standards may be appropriate. A very large library may have many internal budgets subsumed under its overall budget. Another complex step is combining and coordinating subsidiary budgets. It certainly involves more than just totaling the smaller budgets. It must represent a total program that is consistent with the library's objectives. For this reason, very large libraries often have a person whose sole job is budget coordinator who must see the "big picture."

Finally, budget officers compare the actual performance (what has been accomplished, the volume of work, and so forth) against the expected results. Managerial leaders must consistently assess existing circumstances in order to decide whether a major or a minor shift in budget allotments is necessary or desirable. By doing this every few months throughout the fiscal year, you can help control unpredictability. This step is most important because budgets are often prepared 12 to 18 months before they are approved and thus may represent predictions two years old at the time of review.

Library budgets normally are of two types: operating and capital. Operating budgets/expenses identify amounts of money the library expects to expend on basic activities, and they cover a specific timeframe—a fiscal year, which is usually 12 months long. The fact that different organizations use different fiscal years (some examples are January 1 to December 31, June 1 to May 31, July 1 to June 30, and October 1 to September 30) as well as budget preparation cycles can cause surprising problems for library consortia and their cooperative project funding.

Funding bodies can, and occasionally do, change their fiscal year. This can cause the library difficulty, especially in maintaining subscriptions. The problem is not too great when the funding body shortens the fiscal year by a month (at

---

AUTHORS' EXPERIENCE

Evans worked at one private university where the institution changed its fiscal year three times in the space of five years, both lengthening and shortening the year. The library had great difficulty meeting its outside commitments—consortial, maintenance/service contracts, and subscriptions, for example. At the end of the swings, the institution returned to its original fiscal year as the assumed benefits of the changes were never realized.

---

some point in time it will be necessary to address any funding shortfall). When the funders extend the fiscal year by a month or more, the problem may be acute because of lack of funds.

Capital budgets are for expenditures on equipment (usually items expected to last two or more years). Expenditures for technology (hardware and infrastructure) usually fall into the capital expense category. The other major expense is for new construction or remodeling projects.

BUDGET CYCLE

There is a budget cycle, regardless of the fiscal year time frame. That cycle plays a role in the control aspect of budgeting. Budget managers normally deal with at least four fiscal years. Those are last year's, this year's, next year's, and the year after that. Figure 17.1 (p. 430) is an example of a budget cycle. Let us assume the library's fiscal year is July 1 to June 30. Look at the budget cycle and you will see the reason for the four different fiscal years.

For the current year, the manager must monitor expenditures, compare what has occurred against expectations, and make appropriate adjustments. A common practice requires senior managers to provide additional justifications to the funding body for the requested budget for the coming fiscal year. As part of that process, the person is likely to have to respond to questions about the expenditures in the current and past fiscal year. Because budgets are estimates,

Past Fiscal Year		Current Fiscal Year		Future Fiscal Year 1		Future Fiscal Year 2		
July	Dec	July	Dec	July	Dec	July	Dec	July
X		***X***	†††∞∞	X		X		X

Key:
***, Submit coming fiscal year budget.
†††, Defend coming fiscal budget.
∞∞, Plan future fiscal year budget.

Figure 17.1 Sample Budget Cycle

funding bodies usually look at how well the requesting unit actually used its prior appropriations. Senior management must be ready to defend past expenditures, explain how the library is doing with current funding, and justify why extra funds are necessary for the coming fiscal year. During the latter part of a fiscal year, many organizations ask for the initial request for the upcoming fiscal year.

BUDGET PREPARATION

From a legal point of view, the library's senior manager is responsible for use of the budget as well as its preparation, regardless of how she or he may have delegated authority to expend the funds. Only in the smallest library is the senior manager solely responsible for handling the operational budget. Almost every medium- and large-sized library, with several units and departments, usually has delegated some discretionary spending power to units. Even when there is no budget officer, an effective senior manager, whenever possible, delegates some budgetary responsibility to unit heads.

Budget delegation accomplishes several things. First, it places the day-to-day budget decisions close to user services, making it easier to respond to changing needs. Second, it indicates to unit managers that the senior manager has a high level of trust in them and their abilities. Third, it provides middle managers with an opportunity to gain an understanding of budgeting. It also provides senior management with an opportunity to assess middle managers' potential for promotion to higher levels, which generally carry greater budgetary responsibility. Finally, it gives the senior manager more time to maintain overall budgetary oversight.

During the early years of your career, you are unlikely to have major budgeting responsibilities. You may be asked for information, even to provide dollar figures about what you think are the budgetary needs for your work area. The majority of the budgetary process activities are in the hands of senior managerial leaders. That is very reasonable as they, especially the most senior persons, are accountable and responsible for everything that takes place in the library. It is the funding that provides the base for all services and activities. As you progress in your career, you should take every opportunity to learn more and more about library budgeting and how the budget request process operates.

In a delegated environment, initial budget preparation should begin with the managerial leaders having such responsibility. They provide their estimates of their funding needs and pass the proposal on to the next level or senior managers. Each level further combines and adjusts the requests. Finally, senior management assesses the information and drafts the final request.

Every library hopes to have a stable or, at best, a predictable fiscal environment. To some extent, the planning cycle assists in creating such an environment. One of the elements involves the senior managers monitoring the library's economic and political environment. By setting up a budget planning committee, senior management accomplishes several things. First, it involves more people in the monitoring activities. Second, it involves others in thinking about future needs of the library. Third, it provides lower level managers with solid budgetary planning and development experience. Finally, it can build commitment to the library as well as generate some understanding of the limits of budgetary freedom.

Having a contingency plan for possible budget shortfalls is part of a stable environment. It will help avoid making hasty decisions that may be as harmful as the loss of funding. In cutting back, the people most affected, at least initially, are staff.

Some short-term tactics for dealing with fiscal distress include hiring freezes, staff reductions through attrition, across-the-board cuts, and deferred maintenance and equipment replacement. The *American Libraries* (2010) article cited in one of our opening quotations listed eight possibilities for dealing with budget shortfalls or tight economic times: impose across-the-board cuts, reduce library staff, "gut" the materials budget, reduce the number of service points, reduce library hours, raise fines and fees, seek outside support (money, in-kind services, or volunteers), and "stop doing something you know you shouldn't be doing anyhow" (pp. 16–17). Some of these suggestions might be short term in character, as they could be rescinded when times improve; others, such as gutting the materials budget, could have long-lasting impacts, especially if the tough times are long lasting. Fiscal distress for libraries is not always a short-term problem. In the long term, band-aid solutions will not work, and their use often severely damages support from both staff and users.

Glen Holt (2005) wrote an article about "getting beyond the pain" in which he begins with a depressing list of budgetary woes at the state and national levels. He noted that the American Library Association estimated there had been $111 million cuts in public library funding between 2004 and when he wrote the article. Holt provided some ideas for addressing the situation: demonstrate the critical nature of the library (or some of its elements), demonstrate the library benefits, think broadly about possible funding sources, place greater emphasis on being a user/client-focused library, and recognize that globalization does have an impact

---

CHECK THESE OUT

L. S. Moyer published an article in 2005 outlining how one small public library responded to budget cuts: "Library Funding in a Budget-Cut World" (*Bottom Line* 18, no. 3: 112–115).

For an academic library perspective, read Samuel T. Huang's article "Where There's a Will, There's a Way" (*Bottom Line* 19, no. 3: 146–151, 2006).

In terms of a corporate environment, review Gitelle Seer 's article "No Pain, No Gain: Stretching the Library Dollar" (*Bottom Line* 17, no. 1: 10–14, 2004).

on the international marketplace for information. Holt (2005) concluded that "At the same time however, we must recognize the drastic changes that we will have to make to keep up with new ways of working and funding" (p. 189). One of the probable "new ways" of funding is touched on by John Buschman (2003), who suggests that at least in North America the public (taxpayers) have decided that some public sector libraries, if not all, deserve less public support.

Gitelle Seer (2004) made an important point: "Do not confuse short-term belt tightening with long-term financial strategies. It is sometimes hard to tell the difference, and your organization's management may give you few, if any, meaningful clues" (p. 10). Seer's advice, as is ours, is to monitor the internal and external environments like a hawk.

DEFENDING THE REQUEST

Preparing a budget request is often easier than defending it. This stems from the fact that most agencies compete for the limited pool of funds, and each seeks to prove that its needs are the most urgent. Thus, the more care that you put into the preparation of a budget request and the reasons for requested increases, the more likely you are to secure the amount sought. Those agencies that do win the "battle of the budget" are usually the ones that recognize and act on the fact that budgeting is a very political process. All U.S. library managers ought to read the classic book by Aaron Wildavsky, *The Politics of the Budgetary Process.* His first edition appeared in the 1960s, and the fifth edition, *The New Politics of the Budgetary Process,* has a coauthor, Naomi Caiden (Wildavsky and Caiden, 2004). Some librarians, especially students, have difficulty accepting Wildavsky's ideas, as the text deals with the U.S. government and, to a lesser extent, state governments. They see libraries as cultural havens somehow removed from the "ugliness" of politics. Most graduates who read some or all of Wildavsky as students quickly see the connection when they take their first positions.

In addition to the budgetary politics with external agencies, there are internal politics that arise from time to time. The elements are almost identical in the two instances; however, there is, very often, the added dimension of interpersonal relationships to take into consideration. Personal "baggage" makes it that much harder to resolve. "Why did reference get the biggest increase?" "How come department X got the new FTE? We obviously need the help more than it does!" These are samples of the internal politics that can go on. Personal interests in gaining status, authority, influence, and so forth are often underlying issues. Such issues go well beyond true budget concerns; they are very difficult to address, and senior managers must not let them get in the way of the overall budget process.

Wildavsky and Caiden's (2004) book contains many useful ideas. We drew the following material from it, but this discussion is no substitute for reading the book. Despite all the press given to concepts such as program and planning budgeting systems (PPBS) and zero-base budgeting (ZBB), most organizational budgets are basically line budgets (see next section). Organizations often find that when they do move to one of the "newer" budgeting modes, the end result is much the same—an incremental budget—because, after an initial start-up, people use the past year as their starting point.

Exceptions to the incremental pattern do occur. If an agency is "under fire," depending on how serious the situation is, the funding body can use budget cuts to show displeasure. The largest cuts are usually in those deemed "nonessential" programs, such as libraries, museums, schools, and cultural activities. Police and fire protection usually are the last to face reductions. This is clear evidence that government budgeting is a highly political process, reacting to voter concerns. What politician would want to explain to voters the decision to close the local fire station rather than the library?

The incremental approach is present in most library budgets because of the long-term commitments (salaries, retirement programs and pension payments, and database and serial subscriptions). Also, if the user base increases, there will be pressure to hire additional staff. In jurisdictions with strong collective bargaining units, a workload agreement clause can cause a significant increase in staffing costs. Annual salary step and cost-of-living increases are difficult to control, because the withholding of such increases is only temporary. Staff pressure will mount to make up for the losses they believe they suffered.

Like it or not, "lobbying" is part of the library's budget presentation. Perhaps a label that carries a less negative connotation is "advocacy." Both terms relate to the process of influencing people about the importance or value of an issue or cause. Gloria Meraz (2002) describes three areas that librarians can focus on in terms of lobbying—positioning themselves to be effective lobbyists, achieving the most from lobbying sessions, and understanding the lobbying arena. One of her telling points is that "decision makers tend to allocate funding to departments or agencies that are in trouble (crisis). . . . [W]ithout showing some sort of crisis, libraries are not likely to receive large allocations of resources" (p. 68). She notes that most libraries do not have to make up the crisis; all they need to do is show it.

One part of the advocacy process is to draw on the user base, which will be as vocal or as silent as the library leads users to believe they should be. A large user base is fine, but if users are silent during budget crunches, they are not politically useful. A little extra help extended to users—especially to politically influential groups—can go a long way at budget request time. There is nothing wrong with saying, "Look, we seem to be doing a good job for you, but with a little help and a little more money, we could really show you a quality library!" People who are willing to speak for the library at budget hearings can have a positive effect on funding agencies. The "letter to your legislator" approach can be very useful, especially if it occurs year round and creates a strong positive attitude in funders' minds before they begin thinking about budgets with the library in mind.

Some years ago, Jennifer Cargill (1988) wrote a short but to-the-point article about "getting the budget message out." At that time, and as it still remains today, one of the most difficult messages to convey to funding authorities, as well as to users, is the high rate of inflation of library collection resources. Finding a short, simple, accurate, way of explaining to nonlibrarians why such price increase percentages are so large is a challenge.

Developing a good working relationship with the staff members of those who have funding authority is an excellent idea, especially with the staff of the person who heads the committee that first hears the library's budget request. If your relationship is a year-round one, it will be easier to maintain and your chances of success improve further. Keeping in touch, finding out what will be needed for the hearings (well in advance), identifying possible areas of concern, and offering assistance within reasonable limits are all methods of developing a good working relationship. You must be careful to keep the relationship on a professional basis so that there is no hint of personal favoritism.

There is nothing wrong with inviting influential funding officers to attend special library functions (holiday parties, for example) at which a number of users and other influential persons will also be present. They may or may not attend, but they will have the library in mind as something other than a bottomless money pit. Study the mood of the people and the funding authorities with an eye on adjusting your approach as moods shift. During "hold the line on spending" periods, let your request demonstrate how well you are cooperating. Do not try to paint too rosy a picture—play it straight, and do not try to "put one over" on them. You may fool people once or twice because of all the other matters they have to consider, but eventually they will catch up to you. And when they do, you will lose any goodwill you developed over time, and the library will probably suffer for a long time to come.

When presenting plans for new programs, be cautious in what you promise. Do not promise more than you know you can deliver, even when you think you can do much better. It is better to underpromise and overdeliver. As tempting as it may be to make promises in order to get money, resist! Funding officers'

AUTHORS' EXPERIENCE

Evans was able to develop a strong relationship with the academic vice president (AVP) at his last university. The relationship was based on trust that funds requested would deliver the expected results for the university. After a few early tests the AVP knew that requested funds would cover the costs of the project, service, activity, and so forth and that there would be some amount left over. Not much in most cases, but some amount.

The AVP was invited to and attended most of the library's social events and almost always talked to the staff about his appreciation of their being "the people who deliver." Some other campus units believed there was favoritism when it came to budget requests. Perhaps there was, but if there was it was based on "delivering the goods" and on underpromising and overdelivering.

CHECK THIS OUT

A solid article that addresses most of the fiscal issues we covered is Peter Clayton's "Managing the Acquisitions Budget: A Practical Perspective" (*Bottom Line* 14, no. 3: 145–151, 2001).

memories are long and detailed when necessary, and failure to deliver on past promises raises serious doubts about current promises.

Does all of this sound too political for a library? It should not, because it reflects the unwritten rules by which governments and other funding bodies play the budget-politics game.

BUDGET TYPES

For libraries, the operating expense (OE) is the primary budget regardless of format (line, performance, etc.). Within the total operating budget there is a series of budgets covering specific items of expenditure. These are generally interconnecting and include the following:

- A materials budget
- A personnel budget
- A distribution/expense budget
- An administrative expense budget

A *materials budget* takes the form of funds for collection building and online access services. It must take into account producers' price increases and other anticipated costs, such as currency evaluation.

A *personnel budget* (salaries and benefits) specifies the amount of direct staffing needed to meet service objectives for the year. When thinking about the personnel costs you may want to consider the difference between employing salaried as compared with hourly wage employees and permanent as compared with contract staff, because the benefits may vary. For public libraries, doing this type of thinking in advance of talks of privatization may pay off in keeping the public library public. Some institutions may require the involvement of the human resources office to ensure that they budget for the proper "type" of employee.

The *distribution/expense budget* takes into account the estimated costs of a library's delegating or allocating parts of the overall budget, for example, to branch operations. An *administrative expense budget,* as the name implies, details those expenses that result from performing general management functions. This might include senior and other administrative salaries, travel expenses, professional library fees, and office expenses.

What are the typical categories of expenditures included in an OE? For libraries, the largest category is staff salaries, often representing as much as 60 to 65 percent of the total budget. This is one category of expense that most libraries cannot move funds to or from or change during a fiscal year. Usually the only way you can use salary monies for some other purpose is by giving up an FTE or at least part of an FTE. Some libraries, in an effort to secure funds for technology, give up several FTEs. While the practice may secure needed funding, you must be certain the technology will reduce personnel costs.

Funds for building collections (electronic and print) are the second largest OE category. These funds may account for 25 to 30 percent of total budget. Like salaries, these funds tend to grow more quickly than most of the other categories.

Generally, there is less than 15 percent of the budget left for all other expense categories. Office supplies, equipment, technology, and maintenance contracts are all essential and take substantial portions of the remaining funds. Telephone, postage, utilities (in some cases), facilities maintenance (in some cases), printing/promotional activities, membership fees, library charges (such as OCLC), administrative and professional travel, bindery charges, and insurance are all categories that many libraries must consider. Is it any wonder that few libraries have much money left for covering professional development and staff training costs and a host of other desirable needs?

The following are subcategories of the categories mentioned and indicate the range of activities the remaining 15 percent must cover: small equipment items, such as book trucks, step stools, office chairs, and desks—perhaps to meet changing health and safety standards; exhibit supplies; "security targets" for items in the collection; guidebooks and bibliographic instructional material; interlibrary loan or document delivery fees; and vehicle repair and licenses. The list could go on and on, but the foregoing provides a sense of the budgetary challenges.

Funds raised outside the parent organization for OE purposes are less constrained in terms of usage. There are times such funds are restricted by the donor to a specific purpose. You are likely to encounter *restricted* and *unrestricted* funds. The OE is unrestricted; that is, you may spend OE collection funds for any appropriate item. A restricted collection-development fund might require you to buy items only on Middle Eastern archaeology. It is not uncommon for a donor to restrict the expenditure of the gift to areas in which she or he has a special interest. As experienced fundraisers know, securing an unrestricted gift is difficult, as "no one wants to give money for light bulbs and toilet paper."

FOR FURTHER THOUGHT

Review the operating expense budget and its component parts, bearing in mind a library you know. Would you expect this library to have a materials budget, a personnel budget, a distributive/expense budget, or an administrative budget? If not, why might there be a variation?

BUDGET FORMATS

Before exploring the major budget formats, we need to briefly mention two variations you rarely encounter—lump sum and site budgets. A *lump sum budget*, as its name implies, is a single allocation, and the funds are not tied to any category of expenditure. You have the freedom to use the funds as needed or, at least, as your governing board deems appropriate. The freedom is wonderful until it comes to accountability, when it becomes akin to wrestling an angry bear with one hand tied behind you.

Site budgets are allocations tied to a specific location (a branch, for example) and that all categories of expense. They can be a good method for giving more professionals early experience with managing an entire budget.

Another type is the *formula budget.* You most commonly encounter a formula budget in educational settings, where student numbers are linked to a funding amount—more students translate into more money. Some public libraries may have something similar, with a per capita figure or percentage of taxes.

In an academic library, you are likely to encounter a subbudget that is formula based—acquisitions. Academic libraries have used a variety of formulas in an effort to help achieve some balance in spending in support of the teaching departments. Such efforts have never fully satisfied all the faculty members.

LINE-ITEM BUDGET FORMAT

The *line-item budget* is the most common format. It has a long history of use and allows for easy comparison of expenditure categories from year to year. Figure 17.2 illustrates how the comparisons often appear in documents from funding authorities. The listing of requested and actual expenditures may cover as few as three years or as many as five or six.

Line-item budgets focus on classes of expenditures, with each class representing a "line" in the budget. Each major unit in a large organization, such as a library or a police department, has an identifying budget number. In Figure 17.2, the budget number in the upper left corner identifies the library. That number is permanent as long as the parent organization uses a particular fiscal management system.

Within each budget number are lines representing the classes of expenditure the funding authority wishes to track. Frequently, the lines also have a number associated with it. Figure 17.2 illustrates the labels that categorize expenditure as

---

CHECK THIS OUT

An interesting assessment of formula usage in academic libraries is Roger Cross's "Budget Allocation Formulas: Magic or Illusion?" (*Bottom Line* 24, no. 1: 63–67, 2011).

Account: 056739 Jackson Public Library							
		Budget	Actual	Budget	Actual	Budget	Actual
Code	Description	FY 06/09	FY 05/10	FY 06/10	FY 05/11	FY 06/11	FY 06/12
422	Telephone	6,377	6,570	6,377	7,595	6,377	8,207
465	Travel	2,565	3,053	2,565	2,961	3,250	3,057
466	Postage	1,100	975	1,100	1,000	1,500	1,325
510	Office supplies	4,217	4,198	4,275	4,279	4,500	4,482
511	Other supplies	2,500	2,483	2,500	2,608	3,000	2,956

Figure 17.2 Sample Line-Item Budget

codes. Thus, in Figure 17.2, code 465 identifies expenses associated with travel. Whatever the label used for line items, the purpose is to allow for easy tracking of expenditures. If the funding body wants to know how much the organization as a whole spent on office supplies, all it needs to do is add up all of the "510" lines in the active account numbers. There is no "standard" number of expenditure classes for line items. The number varies from organization to organization.

Line-item budgets are the least complex to manage. A budget request usually starts with last year's allocation and builds from there. More often than not you will have received some "guidelines" from the parent body about its overall plan for the budget. These will almost always indicate how much, if any, inflation you may add to which lines. You may be encouraged to shift monies from one line to another to better reflect your operating needs (an exception here is that you rarely have freedom to shift salary monies).

PERFORMANCE BUDGET

Some scholars don't think line-item budgets are as good as other budget formats from an efficiency and effectiveness point of view. One reason for this is that line budgets are highly susceptible to incremental increases or, as critics say, "Once a line always a line, and once a mistake always a mistake." Another issue is that the lines focus on categories of expense, not on effectiveness of the expenditure. There is no easy way to relate expenses to a library's mission, goals, or objectives. Thus, there is no identifiable relationship between expenditure and achievement. The other formats do link expenditure and achievements.

Some people view performance budgets as *the* tool for fiscal control. *Performance budgets* focus on tasks rather than on classes of expenditure (see Figure 17.3). A performance budget is an expansion of a line-item budget, but using it gives managers and funding authorities a means to assess the unit's performance in terms of quantity and unit costs.

The major drawback to the performance budget is that it is of little value in assessing quality. Thus, while closer to relating expenditures to the mission, goals, and objectives, it still does not clearly show the relationship to quality. One

	Acquisitions	Cataloging	Reference	Circulation	Administration
Salaries	$XX	$XX	$XX	$XX	$XX
Materials	$XX	$XX	$XX	$XX	$XX
Postage	$XX	$XX	$XX	$XX	$XX
Telephone	$XX	$XX	$XX	$XX	$XX
Office supplies	$XX	$XX	$XX	$XX	$XX
Etc.					
Total	$XXX	$XXX	$XXX	$XXX	$XXX
Grand Total					$XXXX
Percentage*	X%	X%	X%	X%	X%

*Total of all percentages should equal 100%.

Figure 17.3 Sample Performance Budget

reason you might want to employ a performance budget internally, regardless of what the parent organization's budget format is, is for staff development. In essence, you can give functional department heads their own budget to manage. It will usually result in more realistic budget requests from the department heads as they gain an understanding of budgetary issues.

PROGRAM BUDGETS

Program budgets relate the expenditures to the activities and programs the library provides and links monies spent on them to the library's mission, goals, and objectives. Needless to say, such budgets require substantially more time to prepare. The extra time requirement may account for the lower usage of this format. A program budget takes more time to prepare because staff time has to be allocated to each activity (cataloging or reference, for example). While some staff may devote 100 percent of their time to a single program, others may have responsibilities in several programs. The question for such individuals is, how much time to attribute to each program?

How a library defines its programs will depend on how it defines its mission, goals, and objectives. Whatever the case may be, implementing a program budget requires introducing three major operational concepts:

- Developing an analytical ability for examining in-depth library goals and objectives and the programs designed to meet them
- Creating a five-year programming process plan combined with a sophisticated management-information system
- Creating a budgeting mechanism that can take broad program decisions, translate them into refined budgetary decisions, and present the results for action

The following steps are necessary to accomplish the third task of identifying fiscally efficient operational programs that meet broad goals:

1. Identify library objectives.
2. Relate broad objectives to specific library programs.
3. Relate programs to resource requirements.
4. Relate resource inputs to budget dollars.
5. Relate inputs to outputs.

These steps not only provide a quick overview of the program budget process but they also indicate the interrelated nature of management activities. They also provide another indication of why program budgeting is time-consuming.

The next step is to determine appropriate work programs: groups of related activities that produce products (items cataloged, items circulated, for example). You then assign to each work program a cost. Each work program has a unit justification, which states that program's general objectives and its scope of activities.

You can assign each activity a time and cost factor. You then combine these factors in work measurements to determine how much time and money are needed to do each element of an activity as well as the whole job.

To determine staffing needs, you multiply the number of units of work programs by the time factor per work unit (usually work hours) and then divide by the number of hours a person works per year. You determine the cost by dividing the work-hour cost of producing a measure of work by the annual number of work units and then multiplying that cost by the number of work units anticipated for the coming year.

This quantitative emphasis may present problems. First, how do you determine work-unit measurements? Is cataloging measured by titles or by volumes processed? It cannot be both. Also, there is the problem of applying standards when they are amorphous or nonexistent. A related problem is that measuring library activities qualitatively is difficult at best. If unit production drops but quality of service increases, how do you measure that aspect? Can you measure the quality of the materials being used? What is the relative use of materials within the library, and how is that measured? These problems underline the necessity of clearly stated objectives at the outset.

The ultimate objective of the costing and work measurement is to develop a standard cost and performance for various functions, activities, and subactivities. The standard is simply an average based on past performance; you adjust it as new data become available. Figure 17.4 (pp. 442–443) provides an example of some of the major components of a program budget using a nonlibrary department as the example.

The primary weakness of the program budget lies in its emphasis on the quantification of library activities. Comparative evaluations will involve qualitative judgments, which are difficult to reflect in the quantitative elements in the budget.

ZERO-BASE BUDGET

The budgeting wave of the future during the 1960s and early 1970s was thought to be program budgeting; however, problems in measuring the library and the amount of time it took to gather information reduced the wave to a ripple.

The next candidate for such a wave arrived in the form of *zero-base budgeting* (ZBB) in the 1980s. It is currently little more than a ripple on a small pond. Supporters claimed ZBB was a possible replacement for the line, performance, and program formats. When taxpayers have major concerns about their tax burden, ZBB has widespread appeal, if not application. Given the current general feeling about governments and their costs, we may see an upswing in requiring agencies to use the ZBB format regardless of how time-consuming it may be. Thus, we decided to provide a brief overview of the concept.

The term "zero base" comes from the first step in the process; that is, the submitting agency is to assume that it is beginning operations for the first time (point zero). Thus, the focus of the planning and development of the ZBB is on the purpose and functions it should perform in order to meet its mission. In theory, an organization that uses ZBB would become more cost-effective by continuously reviewing its purposes and attempting to remove unneeded activities. From a taxpayer's point of view, if ZBB was practiced, the existing tax base would produce the maximum service at the lowest cost.

Several phases of ZBB are necessary in order to implement the system: construction, planning, budgeting, and control. *Construction* is a time-consuming part of the process. It is during the construction phase that the budget preparer assumes that the unit is starting at zero activity.

Assume you are the head of an archive unit, and you are to prepare a ZBB request. As part of the construction phase you might identify two functions (there would be more; two will illustrate the point): "to ensure that users receive accurate assistance in their search for primary materials" and "to ensure that users receive proper instruction in the use of archival resources, especially publishing rights." The function outcome statements would be "accurate assistance" and "users instructed in the use of archival resources."

You then need to divide functional statements into a series of subfunctions, thereby creating a hierarchy of activities. Under the function "users instructed . . ." you might list a set of the subfunctions such as "to ensure the understanding of residual property rights" (outcome: identified skill), "to ensure that users who need assistance are identified" (outcome: users identified), and "to ensure that users learn archival research skills" (outcome: knowledgeable customer). One could go further and divide each subfunction. For example, the "identified skills" subfunction might have divisions such as "to ensure that users know how to differentiate between primary and secondary materials in an archival collection" and "to ensure that users know how to properly credit archival materials." Our limited example illustrates just how time-consuming such a process would be for a library; remember that, in theory, this is an annual process.

When you think about an entire organization, it is not surprising that a very large percentage of the budget process is spent on "construction." No one disagrees that such a careful review of functions is valuable from time to time. But after their first "construction," very few individuals revisit their initial statement, which defeats a major purpose of ZBB.

Sample Program Budget Request—Fiscal Year 2012

Goals:
I. To provide access to significant fish and wildlife research information developed under the Federal Aid in Fish and Wildlife Restoration program.
II. To provide access to non-Federal aid, state-sponsored research.
III. To provide access to Federal aid and non-Federal aid research for the staff of noncontributing and private agencies.

In order to accomplish these goals the following objectives (services) have been determined:

A. Input (Indexing Services)
To acquire, evaluate, index, and process research reports produced by the Federal Aid in Fish and Wildlife Restoration program. In addition, not to exceed 75 manuscripts submitted by the American Fisheries Society during 2012.

1. Acquisitions will be arranged by the U.S. Fish and Wildlife Service and coordinated by the Project Manager and Indexing Specialists. Five trips, one to each regional office of the Fish and Wildlife Service, will be planned for the purpose of promoting the acquisition of Federal Aid and non-Federal Aid reports.

Personnel	$21,114.71
Travel	4,800.00
Telephone	432.00
Total	$26,346.71

2. Evaluation of 1,200 reports

Consultant	$6,800.00

3. Indexing of 650 reports will be done according to established selection criteria policies for bibliographic description and classification by subject content.

4. Processing entries for reports, including theses, for computerized storage, according to the most efficient mechanism, will be done by the indexing specialists.

Personnel	$11,271.07
Data processing	3,600.00
Digital copies	500.00
Total	$15,371.07

B. Output
To provide customized retrospective literature searching to Fish and Wildlife Reference Service cooperators and clients.

1. Literature searching will be done according to established search strategy policy.

Personnel	$12,484.87
Consultant	520.00
Data processing	2,762.00
Postage	950.00
Telephone	3,388.00
Total	$20,104.87

2. State indexes will be provided by the reference staff, when bibliographies are not appropriate to answer requests. Updated fish and wildlife indexes for each state will be produced and distributed once a year to each state fish and game headquarters.

Personnel	$6,326.07
Data processing	600.00
Total	$6,926.07

Figure 17.4 Sample Program Budget Request—Fiscal Year 2012

3. Reproduction and dissemination of reports to fulfill requests will be done by photocopying original reports (est. 600,000 pages) or digital copies (est. 4,000).

Personnel	$31,412.31
Digital copies	2,200.00
Equipment rental	19,087.10
Supplies	5,400.00
Postage	5,200.00
Printing	6,445.50
Total	$69,744.91

C. Fish and Wildlife Reference Service Newsletter
To make known the services available from the Fish and Wildlife Reference Service to potential users in cooperating agencies and others by mean of a quarterly Newsletter.

Personnel	$28,563.26
Printing	6,006.80
Postage	2,000.00
Maintain mailing list	2,000.00
Total	$38,570.06

D. Administration and Other Costs
This covers personnel time and other costs needed to administer the program of the agency. This includes training, supervision, representation at meetings, planning, budgeting, billing, space rental, miscellaneous office equipment and supplies, and part of the telephone and postage costs.

Personnel	$19,423.16
Other costs	9,336.00
Total	$28,759.16

E. General and Administrative Expense, or Overhead
General and administrative expenses are calculated to cover certain expenses incurred by the city public library.

F. Income
Charges are made to clients for all services and to cooperators for some duplication of materials. Estimated income is credited to the contract.

Summary of Program

Program	$ Amount	% of Total
A. Input	48,517.78	19.50
B. Output	96,775.85	38.90
C. FWRS Newsletter	38,570.06	15.50
D. Administration	28,759.16	11.56
E. General Administrative Expense		
@ 17% of A through D	36,145.88	14.53
Grand Total Cost	248,768.73	100
F. Credits/Income	35,000.00	
Net Cost	213,768.73	

Decision packages are the ultimate goal of the construction and planning phases of ZBB. As part of the construction process, you must establish a quantitative value and calculate the financial resources required to achieve each outcome statement. Normally, you calculate the quantitative figure and total cost on the basis of annual output rather than unit cost. These costing activities are very similar to those of program budgeting. The outcome statement with costs becomes a decision package.

The last step in preparing the decision package(s) is to rank each option and package in terms of their decreasing benefit to the organization. Needless to say, a high percentage of the options suggesting increases rate higher than those with decreased support. In theory, the frontline managers have the opportunity to prioritize their activities.

Clearly, the time necessary to prepare a comprehensive ZBB on an annual basis is enormous; few organizations that still employ some variation of ZBB revisit the construction annually. In addition, ZBB forces senior managers to review piles of paper. Most of the organizations that used ZBB decided the information overload at the most senior levels was too great. As a result, they terminated the ranking process one or two levels below the top.

FUND ACCOUNTING

Because the majority of libraries are part of nonprofit organizations, we include a brief section on fund accounting. This is a complex topic, and we can provide only some highlights. *Fund accounting* is peculiar to nonprofits. Accountants developed the system as a result of nonprofit characteristics of the users and the uses of information. Four of the nonprofits' "special" characteristics follow:

- The focus on social benefits
- The relative absence of profit-motivated behavior on the part of resource contributors (public and private)
- The special government- and constituent-imposed constraints on their activities
- The lack of generating a profit (this is not the same as generating income)

Users of fund accounting information are a diverse group, both internal and external to the organization.

There are similarities between fund accounting and for-profit accounting systems. However, profit enterprises use a single-entry focus, while fund accounting usually involves many fragmented financial reports. Such reports focus on separate individual funds and the flow of liquid assets rather than income.

The general fund exists to account for the unrestricted resources as well as resources not accounted for in any other group of accounts. *General fund* operating statements show revenues, expenditures, and encumbrances, as well as changes in fund balances. *Debit funds* track resources segregated for paying interest and principal on a general obligation debt. Many libraries have new facilities paid for

CHECK THESE OUT

Smith, G. Stevenson. 2002. *Managerial Accounting for Libraries and Other Not-for-Profit Organizations.* 2nd ed. Chicago: American Library Association.

Turner, Anne M. 2007. *Managing Money: A Guide for Librarians.* Jefferson, NC: McFarland and Company.

in full, or in part, by bond issues—a general obligation debt. *Capital project funds* control resources for the purpose of acquiring major fixed assets. Reports on capital project funds seek to list sources, uses, and available resources for individual projects. Most library facilities projects are a combination of monies from public and private sources; such monies would be part of the capital project fund.

A *special-revenue fund* accounts for, and reports on, resources that come from special sources—for example, a library foundation—or that carry restrictions on their use. Some libraries have endowments that would fall into this category. Some municipalities, and some academic institutions, engage in some form of commercial activities. *Enterprise funds* control activities that provide goods or services to the general public (Friends of the Library merchandise, for example) or user charges (photocopy charges are common). Library photocopy income would be part of the enterprise fund. *Internal library funds* are similar except the "customer" is part of the organization. You may encounter "chargeback" situations in which a nonlibrary unit charges the library a fee for its services; two common chargeback areas are computing and building maintenance.

While library managers may have little direct involvement in fund accounting, they do have substantial indirect contact, whether they know it or not. Having some knowledge of fund accounting will assist in working more effectively with funding authorities.

AUDITS AND AUDITORS

With deep apologies to Robert Frost we must report:

> As we sigh and vent
> Indeed you must account for
> When and where each cent was spent.
> Those who gave or lent
> The funds you begged on knees bent
> Expect you'll have a statement
> True and fair of every cent.
> Beware, should you fail
> Expect a sad event
> For off to jail you may be sent.

Poets we are not, but the sentiments expressed are all too true. The accounting or accountability of how you spent those cents falls under the purview of auditors.

Without question, fiscal accountability is a concern to supporters and budget officials. Essentially, an audit is a post-action review by an independent appraiser. There are several types of audit, not all of which are financial in character; however, the majority of audits do have finances as the underlying concern.

External and internal audits are the two broad categories. Almost every for-profit and nonprofit must have an annual *external audit* conducted by an independent auditor. Normally, an independent auditor is a certified public accounting (CPA) firm. There are two major purposes of the annual audit. The first is to ensure that financial accounts and statements are accurate. Second is to ensure that the organization is following generally accepted accounting principles. Such audits, because of their legal implications, are very thorough. A library that is part of an organization that must have an annual external audit may expect occasional, if not annual, visits from the independent auditor. You never know exactly what the auditors will want to review until they arrive; however, more often than not, it will be the collection-development fund accounts. This is because there are so many financial transactions involved in acquisitions work.

Internal audits, or operational audits, may or may not be fiscal in nature. Some of typical audits are these:

- Financial records (records must be accurate, proper, and in order)
- Compliance (reviews both internal and external policies and procedures)
- Operational (evaluates effectiveness and/or efficiency of an operation)
- Performance (purchasing, receiving, and payment records must follow proper fiscal and accounting regulations)
- Fact finding (official job classifications and descriptions must accurately reflect the work being done)

More often than not, parent body employees conduct the internal audit. These employees usually report to the chief operating officer of an organization in order to ensure their independence of judgment. Compliance and opera-

FOR FURTHER THOUGHT

Reflect on the nature of the records that might be audited, and check the auditing requirements for libraries in your state.

AUTHORS' EXPERIENCE

Alire, as soon as she arrived as the new library dean, would call for a formal financial audit. The audit would be external to the library but internal to the university. The audit was formal in that she would request it in writing to the chief financial officer (vice president for administrative services or vice president for finance, for example). Because these audits are very thorough and time-consuming, the vice president would have to assign a staff member from his or her office to conduct the audit within a certain time frame.

Alire would explain to the university's chief financial officer, the provost, her management team, and the entire library staff that the reason for the audit was not because she thought there were any financial issues (which is why she called for the audit within a month or so of her arrival). She explained that she wanted all the fiscal matters for which she was responsible in her tenure as the new dean to be identified with her tenure there. This meant that if the auditor listed "any findings" (usually procedural) Alire and her budget manager along with her new management team would correct those findings and start with a clean slate. Any financial issues that occurred during Alire's tenure would be her issues and not the issues inherited from her predecessor.

Because her first financial audit was so successful, Alire, in subsequent deanships, called not only for a financial audit but also for personnel (procedures) and security audits for the same reason as mentioned.

tional audits may use outside consultants in order to have the depth of knowledge needed to make judgments about a particular area.

You may hear a unit managerial leader say something like "Auditors are arriving tomorrow" with some degree of apprehension. Thoughts such as "Did I do everything right?" "Can I remember why I signed the requisitions 11 months ago?" "Does the proper 'paper trail' exist?" or "Am I in some type of trouble?" are common concerns. Auditors and audits generate almost as much anxiety as do performance appraisals, even in people with prior successful experience with the process. Too often, the reaction to auditors is that they are "snoopers" and "busybodies" who only create extra work. They do create extra work, but they provide an essential stamp of approval indicating sound accountability. Sound accountability is a major factor in receiving adequate funding for your operations. Jennifer Cargill (1987) offered good advice some years ago in an article titled "Waiting for the Auditor." She ended her article with, "Following the Ps—Proper Prior Planning and Preparation—will make them Painless" (p. 47). Doing so may not make it painless, but it will make it at least less painful.

BUDGET REPORTS

There are types of budget reports that you will need to become familiar with as your career moves forward. There is of course the *annual budget form* that shows the allocations. There is the *monthly reconciliation report* (often internal to the library) showing balances for what has been expended and encumbered and what remains (free). Acquisitions, collection-development personnel, as well as senior managers are interested in what these reports show. There is something similar from the parent financial office showing the differences between allocated and expended amounts (variance). Such reports are useful for many categories of expenditures, such as supplies and salaries. More important, they are terribly valuable for collection funds and other categories where encumbrances are key to knowing where you stand with the budget. G. Stevenson Smith (2002) illustrated the importance of variance when he wrote: "Variances provide different information for the manager. The *cost variance* is the difference between the legally approved budget appropriation and accrual-based expenses during the year. . . . The *expended variance* shows the effect of outstanding encumbrances on the cost variance" (p. 85). An advantage of the variance data is that at year end, assuming you have the authority to do so, you can think about shifting funds from an underexpended category to a different category in the coming fiscal year.

Another type of report is the *targeted report*. Such reports allow you to assess the costs in a specific area. Again for collection management, the library may have a single budget category from the parent institution for collection development. You might do a targeted report to determine how much of that large pool has been spent on children's books, electronic resources, media, and so forth. This type of information is very useful in planning the new budget request, making adjustments during the fiscal year, and allocating funds to departments in the case of an academic library.

INCOME GENERATION

Today, few libraries can expect to receive all the funds they need from their parent institutions or, at least, not enough to operate the way they would like. This is why ALA Treasurer Jim Neal's comments on income generation at the beginning of this chapter are so important.

CHECK THESE OUT

Two useful publications to read to get more in-depth information on income generation are *Becoming a Fundraiser,* 2nd ed., by Victoria and Stephen Elder (Chicago: American Library Association, 2000) and "Ten Principles for Successful Fundraising" by Gary Hunt and Hwa-Wei Lee (*Bottom Line* 6, no. 3/4: 111–121, 1993).

Developing and maintaining a positive image is important for all libraries—and it is essential for fundraising. There will be no opportunity for securing funds if the library's image is anything but positive. However, having a positive image is not enough. You must communicate that image to users, the general public, as well as to prospective sources of new funding. Granting agencies are just as interested in the image of their grantees as are individual donors.

We indicated earlier that finding sources of funding, other than the parent institution, for "light bulbs and toilet paper" is a challenge. Most foundations, donors, and other grant-giving organizations are interested in funding only special projects that have a very high probability of success. Securing funding for this activity may free up general operating funds for important or special activities that are underfunded. There will be competition from other libraries and other organizations seeking extra funding, and it will require an investment of time and collaboration within the organization if it is to be successful.

Fundraising, while it may have to be a part-time activity, requires planning and leadership. It will not be effective if it is a matter of "I'll do it when I have time." Only the very large libraries have the luxury of a full-time fundraiser. Most must depend on the efforts of several people who devote some of their time to fundraising—a team approach. As with any team, there needs to be one person in charge to call meetings, set agendas, propose ideas, implement plans, push the initiative forward, and monitor outcomes—in essence, provide the leadership. Generally, that person is the senior or next-most senior manager of the library. One reason for this is because donors want to know they are working with the decision makers.

Regardless of source, income generation is largely a matter of "the right person asking the right source for the right amount for the right project at the right time and in the right way." As you might imagine, getting all those "rights" correct takes planning, practice, preparation, and practical experience. Workshops help, but only real-world experience, and a few disappointments along the way, will translate theory and ideas into "money in the library's bank."

One long-standing internal revenue source for libraries is the sale of duplicate or otherwise unwanted gifts and donations. "Gifts in-kind" to libraries are very common; how libraries dispose of such items varies. Publicly supported libraries need to be aware of any regulations regarding the disposal of "public property." Donors may benefit from a tax deduction for donations in cash or in-kind to charitable or public bodies.

Many libraries impose fines for rule infractions and for lost or damaged items, all of which generate income. How the parent body treats such income can have an impact on your budget; many jurisdictions require that fines go into the general operating fund, not credited to the collecting agency. As you might guess, not getting monies paid for a lost or damaged item can become a drain on your budget, particularly if you must repair or replace the item. This in turn puts more pressure on you to raise monies from somewhere. A similar situation may exist for fees charged for library services, although it is more common that the library retains all or most of that income.

Another quasi-internal source is through activities undertaken by non-staff people (a support group) on behalf of the library—"Friends of Anywhere Library," "Library Associates," "Supporters of . . . ," or a similar title. That group may be no more formal than some volunteers who handle an ongoing book sale or may be a formal legal entity, a 501(c)(3) organization. In some situations, governing board members may be expected to make an annual contribution to the library. There can also be special types of "internal" funds, such as endowments, wills, trusts, and living trusts.

A major reason for having a foundation is to raise funds that are generally not taken into consideration by the library's parent body when setting the library's budget allocation. Another plus is that the foundation may invest the funds raised to generate still additional income. Without doubt, such bodies can be very effective fundraisers, as they are almost always composed of individuals who strongly support the library and its programs.

The significant difference between a support group and a foundation is the support group may not have the IRS 501(c)(3) status. This means that they may engage in political activity and lobbying but not indicate that donations are tax deductible. Even if they do not engage in political activities, they can be a significant source of extra funds for academic, public, and school libraries. Such groups have been raising a great deal of money for libraries over the years; even though many of their events raise only a small sum, the annual total is impressive.

There are also some rare and, in the past, overlooked opportunities to raise some substantial amounts of money locally—wills, trusts, and planned giving. Clearly bequests in a will become a source of funds only at death; however, today many nonprofit groups actively work with people to have the library included in a will. Trusts, on the other hand, come in many shapes and sizes. Some may

---

AUTHORS' EXPERIENCE

Evans has vivid memories of maintaining a long-term relationship with a donor who had a provision in her will that would give the proceeds from the sale of her home to the library after she died. On assuming his position as director, he was told about the need to maintain this donor/library relationship. He should go to her house twice a month on Sundays to talk with the lady. He was further advised to take some bakery "goodies." Shortly after starting the visits he decided to bake a cake for a visit. He was very surprised to find out the lady had once supervised Julia Child and remained a close friend with Child. The lady appreciated Evans's cake-baking efforts but suggested he buy one of Julia's dessert cookbooks. You need to do almost anything to maintain good donor relations.

The cakes may have helped, but the main concern for the lady was her lack of complete trust that the institution would honor her wishes that the sale proceeds would go to the library. Every meeting was spent going over what had and could be done to allay her fears. Evans can report that, when the time came, the institution did honor her wishes.

You must continue to maintain and perhaps improve the library's relationship with such individuals who have made a provision in their wills to benefit the library.

---

generate income for the library only during the donor's lifetime; others may generate income for both the donor and library during the donor's lifetime, while others become effective only at the donor's death. These are likely to increase in importance for libraries over the coming years.

Partnerships with a business are one of the newer fundraising approaches for libraries. Many libraries prefer to use the term "collaboration," as it seems less profit oriented. Glen Holt (2006) listed several reasons for seeking "corporate partnerships." His last reason, in our opinion, is the most telling: "Co-funding through sponsorships can be a great way to build and share current and potential audiences between the public and private sector" (p. 35). What you need to do is think broadly or imaginatively to find sponsorship possibilities. Partnerships with business can be extended to acquiring expertise that is not available within the library. Local radio and TV stations may provide airtime, local newspaper reporters can brief staff on how to write good copy, and public relations companies may well be prepared to offer their help to nonprofit libraries.

Grants and "gifts" from foundations and government agencies is our final "other funding" source category. The art of grantsmanship is something you can develop, but like any art it takes practice and then more practice before you have consistent success. Seeking grants is usually project focused—seed money for a new program, partial support for a facilities project, funds for new or replacement equipment, and so forth. As such it requires carefully thought-out plans.

An important step, in fact a key step, is to be certain you know what a foundation's or agency's current funding priorities are. Although their broad interest seldom changes over time, their annual funding priorities within a broad area may in fact vary from year to year. Do your research before making a call or sending a letter of inquiry. Most granting agencies have websites where you can do a substantial amount of research about mission, priorities of the current funding cycle, what the funding cycle is, proposal guidelines, deadlines, and much more. Most grant-giving agencies are willing to talk by phone to explore projects. This can save the time of the agency and the library.

If you have no prior experience in grant proposal preparation, signing up for a workshop or two is well worth the time and expense. Some grant-giving agencies organize workshops to outline their requirements. Also, when possible seek the assistance of an experienced grant writer. Be prepared to fail to get a grant on your first few efforts; however, keep trying and you will succeed. The good news is that, with many foundations, once you are successful your chances of getting later grants go up—assuming you have delivered on the first grant.

Even if fundraising is a part-time activity, there is an institutional cost. Time spent on fundraising is time not spent on library operations. The library's position as part of a larger whole usually means that it must get approval before undertaking fundraising activities. Senior managers may not approve such activities if they believe funds raised would not outweigh the time and effort expended or would be in conflict with other "broader" fundraising activities. Additionally, many funding groups and agencies require matching funds. That is, the library has to demonstrate that it will provide a certain percentage of funds to the proposed project or program if it funded. These funds can be actual dollars allocated, in-kind funds, or a combination of both. Senior managers must be aware of these funding stipulations and the funds being proposed as matching funds before they approve the proposal for advancement.

It is important to coordinate fundraising activities and not have several units from the institution approaching a single source with different projects. One reason is that one proposal may already be in front of the source and another proposal might cloud the issue. In addition, input will be required from the parent institution to ensure that it has been properly costed and that the parent institution is fully aware of what the library plans to do.

CHECK THIS OUT

A book to consult, regardless of library type, is Amy Sherman and Matthew Leher's *Legacies for Libraries: A Practical Guide to Planned Giving* (Chicago: American Library Association, 2000).

KEY POINTS TO REMEMBER

- Fiscal management is about securing, expending, and accounting for the essential monies to operate the best possible library.
- Budgeting is more than managing this year's allocation; it is thinking about what you will need in the future as well as how well you managed previous allocations.
- Budgeting is a political process that involves careful monitoring of your library's environment if you hope to secure adequate funding.
- You seldom have a voice in the type of budget to use—line, performance, for example—so your goal is to make the most effective use of what type is in place. This requires some study of the type's theory and methodology as well as assessing the organizational culture of the parent/funding body.
- Gaining an understanding of accounting and financial terminology will aid in developing sound relationships with those who devote their full-time attention to money matters in the parent organization.
- Income generation from sources other than the parent body will become an increasingly important part of a library's fiscal management activities.

References

American Libraries. 2010. "Tough Times and Eight Ways to Deal with Them." *American Libraries* 41, nos. 1/2: 16–17.

Buschman, John. 2003. *Dismantling the Public Sphere.* Westport, CT: Libraries Unlimited.

Cargill, Jennifer. 1987. "Waiting for the Auditor: Some Interim Advice." *Wilson Library Bulletin* 67, no. 9: 45–47.

———. 1988. "Financial Constraints: Explaining Your Position." *Wilson Library Bulletin* 68, no. 4: 32–34.

Cottrell, Terry. 2011. "Moving On: Salaries and Managing Turnover." *Bottom Line* 24, no. 3: 187–191.

Hartmann, Meg Klinkow. 2011. "Show Me the Money: Privatization and the Public Library." *Illinois Library Association Reporter* 29, no. 1: 4–7.

Holt, Glen. 2005. "Getting Beyond the Pain: Understanding and Dealing with Declining Library Funding." *Bottom Line* 18, no. 4: 185–190.

———. 2006. "Economics: Corporate Sponsorship." *Bottom Line* 19, no. 1: 35–39.

Linn, Mott. 2010. "Cost–Benefit Analysis: A Primer." *Bottom Line* 23, no. 1: 31–36.

Meraz, Gloria. 2002. "The Essentials of Financial Strength through Sound Lobbying Fundamentals." *Bottom Line* 15, no. 2: 64–69.

Neal, James G. 2012. E-mail communication sent to Camila A. Alire, February 21.

Seer, Gitelle. 2004. "No Pain, No Gain: Stretching the Library Dollar." *Bottom Line* 17, no. 1: 10–14.

Silverman, Emily. 2010. "Planned Giving: Preparing for the Future." *Bottom Line* 23, no. 3: 132–134.

Smith, G. Stevenson. 2002. *Managerial Accounting for Libraries and Other Not-for-Profit Organizations*. Chicago: American Library Association.

Wildavsky, Aaron, and Naomi Caiden. 2004. *The New Politics of the Budgetary Process*. 5th ed. New York: Pearson/Longman.

Launching Pad

Casey, Anne Marie, and Michael Lorenzen. 2010. "Untapped Potential: Seeking Library Donors among Alumni of Distance Learning Programs." *Journal of Library Administration* 50, nos. 5/6: 515–529.

Cottrell, Terrance. 2012. "Three Phantom Budget Cuts and How to Avoid Them." *Bottom Line* 25, no. 1: 16–20.

Hallam, Arlita W., and Teresa R. Dalston. 2005. *Managing Budgets and Finances: A How-To-Do-It Manual for Librarians and Information Professionals*. New York: Neal-Schuman.

Kepler, Ann, ed. 2012. *The ALA Big Book of Library Grant Money*. 8th ed. Chicago: American Library Association.

Kirk, Rachel, and Kelli Getz. 2012. "Accounting Techniques for Acquisition Librarians." *Serials Librarian* 62, nos. 1/4: 17–23.

Price, Lee. 2011. "Wanted: High Net Worth Donors." *Public Libraries* 50, no. 3: 28–31.

Rossmann, Doralyn, and Elizabeth A. Shanahan. 2012. "Defining and Achieving Normative Democratic Values in Participatory Budgeting Processes." *Public Administration Review* 72, no. 1: 56–66.

Silverman, Emily. 2008. "Building Your Base: Identifying Library Donors." *Bottom Line* 21, no. 4: 138–141.

Smith, Debbie A. 2008. "Percentage Based Allocation of an Academic Library Materials Budget." *Collection Building* 27, no. 1: 30–34.

Steele, Kirstin. 2008a. "Are Budget Limitations Real? Perspective, Perceptions, and a Plan." *Bottom Line* 21, no. 3: 86–87.

———. 2008b. "Budgeting for Libraries: Space Equals Money." *Bottom Line* 21, no. 4: 122–123.

Technology changes rapidly through new products offering new ways of doing familiar things and opportunities to do new things. Every library staff needs at least one technology scout, someone who continually scans the technology horizon. The scout explores opportunities, brings them to the attention of colleagues, and suggests ways the library can exploit them to improve services and users' experiences in seeking and using information. A good technology scout is enthusiastic about technology's potential, tests its capabilities, and always judges it from a user's point of view. The scout articulates and applies evaluative criteria and declares a technology "cool," not at first sight, but after it truly demonstrates its coolness. Because not every colleague has the same curiosity about and enthusiasm for technology, an effective technology scout knows how to meet them at their comfort level when exploring with them ways they can benefit in their work by adopting, even if not passionately embracing, a new technology or tool.

—Jim Rettig, ALA President, 2008–2009 (2012)

You truly realize the role library technology plays in today's world when you overhear your cleaning lady talking on her cell phone and telling someone how useful the public library's Internet connection is for helping her get and keep customers. Ending the conversation with "And it is FREE."

—G. Edward Evans (2012)

The future is here! At press time, the Flagstaff City–Coconino County Library was working hard to establish a new service for our library customers; Downloadable audio books and electronic books!

—City of Flagstaff (2011)

Sometimes an intellectual understanding of change is not the same as a visceral one. Managers all *know* that information sharing and collaboration are potent paths to innovation, but do they *feel* it? Especially as new generations of employees arrive, generations that were "born and raised with technology in their hands," do managers really understand "the huge sea change in how the young work force is wired" and what that means.

—Michael S. Hopkins (2010)

18

MANAGING TECHNOLOGY

This chapter focuses on the following:

- Centerpiece for today's library services
- Staff skills
- Planning and controlling costs
- Technology issues
- Cloud computing
- Social media
- Collaboration

TECHNOLOGY, ALTHOUGH a "thing," is almost as challenging to manage as people. In many ways some librarians, at least those of us who are older, may wish that library technology was still only about audio, video, and other equipment we made available to the public, as these were less complex to manage. This is no longer the case; some of the older "technologies" remain, but the reality is that technological consideration pervades library operations.

Our opening quotation about the Flagstaff Public Library illustrates the challenge; its 2011 announcement of a "new service" was for a service many public libraries had offered for several years. The challenge of being at even the midpoint of the technology curve is daunting. Slowly but surely the cost of technology is getting closer and closer to the total of a library's materials budget; in many cases, it has already surpassed that amount. Almost every day you can read about some new technological development that may have potential in a library setting. There was a time, not all that long ago, when a five-year replacement cycle for library IT equipment seemed short. Now it seems to have become nanoseconds.

Michael Hopkins, in another of our opening quotations, makes an important point about the expectations of younger employees regarding technology. Had he been thinking about libraries when he wrote the opinion piece, he well might have written "as new generations of employees and *customers* arrive, generations that were 'born and raised with technology in their hands,' do managers really understand 'the huge sea change in how the young people are wired?'" To survive today, libraries must embrace technology in almost all its forms. Finding the funding to do that and maintain other library services desired by our users tests our creativity and ingenuity. Being an effective steward of funds and balancing all of your users' needs and wants against available resources will be one of your ongoing challenges.

Library technology also generates some collaboration challenges, as there is interdependency between the library and the parent organization's IT unit. Libraries are not self-sufficient when it comes to ICT (information and communication technology). Library managerial leaders must collaborate with IT colleagues to arrive at the best solution that meets the needs of the organization as a whole. There is also the need to collaborate with other libraries in order to achieve maximum results from our technology dollars. We explore this issue later in the chapter.

TECHNOLOGY'S ROLE IN LIBRARY OPERATIONS

Contrary to what some people think and write about libraries in a digital world, libraries and their staff are not backward looking; libraries are reasonably quick to adopt new technologies. In some cases, they may be too quick to try something new; one example is e-books when some libraries moved quickly into that area only to find the technology was not ready for the mainstream. As a result, they lost money, time, and effort for being on the "bleeding edge" of technology's curve (for a discussion of early e-books and libraries, see Hage and Sottong, 2000; Sottong 2001). Nevertheless, the stodgy library image of not adopting technology remains strong in some minds.

A 2011 example of the misconception about libraries and technology appeared in an op-ed piece in the *Los Angeles Times*. In the October 26 issue (http://opinion.latimes.com/opinionla/2011/11/saving-libraries-but-not-librarians-blowback.html), Dan Terzian, an attorney with no identified background in librarianship, suggested librarians and many libraries were no longer necessary. Some of his comments were: "The digital revolution has made many libraries obsolete"; "All but the most heady research can be performed by a Google, Google Books, or Google Scholar search"; and "Libraries should embrace the digital revolution, even though it entails the loss of librarians." Feedback to his opinions was swift and negative; apparently many librarians and library supporters have at least embraced some aspects of the digital revolution and know how to post comments on websites.

We included this example because we believe it makes an important point. We, librarians, still have significant work to do in getting the message out—that libraries have indeed embraced technology and that librarians and libraries have a positive impact (intellectually and economically) on society. For example, libraries are creating digital archives (local history, institutional, and rare book/special materials), something that no for-profit organization would ever consider. This is another example of the library's very special role and place in society.

There are many components to libraries and technology; however, there are two broad aspects. From a daily work point of view, ICT has been fully integrated into library operations. Service to the users is equally dependent on ICT. Almost every library, from school libraries to the Library of Congress, employs technology for daily work activities and service and has been doing so for some time.

In terms of the "digital revolution," libraries have a long history of adopting technological advances. The Library of Congress developed work applications for the first-generation computer systems. Other libraries began using similar variations, many "homegrown," in the 1960s. Libraries are a prime example of organizations that quickly shifted from dependence on manual systems to almost total dependence on technology. The 1960s mainframes were the base that shifted to minicomputers in the late 1970s, to the client/server model in the 1980s, and then to web-based technology in the 1990s. It appears that in the 2000s they will shift yet again, this time to the "cloud."

Librarians demanded ever-growing functionality in the systems that they acquired so that by the mid-1980s the terms "integrated library system" and "turnkey system" filled the professional literature; and more and more digital material became part of their collections. In today's libraries when the servers go down (it does not happen all that often), staff ask if they can go home as they cannot do their work; and users become rather upset that much of what they wish to do in the library is not possible.

The design of integrated systems was based on traditional library functions; although the systems handle print material well, they are not as effective for electronic content. Slowly but surely practices have shifted to reflecting the capabilities of technology rather than only employing part of its capabilities. Traditional organizational structures and operations have and continue to change. The tools to deliver e-content have fallen behind service needs (for a discussion of the shortcomings of ILS and digital materials, see Breeding, 2006).

One issue that is important in any networked library environment is server "up" time. With most libraries operating 24/7 for remote access, the need for reliable servers is an important issue. To achieve that goal, servers must be operational 99.9 percent of the time. Four of the major benefits of operating some form of a client/server environment are these:

- The capability of sharing files and interacting with other systems accessible through a local or wide area network
- The capability to move computing functions from a large central system to local servers and workstations/terminals
- The capability to reduce end user training by providing graphical interfaces with point-and-click technology

> **TIP**
>
> Keep abreast of technological changes by following Lorcan Dempsey's weblog (http://orweblog.oclc.org/) on libraries, services, and networks. Lorcan is Vice President of Research and OCLC's Chief Strategist.

- The capability to employ multiple applications from a single workstation (additionally, because libraries are usually part of a larger organization, the parent body may require going with a client/server environment)

The following are technological implications for service delivery:

- The need for a robust infrastructure backed up by ready access to skilled technical support
- 24/7 access
- Efficient information security policies
- Excellent relationships with vendors and providers of outsourced services
- A realistic budget for maintenance, licenses, and upgrades
- An investment in staff and user training
- Effective environmental scanning of potential impacts on the library

However, having the technologies is only part of the picture; it must be backed up by staff members who understand the needs of the user community, anticipate these needs, know the relevant sources, and deliver the required information in the preferred format at the right time. Information delivery still requires human intervention.

STAFF BACKGROUND AND TRAINING

Jim Rettig's statement about the internal role of the *technology scout* at the beginning of chapter is so relevant when talking about library staff. The scout is the person who introduces the new technology and its applications to library staff. Once this is done and the technology is adopted, then the scout hands off the training of the staff to another techie.

One aspect of managing technology involves making certain staff at every level have the necessary background and training to handle the technology in place, as well as the technology it plans to acquire. Funding for staff development opportunities for the professional side of information work is usually limited. The challenge is to decide how to allocate the funds available.

With new applications or a major upgrade, having staff do training on their own with a user manual is not good use of their time. Library technology ven-

CHECK THESE OUT

Jennings, Anna. 2005. "Determining and Meeting Personnel Training
    Needs." *Computers in Libraries* 25 (8 September): 13–15.
Quinney, Kayla L., Sara D. Smith, and Quinn Galbraith. 2010. "Bridging the
    Gap: Self-Directed Staff Technology Training." *Information Technology
    and Libraries* 29, no. 4: 205–213.

dors usually offer some level of training for their products. It is often more effective to build training costs into the price of acquiring the system than trying to secure separate funding. Some software vendors offer training packages that are built into the application ("tutoring" programs) often accessed online.

Managers should plan for three types of training: entire staff for a new application, new staff members, and the end users. With this in mind, it is evident why training costs should be an item in the annual technology budget. Sometimes it is possible to use a mentor approach for librarywide training. One advantage is that the mentor is better able to relate to the special needs of her or his coworkers than is a general trainer. Training in groups is more cost effective than the one-on-one approach—this is true for both staff and end users. Two widely used training technologies are multicasting and video-on-demand, which can be implemented on local area networks, corporatewide area networks (intranet), or the Internet.

While multicasting and video on-demand have their individual strengths, in combination they provide a rich environment for delivering training. The ability to be implemented across networks makes them easy to manage, provides economies of scale, and permits personnel savings. Some libraries now set aside a space for training purposes. RSS feeds and the iPod are useful for delivering instruction to individuals cost effectively.

Another training cost is the help desk function that the staff provides. With remote access, users will ask both information-related questions and questions about accessing the system. Bell and Shank (2004) have described the role of the "blended librarian." There is a need for specialists who can handle the traditional requests for information and also "walk through" the technical problems with the users. It requires subject knowledge, awareness of the many technical problems users may encounter, and the communication skills of a call center operator. While today's education of librarians provides a good background in the basic areas such as database management and networking issues, support staff are less likely to have an educational background in ICT, so you need to provide that background.

In Chapter 9, we looked at change and resistance to change and suggested you cannot always predict when, or if, resistance will occur. However, among the types of change in technology that has a high potential for resistance is replacing a system or a major upgrade. In 1970, Dickson and Simmons identified nine areas of staff concern or reasons for resisting technology that still hold today:

- Threats to economic security
- Threats to status or power
- Increased job complexity
- Uncertainty or unfamiliarity
- Changed superior–subordinate relationships
- Increased rigidity or time pressure
- Role ambiguity
- Feelings of insecurity

Some of the resistance can be overcome through training. However, communication is the key to success for those planning and implementing technology changes. Encouraging staff input concerning their technology needs and determining the best time to make the changes will also help overcome resistance.

There is one other technology-related staff issue for managerial leaders—"technostress." One element of such stress is physical, as staff members spend more and more time using an e-workstation. Poor posture, equipment, lighting, and physical arrangement can lead to a variety of physical or health problems, ranging from mild headaches and eye strain to carpal tunnel syndrome. Managers must take ergonomic factors into account, and a number of countries, such as the United States, have legal requirements that must be met. Staff personnel need information about posture and exercises to release tension and about how to plan their work so that they do not spend long uninterrupted hours at a workstation. Getting away, even for a few minutes every hour, reduces technostress. Build into tasks a mix of technology- and nontechnology-based activities so that staff can take a break.

The second aspect of technostress is mental, which can be experienced by staff, managers, and end users. Managers know that changes in technology will result in tension and/or stress even if there is no resistance. Part of the tension/stress reduction process is having ample and adequate training for the changes; scheduling ample lead time and getting written information to the staff about the change and the technology reduce stress when the change actually occurs.

Working with vendors to produce user-friendly paper documentation and online manuals can reduce technostress. Nothing builds stress more quickly than facing some deadline that requires the use of a new technology or software and not being able to make it work after following every step in the vendor-supplied documentation. Talking with other libraries and using the product before making the purchase decision are always good practices. Among the questions to ask are "How good is the documentation?" and "How good is the vendor training or support?" Knowing what to expect allows you to anticipate and prepare solutions before the problem arises.

These are some personal factors that managerial leaders should think about in terms of stress:

- Is it really essential that I have the same technology and applications at home as in the office?
- Is it really essential that I do this work at home?
- Is it possible that I could make better use of office time so I do not have to take work home?
- Is it really essential that I check my office e-mail from home at night, on the weekend, at a conference, or even on vacation?
- Can I turn my phone off when I leave the office?
- Is it necessary that I become the "techie of techies" in my organization when that is not my area of responsibility?

Some management gurus consider technology as the driving force and should be the primary managerial focus. However, managers have a long history of operating without computers; and there is a body of principles and practices that are technology independent. Technology is a management tool, not an end in itself. If it provides more data, alternatives, and models more quickly to aid decision making or any other basic management function, that is welcomed. However, you must still understand how to assess the data and the decision-making process (or other function) in order to take effective action. Technology should not, and in most cases cannot, replace human judgment and assessment.

While managerial leaders at all levels understand that the useful life of technology is getting shorter and shorter, some funding officials do not yet accept this fact.

TRY THIS

With a specific type of library in mind, list all the causes of technostress that you can think of. Then, in a second column, list ways of overcoming them.

They think, "If we provide X amount of money for technology equipment this year, we will not have to deal with this again for four or five years." Managerial leaders face several challenges: planning for technology, acquiring the technology, controlling technology costs, and ensuring that higher-funding authorities understand the nature of ICT costs and rates of change.

TECHNOLOGY PLANNING

A key factor in maintaining a successful ICT program is careful long-range planning. Accurately predicting future changes in technology direction and the timing of those changes is almost impossible much beyond 12 to 24 months. Nevertheless, the best insurance for managing technology, in the most cost-effective manner possible, is developing a long-term plan.

By treating the process as a rolling plan, you gain the benefits of long-term planning while maintaining the flexibility to adjust the plan in a changing environment. A rolling plan is one that you review and revise each year. All of the planning elements discussed in Chapter 4 apply. What makes long-term technology planning somewhat different from other planning is the almost certain knowledge that the plan will probably never be fully implemented—each passing year some element(s) will be modified as technologies change.

Managerial leaders must plan for ICT from at least four viewpoints. Most important are the strategic considerations: factors such as competitive differentiation, overall improvement in decision making, and improved operational processes. Thinking about technology both offensively and defensively are also useful exercises. From an offensive viewpoint, considering how to achieve or realize maximum benefit from the use of ICT is vital. Defensively, think in terms of controlled growth and what is happening in other libraries. The fourth point of view that underlies most of the other aspects is cost justification.

Critical success factors (CSFs) are the library activities in which "things have to go right" or "failure will hurt performance the most." CSFs are very useful in technology planning. From a library point of view, one of the technology CSFs is network reliability—both intranet and Internet. Another CSF is the reliability of the ILS. An additional example of a technology CSF is the integrity of the customer database. Such factors become useful in planning the architecture and long-term technology needs.

There are a number of planning models; we favor Emberton's (1987) holistic planning approach. The first step is to gain agreement on, or verify, that the current statement of the library's mission and goals reflects the actual desires of senior management and governing bodies.

One advantage of starting with mission and goals is that they are both general in character, which means the uncertainty about future directions of technology is less of an issue. Using objectives, which are much more specific and which reflect the purposes of current functions and activities, allows you to plan technology requirements realistically.

Another step is to examine each goal, objective, function, and activity and ask the question, "Could ICT assist in its performance or achievement?" Related questions are, "What type and how much technology would, or could, be appropriate?" and "What problem does the technology address?" One example of a goal is "To provide 24-hour access to library resources." By using a general statement, you can develop a long-range plan without too much concern about unexpected technological changes. You are not necessarily locked into a particular technology solution long term. (Some of us remember the days when libraries provided access to digital information through CDs and CD towers and worried about PC and Mac compatibility.) It also makes it easier for the decision makers to look at today's state-of-the-art technology and consider experts' opinions about future trends when deciding what to do during the next 12 to 18 months.

Basic technical issues also play a key role in a successful planning process. It becomes important to have answers to questions such as these:

- Are there any organizational policies that influence decision making?
- What types of data are required to reach an informed decision?
- Which technology offers the greatest payoff in relation to service goals and objectives?
- What are the functional advantages, if any, of the new technology?
- What are the technical prerequisites for using a specific technology?
- If different objectives require different technologies, what are the compatibility issues?
- Does the library have the infrastructure to support the new technology?
- Is the technology an "open system" or proprietary? If proprietary, how difficult would it be to migrate to another system in the future?
- What technical strategy will be most effective: network or stand-alone?
- How will staff and users be affected?
- What are the staffing and training requirements?
- What are user education requirements?
- What are the short- and long-term implications?

Beyond technical considerations, here are some political and end user issues to consider:

- What is the parent institution's attitude toward expenditures on technology? Is it a long-term or a short-term view?
- Is there an organizational policy to centralize ICT services, or are they decentralized?
- Will the expenditure for and implementation of the technology create relationship problems with other units in the parent institution or collaborating services?

- What is the library's track record with funding authorities when it comes to implementing technology?
- Will all end users be able to access and/or benefit from the proposed technology?
- Is there an issue about differing end user platforms or "average" users' system capabilities?
- Does the proposed technology relate to or meet immediate- and long-term needs of end users?
- Does the proposed technology restrict or constrain end user creativity in using technology?
- Is the system flexible enough to meet all end users' needs?
- Are there any end user training implications?

The planning must involve functional, institutional, usage, risk, and staffing analyses as well as take into account implementation and hardware assessment. Remember that technology planning is more than about hardware and software; it requires understanding the organization, its purpose(s), and its customers. What your goal should be is to create an information environment appropriate for the library while meeting the parent organization's needs—not to add technology for technology's sake or to "prove" the library is up-to-date. In essence, technology development follows a five-stage process: problem definition, data collecting, conceptual design, detailed design, and implementation.

CONTROLLING TECHNOLOGY COSTS

Controlling technology costs is a managerial leader's challenge and a budget officer's nightmare. Traditionally, libraries have had two categories of expense that are ongoing and always increasing: salaries and journal subscription costs. There are some techniques for controlling salary expenses, such as not granting additional staff positions, limiting annual salary increases, imposing hiring freezes, and, occasionally, cutting existing positions. Options for controlling subscription price increases are generally fewer, because they are outside your and the parent institution's control. Many libraries have joined consortia to gain bargaining power with publishers in order to limit the size of price increases. This really only helps keep the increases down. However, to stop the escalation, you must cancel titles.

TRY THIS

List six areas of expenditure on information and communications technology. Which do you expect to increase in the next five years, and which may decrease?

AUTHORS' EXPERIENCE

Alire would always inform university administrators that information technology was not less expensive to implement and maintain. It did, however, allow the library to be more efficient and effective in terms of providing 24/7 access to library materials. Efficiency was based on better use of staff, facilities, and time. Effectiveness was based on providing access to information for students and faculty anytime and anywhere.

Today, technology costs are the third component in the ever-increasing costs for most libraries. They are also beyond your control. Unlike journals, you rarely are able to "cancel" technology. Today's libraries, and their users, are too dependent on technology to delay expenditures on upgrades and replacements. When a vendor no longer supports a product, you need to either upgrade or face the costs and frustration of attempting to maintain the existing technology on your own. The two most effective tools for controlling technology costs are having a rolling five-year plan and developing a clear understanding of which functionalities are absolutely essential and which would be just "nice" to have.

These are important cost concerns, but the one that makes ICT increasingly expensive is the demand for ever-increasing functionality. Functionality requires development by the vendors—the cost of which they incorporate into the new price. Library managerial leaders who have been involved in several ILS acquisitions often liken the process to buying a new automobile. It seems as if everything is an "option at an additional cost." Establishing a set of system requirements prior to starting a search is useful in controlling the costs.

FROM THE AUTHORS

Evans worked at a university that struggled with controlling institutional ICT costs. The university president made a surprise announcement on a Friday afternoon that all of the ICT services were to be outsourced the following Monday. ICT staff had the weekend to decide if they would accept a position with the outsourcing firm. In any event, they would cease being a university employee at 5:00 p.m. that day. The president also announced he had signed a seven-year contract with the company.

Four years later, the university canceled the outsourcing contract. That decision led to additional problems for campus IT users.

CHECK THESE OUT

Matthews, Joseph R. 2002. *Internet Outsourcing Using an Application Service Provider: A How-To-Do-It Manual for Librarians.* New York: Neal-Schuman.

Pantry, Sheila, and Peter Griffiths. 2004. *Managing Outsourcing in Library and Information Services.* New York: Neal-Schuman.

Rivard, Suzanne, and Benoit A. Aubert. 2008. *Information Technology Outsourcing.* Armonk, NY: M. E. Sharpe.

Owning a home computer demonstrates the problem of the constant need to upgrade memory and storage capacity. Just when you think your computer is up-to-date and you go to buy a new software program, the program lists system requirements that exceed the computer's capability. In an institutional setting, this scenario repeats itself over and over again with every employee who has a workstation. End users request additional features and functionality; software producers create a new product meeting those desires; and system requirements escalate along with costs.

Given this reality, we do not think that libraries should attempt to be on the forward slope of the technology curve. Too often, significant problems exist in "leading edge" products, and some products never do mature. We suggest that the prudent manager should aim to stay only near the top of the curve or just slightly behind. Let someone else work through the inevitable bugs. In most cases, securing equipment funding is difficult, and spending it on unproven products is risky. Working with staff to keep technology expectations at a reasonable level is essential in managing technology.

Personnel assigned to ICT administration are often not additional staff but reassigned existing staff. Technology rarely reduces workloads or costs—it does assist staff to accomplish more work and often creates unexpected opportunities. Hence you face the challenge of balancing traditional activities and newer systems administration responsibilities with few, if any, additional personnel.

A continuing trend in many organizations is to outsource services to control costs. Providers of specialist services are able to employ a wide range of expertise and amortize costs over a number of customers, perhaps moving some tasks offshore. ICT services have the potential for outsourcing, particularly in small organizations. It requires a clear understanding of expectations on the part of the customer and supplier, a consideration of what would happen if the supplier fails, a careful examination of internal costs and outsourcing, a legal contract, and close monitoring of the quality of service provided.

TECHNOLOGY ISSUES AND LIBRARIES

DIGITAL CONTENT

Perhaps the biggest "technology" issue you, as a library managerial leader, have to handle is digital content. Not many other organization managers have this type of responsibility in addition to their normal technology duties. You must manage the content as well as the hardware and software to which end users must have access. This introduces issues of evaluation, selection, acquisition, and usage of e-resources. In most libraries, the collection management duties are shared, and part of the evaluation process for e-materials involves assessing the technology requirements. Collection management is a subject that is a full course in library schools, and this is not the place to go into details. For a full discussion of the topic, see G. Edward Evans and Margaret Saponaro's (2012) *Collection Management Basics.*

From a management perspective, there are legal questions as well as questions of ownership and permitted usage. In the past, when a library collection consisted primarily of printed materials and media such as videos and audio materials, it was only a question of complying with copyright law. Not that copyright compliance was a minor matter or easy—it's just that it was the only significant legal issue related to the use of collections.

Now, in addition to the long-standing copyright issues, the Digital Millennium Copyright Act (DMCA, http://www.copyright.gov/legislation/pl105-304 .pdf) further complicates your managing digital materials and providing access to the Internet. DMCA amended U.S. copyright law to comply with WIPO (World Intellectual Property Organization, http://www.wipo.int/portal/index .html.en) treaties on such matters as term of coverage. It did more than that; it also addressed a great many of the technology aspects of copyright. One of the education/library community's concerns was about the decline of fair use rights related to section 1201. This section prohibits gaining unauthorized access to material by circumventing any technological protection measures a copyright holder may have in place. Section 1201 is not intended to limit fair use, but fair use is *not* a defense to circumventing technological protection measures.

Section 1202 prohibits tampering with "Copyright Management Information" (CMI). The DMCA identified the following as constituting CMI:

- Information that identifies the copyrighted work, including title of the work, the author, and the copyright owner
- Information that identifies a performer whose performance is fixed in a work, with certain exceptions
- In the case of an audiovisual work, information that identifies the writer, performers, or director, with certain exceptions
- Terms and conditions for use of the work

- Identifying numbers or symbols that accompany the above information or links to such information, for example, embedded pointers and hypertext links
- Such other information as the Register of Copyrights may prescribe by regulation, with an exception to protect the privacy of users

One aspect of the DMCA that is very important for most libraries is "Title II: Online Service Provider Liability." The reason for this is that the DMCA defines "online service provider" (OSP) very broadly. Libraries that offer electronic resources or Internet access are considered OSPs. The law creates some "safe harbors" for certain specified OSP activities. When an activity is within the safe harbor, the OSP qualifies for an exemption from liability. One aspect of the liability relates to illegal activities such as misuse of copyrighted digital materials. This is of particular importance for libraries supporting educational activities, distance education, course reserves, and other online course materials, for example.

When subscribing to a print journal or purchasing a book, there is no question about ownership. Nor are there issues about who can use the material or how often it can be used. If a journal has 12 issues and 12 individuals want to read one of the issues all at the same time, there is nothing to keep them from doing so. Access to web-based information products comes with a license that may impose limitations on library use.

Vendors of electronic products view licenses as a means of controlling use of their products and protecting their investment, as well as more likely ensuring them a profit. All too often libraries treat the "opening of this seal is taken as accepting the licensing agreement" statement that usually accompanies a software product in the same way most people do the contract they sign when they rent a car at an airport—they accept the agreement without reading it. If the person renting a car read and understood the rental agreement, there would probably be very few vehicles rented. The same is true for licenses accompanying electronic products for library use.

The failure to read and modify library vendor agreements can result in loss of, or limitations on, the "rights" that exist for paper products—for example, fair use, interlibrary loan, and multiple copies for face-to-face educational use. The license can impose limits on who may use the material that are impossible for the library to control or monitor in any cost-effective manner. Very often the license contains a clause that would impose on the library the legal responsibility for controlling how the end user uses the materials—clearly an impossible task. Occasionally there will be some limitations on the frequency of use or the number of simultaneous users. We are not aware of a vendor actually attempting to "seek a remedy" for a library failing to comply; however, this does not mean it will not happen.

A lawyer need not review every contract; however, what is necessary is a plan for dealing with electronic licensing that has input from the library's parent organization's legal counsel. You should have a document that outlines what rights are essential for library service (such as retaining downloading rights, interlibrary loan usage, and copying), what are highly desirable, and what are of little or no concern.

The library's and parent organization's goals should be that end users have as much freedom to access and use the material under the license agreement as they do under print copyright. If they do not, there is something wrong. In some cases, "user" carries a very limited meaning in the license when compared to the library's definition. Another problematic term is "lending"—most licenses tightly control, if not prohibit, lending. What remote access is possible? Any library supporting distance education, training, or other geographically widespread activity has a vested interest in remote access.

There is a virtual alphabet soup of technical implications for e-materials to understand—some of which are DC, DLF, DOI, DRM, EAD, ERMI, PURL, SFX, and XML. All of these, and more, relate to managing library e-resource content in one way or another.

DC (Dublin Core, http://dublincore.org/) is something you know or will learn more about during the course of your degree program. DC's metadata initiative focuses on providing standards to assist in finding, sharing, and managing digital information. Many of the standards underlay numerous e-products a library provides access to and the manner in which the library provides that access.

DLF (Digital Library Federation, http://www.diglib.org/) is under the umbrella of the Council on Library and Information Resources. Although the membership is primarily composed of research libraries, its initiatives benefit any library engaged in creating and maintaining e-resources. One such effort is ERMI (Electronic Resource Management Initiative, http://www.diglib.org/standards/dlf-erm02.htm), which address managing licensed products.

DOI (Digital Object Identifier) is a system somewhat like ISBN and ISSN. The DOI website spells out the following:

> The DOI System provides a framework for persistent identification, managing intellectual content, managing metadata, linking customers with content suppliers, facilitating electronic commerce, and enabling automated management of media. DOI names can be used for any form of management of any data, whether commercial or non-commercial. The DOI System is an ISO International Standard. (http://www.doi.org/)

Some libraries use the DOI, when available, rather than a URL, as it provides a more stable link to the material.

DRM (Digital Rights Management, http://www2.safenet-inc.com/) is a set of "technologies" that e-producers (books, games, music, serials, and video) can employ to control access to and use of their copyrighted material, especially copying, by third parties. From a library resource point of view, the use of DRM technologies can and may prevent legal fair use activities of end users. Knowing what, if any, DRM technologies are embedded in a product or service is important.

EAD (Encoded Archival Description, http://www.loc.gov/ead/eaddev.html) is now part of the Library of Congress's service program. It is a standard for machine-readable finding aids for e-materials created by archives, libraries, museums, and repositories. The standard employs SGML (Standard Generalized Markup Language) and XML (eXtensible Markup Language) as the base for encoding information.

OpenURL, the very familiar "web address," was developed by the National Information Standards Organization (NISO), a component of the American National Standards Institute (ANSI) as standard Z39.88. OCLC (http://www.oclc.org/research/activities/openurl/default.htm) is the current body for maintaining the standard.

PURL (Persistent Uniform Resource Locator) helps address the problem of disappearing URLs: "PURLs provide a level of indirection that allows the underlying Web addresses of resources to change over time without negatively affecting systems that depend on them. This capability provides continuity of references to network resources that may migrate from machine to machine for business, social or technical reasons" (http://purl.oclc.org/docs/index.html).

SFX (http://www.exlibrisgroup.com/category/SFXOverview) is an OpenURL link resolver. As you will see when you visit the website, SFX is a proprietary program. Many libraries use SFX as it provides extra benefits, such as e-usage data. Having sound e-usage data is critical when it comes to evaluating e-resources.

CHECK THESE OUT

The following are useful guides to the complex issues of copyright and compliance:

Bebbington, Laurence W., ed. 2011. *Information Law and Intellectual Property Rights in a Digital Landscape.* New York: Neal-Schuman.

Behrnd-Klodt, Menzi L. 2008. *Navigating Legal Issues in Archives.* Chicago: Society of American Archivists.

Butler, Rebecca P. 2011. *Copyright for Teachers and Librarians in the 21st Century.* New York: Neal-Schuman.

Crews, Kenneth D. 2011. *Copyright Law for Librarians and Educators: Creative Strategies and Practical Solutions.* Chicago: ALA Editions.

Harris, Lesley Ellen, ed. *The Copyright and New Media Law Newsletter.* Quarterly. Chicago: ALA Editions.

Lipinski, Tomas A. 2013. *The Librarian's Legal Companion for Licensing Information Resources and Services.* Chicago: American Library Association.

Padfield, Tim. 2010. *Copyright for Archivists and Records Managers.* 4th ed. London: Facet.

Russell, Carrie. 2011. *Complete Copyright for K–12 Librarians and Educators.* Chicago: ALA Editions.

XML (eXtensible Markup Language, http://www.xml.com/) is one of many document markup languages. With any full-text material, whether book or serial, one issue to consider is the way the text was digitized: ASCII, Adobe, HTML, or SGML. ASCII is the oldest and in many ways the easiest approach. Adobe Acrobat PDF (Portable Document Format) is currently a common format on the Internet. HTML (Hypertext Markup Language) is probably the most common method used on the World Wide Web. It is a sublanguage of SGML (Standard Generalized Markup Language). Many organizations used SGML to digitize their internal documents; currently the favored standard is XML.

These are just a sample of the alphabet soup that confronts the library staff's management of e-resources. End users don't really care about the technology side of having e-resources; they just want them available 24/7—the how that takes place is the library's concern. Your job is to manage them so that technical issues do not get in the way of the users.

SECURITY

Technological security has both a physical and an intellectual aspect. You don't want your investment in technology to be stolen or its functionality compromised by malicious behavior. On the intellectual side, you must address concerns about personal privacy as well as intellectual freedom (filtering). To a degree, the physical security aspects are the easiest to manage.

Broadly speaking, there are four types of control that will help ensure quality and security:

- Information system controls
- Processing controls
- Storage control
- Physical facility controls

Information system controls attempt to ensure accuracy, validity, and propriety of system activities. Many relate to input as well as to output data. Some of the data entry controls are passwords (or codes) for different levels of staff, formatted data entry screens, and audible error signals. Another type of information system control is control logs, which preserve evidence of all system input.

Processing controls help ensure that correctly entered data goes through processing properly. Some processing controls identify errors in arithmetic, calculations, or logical operations, or data not processed, or data lost. These controls are for both hardware and software. For hardware, such controls include malfunction detection circuitry, circuitry for remote diagnostics, and redundant components. In terms of software, checks for internal file labels, "checkpoints" within a program that assist in building an audit trail, and system security monitors are examples of processing control.

System output is another area of concern for procedural controls. One example is logging of output documents and reports and where those reports went. Control listings are a means of providing hard-copy evidence of all output produced. Distribution lists help personnel responsible for control ensure that only authorized users receive output.

Storage control is also important. Someone must be responsible for maintaining and controlling access to databases. You can control access through passwords and codes assigned to end users or through identification verification. The typical system has a three-level security procedure: user logon, user password, and unique file name. Essential security measures for storage are file backup of data and programs and storage of backup material in another location.

Physical facility controls involve a variety of security measures, from simply a locked room out of the public area to a high-security facility with elaborate environmental controls. In a distributed-technology environment, physical security of equipment becomes more difficult and complex, but you must attempt to provide some security, if nothing more than equipment "lockdowns."

Another important security element in the Internet environment are "firewalls" that protect the network from unwanted access or intrusion by serving as a safe transfer point to and from other networks. Its function is to screen network activity and allow only authorized transmissions in or out. Unfortunately, firewalls are able only to deter, not completely prevent, unauthorized access. Problems of hacking will continue for the foreseeable future. One security solution will be in the growing area of biometrics. Security systems using biometrics assess physical traits that make a person unique: voice verification, fingerprints, hand shape, keystroke analysis, and eye/retina scanning are some examples. A digitized biometrics profile is created for each user; special sensors then measure the person wanting access, and, if there is a match, access is allowed.

You must expect public-access PCs will have malware, viruses, and worms from time to time. All of these can be problems for staff machines; however, they are certainly problems for public machines. Some "infections" are just a nuisance, while others can destroy contents of memory and hard disks. They often migrate from one computer to another by means of the Internet, e-mail, or intranet. Having effective and up-to-date virus checking/cleaning software is important, as is using it on a regular basis. A virus-checking program that automatically scans any file downloaded from the Internet or an intranet is highly desirable.

INTELLECTUAL SECURITY

There are three major user privacy issues for libraries. One relates to personal information the library collects about a person as part of its normal business practices (such as basic contact information for borrowers and what they borrow). The second issue is who can access that information and under what conditions. The third issue is what vendors can collect from library users.

Although a much broader issue than technology, user privacy is part of managing library technology. Most libraries have a confidentiality policy, and the ALA's "Policy on Confidentiality of Library Records" (http://www.ala.org/ala/aboutala/offices/oif/statementspols/otherpolicies/policyconfidentiality.cfm) offers guidance in formulating or revising such a policy.

CHECK THESE OUT

The following items explore in more detail the issues of privacy, libraries, and the digital environment:

Barnes, Susan B. 2006. "A Privacy Paradox: Social Networking in the United States." *First Monday* 11, no. 9. http://firstmonday.org/htbin/cgiwrap/bin/ojs/index.php/fm/article/view/1394/1312.
Woodward, Jennette. 2007. *What Every Librarian Should Know about Electronic Privacy.* Westport, CT: Libraries Unlimited.

One part of library privacy relates to the personal information the library collects about its registered users, such as name and contact information. Making certain there are security measures to help ensure only authorized individuals gain access to this information is vital. Also, the staff must receive training in understanding who may gain access without a court order (such as, can law enforcement officers, parents, or parent organization officials have access?). We addressed the question of user privacy in some detail in Chapter 3.

Another aspect of privacy is usage of library resources (print, digital, and other formats). In terms of materials a user borrows, most libraries require the staff to eradicate past circulation data in order to preserve user confidentiality. Today's ILS systems normally break the link between the borrower and the item(s) upon return and payment of any required fees. If the circulation system used in a library requires that the name of a borrower appear on a book card or some other traceable record, staff should render the name illegible as part of the discharging process.

Who may have access to information about what a person uses or has used has become complicated since 9/11. As long as libraries have existed, police, government officials, ministers, parents, spouses, and others have asked libraries about the reading habits of borrowers. In the past, such access required a court order. After 9/11, there was a change regarding access to library records, at least for federal law enforcement officers. The USA PATRIOT Act authorized warrantless searches and the requirement that the library not communicate to anyone that such search occurred or was underway.

What data might be available from library records that law enforcement officials might not more easily access elsewhere? Actually, not all that much. What a suspect might have been interested in that relates to law enforcement's concerns may well be available in more detail from those who know the person. Karl Gruben (2006) wrote, "In actuality, the Department of Justice does not have as much interest in what Johnny is reading as it does in what he is looking at or emailing or Instant messaging on the Internet, particularly since there is suspicion that the 9/11 hijackers communicated through Internet terminals in public libraries" (p. 303).

Filtering access to the Internet has been a hot topic for the general public, government officials, and libraries. Public and school libraries appear to be "caught between a rock and a hard place" on this issue, as long as they offer Internet access to the public and are short of funds for providing that access. Some of the general public, governing boards, and elected government officials want libraries to use filtering software that will deny access to certain types of sites. Others, believing in free speech (the First Amendment), do not want filtering. The primary reason for filtering is to keep children from having access to "unacceptable" sites.

The Children's Internet Protection Act (CIPA), enacted in 2000, requires public libraries and schools to install filters on their Internet computers if they want federal E-Rate funds for Internet connectivity. The penalty for not doing so is loss of federal funding. Public and school libraries have developed various policies on implementing CIPA, from installing filters on all public stations, installing filters on some stations designated for children, to declining to install filters at all. Some public libraries take a middle ground, either designating certain stations without filters as "adults only" or disabling filters upon requests by adults (allowed by CIPA). A rather large number have chosen to forego E-Rate funds in the name of intellectual freedom and professional ethics. Again, we looked at this issue in detail in Chapter 3.

Filtering is yet another technology management issue you must address if you work in a public or school library. Staff must understand the filtering policy and, in public libraries, be able to quickly turn on and off the filtering software if that is allowed. They must also understand just what is and is not filtered by the software; different vendors employ different sets of "stop words."

CLOUD COMPUTING

You have probably seen and read articles about cloud computing. Is it a passing flavor of the year, or is it a long-term change in how organizations handle their computing and technology needs? It is too soon to know the answer, but it appears as if it will be another technology issue for librarians to seriously think about and assess for its potential for their library. Marshall Breeding (2011) suggested, "We're now entering into a new phase of the history of library automation characterized by new technology underpinnings, including cloud computing, fully web-based systems, and service-oriented architecture and fresh approaches to functionality that recognize current library realities" (pp. 33–34).

According to the *Harvard Business Review* (2011), "Cloud computing enables access through the Internet to a shared pool of computing resources (hardware, software, etc.) that can be tapped on demand and configured and scaled up or down as needed" (p. 1). The basic concept of "the cloud" is to shift applications from local servers to remote servers that are used by many organizations—a form of collaboration in a sense. One example of cloud computing is described by Courtney Greene and Elizabeth Ruane in their 2011 article "Collaboration in the Cloud" in which they detail their coauthoring of a book using "exclusively cloud-based applications and services." Perhaps the best library example of cloud applications for libraries is OCLC's WorldShare Management Services (http://www.oclc.org/worldshare-management-services.en.html/). The webpage succinctly spells out the concept: "OCLC WorldShare Management Services provide a unified, Web-based environment that streamlines cataloging, acquisitions, license management and circulation and offers a powerful discovery and delivery tool for library users." The page goes on to list various benefits, most of which relate to cost control and increased efficiency.

We believe that more and more libraries will add planning for cloud applications to their regular technology planning process. Certainly it will be examined carefully as a possible cost containment solution, as almost all ILS systems have annual maintenance costs as well as staffing issues, even when much of the work is done remotely by the vendor.

SOCIAL MEDIA

Social media are now part of a library's activities, at least to some degree. There are two primary reasons for libraries to make use of these media. The first reason is to increase awareness (marketing) of its services, programs, new resources, and other activities for users. The second reason is to build or create relationships with its service community.

One clear advantage of social media is its interactive nature, which is highly valued by younger people. There can be quicker feedback than from print and other less interactive media on library issues and ideas (instant messaging, tagging, and Facebook are examples of the faster potential). The range of social media possibilities will only expand over the coming years.

This is not the place to explore all the potential and actual uses of social media. We provide some useful resources on such matters in the Check These Out box on p. 478. However, there are some significant management issues related to the library's use of social media that we want to highlight. First, and perhaps foremost, there must be senior management support for the activity. A "let's try this and see what happens" approach is more than likely to lead to failure just as with any other project. Senior managers must have a commitment to succeeding. Lacking such commitment means there may not be enough resources, especially time, for the effort to be effective.

CHECK THESE OUT

These books provide an overview of the organizational use of social media, its costs and benefits, and its use in libraries:

Blanchard, Oliver. 2011. *Social Media ROI: Managing and Measuring Social Media Efforts in Your Organization.* Indianapolis: Que.

Qualman, Erik. 2009. *Socialnomics: How Social Media Transforms the Way We Live and Do Business.* Hoboken, NJ: Wiley and Sons.

Solomon, Laura. 2011. *Doing Social Media So It Matters: A Librarian's Guide.* Chicago: American Library Association.

When the project is just the result of a staff person's interest in blogging or starting a library Facebook page, for example, the chances are it will be effective as long as that person stays an employee. When that person leaves, if there is not a library commitment, the activity will wither away. We believe it is better not to start using social media than to do so intermittently or ineffectively—to create a positive library image takes time, money, effort, and commitment.

A small word, "workload," is the key to most successful library activities. As we noted in Chapter 16, job descriptions are important. The common phrase "other duties as assigned" can become a workload nightmare for employees. Getting a new position (full- or part-time), or even retaining an existing one, is often a great challenge, especially if the specific duties listed constitute a full workload for the position. Adding other duties later, such as looking after the library's blog, without taking something away usually results in something getting less attention. For the individual, there may be performance consequences—poorer performance on one or more of the duties—or extended hours. A supervisor may not see the new duty as relevant to her or his unit's activities, thus adding to the stress of everyone involved.

Few of today's libraries have much in the way of staffing "fat." This makes it imperative that you look at what the top priorities are for meeting the users' needs and consider what may no longer be needed or may be consolidated. Social media activities are important for libraries, but just adding them to existing workloads is not a good practice.

COLLABORATION

Library technological collaboration revolves around two broad categories—intraorganizational and extraorganizational. If you have to choose just one area to focus on it should be intraorganizational, as most libraries are dependent on the parent organization's ICT unit for the infrastructure that is necessary to provide web services. Working with library consortia is a means of helping control technology costs—both hardware/software and digital content.

Prior to moving to web-based services, many libraries' ILSs and some degree of networking for the staff were more or less technological islands. The major reason for having to go outside the library was to have access to OCLC services, often through a dedicated telephone line or two. Larger libraries had an IT unit, with a modest-sized staff who handled almost all of the technical needs. Fewer and fewer of today's libraries have more than one "technical" (non-MLS) person on their staff.

As the parent organization became more dependent on technology, it became more cost effective to have an organizationwide ICT unit rather than multiple departmental units. Costs and coordination of activities became critical. In time, positions such as Chief Information Officer (CIOs) appeared. At times, a chief librarian became the CIO; in other cases it was a computer science person. The critical and challenging role of the CIO is described by Broadbent (a former librarian now at Gartner Inc. and the Melbourne Business School) and Kitzis (2004). For example, how does a CIO balance the concepts of "service" and network "security." Often for the latter, the CIO wants as tight a firewall (security) as possible, while the librarians want it as open (sharing) as possible.

As is true of budgeting, there are institutional technology politics. Most institutional CIOs, regardless of what their overall background is—such as being a librarian—face a host of competing demands. "We need new hardware and software for this project, *now*" and "We need you folks to modify this aspect of the system so we can. . . " are two examples of the many "We need it now" requests that come into ICT departments on a daily basis. Just like the library, ICT must prioritize its responses to such requests. The challenge for the library is to understand how the priorities get set and how to move up the list. We librarians sometimes do not fully understand just how complex the technology infrastructure is that underlies our activities. Working collaboratively is the best political approach. Taking time to understand at least the basic infrastructure is also a good idea. You can demonstrate some awareness of the fact that it is rarely just a matter of adding this or that software. The ultimate goal of the collaboration should be agreement that ICT supplies the means and the library provides the content for the end users.

There are signs of a growing trend in collaboration among independent software vendors in libraries rather than the fierce competition that formerly existed. The aim is to lower the cost and technical barriers for services, making it easier to share data more easily.

The next developments in collaboration will bring together services across sectors, as government policies encourage linkages between archives, libraries, and museums. This will bring some exciting benefits for users crossing the boundaries—for example, between information and cultural services. It creates the need for e-leaders.

KEY POINTS TO REMEMBER
- Technology provides access to information for users and generates management information to aid decision making.

- Technology improves productivity and assists in data collection, analysis, and use.
- Technology can help free up staff time, and it can make a service operate more cost effectively.
- Managers require enhanced technology skills.
- The proportion of the budget spent on the initial investment and associated recurrent costs will continue to increase and dominate annual expenditures.
- A major investment is needed to train staff to work effectively and efficiently.
- Users benefit from coaching to help them access information effectively.
- Rapid change will continue.
- Increasing attention is being paid to legal and security issues.
- Technology requires careful planning and control.

References

Bell, Steven J., and John Shank. 2004. "The Blended Librarian: A Blueprint for Redefining the Teaching and Learning Role of Academic Librarians." *College and Research Libraries News* 65, no. 7: 372–375.

Breeding, Marshall. 2006. "Musing on the State of the ILS in 2006." *Computers in Libraries* 26, no. 3: 26–28.

———. 2011. "A Cloudy Forecast for Libraries." *Computers in Libraries* 31, no. 7: 32–34.

Broadbent, Marianne, and Ellen Kitzis. 2004. *The New CIO Leader: Setting the Agenda and Delivering Results.* Boston: Harvard Business School Press.

City of Flagstaff. 2011. *Cityscape*, Fall: 21.

Dickson, G. W., and J. K. Simmons. 1970. "The Behavioral Side of MIS." *Business Horizons* 13 (August): 63–71.

Emberton, John. 1987. "Effective Information System Planning and Implementation." *Information Age* 9, no. 7: 159–162.

Evans, G. Edward. 2012. Comments based on a telephone conversation overheard by author in 2011.

Evans, G. Edward, and Margaret Saponaro. 2012. *Collection Management Basics.* 6th ed. Westport, CT: Libraries Unlimited.

Greene, Courtney, and Elizabeth Ruane. 2011. "Collaboration in the Cloud" *College and Research Libraries News* 72, no. 8: 454–459.

Gruben, Karl T. 2006. "What Is Johnny Doing in the Library? Libraries, the U.S.A. Patriot Act, and Its Amendments." *St. Thomas Law Review* 19, no. 2: 297–328.

Hage, Christine L., and Stephen Sottong. 2000. "Should Libraries Jump on the E-book Bandwagon?" *American Libraries* 31, no. 7: 61.

Harvard Business Review. 2011. *How the Cloud Looks at the Top: Achieving Competitive Advantage in the Age of Cloud Computing.* Special Report. Cambridge, MA: Harvard Business Review Press.

Hopkins, Michael S. 2010. "The Digital Natives and You." *MIT Sloan Management Review* 51, no. 3: 96.

Rettig, Jim. 2012. E-mail communication sent to Camila A. Alire, February 2.

Sottong, Stephen. 2001. "E-book Technology: Waiting for the 'False Pretender.'" *Information Technology and Libraries* 20, no. 2: 72–80.

Launching Pad

Agosto, Denise E., Andrea Forte, and Rachel Magee. 2012. "Cyberbullying and Teens: What YA Librarians Can Do to Help." *Young Adult Library Services* 10, no. 2: 38–43.

Andrews, Judith, and Derek Law. 2004. *Digital Libraries: Policy, Planning, and Practice.* Burlington, VT: Ashgate.

Bielefield, Arlene, and Lawrence Cheeseman. 2007. *Technology and Copyright Law: A Guidebook for the Library, Research and Teaching Professions.* 2nd ed. New York: Neal-Schuman.

Brynko, Barbara. 2012. "Libraries: Coping With 'Digital Squeeze.'" *Information Today* 29, no. 4: 1–36.

Cervone, H. Frank. 2010. "An Overview of Virtual and Cloud Computing." *OCLC Systems and Services* 26, no. 3: 162–165.

Kaufman, Paula. 2012. "Let's Get Cozy: Evolving Collaborations in the 21st Century." *Journal of Library Administration* 52, no. 1: 53–69.

King, David Lee. 2011. "Facebook for Libraries." *American Libraries* 42, nos. 5/6: 42–43, 45.

Konshak, Peter. 2009. "Using Text Messages to Communicate with Patrons." *Computers in Libraries* 29, no. 1: 11–13, 44.

Mardis, Marcia A., Teralee El Basri, Sylvia K. Norton, and Janice Newsum. 2012. "The Digital Lives of U.S. Teachers: A Research Synthesis and Trends to Watch." *School Libraries Worldwide* 18, no. 1: 70–86.

Matthews, Joseph R. 2004. *Technology Planning: Preparing and Updating a Library Technology Plan.* New York: Neal-Schuman.

Price, Lee. 2011. "Social Media Brings in the Money." *Public Libraries* 50, no. 2: 24–27.

Renfro, Patricia, and James Neal. 2012. "The Integration of Libraries and Academic Computing at Columbia: New Opportunities for Internal and External Collaboration." *Journal of Library Administration* 52, no. 2: 162–171.

Shkolnikov, Tanya. 2002. "To Link or Not to Link: How to Avoid Copyright Traps on the Internet." *Journal of Academic Librarianship* 28, no. 3: 133–140.

Stanton, Jeffrey M., and Kathryn R. Stam. 2006. *The Visible Employee: Using Workplace Monitoring and Surveillance to Protect Information Assets—Without Compromising Employee Privacy or Trust.* Medford, NJ: Information Today.

The dawn of the digital or electronic age, with increasing access to e-resources rather than print, was heralded by many as marking the end of the physical library as a key building type. . . . If anything the profile of libraries has been raised and the continuing need to house collections, while at the same time providing a supportive environment for navigating the world of information beyond the library's walls, has meant that library design is again a hot topic.

　—Karen Latimer (2010)

One of the challenges of managing a public library is dealing with maintenance issues and emergency situations

　—Kathryn Ames and Greg Heid (2011)

The awesome and inspiring spaces are also by nature shared spaces; most libraries are designed to serve multiple user populations and multiple users. The physical library is a space where individuals come together.

　—Jeffrey Pomerantz and Gary Marchionini (2007)

Our libraries are designed to have pretty flexible space. . . . I would say about 35% of the public space is dedicated to children and teens and this can grow to about 60–70% depending on the day and the projects and programs. . . . We used our inspiration from our original vision: our libraries needed to be majestic, soaring, natural, whimsical, playful, inspiring, to name a few. . . . Our spaces needed to be flexible and accommodate the way people use our spaces.

　—Pam Sandlian-Smith (2012)

19

MANAGING AND PLANNING PHYSICAL FACILITIES

This chapter focuses on the following:

- Library as "place"
- Managing the facility
- Risk management
- Disaster management
- Sustainability
- Planning new space
- Moving to a new location

SOMETIME IN THE future it may be that something like a combination of IBM's Watson (an artificial intelligence computer system) and the *Starship Enterprise*'s LCARS (Library Computer Access and Retrieval System) will make archives, libraries, museums, and perhaps even some types of brick and mortar stores obsolete. However, even Watson and LCARS require some physical space. Such a scenario is not likely to take place in your lifetime or perhaps even in your children's children's lifetimes. Until that does occur, the library as a physical space will continue to exist. And, as long as this is the case, librarians will have to manage the space.

People have been predicting the demise of print materials and libraries for some time now. As a young librarian interested in library design and renovation, one of the authors participated in a meeting in the late 1960s on the future of library building design. Several of the participants were adamant that in less than 20 years there would be no need to design new buildings, and existing libraries would be just seldom-visited museums because of technology. However, little has changed over the past 45 plus years—books, magazines, and newspapers are still available in print form, libraries continue to acquire such items every year, and new buildings and additions are being built to house the growing collections. Will this pattern continue indefinitely? Probably not, but the library as a physical space is highly likely to do so.

Libraries have and certainly will continue to evolve as technology and society change. There is ample evidence of this evolution today. One example appeared in a newspaper article in 2011 that described the changing design ideas of library space for teenagers. It reported on a joint project funded by the Institute of Museum and Library Services (IMLS) and the MacArthur Foundation focusing on libraries and young people. It opened with, "Imagine walking into a public library filled with PlayStations, Wii game consoles, and electronic keyboards pumped up to maximum volume. . . . That is exactly how one enormous room on the ground floor of the Chicago Public Library's main branch functions" (http:// www.edweek.org/ew/articles/2011/11/29/13thr_libraries.h31.html). What about print materials in such a wired space? According to Amy Eshleman, an assistant commissioner at the library, there was a fight over designing space for books between the library staff and the designers and funding agencies. The library's desire to move its YA collections into that space prevailed, and "book circulation has gone up by about 500 percent since the space opened." The article also indicated that public libraries in Houston, Miami, New York, Philadelphia, San Francisco, and many smaller towns across the country would be designing similar spaces.

Pam Sandlian-Smith, Library Director at Anythink Libraries in Adams County, Colorado, whom we quoted at the beginning of this chapter, believes in the power of library as place. When she arrived as the new director, she discovered that the architect had already drawn up plans for some of the library system's new library buildings. However, Pam was able to get everyone to go back to the drawing boards to rethink the new spaces and buildings. She did not want shelving to drive the space. Unlike many typical building programs that create space mainly for fairly large collections, Anythink Libraries made their bookshelving fit around activities and services. This allowed for "amazing flexibility" where they could remake their space fairly easily by rearranging shelving. Anythink Libraries now physically accommodate noisy and quiet collaborations, media experiences including gaming and movies, comfortable seating for individuals and for groups, quiet study areas, popular materials and displays designed for impulse purchases, activity areas for messy work in the children's spaces, craft areas, spaces for families with babies and toddlers, iconic spaces (tree houses!), bookstores, convenient and fast checkout, computers and computer labs, program and learning spaces, book clubs, and more. They are presently working on an IMLS YouMedia project for teen space at their central library that includes adding an editing studio, some additional acoustical insulation, and doors. As the percentage of young people in a library's service population grows, you will see more and more space designed to meet interactive needs as well as quieter spaces for more contemplative activities, including using print materials.

A second article, appearing on the same day as the aforementioned one looked at school libraries and noted, "The new emphasis on collaborative learning and the use of digital tools to produce dynamic research projects leads to a louder, more hands on environment. . . . The shift to a noisier and more interactive library model is relatively new in U.S. school systems" (http://www.edweek .org/ew/articles/2011/11/29/13thr_theunquietlibrarian.h31.html).

ADVISORY BOARD EXPERIENCE

Virginia Walter provided this information about a new public library that is having an impact on library facilities and their design.

> A new movement is for Early Childhood and Family Spaces. In fact, Family Place is the name for a national movement that started at the Middle Country Library in New York and has spread throughout the country. Participating libraries pay to be trained in the principles of a Family Place Library, which include elements of programming, collection development, and space planning. An early childhood area is created that is designed for caregivers to spend time with their children ages 0 to 3. It includes age-appropriate toys and games that would not be out of place in a well-equipped nursery school. There is a focus on creative play as critical to early childhood development and to the acquisition of early literacy skills. The goal is for families to come and spend time interacting with their very young children instead of grabbing some picture books and leaving.
>
> The newly revised initiative from ALSC (Association for Library Service to Children) and PLA (Public Library Association), Every Child Ready to Read @ Your Library (ECRR), is a program designed to train parents and caregivers to give their young children essential early literacy skills. Like Family Place, it recognizes the importance of play in literacy acquisition so many libraries are adding an array of toys that foster play to their picture book areas. Among other issues, it raises the need to keep the toys clean.

The authors wish to note that the above is something new for U.S. public libraries. The concept has been in practice elsewhere, such as the Nordic countries, for a very long time.

LIBRARY AS PLACE

As we suggested earlier, even technology requires physical space. Accessing the content of the digital world requires equipment and space somewhere. Some people also require assistance, at least to achieve the best results, which adds still more space requirements.

Throughout the thousands of years of their existence, libraries have been places where people congregate, think, and collaborate. This is unlikely to change in the foreseeable future. Although what they work with may change in format, it will still be content that has to be acquired and made available in some manner. All this implies is that there is a need for some physical space.

Often one of the library design functions, especially in larger libraries, is to inspire thinking and learning. The notion of libraries as social places has been with us almost as long as libraries. Early examples of incorporating the idea of social space into library design can be seen in Nordic country libraries, which have done this for a very long time. Most of the large public libraries have had restaurants and cafés in their facilities for more than 50 years. Also, many are part of the community's cultural complex—libraries, meeting halls, museums, and theatres.

Having a café associated with or in a library is becoming more common in new U.S. library buildings. As library collections become increasingly digital, there is less concern about having a "no food in the library" policy. The underlying reason for such policies was concern about insect infestations and their potential health issues for both people and collections.

Michelle Twait (2009), in writing about an experience teaching a course on library as place, noted the following from her students when asked what they would like in a library. All of the students were self-acknowledged nonlibrary users:

Natural lighting, a café, traditional reading rooms, a 24/7 space, a conference room, individual lamps in study carrels, longer couches (the library's current "love seats" were not long enough to stretch out and sleep on), more individual study rooms, and a "grand entrance." They talked about softer, more indirect lighting, warm colors, comfort, rooms that inspire and welcoming spaces. (p. 22)

Essentially they wanted both group/social and individual comfortable spaces with some degree of individual control. Perhaps they assumed a wired environ-

AUTHORS' EXPERIENCE

Alire, while dean at the University of New Mexico, and her management team wanted to expand a coffee cart in the main library, much to the chagrin of some staff members who didn't want to give up valuable space. When doing focus groups, the library learned that while students appreciated 24/7 remote access to library materials, they also wanted "library as place" where they could meet for group study and group projects and where they could enjoy a café atmosphere. The final result was the installation of the first full-service Starbucks located in an academic library in the United States. The goodwill between the library and the campus—students, faculty, and staff—far exceeded the concerns of the naysayers.

ment as technology was not mentioned, or they believed they already had access to what they required. In any case, their "wish list" is not far removed from what architects and librarians attempt to achieve in new buildings.

We agree with Alistair Black and Nan Dahlkild's (2011) statement regarding ongoing shifts in thinking about the library as physical space:

> Library domains have been rebranded—as idea stores, learning cafés, discovery centers, media spaces, and learning resource centers to give just a few examples. Further, while it is true that the emergence of and increasing sophistication of digital ICTs has sharply increased fears of a library- and print-culture Armageddon, the physical library building has accommodated, with some success, the proliferation of virtual technologies. Indeed, the computer has in many respects enhanced the operations of the traditional library, bestowing upon it a new flexibility, not least in terms of greater opportunities and creativity in the organization of physical space, as materials are miniaturized and digitized. (p. 1)

As we noted in Chapter 18, on technology, librarians have a substantial amount of work to do to get the message out that libraries have and will continue to adapt to and embrace the digital world as well as be a major social asset. We like Terence Huwe's (2010) view of the issue:

> People love to study and commune together. With respect to understanding that basic human need, we have been remarkably effective in the battle for the hearts and minds of our communities. Of course, the digital era has revolutionized society's perception of space. Even so, against this backdrop, the struggle to preserve and enhance library space is a battle for the hearts and minds of communities. It is ongoing and will never end. (p. 29)

A final thought, or caution, about the library as place is that some libraries, especially academic and school, face the challenge of a senior institutional manager having the notion that "everything is digital, so the library does not need all that space." Space always seems to be in short supply; just think about the last time you looked for a parking spot. Senior managers receive more requests for additional space than is available or likely to become available through construction. Fighting to keep what you have is hard, but there is ample material available to help you win that struggle.

The issue goes beyond "digital." One of the authors, when working on the design of a new library, had a facilities manager who was very upset at the idea that the building would have a substantial amount of empty shelving on opening day and for some time to come. "We can't have that. People will think we lied about what was needed." Eventually, the notion that library collections grow annually, services and user populations also increase, and the reason for the new facility was the library had outgrown its current space was accepted—more or less.

MANAGING THE FACILITY

There are two broad aspects to managing the library as a building. First, there are the daily issues of keeping the facility safe, healthy, and inviting for users as well as protecting the community's investments (collections and equipment). The second is something you may become involved in some time during your career—renovating or designing a facility. As you might expect, changes in the operating environment increase the responsibility and accountability you have for the building/space. These include the following:

- Greater attention being given to environmental factors resulting from global warming and the need for buildings to be energy efficient
- Concerns regarding the health and safety of staff and users
- The need for increased security of people, documents, and electronic data
- The impact of technology in the workplace, focusing attention on layout and design together with health and safety issues
- The pressure to keep overhead costs down and the cost implications of poor maintenance

As Ames and Heid stated (2011), "A safe and clean facility is the responsibility of all the staff" (p. 10). Library service hours are generally longer than any one staff member's workday. Often service is provided seven days a week and sometimes 24 hours per day. Inevitably some facility issues arise when few, if any, senior members of staff are on duty. You need to have plans in place for handling issues ranging from minor ones such as leaking faucets to major ones such as a fire or earthquake—as well as train the staff in how to implement the plans.

HOUSEKEEPING MATTERS

Our opening quotation from Ames and Heid mentioned only public libraries; however, their point applies to any type of library. With the exception of school and corporate libraries, most libraries are stand-alone facilities. This means the library staff have more responsibility for the space than in other types of employment. Today it is rare for a library to have full-time maintenance/custodial per-

---

CHECK THESE OUT

Cotts, David G., Kathy O. Roper, and Richard P. Paynet. 2010. *The Facility Management Handbook*. 3rd ed. New York: American Management Association.

Trotta, Carmine J., and Marcia Trotta. 2001. *The Librarian's Facility Management Handbook*. New York: Neal-Schuman.

TIP

Management by "walkabout" or "showing the flag" is one way to spot housekeeping problems. Take a notebook, palm pilot, iPhone, or iPad with you to note problems.

sonnel on duty. Parent organizations usually find that sharing the services of such personnel is more cost effective than assigning full-time FTEs to a single facility.

On a daily basis, housekeeping is an issue. Poor housekeeping can affect the health and safety of staff, users, and collections. It starts with basic questions about such tasks as who picks up litter and empties wastebaskets and how frequently. How often are restrooms cleaned and provisioned, especially those for the public? Does custodial staff have responsibility to dust the books and shelves? How often and who vacuums/cleans the floors? Does anyone have the responsibility? These may seem like small problems, but there are health issues involved—more for staff than for users.

Staff can become sick from extended exposure to "collection dust"—a fact certified by medical professionals. In extreme cases, the person may be unable to return to work. Beyond the health issue, which is serious but not that common, there is the health of the collection to consider. Dust and dirt on the shelves act as a very fine abrasive on materials as users and staff pull them off and replace them on the shelves. Over time, the small damage from such cycles accumulates to the point that the item needs repair or replacement. You have to balance the annual cost of such repairs and replacement against the cost of having shelves dusted. Dust also plays havoc with computers, photocopiers, and other equipment.

Other housekeeping issues are burned out lights, problems of temperature and sun control, plumbing, leaky roofs, cracked sidewalks, and wet floors. The list could go on at some length, but you can probably see our point. Essentially any building component can cause a problem sometime in its lifetime. What happens when a user, late on a Saturday afternoon, reports that a water faucet in the restroom will not shut off and water is spilling over the floor? Is there someone or someplace to call? Will someone fix it before the start of the next shift? What does the staff do until the problem is resolved? In Chapter 3, on legal

CHECK THIS OUT

One example of the daily issues is discussed by Missy Henriksen in "Pest Management" (*American School and University* 83, no. 3: 220–223, 2010).

issues, we noted the liability concerns regarding the library and users. Clearly you need to be certain staff understand how to handle facility problems and how to keep the liability exposure as low as possible.

Fixing matters related to housekeeping or to the building is not the responsibility of the library if there is a parent organization. A facilities manager arranges contracts and organizes the work of specialist maintenance staff such as plumbers and electricians. They, like librarians and libraries, face severe budget problems. Mike Kennedy (2011) wrote, "In the funding climate that schools and universities find themselves, building managers will be fortunate to hang on to the budget they have, let alone receive the resources they need to address short- and long-term maintenance requirements" (p. 32).

Generally custodial staff members are not library employees. If they are, there is a high probability they are unionized and have a contract clearly delineating the services provided. Whether they are union or not, there will be a contract spelling

AUTHORS' EXPERIENCE

The following are two examples from Evans's experience in the area of building housekeeping. The first was a case in which the contract specified the custodians were to vacuum the floor of the library on a daily basis. He noticed that often it looked like the carpeted stairways were not vacuumed; as a test he placed some threads on each of the stairways. Two weeks later the threads were still there. A discussion with the custodial staff supervisor indicated the contract indicated "floors" with no mention of "stairways." Therefore the custodians had no responsibility to do such vacuuming. The supervisor would vacuum the stairs but at an extra fee. Hence the issue became part of the next contract negotiations. Although it is a minor matter, it takes time and generates occasional negative comments from users and staff. Who would have thought that becoming a librarian would lead to spending time debating who cleans stairways?

The second example is one that is an issue in most libraries—dusting books and shelves. This task is rarely covered in a custodial contract, or, if it is, it substantially increases the cost. Evans asked for a quote from the company providing custodial service for such a project. The price was just over $225,000, roughly 50 cents per volume for a one-time cleaning. That was far beyond the library's means and that of the parent organization. As an alternative the library tried using work-study students. That did work, but student turnover was very high, and the staff time to train a new student added to the overall cost of what became a never-ending activity.

Understanding what is and is not part of custodial contracts takes time but is vital to the proper management of the building.

out the services provided. Anything not covered in or going beyond contractual limits may be available but only at an additional charge. With tight budgets, extra charges are difficult, if not impossible, to handle.

RISK MANAGEMENT

Risk management is an essential part of managing a building safely. Most parent organizations have some type of insurance that covers losses, such as those resulting from fires and floods, and liability coverage; they have both only to some degree. (It is rare for insurance to fully cover losses, as there is usually some type of deductible to pay.) Insurance firms are usually happy to help you analyze the building's potential health and safety issues. If they can get the insured to address potential problems, there are going to be fewer claims to pay.

A risk management program identifies potential problems, possible solutions and their likely costs, and how to keep new problems from arising. In terms of potential issues, having a disaster or crisis management team prepare scenarios of possible events and how to address them when/if one does occur may take staff time but will pay dividends should the worst happen. Crisis management recognizes that there is a "golden hour," the period during the earliest stages of managing a crisis when critical decisions are taken.

HEALTH, SAFETY, AND SECURITY

Library health, safety, and security are critical issues for everyone—staff, users, and even collections. A surprising number of hazards can emerge in operating a public facility such as a library. As a managerial leader, you have a duty of care for the staff, users, and collections. Involving all members of staff in identifying risks is a good exercise and makes people aware of potential hazards. They will also be able to offer good suggestions based on their daily experiences.

An increasing challenge is maintaining a comfortable working environment as we experience the effects of global warming. One constant issue is controlling temperature and humidity levels. Probably every manager has wondered from time to time, "Why, if they can send people into outer space and not have them freeze or burn to death, can they not design a building heating, ventilating, and air conditioning (HVAC) system for earth that works?" One reason for the complaints is the variations in people's inner thermostats; some people need cool temperatures, while others need warmer. In addition to individual preferences,

---

CHECK THIS OUT

Breighner, Mary, William Payton, and Jeanne Drewes. 2005. *Risk and Insurance Management Manual for Libraries.* Chicago: American Library Association.

over time systems break down, need to be taken out of service for maintenance, and simply wear out. As with custodial work, staff responsible for HVAC are rarely part of the library staff. This makes issues of response time and level of service matters of discussion and complaints.

A great challenge is balancing concerns for people and for the collections. What is good for people is not ideal for the collections and equipment. Two big subchallenges are temperature/humidity control and safety issues. Safety is divided into three major areas: safety from physical harm, safety of belongings, and psychological safety. You must address all these areas and balance the needs of people, collections, and technology.

For libraries with significant preservation responsibilities, such as archives, research libraries, and national libraries, one balancing act is among people, technology, and materials, all with different ideal climatological requirements. Both staff and customers generally prefer a working temperature at or near 72°F (22°C) with 50 to 60 percent humidity. Ideal storage conditions for collections are 60°F (15°C) and 50 percent or less humidity. This means compromise, usually in favor of people and technology, if the goal is to mix people and materials. Separation may or may not be feasible or affordable, as it probably requires two HVAC systems or modification of a single system into the equivalent of two systems.

To gain an overview of safety issues, conduct a security audit as part of the risk management program. One way is to create a security checklist, drawing on the expert advice from the parent organization's facilities manager, and then carry out a survey. If expertise is not available from within the organization, then the local police and/or fire department and the insurance company will usually provide professional advice, as they have an interest in seeing that safe conditions exist and generally welcome inquiries. Basics about existing fire protection equipment and emergency exits will be part of a survey.

Unfortunately, people and "thing" safety concerns can conflict in another area as well. In any library, except one-room facilities, there are likely to be one or more emergency exits located in areas not visible to the staff. Emergency exits are usually mandated by fire protection and building codes. Their location is a function of distance between exits, the number of persons in an area, and the activities in the area. While emergency exits provide for people's safety during a crisis, they also provide a means by which people may leave unseen at other times and take library materials with them. One method of controlling this problem is, during the initial design stage, to place staffed service points within sight of all exits. However, even in modest-sized buildings, this is almost impossible to accomplish. Another method is to install alarms so that opening the door sets off the alarm. Usually the best that happens in this case is that staff are alerted to the unauthorized use of the exit; but by the time staff get to that door the person is no longer in sight. Higher levels of security may be necessary, such as CCTV (closed-circuit television) cameras or designated security staff; you have to weigh the benefits against the installation and operational costs.

Collection documents have a way of "growing legs" and walking out without being checked out. Many libraries install a security system similar to that found in shops in the form of strips or "targets" attached to items in the collection and an exit control unit that sounds an alarm if the item has not been properly discharged. These systems are expensive to purchase, and the annual costs for targets can also be substantial. Is it worth the cost? The answer is, it depends on local circumstances. In making a decision about investing in a security system, you should:

- Collect data on lost and missing items
- Collect user complaints about mutilated materials
- Collect data on users "forgetting" to check out items
- Collect data on the amount of money spent annually on replacements
- Collect data on the cost of the security system for installation and maintenance, and estimate the annual cost of targets

With these data in hand, a decision can be made about the cost/benefit of installing a collection security system. ICT equipment also presents challenges similar to the collections.

CRIME

We live in a society where crime seems to increase yearly. In the workplace and where members of the public are present, organizations have had to increase security. The threats range from lower level crimes, such as thefts of personal belongings from staff and users, to acts of violence experienced even in school libraries as well as rapes, gang violence, and even murder in public libraries.

User spaces in isolated or remote parts of the building are higher risk areas than those in large open areas, which have many user spaces. Poorly lit and remote staircases are also high-risk areas. You have a number of options that range from:

AUTHORS' EXPERIENCE

Because the University of New Mexico's main library was a block away from a main road in the city where a lot of homeless people congregated and because many staff members working nights and weekends were women who had personal safety concerns, Alire and her management team made the decision to find the funds (robbing Peter to pay Paul) to contract with a security agency to have security officers staff the official entrances to the main library and "make the rounds" during the day and just before closing.

- doing nothing (this will raise the library's liability risk),
- devoting some staff time to patrolling the building (which reduces time for other work),
- hiring security staff or a firm to patrol the building (a costly but effective option), to
- installing a variety of electronic surveillance equipment (costly and could carry unexpected legal consequences, e.g., questions of privacy).

It is a matter of taking action to protect both users and staff. Often at closing time there are only two or three staff members on duty to shut down the facility. Some libraries may be in areas where the crime rate is high and/or geographically isolated, making the staff vulnerable, particularly during night shifts. Few, if any, staff decide to work in a library because they want to be police officers. Management decisions are difficult at best, but, generally, some action is necessary and should be discussed with the board or senior management of the organization, staff, and representatives of the user community.

These are some of the daily facility management issues—enough to make the point that the physical facility requires managing and monitoring just as much as people and collections do.

CHECK THESE OUT

Cravey, Pamela. 2001. *Protecting Library Staff, Users, Collections, and Facilities: A How-To-Do-It Manual for Librarians.* New York: Neal-Schuman.

Kahn, Miriam. 2008. *Library Security and Safety Guide to Prevention, Planning, and Response.* Chicago: American Library Association.

O'Neill, Robert. 1998. *Management of Library and Archival Security: From the Outside Looking In.* Binghamton, NY: Haworth Press.

EMERGENCY AND DISASTER MANAGEMENT

Emergencies happen. For the staff, few events are more stressful than at night or on the weekend when a person comes to the desk as says, "I'm not sure what is wrong, but there is a person on the floor not moving" or "I just saw a man on the third floor holding a gun." You may never hear either of these statements; however, there is a very good chance you will hear something equally upsetting.

Having both an emergency and a disaster preparedness plan ready to put into action when necessary will make both the staff and the users safer. Consider separating the two documents to make it easier for the staff to find the appropriate information, if they don't already know what to do. Working with local police and institutional security officers, fire departments, and emergency medical technician groups about what to and not to do gives the staff a greater sense of confidence. Knowing what to do leads to more confidence and less stress and very likely a more positive outcome.

Disaster preparedness teams attempt to identify the major risks (fire, floods, earthquakes, etc.). During the course of your career, you are likely to have to deal with one or more major facility disasters. Having a plan for handling such events will help reduce some of the stress the event(s) bring. Developing such plans requires time and effort but is essential. All library departments must be involved in creating the plans. Using a steering committee composed of representatives from each department is an effective method for developing and, importantly, periodically updating the plan. A successful plan will include the following:

- A realistic assessment of potential disasters
- A consideration of the differences between handling a library disaster and handling one that is part of a larger local or regional disaster
- A determination of collection salvage priorities
- A determination of insurance coverage and authority to commit funds for recovery

SOMETHING TO CONSIDER

Alire and her management teams (at Colorado State University and University of New Mexico) experienced a series of disasters and recoveries during her tenure as library dean. These included a major natural flood disaster (CSU), the flooding of an underground branch library building because frozen pipes burst (UNM), a major fire in the main library (UNM), and a mitigated potential disaster in the special collections center (UNM). The disaster planning and emergency response manuals at both university libraries were critical. Each disaster came with a different set of emergency response and recovery measures than the previous one. Nonetheless, the manuals were sound points of reference.

- Procedures to activate when a disaster, or incident, occurs
- Staff training to ensure that the procedures work and that staff are aware of them
- A telephone tree for emergency telephone calls, starting with the person who will direct the recovery efforts
- Skeletal forms on the library's website that can be completed immediately upon the disaster occurrence that informs staff and users and updates them on a daily basis (The staff form must be on the library intranet, whereas the information for the community is on the Internet.)
- A list with telephone numbers of recovery resource vendors and service providers
- Creating a schedule for regular review of the operation of the plan and updating information
- Developing a partnership with a local library to which users can be directed when a disaster strikes

Perhaps the most common disaster is water damage and not just from major storms or firefighting efforts. Water pipes and radiators break, and this may happen when the library is closed and a day will pass before anyone notices the problem. Even an unremarkable rainfall can cause damage if building maintenance has been deferred for too long.

Almost every organization has a growing list of deferred maintenance projects. Mike Kennedy (2011), in writing about educational institutions' maintenance issues, noted: "In the funding climate schools and universities find themselves, building managers will be fortunate to hang on to the budget they have, let alone receive the resources they need to address short- and long-term maintenance requirements" (p. 32), pointing out that in 2010/11 32 percent of the institutions deferred maintenance and 60 percent expected to do so in 2011/12. Deferring maintenance projects is something we all do—if nothing more than deciding to vacuum the floor tomorrow. Almost every deferred project will cost a little more—perhaps five or ten minutes longer to get the vacuuming done properly. Most deferred activities are not all that costly, but some can become major funding and loss issues. When it comes to significant building repairs, a year's delay will mean a greater cost; if nothing else there will be an inflation factor. Almost every library has one or two deferred projects.

AUTHORS' EXPERIENCE

Evans experienced one such deferred maintenance case. He looked after a library that was a combination of old and new construction. Over the years the collections had grown, been shifted, and been rehoused to handle new materials. He discovered that although 85 percent of the shelving units met existing seismic building codes a substantial number of the original shelving did not meet codes. For five years he submitted a request for $32,000 to bring the shelving into compliance. Each year it was placed at the top of the deferred maintenance list—"we will do it, if there is any money left after we do the major projects."

Early on a January morning in 1994 the Northridge earthquake struck. Evans's library was more than 15 miles from the epicenter. However, as you might guess, all of the noncompliant shelving went down—not just tipped over but sheared off—and thousands of bound periodicals were also damaged beyond repair. What had been a $32,000 deferred maintenance project escalated into a $187,000+ effort. Had the work been done when first proposed it seems likely the problem would not have occurred. With shelving that did meet current codes, no damage was sustained beyond the books and other items on the floor, and some of that damage was repairable.

For institutions, it is a matter of weighing risks when it comes to maintenance, and perhaps some finger crossing that the worst will not happen. You will have to do your best to keep major deferred projects from becoming long-term issues, but you will have to accept that there will be some projects delayed for longer than you'd like.

Recovery plans for various natural disasters—earthquakes, hurricanes, tornadoes, and typhoons—will vary with the type of disaster, its expected frequency, and the amount of damage expected. Other factors are the age of the facility (newer structures are more likely to reflect higher building standards) and what, if any, disaster recovery plans may exist in the parent organization.

One thing is certain about a major disaster: not everything will be salvageable. Some documents will be destroyed and many will have some damage, and there will not be time or money to save everything. Thus the value of setting priorities before the disaster strikes becomes apparent. What is irreplaceable (first priority); what is expensive and perhaps difficult to replace but is replaceable (second priority); and what is easy to replace (last priority)? Setting these priorities will prove more difficult than you might expect, as staff members will have differing views depending on their primary responsibilities. Checking with users and perhaps with the parent institution may indicate that staff views and public views do not always agree. You may have to spend a substantial amount of time explaining and justifying the priorities and, eventually, reducing the size of the first and second priority categories.

A recovery plan must also address the financial aspects of the situation. Time is of the essence in the recovery of documents. Waiting 72 hours or more to process wet paper materials may mean that there is little point in trying to recover them. Waiting to get approval to commit money to handle recovery efforts until after disaster strikes will probably mean missing the window of opportunity to save paper-based materials. The senior managers are unlikely to have unlimited emergency spending authority, but having a reasonable upper-limit spending power is essential.

Establishing a disaster recovery team is essential. When the library designates a person responsible for preservation activities, that person should be a member of the team, if not the team leader. Whoever the team leader is, that person needs to be able to stay calm and think clearly in times of high stress. Managers, the team leader, and the team need to have cell phones, and those numbers must be known by all. It helps to practice the plan and to have some basic recovery supplies on hand.

A telephone tree provides name, landline and cell phone number, home e-mail address, and the order in which staff should receive calls regarding the disaster. An event occurring during operational hours is one matter but another if it happens after hours. Even with a practiced plan, it takes some time to get it operational. Well-meaning staff who are not part of the recovery team can get in the way or create more problems than already exist. Being able to call in personnel when needed is much easier and effective than having people standing about wanting to do something. And remember that almost everyone wants to help when a disaster strikes.

CHECK THESE OUT

Alire, Camila. 2000. *Disaster Planning and Recovery Handbook.* New York: Neal-Schuman.

Halsted, Deborah, Richard Jasper, and Felicia Little. 2005. *Disaster Planning: A How-To-Do-It Manual with Planning Templates on CD-ROM.* New York: Neal-Schuman.

Jones, Virginia, and Kris E. Keyes. 2001. *Emergency Management of Records and Information Programs.* New York: ARMA International.

Kahn, Miriam. 2012. *Disaster Response and Planning for Libraries.* 3rd ed. Chicago: American Library Association.

Wilkinson, Frances C., Linda K. Lewis, and Nancy K. Dennis. 2009. *Comprehensive Guide to Emergency and Disaster Preparedness and Recovery.* Chicago: Association of College and Research Libraries.

Another aspect of disaster management is dealing with the emotional responses that the staff and users will have (Klasson, 2002). The feelings that are often experienced need to be understood. It is sensible to be aware of counseling services that can be speedily contacted if required, because the full impact of the incident may not be immediately evident.

Having a plan and failing to review it at regular intervals or not practicing its implementation is almost pointless. Practice will mean some time lost to information work, but it will be well worth the investment. Also, copies of the plan— as well as appropriate insurance, police, fire, and security agency numbers—must be in the hands of all key personnel, both at home and in the workplace.

SUSTAINABILITY

"Sustainability" is a word used widely in both the popular and the professional press. We placed our discussion of the concept here as it applies to both existing buildings and the design of new facilities. The concern about saving energy is not a new issue. As James Qualk (2011) noted, "The idea that a new or existing building can be capable of using very little, if any, grid energy or water while serving as a healthy place for people to live and work is now commonplace. But this is just one of many ways buildings still fall short of their true potential" (p. 75). Brian Edwards (2011), in writing about library building design, illustrated the overall issues in sustainability:

> Concerns over climate change and the consequent drive for energy efficiency is leading to new approaches to the design of libraries and reshaping of existing ones. Greater attention is being paid not just to fossil fuel energy consumption but to a wider range of environmental and ecological issues. In many ways the architectural approach to the twenty-first century library is returning to the roots of the modernist library found in Scandinavia with its emphasis upon high levels of daylight, natural materials, social harmony, and contact with nature. (pp. 190–191)

Facility managers, usually from the parent organization, not the library, have been engaging in energy-saving efforts for 40+ years. Their efforts and the library's purpose, especially for libraries with major preservation responsibilities, can come into conflict. Earlier we noted that one of your challenges in managing a library building is that peoples' comfort levels in terms of temperature and humidity and what levels are good for collections are rather different. Items in the collections are made up of a composite of materials (paper, acetate, emulsions, plastic, glues, cloth, cardboard, thread, etc.). Each component expands and contracts at rather different rates as the temperature and humidity change. Every expansion and contraction stresses the item and shortens its useful life. The greater the swing in temperature and humidity, the greater the stress on the item. When facility managers, as they often did and still do, turn off the heating or air conditioning during nonservice hours to save energy,

AUTHORS' EXPERIENCE

Evans was involved in designing a collection storage facility for a museum. The archives were to go into the new building; unfortunately, there was not enough money to include the library collections. The building earned a platinum-level LEED award. The sloped roof has native plants as the top level, and rain water is collected to irrigate the plants. Essentially the building is for storage with very limited office space. Researchers use materials in other buildings. The interesting aspect of the project was that meeting LEED criteria did not materially increase the cost of the building.

the library collections experience "roller coaster" swings in temperature and humidity.

There are times when some librarians do not like to discuss collections as capital goods (requiring appreciation, depreciation, capitalization, etc.). However, when it comes to roller coaster temperature and humidity swings and trying to make the point that a more constant 24/7 environment will protect the parent organization's investment, it is time to start talking about collections as capital goods. Both authors have had to make this point one or more times during their careers.

The foregoing is, or should be, a problem just for existing buildings. New buildings can be both environmentally appropriate and energy efficient. This is particularly true if the facility can become LEED certified. The U.S. Green Building Council (http://www.usgbc.org/) developed the LEED (Leadership in Energy and Environmental Design) rating system. It is a third-party certification process using a point system. The rating system has a maximum of 110 points assigned to seven categories:

- Sustainable sites, 21 (emissions)
- Water efficiency, 11
- Energy and atmosphere, 37
- Materials and resources, 14
- Indoor environmental quality, 17
- Innovation in design, 6
- Regional priority, 4 (varies by region of the country)

Earning 40 points gets a building certified; 80+ is a platinum rating, 60+ is a gold rating, and 50+ is a silver rating. It seems likely that this system will become a standard part of the design process over the coming years.

PLANNING FOR NEW SPACE
Only a few librarians will experience active involvement in planning a major addition, remodeling project, or totally new facility. Many librarians look for-

ward to such a project, but only a few look forward to doing it a second time. Perhaps the major reason for the less positive view is that almost all building projects become a series of compromises, some the library wins and many the parent organization, architect, and/or budget managers win. This is especially true when attempting to plan a facility capable of handling growth for 20 years or more and predicting the changes that may happen in that time. Perceived needs far exceed the funds available, resulting in a downsizing of the facility size or in the fit-out and equipment installed—and sometimes in all of them. The longer the time between funding the project and its completion, the greater will be the downsizing, as costs generally escalate. The process is often labeled "value engineering"—a fancy way of saying cost cutting.

In an ideal situation, a new facility should be:

- Flexible
- Adaptable
- Expandable
- Accessible
- Compact
- Stable in climate control
- Secure
- Attractive
- Economical to operate and maintain
- Comfortable
- Varied

To address just a few of these—flexibility is essential because the use of the space is likely to change at some point. For example, the volume of technical services work is declining as a result of outsourcing. Changes in the way reference work is done means that formerly desk-bound staff are frequently moving about the facility (Warnement, 2003). A modular building with few, if any, internal weight-bearing walls is typical of a flexible design. Internal walls that are weight bearing cannot be moved as needed without causing structural damage or requiring very complicated and costly work

Adaptability is not always the same as flexibility. For example, public and special libraries and records management centers need to be located where their users gather naturally, but this can change over time as the parent organizations change. So the premises may need to be planned so that they can be adapted for other uses.

Given the inevitable growth of archives and libraries, having a facility that can be expanded is highly desirable. Funds for an addition or remodeling are easier to raise than for an entirely new building. The designer must consider where the future expansion space might be and how that relates to the existing structure. It is not uncommon for the area labeled "future expansion" on the original plans to turn out to be unsuitable, for various reasons, when the time comes to expand.

Ideally, the project consists of a primary planning team of five or more persons: architect, library representative, specialist space planning consultant,

CHECK THIS OUT

Donald Beagle provides some idea of the range of issues related to adapt-ability in his "The Emergent Information Commons: Philosophy, Models, and 21st Century Paradigms" (*Journal of Library Administration* 50, no. 1: 7–26, 2010).

interior designer, representative of the parent institution, and, in some circum-stances, a user. Larger teams are possible, but the larger the group, the longer the process takes. Clearly many people will need to have input at different stages of the project, but having everyone involved in every aspect of the project slows the planning activities.

The need for an architect is apparent. The library representative will most likely be a senior manager, if not the senior manager, because decisions need to be taken reasonably quickly, especially in the latter stages of the project. Parent institution representation is necessary if for no other reason than to monitor the cost of the project, and it is also helpful to ensure that the design will fit into any existing architectural master plan.

Planning any new building is a complicated task involving highly detailed data, down to the required nail and screw sizes. Archives and libraries are very complex building types, almost as complex as a hospital. Few librarians have experience with designing a new library, and even fewer have that experience more than once. Also, there are few architects with library design experience, although the numbers seem to be increasing. Thus, having an experienced per-son (library building consultant) is highly advisable. The consultant is usually the person with the greatest experience in developing effective designs for library operations. A consultant's role is to ensure that the interior design will be func-tional with the appropriate level of detail required for an effective and efficient archive or library.

The input of an interior designer is useful, as he or she can take the vision, image, and ambiance that the library seeks to project and translate it into the finished space. (Think about what Michelle Twait's students indicated they want in a library that they would use, as listed earlier.) The interior designer works

TIP

Professional journals such as *American Libraries* and *Library Journal* pub-lish annual reviews of new and renovated archives and library premises that are sound sources of information about trends in design and architec-tural practices.

CHECK THIS OUT

Bringing users and staff together in focus groups provides helpful advice and gives them involvement in the project. A good article related to user input is Marcus Vaska, Rachel Chan, and Susan Powelson's "Results of a User Survey to Determine Needs for a Health Sciences Library Renovation" (*New Review of Academic Librarianship* 15, no. 2: 219–234, 2009).

closely with the architect and space consultant to ensure that the most effective use of space emerges at the fit out stage.

The building program is the key planning document. It is the outcome of the joint efforts of the library, the consultant, and the users. It provides the architect with the information needed to design the facility. Often it is also used to raise money for the project. To that end, it normally includes information about the existing services, collections, staff, and service population along with data about the parent organization. At the heart of the program, and essential for the architect, are data sheets for all the activities and units to be built into the new facility. Data sheets cover not only the equipment and the people who will occupy the space but also the relationship of that space to other spaces in the facility.

There are several stages in the design phase of the project. The first phase yields conceptual drawings reflecting several different exterior designs and some blocks of interior space indicating work areas, collection space, and so forth. Selection of the exterior design and shape of the facility occurs at this point and can have major implications for the project. A plain square or rectangular building is the least costly. As the exterior walls become more complex (L shaped, curved, or irregular in some way), the cost of the exterior rises, possibly leaving less money for the interior.

Very often, major archives and libraries holding national or university collections become symbols or monuments for the parent organization; these usually require dramatic architecture or an architectural statement. A cube or a shoebox does not usually make much of a statement. Conflicts over exterior statements

CHECK THESE OUT

John Moorman's "Library Buildings: Planning and Programming" (*Library Trends* 60, no. 1: 215–226, 2011) provides details and values of building programs in the design process, as does Ann M. Martin, Douglas D. Westmoreland, and Angie Branyon's "New Design Considerations That Transform the Library into an Indispensable Learning Environment" (*Teacher Librarian* 38, no. 5: 15–20, 2011).

REMEMBER

Spectacular buildings can present challenges for users. The Seattle Public Library opened in 2004 in a glass and metal-mesh structure with offset levels and spiraling rows of books. It won rave reviews from architects and librarians, but users and tourists kept getting lost. The designers intended to provide subtle hints that would guide people through the space, but the library had to employ a professional to install "wayfinder" signage.

versus the requirement for adequate functional interior space can emerge at the exterior design stage.

The second stage yields the schematic drawings reflecting the architect's interpretation of the building program. They start to reflect building and safety codes. Staff and user inputs are critical at this stage, as they will have to work in and use the space. The planning team should listen carefully to their comments and, whenever possible, incorporate them into the final design. It is at this stage that major adjustments in the location of this or that activity is the easiest to make, before the detailed drafting that follows later. An important consideration at this stage is the estimate of the operating cost for the facility and how it has been minimized.

Final working drawings are the last design stage. Here the drawings are complete to the last detail—which way a door opens, how wide it is, what it is made of, what color it is, and so forth. They reflect all aspects and specifications of the building, and they become the basis for the contractor's bid construction. There is a review and approval process for the final working drawing by the "owners"—the library and its parent institution—that in essence states, "Yes, this is actually what we want built in all its detail." The reason this is important is because anything overlooked in the final drawing may be corrected or added, but for an additional charge. In the United States, such corrections are known as "change orders"; the more change orders, the less money will be available for furniture and equipment. So a thorough review of the construction documents is critical to the level of funding available to finish the project as planned.

With the trend toward the development of joint-use libraries, for example, community libraries incorporating public and school libraries, or university and public libraries joining together, the planning of facilities includes even further considerations. The needs of all users and staff must be taken into account—and there can be conflicting interests. But good communication, a positive approach to planning, and goodwill can overcome difficulties, and a cost-effective solution can emerge.

MOVING TO A NEW LOCATION

Moving a collection to its new location can be challenging for the staff. Somehow, moving costs, probably because they are incurred during the last stage of the process, never seem to be adequate for the job at hand. Extras along the way have eaten into the project funds. So the staff has a dual challenge. The first is moving the materials from point X to point Y and maintaining the proper sequence for the materials—not as easy a planning task as it might seem. The second is to complete the first task with the funds available. The ideal solution is to employ professional movers who have experience in moving collections. Options beyond that are many, all the way up to trying to get enough volunteers to do the job for free (or, at most, for the cost of food and drink for the day). When considering all the options in cost terms, it is vital to calculate increased staff costs in the supervision of putting things back in order after the move is complete. Munde (2003) reviews the after-costs for the Leid Library at the University of Nevada

Having completed the move, a post-occupancy evaluation should be carried out, recording the outcomes for both the stakeholders and the colleagues planning the new premises. Oder (2001) reported the challenges facing the San Francisco Public Library when its post-occupancy evaluation indicated dissatisfaction on the part of users and staff.

Occupying a new facility is a major change for staff and users alike. There will be high expectations for the new facility; most will be realized, but a few will not. Change is stressful, and sometimes some of the compromises required generate staff unhappiness. The staff actively involved in the planning process must make a major effort to communicate quickly, frequently, and accurately to the rest of the staff about progress, changes, and the reasons for change.

KEY POINTS TO REMEMBER
- Library buildings are likely to continue being built for some time to come.
- Housekeeping matters—for both collections and people.

- Business continuity is vital.
- Risks must be assessed for the purposes of safety and insurance.
- Health, safety, and security are of growing concern.
- Disasters happen; all libraries need a disaster management plan that is regularly updated.
- Building and remodeling projects are complex and require professional assistance.
- The most successful new libraries are the result of a collaborative team effort that involves users' views about the new space.
- Sustainability will become an ever-growing factor in managing a facility.
- Moving a collection is a staff challenge.
- A post-occupancy evaluation records outcomes for the stakeholders and professional colleagues.

References

Ames, Kathryn, and Greg Heid. 2011. "Building Maintenance and Emergency Preparedness." *Georgia Library Quarterly* 48, no. 1: 10–13.

Black, Alistair, and Nan Dahlkild, 2011. "Library Design: From the Past to Present." *Library Trends* 60, no. 1: 1–10.

Edwards, Brian W. 2011. "Sustainability as a Driving Force in Contemporary Library Design." *Library Trends* 60, no. 1: 190–214.

Huwe, Terence K. 2010. "Hearts, Minds, and the Library's Physical Space." *Computers in Libraries* 30, no. 8: 29–31.

Kennedy, Mike. 2011. "Maintaining Perspective." *American School University* 83, no. 10: 32–35.

Klasson, M. 2002. "Rhetoric and Realism: Young User Reactions on the Linköping Fire and Its Consequences for Education and Democracy." *Library Review* 51, nos. 3/4: 171–180.

Latimer, Karen. 2010. "Redefining the Library: Current Trends in Library Design." *Art Library Journal* 35, no. 1: 28–34.

Munde, Gail. 2003. "After-Costs of Library Construction: A Case Study of Leid Library at the University of Nevada, Las Vegas." *Bottom Line* 16, no. 4: 143–150.

Oder, N. 2001. "SFPL Faces a Host of Challenges." *Library Journal* 126, no. 10: 60–62.

Pomerantz, Jeffrey, and Gary Marchionini. 2007. "The Digital Library as Place." *Journal of Documentation* 63, no. 4: 505–533.

Qualk, James D. 2011. "Building 'Shall Be Capable Of.'" *Environmental Design and Construction* 13, no. 11: 75–76.

Sandlian-Smith, Pam, Library Director at Anythink Libraries in Adams County, Colorado. 2012. E-mail communication sent to Camila A. Alire, April 20.

Twait, Michelle. 2009. "If They Build It They Will Come: A Student-Designed Library." *College and Research Libraries News* 70, no. 1: 21–24.

Warnement, Mary. 2003. "Size Matters: The Debate over Reference Desk Height." *portal: Libraries and the Academy* 3, no. 1: 79–87.

Launching Pad

Aldrich, Rebekkah Smith. 2011. "A Whole Systems Approach: Why Integrated Building Design Spurs Better, More Sustainable Projects from Start to Finish." *Library Journal* 136, no. 15: 30–33.

Barclay, Donald, and Eric D. Scott. 2011. *The Library Renovation, Maintenance and Construction Handbook*. New York: Neal-Schuman.

Bazillion, R. J. 2002. "Academic Library Construction: Managing the Design to Build Process." *Journal of Library Administration* 36, no. 4: 49–65.

Beagle, Donald Robert. 2006. *The Information Commons Handbook*. New York: Neal-Schuman.

Calzonetti, Jo Ann, and Victor Fleischer. 2011. "Don't Count on Luck, Be Prepared: Ten Lessons Learned from the 'Great Flood' at the University of Akron's Science and Technology Library." *College and Research Libraries News* 72, no. 2: 82–85.

Council on Library and Information Resources. 2005. *Library as Place: Rethinking Roles, Rethinking Space*. Washington, DC: Council on Library and Information Resources.

Danks, Richard. 2010. "O&M for Green Buildings: Are Operators Prepared?" *ASHRAE Journal* 52, no. 9: 92.

Erickson, Paul W. 2011. "Maintenance Needs." *American School and University* 83, no. 8: 26–28.

Hauke, Petra, and Klaus Ulrich Werner. 2012. "The Second Hand Library Building: Sustainable Thinking through Recycling Old Buildings into New Libraries." *IFLA Journal* 38, no. 1: 60–67.

Jankowska, Maria Anna, and James W. Marcum. 2010. "Sustainability Challenge for Academic Libraries: Planning for the Future." *College and Research Libraries* 71, no. 2: 160–170.

Kohl, David. 2006. "Where's the Library?" *Journal of Academic Librarianship* 32, no. 2: 117–118.

Latimer, Karen. 2011. "Collections to Connections: Changing Spaces and New Challenges in Academic Library Buildings." *Library Trends* 60, no. 1: 112–133.

Leighton, Philip D., and David C. Weber. 2000. *Planning Academic and Research Library Buildings*. 3rd ed. Chicago: American Library Association.

Maxymuk. John. 2010. "Library as a Place in Space." *Bottom Line* 23, no. 3: 128–151.

Miller, William, and Rita M. Pellen. 2006. *Dealing with Natural Disasters in Libraries*. Binghamton, NY: Haworth Press.

Mueller, Charles G. 2012. "The Once and Future Library." *American Libraries* 43, nos. 3/4: 39–41.

Niegaard, Hellen. 2011. "Library Space and Digital Challenges." *Library Trends* 60, no. 1: 174–189.

O'Donnell, Patrick. 2010. "Integrate Your Plans for Energy and Maintenance." *Buildings* 104, no. 12: 40–44.

Persily, Gail L., and Karen A. Butler. 2010. "Reinvisoning and Redesigning 'a Library for the Fifteenth through Twenty-First Centuries.'" *Journal of the Medical Library Association* 98, no. 1: 44–48.

Shepherd, F. 2002. "Diary of a Move." *Records Management Bulletin*, no. 109: 107–109.

Tooey, Mary Joan. 2010. "Renovated, Repurposed and Still 'One Sweet Library.'" *Journal of the Medical Library Association* 98, no. 1: 40–43.

Wayne, Richard. 2010. "Three Library Building Blocks for Planning for the Future." *Texas Library Journal* 86, no. 4: 122, 124–125.

PART V

MANAGING YOURSELF AND YOUR CAREER

I have a dog-eared stenciled piece of paper that I have taped to my office wall in each position I have held. I don't even recall where I found that piece of paper. However, the saying on the paper is: "Once you lose your integrity, everything else is a piece of cake."

  —Camila A. Alire, ALA President, 2009–2010

Codes of ethics can serve three major purposes in organizations. These include demonstrating a concern for ethics by the organization, transmitting ethical values of the organization to its members, and impacting the ethical behavior of those members.

  —Thomas R. Wotruba, Lawrence B. Chonko, and Terry W. Lee (2001)

It is well documented that people see what they want to see and easily miss contradictory information when it's in their interest to remain ignorant—a psychological phenomenon known as motivational blindness. This bias applies dramatically with respect to unethical behavior.

  —Max H. Bazerman and Ann E. Tenbrunsel (2011)

It is an unfortunate but inescapable fact of business life that working people engage in unethical work behaviors which threaten the legitimate interests of organizational stakeholders.

  —Bennett J. Tepper (2010)

There will undoubtedly be challenges ahead where the ethical neutrality of the librarian is challenged, both positively and negatively. To face such situations we need to know what we stand for as a collective, and ensure it is never forgotten.

  —David McMenemy (2007)

20

ETHICS

This chapter focuses on the following:

- Organizational and professional ethics
- Why ethics matter
- Professional standards, values, and codes
- ALA's Code of Ethics

SOME PEOPLE HAVE the opinion that "management ethics" is an oxymoron. Certainly there are some examples that support such a view; however, what is overlooked are the tens of thousands of examples that get no notice as organizations go about doing their business in an ethical and socially responsible manner. As one of our first opening quotations indicates, organizational ethics serve several purposes, and when those working in an organization implement its ethical values it usually goes unnoticed. What we notice is the unethical actions and behavior of organizations.

Ethics, values, and social responsibility are not identical concepts, but they are interrelated. They apply to all organizations, including libraries. Certainly ALA has demonstrated an interest in all three for a great many years, as seen in the existence of its code of ethics, standards of service, and the work of the Social Responsibilities Round Table (SRRT; http://www.ala.org/srrt/).

Management ethics deal with right and wrong actions and activities. The difference between social responsibility and management ethics is that the focus of the former is on organizational action and activities while the latter focuses on personal actions. Although the definition appears clear-cut, it is seldom so in practice. A study published in the 1980s indicated that frontline supervisors (41 percent), middle managers (26 percent), and top managers (20 percent) all believed they had to compromise personal principles in order to conform to organizational expectations (Schmidt and Posner, 1982).

A key to keeping ethical conflict to a minimum is for senior managerial leaders to behave in clearly ethical ways and to recognize that conflicts may exist in the minds of subordinates. A very simple example of how such a conflict could arise would be in a library with a policy that the collection should contain all points of view on subjects. Do the collection-development officers face a possible conflict between personal values and organizational expectations? The answer is often yes, depending on the subject and on an individual's religious, political, and other beliefs.

One of the ways to help reduce conflict is to have in place codes of ethics, both professional and organizational. Codes assist staff in thinking about ethical issues and assist top management in identifying possible areas of conflict. Most national professional associations have such codes. However, in order to be truly effective, codes need to have some sanctions attached to violations of them. Failure to include sanctions turns a code of ethics into a public relations statement. Social responsibility and ethics are probably two of the concepts that will differ from organization to organization.

Ethics is about choices, as is social responsibility. What is important? What should be done in this situation? The basis for making the choices, from an academic point of view, comes from a branch of philosophy called "normative ethics." Within this field are three groups of theories—utilitarian, Kantian, and social contract—that provide the manager with some guidance in making a choice.

Utilitarian theories hold that the outcomes of actions or decisions should be the basis for judgment as to the rightness or wrongness of a choice. John Stuart Mill is perhaps the most notable writer in this area. His idea was that moral choices that produce the greatest good for the greatest number of people are nice, but determining the "good" is a complex and often impossible task. Perhaps it is easier to identify unethical choices; most people would agree that a decision that enhanced only the position of the decision maker at the expense of others is unethical.

Kantian ethics, as the name implies, rest on the ideas of Kant about nonconsequential theory. Essentially, and most simply, the idea is to act or decide in a way that people are never the mere means to an end but that they are the end in themselves. At several points in this text we have mentioned that it is good to have user advocates for your library. There is a possibility of an ethical issue when you ask or employ those advocates to support efforts to increase staff salaries. Will the users actually get any "good" if there are salary increases? Are you employing them as a means rather than an end?

Social contract ethics are principles that form the basis of many social contract theories. Two examples are principles of opportunity and principles of justice. Opportunity, as you might guess, relates to equality in access to society's benefits (economic, education, etc.). Justice rests on the notion that "goods" are distributed so that even the least advantaged members of society get some benefit from those goods. You probably can see how these two concepts relate to library operations. ALA's Freedom to Read Statement (http://www.ala.org/offices/oif/statementspols/ftrstatement/freedomreadstatement) and the profession's concern about a digital divide are examples.

WHY ETHICS MATTER

Do ethics matter? The answer is a very definite yes! Librarians have been concerned with professional values and ethics for more than 100 years. ALA published its first code of ethics in 1938, although there was discussion of professional values, responsibilities, and ethical behavior of librarians starting in the early twentieth century. The latest revision of the code occurred in 2008. The code touches on collections, services, access, intellectual freedom, intellectual property, personal/professional values, and personal interests and user needs (see Figure 20.3, p. 521, for the full text of the code). It is a mix of social responsibility (organizational) and personal behavior (ethics). One element it does lack is any sanctions for not following the guidelines, for that is what the code is— guidelines. It is up to each library to implement the guidelines and decide what to do, if anything, if it sees a problem. Other library profession associations, such as the Medical Library Association and Special Library Association, have their own codes of ethics.

Jean Peer (2008) made this point:

> Ethics is about choices. As a system of principles determining right or wrong conduct, ethics defines the parameters of those choices. . . . Indeed, ethics relates to "custom," the word deriving from ethos, the way things are done. . . . In the years before publicly-funded libraries, librarians had no transcendent obligation to the local community, to the larger society, to their profession, or to the values it embodied. (pp. 1–2)

Her book, *Library Ethics*, provides a detailed look at our professional values and the ethics that do, or should, underlie how libraries operate.

Earlier we noted that managerial leaders can help staff members behave ethically by modeling such behavior. One reason ethics matter is that managerial leaders can also, perhaps unknowingly, cause staff to behave unethically. Bennett Tepper's opening quotation should raise some concerns about ethical behavior in organizations. There is no doubt that people are motivated, in large part, by their personal values. Some people have very, very strong value views (religious or political, for example) and believe it is a responsibility to convince others their values are the correct values. If such a person is the senior managerial leader of a library, what are the chances that staff members would act in ways that went against the leader's articulated values? Would they have the moral courage to at least quietly follow the ALA ethical guidelines, such as adding items to the collection that they know are contrary to the director's beliefs? According to Tepper (2010), "A compelling body of empirical research evidence suggests that it is disturbingly easy for authority figures to put their direct reports in positions where unethical choices are preferred over ethical choices" (p. 592). Some of the empirical studies that support Tepper's point are Stanley Milgram's (1974) *Obedience to Authority*, Thomas Blass's (2000) *Obedience to Authority: Current Perspectives on the Milgram Paradigm*, and Kerry Patterson, Joseph Grenny, David Maxfield, Ron McMillan, and Al Switzer's (2008) *Influencer: The Power to Change Anything*.

Wotruba, Chonko, and Lee (2001), authors of one of our opening quotations, made a further point that "the ethical climate of an organization is a composite of

FOR FURTHER THOUGHT

Locate a copy of the code of ethics or statement of values from a professional area you are interested in. (If one has not been issued, then look at the ALA code; see p. 521.) Does the document provide practical guidance that you can act on as a managerial leader? What do you consider to be the most difficult ethical or moral dilemma that you are likely to encounter today?

formal and informal policies of that organization as well as the individual ethical values of its managers. In this context, an ethics code as a formal policy would be one building block of the organization's ethical climate, representing a statement of corporate ethical values" (p. 60). We suggest that the ALA Code of Ethics be discussed with each new library employee as part of his or her orientation program. This approach serves to emphasize for the new employee, as well as for existing staff, that ethics do matter and to clarify just what those ethical values are.

Dave Anderson (2011) wrote about a very common ethical issue—"little white lies." He suggested, "White lies are like the gateway drug to bigger offenses. . . . And in a business world that is already unstable, it's not a risk you should be willing to take" (p. 22). Most of us do tell white lies from time to time. On a personal level, we say we "have a prior engagement" when we don't want to attend an event. At work, we say we are "sorry but I cannot do that" when the fact is we could but wish to avoid the issue. Anderson (2011) suggested there are four little words we often use that are a tip-off that we are being less than ethical in our work activities: "just tell them that. . . . Any sentence that begins with that phrase is usually followed by a lie" (p. 22). Sometimes there is good reason for asking a staff member to say that—you are in a meeting and will get back to the person quickly. At other times it is avoidance. Certainly not all avoidance is unethical, but sometimes it is.

Sometimes professionals find that a conflict arises between a code developed by their professional association and an instruction issued by their manager. Such issues can occur in terms of access to certain services or information. Divided views of ethical behavior are probably the greatest challenge that managerial leaders encounter.

STANDARDS, VALUES, AND CODES

There are a variety of library standards, guidelines, statements, and codes promulgated by the ALA and other professional organizations that in some way touch on professional ethics, values, and behavior. We have mentioned standards and guidelines in other chapters in this book. You can check out the wide range of ALA standards and guidelines at http://www.ala.org/tools/guidelines/standardsguidelines. An interesting document on the ALA list is the Association of College and Research Libraries' (ACRL) *Standards for Libraries in Higher Education* (adopted in 2011, http://www.ala.org/acrl/standards/standardslibraries). What makes this document particularly interesting is that it includes a mix of both operational standards (institutional effectiveness) and professional behaviors (professional values).

A good example of library values is ALA's Freedom to Read Statement (Figure 20.1, pp. 516–519). Its seven propositions cover many of the long-held values of librarians, publishers, and booksellers. The fact that both for-profit and nonprofit organizations put forward the values carries greater weight in society than if just one organization did so. This does not, however, mean there are not challenges to carrying out these values.

Likewise the ALA's Library Bills of Rights (Figure 20.2, p. 520) is a statement of values that has ethical implications. It is likely you will have more than one occasion during your career when both the Freedom to Read Statement and the Library Bill of Rights will come in handy. They may not solve your ethical dilemma, but they will provide you with serious food for thought about what choice to make.

ALA'S CODE OF ETHICS

Turning to ALA's Code of Ethics (Figure 20.3, p. 521), we will cover the first seven points of the code. The final point, professional development, is a function of your career motivation and desires rather than an ethical concern. (We explore career development in the next chapter.) Some people might and do say that privacy (point III) and intellectual property (point IV) are matters of law rather than ethics. Both certainly are matters of law. However, unless you take the strictest approach to the law, there are times when there are grey areas and when ethical choice(s) come into play.

ACCESS

Point I of the code relates primarily to access to library services and programs, while the final clause addresses personal conduct with users. You should not be surprised to learn that, in addition to the code, ALA has a number of guidelines about access. One example is "Economic Barriers to Information Access: An Interpretation of the Library Bill of Rights" (adopted in 1993; http://www .ala.org/ala/issuesadvocacy/intfreedom/librarybill/interpretations/econom- icbarriers.cfm). One outcome of that document and professional concern is seen almost daily across the country as people line up to use the Internet-access computers in public libraries, many of who cannot afford the equipment or cost of connectivity. As more and more agencies, in all levels of government, require some or all interaction be done through the Internet, this increases pressure on libraries to maintain and expand such access. Doing that will place a burden on already tight budgets and force the library staff and governing boards to make hard choices. Some of those decisions will be ethical in nature.

As a friend of the authors once said, "So many ethical choices are so d——relative." Point I of the code provides an example of the relativity issues.

THE FREEDOM TO READ ACT

The freedom to read is essential to our democracy. It is continuously under attack. Private groups and public authorities in various parts of the country are working to remove or limit access to reading materials, to censor content in schools, to label "controversial" views, to distribute lists of "objectionable" books or authors, and to purge libraries. These actions apparently rise from a view that our national tradition of free expression is no longer valid; that censorship and suppression are needed to counter threats to safety or national security, as well as to avoid the subversion of politics and the corruption of morals. We, as individuals devoted to reading and as librarians and publishers responsible for disseminating ideas, wish to assert the public interest in the preservation of the freedom to read. Most attempts at suppression rest on a denial of the fundamental premise of democracy: that the ordinary individual, by exercising critical judgment, will select the good and reject the bad. We trust Americans to recognize propaganda and misinformation, and to make their own decisions about what they read and believe. We do not believe they are prepared to sacrifice their heritage of a free press in order to be "protected" against what others think may be bad for them. We believe they still favor free enterprise in ideas and expression.

These efforts at suppression are related to a larger pattern of pressures being brought against education, the press, art and images, films, broadcast media, and the Internet. The problem is not only one of actual censorship. The shadow of fear cast by these pressures leads, we suspect, to an even larger voluntary curtailment of expression by those who seek to avoid controversy or unwelcome scrutiny by government officials.

Such pressure toward conformity is perhaps natural to a time of accelerated change. And yet suppression is never more dangerous than in such a time of social tension. Freedom has given the United States the elasticity to endure strain. Freedom keeps open the path of novel and creative solutions, and enables change to come by choice. Every silencing of a heresy, every enforcement of an orthodoxy, diminishes the toughness and resilience of our society and leaves it the less able to deal with controversy and difference.

Now as always in our history, reading is among our greatest freedoms. The freedom to read and write is almost the only means for making generally available ideas or manners of expression that can initially command only a small audience. The written word is the natural medium for the new idea and the untried voice from which come the original contributions to social growth. It is essential to the extended discussion that serious thought requires, and to the accumulation of knowledge and ideas into organized collections.

We believe that free communication is essential to the preservation of a free society and a creative culture. We believe that these pressures toward conformity present the danger of limiting the range and variety of

Figure 20.1 ALA's Freedom to Read Statement

inquiry and expression on which our democracy and our culture depend. We believe that every American community must jealously guard the freedom to publish and to circulate, in order to preserve its own freedom to read. We believe that publishers and librarians have a profound responsibility to give validity to that freedom to read by making it possible for the readers to choose freely from a variety of offerings.

The freedom to read is guaranteed by the Constitution. Those with faith in free people will stand firm on these constitutional guarantees of essential rights and will exercise the responsibilities that accompany these rights.

We therefore affirm these propositions:

1. *It is in the public interest for publishers and librarians to make available the widest diversity of views and expressions, including those that are unorthodox, unpopular, or considered dangerous by the majority.*

Creative thought is by definition new, and what is new is different. The bearer of every new thought is a rebel until that idea is refined and tested. Totalitarian systems attempt to maintain themselves in power by the ruthless suppression of any concept that challenges the established orthodoxy. The power of a democratic system to adapt to change is vastly strengthened by the freedom of its citizens to choose widely from among conflicting opinions offered freely to them. To stifle every nonconformist idea at birth would mark the end of the democratic process. Furthermore, only through the constant activity of weighing and selecting can the democratic mind attain the strength demanded by times like these. We need to know not only what we believe but why we believe it.

2. *Publishers, librarians, and booksellers do not need to endorse every idea or presentation they make available. It would conflict with the public interest for them to establish their own political, moral, or aesthetic views as a standard for determining what should be published or circulated.*

Publishers and librarians serve the educational process by helping to make available knowledge and ideas required for the growth of the mind and the increase of learning. They do not foster education by imposing as mentors the patterns of their own thought. The people should have the freedom to read and consider a broader range of ideas than those that may be held by any single librarian or publisher or government or church. It is wrong that what one can read should be confined to what another thinks proper.

3. *It is contrary to the public interest for publishers or librarians to bar access to writings on the basis of the personal history or political affiliations of the author.*

No art or literature can flourish if it is to be measured by the political views or private lives of its creators. No society of free people can flourish that draws up lists of writers to whom it will not listen, whatever they may have to say.

4. *There is no place in our society for efforts to coerce the tastes of others, to confine adults to the reading matter deemed suitable for adolescents, or to inhibit the efforts of writers to achieve artistic expression.*

To some, much of modern expression is shocking. But is not much of life itself shocking? We cut off literature at the source if we prevent writers from dealing with the stuff of life. Parents and teachers have a responsibility to prepare the young to meet the diversity of experiences in life to which they will be exposed, as they have a responsibility to help them learn to think critically for themselves. These are affirmative responsibilities, not to be discharged simply by preventing them from reading works for which they are not yet prepared. In these matters values differ, and values cannot be legislated; nor can machinery be devised that will suit the demands of one group without limiting the freedom of others.

5. *It is not in the public interest to force a reader to accept the prejudgment of a label characterizing any expression or its author as subversive or dangerous.*

The ideal of labeling presupposes the existence of individuals or groups with wisdom to determine by authority what is good or bad for others. It presupposes that individuals must be directed in making up their minds about the ideas they examine. But Americans do not need others to do their thinking for them.

6. *It is the responsibility of publishers and librarians, as guardians of the people's freedom to read, to contest encroachments upon that freedom by individuals or groups seeking to impose their own standards or tastes upon the community at large; and by the government whenever it seeks to reduce or deny public access to public information.*

It is inevitable in the give and take of the democratic process that the political, the moral, or the aesthetic concepts of an individual or group will occasionally collide with those of another individual or group. In a free society individuals are free to determine for themselves what they wish to read, and each group is free to determine what it will recommend to its freely associated members. But no group has the right to take the law into its own hands, and to impose its own concept of politics or morality upon other members of a democratic society. Freedom is no freedom if it is accorded only to the accepted and the inoffensive. Further, democratic societies are more safe, free, and creative when the free flow of public information is not restricted by governmental prerogative or self-censorship.

7. *It is the responsibility of publishers and librarians to give full meaning to the freedom to read by providing books that enrich the quality and diversity of thought and expression. By the exercise of this affirmative responsibility, they can demonstrate that the answer to a "bad" book is a good one, the answer to a "bad" idea is a good one.*

The freedom to read is of little consequence when the reader cannot obtain matter fit for that reader's purpose. What is needed is not

Figure 20.1 ALA's Freedom to Read Statement *(continued)*

only the absence of restraint, but the positive provision of opportunity for the people to read the best that has been thought and said. Books are the major channel by which the intellectual inheritance is handed down, and the principal means of its testing and growth. The defense of the freedom to read requires of all publishers and librarians the utmost of their faculties, and deserves of all Americans the fullest of their support.

We state these propositions neither lightly nor as easy generalizations. We here stake out a lofty claim for the value of the written word. We do so because we believe that it is possessed of enormous variety and usefulness, worthy of cherishing and keeping free. We realize that the application of these propositions may mean the dissemination of ideas and manners of expression that are repugnant to many persons. We do not state these propositions in the comfortable belief that what people read is unimportant. We believe rather that what people read is deeply important; that ideas can be dangerous; but that the suppression of ideas is fatal to a democratic society. Freedom itself is a dangerous way of life, but it is ours.

This statement was originally issued in May of 1953 by the Westchester Conference of the American Library Association and the American Book Publishers Council, which in 1970 consolidated with the American Educational Publishers Institute to become the Association of American Publishers.

Adopted June 25, 1953, by the ALA Council and the AAP Freedom to Read Committee; amended January 28, 1972; January 16, 1991; July 12, 2000; June 30, 2004.

Source: http://www.ala.org/offices/oif/statementspols/ftrstatement/freedomread statement.

There is a little word in that section that is loaded: "equitable." Just what that means is open to wide-ranging debate. If you look up "equitable" in a thesaurus, the first synonym usually listed is "fair." Equitable and equal are not one and the same, although some people would argue they are. More often than not what is viewed as equitable or equal depends on your point of view. The reality is that it is impossible for libraries to provide equal service to its entire service community—the funding simply does not exist to do that. That would require that a user group of 100 would receive an equal amount of support as a group of 1,000. Educational libraries, in particular, face the question of equitable/equal support each year when it comes to allocating funds for subject and teaching department collection development. Would it be equitable to allocate as much funding to an honors program as to a subject area? Would it be equitable to spend less? As you might expect, those little words, *equitable, equal,* and *fair,* can generate debates about choices that have to be made.

INTELLECTUAL FREEDOM

Intellectual freedom (IF) is a long-standing concern for librarians. It has been a centerpiece in legal actions between members of the service community and

LIBRARY BILL OF RIGHTS

The American Library Association affirms that all libraries are forums for information and ideas, and that the following basic policies should guide their services.

I. Books and other library resources should be provided for the interest, information, and enlightenment of all people of the community the library serves. Materials should not be excluded because of the origin, background, or views of those contributing to their creation.

II. Libraries should provide materials and information presenting all points of view on current and historical issues. Materials should not be proscribed or removed because of partisan or doctrinal disapproval.

III. Libraries should challenge censorship in the fulfillment of their responsibility to provide information and enlightenment.

IV. Libraries should cooperate with all persons and groups concerned with resisting abridgment of free expression and free access to ideas.

V. A person's right to use a library should not be denied or abridged because of origin, age, background, or views.

VI. Libraries that make exhibit spaces and meeting rooms available to the public they serve should make such facilities available on an equitable basis, regardless of the beliefs or affiliations of individuals or groups requesting their use.

Adopted June 19, 1939, by the ALA Council; amended October 14, 1944; June 18, 1948; February 2, 1961; June 27, 1967; January 23, 1980; inclusion of "age" reaffirmed January 23, 1996.

Source: http://www.ala.org/advocacy/intfreedom/librarybill/.

Figure 20.2 ALA's Library Bill of Rights

libraries. You have undoubtedly read about and discussed this concern in one or more of your LIS classes. IF and censorship are interrelated just as they are in point II of the code. IF is much broader in scope than censorship and is tied to the First Amendment of the Constitution. This is not the place to explore the complexities of IF. We will briefly look at censorship, ethics, and you.

In today's world of tight library budgets and lean (almost skeletal at times) staffing, it is common for librarians to have some collection management responsibilities in addition to several other significant library obligations. Should you experience that situation, you will find yourself stretched for time and energy to do everything as well as you would like. Any extra work activity, such as a committee assignment or presentation, is an added burden. Suppose you are reviewing possible additions to the collection and see an item that could be useful in

CODE OF ETHICS OF THE AMERICAN LIBRARY ASSOCIATION

As members of the American Library Association, we recognize the importance of codifying and making known to the profession and to the general public the ethical principles that guide the work of librarians, other professionals providing information services, library trustees and library staffs.

Ethical dilemmas occur when values are in conflict. The American Library Association Code of Ethics states the values to which we are committed, and embodies the ethical responsibilities of the profession in this changing information environment.

We significantly influence or control the selection, organization, preservation, and dissemination of information. In a political system grounded in an informed citizenry, we are members of a profession explicitly committed to intellectual freedom and the freedom of access to information. We have a special obligation to ensure the free flow of information and ideas to present and future generations.

The principles of this Code are expressed in broad statements to guide ethical decision making. These statements provide a framework; they cannot and do not dictate conduct to cover particular situations.

I. We provide the highest level of service to all library users through appropriate and usefully organized resources; equitable service policies; equitable access; and accurate, unbiased, and courteous responses to all requests.

II. We uphold the principles of intellectual freedom and resist all efforts to censor library resources.

III. We protect each library user's right to privacy and confidentiality with respect to information sought or received and resources consulted, borrowed, acquired or transmitted.

IV. We respect intellectual property rights and advocate balance between the interests of information users and rights holders.

V. We treat co-workers and other colleagues with respect, fairness, and good faith, and advocate conditions of employment that safeguard the rights and welfare of all employees of our institutions.

VI. We do not advance private interests at the expense of library users, colleagues, or our employing institutions.

VII. We distinguish between our personal convictions and professional duties and do not allow our personal beliefs to interfere with fair representation of the aims of our institutions or the provision of access to their information resources.

VIII. We strive for excellence in the profession by maintaining and enhancing our own knowledge and skills, by encouraging the professional development of co-workers, and by fostering the aspirations of potential members of the profession.

Adopted at the 1939 Midwinter Meeting by the ALA Council; amended June 30th, 1981; June 28th, 1995; and January 22, 2008.

Source: http://www.ala.org/advocacy/proethics/codeofethics/codeethics.

Figure 20.3 ALA's Code of Ethics

the collection. You also know from reading the current literature that the item has caused a number of libraries problems with complaints and, in at least one case, a lawsuit. Challenges are time-consuming, stressful, and frustrating regardless of their outcome.

What should you do? To top things off, you are due to have your annual performance review in a few weeks, and there are a couple of small projects you want to get finished in order to have accomplished the goals you and your supervisor set a year ago. You can avoid the potential work from dealing with a challenge by not ordering the item. Is that ethical professional behavior? You can always explain not adding the item on the grounds of a limited budget and/or some better item might be available later. Who will know you made the choice not to add the item for personal reasons, other than yourself? It is easy to say you would never do such a thing when sitting in a classroom and quite a different matter when you are in the real work world.

As much as the profession might wish otherwise, librarian self-censorship is a very real issue. Debra Lau Whelan, (2009) in writing about self-censorship, stated:

> It's a dirty secret that no one in the profession wants to talk about or admit practicing. Yet everyone knows some librarians bypass good books—those with literary merit or that fill a need in their collections. The reasons range from a book's sexual content and gay themes to its language and violence— and it happens in more public and K–12 libraries than you think. (p. 27)

The issue is long standing and goes beyond the topics Whelan mentioned.

Some in the profession have been and are willing to raise the issue, and there is evidence of self-censorship in the literature. Perhaps the first book on the topic was Marjorie Fiske's 1959 *Book Selection and Censorship*. Her work was commissioned by the California Library Association in response to heavy pressure from individuals and groups to remove anything that could be considered communistic or socialistic. In her report, she noted librarians often waffle or weasel-worded their view about avoiding adding "potentially objectionable" items to the collection. Fiske (1959) illustrated the problem by quoting a librarian in her study: "We haven't been censoring but we have been 'conservative.' After all, this is a conservative community and that is how parents want it to be" (p. 62). You almost always have one or more rational reasons to justify your negative decision regarding an item. The question is, is the decision ethical?

PRIVACY
We explored the technical and legal aspects of privacy and confidentiality (point III) in Chapter 18. There is an ethical side to the topic as well. Some questions to ponder include whether or not you or the library has an ethical obligation to (1) inform users that "personalization" of library database sites can provide the vendor with more personal and marketable information than the person might

like; and (2) inform, and if necessary stand firm, with database vendors that they must comply with library privacy and ALA confidentiality policies, if they wish to retain your library's business? You can review ALA's Policy on Confidentiality of Library Records at http://www.ala.org/ala/aboutala/offices/oif/statementspols/ otherpolicies/policyconfidentiality.cfm. Some of the other standards and guidelines also contain recommendations regarding user/patron confidentiality.

Another potential issue that is likely to arise in some corporate library settings is that some firms view material in their library as proprietary, even if the material is from the open literature. Such situations will call for yet another recalibration of traditional professional ethics.

There are times when the sections of the code can present you with the dilemma of choosing between competing ethical areas in the code. One example is between privacy (point III) and intellectual property (IP; point IV). Over the years IP laws have become ever broader in scope and more restrictive of what you may freely use without permission (fair use).

Assume you are assisting a student with a class report or term paper. The student wants to find an online image to include in the project and has asked for help. After some time, the two of you find something the student likes and copies it and saves the web address for the image. Just before closing the page you notice the image is copyrighted. You decide to take the opportunity to briefly talk about copyright and permissions, indicating that using the desired image would require such permission. As you see eyes glazing over and a fair degree of restlessness, you wonder if the student will ask for permission.

You know that there is widespread belief that everything on the web is free to use as a person wants. Furthermore, you know that the notion that permission might be required is almost nonexistent. So what should you do? Ignore

ADVISORY BOARD EXPERIENCE

Representing the corporate library management sector, one advisory board member, Sachi Yagyu commented on ethics:

> This is an especially interesting chapter for me that requires more thought. The move from a university setting to a corporate one has involved a recalibrating of some ethical issues. Ostensibly, library books are for use for work purposes. It is an approved practice to share information about who has a book if asked. This is still very difficult information for me to share although I understand the various reasons that dictate the need. I find it odd that no one has ever complained. I now share this information with new staff during the library orientation process.

the matter, because no one will know the difference and chances of the copyright holder finding out and tracking the use of the image to a library IP is almost nil? (Do remember that in the United States any organization allowing Internet access is considered to be an Internet service provider [ISP] and may have some liability for a proven infringement if a user accessed the material through that ISP.) Do you have an obligation to follow up with the student regarding getting permission? Do you have a responsibility to check with the student's instructor about the project and image usage? Do you have any obligation to the copyright holder? You face some difficult choices, and the code will provide only a little guidance.

Looking at the two relevant sections of the code, you see they are in conflict as in the above situation. So, where do you go for guidance? You could check websites such as ALA's Copyright Advisory Network (http://librarycopyright .net/). Probably your best option is to go to your mentor, if you have one, or to a trusted experienced colleague for advice or just to talk out the options and issues. Such people may have had similar experiences and will talk about the outcome(s) of their choices

COWORKERS
Point V covers ethical coworker behavior. Obviously all the aspects of ethical interpersonal relations apply to coworkers. We mentioned earlier in the chapter an added aspect for managerial leaders—their impact on subordinates regarding ethical behavior. Aline D. Masuda (2011), in summarizing earlier findings on the topic by Raskin, Novacek, and Hogan (1991), noted that "individuals with an unhealthy self-concept are likely to use power-seeking strategies to regulate self-esteem. Because these individuals' source of esteem is power, they would not mind violating moral values" (p. 6). Her point, as well as ours, is that there are individuals who, especially in an organizational setting, can be unethical in their behavior as a means of securing increased power or authority. They may also influence others to behave in a similar manner in their quest. It is something to keep in mind as you begin to think about seeking a more influential position.

SELF-INTEREST
Self-interest at the expense of the library or its service community is the subject of point VI. Just what constitutes self-interest is sometimes a matter of debate. One of the arguments has to do with accepting or rejecting vendor "gifts." Some individuals believe vendor gifts, be they boxes of candy or other edible items at the holidays or a meal at a meeting, are nothing but bribes. They think accepting such gifts harms the library and its service community, because the cost of the gift gets incorporated into the price of the vendors' products. In one sense they are right; the vendors do factor in all their costs when setting a price. However, the price is not going be less because libraries do not accept such gifts. You can refuse vendor gifts, but your prices will not be

You can probably think of similar situations. List four and outline the potential ethical challenges for each. Share your thoughts with some classmates. Do they agree with your assessments?

lowered because of that fact. From the vendors' perspective, the holiday gift is simply a marketing tool and a small means of saying thank you for your business. They do not believe it changes your mind about the company, and they understand such judgments will be based on the firm's performance. Furthermore, the dollar amounts are so small, even in aggregate, that they would not reduce the price of the product. In the case of meals at a meeting or when vendor representatives visit the library and offer to take one or more staff to lunch, the vendors view this as market research. They know few, if any, individuals are going to make a business decision based on getting, or not getting, even the most elegant lunch or dinner. We do not believe this is a serious ethical issue for librarians, although some people do.

There are much more serious ethical self-interest concerns. Suppose you are given the assignment to work with a contractor on one of what will be several library renovation projects. Near the end of the project you say to the contractor, "I have enjoyed working with you on this project. I hope we can do so again in the near future. I have a question for you. I have a small remodeling project at home. Could you recommend any contractors I might contact who are reputable?" Is that question ethical under the circumstances? How would the library or its users be harmed if the contractor did undertake the project? Would you be obligating the library to giving the contractor one or more of the remaining library projects?

Perhaps a more common issue is using library funds or services for personal interest(s). The authors know of several instances when collection development funds and income from the sale of duplicate items were directed toward

A good article that provides eight ethical situations to think about is Helen R. Adams's "Reflections on Ethics in Practice" (*Knowledge Quest* 37, no. 3: 66–69, 2009). The situations depicted in the article are set in a school library media environment; however, it is easy to see how each one could occur in any type of library.

acquiring items outside the library's collecting scope and directly related to a librarian's research or hobby interest. Certainly the funds go to acquisition of items that go into the collection, so does that make it ethical? What if the person claims the purchase is to begin a new collecting area for the library? As a staff member not involved in the activity, do you have an obligation to report any behavior that you believe to be unethical to the governing board or to the office of the CEO of the parent organization—assuming you are certain of the facts? If you don't do so, are you behaving ethically?

Many years ago, Douglas J. Foskett (1962) wrote *The Creed of a Librarian: No Politics, No Religion, No Morals*. In it, he made the case for professional practice that is neutral, noting that "the librarian ought virtually to vanish as an individual person, except in so far as his personality sheds light on the working of the library. . . . He must put himself in the reader's shoes" (p. 10). This is what point VII of the code identifies as ethical professional practice.

It is a simple-sounding goal, but one that is very difficult to put into practice day in and day out. We mentioned one challenge earlier in this chapter—not selecting a certain item in order to avoid a possible challenge. The same set of questions we listed then applies to almost any item—you don't like the author's style, the author's philosophy, religion, politics, and so on. It can come up in your service activities as well. One frequently encountered situation is that of homeless individuals in the library. Homeless people may be dirty and smell, and some libraries even have policies regarding body odor (e.g., see the 2006 *American Libraries* article "Stir Raised by Dallas Body Odor Rule"). We have included several references in the Launching Pad section that provide additional examples.

AUTHORS' EXPERIENCE

Alire, when leading a major library disaster, was asked by the university president to announce to the campus community that the library was totally recovered and to do it "with conviction." This was so far from the truth that Alire knew to agree to do so would be to compromise her integrity with her staff (who would also know that it was an untruth), the students and faculty, and herself. This was an ethical dilemma for her. However, Alire knew the minute she walked out of the president's office that she would have to resign rather than deceive.

Her personal dilemma was leaving a job without having another job waiting. That would be compromising her work ethic. Which dilemma was solved? Alire resigned her position because the ethical dilemma was much greater than the work ethic one. This is why her quote at the beginning of this chapter is so important and personal.

We conclude with two quotations that reflect the challenges involved in professional practice:

It is evident that the professional ethics and principles of an organization may often conflict with societal and personal ethics. In fact, professional ethics and principles often have internal conflicts. These conflicts are interwoven into professional responsibilities of information science professionals. (Jefferson and Contreras, 2005, p. 66)

Woodward, Davis, and Hodis (2007), in paraphrasing Trevino and Youngblood (1990), wrote:

Individuals throughout life's experience will struggle with feelings about what is right and what is wrong. More adept individuals at ethical reasoning are more likely to make judgments based on principles they choose as opposed to those gained through peer pressure and other outside influences. Individuals with higher levels of moral development are less likely to engage in unethical behavior. (p. 195)

KEY POINTS TO REMEMBER
- Ethical behavior is a matter of choices.
- Organizational ethics rest on three types of philosophical theories—utilitarian, Kantian, and social contract.
- Ethical professional behavior is your responsibility.
- Library professional codes of ethics have no sanction powers, so there is danger of facing penalties should you chose to ignore the code(s). There is just your conscience to guide you.
- ALA's Code of Ethics addresses just about all aspects of library activities that you carry out on a regular, if not daily, basis.
- As a leader-manager you have the extra responsibility of not placing those who report to you in awkward ethical positions by your actions or suggestions, for example, "just tell them that _____."
- There will be times when the ethical choice will not be clear-cut and will be difficult to make.

References
American Libraries. 2006. "Stir Raised by Dallas Body Odor Rule." *American Libraries* 37, no. 2: 11.

Anderson, Dave. 2011. "Leadership and Little White Lies." *Public Management* 93, no. 10: 22.

Bazerman, Max H., and Ann E. Tenbrunsel. 2011. "Ethical Breakdowns." *Harvard Business Review* 89, no. 4: 58–65.

Blass, Thomas. 2000. *Obedience to Authority: Current Perspectives on the Milgram Paradigm.* Mahwah, NJ: Lawrence Erlbaum Associates.

Fiske, Marjorie. 1959. *Book Selection and Censorship*. Berkeley: University of California Press.

Foskett, Douglas J. 1962. *The Creed of a Librarian: No Politics, No Religion, No Morals*. Library Association Occasional Papers No. 3. London: Library Association.

Jefferson, Renée N., and Sylvia Contreras. 2005. "Ethical Perspectives of Library and Information Science Graduate Students in the United States." *New Library World* 106, nos. 1208/1209: 58–66.

Masuda, Aline D. 2011. "Power Motives and Core Self Evaluation as Correlates of Managerial Morality." *Academic Leadership: The Online Journal* 9, no. 1. http://academicleadership.org/article/power-motives-and-core-self-evaluation-as-correlates-of-managerial-morality.

McMenemy, David. 2007. "Librarians and Ethical Neutrality: Revisiting *The Creed of a Librarian*." *Library Review* 56, no. 3: 177–181.

Milgram, Stanley. 1974. *Obedience to Authority*. New York: Harper and Row.

Patterson, Kerry, Joseph Grenny, David Maxfield, Ron McMillan, and Al Switzer. 2008. *Influencer: The Power to Change Anything*. New York: McGraw-Hill.

Peer, Jean. 2008. *Library Ethics*. Westport, CT: Libraries Unlimited.

Raskin, Robert, Jill Novacek, and Robert Hogan. 1991. "Narcissism, Self Esteem and Defensive Self Enhancement." *Journal of Personality* 59, no. 1: 19–38.

Schmidt, Warren H., and Barry Z. Posner. 1982. *Managerial Values and Expectations*. New York: American Management Association.

Tepper, Bennett J. 2010. "When Managers Pressure Employees to Behave Badly: Toward a Comprehensive Response." *Business Horizons* 53, no. 6: 591–598.

Trevino, Linda K., and Stuart A. Youngblood. 1990. "Bad Apples in Bad Barrels: A Casual Analysis of Ethical Decision-Making Behavior." *Journal of Applied Psychology* 75, no. 4: 378–385.

Whelan, Debra Lau. 2009. "A Dirty Little Secret: Self-Censorship is Rampant and Lethal." *School Library Journal* 55, no. 2: 26–30.

Woodward, Belle, Diane C. Davis, and Flavia A. Hodis. 2007. "The Relationship between Ethical Decision Making and Ethical Reasoning in Information Technology Students." *Journal of Information Systems Education* 18, no. 2: 193–202.

Wotruba, Thomas R., Lawrence B. Chonko, and Terry W. Lee. 2001. "The Impact of Ethics Code Familiarity on Manager Behavior." *Journal of Business Ethics* 33, no. 1: 59–69.

Launching Pad

Beall, Jeffrey. 2011. "Librarians and the Threat to Free Political Speech." *American Libraries* 42, nos. 9/10: 33.

Budd, John M. 2006. "Politics and Public Library Collections." *Progressive Librarian*, no. 28: 78–86.

De Hoogh, Annebel B., and Deanne N. Den Hartog. 2009. "Ethical Leadership: The Socially Responsible Use of Power." In *Power and Interdependence in Organizations*, edited by Dean Tjosvold and Barbara Wisse, 338–354. Cambridge, England: Cambridge University Press.

Dole, Wanda V., Jitka M. Hurych, and Wallace C. Koehler. 2000. "Values for Librarians in the Information Age: An Expanded Examination." *Library Management* 21, no. 6: 285–297.

Grojean, Michael W., Christian J. Resick, Marcus W. Dickson, and D. Brent Smith. 2004. "Leaders, Values and Organizational Climate: Examining Leadership Strategies for Establishing an Organizational Climate Regarding Ethics." *Journal of Business Ethics* 55, no. 3: 223–241.

Hauptman Robert. 2002. *Ethics and Librarianship.* Jefferson, NC: McFarland and Company.

Hill, Rebecca. 2010. "The Problem of Self-Censorship." *School Library Monthly* 27, no. 2: 9–12.

Janes, Joseph. 2012. "Data, Data Everywhere: As the Big Data Beast Fattens, Will Privacy and Ethics Get Gobbled Up?" *American Libraries* 43, nos. 5/6: 42.

Jones, Barbara M. 2012. "Controversy in Fifty Shades of Grey." *American Libraries* 43, nos. 5/6: 21.

Koehler, Wallace. 2006. "National Library Associations as Reflected in Their Codes of Ethics." *Library Management* 27, nos. 1/2: 83–100.

Library Administrator's Digest. 2012. "Ethics for Trustees." *Library Administrator's Digest* 47, no. 3: 22–22.

Manley, Will. 2010. "Conservatives among Us." *American Libraries* 41, no. 10: 56.

Martin, Ann M. 2009. "Leadership: Integrity and the ALA Code of Ethics." *Knowledge Quest* 37, no. 3: 6–11.

Moellendick, Cora McAndrews. 2009. "Libraries, Censors, and Self-Censorship." *PNLA Quarterly* 73, no. 4: 68–76.

Perego, Martha. 2011. "Rewind: Taking Steps to Undo the Unintentional Ethical Misstep." *Public Management* 93, no. 10: 2–3.

Posner, Beth. 2012. "The Ethics of Library Resource Sharing in the Digital Age." *Interlending and Document Supply* 40, no. 2: 119–124.

Spackman, Andy. 2010. "Our Conservative Ideals: The Profession's Values Are Not Solely Liberal Ones." *American Libraries* 41, no. 4: 25.

Strickland, Ruth Ann, and Shannon K. Vaughan. 2008. "The Hierarchy of Ethical Values in Nonprofit Organizations." *Public Integrity* 10, no. 3: 233–252.

Usherwood, Bob. 2007. *Equity and Excellence in the Public Library.* Aldershot, UK: Ashgate.

Woolwine, David E. 2007. "Libraries and the Balance of Liberty and Security." *Library Philosophy and Practice* 9, no. 2: 1–17.

Proactive career behaviors include deliberate actions undertaken by individuals in order to realize their career goals.

—Ans De Vos, Inge De Clippeleer, and Thomas Dewilde (2009)

Midcareer is a perfect time for self-assessment and renewal.

—Cory Tucker (2008)

Finally, your professional career doesn't stop with getting a job. It starts there. To all my fellow IS and LS graduates, once you land that first job, continue to network with coworkers, clients, and former classmates. . . . You never know when it will come in handy.

—Kristen Centanni (2011)

21

PLANNING
YOUR CAREER

This chapter focuses on the following:

- Thinking ahead regarding your career
- Career-planning process
- Professional development
- Marketing yourself
- Work/life debate
- Factors that contribute to success

FEW LIBRARIANS MAKE a career of their first job; getting the first job may seem a daunting task, and doing it again seems like more than you want to think about at the moment. In this chapter, we look at both getting the first position and planning your long-term career goals. Getting the first and later positions draw on many of the same skills. In both cases you need a plan, and the sooner you start thinking about the plan, the better it is.

Why bother thinking about your long-term career plans before you have your first position? A major reason for doing so is that it helps you decide what to seek in the first position. Often the first position sets the course for your career without your meaning for it to do so. You may recall in Chapter 4 we quoted (from *Alice's Adventures in Wonderland*) Alice and Cat's exchange regarding directions: "'Would you tell me, please, which way I ought to go from here? 'That depends a good deal on where you want to go,' said Cat. 'I don't much care where,' said Alice. 'Then it doesn't matter which way you go,' said the Cat." So it is with your career; lacking a plan probably may result in a less satisfying work life.

One reason for planning is generally librarians substantially increase their salaries through taking on greater and greater managerial leadership responsibilities. However, "up" is not the only way to do so, assuming you know such responsibilities are not something you want. Also, flattening of library organizational structures means there will be fewer "up" opportunities. We provide some suggestions in the Launching Pad section that describe opportunities for using your LIS skills in a variety of settings.

SOMETHING TO CONSIDER

It is true that in most cases it is a matter of moving up in managerial leadership responsibility in order to increase your librarian salary by a significant amount. However, in some academic libraries there are promotion systems in place where a person can stay in a job he or she really likes and still be promoted and granted major salary increases. Few other types of libraries have such systems. Those academic libraries with such systems are usually based on faculty status or something very much like the faculty system. What that means, in most cases, is that you must have an inclination for and find time to engage in research and scholarly/publication activities. It may also entail earning an additional graduate degree or two. These are interests that not everyone has and something to keep in mind when job seeking and making career plans in terms of academic libraries.

Yet another reason for planning and periodically reassessing the plan is that we all know that technological knowledge and skills change rapidly; and today's knowledge may be obsolete tomorrow. Monitoring the changes, even if not required in your current position, will help you assess what new skills to develop in order to meet long-term career goals. Elías Tzoc and John Millard (2011) listed 21 different categories of "digital library" career opportunities. While the categories are likely to remain constant for some time, the skills to perform the jobs are very likely to change. Keeping a watchful eye on such changes may well pay dividends down the road.

In today's economic conditions, almost no one's job is totally secure. We hope that when you read this chapter the conditions are very much better than they were when we wrote it; however, economic conditions have a way of swinging back and forth. Having a plan for dealing with the "unthinkable" job situation (such as being laid off) will help make the unthinkable a little less stressful.

There is in today's workforce both a lack of trust of employers and, for many, a feeling of work stagnation. With unemployment at high levels, people tend to stay in jobs they would like to leave. In 2009, *The Economist* published "Hating What You Do" and noted:

> A survey of the Center for Life-Work Policy, an American consultancy, found between June 2007 and December 2008 that the proportion of employees who professed loyalty to their employers slumped from 95% to 39%; the number voicing trust in them fell from 79% to 22%. . . . More than half of the respondents described their jobs as "stagnant," meaning they had nothing interesting to do and little hope of promotion. Half of these "stagnators" planned to look for another job as soon as the economy improved. (p. 70)

You can believe your job is stagnating and/or there is little hope of promotion regardless of the economic conditions; having a plan for how to change that will make "moving on" less painful and drawn out.

CAREER-PLANNING PROCESS

In our view, there are five steps in creating a useful career plan—self-assessment, knowing career options, mentoring/networking, having a "life plan," and having a professional development plan. Self-assessment is the first and, in many ways, the most important. It requires you to take a very hard look at yourself—where you currently are, not where you would like to be—and at your strengths and weaknesses. Ask yourself questions such as, "What is my personality (outgoing, shy, etc.)?" "Am I passive/assertive or rational/emotional?" "How do I prefer to learn (self/group, hands on, academic, etc.)?" "What are my skills (both work and nonwork related)?" "What do I value (friends, status, money, time, etc.)?" "What do I want in a job (learning opportunities, satisfaction in doing something well, etc.)?" "What did I like and dislike about past work situations?" Another key question is, "How much risk can I tolerate?"

Another part of the planning process is to assess what the available career options are, both with your existing LIS skill set and with other knowledge and skills you possess. You may be surprised by the range of possibilities for the MLIS skills that are not in a library setting. Joanne Gard Marshall and colleagues (2009), looking at MLIS graduates from 1964 to 2005, found that just over 14 percent were using the degree skills in nonlibrary settings (some examples are jobs with database/content providers, ILS system vendors/developers, and database management firms). Your other existing skills and the MLIS may open unexpected opportunities as well, so investigating some of the possibilities will help you make an informed career plan. A good website to visit for more information is Real Job Titles for Library and Information Science Professionals (http://www.michellemach.com/jobtitles/realjobs.html).

Librarians have USPs (unique selling points) that rest on their abilities to understand subject analysis; recall with relevance and precision; and know where to find information, how reliable it is, and how it can be retrieved and packaged to satisfy user needs and communicated effectively and efficiently. And as new challenges emerge, so many of the former ones will remain. All these skills can and do apply to many nonlibrary work environments.

CHECK THIS OUT

A good book that covers a variety of employment possibilities is Linda P. Carvell's *Career Opportunities in Library and Information Science* (New York: Ferguson, 2005).

When you identify a subject area that looks interesting, try to locate people who are working in the field and see if they are willing to talk to you about opportunities and to provide a firsthand perspective of the work. Even better, assuming they are local, see if you might "shadow" them in their workplace for a day or two or volunteer with them. There is nothing like having experience in another area without having to leave your current position.

Part of the planning process is thinking about "what would I like to be doing five or ten or more years from now." Another decision to make, once you have identified your long-term goal(s), is what you need—knowledge, skills, experience, and so forth—to achieve that goal. Professional development is your responsibility. Yes, your current employer may be willing to pay for some development activities, but almost always the activities will relate to your current position. Needless to say, few employers are willing to underwrite activities that are likely to lead to your going somewhere else. How you go about developing the requisite skills for the long-term objective is a matter of your preferred learning style.

Finding a mentor is part of most successful career plans. A mentor provides help in a great many ways. However, to be effective, both of you must be willing and able to spend time getting to know one another. A mentoring relationship is relatively long term. Mentors are great as "sounding boards" about current job situations: "I would think about doing that just now," "That sounds like an excellent plan," "I would sleep on that," and "Have you thought about . . . " are the kinds of comments we received from our mentors and gave to our mentees over the years. When the mentor gets to really know you, she or he can be very helpful in reviewing your self-assessment results. Mentors can be

---

TIP

When it comes to finding a mentor, you should not expect your supervisor to play that role. That person may do so but only rarely. It is up to you to find one. Two good places to start the search are former teachers and people you meet through professional associations. A key to a good mentoring relationship is finding an individual who has similar work values, whom you respect, and who has achieved something you would like to achieve. Sometimes a mentoring relationship just develops. However, more often you will need to approach the person and ask if she or he would be willing to be your mentor. Have a plan in mind for what you are seeking in such a relationship so that the person can assess whether she or he has the knowledge, time, and so forth to undertake the desired activity.

Perhaps the biggest challenge for the mentee is being able to "hear" some things that are discomforting. However, a good mentor should and will point out areas where improvement would be good.

invaluable when it comes to job changes, and they may even push you to make a move when you are not sure you are up to the new responsibilities.

Beyond working with a mentor, you will want to follow Kristen Centanni's advice in her opening quotation in this chapter—start networking while in your MLIS program. Network contacts can be as helpful as your mentor throughout your career. They can indeed be sounding boards, informants about job prospects, and so forth. Like mentoring, networking is about building relationships and trust. As is true of good work relationships, you need to be as good a listener as you are a talker. Certainly social media is now a key part of networking and is a place where "me" can be dominant, unlike in face-to-face interactions where "me" should be less prevalent.

Something to keep in mind is what you put on your public social media accounts, as prospective employers may well check what you have posted. More specifically, candidates for employment have been asked for their passwords to their social media accounts, like Facebook and Twitter. Some companies are more subtle about their requests. They ask the candidate to "friend" a particular company employee so that they can access the candidate's pages, or they ask the candidate to access his or her social media account on their company computer during the interview (Valdes and McFarland, 2012). Many see this as an invasion of privacy; the potential employer sees it as learning more about the candidate.

As reported on a popular human resources website, in 2012 Maryland was the first state to pass legislation prohibiting employers from requesting or requiring employees or job applicants to provide access to their personal social media accounts. The expectation is that many more states will do the same (HR.BRL.com, 2012). The bottom line here is, as with e-mail, don't put up something that you would not want to see on the front page of the newspaper

TRY THIS

Preparing a career plan may seem daunting. We suggest a good way to begin the process is to do the following by picking just your top three priorities for each category:

- Your personal skills
- Your professional skills
- Your work values—"must haves"
- Work areas of interests—"really like"
- Work areas of low interest—"really draining"
- Possible career options
- New skills you would like to have

Finally, once you have thought through your long-term career goals (life plan), it is time to consider what you need to do to achieve those goals. Most likely it will entail some form of professional development. The vast majority of us in the field have a commitment to life-long learning in all its forms, not just professional.

You have a variety of options for professional development. National professional association meetings are a major source through both general presentations and specialized workshops. Such meetings are also an important part of the professional networking process; so attendance at such meetings need not always have a professional development motive. Local, regional, and online professional development opportunities also exist. Of course, there are course and degree program options as well as independent learning. Just remember, only you are responsible for your professional development.

MARKETING YOURSELF

Whether you are seeking your first professional position or a new job, you are marketing yourself to prospective employers. We looked at recruiting staff in Chapter 16 from the point of view of employers; here we discuss the process from the applicant's perspective.

APPLICATION PROCESS

The application process and how you approach it is critical to getting to the next stage—an interview. It starts with your résumé. Sometimes we forget to add new information to it and send it off as it exists; don't forget to keep it fresh. Also, understand that your résumé performs two roles. First and foremost, it acts as a record of your milestones and achievements. It is all too easy to forget dates, and even events, that were important in your career as the years roll by. An ongoing record is the foundation for future applications for employment, volunteer work, appointments to professional association committees, further study opportunities, travel scholarships, and the like. Second, it can be adapted for each application, containing only the information that is appropriate and relevant to that position.

You probably know the basic components of a sound résumé/curriculum vitae (CV). Just in case you don't recall the elements, here they are:

- Name, address, phone number, fax number, and e-mail address
- Date, place of birth, nationality—if you are happy to provide this information
- Education: high school, university—with marks, distinctions, and awards
- Professional courses: university, title of program, specialist papers, awards, and scholarships
- Courses that develop additional skills, such as IT, languages, or communication
- Work experience to date (including all that preceded entry to the profes-

sional course—remember that any work with the public, even in supermarkets, for example, will have helped you develop communication and
team skills)
- Membership in relevant organizations, particularly professional bodies
- Attendance at professional conferences
- A brief note of interests and hobbies—to provide a talking point at interviews

As your career develops, adding attendance at professional development courses,
papers presented at conferences, and other publications, professional awards,
and so forth may provide just the essential pieces of information to get an interview. Your mentor can provide good advice on what to include in a CV and in
turn will be better prepared to write references on your behalf. In a competitive
job market, you could turn to a professional résumé writer. These writers are in
touch with employers and know what the current approaches are, and they are
skilled in the design and layout of compelling documents. You can be sure that
the finished product will not contain errors that a spell-checker can miss.

Tailoring the résumé to the particular vacancy description can be effective;
we strongly recommend you take the time to do that tailoring. In tight economic
times, most vacancy announcements generate a large number of applicants. The
search committee will look for applications that "jump out" because the applicant has skills matching their needs. A less tailored CV may have the requisite
skills embedded in it, but they are hidden in a wealth of other information. Ideally that should not matter, but the reality is that being on a search committee is
an extra task and takes time away from other work activities, and thus haste to
finish the first review may cause something to be missed. A targeted CV is less
likely to get overlooked.

Check with people you list as references to be sure they are still willing to do
so and that you have their current contact information. One way to do this is
to send them the job announcement so they have a chance to assess what they
can, or can't, do as a reference. A professor who you had for "kiddie lit" may be
willing to be a reference but perhaps not all that useful when applying for an
electronic resource librarian position.

THE INTERVIEW

So, you have an interview scheduled; what next? Do your homework on the institution and its location. You can gain a general sense of the employer from the Internet,
but only a general sense. Ask your mentor and network what they know about the
institution. They may even know someone who worked there and who might be
willing to talk to you. Spend some time preparing a list of questions to ask, if they
are not covered during the interview. Most job interviews include or end with some
variation of "Do you have any questions for us?"

In the past, libraries prepared a very short list of candidates—three or four—
to invite for on-site interviews. The cost of bringing in more individuals was

SUGGESTIONS FOR INTERVIEWEES

- Research the library and parent organization ahead of time (go online).
- Develop a few questions to ask the interviewer(s) about the institution.
- Request a position description, and develop a question or two about the position.
- Think about the answers you might give to questions that are likely to be part of the interview. (What interests you about this particular position? What do you consider your strengths and your weaknesses? What does the term "service" mean to you?)
- Dress appropriately.
- Be on time.
- Be certain to have the interviewer's/chairperson's name and learn the correct pronunciation.
- Remember that your "body language" also reflects your interest and attentiveness.
- Brief pauses before answering complex questions are appropriate— thinking before speaking is always a good idea.
- Respond to all parts of a multipart question; asking for clarification or for repetition of a part of such questions is appropriate.
- Asking how any personal or potentially illegal question(s) relate to job performance is appropriate; however, ask it in a nonconfrontational manner, as the question may be job related.
- Thank the interviewer(s) for the opportunity to interview for the position.
- Ask about the anticipated time frame for deciding on who will be hired; this is appropriate.
- Making post-interview notes about some of the high and low points of the interview can be helpful in the future.

too high in terms of both money and time. Today libraries, like many other organizations, are using telephone or video conferencing (such as Skype) interviews to do an initial screening of a larger pool of applicants before making the final selection for on-site interviews. As Jahna Berry (2011) noted, "With video, companies can get an early impression of key factors, such as a job seeker's personality and communications skills, which helps narrow the applicant pool. But candidates must make careful preparation to ensure making a good on-camera impression" (p. D1).

CHECK THESE OUT

Richard Nelson Bolles's *What Color Is Your Parachute? A Practical Manual for Job Hunters and Career-Changers* (Berkeley, CA: Ten Speed Press, 2010) and *The Job-Hunter's Survival Guide: How to Find Hope and Rewarding Work Even When "There Are No Jobs"* (Berkeley, CA: Ten Speed Press, 2010) provide more in-depth information on how to find and land the right job. His website (http://jobhuntersbible.com/) contains career and personality tests, articles, and practical advice for job seekers.

Jeanette A. Woodward's *A Librarian's Guide to an Uncertain Job Market* (Chicago: American Library Association, 2011) is another helpful resource. For those of you wanting to work in academic libraries, consider Teresa Y. Neely's *How to Stay Afloat in the Academic Library Job Pool* (Chicago: American Library Association, 2011).

The basic preparation for such an interview is no different than for any other interview. However, there are some added elements; and Berry (2011) provided several tips for preparing for a video interview. One obvious need is not only to have the proper equipment and connectivity but also to test it well before the interview. Be sure to check that the room you plan to use is echo free—echoes can be very distracting for everyone. Another room/space issue is the background; a cluttered or highly patterned background can be distracting or, in the case of clutter, send the wrong message. Lighting can be an issue; you may need more light but out of the camera's line of sight. What you wear is also a bigger factor with video than it is with in-person interviews; patterned blouses or shirts are not recommended, and check the plain colors to determine how they come across on video. Keep family, friends, and pets out of the room and listening distance; they can be a distraction for you. Eye contact is always a factor in interviews but becomes critical in video interviews, as it is easy to tell when your eyes do wander—look straight into the camera. If you can see yourself on the screen try not to look at yourself or cover that part of the screen. Finally, and just as for in-person interviews, rehearse, rehearse, rehearse; if possible, record the rehearsal(s) so others can assess the performance and make suggestions for improvement.

Regardless of the interview format, thinking about and rehearsing your answers to some of the typical questions is worth the time and effort. We covered many of the general interview questions in Chapter 16; here a few of the common ones:

- What interests you about this position?
- What are your work strengths?
- What are your work weaknesses?

- What do think your supervisor/friend would say about your work ethic?
- What was your favorite job, and what made it so?
- What was your least favorite job, and what made it so?

There are many other such questions you might expect, and spending some time thinking about the specific job skills and your background can pay off in a job offer.

FLEXIBLE WAYS OF WORKING

Before taking your career in a new direction, examine the range of flexible working practices available in organizations today. Because libraries generally operate over extended hours, flexibility is often easier to arrange than in many other types of organizations.

Part-time posts may be available. A job-share is one way of retaining professional expertise while an employee moves into a new field. These arrangements can bring benefits to the employer by having a well-qualified and motivated staff member for some hours rather than losing this employee altogether.

The growth of the Internet has introduced another flexible way of working, which is to telework or telecommute. Jassin and Moe (2005) discuss the ways in which librarians can compete with other workers by developing their own telecommuting jobs. Working from home on a freelance basis can be effective for an increasing number of areas of professional practice. It has been common for indexers and abstractors to work in this way for many years, and the practice now extends to handling inquiries, performing marketing and public relations tasks, and using information brokers, consultants, and editors. Working in this way requires good organization and communication skills and close attention to customer care. Professional associations are generally able to offer advice on the professional indemnity insurance that is essential to have when working independently in the information field.

Another option is to take a temporary or contract post. Changes in the labor market have resulted in a greater number of people being employed on limited-term contracts. Contract working provides an opportunity to experience subject areas with a range of employers or in a variety of specialty posts. The employment agencies can assist an individual to manage a career based on contract posts, particularly in the private sector. A number of writers in the management field have suggested that all professionals will develop portfolio careers in the future that involve greater flexibility and more switching between jobs. But there is one precaution to take if stepping back from a permanent or full-time position and that is to consider the vital pension plan, health insurance, and other insurance you will lose. This may not seem important to you when you are in your twenties or thirties, but it can have an impact later in life.

CAREER BREAKS

Career breaks benefit both the employee and the employer. In some occupations and countries, the need for a break is recognized in the conditions of employment. Academics may be granted study leave. The employer gains benefits, because the person who enjoys a break comes back refreshed and reinvigorated. Another benefit for the staff development program is that another member of the staff has an opportunity to demonstrate her or his skills in a different post. This assists the employer to assess her or his suitability for promotion.

Developmental internships or fellowships may be available for those designated as "high flyers"—for example, the developmental opportunities organized by the Association of Research Libraries. In some universities, staff may be eligible for a sabbatical to pursue their personal research in order to maintain subject knowledge.

Traveling overseas may be a choice at any stage in a career. Travel scholarships for short periods of time are offered by a number of organizations. Exchanges with professionals in other parts of the world can be set up with facilitators through exchange registers that list people seeking an exchange in all types of organizations and in a number of countries around the world. Most are for three or six months and often involve a swap of job, house, and car. Voluntary service overseas was, at one time, the province of the new graduate, but now, as more people take early retirement or a career break, their skills and experiences can be of value in other countries.

Breaks for family responsibilities, such as maternity or paternity leave, are becoming part of established employment policies and practices. This can help parents to enjoy, and more fully participate in, the early stages of their child's life. The length of time available, paid or unpaid, varies from one employer to another.

THE WORK/LIFE DEBATE

The general management literature demonstrates a continuing concern about the pressures that are being placed on managers and their staff as organizations strive to cut operating costs and as ICT changes the way in which work is done. Much has been written about the negative effects of stress that can affect anyone within an organization, regardless of age, gender, or job level. Progressing in a career can increase the susceptibility to stress. Learning a new job can mean taking work home and acquiring new knowledge, qualifications, or skills. E-mail, the Internet, and intranets can add to the pressures of daily life, resulting in a situation where it is hard to break away from work, always needing to "catch up." In its most serious manifestation, excessive eating, drinking, or smoking can be the individual's answer to the problem. But stress can damage physical and psychological health and reduce the effectiveness of a person's performance, which, in turn, impacts on the work of their colleagues. Recognizing the symptoms may

---

CHECK THIS OUT

Richard Boyatzis and Annie McKee's *Resonant Leadership* (Cambridge, MA: Harvard Business School Press, 2005) helps leaders and potential leaders deal with or avoid stress and challenges through employing certain techniques.

---

be unpalatable to the employee and difficult for the employer. Organizations that provide in-house counseling, such as universities, may have a better way to help staff—and themselves. The remedy lies with the individual, who should limit the amount of overtime worked, take all of a leave allowance, enjoy a holiday, have a leisure-time interest, and enjoy time with family and friends for a full life.

FACTORS THAT CONTRIBUTE TO SUCCESS

We believe the following factors will contribute to your success in whatever direction your career takes:

- Know yourself, both your strengths and weaknesses.
- Have high standards, both personal and professional, and demonstrate them in your daily work.
- Demonstrate commitment to whatever job you have.
- Cultivate clear thinking, and maintain an objective viewpoint.
- Be reliable.
- Be adaptable.
- Cultivate and never lose your sense of humor.
- Understand the ways that others think.
- Show a concern for others in your professional and personal life, but in unobtrusive ways.
- Keep at the cutting edge of change.
- Develop good communication and influencing skills.
- Acquire political skills.
- Extend your managerial knowledge, and know what the best practices in management thinking are.
- Ensure that you are working effectively as a member of a team at all stages in your career.
- Know how to make decisions, and change them if the situation demands.
- Delegate.
- Maintain control over your own time.
- Recognize mistakes that you have made, and learn from them.

> **AUTHORS' EXPERIENCE**
>
> Serving as a mentor in several relationships, Alire works hard to provide her protégés with advice and reasons for that advice. They can choose to heed or not heed her words as they see fit. In some cases, she has had to be brutally honest but with compassion and encouragement. These relationships have withstood the test of time, and the protégés have moved into academic library directorships.

- Believe in yourself.
- Understand that career development requires an investment of time and money.
- Enjoy the job you are doing. If you don't enjoy the one you are in, find another.

Moving from a professional program to a first job is likely to produce culture shock, as the fundamental purpose of professional education is not to train students for a first job but to prepare them for a professional career (Holley, 2003). It is important to understand that the program's purpose is preparation for the longer term. The theory and principles learned support professionals throughout their careers.

The direction a career takes is often conditioned by factors outside your control. These include economic, political, social, and technological change and the state of the labor market. But there is a range of opportunities, and you do have choices in deciding in which direction to move. Career development depends on keeping well-informed. Information-handling skills are transferable skills, and they can be used in many occupations outside the mainstream of the information professions.

We have enjoyed our careers in library and information work and in management but couldn't have predicted the paths they would take when we started. We have both had wonderful experiences as librarians and library educators; however, it is also true that there have been one or two less than good experiences. So we'd like to pass on some advice: Monitor change and keep abreast of events, not only within librarianship and information work but also in what is happening in the wider world, that might affect your career. For example, where will librarians fit into the growing market for knowledge managers? Continual self-appraisal and self-assessment will identify emerging education and training needs.

A mentor who knows you well will provide objective advice on your strengths and weaknesses and on whether you should apply for that post that caught your eye. And sometimes she or he will give reasons why you shouldn't. Career goals are important, but flexibility is essential. Remember that realistic self-promotion will move a career forward. Finally, a key factor in any job is the level of enjoyment and reward, both extrinsic and intrinsic, that it provides.

References

Berry, Jahna. 2011. "Get Acquainted with Your Future Boss: More Employers Using Internet Video Conferencing in Interviews." *Arizona Republic*, November 4: D1–D2.

Centanni, Kristen. 2011. "Making the Most of It." *Library Journal* 136, no. 16: 31.

De Vos, Ans, Inge De Clippeleer, and Thomas Dewilde. 2009. "Proactive Career Behaviors and Career Success Planning during the Early Career." *Journal of Occupational and Organizational Psychology* 82, no. 4: 761–777.

The Economist. 2009. "Hating What You Do." *The Economist* 393, no. 8652: 70.

Holley, Robert P. 2003. "The Ivory Tower as Preparation for the Trenches." *College and Research Libraries News* 64, no. 3 (March): 172–175.

HR.BLR.com. 2012. "Maryland Becomes First State to Enact Password Privacy Protection Bill." HR.BLR.com. May 15. http://hr.blr.com/HR-news/HR-Administration/Electronic-Monitoring/Maryland-Becomes-First-State-to-Enact-Password-Pri.

Jassin, Marjorie, and Tricia Moe. 2005. "The Flat Track to New Career Options for Librarians." *Online* 29, no. 5: 22–25.

Marshall, Joanne Gard, Victor W. Marshall, Jennifer Craft Morgan, Deborah Barreau, Barbara Moran, Paul Solomon, Susan Rathbun-Grubb, and Cheryl A. Thompson. 2009. "Where Will They Be in the Future? Implementing a Model for Ongoing Career Tracking of Library and Information Science Graduates." *Library Trends* 58, no. 2: 301–315.

Tucker, Cory. 2008. "Development of Midcareer Librarians." *Journal of Business and Finance Librarianship* 13, no. 3: 241–248.

Tzoc, Elías, and John Millard. 2011. "Technical Skills for New Digital Librarians." *Library Hi Tech News* 28, no. 2: 11–15.

Valdes, Manuel, and Shannon McFarland. 2012. "Employers Ask Job Seekers for Facebook Passwords." *Associated Press*, March 22. http://news.yahoo.com/employers-ask-job-seekers-facebook-passwords-170500338.html.

Launching Pad

Carven, Beth N. 2011. "Online Group Mentoring: A Solution for Today's Socially Addicted Employee." *T&D* 65, no. 12: 18.

Czarnecki, Kelly. 2011. "Help Wanted: How to Turn a Passion for Gaming into an Exciting Career." *School Library Journal* 57, no. 2: 20–21.

Gordon, Shannon. 2010. "Once You Get Them, How Do You Keep Them?" *New Library World* 111, nos. 9/10: 391–398.

Keener, Molly, Vicki Johnson, and Bobbie L. Collins. 2012. "In-House Collaborative Mentoring." *College and Research Libraries News* 73, no. 3: 134–146.

McGhee, Marla W. 2012. "A School Library Work Plan." *School Library Monthly* 28, no. 6: 32–34.

Mullins, John. 2009. "Career Planning: The Second Time Around." *Occupational Outlook Quarterly* 53, no. 2: 12–15.

Newlen, Robert R. 2006. *Resume Writing and Interview Techniques That Work: A How-To-Do-It Manual for Librarians*. New York: Neal-Schuman.

Next Step Magazine. 2011. "Ten Social Media Tips to Help You Land a Job." *Next Step Magazine,* Nov./Dec.: 29.

Weech, Terry L., and Alison M. Konieczny. 2007. "Alternative Career for Graduates of LIS Schools." *Journal of Librarianship and Information Science* 39, no. 2: 67–78.

Younghee, Nor. 2010. "A Study Analyzing the Career Path of Librarians." *Journal of Academic Librarianship* 36, no. 4: 329–346.

INDEX

You may also be interested in

EVERYDAY HR
A Human Resources Handbook
for Academic Library Staff

GAIL MUNDE

Readers will find Munde's handbook an effective atlas of the most traveled regions of the HR terrain.

ISBN: 978-1-55570-798-9
200 pages / 6" x 9"

ACADEMIC LIBRARIANSHIP
CAMILA A. ALIRE AND
G. EDWARD EVANS
ISBN: 978-1-55570-702-6

CHALLENGES IN
E-RESOURCE MANAGEMENT
A Practitioner's Guide
LOUISE COLE
ISBN: 978-1-55570-935-8

THE NEW
PROFESSIONAL'S
TOOLKIT
BETHAN RUDDOCK
ISBN: 978-1-85604-768-5

MARKETING YOUR
LIBRARY'S ELECTRONIC
RESOURCES
MARIE R. KENNEDY AND
CHERYL LAGUARDIA
ISBN: 978-1-55570-889-4

MARKETING CONCEPTS
FOR LIBRARIES AND
INFORMATION SERVICES
Third Edition
EILEEN ELLIOTT DE SÁEZ
ISBN: 978-1-85604-870-5

COMMUNICATING
PROFESSIONALLY,
Third Edition
CATHERINE SHELDRICK ROSS
AND KIRSTI NILSEN
ISBN: 978-0-8389-1170-9

Order today at alastore.ala.org or 866-746-7252!

ALA Store purchases fund advocacy, awareness, and accreditation programs for library professionals worldwide.